I0819628

Lafayette IN AMERICA in 1824 and 1825

Journal of a Voyage to the United States

WELCOME
LAFAYETTE

Lafayette IN AMERICA in 1824 and 1825

Journal of a Voyage to the United States

By Auguste Levasseur

Translated by Alan R. Hoffman

LAFAYETTE PRESS, INC.
MANCHESTER, NEW HAMPSHIRE

Originally published in French in 1829
as *Lafayette en Amérique, en 1824 et 1825*
by Auguste Levasseur

Published by
Lafayette Press, Inc.
Manchester, New Hampshire
Second, third and fourth printings produced by Peter E. Randall
Publisher, Portsmouth, New Hampshire

First edition, second printing, 2007; third printing, 2016;
fourth printing, 2024
Printed in the United States of America
ISBN-13: 978-0-9787224-0-1
ISBN-10: 0-9787224-0-X

ebook ISBN: 978-0-9787224-1-8

Library of Congress Control Number: 2006933750

Director/Publisher: Jay Girard
Designer: Betsy Bailey
Copyeditor: Mary K. Tetreau

This book is printed on acid-free paper.

To my dear children, Adam and Elena,
in the hope that you will read this book
some day and be inspired.

CONTENTS

VOLUME ONE

VOLUME TWO

ILLUSTRATIONS

Frontispiece: Anonymous (American), "Welcome Lafayette" (detail), c. 1824, engraving on silk scarf, 30 x 33 inches, David Bishop Skillman Library, Lafayette College, Easton, Pennsylvania.

Facing page:

Attached to back cover: Map of Lafayette's Trip

The illustrations and the map are from Levasseur's original 1829 edition. Eight of the engravings signed "Couché fils" are by Louis-François Couché. The Washington's Tomb, Statue of Washington and Brandywine Cup engravings are unsigned. The copyright has expired on these illustrations.

PREFACE TO THE THIRD PRINTING

Why a Third Printing? There are three reasons. First, the supply of books from the Second Printing is exhausted; and I did not want the only unabridged translation of Levasseur's *Lafayette en Amérique en 1824 et 1825* to be out of print. Second, my good friend, Veronica Eid, formerly Adjunct Professor of French at the University of Delaware, had volunteered to copy-edit the book. Her work in this regard took place over a period of years, and we used to meet to discuss her proposed changes at Yorktown, VA at the time of the Surrender Day exercises in October on an almost annual basis. Our meetings over coffee and sometimes ice cream were productive as we debated each one of her proposed edits, and I usually concluded that she was correct. In the summer of 2015, I asked her if she could complete her work soon as we were running out of books from the Second Printing. She agreed, and over a period of weeks she sent me her edits of the last third of the book by e-mail, the last set of edits having been sent at 12:38 a.m. on July 28, 2015. Thank you, Veronica, and, to the extent that the Third Printing is improved, you are clearly most responsible.

The third reason is that in the eight years since *Lafayette in America in 1824 and 1825* appeared, I have found a number of errors. While at least one was brought to my attention by a reader, I discovered the others myself. Perhaps the most embarrassing is my failure to realize that when Levasseur's text recounted how they arrived at "Boston" where they spent the night, he could not have meant Boston since they had left that city in the morning. I learned of the error as I prepared to give a book talk at the *Bolton* Historical Society! While the substantive errors were few, I wanted the opportunity to correct them.

In the course of preparing the manuscript for the Third Printing and reviewing Veronica Eid's proposed edits, I re-read the book and re-entered early 19th-century America. I found it even more enjoyable than my first read as I was not grappling with every word or phrase. However, when I found a particular phrase or clause that was awkward or unclear, I went back to Levasseur's book and endeavored to improve on it. I do believe that the combination of Veronica's and my edits has made the Third Printing a more accurate and readable version of Levasseur's work.

The First Edition appeared on the cusp of an important year – 2007 – for the commemoration of Lafayette's life and career. This was the year of

Lafayette's 250th birthday, and this milestone was celebrated by an exhibition, which included numerous objects from the Farewell Tour. The exhibition traveled from Mount Vernon to Lafayette College and to the New-York Historical Society where it stayed until the middle of 2008. Other places joined in celebrating and commemorating Lafayette's life and career. In Fayetteville, North Carolina, the Lafayette Society commissioned a movie starring Lafayette reenactor Mark Schneider and produced a wonderful comic-book biography of Lafayette, which it still distributes to the schools in Cumberland County, NC. The City of Lafayette, Louisiana had a year-long calendar of events – it was nearly an event a day – and an art exhibition open the entire year that included works on loan from France. I attribute the fact that the First Edition was exhausted by the fall of 2007 in part to this renewed interest in Lafayette.

In 2015, there was another burst of enthusiasm for Lafayette's life and career. The voyage of the replica frigate *Hermione* was the reason. The *Hermione* arrived in America in early June and travelled up the coast where it was greeted by thousands at Yorktown and Alexandria, VA, Annapolis and Baltimore, MD, Philadelphia, New York City, Boston, MA, and Castine, ME. The original *Hermione* brought Lafayette back to America on his second voyage in 1780 with the news that a French Expeditionary Force and a small fleet would be arriving to support our Revolution. This event turned out to be the beginning of the end for British rule in the American Colonies.

While the highlight of these port visits was the opportunity to tour the ship, the Hermione-Lafayette Association also provided historical exhibits, which included materials on Lafayette's life and role in the American Revolution. Thus, as in 2007, interest in Lafayette was reignited, and I believe that this interest played a role in depleting the inventory of the Second Printing.

Although Levasseur is still not a household name, he has achieved a certain level of recognition, if not celebrity. Auguste Levasseur now has his own entry in Wikipedia (not created by me, I might add). Moreover, a number of reprints of the abridged 1829 American translations have now appeared in competition with this translation. However, neither of the two 1829 English translations is complete—one is more severely redacted than the other—and neither contains the original illustrations or the Farewell Tour route map.

Following in Levasseur's footsteps, I will end this preface with an anecdote. As I was grappling with one particularly irksome phrase in Chapter VIII of Volume I, I decided to consult the 1829 translation published in

Philadelphia, which I had acquired several years ago. As I was paging through it to find Dr. Godman's translation of the phrase – John D. Godman, M.D. was Charles Willson Peale's son-in-law – I came across a long paragraph about hotels in America that I did not remember seeing in my translation. I went back to my book, and, sure enough, it was missing. My first thought was something like this: "Oh no; is my translation incomplete? How could I have missed this?" Immediately I opened Levasseur's book and determined that the section on hotels was not there either. I breathed a sigh of relief.

Next I decided to audit the Chapter headings. Chapter VIII in Levasseur's original and my translation reads "New York." It is the only heading without a series of topics. In the Godman translation, the following appears for Chapter VIII:

> Streets of New York: drunkenness: prostitution: lotteries: hospitality: bankruptcy: women and young girls: luxury: hotels: police: anecdote: number of passengers arriving at New York, from 1818 till 1819.

I then consulted the other 1829 translation, which was published in New York, and this version has the Chapter heading "New York" and, like my translation, does *not* contain the section about hotels.

My working hypothesis is that Dr. Godman had an early manuscript of the French text, which Levasseur later changed in at least two respects. First, he omitted the topical chapter description for Chapter VIII, perhaps because it appeared too negative to him. Second, he deleted the long paragraph about hotels which, however, is not nearly as negative as some of the other parts of Chapter VIII. That Dr. Godman may have received an early manuscript is plausible because he credits Peter Du Ponceau for helping him with the translation. Du Ponceau, who knew Lafayette from the American Revolution and spent considerable time with him during the Farewell Tour when Lafayette was in Philadelphia, corresponded with Lafayette and to a lesser extent with Levasseur after they had returned to France. He may well have been the conduit for the early manuscript. In any event, for the sake of completeness, I have appended Dr. Godman's section on "hotels."

Alan R. Hoffman
Londonderry, New Hampshire
October, 2015

APPENDIX*

If luxury have invaded the dwelling of the banker; if she be seated at the table of the manufacturer, or penetrated even to the cabinet of the man of science, she has not yet crossed the thresholds of the hotels. Nothing can be more simple, nothing can be more modest, I might almost say more incommodious than the boarding-houses of New York, and indeed of all the other cities of the union. The bed-rooms are commonly large halls, containing seven or eight beds, placed not more than three or four feet apart, in which travelers go to rest at night, and quit them very early in the morning. Every one dresses and undresses himself in silence, and as it were in public, as there are neither screens nor curtains to conceal the business of the toilet. Three meals are offered daily to the boarders; in the morning at 8 o'clock, breakfast, composed commonly of bread and butter, eggs, fish, smoked meats, with tea and coffee for beverage: the dinner is amply supplied with large pieces of boiled and roast meat, accompanied by some pastry, and a few unseasoned vegetables; the whole washed down by a large quantity of wines, and other liquors; supper is exactly like the breakfast. These meals are always announced at fixed hours by the ringing of a bell, at the sound of which the boarders move with precipitation to seat themselves at table, at which, with still greater precipitation they take their food, and nothing is heard but the clattering of knives, forks, and dishes, as conversation is rarely carried on between persons entirely unacquainted, unless they have been introduced to each other by a common acquaintance. The parlour, or hall, which the inmates frequent in the intervals of the meals, is commonly a great compensation for the community of the bed-chambers, and the silent precipitation of the dining-room. Here one finds the newspapers; sometimes a piano, and often a select society, the honours of which are almost always gracefully done by the lady of the house, whose education and manners differ essentially from those of boarding-house keepers in Europe. It is especially in the relations of host and hostess, with the guests, that the feeling of equality which here animates all ranks, displays itself with all its force, and it is not in the least degree more affected by the act of receiving than that of paying money. Servility and arrogance are as uncommon in the boarding-houses of New York as they are said to be frequent in those of London. The mean price of boarding and lodging in New York is about a dollar and a half per day. No deductions are ever made for meals of which the boarder may not have partaken.

*From Volume I, Chapter VIII of the Godman translation

PREFACE

Four years ago, I read *America's Jubilee: How in 1826 a Generation Remembered Fifty Years of Independence,* by Andrew Burstein. Chapter One, entitled "An Esteemed Friend Twice Touches Hearts," caught my attention. It described General Lafayette's Farewell Tour of all 24 of the United States in 1824 and 1825.

Upon reading about the festivals, banquets and balls in Lafayette's honor, his honorary participation in the laying of cornerstones of public monuments and buildings and the unadulterated adulation with which the American people celebrated the visit of the last surviving Major General of the Revolutionary War, I asked myself: What was all the fuss about? Although I majored in American history and had pursued an avocational interest in the period of the American Revolution, my knowledge of Lafayette was very limited. So I resolved to learn more. In the fall of 2002 I acquired and devoured a recent biography, *Lafayette*, by Harlow Giles Unger, and a catalogue, with three scholarly essays, of a 1989 traveling exhibition centered on the art generated by Lafayette's Farewell Tour, *Lafayette, Hero of Two Worlds.* I was hooked.

I have continued to read widely about Lafayette and, more recently, his wife, the remarkable Adrienne. I have concluded that he was the noblest, most consistent, most principled and, in many respects, the most modern of all of our Founding Fathers, and one of the greatest men of his time. At a certain point in my studies, I wanted to read the book that Burstein and other authors had referenced in describing the Farewell Tour, Levasseur's *Lafayette in America in 1824 and 1825,* written by Lafayette's private secretary who accompanied him on his trip. Initially, I tried to obtain an English translation without success. I learned that two English translations had appeared in 1829, neither of which was complete, and that one of them was reprinted in 1970. I finally located the original 1829 publication in French at the Brattle Book Shop in Boston. When I looked at Levasseur's Foreword, I found that I understood it. I had studied French and Latin extensively in school and, to my surprise, had retained the ability to read French.

At that moment I decided to translate the book. For approximately two years – in the evening and on weekends – I sat at our dining room table with dictionaries at hand and traveled to 19th century America. It was truly a labor of love. In the past year, I arranged for a manuscript to be produced and spent my leisure time editing, re-editing and attempting to find "le mot juste" for every phrase in the book.

My primary goal in publishing this book is to restore Lafayette to his rightfully high place in the pantheon of American heroes. The ecstatic response to him in 1824-1825 was a reflection of the gratitude of the American people for his role in our Revolution, which they believed was responsible for the republican institutions and prosperity they enjoyed. In the first half of the 19th century, Lafayette was a superstar. When state banks printed legal tender during this period, there were bills with Lafayette's image in more states than those of any other person except George Washington. One can get a sense of his importance by the number of American cities, towns or counties named for him – about 80 – by the innumerable streets, squares and parks named for him, by the numerous statues and public monuments which memorialize him, by Lafayette College in Easton, Pennsylvania, and by Mount Lafayette in the White Mountains in my home state of New Hampshire.

Lafayette's reputation was revived in the run-up to World War I when his contributions to our successful Revolution were used to justify America's coming to the aid of France and her allies. In 1917, General Pershing led the American Expeditionary Force to France. On July 4, at Picpus Cemetery in Paris, where Lafayette is buried in soil from Bunker Hill, Pershing's aide, Colonel Charles E. Stanton, said: "*Lafayette, we are here.*" Also in 1917, Robert Underwood Johnson published "The Sword of Lafayette," a stirring poem that ends: "Forget us, God, if we forget / The sacred sword of Lafayette."

More recently, there have been at least three commemorative stamps that depict Lafayette: in 1952, the 175th anniversary of his arrival in America to join our Revolution; in 1957, the 200th anniversary of his birth; and in 1977, the 200th anniversary of his arrival in America.

However, today most adults and almost all of our children have no idea who Lafayette was. (My daughter's high-school American-history text had one paragraph that condescendingly referred to him as a young adventurer.) The time has come to restore Lafayette's reputation and to ensure that his important role in our Revolution is recognized. This role included not only his military exploits, especially the Virginia Campaign and the victory at Yorktown, but also his intense lobbying on our behalf in France in 1779 and early 1780. His lobbying was a major factor in the decision by the French Ministry to send 5,000 troops and a portion of the French fleet to Newport in 1780 and to dispatch the French fleet from the West Indies with additional troops in 1781. Without these forces, there would have been no victory at Yorktown.

In this translation I have endeavored to remain as faithful as possible to the original text. Thus, I disclaim responsibility for Levasseur's obvious love of the semicolon and consequently overlong sentences. Spelling of names and places was a challenge. In this regard, I have used the modern spelling whenever possible. On rare occasions I corrected an obvious error made by the author. For example, when he identified "Samuel Hancock" and "John Adams" as the only patriots who were exempted from British General Gage's proposed 1775 amnesty in one of his historical flashbacks, I could not resist correcting Levasseur's transposition of their first names in the text. The footnotes appearing at the bottom of the pages, the plates and the map insert are reproduced from Levasseur's original edition. Neither the plates nor the map appeared in the two 1829 English publications.

It dawned on me as I worked that I was frequently translating back to English what Levasseur had originally translated from English to French. This was true with regard to the numerous speeches and toasts that the author reports. However, in only two instances did I consult an English text. The first was Daniel Webster's great oration on June 17, 1825 at the laying of the cornerstone of the Bunker Hill Monument in Charlestown, Massachusetts, which is the climax of the book. The second was John Quincy Adams' farewell address to Lafayette and Lafayette's reply in September 1825. As to the former, I had acquired a copy of Webster's speech that I consulted, but I did not substitute it for an original translation of Levasseur's version. As to the latter, it became apparent to me that Levasseur was translating directly from a newspaper account of the farewell speeches that I had also acquired. In this one instance, I substituted a newspaper account for an original translation.

I believe that this publication, which is being released in time for the 250th anniversary of Lafayette's birth on September 6, 2007, is the first *unabridged* translation of Levasseur's work in the English language. The two English translations I am aware of are not complete. One translation contains only a few of the numerous addresses given to Lafayette and his replies, which best capture the spirit of the times and the love affair between the American people and Lafayette; the other also omits important sections of Levasseur's work. It is my hope that the publication of *Lafayette in America* at this time contributes, along with other publications, events and exhibitions that are being planned to coincide with Lafayette's 250th birthday, to restoring this great man to his proper place in America's history.

INTRODUCTION
Setting the Scene

On the invitation of Congress and President James Monroe, General Lafayette sailed from Le Havre, France on the American merchant ship *Cadmus* in July 1824 for the United States of America, his adoptive country. Although he had last visited these shores in 1784 after the Treaty of Paris formally ended the American Revolution which he had shared the glory of winning on the battlefield, this visit – 40 years later – produced a fervid outpouring of affection from the American people for the last surviving Major General of their Revolution. During his 13-month "Farewell Tour," he visited all 24 states, where he was celebrated and honored on an almost daily basis. There were parades of militia and children, festivals, banquets, speeches, balls, triumphal arches built in his honor, dedications of public monuments – he helped to lay the cornerstone of the Bunker Hill Monument in Charlestown, Massachusetts in June 1825 – and "meet and greets" with the people who came to pay their respects to and to touch the "Nation's Guest" as he was commonly called during his extended visit.

Who was Lafayette? Why did his visit generate the outpouring of emotion that it did? Gilbert du Motier de Lafayette was born to an aristocratic family on September 6, 1757 in the Auvergne region of France. He came from a long line of military figures: an ancestor fought in the Crusades, another fought with Joan of Arc against the British, and his father had been killed by the British in the Seven Years' War in 1759. Having received a classical education and being inspired by our Revolution and its republican ideals, Lafayette obtained a commission in the Continental Army from Silas Deane, America's representative in Paris, in late 1776. In April 1777, not yet 20 years old, Lafayette sailed for America on a ship purchased and provisioned with his own funds. Commissioned as a major general, he met Washington in Philadelphia in the summer of 1777 and joined his ragtag troops in Pennsylvania.

In his earliest involvement in the Revolutionary War, Lafayette displayed prudent judgment in war councils and courage on the battlefield, and he quickly became a dear friend and trusted confidant of Washington. In September 1777 shortly after his 20th birthday, he was wounded at the Battle of the Brandywine, Pennsylvania, where he impressed his American comrades with his personal courage and sangfroid. These qualities led Washington to petition Congress to grant Lafayette command of a division in the Continental Army, and Congress authorized the command in December 1777. Washington also relied on Lafayette's diplomatic skills. In the summer of 1778, during the Rhode Island campaign, Lafayette mediated a "truce" between feuding allies, after New Hampshire's General John Sullivan accused General-Vice Admiral Charles-Henri, Count d'Estaing, who had arrived with a French naval squadron of leaving the scene of an invasion.

During a lull in the War, Lafayette returned to France in early 1779 to lobby King Louis XVI and his ministers for more material aid, loans, French troops and the return of the French fleet to the United States. The French Ministry eventually approved his plan, and Lafayette returned to America in 1780. He was followed by General Rochambeau and 5,000 French troops, who arrived in Newport, Rhode Island with a small naval squadron in July 1780. In April 1781, Lafayette brought the 1,200 continental troops under his command to Virginia. In his famous "Virginia Campaign," he began a lasting friendship with Thomas Jefferson, removed the stores of munitions from Richmond just before the arrival of British forces and harassed Cornwallis' superior forces in a war of skirmishes until, at long last, major help arrived in September 1781. At this time Lafayette was joined by Washington and the troops under his command, French forces under General Rochambeau and the French West Indian fleet, having arrived from the West Indies with additional French troops. Together they defeated the British Army at Yorktown and effectively ended the shooting war.

Now, 43 years after Yorktown and 40 years after his last visit to the United States, Lafayette, "Hero of Yorktown," was returning to his adoptive land. The interim period had not been so kind to him. One of the leaders of the early phases of the French Revolution – co-author of the French Declaration of the Rights of Man and Citizen and head of the National Guard in Paris – Lafayette was forced into exile by the Jacobins and imprisoned in Prussia and in Olmutz, Austria from 1792 to 1797. His freedom won by Napoleon and American officials, he lived as a gentleman farmer at La Grange, his wife's chateau east of Paris. After participating in the legislative assembly during the 100 days of Napoleon's return in 1815, he was in and out of French politics as one of the Liberals elected to the Chamber of Deputies during the Bourbon Restoration and supported revolutions at home in France and in Greece and Poland. In early 1824, as the Government of France became more ultraroyalist, Lafayette and most of his Liberal colleagues in the Chamber lost their seats and he was distinctly "out." (He was to be "in" in 1830 when, at 72, after the Bourbon Monarchy was again overthrown, he turned down the Presidency of a French Republic in favor of the coronation of Louis-Phillipe, who he believed would be a constitutional monarch, and assumed command of the National Guard.)

Thus, President Monroe's 1824 invitation came at a propitious moment, and Lafayette accepted it readily and sailed for America. His was a party of four: the General; his son, George Washington Lafayette; his private secretary, Auguste Levasseur; and his valet, Bastien. Levasseur, a young French officer who had been involved in conspiratorial activities against the Crown in the early 1820s, was engaged to send dispatches to Lafayette's Liberal friends in France. It was hoped that the publication of these dispatches showing the success of the American experiment would revive the Liberals' political prospects. Levasseur also kept a journal of the trip and published it in 1829 under the title *Lafayette in America in 1824 and 1825*.

Why did the "Nation's Guest" engender such a great outpouring of love and admiration during his visit? There were a number of reasons. The time was right. It was the "Era of Good Feelings," James Monroe's mostly successful Presidency, perhaps the most successful term in office since Washington's. It was a time of great optimism and pride in the successes that the liberated American Colonies had achieved, particularly in the North and the West. As Levasseur described it, there was tremendous pride in population growth along with the growth of manufacturing, agriculture, commerce, the arts and sciences and the spread of public education. It was thought that the republican institutions that the Revolution ushered in were the most important cause of the great progress that America had made. Thus, there was an intense feeling of gratitude towards the military and political leaders who had won the Republic. Moreover, preparations for America's Jubilee, the 50th Anniversary of Jefferson's Declaration of Independence, had commenced.

At this time of retrospection and celebration, enter General Lafayette who had risked his life, his fortune, and his sacred honor and spilled his blood at Brandywine for America's cause. Unlike the great living American leaders whose early brilliance had been dimmed by controversial political careers – John Adams, Jefferson and Madison all fall into this category – Lafayette burst on the American scene with his reputation largely intact and unsullied. As reflected in many of the welcoming speeches addressed to Lafayette, Americans were aware of the vicissitudes of Lafayette's long career – his role in the French Revolution, his imprisonment in the imperial dungeon at Olmutz and his more recent support for European and South American revolutions – and they viewed Lafayette's actions sympathetically and with approval. Thus, his 1824–1825 visit became a renewal of his love affair with the American people.

Just prior to a five-month trip he made to America in 1784, which was also marked by displays of the American people's great affection for him,

Lafayette wrote a letter which he could as easily have written about his 1824-1825 visit:

> As to my going to America, I first went to join the Revolution and not for the war… which in support of the Rights of Mankind had become necessary. Now I am going for the people, and my motives are, that I love them, and they love me…. How could I refrain from visiting a Nation whose [sic] I am an adoptive son, and where I have experienced so many marks of affection and confidence?[1]

Lafayette in America covers the General's 13-month marathon tour through each of the 24 States. From the time of his arrival at New York Harbor and the spectacular reception that he received in New York City in August 1824 to his departure from Washington City in September 1825 and the farewell address of President John Quincy Adams, Levasseur chronicles Lafayette's pilgrimage and the ecstatic response of the American people to his noble persona. The speeches were moving, affectionate tributes to this great adoptive American and to the country that he had helped to found. The parades, the banquets, the balls and the triumphal arches all attested to his unmitigated popularity. However, the anecdotes are most telling: for example, the near riot in Newburgh, New York after the people learned that Lafayette would have to depart without joining in the festivities that they had prepared for him due to the delay caused by his ship's running aground earlier in the day.

Levasseur's journal does more than chronicle Lafayette's triumphal tour. It contains numerous digressions from the General's journey that depict a country bursting with pride in its revolutionary past and republican institutions and brimming with optimism born of the great successes that the last half-century had produced, but with the bane of slavery, which Lafayette had consistently opposed for more than 40 years, looming like a dark, threatening cloud.

The journal includes detailed descriptions of most of the states that Lafayette visited including their history, geography, population, constitution and customs. There are numerous flashbacks to the founding of the Colonies, the Revolution and the War of 1812.

---

1. Idzerda, Stanley J., ed., *Lafayette in the Age of the American Revolution: Selected Letters and Papers, 1776-1790* (Ithaca, New York: Cornell University Press, 1977-1983), V, p. 214.

There are sympathetic descriptions of the plight of Native Americans – particularly in the South and the West – who, like America's Blacks, loved Lafayette. There are poignant accounts of Lafayette's visits with the ex-Presidents Adams, Jefferson, Madison and Monroe after his retirement. There is a description of Lafayette's extended stay at the White House with John Quincy Adams and his family. There is an account of Lafayette's passage on the newly constructed Erie Canal. There is even a harrowing account of the shipwreck of Lafayette's steamship on the Ohio River! To sum up, *Lafayette in America* can be seen as a kaleidoscopic series of snapshots of America 50 years after its birth.

WHO WAS LEVASSEUR?

Unlike his contemporary Alexis de Tocqueville who visited America less than a decade later, Auguste Levasseur never became a household name either in America or in France. However, from various sources, I have gleaned enough information about him to provide the bare outlines of his career.

It is clear that Levasseur was a military man. In Lafayette in America, he displays an avid interest in military matters such as caliber of weapons, uniforms, precision in marching and handling of weapons and militia regulations. Prior to the Farewell Tour, Levasseur served as an officer in the 29th Regiment stationed at Neuf-Brisach.[2] In contemporary newspaper accounts of the 1824-1825 trip, he is sometimes referred to as "Colonel Levasseur."

It is known that Levasseur had been involved in the Carbonari conspiracy against the French Monarchy in the early 1820s. He participated in the Belfort plot, an attempt to subvert the garrison in the fortified city of Belfort in Eastern France.[3] Thomas Jefferson adverts to this aspect of Levasseur's early career. In a letter to Lafayette shortly before Lafayette visited Monticello in 1824, Jefferson writes: "[A]nd the revolutionary merit of M. leVasseur [sic] has that passport to the esteem of every American, and, to me, the additional one of having been your friend and co-operator, and he will, I hope, join you in making head-quarters with us at Monticello."[4]

In Levasseur's Foreword, he states that he continued to serve as Lafayette's private secretary for more than three years after their return to France and had entered into a career in industry as of 1829. His revolutionary career, however, had not ended; he participated in the Revolution of 1830 that overthrew the Bourbon Monarchy.

According to Dr. Cloquet, Lafayette's physician who also treated Levasseur: "This brave man [Levasseur] received a ball on the foot, which broke the bones of the tarsus in the attack upon the Louvre in the Revolution

---

2. Neely, Sylvia, *Lafayette and the Liberal Ideal 1814-1824,* (Carbondale, Illinois: Southern Illinois University Press, 1999), p. 257.
3. Ibid., pp. 195, 257.
4. Peterson, Merrill D., ed., *Jefferson Writings,* (New York: The Library of America, 1984), letter of Jefferson to Lafayette, October 9, 1824, pp. 1497-1498.

of 1830."[5] He recovered from his wound and, as of 1834, he was serving as French consul at Trieste.[6]

That Levasseur was a genuine liberal and an exponent of Lafayette's archetypically liberal positions is clear from this book. In *Lafayette in America,* he shares and expounds Lafayette's long-held opinions on the evil of "Slavery of the Blacks" and Lafayette's practical solution of education and gradual emancipation. His treatment of Native Americans mirrors Lafayette's always sympathetic views. His observations on France also appear to reflect Lafayette's well-known political opinions. Like Lafayette, Levasseur considered Napoleon "The Usurper" and was extremely critical of Restoration France under the Bourbon Monarchy. Tellingly, he receives the news of Louis XVIII's death from then Secretary of State John Quincy Adams in 1824 without comment.

The principal reason that Lafayette employed Levasseur as his private secretary in 1824 was to provide dispatches to liberal associates in France for publication in sympathetic French newspapers and journals.[7] This was deemed necessary to fulfill the main purpose of the Farewell Tour – to revive the Liberals' political prospects in France by publicizing the lessons that the successful America experiment in republicanism could teach Europeans.[8] Thus it was that Levasseur came to keep a journal of the Farewell Tour. This journal, I believe, is a perceptive and too-long ignored portrait of America 50 years after its founding.

Alan R. Hoffman
Londonderry, New Hampshire
August 2006

---

5. Cloquet, Jules, M.D., *Recollections of the Private Life of General Lafayette*, (New York: Leavitt, Lord & Co., 1836), I, pp. 41-42.
6. Ibid., p. 42.
7. Neely, p. 257.
8. Ibid.

FOREWORD
by Auguste Levasseur

In publishing the journal of the trip that I made with General Lafayette at this late date, I believe that it is my duty to render an account of the circumstances which have delayed this publication for so long a time.

The functions of private secretary that I fulfilled for General Lafayette continued more than three years after our return. During all this time, I thought that the closeness of my relations with him imposed on me a duty of delicacy not to dispatch from his office a narrative of which he must necessarily be the principal subject. Ruled by this opinion, I resisted the solicitations of my friends, and I persisted in waiting for the time when, having become totally independent by entering into a career in industry, I would be able to publish my Journal, without any person being liable to sharing with me the responsibility for the opinions or the facts which are written there. Today, this time has arrived, and I do not find it inconvenient any more to deliver to the public some details that are not at all foreign to it, but which are found nowhere else as complete as in the Journal, and which, besides, offer the characteristic of authenticity that it would be difficult to dispute because, apart from the fact that I would be able to invoke the testimony of several million witnesses if necessary, I am able to state, moreover: *All that I tell I have seen.*

Although I need not say it, in offering to my friends and to the public the details of a triumph that honors the nation that conferred it as much as the man who was its subject, the recitation of which will be one day, I hope, the greatest encouragement that one would be able to offer to the sincere friends of a wise liberty, I am less concerned with embellishing my narration than I am with preserving that characteristic truthfulness that will be its greatest, and perhaps even its sole, merit. Carried along for 14 months in the middle of the whirlwind of popular festivities that followed uninterruptedly on the footsteps of Lafayette in the 24 States of the Union, I was able to write my Journal only during the brief hours of the night, and, if I may say so, even in the presence of the events of the day. It must necessarily have felt the effects of this extreme restlessness; however, I did not believe that I should cause it to undergo any change except for a division into a certain number of chapters, of which each forms a series of facts that are more intimately linked either to a time period or to a locality. This division appeared to me to be so much more suitable, as it has allowed me to leave out all the dates which obstruct the narrative, and a crowd of details which would not have any interest except for a small number of individuals.

VOLUME ONE

G.al LAFAYETTE.

Chapter I

Invitation of the United States Congress to General Lafayette – Departure from Le Havre – Crossing – Arrival at Staten Island – Entering New York – Review of the Militias – Festivities Given to Lafayette – Statistics of the State of New York – Its Constitution, etc.

Nearly a half a century had elapsed since Lafayette, inspired by love of glory and of liberty, had torn himself from the sweet affections of his family and from the dangerous charms of the Court, to offer the support of an illustrious name and a mighty fortune to a nation which was fighting courageously, it is true, for its independence, but whose weakness seemed destined to cause its complete ruin in a struggle apparently so unequal. Since his return to France, Lafayette, although entirely occupied by the French Revolution, for the success of which he sacrificed his fortune and his tranquillity, and sometimes risked his life and his popularity, often looked back at his recollections of America; and in the prison of Olmutz, under imperial despotism, he consoled himself with the thought that, at least, the tree of liberty which he had helped to plant was bearing fruits as sweet as they were plentiful, and that there existed a people both happy and worthy of it, who maintained toward him a lively sense of gratitude; but restrained by reasons of more than one kind, he could only harbor the desire of seeing America again without foreseeing, however, whether he would be able to return there one day.

The trust of his fellow citizens, who, after the events of 1815, called him back to the political scene, seemed to be still another reason for him to stay in France; however, in 1824, the intrigues of a Government, as corrupted as it was corrupting, having removed him from representation of the Nation, he was free at the moment that the President of the United States addressed to him the following letter:

> Washington City, February 7, 1824
> My dear General, about 15 days ago, I wrote you a letter that I entrusted to Mr. Brown and in which I expressed to you my desire to dispatch, in the French port that you will indicate to me, a frigate to bring you here, in case you may be free to visit the United States now. Since that time, the Congress has passed a resolution on this subject in which it expresses to you the sincere attachment of the entire Nation, which ardently desires to see you again in its midst; the time in which you believe that you can respond to this invitation is left totally to your choice; but know that, whatever your decision may

be, it will suffice to have the kindness to inform me so that, as soon as possible, I may give the orders for a vessel of the State to pick you up at the port which you indicate and bring you to this adopted country of your youth, which has always retained the memory of your important services. I am sending to you herewith the resolution of Congress, and I add to it the assurance of my high esteem and affectionate feelings.

James Monroe

Lafayette could not refuse an invitation so honorable and pressing, and his departure was fixed in the month of July. He refused the offer of Congress which wanted to send him a ship of the Nation to transport him more securely and more comfortably. He also had to repel a crowd of demands of his fellow citizens, who, believing perhaps that it was a question of a new expedition in favor of liberty, wanted to share the perils and the glory with him; and without any travelling companions except his son and the author of this Journal, he left Paris on July 11 and arrived at Le Havre on July 12, where the American merchant ship, *The Cadmus*, had been waiting for him for several weeks.

The patriotic citizens of Le Havre had prepared a reception very capable of touching his heart; but the disposition of the authorities, which was ridiculously easy to offend, interfered with the celebration, and would have transformed it into a scene of disorder and perhaps of blood, if the inhabitants had been less wise. Agents of the police, militia and Swiss mercenaries contended with the zeal of the citizens expressing their noble sentiments during the short time that General Lafayette stayed among them. However, it was in the presence of the entire population and in the midst of the most lively demonstrations of public spirit that he embarked on the 13th at noon.

The perfectly calm sky and sea permitted us to pass easily aboard our ship, which was at the dock. All the crew, lined up on the deck, waited for the arrival of the General with an expression of joy mixed with a noble pride. At the moment when he passed under the American flag, which owed to him such a great part of its glory and its independence, the crew greeted him with a triple *huzzah*, to which all the boats in the port responded, as well as the crowd which had remained ashore. Some special friends of the General, who had accompanied him on board *The Cadmus*, received his last farewells. Almost immediately, a strong breeze, filling our sails, carried us out to sea, and made us lose sight of this cherished land, on which, no matter what they may say and do, virtue and patriotism shall always find courageous defenders.

With a good ship as skillfully commanded and maneuvered as was *The Cadmus*, we could only have a favorable crossing. The blast of wind which beset us the next morning, and which broke two topgallant masts, only resulted in furnishing us another occasion to admire the equanimity of our excellent Captain Allyn in his command, and the vigor of his crew in carrying out his orders.

On August 1, the wind died off suddenly; the sea became immobile, and our trip was suspended. Gathered on deck with four young American passengers around the General, we were contemplating with pleasure the smooth surface of the sea, which moved not at all, when suddenly, near the horizon, we caught sight of a black dot which seemed to advance toward us. For nearly a half hour, we lost ourselves in conjecture about what this object, which was evidently approaching us with sufficient speed, could be; finally, before long, the movement of oars revealed to us a longboat; and the sound of a bugle[1] made us suspect that it was carrying soldiers.

We were not deceived. In less than a few minutes, the light skiff carrying seven uniformed men, of whom two were armed with rifles, drew up near our ship. The head of this adventuresome troop, measuring with a bold look the elevation of the side of the ship, demanded the rope-ladder in order to arrive among us; it was thrown to him, and soon he and his companions were on deck. In a slightly cavalier tone, they announced that they were English officers, that a transport ship, which they pointed out to us on the horizon and which, like ours, was delayed by the calm, was transporting them to Halifax (Nova Scotia), where they were going to be stationed; and lastly that the beauty of our ship, boredom and curiosity had spurred them to come to visit us. Our Captain greeted them with a cold politeness, our sailors hardly turned away from their work; but their appearance as well as their boastfulness seemed to remind our young American passengers of the burning of the Capitol.

Despite this not very encouraging reception, the English officers now began to multiply their questions, when Captain Allyn, as his only answer, pointed out to them General Lafayette by name; at this name and at this unexpected sight, their manners changed entirely. They took off their hats, and they received with respect the hand which he cordially offered to them. Then, they were invited to descend into the cabin, where they were served refreshments. They were engaged in conversation; but often during the conversation, they extended their gazes at one time toward the General, at another toward all the admirable details of the ship and the crew, and this examination seemed to throw them into a great preoccupation. Indeed, what memories must the sight

1. A horn with keys invented in England.

of these Americans, yesterday their dependents, today their formidable rivals, conducting in their midst the man who so powerfully aided them in that courageous and just struggle for liberty and against oppression have awakened in them! After a half-hour of conversation, they left us while accepting with good grace some bottles of Bordeaux and Madeira which our Captain had brought to their longboat.

We continued our trip without another important incident, up to the 14th, the day when we finally detected land. On the 15th, at daybreak, the pilot was alongside us, and some hours later, we could easily make out the fresh verdure which adorns Staten Island and the charming white cottages which enliven it, and the movement of its citizens whom the anticipation of a great event caused to descend to the shore with all possible speed. Already the sea around us was covered by a throng of longboats, narrow and light, steered by some vigorous and agile sailors, of whom the neatness of their clothes and the modesty of their expressions contrasted remarkably with the idea which the sight of simple seamen generally gives rise to in Europe.

When one of the boats arrived near our ship, it slackened its motion; its drivers, casting a worried look toward our deck, inquired of our crew if they had Lafayette on board; as soon as they had received an affirmative response, joy burst out on all their faces; they threw themselves toward one another, while shaking each other's hands, and while congratulating each other on the good fortune which they were going to enjoy; and then, turning back toward the vessel, they asked a thousand questions on the health of the General, on the manner in which he had borne the crossing, etc.; but without shouts, without disorder, without impatience. We listened to them rejoice among themselves that Lafayette's voyage had been gentle and speedy, that his health had not been disturbed, that, finally, the wishes of their fellow citizens were going to be fulfilled; and all that as if a family which rejoiced at the return of a dear and long-awaited father had said it.

While I contemplated this scene so interesting and novel for me, the noise of a cannon caught my attention from another side; it was the artillery of Fort Lafayette, which was announcing the arrival of *The Cadmus* to the City of New York. At the same time, a steamboat came alongside us, and we received a delegation on board, at the head of which was young Tomkins, son of the Vice President of the United States. He came to announce to the General that, this day being a Sunday, the City of New York, which desired to make a brilliant reception for him, but which did not wish to disturb the Lord's Day, and which besides had still some preparations to complete, requested that he postpone his entry until the morrow; the Vice President was inviting him to come to his house on Staten Island while he waited. The General accepted the invitation, and in a little while we were on the shore, where we found the Second Magistrate of a great republic, on foot in peaked cap and jacket, who, cordially, welcomed his old friend, who on the next day was going to commence, in the midst of 12,000,000 free men, the most brilliant and the purest triumph. Mr. Tomkins showed us to his house, where we were received by Mrs. Tomkins and their daughter. But the news of Lafayette's arrival spread quickly into the vast City of New York, and the Bay was already covered with boats, which were carrying a crowd of citizens who were rushing toward Staten Island in order to address to him these first greetings, this *welcome*, which was enthusiastically repeated afterwards by the entire Nation.

On the next day, the 16th, the preparations to welcome the General in New York had been completed; and at the same time, at Staten Island, he received a delegation of the City – several members of the municipal body, and the Commanding General of the militias, who came to announce the arrival of the Steamship, *The Chancellor Livingston*, which was to carry him to New York. At one o'clock, the cannon of Fort Lafayette gave the signal for the departure. Immediately, we descended to the shore, where we found several steamships, like floating palaces. On board *The Chancellor Livingston*, which received us, were diverse delegations of the City, some generals and officers of the militias, the army and the navy, a detachment of infantry, and more than 200 principal citizens of New York, among whom the General recognized several of his former comrades-in-arms who came to rush headlong into his arms, while congratulating themselves on seeing him again after so many years and so many dangers had passed. During these touching scenes of remembrance and of joy, a charming band played the French tune *Where can one be better than in the bosom of his family*, and the flotilla put out to sea.

It is impossible to describe the majesty of this sail towards the City. The sea was covered with boats of all kinds, elegantly decked out, and loaded with an innumerable throng. These vessels, all of whose movements were of an inconceivable lightness and speed, seemed to fly about around us. *The Cadmus*, which followed in our wake, appeared to have been carried in triumph rather than towed by the two steamships which accompanied it. As we advanced, the forts which protected the harbor, and then the houses which ran along the embankments, assumed a form more distinct to our eyes. Soon we were able to recognize the crowd which covered the shore everywhere, discern its excitement and make out its shouts of joy. Finally, at two o'clock, the General disembarked in the Battery, in the midst of acclamations of 200,000 voices, which hailed and blessed his welcome. *The Lafayette Guard*, clad in a uniform both elegant and simple, and wearing on their breasts the portrait of their General, rushed him into their midst and accompanied him up to the front of a long battle line formed by the militias which were waiting for them. Accompanied by a chief of staff, he traversed the front of the line, which was numerous and gleaming. As he advanced, each corps tilted its flag and arms before him; all were arrayed with a ribbon imprinted with his portrait and with this inscription: *"Welcome, Lafayette."* These words were found written everywhere and were repeated by every mouth. During this review, the cannons reverberated on the shore, in forts and on all the warships. "Ah, may this *cannon of welcome* resound in Europe," a young American officer who accompanied us said to me. "May it inspire in the powerful who govern you the love of virtue and in the people the love of liberty." These wishes, which were like those of my heart, brought my thoughts back towards my Fatherland, and I could not hold back a sigh.

At the end of the battle line were carriages which awaited us. The General was placed on a chariot harnessed to four white horses; and, in the middle of a crowd which pressed upon it on all sides, we proceeded to City Hall. On this passage, all the streets were decked out and adorned with bunting; and from the crossroads, the people threw flowers and wreaths. Having arrived at City Hall, he was greeted by the Municipal Council, at the head of which was the Mayor, who addressed to him the following speech:

> General, as the voice of the authorities and the people of New York, I come to express to you the pleasure which we have in seeing you arrive in a land which owes you, in part, its success and its freedom. Your companions-in-arms, of which only a very small number still live, have not forgotten, and their descendants will never forget the young, brave Frenchman who dedicated his youth, his talent and his fortune in defending their cause, and who risked his life and spilled his blood for their well-being and their independence. As long as they will be worthy of the liberty which they enjoy, they will remember that you appeared on these shores, at the most threatening moment of their Revolution, and that you made common cause with them at the time when their cause appeared to be desperate. A half a century has elapsed since these great events, and, during this interval, your name has become as dear to the friends of liberty of the old continent as it was already to those of the new. The people of the United States regard you as one of their most beloved sons, and I hope, General, that their conduct will prove the error of those who claim that a republic is always ungrateful to its benefactors.

After the General had expressed gratitude for the honorable reception which he had just received, and for the wonders which he had just witnessed, they led us on to the colonnade of City Hall to see the very same army of militias, which we had found in battle array in the Battery, march by. We could easily observe its composition and its dress. Its composition is that of a truly national army, that is to say formed all of young citizens, vigorous, capable of bearing arms and withstanding fatigue, without discrimination on account of wealth or birth. The confident march of the divisions and the martial appearance of the men appeared to me proof of the care with which each one had prepared himself to be a firm defender of his country, if necessary. The artillery, which marched after the infantry, was formidable in number, but I believe that it was far from fulfilling the conditions necessary to make a good light artillery. The variety of caliber of firearms was necessarily an impediment for the provisioning of ammunition in a campaign. This disadvantage will disappear soon, they say, because the Government has now committed to furnish gunnery to each new company which is organized, and it has approved only a very small number of calibers.

After the army had marched by, we entered a large room of City Hall, which was decorated with portraits of many men who, by their talent and their courage, have rendered some service to the Fatherland; among these portraits was one of General Lafayette. The doors of the hall stayed open to the public, which rushed in; and the General was, as it were, delivered up to the admiring people for over two hours. Some mothers surrounded him while presenting their children, for whom they requested his blessing; and after it was secured, they carried them away, while embracing them with a new tenderness. Some feeble old men seemed to be revitalized by speaking of the numerous battles in which they had joined with him in the conquest of liberty. Some men of Color reminded him with tenderness of his philanthropic efforts at various times in order to remove them from the ranks of those whom frightful prejudices still oppress in some regions. Some young men, whose rough and blackened hands announced the necessity of working, stopped in front of him and said to him with pride: "We also are of the number of ten million who owe to you our happiness and freedom . . . !" Many others wanted to speak to him, but were prevented by their tears of emotion. Those who could not approach him attempted to compensate by addressing George Lafayette, whom they took pleasure in pressing into their arms, while telling him of their admiration for his father.

Finally, at five o'clock, the General tore himself away from the embraces of his numerous friends with difficulty and was brought to the City Hotel, which had been readied magnificently to welcome him. The national flag hanging above the door indicated from afar the residence of the *Nation's*

Guest, a glorious and touching title by which he was greeted with cheering when he entered. A splendid dinner party, which all the civil and military authorities attended, concluded this day, which alone could be considered as a beautiful reward for the greatest of sacrifices and which, however, was only the prelude of the unique triumph reserved for Lafayette.

During the four days that followed, the General had great difficulty dividing his time in a manner to satisfy the wishes of everybody. He devoted two hours each day to the public in the large room of City Hall, into which the crowd thronged as it did on the first day, and where he received numerous delegations from the surrounding towns, or from different States, who expressed the desire and the hope to receive a visit from him. The rest of the time was absorbed in fetes that the learned societies of the City offered to him.

The Historical Society, having convened an extraordinary assembly under the presidency of Dr. Hosack, received the General and his son as honorary members of the Society. The Bar, the Society of the Cincinnati and the French residents of New York arrived to congratulate him. These latter, numbering more than 200, joined together under the Presidency of Mr. Monneron, expressed to him warmly the feelings that the triumph of their compatriot aroused in them. "General," they said to him,

> It is in the name of the French who have settled in this City that we come to congratulate you on your joyful arrival on this hospitable soil, on this land, the sight of which must have awakened in you such sweet sentiments; where you cannot take a step without encountering a memory which must be dear to you. For a soul such as yours, there is no purer pleasure than to see the principles that you have defended in the field of honor and in the parliament sanctified by the happiness of an entire people. The freely given and spontaneous homage of this generous and enlightened people is a striking lesson for the mighty of the earth. It teaches them that, even if a nation forgets its oppressors or remembers them without indignation, it leaves the names of a Washington and a Lafayette as a legacy to the gratitude of its descendants. We do not even try to express to you the emotion that we feel in seeing you as the Guest of America. We cannot refrain from making a wish that is worthy of you. It is that this beautiful France, our common Fatherland, which has founded some free institutions also, be forever a stranger to the intrigues and the passions of despotism.

At the end of this speech, a little girl carried by her father came to embrace the General and placed a wreath of perennials on his head. "This is great honor for me," he responded with deep feeling.

> It is a great honor for me, on my arrival in this land of liberty, to receive the compliments of my compatriots. Already, at the moment of my departure, the displays of kindness of the good City of Le Havre had left some very sweet memories in my heart. I love sharing with you the emotions that I am experiencing in this happy American land to which I am attached by so many bonds. We patriots of 1789 also wanted to establish the dignity, the prosperity and the happiness of our beautiful France on the sacred foundations of liberty and equality; and, despite our miscalculations and our misfortunes, the contemporaries of this period, especially your respected President, will tell you that the Revolution of '89 has greatly improved the lot of the vast majority of the people . . . .

At this recollection of the beautiful days of our Revolution, everyone was moved; each came to clasp the hand of the General, while saying to him: "Yes, the lot of the vast majority of the people has been improved. Let France preserve what remains to it of the public freedoms won by the Revolution!"

On the 18th, the National Navy wanted also to hold a festival for the Nation's Guest, who crossed the East River on a steamship in order to reach Brooklyn, where the naval construction yard and dockyard stood. In this short crossing, the General was saluted by artillery fire of several frigates and men-of-war which were in his path. This trip, which the naval officers surely made at one and the same time agreeable and interesting, furnished us the occasion of visiting a beautiful steam frigate. This formidable machine resembled a floating fortress; its sides, supported by strong masonry, are cannon-proof; its movement, necessarily very slow, does not permit it to maneuver on the high seas, but leaves it no less appropriate for the defense of the coasts where she could, at will, cover the places menaced by the enemy while putting herself under the protection of the shore batteries. They say that the Government intends to complete its system of maritime defense by the construction of several similar frigates.

From Brooklyn, we could easily catch sight of New York, of its Port and of its immense Bay; it is difficult, I believe, to see anything more picturesque and, at the same time, more imposing. The Hudson River and the East River, which is only an arm of the sea which runs between Long Island and the continent, wash two sides of a vast triangle which encloses the City, and they come in front of the Battery to merge their waters into the deep Bay which shapes Long Island and Staten Island; from the wide embankments which run along these two watercourses, one sees, in all seasons, a forest of masts which display to the eyes the flags of all the nations. The City, which in 1615 was only a small fort built by the Dutch, is today the most populous, largest, richest and most powerful city of the New World. With the exception of City Hall, there is not in New York a single public monument which merits the attention of an artist; but, on the other hand, the width of the streets, the beauty of the walkways, the neatness of the homes, all these are, in a word, perfectly calculated for the health and convenience of the inhabitants. Its size and population have increased each year in a remarkable manner. In 1820, it contained 128,916 residents. One counts 170,000 today. It is necessary to include in this number the population of Brooklyn, which ought to be considered a suburb of New York.

Despite the great advantages of its situation, its commerce and its vigor, New York is not, however, the seat of government of the State of the same name. In this fortunate country, where all is very much more calculated for the advantage and well-being of the citizens than for the satisfaction of the authorities, it is necessary, before all, that the town to be chosen as capital be as much as possible at the center of the State, and New York is at one of its extremities. Besides, this City combines enough other advantages without that one. The safety of its Port, the vastness of its Bay, which could hold all the fleets of the entire world, the ease of its interior communications by navigation of the Hudson, and especially by that great canal which joins the waters of Lake Erie with the Ocean, will always make it one of the most important commercial localities.

More than 80 steamships, ever ready to brave adverse winds, carry the products, not only of New York State, but also of the neighboring States, in all directions. In 1820, the export trade made by the Port of New York was about $13,162,000, of which $7,899,000 originated from the particular products of the State. These details, which were given by a naval officer while I was letting my eyes roam over the imposing scene which surrounded me from Brooklyn Heights, piqued my curiosity deeply and caused me to resolve to seize the first favorable opportunity to get some fuller particulars about a city and a state which appeared to me, all of a sudden, to have so much grandeur and prosperity.

I did not have to wait long for this opportunity: the same evening, after a dinner which had been enlivened by the presence of a large number of distinguished men of New York, I found myself beside Mr. M....., an old man whose conversation, always interesting and instructive, had taught me that, after having dedicated his youth to the conquest of independence for his country, he had not ceased, afterwards, to apply his thoughts to the means of enhancing the well-being of its citizens. Despite the circumspection that I brought to my initial questions, he soon divined my wish and, having made me sit in a corner of the room, he said:

> I hope that, although our Country may still be very young and that it may not yet have received the benefits of a lengthy civilization like Europe, you will not have any less pleasure in visiting it. You will not find here, as in France, the Arts and Sciences carried to that high stage which is the talk of all the nations; but you will encounter everywhere peace, abundance and liberty; everywhere you will see a large and active population, easily obtaining the necessities by an industry which the authorities never have the right to fetter; and this picture is rare enough, I believe, in Europe to attract your attention here. But without going into the details, which it is better that you gather yourself during your trip, I want, by a brief account of the history and the statistics of this State, to show you some results in which you will probably be forced to acknowledge the influence of our institutions which we are not vain enough to consider to be perfect, but which we believe still to be superior to those of all the nations which have preceded us in the immense course of civilization. Our origin is not lost like yours in the night of the ages, and the gods have not taken the trouble to mark the interest which they took in our first settlements by miracles; also Science and History are not with us the monopoly of some chosen few. They are in the national domain, of which the boundaries, still very recent, can easily be explored and recounted by each one of us.
>
> It was in 1609 that the Hudson River was discovered by a seafarer who gave it his name. Already in 1610, some Dutch had built their huts alongside Indian dwellings, but it was only in 1619 that the settlements acquired stability. Soon after, the English came to contend with the Dutch for a land which belonged to neither the one nor the other and the ground was stained with blood and covered by fortresses. Finally, in 1674, a treaty was signed, about which the legitimate landowners were surely not consulted, assuring peaceful possession to the English. In 1683, the Colonists first convened a house

of representatives to regulate their interests; but three years later, James II of England was frightened by the representative system and by the publications of the press, and outlawed both. The reign of Mary, who took the throne in 1689, restored liberty to the Colonists, who convened their representatives again in 1691. Then, the population was increased considerably by immigrants from Germany, who came in great numbers to settle in the province. The first newspaper published in the Colony was printed in 1733; but the following year the press was curtailed anew, and the Colonists fell under arbitrary rule again. In spite of the despotism which weighed on the Colony for the following 20 years, the people were nonetheless very attached to England and took a very active part in the war which this power made with France in 1754. Finally, in 1765 the patience of the people was pushed to its limit; they burned the law which established stamps; they refused imports from England, and they fervently engaged in revolutionary warfare. The State of New York was the theater of operation during the whole time that this war lasted, and the City was almost constantly in the control of the enemy; but the ardor of the people did not abate. I will not go into each of the details of this glorious campaign which had our liberation as its result. Situated as you are near the man who shared in the works of our immortal Washington, you have, no doubt, the opportunity to garner often from his lips more exact and more interesting accounts of these events than I would be able to give you. I am going, therefore, to pass immediately to the picture of our present situation.

Since the peace of 1783, our State has made all kinds of astonishing progress; our territory has been enlarged considerably; and our boundaries have been fixed by treaties with the neighboring States. Now we are bordered on the *North* by the States of Vermont, Massachusetts and Connecticut; on the *South* by New Jersey and Pennsylvania; on the *West* and *Northwest* by upper Canada, from which we are separated by Lake Erie, Lake Ontario and the Niagara and St. Lawrence Rivers. So limited, our territory has an area of 46,200 *miles*. So at most 80,000 people populated this immense area at the beginning of our Revolution; in spite of the Revolutionary War, which lasted nearly eight years, the number of inhabitants increased, and, at the peace of 1783, it was about

200,000, a number a little higher than the current population of the City alone. Since that time, growth has taken place in a progression which suffices alone, I believe, to demonstrate the superiority of our institutions over the Colonial regime which we were rid of. In 1790, the general census found us with a population of 349,120; in 1800, 586,050; in 1810, 959,040; in 1820, 1,372,812; and, finally, today we count a population of 1,616,000.

Our Agriculture, our Manufacturing, and our Commerce have expanded by reason of the increase in our population. Wheat is the principal product of the Southern part of the State; and, in the West, we harvest hemp in great quantities. At least 280,000 people are employed in Agriculture, and they keep 7,160,967 acres of good land in full productiveness. We would easily be able to find in the State 1,530,421 horned animals; 3,496,628 horses; and 1,467,573 pigs. Nearly each county has a Society of Agriculture created by the most enlightened men, and they attend successfully to the progress of Agriculture, and even the Arts and Sciences.

Capital of more than $15,000,000 and about 70,000 people are employed in manufacturing of all kinds, which are principally located in the environs of New York City, on the banks of the Hudson, near Utica, and in the fertile regions of the West. One of the last censuses informed us that we have 170 iron works; 125 oil crushing mills; 2,000 potash mills; 250 wool and cotton mills; 1,222 cloth mills; 1,129 distilleries; 1,584 carding machines; 2,264 flour mills; 5,195 sawmills . . . .

"But I see," my obliging guide said, while breaking off his discourse, "how I astonish you by all these details. You believe perhaps that I exaggerate, or that my memory, enfeebled by age, recalls imaginary numbers . . . . Well, you can easily convince yourself of the correctness of my calculations; take the excellent work of Melish, entitled *Geographic Description of the United States*, a book written with care and from the most authentic documents, and you will find there many other tables which escape my memory for the moment; and which will increase your astonishment far more. If you knew our institutions," he added, becoming animated, "you would understand better how, with us, each person enhances his prosperity and success every day, inevitably redounding to the benefit of the community. Our Government, simple and economical, does not need, like yours, to seize the necessities from the citizens often in order to defray the expenditures that no one has the power or the courage to control. What each of us earns by his work in a year remains with him and increases his habits of industriousness for the following year; from this comes the rapid growth of wealth which surprises you so greatly." He continued as follows:

> It remains for me now to speak to you about the form of our Government. I will be very brief because it is late, and I believe that you must renew, by some hours of sleep, the strength which you will need to combat the fatigue of the festivities that you know have been prepared for a long time on the route which General Lafayette is to travel.
>
> The Constitution of the State of New York was adopted in 1777; it was amended in 1801 and again in 1821. The authors of our first Constitution thought, with reason, I believe, that a people ought always to have the right to modify its laws as its situation and needs change; and we have already taken advantage of this right twice, as I have just told you, and it is assumed that our children, taking advantage of our experience and their enlightenment, will yet perfect this work of their ancestors. This Constitution thus revised approximates very much those of the other States of the Union and establishes three powers in the State. These three powers deriving from the people are: the legislative, the executive and the judicial powers. The legislative power is entrusted to a Senate and a House of Representatives. The Senate is composed of 32 members chosen for four years, and a quarter of it is renewed each year. In order to be a Senator, one must be 30 years old and be a landowner. The House of Representatives is composed of 128 members chosen every year by the different counties, proportionally to their population. The executive power is entrusted to a Governor chosen every two years. The Governor has the right to appoint all the public employees, but his choices must be approved by the Senate.
>
> The judicial power resides in a Court of Appeals composed of the Senate, the Chancellor and some Judges of the Supreme Court. The Judges of the Supreme Court, like those of the District Courts, are not removable, but cannot serve any more after the age of 60.

"What," I exclaimed. "At 60 years a judge is declared to be incapable! Do you believe, then, that the faculties of man have such near limits, or, indeed, that this premature incapacity is one due to your climate?" "Neither the one nor the other," he answered. "It is simply a great mistake committed by the authors of our political code. It will be fixed, I hope, at the next revision of our Constitution. It is absurd, as a matter of fact, to dismiss a judge at the moment when time and experience have enlightened his mind and ripened his judgment; it is cruel also to retire him at an age when there is not left to him enough time any more, nor enough strength, to embark on a new career, and to expose him, consequently, to end in misery that which he had so honorably begun in serving his country." He continued:

> Every White man having attained the age of 21, having resided for six months in the State, and paying any tax during the electoral year, has the right of suffrage. Every Colored man 21 years old, enjoying the right of citizenship for three years, a landowner, and paying a tax of $250, also has the right to vote. This distinction between the colors must surprise you; I will not undertake to justify it; I will content myself with begging you to wait to condemn it until you have traversed the entire Union to judge the respective situations of the two races.
>
> This Government, which satisfies all our needs perfectly, is not expensive: for it and its principal employees we do not spend 300,000 francs per year; the revenue alone of our salt works of the West exceeds this sum, so that the money coming from the sale of our national land, from our funds deposited in the banks, from the different hiring out of public or private institutions, is put in reserve for the expenses of the State; so that, when we have some extraordinary expenses, such as the purchase of arms, of military equipment, construction of arsenals, provision of stores, etc., we are not obligated to increase our taxes, which since 1800 have not changed, and which are so small that they do not exceed the thousandth part of the value of property.
>
> Thanks to its economy and its good management, the Government has found a way to apply a fund of $1,730,000 to public education. This year, moreover, the treasury has spent $200,000 for the schools, which have also received more than $850,000 by way of private subscriptions; so that, at this time,

> 7,642 public schools, established in the different districts, combine in the education of 403,000 children and young people; that is to say, a quarter of the population....

The clock struck midnight: everyone had quit the room, and I continued to take in the precise details which Mr. M..... was providing to me, avidly and without thinking of sleep, when suddenly we were interrupted by a great uproar of voices to which were joined almost immediately the sound of bells and the resounding noise of fire trucks which were rolling rapidly over the pavement. "Here is an opportunity that you must not miss," cried Mr. M....., "a fire is breaking out in one of the neighborhoods of the City; go there. By what you will see there, you will learn more about our practices of discipline and policing than all that I would be able to tell you for the rest of the night." This advice was nearly superfluous because, as soon as I could recognize the cause of the uproar, my first movement was to rush headlong toward the door. On the staircase, I encountered George Lafayette, who was descending with the same alacrity as I was. Arriving in the street, we had only to be swept along by the surge of the people in order to arrive promptly at the place of the incident.

After a rather long run, we arrived at the end of a street looking out on the wharves of the East River. It is there that the fire had broken out. The fire had started first in a store filled with combustible materials, and in some homes built of wood. The flames, which rose violently, allowed us to see the scenes of the fire and the crowd which gazed at it distinctly. Five or six thousand people, arrayed on the wharves or having climbed the masts or the yardarms of the vessels which abutted them, kept motionless and nearly silent, as if they were attending a theatrical performance. This silence was interrupted only by the horrible crackling of beams which were at each moment engulfed by the flames, by the monotonous and rhythmical sound of the fire trucks and by the commands of the fire chiefs.

In order to arrive at the foot of the burning homes, we had to cross a large part of the crowd which surrounded them, and that was difficult. But in the gleam of the flames we were recognized by some persons who were near us and who mentioned the name of Lafayette. This name, repeated by each mouth on our passage, was the good luck charm which allowed us to arrive at the spot which we wanted to reach. There, in a vast space left free by the crowd, there were more than 35 trucks, of which only some worked on the fire, the others supplying them by long interconnected fire hoses. Each of these fire trucks carried, on a kind of platform, its chief, armed with a speaking-tube, who was giving commands to a score of men arranged for the maneuver. When the men of a fire truck were worn out, they were instantly replaced by others coming out of the crowd at the command of the chief who cried out in a loud voice: "So many men of such and such company, advance." At once, the number of men requested sprang toward the fire trucks which needed help, and the exhausted men withdrew into the crowd, where they became quiet spectators.

At the head of this crowd were some police officers, who could be recognized by their long white stick, with the aid of which they maintained order, by placing it horizontally in front of the most impatient, and by letting pass only the men requested by the fire chiefs. We recognized, then, that this crowd, so calm and so obedient, was nothing other than the youth enrolled in the fire companies. One of the police officers, who had dined with us the same evening, recognized us and greeted us. "We take very keen interest in the misfortune which necessitates your presence here," said George Lafayette to him, "and we would consider ourselves happy if our feeble services could be useful to you." "We thank you for it," he responded. "You see yourself how their needs are few. However, if you desire to draw nearer in order to judge the result of our efforts better, you can follow me."

He led us to the middle of the fire trucks, and there we saw with what courage and skill these young volunteers dedicated themselves, in the face of the greatest dangers, to preserve the property of the citizens. We stopped for a moment near the fire truck closest to the burning buildings. We offered our arms in service; they accepted, but in a manner which proved to us that it was only out of politeness. After five minutes, the young men who had yielded their places came to take them back, after having shaken our hands fondly. The fire, in spite of its force, had been made to recede by the efforts of so many fire trucks so skillfully operated, and soon we recognized that the danger was entirely removed. As we withdrew, we could not refrain from expressing to the police officer our admiration for the order and the calm that had ruled constantly in the midst of the crowd, which a few officers are sufficient to keep in check and direct, without the aid of a single bayonet or a uniform; and, upon returning to the City Hotel, we agreed that the sight of such an unparalleled scene sufficed to prove to what degree the rule of order holds sway over people who make their laws themselves.

Chapter II

Departure from New York – Route from New York to Boston – Arrival at Boston – Visit to the University at Cambridge – Visit to Charlestown and Bunker Hill.

On August 20, in the morning, we left New York to proceed to Boston in the State of Massachusetts. From daybreak, several militia corps were in battle array in front of the door of the hotel, waiting to accompany the General up to the exit from the City, where the farewell salute was given to him by a battery of six cannons, two of which had been taken from the English at the siege of Yorktown in 1781. A large number of citizens on horseback or in carriages accompanied him up to New Rochelle, where we stopped for some moments to give him the time to receive some of his old companions-in-arms, who, not having been able to come to New York, were assembled to meet with him and shake his hand on his way.

At SawPitts, we met an escort of cavalry which joined with the escort from New York, which wanted to continue its service up to *Putnam* Hill, where a triumphal arch had been built by the toil of the young girls of the neighboring villages; they had decorated it with the greatest possible care and had placed on it an inscription which expressed their gratitude to Lafayette and recalled the audacious flight of Putnam. From the base of the triumphal arch, they pointed out to me the extremely steep slope down which this fearless man rushed headlong to break free of the English, who were nearly overtaking him and who dared not follow him on a road so frightening and so dangerous.

Putnam, having appeared on the scene of the Revolution in which he played a glorious role, had already left the obscurity to which his agricultural life seemed destined to condemn him. Barely an adolescent, he had established a great reputation for strength and fearlessness among his young comrades by going to attack, right into the cave where she had retired, a she-wolf which for several years had become the terror of the district where he lived. In 1755, at the age of 37, he left the plough for the sword and took command of a company of a provincial regiment. In the war which broke out in America between France and England, he earned the admiration and the astonishment of his companions-in-arms as chief of the partisans. One man alone could then be compared to him; and this man was French; his name was Molang. In an encounter between these two leaders, Putnam was beaten and seized. He owed his very life to Molang, who snatched him from the Indians who were making ready to burn him alive; but his reputation did not suffer from this defeat, because he had, by prodigious feats of valor and skill, vigorously contested the victory with Molang.

The news of the battle of Lexington tore him again from the life in the fields which he had resumed for so long a time. His ancient fame very soon rallied under his command a great number of fellow citizens, at the head of which he appeared at the Battle of Bunker Hill. From this day up to the end of the campaign of 1779, a time at which an attack of paralysis forced him to leave the army, he did not let any chance to prove that he had dedicated his life to the cause of liberty escape. His integrity had become proverbial, and the following anecdote will give an idea of the quality of his character. In the Spring of 1777, he had command of a particular corps in New York State. A man named Palmer, a lieutenant of newly levied Tory troops, had been found in his camp; the English Governor, Tryon, claimed him as an officer in the service of the King, and threatened Putnam with all his wrath if he did not return the man to him on the field. Putnam responded with this note:

> Sir: Nathan Palmer, lieutenant in the service of your King, has been arrested in my camp as a spy, judged as a spy, condemned as a spy, and will be hanged as a spy.
> *P.S.* Afternoon. He is hanged.

By the good offices of the public body of New York, three of whose members had been designated to accompany us until our return, numerous excellent relays of horses had been placed at our disposal on the entire route. In spite of this wise precaution, our trip was very slow because we could not pass a hamlet without being kept there for some time by the greetings of the population having rushed there from 20 miles around. Each village had raised its triumphal arch, on which we almost always saw the names of Washington and Lafayette joined, or the date of the Battles of Brandywine and Yorktown. Everywhere announced by cannon fire, everywhere received and complimented by the magistrates of the people, everywhere obliged to set foot on land to receive displays of the love of the entire population, it was only after five days and nearly five nights, that the General was able to arrive in Boston, which was, however, only 200 miles from New York.

I say nearly five nights with reason, because we traveled constantly up to nearly midnight in order for us to set out again at five o'clock in the morning. However, in the middle of these touching and sublime scenes of gratitude of all the people, we were not allowed to think of fatigue: even our travels at night had a charm which made us forget it. The long line of carriages, escorted by horsemen equipped with torches; the fires lit at intervals on the summit of the hills, around which were some family groups which the desire to see their guest had kept awake; the slightly wild sound of the bugle of our escort, repeated several times by the echoes of the valleys; the view of the sea which appeared to us from time to time to our right; the faraway and diminishing sound of the bells which had announced our passage; all, in a word, made an attractive and picturesque scene around us worthy of Cooper's pen. It is in this way that we traversed Fairfield, New Haven and New London in Connecticut, Providence in Rhode Island and, finally, the route from Rhode Island to Boston.

New Haven is the largest city of the State of Connecticut; it is, alternating with Hartford, the seat of government. Its population is more than 7,000; its site on a small bay formed by the East River is pleasant. The short stay that we had there permitted us only to hurriedly visit its college, which enjoys a great reputation, not only in the State of Connecticut, but also in the entire Union. It was founded in 1701, under the name of Yale College, in honor of Elihu Yale, Squire of London, its principal benefactor, then Governor of the Company of the East Indies. The favor which the people have constantly accorded to it has made the college an eminent institution. Today, it contains more than 400 students; there are a President, four Professors, six teachers and a Treasurer. The college is managed by a corporation composed of a Governor, a Vice-Governor, six senior members of the Board and ten faculty members, all members of the clergy. The business of the College is handled by a committee of three or four members who meet four times a year. The courses which are taught are: 1. Theology, which is taught by the President; 2. Mathematics and Natural History; 3. Chemistry and Mineralogy; 4. Languages and Ecclesiastical History; 5. Law.

In order to enter into the first class, the candidate must be capable of translating the Old Testament from the Greek, Virgil and Cicero, and be capable of writing in Latin according to Clarke's Rules; he must also know Arithmetic. The price of board is about two dollars per week.

The library contains more than 6,000 volumes, and a fund producing $200 per year has been allocated to it. The greatest part of academic books, which have great value, came from gifts of the celebrated Berkeley, Bishop of Cloyne in Ireland, who furnished about 1,000 volumes estimated at 400 pounds sterling.

The Chemistry laboratory is remarkable for the number and the selection of its instruments. The Mineralogy collection, which contained to begin with 2,500 specimens, has been enriched considerably by General Gibbs, who bequeathed to it 24,000 for the use of the students. These 24,000 specimens are valued at $20,000.

There is also in Yale College a medical institution whose teachings revolve around the following matters: 1. Theory and Practice of Medicine; 2. Surgery and Obstetrics; 3. Anatomy; 4. Chemistry, Pharmacy and Mineralogy.

The President of the College, its Professors and Administrators led us into all parts of the institution and gave us some details with a kindness and a precision which earned all our gratitude.

They told us that in New Haven there is a fine arms factory, but the little time which the General could spend did not permit us to visit it.

As in the State of New York, and perhaps even more, public education is the object of the most constant concerns of the people and the Government. Thus, it would be difficult to find in this State a child 12 years old who does not know how to read or write. The law of the State requires that each town have a grammar school; there are everywhere a great number of colleges in which the different branches of human knowledge are skillfully taught at little expense. The City of New Haven alone, besides the great Yale College, has, in addition, 16 public schools and eight private schools.

The funds dedicated to the schools have been increased to $1,500,000, of which the interest, with $12,000 coming from public taxes, is used annually toward the expenses of education. Each town receives in proportion to the total amount of its contribution; and the schools are directed and overseen by a committee chosen by the residents, who do not allow anything so important as public education, one of the first guarantees of liberty, to become the monopoly of a religious community or a single university.

The people of Connecticut are rigidly observant of religious practices, but for a long time they have cast off the spirit of persecution which animated the founders of the Colony, whose first ecclesiastical ordinance after taking possession of the land in 1637 denied the privileges of citizenship to all those who did not submit entirely and without reservations to the formalities of the established religion. Today, as religious liberty is established by the law, mutual tolerance of the different denominations has created a sort of fraternity among them; we had very striking proof of this on the Sunday that we spent in New London.

Upon arriving in this City, General Lafayette, in order not to offend the customs of these excellent people from whom he had received such moving proofs of affection, had expressed the wish to attend a Holy Service. Soon the Congregationalists and the Episcopalians, who formed the dominant denominations of the City, offered him their churches. It was difficult to accept the offer of one without offending the other, and the General said to them that he would go willingly to both of them. This response spread great joy in the City. We went first to the Congregational Church, then to the Episcopal Church. We found both of them surrounded and filled with a crowd without distinguishing congregations. In each Church, the sermon turned upon morality without discussion of dogmas and ended with a eulogy *to the one whom God had conducted so many times across the dangerous Ocean in order to assure the happiness and liberty of America.* These sermons were heard with an equal contemplativeness by all. Upon leaving the churches, the two ministers shook hands cordially and congratulated each other on the good fortune which they had had in receiving the Nation's Guest at their churches.

The State of Connecticut has in itself all the elements of prosperity; its fertile soil offers, at the same time, valuable products of the Vegetable and Mineral Kingdoms. Iron, lead, copper, sulfur, antimony, marble, porcelain clay and coal are found there in large quantities in some districts. In order to give an idea of the number, the variety and the activity of manufacturing, suffice it to say that, out of a population of nearly 280,000, manufacturing occupies more than 18,000. Industry owes to Connecticut several useful inventions, among others *Chittenden's* machine to make the cogs of the wool-carding machines, invented in 1784 and very much perfected since that time. This machine was put in motion by a mandrel twelve inches long and one inch in diameter, at each turn of which they make a cog; they make 36,000 per hour. The machine of *Miller* and *Whitney* separates the cotton from its seeds. Before this innovation, the operation was done by hand, and so slowly that one person was able to produce only one pound in a day; by the new process one can produce more than a thousand pounds daily. The invention of this machine was purchased by the Government of this State for $50,000.

William Humphreys' machine spins the wool by means of water. Twelve spindles of this machine do as much work as 40 simple spindles. The right of constructing this machine was purchased at a price of one dollar for each spindle. *Culver's* machine clears basins and removes sandbars which form at the mouth of rivers. By means of this machine, they have hollowed out the channel of the Thames[2] extensively.

In entering the State of Rhode Island, Lafayette experienced a sharp tinge of regret that he was unable to suspend his triumphal trip for a time. It would have pleased him to visit some places which reminded him of so many memories of his youth.

2. Small river of Connecticut.

In 1778, Lafayette had been dispatched by Washington with two brigades in order to go to the aid of Sullivan, who was trying to seize Rhode Island, which the English had occupied since 1776. In order to better assure the success of the operation, they had awaited the arrival of the Count d'Estaing, who was bringing a French naval squadron, which was carrying a landing party, and offered the double advantage of closing off any retreat by sea from the British, and reinforcing the attack that Sullivan was contemplating against Newport. But unfortunately a misunderstanding took place between the Count d'Estaing and Sullivan; the French troops had not landed, and while Lafayette was forced by mediation to restore peace between the two chiefs, the arrival of the English naval squadron commanded by Lord Howe was signaled. Soon, Count d'Estaing, profiting from a favorable wind, left to attack Lord Howe. The two admirals spent two days in maneuvering to take advantage of the wind. Finally, at the time when they were going to come to blows, a terrible storm separated them and treated the two squadrons so badly that one had to return to New York to find shelter and the other made haste to return to lay up in Newport. After the return of the French fleet, Sullivan hoped to resume his military operations; but the Count d'Estaing declared that, after having sought the opinions of his officers, he had decided to leave for Boston. Moreover, his orders stated that, in case his squadron experienced some damage, where it would be threatened by superior English forces, he must seek to withdraw into this Port.

The damage that he had experienced from the storm and the news of the appearance of a very numerous English fleet on the coast justified his withdrawal to Boston, but this retreat threw Sullivan and his army into despair. Without the aid of the French squadron, it was no longer possible to count on success; the squadron took away with it all the hopes that they had conceived. Generals Greene and Lafayette were sent to Count d'Estaing to contest his baleful resolve; they spoke to him heatedly, both about the glorious advantages which French and American arms would draw from his cooperation against the English garrison of Rhode Island, which could not escape him, and about the unfortunate effects which the abandonment by an ally whose presence had at first caused such joy would produce in the spirit of the American Army. They represented to him both the dangers of his retreat across the reefs of Nantucket, with ships in bad condition, and the advantages which Newport offered to him over Boston; as much to repair his vessels as to resist the encroachments of an enemy emboldened by the superiority of its forces. Finally, they concluded by entreating him not to sacrifice the glory and the interest of two nations joined in the defense of so beautiful a cause because of petty private disputes. However weighty all these considerations were, the Count d'Estaing did not persist any less in his decision and set sail at once.

Thus abandoned by the fleet, Sullivan assembled the general officers of his army to garner their opinions on the two courses which were left for them to take: to try to take the place with brisk force or to evacuate the island, while removing all their stores. The discouragement of the army caused by the departure of the fleet rendered the first way difficult to accomplish; the second was heart-breaking for men who had seemed so close to success. Sullivan's council took a middle course and broke up with the resolution to lift the siege, to retire to the northern end of the island, and to entrench there in order to await events. This was accomplished on the very night which followed, with as much luck as skill. Sullivan then brought up again his hopes about the French squadron, and wanted to make a last attempt toward Count d'Estaing. Full of confidence in the great influence which Lafayette exercised over all those with whom he dealt, he charged him with this delicate mission. The latter accepted and left for Boston, but not without ascertaining how great the cost would be for him to separate from his companions-in-arms at the moment when they could not doubt that the enemy would attack soon. In fact, during his absence, the English tested the American position on several occasions, but without success; these diverse engagements had contributed to restoring the confidence of Sullivan's troops. The negotiation of Lafayette resulted in his obtaining a promise of the return of the squadron after all the damage had been repaired.

All finally seemed to promise Sullivan the reward due his tenacity, when the news of a reinforcement of 4,000 men, brought to the English by General Clinton himself, unfortunately, made it necessary to evacuate the island as soon as possible, in order that he not be obstructed on his way. He prepared his withdrawal with rare skill. The maneuver was about to begin when, to Sullivan's great astonishment because he believed Lafayette was still in Boston, Lafayette presented himself to take command of the rear guard. He had traversed the distance from Boston to Rhode Island, which was about 75 miles, in eight hours. This zeal moved Sullivan deeply, and he left Lafayette the leadership of the rear guard. All was executed with so much prudence that at 2:00 a.m. the maneuver was entirely concluded, and the American troops were positioned in safety on the mainland from Providence to Tiverton.

This withdrawal brought Sullivan the thanks of Congress, which also complimented Lafayette, as *much for the sacrifices of personal gratification which he had made in agreeing to leave the army to serve the interests of the United States at the time of a battle, as for the vigorous command he had maintained in leading the rear guard.*

At the intensity of the raptures which burst out from all parts around us upon our arrival in Providence, it was easy to recognize that the people of this region had not at all lost the memory of the conduct of Lafayette at the time of this glorious retreat. The expressions of recognition of the Congress appeared to have been no longer forgotten, for I heard them repeated by every mouth, I saw them written on all the triumphal arches. Despite the solicitations of the people and their magistrates, the General could stop only for the time necessary to take some refreshments; and we hastened to proceed to the Massachusetts border, where two aides-de-camp of the Governor of that State were waiting for Lafayette with new carriages and a new escort. We met them at sunset. Colonel Harris, the first aide-de-camp of the Governor, displayed such alacrity in commanding our trip that we were in Dedham at one o'clock a.m., and at two o'clock a.m., by the light of torches, we entered Roxbury, a delightful village two miles from Boston, where the house of Governor Eustis, who was waiting for the General with animated impatience, is located. In spite of the advanced hour of the night, everyone was awake in this house, where the windows, garden and carriage drives were illuminated. The reception that the Governor gave to the General was straightforward, simple and friendly, as befit a reception by an old republican soldier delighted to see again a former companion-in-arms whose works he had shared. Two hours of sleep made us forget the fatigue of the day and enabled us to make our entrance in Boston on the morrow.

At daybreak, we were awakened by the sound of martial music. It was that of the light infantry, which was already making an exhibition of its maneuvers under our windows. The sight of the uniform of this troop stirred the heart of the General strongly; he could not divert his eyes from it, and he cried out at each moment: "My brave light infantry, it is just like that that it was clad! What courage! What resignation! So much did I love it!" At that moment, an aide-de-camp of the Governor was admitted into his rooms and presented to him a man still young, but with a melancholy countenance. He carried in his hands a sword, which he presented to the General. "Do you know this sword?" said he – "I think that it at least resembles those that I had procured from France in order to arm the non-commissioned officers of my light infantry." – "It is indeed one of these; my father received it from your hands; he used it gloriously in the conquest of our independence; he conserved it scrupulously in memory of his General and would have been happy to present it to you himself. The day before yesterday he still hoped for it, and this hope eased his last moments; but the day before yesterday, he died . . . . Poor, he has not bequeathed riches; but he left me this sword, which will be for me the most precious of possessions, if you approve the gift that he has made to me." While he was speaking, the General took the sword in his hands; he returned it to him, while saying at the same time: "Keep it, guard it carefully so that, in your hands, it can serve to maintain the rights the conquest of which it had so valiantly contributed to in the hands of your father." The American received the sword rapturously and left while uttering the name of his father and Lafayette with emotion.

Shortly after the procession which was to accompany the General arrived, the cannon gave the signal for departure, and we started out. The gathering of the people who had left the City was so large that the road was obstructed by it, and it took two hours to go two miles. The entire route was bordered by militia on foot and on horseback; the carmen from Boston, clad in gleaming white blouses, formed a numerous corps of perfectly mounted cavalry. About 60 small boys from 12 to 14 years old organized a company of artillery and using two pieces of cannon whose caliber was proportioned to their strength, ran to the head of the procession, stopped from time to time to salute Lafayette with a salvo from their battery, and set out again rapidly to take a new position and salute him again.

At noon we were in the suburbs of Boston. At the gate of the City, under a triumphal arch, we met the municipal body. The Mayor, alone in an uncovered carriage, stopped alongside the General's carriage, which was also uncovered; each saluted the other while rising, and the Mayor, beginning to speak immediately, said to him: "You see this people for whom you have fought, it is happy beyond your hopes; its liberty is assured; it relies now on its strength without fear and without reproach. You have shed your blood for three million men, and ten million move forward to you today. This movement is not one of a populace turbulently excited by the sight of the laurels that a young conqueror has recently won; it is the movement of a great people who yield to an impulse, solemn, moral and wholly intellectual." The calm and modest bearing of the General during this speech, the handsome face of Mr. Quincy, which was animated as he spoke, the triumphal arch which rose above them and the scrupulous silence of several thousand citizens offered to my astonished view at this moment the beautiful ideal of a popular celebration, of a republican triumph.

After the General's response, we crossed the City to go to the State House; during this drive, the displays of affection which the inhabitants of Boston lavished on the General were so touching that we could not hold back tears of emotion. In front of the State House, on an immense lawn, where one saw a sea covered by small islands in the distance, was a long double line of young girls and boys of the public schools; all were decorated by a *Lafayette ribbon*, and lifted their little hands towards the sky while uttering cries of joy.

One of the youngest girls came to offer greetings. They lifted her towards the carriage of the General, she placed a crown of perennials on his head, and embraced him while calling him tenderly by the name father. Finally, we entered into the Senate Chamber, where all the public functionaries, the members of the Society of the Cincinnati, the scholars and as many of the citizens as the hall would hold were joined. At the moment when the General appeared in front of Governor Eustis, who greeted him at the door, the national flag was raised on the dome of the State House and all the militias fired their arms.

After the welcoming speech given *in the name of the Government and in the presence of the citizens of the State of Massachusetts*, the scene at City Hall in New York was repeated; that is to say, the General was detained for more than two hours by the displays of friendship of all those who could reach him. Afterwards, they led us to a hotel at the beginning of Park Street which had been prepared to receive us. The Mayor himself showed us to our rooms, which were richly furnished: "Make yourself at home here," he said, "you will find, I hope, all that which is necessary; if you find there nothing superfluous, remember that you are received by republicans. ..." – These words of Mr. Quincy were, doubtless, quite amiable; but I confess that they gave us much to consider about the meaning of *necessary* to the republicans of Boston, especially when we learned that some very beautiful carriages and some very good horses had been put at our deposal for the entire time of our stay in this City.

In the evening, we went to the Exchange Tavern in order to dine with the Govenor, his staff, the municipal body and the other constituent bodies of the City. The hall was decorated and adorned with slogans which recalled both actions of Lafayette and the recognition that the Americans reserved for the help which France gave to them when their fortune, still undecided, was equally balanced between liberty and oppression. The French and American flags, joined together, waved above the head of the president of the banquet, and Mr. Parker, Chief Justice, made a toast to the memory of Louis XVI, while adding that all those who had favored liberty ought not to be forgotten, even when they had worn the crown.

On the 25th at noon, we went to the University in Cambridge to be present at the distribution of prizes, which was made with a pomp considerably enhanced by the attendance of a great number of women whom the desire to see Lafayette, who they knew was supposed to be there, had attracted.

Cambridge is one of the most beautiful and most wealthy villages of New England; it is situated two and a half miles from Boston and contains more than 3,000 inhabitants. Its university, known under the name of Harvard College, in honor of its founder, has produced a large number of men distinguished in

Letters and in the Sciences; also the citizens of Massachusetts, who are proud of its success, sustain it with a liberality which proves how much the lights of learning are honored in this State. Besides the Chairs of Theology, Anatomy and Surgery, Medical Science, Chemistry, Theoretical and Experimental Physics, Mathematics, Natural Philosophy, Logic, Metaphysics, Latin, Greek and Oriental languages, which have existed for a long time, six new chairs and three faculties were established about 12 years ago, as follows[3]: a Chair of Natural History, founded by a private subscription, for the establishment of a botanical garden and the upkeep of a professor; a Chair of Rhetoric and Oratory established by a gift of Ward Nicholas Boylston; a Chair of Greek Literature, founded in 1814 by a gift of an anonymous donor of Boston; a Chair of Spanish and French languages, founded by a rich merchant of Boston who, for this purpose, bequeathed a sum of $30,000; a Chair founded in 1816 by the Count of Rumford; its object is the application of Physical and Mathematical Sciences to the useful arts; the founding capital raised was $40,000; and a Chair established in 1817 for Natural Theology and Moral Philosophy.

The three faculties which make up programs of instruction are: a Medical School; a School of Theology in which they provide, with the aid of a subscription, for the needs and the education of the students, this subscription being punctually filled by persons motivated by love of the public good; and a Law School for those who intend to join the bar. The library, which is composed of nearly 20,000 volumes of selected works, grows each year with private gifts.

Finally, this University, by its revenues, the richness of its library and its rooms, the merit of its professors, and the means that it furnishes to acquire all kinds of education, has no equal, not only in the rest of the Union, but perhaps in all of Europe.

General Lafayette was received at the door of the chapel in which the prizes were given by the President, Mr. Kirkland, who spoke to him with an eloquence which had its source in a heart that was greatly moved. When the General appeared in the hall, the cheering and the rapture of the entire crowd was such that it was not possible to begin the exercises for a long time; it was a truly fascinating picture, namely, that of the immense benches full of young girls crowned with flowers waving their handkerchiefs above their heads in order to salute the one whom they called their father, their friend, their defender, the companion of their great Washington .... In vain, did the President appeal several times for silence without which it was not at all possible to make himself heard; each time his voice was covered up by applause and shouts of *Vive Lafayette*! Finally, after a half hour, calm was restored, and they were able to begin the

3. *Statistical, Historical and Political Description of the United States* by Warden.

exercises which were often interrupted by the fervor with which all allusions to Lafayette encountered in the speeches given in this session were met.

We returned again on the following day to the University in Cambridge in order to attend, in the same hall and in the presence of the same public animated by the same enthusiasm, a session of the Hellenic Society. The opening speech was given by Mr. Everett, a young professor whose talents and precocious eloquence promise to the national rostrum a very distinguished orator. If my pen were more practiced, I would have tried to reproduce here this speech which, despite its length, was listened to till the end with an avid interest by the audience and was often drowned out by well-deserved applause.

The orator proposed to inquire into *the particular causes which contribute the most to the development of intelligence in the United States*. He proved to us, effortlessly, that they were all in the democracy of the institutions. "Our popular institutions," he said,

> Are favorable to the development of intelligence because they are based on Nature's wish, they do not at all condemn the social body to inaction or to humiliation, and they connect to each member of society that vital nerve by which each great and generous impression reacts with an electric speed on the entire society. They extend the benefits of education to all, they push talent, ignored and apprehensive, into the joyous pursuit of competition; in a thousand different ways they prepare numerous audiences for lips that nature has endowed with the skill of persuasion; they place the lyre in the hands of genius; and they bestow on all those who search for it or deserve it the sole patronage worthy of envy, the *patronage of services rendered to society!*

Having demonstrated at great length but vigorously the superiority of Republican Government, as it is conceived and practiced in the United States, over the Monarchial system which, after having divided a part of the nation into nobles, into privileged priests, into soldiers, always armed, into inquisitorial police, made a class of political pariahs of the rest, the orator concluded by paying his tribute of gratitude to Lafayette. "This year," he said,

> Is going to complete the first half-century of the most important era of human history, the era of our Revolution. During this epoch, time has seen most of the great men to whom we owe our national existence fall in the dust that they had

watered with their blood. Few of them still enjoy the sweet fruits of their works and their sacrifices among us; however, here is one of them who, yielding to the voice of the people, comes at the end of his career to receive the respects of a nation to which he had sacrificed his youth. American history has not at all forgotten that when this friend of our country applied to our Commissioners sent to Paris in 1776 in order to request the means of proceeding to America, they were obliged to answer him (so poor and wretched was our dear country then) that they had neither the means nor the credit to equip a single vessel in all the ports of France. Well, said the young hero, I will equip one myself. And it is a fact literally true that, although America was too miserable to transport him to its border, he did not hesitate, at a still tender age, to leave family, success, riches, and high rank in order to engage in the bloody and doubtful struggle of our Revolution.

Greetings! Friend of our fathers! May you be welcome on our shores! Happy are our eyes to look upon your venerable features! Enjoy a triumph, which is reserved for neither conquerors nor monarchs, the assurance that here in all America there is not a heart which does not beat with joy and gratitude at the sound of your name. You have already received, or you will receive soon, the greetings of this small number of ardent patriots, wise counselors, and intrepid warriors with whom you were associated in the conquest of our liberty; but it is in vain that you will search around you for all those who would have preferred, to years of life, a day like this one passed with their former companion-in-arms. Lincoln, Greene, Knox, Hamilton are dead; the heroes of Saratoga and of Yorktown are fallen before the only enemy whom they could not conquer; and the greatest of all, the first of heroes and men, the friend of your youth, the savior of the country, rests in the bosom of the land that he emancipated. On the banks of the Potomac, he rests in peace and glory. You will visit again the hospitable house of Mount Vernon; but the one whom you venerate will not be on the threshold any more to welcome you; his voice, that comforting voice which reached you in the dungeons of Austria will break the silence no more to offer you a seat at his hearth; but the children of America will greet you in his name and cry out to you: Welcome Lafayette! Three times welcome on our shores, friend of our fathers and of our country!...

On the 27th, rather early in the morning, some carriages, an escort of cavalry, the civil and military authorities, and a great number of citizens came to call for the General in order to conduct him to the Naval Yard situated at Charlestown, which is separated from Boston only by an arm of the sea that one crosses over on a very beautiful bridge, more than a mile long. We were welcomed at the naval arsenal by Commodore Bainbridge, whose name calls to mind more than one glorious battle against the English Navy. After having visited the works, we went up to Bunker Hill.

Bunker Hill is one of those landmarks, unfortunately still too rare on the face of the earth, that recalls the noble exertions of liberty against tyranny and oppression to the most distant posterity. It is at Bunker Hill that, for the first time, the Americans dared, in a regular combat, to brave the arms of their oppressors; it was there that some men, nearly without arms and without discipline, and very much inferior in number to their enemies, but encouraged by their wives, their children, their fellow citizens, who from the hilltops of Boston caused them to hear those magic words – *Independence, Posterity* – withstood, with a courage worthy of heroic times, three successive assaults delivered by battalions of numerous men whom the experience and the science of combat seemed destined to lead to an easily accomplished victory. Forced, finally, to yield to numbers, the Americans retired, but in good order, and leaving behind them bloody proofs of their vigorous resistance.

It was a moment before this retreat, which revealed to the friends of liberty their strength and their hopes, this retreat which was worth a victory, that the young and worthy General Warren fell. Having regard for his courage, death had not dared to strike him during the combat. While returning into the entrenchments that he had left in order to pursue the English who had failed for the third time in their attack, he received a bullet in the back .... He rests now under a simple monument built precisely on the spot where his blood reddened the earth.

It was at the foot of this monument that General Lafayette was greeted by some old warriors, the glorious remnants of the first battle of the War of Independence. In their presence, Doctor A.M. Thompson addressed to the General a speech of congratulations in the name of the inhabitants of Charlestown. "In the midst of the joy that your visit causes us," he said,

> We cannot shield ourselves from a special excitement in receiving you on the storied heights of Bunker Hill. On this sacred ground, immortalized by the death of heroes of our Revolution, and dedicated to their generous spirits, liberty appeared, sometimes bloody and steeped in tears; her chariot

> was carried on wheels of fire. Today, she appears here between peace and glory, escorted by the sweet affections of a happy people, to offer the civic crown to her favorite son who devoted his first energies in her defense.
>
> Permit us, beloved General, to express to you again our ardent prayers that your precious life be prolonged up to the limits ordinarily accorded to humanity; that this land, which you have enriched by the sacrifice of your early youth, be dedicated as a home of your older years; that the country, which today takes pleasure in identifying your glory with that of Washington, be able to see you, during the rest of your long life, enjoy the cares and attentions of a people who have always reserved for you such a lively feeling of gratitude and admiration.

General Lafayette was very moved by this speech, and his emotion was communicated to all those who surrounded him. "It is with profound respect," he replied,

> That I tread upon this hallowed ground, where the blood of American patriots, the blood of Warren and his companions, gloriously spilled, revived the force of three million men and secured the happiness of ten million who live now, and of so many others to be born. This blood has summoned the American continents to republican independence, and has awakened in the nations of Europe the necessity of, and assured for the future, I hope, the exercise of their rights. Such have been the results of this resistance to oppression, which some alleged sages of that era called *imprudence*, although resistance was a duty and a virtue and it has been the signal for the emancipation of the human race ....

This response was drowned out by the applause of the crowd and salvos of artillery. Immediately thereafter, some battalions of young militia, led by Governor Eustis and Generals Brooks and Dearborn, passed before the General to the sound of cannon and the sound of a military band, which played that sublime melody, dear to French patriots, which always reminded them that they also had their Warren, whose generous blood had watered the tree of liberty in the shade of which we would be reposing gloriously today, if it had not been shaken by anarchy and struck in the heart by the sacrilegious sword of an audacious soldier.

A frugal meal, served under a tent, ended this ceremony, after which we returned to the City to visit the arms depot of the militia, the old City Hall, from which the assembled people left in a throng to go to the Port to destroy two cargoes of tea sent by the English East India Company, and the hall where the Declaration of Independence of Massachusetts was signed. In the course of these visits, I collected some details on the history and the current situation of this State which appeared to me to warrant being recorded in the following Chapter.

Chapter III

First Settlements in Massachusetts – Summary of the Events of the Revolution in This Province – Conditions Now Prevailing.

The first settlements formed in that part of North America called Massachusetts owe their origin to the religious persecutions practiced in England under the reigns of Elizabeth, James the First, and Charles the First. The history of the first immigrants who came looking for freedom of conscience, which the *European Philosophy of the 17th Century* refused them, in the midst of the savages of the New World, offers only the sad picture of their continual struggle against the climate, diseases and hunger. It was only in 1630 that a larger and better ordered expedition came to reinforce them and help them to found the cities of Salem, Charlestown and Boston. Cromwell, Hampden and many others who exercised so terrible an influence in the Revolution of 1640 were meant to be on this expedition. They were already on board. They were going to raise anchor and search in the New World for nourishment for their ardent dispositions, which perhaps would have been less developed there than in the presence of tyranny, when Charles the First, as if urged on by fate, seized them and put them back on land.

It is worthy of notice that most of the immigrants who left their country, their friends, their families, in order to escape persecution, who consequently ought to have carried in their heart hatred of their persecutors, remained, however, despite their removal, attached to the English Government, and sanctified in the land of their exile the names of their kings by giving them to the rivers which they discovered, to the cities which they built, and to the monuments which they raised. Was this out of respect for royalty which, in spite of its misdeeds, appeared to them nonetheless as sacred, so much does custom rule over men? Or, rather, was it only to cover up and guard against the weakness of their settlements, with the name of a powerful authority, and to pay, at the same time, a kind of tribute to the English Government, which had constituted itself the proprietor of these vast countries *by right of discovery*, and which would not at all have left the Colonies in peace, if, from the very first, they had appeared to want to break all ties with and all memories of the Motherland? This latter reason appears to me the more probable and is adequately supported by the following document, drafted and signed by the immigrants who landed in New Plymouth in 1620.

> In the name of God: Amen. We the undersigned loyal subjects of Lord James, by the grace of God, King of Great Britain, France and Ireland, defender of the faith, etc., having

> undertaken for the Glory of God and the propagation of the Christian faith, the honor of our King and of our country, a voyage to the north of Virginia to found the first colony there, we constitute ourselves solemnly and mutually, by the present act, in a political body for our administration, our preservation and the propagation of the above-mentioned things; and by virtue of this act, we recognize the right to make and adopt such laws, acts and ordinances which should appear to us to be just and useful to the general welfare of the colony, such as whom to name to the different offices. In witness whereof, we have signed the present instrument.
>
> At Cape Cod, on the 11th of November of the eighth year of the reign of our Sovereign Lord James, King of England, France and Ireland, A.D. 1620.

This act, as they saw it, all the while appearing to recognize the authority of England, nonetheless gave to the Colonists the direct administration of their affairs, and lay the foundations of that spirit of independence which, more than a century later, threw off the yoke of the parent state, when it wished to return to the practice of a despotism which it seemed necessary to prescribe there.

In 1692, under the reign of William and Mary, to assure its right of sovereignty in Massachusetts, the English Government usurped the nomination of the governor of this province, but lost in great part its objective by leaving to the provincial legislature the right to regulate and to pay for the appointments of this governor, who, thereby, found himself without strength and influence. The English Government soon recognized its mistake; it wanted to rectify it; and from that moment there broke out between the Motherland and the Colony those misunderstandings, as a result of which the latter increased its resistance as the former became more demanding.

Soon, the allocations of the different powers were completely confused; the governor was invested by the Crown with the right to organize the tribunals and to name the judges; these privileges were hotly contested by the people who reclaimed them as one of the prerogatives of the legislature. In spite of the attempts of the Crown, the Colony, all the while repulsing them with all its power, did not remain any less attached to the Mother Country, and did not at all hesitate to assist it in the colonial war that it waged in 1754 against France. After this war, which for six years had been suspended and resumed with varying chances of success and reversal, and which ended finally in 1760 with the ruin of the French Colonies, the Colonists hoped that the gratitude of the Motherland for the services which they had rendered would assure them forever the enjoyment of their freedom and their rights, acquired by so many sacrifices of all kinds; but two years had barely passed since peace was concluded when they were obliged to renounce their hopes.

England was then triumphant at land and at sea; its commercial supremacy was felt over all points of the globe and aroused the envy of all the nations of Europe; but it had acquired this glory, with which it was intoxicated, only by draining its treasury and by contracting huge debts. In order to pay these debts and to restore its finances, it was necessary for England to create other revenues, and it looked towards the Colonies.

By their commerce with the West Indies, the Colonies had made a tremendous profit and, with that and good management, had found the means of having a reserve which permitted them at the same time to pay their debts and to increase successively importation of English manufactured goods. It was this prosperity which tempted the greed of the Crown, and from that moment all ministerial skill consisted only of varying the means of snatching money from the Colonists. The commanding officers on the coasts were converted into harsh customs officers, charged with *repressing their commerce and preventing contraband.* These commanders, assured of impunity, since they came only under the jurisdiction of the tribunals of Great Britain, were not at all afraid to make illegal seizures, frequently to their profit. The charges on the importation of English products were so increased that they were nearly the equivalent of a prohibition. It was ordered also that the charges could be paid only in silver or gold, and they rendered the paper put into circulation by the Colonists of no value. Finally, the entire new system introduced by the English Ministry became as ruinous as tyrannical, for at the same time that it required enormous duties, it destroyed the means of paying them.

Emboldened by the Colonists' forbearance, the English Government did not know how to stop any more, and the year 1765 saw come into being that fatal law called the *Stamp Act,* which directed that, in the future, all contracts, wills, civil deeds, etc., had to be made on stamped paper, under penalty of invalidity, and which imposed on the paper a tax intended to cover *the expenses of the late War in America.* As soon as it was understood, this law roused all minds to indignation; in private societies and in public assemblies, it became the subject of all the conversation and all discussions; each person referred back to the past and made, with bitterness, a recapitulation of the outrages which he had received from England; from that moment, as they tell it, the fire of revolution was lit; from supplications and remonstrances which they had been satisfied with up to then, the Colonists passed to threats; the people of Massachusetts, in particular, expressed their resentment forcefully; it was at their instigation that a Congress, formed of deputies of the several provinces, assembled in New York on October 7. This Congress, composed of men respected for their character and their understanding, and which served afterwards as a model for the one which conducted the Revolutionary War so gloriously, then published forcefully a Declaration of Rights of the Colonies, a listing of the offenses of England, a Petition to the King and a Memorial to the Parliament.

These acts of the Congress produced an effect in the English Parliament, which was augmented still by the writings and the presence of Benjamin Franklin, who was then in London, and who was summoned before the House of Commons to examine the complaints of his fellow citizens; he presented himself there with the modesty which was characteristic of him and with a republican simplicity which contrasted conspicuously with the insolent luxuriousness of the instruments of authority, who had rushed in a crowd to this session in the dastardly hope to see the one whom they treated as a rebel humiliated because he dared to speak of the rights of man in the presence of royalty. The calmness of his responses and the depth of his arguments produced a great impression on the assembly, made the promoters of the Stamp Act change their minds and caused them to withdraw this monument to their tyranny and ignorance.

As much as the Americans had felt indignation when this law had been passed and joy upon learning of its revocation, nonetheless, the English Government did not know how to take advantage of this return of the public mind to a more mellow disposition; not only did it allow all the odious restrictions that it had placed on the commerce of the Colonies to stand; but soon it followed the Stamp Act with a tax, no less intolerable, on paper, paints, glass and the tea which the Colonies received from England. But what angered the Colonists everywhere was that the preamble of these Acts stated that the proceeds of these new taxes would be put at the disposal of the Parliament in order to pay the costs of administering the Colonies and, in particular, to pay the governors and the judges who, by this measure, found themselves withdrawn from the authority of provincial legislation and put under the domination of the ministries. In order to collect this tax, a permanent administration was created and established in Boston by an act of Parliament.

The people of Massachusetts could not deceive themselves about the views of the Ministry; accustomed for a long time to discuss and administer their own affairs, the people resolved not to submit voluntarily to the dishonor of being governed by an illegal authority established at a distance of more than 2,500 miles. Consequently, they summoned into session their representatives who, upon being assembled, protested against the taxes and the use that they wanted to make of them, and addressed to the other provincial assemblies a memorandum in which, after having recapitulated their privileges and contrasted the encroachments of them by England, finished by asking them for their cooperation in resisting the tyranny which, each day, grew more burdensome on the Colonies. This step of the assembly was treated as infamy and rebellion by the servants of the Crown, who increased the activity of their vexatious measures. Two English regiments arrived in the Port and, upon the Council's refusal to prepare lodging for them in the City, the regiments disembarked under the protection of their ships, bayonettes on gun barrel, and came to establish a guard-house with two pieces of cannon in front of the assembly chamber, which was in this manner converted into a barracks. From that moment, the City was under the control of the soldiers, who roamed through the streets, insulted the citizens, snatched them from their rest or their occupations, and disturbed them even in practicing their religion by the uninterrupted sound of the instruments of war.

In these circumstances, the House was called together in Boston, but it did not want to assemble there, declaring that it did not believe itself free in the presence of the armed force. Consequently, the session was opened in Cambridge, where the Governor had the audacity to present himself in order to request funds for the pay of the soldiers. The funds having been refused, the House was dissolved.

However, a change of administration in the English Ministry had induced the Parliament to suppress all the fees except the one imposed on tea; but this apparent return to a system of moderation did not alleviate in any way the resentment of the citizens of Massachusetts, who saw in this measure only caprice or a new way employed by the Parliament to establish its right of supremacy in the affairs of the Colonies, and made a firm resolution not to abandon this point of contention.

Soon there occurred in Boston an event which just missed having the most serious consequences. The English soldiers were accustomed to see in the citizens only rebels and treated them harshly. The latter, angered by the abuse which they received without cessation, nourished in their hearts a violent hatred against the former and rarely let the occasion of displaying it to them escape. Finally on March 5, 1770, a detachment under the orders of Captain Preston was accosted by some young men who, they say, threw snow balls at them while uttering insults. In their unreasoning resentment, the soldiers countered by firing on the crowd, in the midst of which five persons were gravely wounded, some others slightly wounded, and three killed on the spot. Soon the alarm bells caused the citizens to take up arms; and, without the intervention of the Governor and the magistrates, the soldiers would have been wiped out without a doubt. On the following day, on the demand of the residents, the troops were removed to a distance from the City. Captain Preston and his soldiers were arraigned for trial; but, such was the sense of justice which always animated the citizens of Boston, that, having been convinced that the soldiers had been provoked, they abandoned the accusation brought against them.

This event concluded by convincing the popular party that an open struggle with the Mother Country was now inevitable and that it was necessary to prepare for it. Consequently, secret Committees of Correspondence were organized in all places in order to regularize the decisions which they would soon be obliged to take. The usefulness of this organization, then called *The League*, was not slow in making itself felt.

Upon the institution of the tax on tea, the inhabitants of Boston had resolved not to use it any more, rather than to take it from the English; and, from that time onwards, the India Company had not received any orders. However, afflicted by the loss of this avenue for trade, the Company had decided to direct several cargoes of tea to agents it had in Boston, who had to pay the tax on it themselves and, in this way, to side-step the obstacles. But the arrival of these cargoes was no sooner known than minds were thrown into great excitement. On the following morning, the following notice circulated widely in the City.

> Friends, brothers, compatriots!
>
> The execrable tea shipment by the East India Company to this Port has arrived. The time for destroying it or vigorously resisting the machinations of tyranny has sounded. All those who love their country, who are jealous of their own happiness, and want to deserve well of posterity are urged to assemble at Faneuil Hall today at nine o'clock (the bells will sound then) to plan an effective resistance to this infamous and destructive measure of adminstration.
>
> Boston, November 29, 1773

The citizens proceeded with alacrity in response to this patriotic appeal. The crowd was so large that the hall could not hold everybody, and they were obliged to chose a more roomy place; the discussions which opened and which were prolonged during that first meeting prevented them from passing any resolution that day; they adjourned until the following day, and 25 persons, under the command of Captain Procter, were charged with seeing to it that they did not unload the tea during the night.

The meeting of the 30th was still more numerous, and the ardor of those who were present there was, moreover, magnified by the proclamation of the Governor who urged them to renounce their plan to resist the law, and to disperse if they did not want to risk their lives. These injunctions of the Governor were rejected unanimously and contemptuously and, afterwards, the assembly proceeded calmly to draft several propositions which were accepted. It was decided that those who had received English tea since the institution of the tax unwittingly would be censured and that those who received it in the future would be declared enemies of their country. The members of the assembly pledged under oath to uphold these different resolutions under peril of their lives and their possessions, after which they passed a vote of thanks to their neighbors from the outskirts of Boston for the zeal with which they had come to join with them and also to Mr. Jonathan Williams for the manner in which he had fulfilled the function of *moderator*. The assembly dispersed after having named a commission to see to it that the ships which were in the Port, filled with tea, would set sail as soon as possible.

Several days passed in negotiations between this commission and the authorities without obtaining the departure of the ships. Finally, on the 15th of December, a meeting of the citizens who were more numerous than at the former ones took place; more than 2,000 persons of the country attended. Samuel Philips Savage, of Weston, was named moderator, and Mr. Rotch, the owner of one of the ships, was summoned before the assembly to render an account of its presence in the Port. He declared that the Collector of Customs had refused up to then to dispatch it. He was ordered to stand ready to depart on that very day at his risk and peril, to *protest* at once against the customs officer and to address himself *directly* to the Governor in order to obtain a permit. The assembly adjourned until three o'clock in the afternoon.

Being reconvened at three o'clock, the assembly waited patiently up to five o'clock without Mr. Rotch reappearing. It was going to dissolve then and adjourn until the following day; but Josiah Quincy, Jr., an influential man of the popular party, endowed with great energy, stopped his fellow citizens while reminding them of their undertaking of the day before, *to uphold all their resolutions on peril of their lives and their possessions*. At 5:45, Mr. Rotch reappeared. The response of the Governor was: "That for the honor of the laws and the respect due to the King, he would not permit ships to leave until after Customs had fulfilled all the formalities freely and legally." This response aroused great excitement in the assembly. Soon a man, who was in the galleries dressed as a Mohawk Indian, uttered a *war cry*; at this cry about 30 people clad in the same manner, who were standing at the door, responded; and the assembly was dissolved as if by magic. The crowd hurried towards the Port; the men dressed as Indians leaped on the boats loaded with tea; in less than two hours, all the boxes filled with this commodity were smashed and thrown into the sea; all the other objects which were found aboard were respected; after this expedition the multitude retired in order and in silence.

This action had taken place in the presence of several warships, and, as it were, under the cannon and under the eyes of the garrison of the fort, however, without the authorities daring to attempt the least resistance, so great and so imposing is the wrath of the people who shake off the yoke of tyranny!

The names of the citizens disguised as Indians were never made public; several among them still live, they say, and enjoy with modesty the good fortune which they had to strike the first blows that shook royal power on the American continent.

The national pride of Great Britain became indignant at the news of this resistance, which they called an outrage to his Royal Majesty! Governors and governed all uttered the same cry: Vengeance! War against the rebel Colonies! And this cry was followed by a host of laws, one more tyrannical then the other, with the aid of which they believed that they could terrify and pressure the Province of Massachusetts. The Port of Boston was banned for an unlimited time; the Provincial Charter was revoked; the citizens were uprooted from their natural jurisdiction; the nomination of magistrates was left to the pleasure of the Crown, which also arrogated to itself the right to have its soldiers take up residence in the homes of the citizens.

Far from allowing themselves to be beaten down or intimidated by this audacity and folly of the English Government, the inhabitants of Massachusetts redoubled their energy. A new assembly of the people was convened in Boston, in which they called on God and the world to witness the injustice and tyranny of England. A call was made to the other Colonies to join with Massachusetts in order to maintain and defend their common freedoms; the other Colonies were not at all deaf to this plea; and most of the legislatures declared that the first of June, the date on which the Port of Boston was closed, would be placed in the number of those unhappy days when the bells would sound in a lugubrious tone. The people ran en masse to bow down in the churches to ask God's protection against those who were contemplating civil war and the destruction of their freedoms.

The assembly of Massachusetts was adjourned to Salem, but Governor Gage prevented it from meeting; then, the members of this assembly transformed itself into an extraordinary society under the title of The League, in which they pledged, mutually and in the presence of God, to suspend all relations with Great Britain until all unjust laws were revoked. This League was declared by the Governor to be criminal and contrary to the rights of the King, and this declaration, in turn, was treated as tyrannical because it was in opposition to that which the people were interested in for their own interests; and the aroused populace, after having forced the magistrates named by the Crown to renounce their functions, swore to obey no longer any authorities other than those which would be created by the Colony and to recognize no longer any laws other than the former laws of the Colony.

The cessation of all commerce in Boston soon plunged the inhabitants into the deepest misery; each day their needs were multiplied and made themselves felt with more force; however, no one thought of entering into a compromise with tyranny. The citizens of Marblehead and Salem, in contempt of the injunction of the English authority, hastened to relieve the suffering of their brothers in Boston; they sent food and money, and offered them the free use of their Ports, their wharfs and their warehouses in order to recapture the commerce which they were unable to do at home, and without which, moreover, it was nearly impossible for them to subsist.

Encouraged by these demonstrations of the approval of their compatriots, the Bostonians hardened, more and more, in the resolution which they had taken to uphold by force of arms the justice of their cause. They prepared themselves without respite; some companies of *minutemen* (men at a moment's notice) were organized in the City and in the Province. At the first stroke of the alarm bell, at the first call of The League or the first report of new violence of the English, these men were to take up arms and attack the aggressors everywhere they encountered them at a moment's notice. Stores of arms and munitions were also amassed with skill and dispatch.

For several months, about 30 young workers had been voluntarily organized in a company, with the intent to monitor all the movements of the English and to forwarn their fellow citizens of them. Towards the Spring of 1775, they redoubled their activity and each night made frequent patrols in the streets, two by two. On April 15, towards midnight, they noticed that all the transport boats were afloat and readied astern the warships, and that the grenadiers and the light infantry were making preparations. Immediately they gave this information to Dr. Warren who dispatched a messenger at once to bring this news to John Hancock and

Samuel Adams, who had left the City to escape the Governor who had, they say, given orders to arrest them.

On the 18th, they obtained new indications of a plan of action. The light infantry and the grenadiers were concentrated on the Commons; and, at ten o'clock at night, 800 men, under the orders of Colonel Smith, embarked and came to take ground at Lechmere Point near Cambridge, from which, after having received a day's provisions, they marched until midnight. The movement had as its objective the destruction of the arsenal that The League had created at Concord. The secret having been kept in the camp, the silence observed during the march made the English believe that no one in Boston suspected their departure. By the light of the moon, they hurried their march and arrived quietly, at daybreak, in Lexington, six miles from Concord.

But here the calm which had surrounded them was disturbed by the sound of drums which resounded in the field and which seemed to call the citizens to arms; and a company of about 60 armed Americans appeared suddenly in front of them. Immediately, the English stopped, closed ranks and loaded their weapons; the Lexington company did the same and received the order of its chief not to abandon the terrain without orders and not to fire first. Hardly had these preparations been completed, when Major Pitcairn, commander of the advance-guard, advanced towards the Americans and, in a vulgar tone, shouted: "Lay down your arms, rebels! Disperse, knaves!" This insolent notice remained unanswered. Then Pitcairn turned towards his men and ordered them to fire; they readily obeyed, and 800 Englishmen shamelessly uttered cries of joy while commencing so unequal a fight, a fight in which 60 citizens offered their lives with zeal in a sacrificial offering to the sacred cause of their Country!

The Americans received this first fire resolutely; one of them, seeing a friend fall at his side, cried out: "You will be avenged!" He fired a shot at the English, and the War of Independence had begun....

The Americans could not hold out for a long time against forces so disproportionate; they abandoned the ground, leaving eight dead and some wounded, around whom the English filed proudly while insulting them with cries of victory.

After having rested for some time from this terrible contest, the proud defenders of the Crown set out for Concord where they arrived at nine o'clock. They found the inhabitants there in a great state of excitement, but ignorant still of the assassination of their brothers in Lexington. A company of citizens occupied the bridge. This time the English made their attack without notice. The citizens of Concord countered vigorously and killed some soldiers and officers of the King, after which, too weak to withstand a battle, they dispersed and abandoned the cache of arms to the English who destroyed it in several hours.

Soon the alarm was general in the countryside; the alarm bell called to arms all those who were capable of carrying them, and in a short time, the English found themselves so encircled that they began to feel that their retreat would not be as easy as their victories. From Concord to Lexington their march was only a disorganized flight; the well-directed and well-supplied fire of the rebels who lay in ambush all along the route in the barns, in the gardens, behind the trees and in the ditches, did not allow them a single moment to stop and defend themselves. Having arrived in Lexington, they found Lord Percy there, who, at the head of 16 companies of infantry and a corps of marines and two artillery pieces, came to save them from complete destruction, but not from shame. In spite of this reinforcement, they were still hard pressed to arrive safely in Charlestown, where they passed the night under the protection of the cannon of their vessels; and in the morning they returned to Boston, after having lost nearly 200 men, as many killed as wounded, in this unfortunate expedition.

It would be difficult to portray the astonishment and humiliation of the English when they saw themselves repulsed by *rebels* and blocked in their retreat by an undisciplined multitude. However, the Royal Army was soon reinforced by 12,000 men who arrived from England under the command of Generals Burgoyne, Clinton and Howe. In order to erase the shame of the Lexington march, General Gage decided to deal a heavy blow to the spirit of insurrection. He began with a proclamation that announced the imposition of martial law, and promised a full pardon to all those who put down their arms. John Hancock and Samuel Adams had the honor of being exempted from this general amnesty. Their ardent love of freedom, their enlightenment, their patriotic virtue and the immense influence which they exercised in the mind of the people, earned them, in a word, this distinction.

The citizens of Massachusetts greeted this proclamation as the promises and threats of a despotism which is beginning to fear for its own existence ought to be received; that is to say they did not take it into account and closed ranks.

Now the English Army found itself confined in Boston and on that spit of land which joins the City to the mainland. Thirty thousand Americans kept the English Army tightly blocked. Their right flank was opposite the road to Dedham, their center in Cambridge and their left wing, particularly composed of militia of Massachusetts, stood in Charlestown, a village separated from Boston by a narrow river that one crosses over a bridge. It was by this passage that the English General resolved to break out of this awkward position; but the Americans discovered his plan and hurried to oppose its achievement. During the night, a thousand men, under the orders of Colonel Prescott, established their position and retrenched on Breed's Hill, a small rise which overlooks both the City of Boston and the Charlestown Bridge. When at daybreak the English caught site of the redoubt which the small troop of Colonel Prescott had built with so much diligence, they attempted, but unavailingly, to destroy it.

General Gage then thought it was very important for the safety of his Army to dislodge the Americans from this formidable position, and, consequently, he made his preparations. Major General Howe, at the head of ten companies of grenadiers, ten companies of light infantry and some pieces of field-artillary, came to take the ground at Morton Point, and arranged his men in battle array; but, observing that the Americans were not at all intimidated by this hostile demonstration, he thought it opportune to await the arrival of a reinforcement which he had immediately requested from Boston. This delay gave the Americans time to receive new forces which were brought to them by General Warren and to complete their system of defense. The English began their attack by burning Charlestown; in a few minutes, this village, composed of more than 500 wooden houses, was devoured by flames.

The inhabitants of Boston and the rest of the English Army were drawn up in tiers on the heights of the City, viewing with equal misgivings this terrible combat, to the results of which their destinies were equally bound.

It was June 17, 1775: it was one hour after noon.

The English line got underway and marched slowly into combat, arms in hand, with a calm that came from long practice of military discipline. The Americans awaited them resolutely with that composure, that resolve that the love of liberty always inspires; now the English were no more than 30 paces from the entrenchments of their adversaries, and yet the sound of gunfire had not yet broken the sinister silence which had presided over their movements, when suddenly they received a greeting of musketry so skillfully aimed that their ranks were shaken by it and broken and that they fled in disorder to the shore, abandoning behind them a large number of their officers killed or wounded.

A second attack had the same result and, at this same time, the English soldiers were stricken with such terror that very many of them had sought refuge in the boats. Their officers could not stop them and rally them by using the most drastic means of military discipline. Finally, a third attack, supported by some artillery pieces and by the fire of several vessels and of two floating batteries, had complete success. The American forces in their entrenchments defended themselves for a long time yet by fighting hand-to-hand and by countering bayonette strokes of their adversaries with blows from their rifle-butts. Their retreat was calmer and more orderly than ought to have been expected of militia without experience. In their last attack, the royal troops displayed a great fearlessness and courage worthy of a better cause; they lost nearly 1,100 men there, as many killed as wounded, among which they counted more than 90 officers. The Patriot Army, which had fought for a long time under cover, did not lose 500 men, but had to mourn the death of one of its most valued leaders, that of courageous General Warren.

The English had paid too dearly for this victory to think of pursuing its advantages on the same day. They were content with possession of the bloodstained field of battle.

The needless burning of Charlestown, which preceded the combat, appeared to all Americans as an act of the most disgraceful barbarity, and aroused a general feeling of horror and indignation; it was at Charlestown that the English, after their defeat at Lexington, had found help for their wounded, and all the attentions of a most generous hospitality for their fleeing men … .

The loss of their position at Bunker Hill did not prevent the Americans from continuing to keep the Royal Army tightly blocked in Boston. Each day, the beseiging army saw the forces, which Washington came to take command of on July 2 in the name of the Congress assembled in Philadelphia, increase. However, nothing of importance was undertaken against this place for the rest of this year. Winter came and made the position of the besieged army horrible; the cold was excessive; heating was lacking and the English only supplied it at the expense of the inhabitants whose houses they demolished in order to extract the wood from it. The plight of the inhabitants moved Washington deeply; he wanted to take advantage of some extremely frozen days that would have allowed him to traverse the waters which separated him from the City in order to make a general assault; but his war council was unanimously opposed to it.

Having received some re-enforcements towards the end of February 1776, he resolved to seize Dorchester Heights from which it would be easy for him to harass the vessels which were in the Port and even the garrison of the City. He hoped, besides, that this endeavor, by drawing the enemy out of inaction, would furnish him the occasion for attaining a general engagement; and he took some measures with very great skill in order to take all possible advantage of it. The occupation of Dorchester Heights was conducted so diligently during the night of March 2 that the return of day showed the besieged army the Americans perfectly established and capable of withstanding an attack in their new position.

General Howe felt at once that his situation had become very critical following this bold movement of the Americans; and, after several fruitless attempts to dislodge them, he decided to evacuate Boston while the sea was still open to him; it was on March 17 that he set sail with his entire army, and his rear-guard was obliged to listen to the cries of joy which welcomed Washington on his triumphant entrance into the City.

From this day, Boston, which could rightly claim the glorious title of the *Cradle of the Revolution*, ceased being the theater of operations of the War. The City and the Province were forever rid of the presence of the enemies of liberty; but, for all that, the citizens of Massachusetts did not appear any less ardent in the achievement of the great work of liberating the Colonies; their contingents were always sent punctually to the Continental Army; their militias kept their excellent reputation for courage and patriotism to the end of the war.

News of peace arrived in Boston on April 23, 1783 and spread an intoxicating joy among the people. The complete abolition of Slavery of the Blacks was proclaimed; Commerce and Industry reappeared more brilliant than before, protected by freedom.

Three years later, Massachusetts had already been given a State Constitution which guaranteed both the rights and the interests of the people; and five years later, after long debates, it accepted the Federal Constitution. This acceptance was published on February 6, 1788, and was welcomed with transports of delight by the people who celebrated this event with splendid festivals and who proceeded in a crowd to the home of each of the representatives to express their gratitude to them.

Since this time, the State of Massachusetts has not stopped growing in wealth and in success; it adjusted and determined its boundaries amicably with its neighbors; now it is bounded on the North by the States of Vermont and New Hampshire; on the East by the Ocean; on the South by the States of Rhode Island and Connecticut; and on the West by New York State. The character of its soil is infinitely varied and its coasts are rich with commodious bays which a large number of pretty, little islands adorn. The seacoasts are generally barren; but the lands of the interior are very productive and cultivated with a care which gives to the whole countryside the look of a cheerful garden. Elegant country homes, beautiful villages and great cities attest at every turn to how numerous the population is. In a word, about 530,000 people cover a surface of 7,800 square miles. In 1790, this population was only 370,787 people. This progression is without a doubt very rapid, but we will find it even more astonishing in the new States.

About 65,000 people are employed in Agriculture; 36,000 in the diverse manufacturing of cotton, wool, cloth, glass, paper, soap, in the foundries, etc.; about 14,000 in Commerce. The number of those employed in fishing is also very considerable; but I have not been able to obtain the precise count. However, this appears sufficient to demonstrate to what point industrial activity is driven in this State; for if even now one added the individuals employed in the different offices of government, in public education, or in the practice of the private professions, such as those of mason, carpenter, tailor, etc. and afterwards one subtracted from the total number of the population the children who cannot yet work, and those as to whom age and infirmity does not permit it any more, one would see how small the number of the unemployed is in this State; also, from this industrial activity, there results a general affluence in households, which astonishes the European who visits this country for the first time.

This general well-being of the people contributes towards increasing the equality which the Constitution establishes between individuals before the law in all classes of society. On Sunday at church or in public meetings, it is impossible to distinguish by the attire and, I should almost say, by the manners, an artisan from one they call in society a *gentleman*; the multiplicity of schools and the *right* which every man has to be engaged in public affairs spreads in this class of artisans an intelligence and rightness of judgment that one searches for in vain among the middle class of France. In Boston, what they call high society, that is to say the assemblies of men of letters, of wealthy merchants, of government officials, of persons practicing the liberal professions, offers the astonishing contrast of exceptional education with a great simplicity of manners.

The excessive austerity of character, which distinguishes the leading inhabitants of New England, is being erased little by little by contact with other nations and, especially, by the introduction of tolerance in religious opinions; the strictness of the Puritans has been replaced by an agreeable harmony among the numerous sects which share, not only New England, but the entire Union.

One should not conclude that indifference has succeeded fervor. Religious practices are observed with a scrupulous exactitude. It would be difficult to find a meeting dedicated to pleasure in Boston on a Sunday. However, the chains which they formerly stretched in front of the churches, during the celebrations of the mysteries of faith, have disappeared little by little.

The authorities cannot in any way intervene in matters of religion; the ministers of the different religions are paid by their parishioners, and if the public have a special respect for those who frequent the churches, at least no one is permitted to persecute those who never appear there. In fact, of the religious tyranny of the first Colonists, there remains only a single trace, and this trace is found, unfortunately, in the Constitution. The first Article of the Sixth Chapter excludes from government office all candidates who do not belong to the Christian religion, and who do not swear that they are convinced of its truth: *"J.A.B. do declare that I believe the Christian religion, and have a firm persuasion of its truth.*"

One has difficulty understanding how, in a society so enlightened, and so free, where the progress of philosophy makes its marks with a new step forward every day, they may still refuse the services of a virtuous and educated man to the state because he is Jewish or Moslem.

ADAMS PÈRE.

Chapter IV

Camp at Savin Hill – Visit to John Adams – Review of the Militia – Regulations Concerning the Militias of Massachusetts.

August 28 – General Lafayette was invited by the Governor to visit the camp at Savin Hill, several miles from Boston. He accepted, and we arrived there at noon. Savin Hill is a very picturesque place on the seacoast. It is there that, during the summer months, voluntary companies of militias of Boston come one after the other to pass some days under tents to devote themselves to military exercises. The camp was then occupied by the company of the Guards of New England. Upon our arrival, we found the company under arms; its young leader came to welcome the General, and, after a short speech, returned to the head of his troops, whom he caused to maneuver with very great precision. After diverse movements of the infantry, the artillery began its gunnery exercises. Most of the gunshots were aimed with great skill towards a shield placed a large distance away at water level. The gunners invited the General to aim one of the cannons which was in the battery; he did it, and the ball struck the shield. This feat of skill, which no one expected of a man of his age, earned him the applause of all the young militiamen, and of the ladies, who ordinarily came to walk in the camp in order to visit their brothers or their husbands, and, on this day, were more numerous in order to see Lafayette.

The artillery pieces which we saw had attracted my gaze from the first moment of our arrival in the camp. After the maneuvers, I approached to examine them with more care, and I was not a little surprised to recognize our French models perfectly reproduced. These were the first that I encountered in the hands of the militia. The officers, who noticed the interest that I was taking in this examination, informed me that they owed this improvement to General Lallemand, whom the banishments of 1815 had forced to seek refuge in America, and who died some years later in New York, with the sorrow of not being able to let his last glances fall on his Fatherland. During his stay in the United States, where his talents and his character had gained public esteem for him, he had yielded to the desire of being useful to the Nation which accorded to him so generous a hospitality. The militias of Massachusetts owed great improvements in their artillery to him; and he had left a treatise in ten volumes on this weaponry, in which he not only reproduced in part, it is true, the regulations already known and practiced in France, but he adapted them perfectly to the needs of those for whom he worked.

He had married in Philadelphia the niece of a Frenchmen, who lived in this City for more than 40 years, where by his skill in commerce he had amassed one of the most considerable fortunes of Pennsylvania. This marriage, however, had not improved the situation of General Lallemand, who died poor. His widow lived in Philadelphia under the care of her uncle.

After the visit to the camp at Savin Hill, the Governor brought us to dine at his country house, and we returned to the City to attend a very splendid ball that Mr. Lloyd, United States Senator, had offered to General Lafayette.

John Adams, whose name is connected with all the great epochs of the American Revolution, and who had the honor of succeeding Washington in the exercise of the First Magistracy of the Republic, was then in retirement and burdened by his 89 years. General Lafayette, who had known him in the past, and who even had been linked to him by a close friendship, did not want to leave without having visited him. A sense of tact, easy to understand, made him desire that this visit be made without all the displays of a triumph with which the people were ordinarily surrounding him thus far at his slightest movements. Consequently, he climbed into his carriage unescorted, accompanied only by two notables of the City, and followed by his son and the author of this Journal.

We arrived at Quincy near two o'clock; our carriages stopped at the door of a small, very simple house, built of wood and brick, having only a single floor. I was a bit astonished to learn that this was the home of the former President of the United States. We found the venerable John Adams in the midst of his family. He welcomed us and embraced us with a touching kindness. The sight of his old friend gave him a pleasure and a sense of well-being which seemed to rejuvenate him. During the whole time of the dinner, he contributed a large share of the conversation with an ease and a freshness of memory which made us forget his 89 years.

The long life of John Adams has been entirely devoted to service to his Fatherland and to the cause of freedom which animated him with passion from his tender youth. He was born in Quincy on October 19, 1735, and studied at Cambridge, from which he left in 1755 in order to give grammar lessons in a school in Worcester where, at the same time, he devoted himself to the study of law under James Putnam. In 1758, he was admitted to the bar.

In 1770, he was chosen as a representative of the City of Boston in the Massachusetts Assembly. When the quarrels between the citizens of Boston and the English soldiers turned bloody, he showed the measure of his character by presenting himself, with Josiah Quincy, Jr. and S. Blowers, to defend Captain Preston and his soldiers, who had fired on the people. He was unwilling for the love of freedom to prevail over the love of justice, and his eloquence helped absolve those unfortunate men who were only blind and ignorant instruments of English tyranny. In 1774, he was chosen as a member of the Council of Massachusetts; but his political opinions, which he had already openly and energetically expressed on a great number of occasions, led him to be spurned by Governor Gage. A few months later, he was sent to the Continental Congress where he showed himself to be one of the most ardent and skillful defenders of liberty.

In 1776 he was entrusted, along with Jefferson, to each produce a draft of the Declaration of Independence. That of Jefferson was preferred over his by the Congress it is true; but, by virtue of his eloquence and his patriotism, he was not deemed any less the soul and the torch of this immortal assembly. A short time after, he was assigned with Dr. Franklin and Edward Rutledge to negotiate peace in the Colonies with Lord Howe. In 1777, he was named Commissioner to the Court of France replacing Silas Deane. In April 1779, the Congress having imposed a censure on all its Commissioners in Europe, one honorable exception was made in favor of John Adams.

In 1779, on his return from Europe, he was chosen a member of the convention assembled to draft the Constitution of Massachusetts. In the month of August of the same year, he was sent to Europe with powers to negotiate a general peace. In 1780, the Congress voted him public thanks for the services which he had rendered in Europe. In 1781, he concluded a treaty with the Dutch Provinces which was very advantageous to his country. In 1785, he was sent as Minister Plenipotentiary to the English Government. It was during this honorable mission that he published his learned summary of all the ancient and modern constitutions under the title *Defense of the American Constitutions*. In more than one passage, this work of profound erudition seemed to indicate a predilection of the author for English institutions, and this attracted to him some vigorous attacks of a great number of patriotic authors, particularly Phillip Livingston, then Governor of New Jersey, who rebutted him with talent in an excellent work which he published under the title *Examination of the English Constitution*. Recalled from England at his own request, he was welcomed to his country with the thanks of its citizens and of Congress.

In 1789, after the adoption of the new Constitution, John Adams was elected Vice President of the United States and was kept in this honorable position during the eight years of the Presidency of Washington, who had great confidence in his talents and his patriotism. In 1797, he himself was named to the First Magistracy of the Republic, replacing Washington who refused a third election. Circumstances were then very difficult. The French Revolution, which at first had had general approbation in the United States, had now become, by the intrigues of royalists and foreigners, an object of horror, even for its warmest partisans. The French Question agitated every mind and had become for the two parties, Federalist and Democrat, a subject of animated discussions and sometimes violent attacks. The maladroit and often less than honest intrigues of our diplomatic agents to the United States to take advantage of these divisions alarmed President John Adams and led to his proposing to Congress, as a means of repression, a law which allowed the suspension of *habeas corpus*. This proposal was in very direct opposition to the sense of the freedom of the American people so that, I should say, it was repulsed, not only with force, but also with indignation. The House of Representatives did not want to even consider this bill, and the popularity of John Adams received such a setback that, at the expiration of the fourth year of his administration, he was not reelected.

In 1801, he retired in his home in Quincy. His fellow citizens very soon forgot the cause of his retirement in order to preserve only the memory of the great and numerous services that he had rendered to his country during his long career. They did not delay to offer him the governorship of Massachusetts, and later they invited him to preside over the commission charged with revising the Constitution of the same State; but he began to feel a need for rest; he thanked them while saying that he begged the *theologians*, the *philosophers*, and the *politicians* to let him die in peace. In spite of this refusal, he did not become insensible of the great interests of his country and when, in 1811, they were menaced by the hateful vexations of England, his patriotic voice cried out from the depth of his retirement that the national honor could only be avenged by war. His eloquence was rekindled in a letter which he wrote to rally to this opinion those who, because of party spirit, had moved furthest away from it. In fact, he made so generous a sacrifice of his personal opinions to the dangers of the moment that his most ardent adversaries could not refuse him the expression of their esteem and their gratitude.

Now, although it might be impossible for him to leave his room, he might be barely able to get up off his armchair, and his hand might refuse to bring the food to his mouth without the help of his children or grandchildren, his heart and his head had no less passion for all that is good; the affairs of his country especially are his most agreeable occupation. He could not tire of repeating how great was the joy that the recognition of his fellow citizens for Lafayette caused him. We left him filled with admiration for the courage with which he bears the pains and the infirmities which a century nearly completed has necessarily amassed on his body.

A large review had been ordered and prepared for the 30th. In the morning, the militias from the areas surrounding Boston arrived under the command of General Appleton. Those of the City had, since the preceding day, pitched their tents on the Common opposite the Capitol, and, at our rising, our glances were struck by the sight of an improvised camp. At noon, about 8,000 men were found arranged in battle array on this vast promenade. A large gathering of ladies adorned the crossroads that dominated it, or had filled up the paths which surrounded it. Some time later, General Lafayette presented himself, accompanied by the Governor and his staff, in front of the battle line, where he was greeted by the cheering of the militias, to which the sound of instruments of war and the applause of the numerous spectators responded. After having traversed the ranks of the young citizen-soldiers, of whom the handsome bearing and fine appearance under arms could delight even eyes accustomed to the regularity of the paid troops of Europe, the General was led to the highest point of the promenade in order to see the war movements which they wanted to show him more easily.

We did not find that scrupulous precision in the handling of arms, to which European officers attach so great an importance, and only obtain by submitting the poor soldier to the sad profession of a marionette for at least four hours a day; but we were forced to admire the promptness of loading, and the cohesion and the speed of firing. Doubtless, the movements of the line left something to be desired in composure and precision; but, on the other hand, it is impossible, I believe, to execute with more speed or intelligence the maneuvers of light troops. This kind of service appears to suit the American character; it is also very well suited to militias called, more especially, to the defense of the localities of which all the resources are known to them, and which are particularly favorable to a war of details. This kind of minor operation, which they executed before our eyes, lasted nearly three hours, and engaged our keen interest.

When it was finished, we passed under a huge tent, where the principal citizens had joined at a table of 1,200 places to receive the farewells of Lafayette, who had to leave the City on the next day. At the center of the table, opposite the places which we were occupying, was a large silver bowl, filled with fragments of arms, shells, and military buttons, etc., collected on Bunker Hill, a long time after the memorable battle of June 17. The Governor was kind enough to offer us some of these fragments; for my part, I accepted with thanks a button which he presented to me. Despite the rust which covered it, nonetheless one easily recognized the number 42. The English regiment which carried this number was one of those which suffered the most from the attack of the entrenched Americans.

The care with which the Americans preserve and revere all the momentos of their Revolution is very remarkable; all that which reminds them of this glorious epoch is for them a precious relic which they honor, with religious worship, as it were. This kind of devotion is very worthy of respect since it contributes to the growth of the sacred flame by which the love of liberty inspires them. It is better, I think, than the *profound veneration* that we have in Europe for the ribbons that the authorities distribute.

During this great review, I had noticed with astonishment the variety of the uniforms in the numerous corps which filed in front of us; I was hardly able to find two companies more or less similar; some were clad with a luxury which perhaps was little suited to the profession of arms; those of the country, to the contrary, were clad with such simplicity that the only things military which they had were the cartridge pouch and the gun. This difference was explained by the formation of that which they call *voluntary companies*. These companies are composed of young people whom the relationships of neighborhood or friendship have joined together, under the authority of the Governor, in a private society. By common consent, they determine the color and cut of their uniform, elect their officers and choose a name by which to designate their company. So organized and constituted, they always remain obedient to the general regulations which govern all the militias; but they assemble very often to devote themselves to military exercises; and, as nearly all of these young people belong to the comfortable class, they can incur some expense for the splendor of their dress, and from that comes this variety which I had noticed.

So from this kind of rivalry of luxury among the voluntary companies, there results a great competition in the service and, as the officers who had the kindness to give me some details on this matter claim, it is a good thing without a doubt. But isn't there the fear that behind this good there are some serious drawbacks! The embellishments and the plumes which today only serve to distinguish one such company from another, will they not serve later to distinguish the son of the rich merchant from the son of the ordinary artisan? And this distinction between the opulent militiamen and the poor militiamen, doesn't it open a door to an aristocracy of wealth, not less the enemy of equality than the aristocracy of titles? American customs and, especially, institutions reduce this danger very much to be sure; but, even if the danger is yet distant, must one ignore it? I do not believe so.

The existence, the organization, the duties and the bases of discipline of the militias of the Union are determined by general laws issued by the Congress. However, as the differences of localities or customs which distinguish the character of the different States which compose the great federation require some modifications in the application of these laws, each State has regulated for its own particular account the formation of its militia corps, their internal discipline, nomination of officers, etc., while having care, however, not to deviate from the main bases put in place by the Congress.

As all these particular regulations of the States differ little from one another, and it would be too long, besides, to make them all known in detail, I believe that I will have satisfied the curiosity of the reader sufficiently by giving here only an extract of the ordinances concerning militias of the State of Massachusetts.

The law of the Congress of the United States calls to the ranks of the militia all the citizens capable of bearing arms, from the age of 18 up to the age of 45. The State of Massachusetts makes an exception in favor of individuals hereafter designated: the Lieutenant Governor of the State; the members of the Executive Council; the Judges of the Supreme Court, Inferior Courts and their clerks; the members of the Legislative Assembly; Justices of the Peace; all the officers charged with enforcement of the civil laws; the Attorney General; Public Prosecutor, the Secretary and Treasurer of the State, as well as their clerks; the Sheriffs; employees of public schools, ministers of all the religions without distinguishing the denominations; all the civil officers commissioned by the United States; and, finally, the Quakers when they present a certificate, signed by two or more elders of the Society, stating that the bearer has belonged to the aforesaid Society and that his religious opinions prevent him from bearing arms. Nonetheless, all the individuals heretofore designated, although exempted from service of the militias, are obligated, so long as they are 18 to 45 years old, to have at their homes and to present at each annual review the arms and war equipment prescribed by the laws of the United States. They must, moreover, pay two dollars per year, which is deposited in the till of the treasurer of the city or canton, in order to be used for the arms and equipment of indigent citizens who cannot arm or equip themselves with their own money.

Section 3. The nominations to the different grades in the militias take place in the following manner:

The major generals are chosen by the Senate and the House of Representatives, and commissioned by the general-in-chief.

The brigadier generals are chosen by the written vote of the staff officers of each brigade and commissioned by the general-in-chief.

The staff officers, by the written votes of the captains, lieutenants and second-lieutenants of the regiments to which they are attached, and commissioned by the general-in-chief.

The captains, lieutenants and second-lieutenants, by the written vote of the non-commissioned officers and the soldiers of the respective companies.

All these nominations must be confirmed by the general-in-chief, who alone delivers the commissions or certificates.

The adjutant general is named by the general-in-chief himself.

The quartermaster general is also chosen by the general-in-chief, but with the advice of the council.

The aides-de-camp are chosen by the generals themselves.

The adjutants, the quartermasters, chaplins, surgeons, etc. are all chosen by the commander of the regiment; and confirmed by the general-in-chief.

Section 4. The non-commissioned officers are named in each company by the captain, with the approval of the colonel.

Section 6. Each major must from time to time give orders to fill, by way of election, all the vacant posts in his division. These replacements are announced at least ten days in advance to all those who have the right to vote. If the voters neglect or refuse to provide the replacements required, the major general informs the general-in-chief of it, who at once, with the advice of his council, fills the vacant posts himself, and immediately delivers the certificates of the positions via the brigadier general. Every officer thus named must declare his acceptance within ten days. His silence prolonged beyond this term is considered a refusal, and they proceed to another choice.

Section 7. Every officer legally appointed and commissioned must, before entering upon his duties, swear and sign the following oath:

> I solemnly swear to be faithful to the State of Massachusetts, and to defend its Constitution;
>
> I solemnly swear; and I affirm, that I will fulfill loyally and impartially all the duties which are imposed on me, while using all my abilities in conformity to the statutes of the Constitution and the laws of this State;
>
> I swear to defend the Constitution of the United States.

These oaths and declarations are signed and recorded before a justice of the peace and attested on the back of the certificate.

Section 9. Every officer, non-commissioned officer and soldier of infantry, cavalry, artillery, grenadiers and sharpshooters must possess arms and equipment prescribed by the laws of the United States concerning militias, unless his financial situation does not permit him to obtain them himself. This incapacity must then be certified each year on the first Tuesday of May, to the general assembly of militias, by the administrators for the poor of the city or village; and then the notables of this city or village must see to it that the indigent militiamen be armed or equipped at the expense of the community. The arms thus furnished to the indigent militiamen are only entrusted to him when he is called into the ranks, and are afterwards put in deposit in a warehouse, under the responsibility of the officers.

Section 11. The uniform, the arms, the equipment of an officer, a non-commissioned officer or soldier of the militias cannot be seized for debts or payment of taxes. An officer, non-commissioned officer or soldier cannot be arrested or cited before a civil tribunal when he is going to carry out, is carrying out or returning from carrying out any duty imposed by his militia service.

Section 18. Every commander of a company must assemble his troop the first Tuesday of May to ensure the good condition of the arms and equipment of its soldiers, to order the necessary repairs, and to adjust for the intervening changes on the rolls. He must also assemble the company three times per year to conduct maneuvers. Any time that a chief of the corps wants to assemble his troop for a review or maneuver, he must communicate the order for it by the non-commissioned officers of each company, and these orders must be delivered orally to each soldier or noticed by a writing or a printed paper left at his home. No order for a review or maneuver will be compulsory if it has not been given four days in advance. But in case of invasion, insurrection or other grave circumstances, every order, however precipitate it may be, is legal and compulsory.

Section 22. Each town and each district of the State must have continuously in a warehouse 64 pounds of good cannon powder, 100 pounds of bullets, each bullet weighing one-eighteenth of a pound, 120 gun flints, three military camp-kettles for each 64 men carried on the militia rolls of the town or district. Each town or district which would neglect these provisionings will be punished by a fine which could vary from $20 to $500, according to the seriousness of the neglect.

Section 23. Each time the corps chiefs want to drill their troops, there is delivered to them, on written request, one-quarter of a litre of powder divided into cartridges for each man. This distribution is made under the auspices of magistrates on the account of the town or district.

Section 24. In case of invasion, insurrection or every other public danger, the militias can be called by the commander-in-chief whenever he judges their presence to be necessary. Each man carried on the rolls, who does not obey these orders in 24 hours, is sentenced to pay a fine of $50 or to furnish a man in his place. Each non-commissioned officer or soldier of a militia corps called to arms must take with him provisions for three days, unless a contrary order should be given to him. Each time the militias of a district are called to arms, the authorities of the district must furnish to the detachment called all campaign equipment and utensils, and, in the case of neglect or refusal, are punished by a fine which can be charged from $200 to $500.

Section 26. Any officer, non-commissioned officer or soldier can be called under arms during the time dedicated to the elections of the governor, the lieutenant governor, the senators of the State, the president, the vice president and the members of the congress of the United States. Any assembly of militia during different times is illegal unless it may be ordered by the general-in-chief *in case of invasion*.

Section 29. The parents, the masters or the guardians of minors are obliged to furnish to the said minors enrolled in the militia the arms and equipment required by the law, unless their indigence certified by the administrators of the poor exempts them from this obligation.

Section 30. If an officer, non-commissioned officer or soldier is killed or wounded while carrying out an order prescribed by the laws concerning militias, his widow and his children have the right to compensation determined by the general court.

Courts-martial are established to judge the officers of the militias. Those who are to judge officers above the rank of captain are named by the commander-in-chief, and take the name of general court-martial; those called upon to judge captains and subordinate officers are named by the major generals or by the commanders of the divisions, and take the name of division court-martial. The first is composed of officers taken from the general roll of the division; the second of officers taken from the roll of a regiment or a battalion. The court is composed of a president, a dozen members and a clerk.

The officer who convenes the court can name, besides, six substitutes intended to replace, in order of grade or seniority, members of the court who should fall ill during the proceedings; the members of the court always take their rank after the seniority of their commission, without regard to the seniority of the corps. Before proceeding to open the proceedings, the judge-advocate gives to the president and the other members of the court the following speech:

> You swear to examine, without partiality, without favor, without attachment, without prejudice, without bias and without hope of reward the cause now pending between the state and the accused. You swear also not to divulge the sentence of the court-martial without its approval, nor to publish at any time or any place the secret of the vote or the opinion of any of the members of the court, unless it should be required of you as a witness by a court of justice by virtue of the law.

Each person called as a witness before a court-martial by a judge-advocate is obligated to appear, short of exposing himself to the penalties charged by the law against persons who render themselves culpable of neglect when they are called as witness in a criminal case. Before the witnesses make their statements, the judge-advocate reminds them of their duties in these terms. "You swear to tell the truth, the whole truth and nothing but the truth in this case, and to do it under the pains of being treated as a perjurer...."

If a member of a court-martial is charged, whether it be by the government or by the accused, the accusation must be made in writing and submitted to the court, which pronounces on its validity. The court never accepts an accusation against more than one member at a time. The accused member cannot vote on the question of the validity of the accusation, but then the president votes with the court in order to maintain the number of votes at twelve.

The accused can be declared guilty only on the determination of two-thirds of the members of the court; the punishment to which he can be sentenced is public censure or discontinuance of his office for a time or forever.

Section 31. Each court-martial is authorized to take measures to ensure its tranquility during the time of its session and to imprison any person who disturbs it during its meetings. This imprisonment, however, cannot last more than eight hours.

Section 32. The commander-in-chief can assemble a council of officers every time he judges it necessary to consider a military question or one relative to discipline. The commander-in-chief, the major generals, and the division chiefs can, each in his division, form a court of inquiry to examine each accusation made by an inferior against a superior. This court of inquiry is always composed of three officers and a judge-advocate, all sworn, and can only take testimony without giving its judgment.

Section 34. Every officer accused of misconduct, negligence, disobedience or of mistreatment of and injustice toward his inferiors is summoned before a court-martial. Every officer convicted of a dishonorable act is at once put under arrest and deprived of all military command until the two legislative chambers should request his return from the governor.

Every officer, before being summoned before a court-martial, is first put under arrest, suspended in the exercise of his duties and receives a copy of the charges brought against him. This copy must be delivered at least ten days before the commencement of the proceedings.

Every captain or commander who refuses or neglects to assemble his company as often as the regulations require, or who refuses to assemble when his superior orders him to do it or who, lastly, promotes the absence of men under his orders is triable by a court-martial.

An officer under arrest cannot tender his resignation.

Every person who desires to be a part of a voluntary company is required to enter into a contract to serve in it for seven years.

Every officer who neglects or refuses to march in his detachment when the order to do so is given to him is immediately arrested and brought before a court-martial. The officer who follows him in rank marches in his place.

The company commanders must, from time to time, distribute cartridges to their soldiers in order to make them perform firearms exercises; but if a commander notices a non-commissioned officer or a solider arrive with his gun loaded, he punishes him with a fine which cannot be below five dollars nor above $20.

Every officer who assembles and makes his company perform manuevers during the time of the elections can be summoned before a court-martial, but in all cases he is obliged to pay a fine of $50 to $300.

Every non-commissioned officer or soldier under arms who injures an officer or incites or takes part in any disorder can be put in prison by the company commander for a time more or less long but never exceeding, however, the time during which the company is assembled. He is, besides, convicted of a fine of five dollars to $20.

Every non-commissioned officer or solider who leaves his post without permission of his officer pays a fine of two to ten dollars.

Every non-commissioned officer or soldier sentenced to a penalty involving loss of civil rights by the ordinary tribunals is immediately expunged from the rolls of the militias.

Every non-commissioned officer who is found guilty of neglect, disobedience or misconduct can be reduced from his rank and placed in the ranks of simple soldiers.

Light fines are imposed on non-commissioned officers and soldiers who neglect to appear at the appointed taking-up of arms or who present themselves there with their arms or their equipment in poor condition.

The non-commissioned officers and soldiers of voluntary companies are punished with a two dollar fine if they should appear under arms without having the uniform of their company.

Every excuse for not being present at a review or a taking-up of arms, legally ordered, must be produced within eight days, without which it is not taken into account.

Every non-commissioned officer or soldier who, after having been legally summoned, does not appear pays a two dollar fine at the election of an officer.

The most senior aide-de-camp of each major general, the major of each brigade, and the adjutant of each regiment must always have the exact roll of their respective division, brigade or their regiment.

Each clause of the regulations concerning the militias must be read in the presence of each company, every year on the first Tuesday of May.

Section 36. The collection of fines legally imposed on non-commissioned officers and soldiers is made by the clerk of each company. These collections cannot be made without the intervention of the justice officers of the district to which the person fined belongs.

Section 37. The clerk of each company retains for himself one quarter of each fine and turns the rest over to the commander of the company who gives him a receipt. This money, received by the captain, is employed towards the needs of the company with the approval of the majority of the officers.

Section 38. The adjutant general, the quartermaster general, the judge-advocates, the brigadier majors, the brigade quartermasters, the adjutants and finally all the officers employed on the military boards, the courts-martial and the courts of inquiry receive compensation in money and rations.

The militias called to active duty receive pay and rations like troops of the United States.

The law of the State relative to the repression of insurrections depends on the intervention of the militias and regulates, at the same time, in a positive manner, relations then established between the civil authority and the armed force. This law and the preamble which precedes it appear to be of such high importance that they will be reported here in their entirety.

> *Law for the prompt and efficient repression of seditions and insurrections in the State.*
>
> Considering that in a free government where the people have the right to be armed for the common defense, and where the military power is always subordinate to the civil authority, it is necessary, for the safety of the State, that all good citizens be ready constantly to lend their support to the government, and to oppose efforts of the factious or the ambitious, who would attempt to overthrow the laws and the Constitution of their country; considering that the least delay in the repression of sedition or insurrection, in any part of the State that it might be delayed, can have dangerous and alarming consequences, the Senate and the House of Representatives assembled in the General Court have decided:
>
> Section 1. Every time that an insurrection breaks out in some part of the State, with the intent of obstructing the course of justice and of opposing the legal execution of the laws, or there should occur even the presumption that an insurrection of this kind is being contemplated, it will be the duty of the civil officers, of the sheriff and the judges of the different courts of the places threatened by it to give their opinion to the governor. Immediately, the latter must use the powers invested in him by the Constitution. He will give immediate orders to the major general or to the officer commanding the division

in the territory in which the insurrection has broken out to march with the forces necessary to support the civil authority. He will be able even to give this order to the officers commanding the adjacent divisions, if their aid appears necessary.

Section 2. If, in the opinion of the sheriff and of two justice officers, it was urgently necessary, in order to repress the insurrection, known or presumed, to appeal at once to arms, and if by reason of the distance it was impossible to obtain from the commander-in-chief necessary aid soon enough, it will be the duty of the sheriff and the justice officers to apply to the officers commanding the most adjacent divisions, in order to obtain the forces deemed indispensable in the defense of the civil authorities and in the repression of the insurgents, excepting that they are to inform the commander-in-chief of it as soon as possible. The commanders of the divisions must immediately set the forces requested in motion. The militia raised, armed and equipped according to the law, will be under the orders of the civil officer or the magistrate.

Section 3. If a commissioned officer of the militia refuses or neglects to execute the orders which he shall have received from his superiors to march with a detachment which shall have been entrusted to go to defend the civil authority or to repress sedition, this officer will be punished, besides the punishment directed by the regulations of the militias, with a fine which could not exceed 50 pounds, and will be declared incapable of fulfilling his duties for a time which could not last beyond ten years; according to the seriousness of the transgression or the validity of the excuses offered by the accused, one of the two penalties or both of them will be imposed.

Section 4. If a non-commissioned officer or a soldier belonging to a detachment commanded for the defense of the civil authorities or the repression of insurrection neglects or refuses to march, to arm himself, to equip himself, as he shall have been ordered, or withdraws before having permission for it, should he be convicted before the supreme court, he shall pay a fine fixed by the court, but which cannot exceed ten pounds.

Section 5. Every person who, by public or private speech, or in other ways, attempts to prevent an officer or a soldier belonging to a detachment advancing against an insurrection from doing his duty or urges him to abandon his post, is punishable by payment of a fine which cannot exceed 50 pounds and by the posting of a bond during a term which cannot last beyond three years.

Section 6. Compensation is granted to the detachments which serve in the circumstances determined by this act.

In outlining here the code of militias of the State of Massachusetts, I have omitted a large number of articles which are only prescribed for internal discipline, but that which I have reported will suffice, I hope, to demonstrate upon which principles this formidable organization of the armed force is based.

These sacred principles, which can be doubted only by men interested in upholding despotism, are:

1. That every individual belonging to a society from which he has the right to expect protection in the enjoyment of his life, his liberty and his property must, in return, contribute to the cost of this protection by his personal services or by an equivalent;

2. That the people have the right to bear arms for the common defense;

3. That in times of peace a numerous, permanent army can only be dangerous for liberty; and

4. That the military power must always be subordinated to the civil authority and be governed by it.

It is on these very principles that the worthy Parisian National Guard, the conduct of which was so honorable during the thunderstorms of our Revolution and which so often made the anarchists fall back and the counter-revolutionaries grow pale, was created and organized. Also, it should be noted that there are an infinite number of points of contact between the formation of the American militias and that of the French National Guard, organized by the law of September 29, 1791. The fate of this wise institution, protective of the liberty of which it is the child, has been very different in America than in France, on the other side of the Ocean. In the former, it has been maintained and fortified in the shade of popular institutions which leave to each man his dignity and which guarantee all his rights. In the latter, distorted at first by anarchy, it has disappeared under the despotism which has taken away all of our liberties.

Chapter V

Route from Boston to Portsmouth – Stay at Portsmouth – History, Constitution and Statistics of New Hampshire – Route from Portsmouth to New York – Description of Long Island.

The State of New Hampshire had dispatched a delegation to General Lafayette to invite him to come to Portsmouth to visit the maritime institutions. On August 31, we set out to proceed there while tracing our route via Lexington, Concord, Salem, Marblehead and Newburyport. We stopped for a little while in Lexington, but we started out again from there very much affected by the touching scenes which we had witnessed and the historical memories which we had found there.

They recalled how, in 1775, some countrymen were assassinated by an English battalion on Lexington Square. It was at this very place that General Lafayette was greeted by the people, both free and happy, who came to meet there to celebrate his arrival. Through two lines of beaming militias, we arrived at the foot of the pyramidal monument which marked the spot where the first martyrs of freedom fell and rest. There, two old men told us about this first scene of the great revolutionary drama. They had been participants in it, and this circumstance gave their narrative a powerful spell which captured our attention. They were delighted to tell the least particulars of this action; they repeated with heated indignation the abusive and menacing words which the savage Pitcairn addressed to them while calling on them to disperse; and the smile of anguish and of scorn distorted their lips when they explained to us how 800 English had fired on some countrymen. Then, they named with emotion those of their companions and friends who had been struck dead at their side; in naming them, their eyes, full of tears, cast down on the hillock that we stood on, and our eyes, also, involuntarily proceeded to this last resting place of these citizen-heroes and paid them a tribute of remembrance and admiration. After some minutes of solemn silence, one of the two old men cried out: "We weep still for our brothers, but we do not pity them; they have died for their country and for liberty!" At these words of country and liberty, the crowd, profoundly moved, responded with the cries of "Long live Lafayette" and for a long time it was difficult to restrain this outburst of public recognition.

All the militias of the District had been assembled on the square at Lexington; they filed before the pyramid and Lafayette; they bowed before these two monuments of their Revolution. On their standards was depicted the death of their fathers, the memory of which perpetuated hatred of despotism and of English domination among these citizen-soldiers.

At the moment when we were going to withdraw from the monument to get back to our carriages, a young man appeared before us, carrying in his hands a long, coarsely formed gun covered with rust; he presented it to the General with a solemnity which led us to presume that this instrument of death was entitled by some special circumstance to the veneration with which he carried it. In a word, we learned that this gun was the one which first answered the fire of the English at this place in Lexington. "My father carried it on *April 19, 1775*," the young man said to him. "It is in his hands that the work that you and Washington so gloriously finished began; I am very glad that it makes your acquaintance… ."

The General took the gun and examined it with pleasure; each of us also wanted to touch it. In returning it to the young man, the General counseled him to inscribe on the grip the date of April 19, the name of the brave citizen who made so beautiful use of it, and then to place it in a box in order to preserve it from the ravages of time. The young man was touched by this advice and promised to follow it.

Although the distance from Lexington to Concord is very short, we were nonetheless obliged to stop in this latter Town. The people of the environs had gathered together on the public place where they had set up a tent of flowers and greenery under which a troop of girls, radiant with freshness and beauty, offered some refreshments to the Nation's Guest, who was invited to take his place at the center of an elegantly set table, around which only the ladies had been admitted. Some girls crowned with flowers circulated around this table and did the honors there with an ease and charm which was moving; but it was especially toward the General that their entire attention was drawn, and that all their most tender solicitude was concentrated. All was cheerful, all was gracious in this picture of happiness and joy which we had before us; but at the same time, our glance was struck by a remarkable contrast; opposite the tent, at the other end of this place, we noticed on the hill which bound it a jumbled heap of funeral stones; we recognized that this was a place consecrated to eternal rest. Very many of these monuments were already blackened by age; some were brilliantly white. Near one of the latter a woman and two children clad in black prostrated themselves; their grieving demeanor seemed to tell us that festival days are not the end of days of mourning; but not one of the table-companions appeared to entertain this view; all were too happy to notice how narrow the space was which separated them from the place where all return to nothingness.

At Marblehead, I was dragged out of the profound reverie into which the scene at Concord had immersed me by the noise of the cannon and the shouts of the people who came running before General Lafayette. Some brilliant preparations had been made to receive him in this Town, where they knew, however, that he could not stop to eat. While ascending *Washington Hill*, he encountered the students of 11 public schools and 20 private schools, escorted by their teachers and the president of the education council. Girls and boys, they were 900 in number. A delegation formed of one representative of each school approached his carriage and presented him an address in which they expressed the gratitude of the children for the services which their fathers had received from him.

Salem is only 14 miles from Boston, and yet we arrived there after noon because, at each step, General Lafayette was obliged to stop to receive displays of affection from all those he met on his route. At the entrance to the City, he was received by the magistrates and by a procession of numerous citizens. Several militia corps were in battle array during his passage, and his arrival was announced by salvos of artillery and ringing of bells. In spite of the rain which was falling in torrents, the streets were entirely filled with a throng which rushed headlong upon his passage and which heaped benedictions upon him. We traversed the whole City at a walking pace in order to pass beneath a great number of triumphal arches which were decorated with emblems and inscriptions. On one we read: *"Honor to Lafayette! Honor to the one who fought and spilled his blood for the peace and happiness which we enjoy."* On another: *"Lafayette, friend and defender of liberty, welcome to your favorite land!"* On another, finally: *"At the time of our adversity, you helped us; in our prosperity, we recall your services with gratitude."* The dining hall and the dinner itself had been decorated by a great number of women from the City. Opposite the place which the General occupied at the table, in the middle of garlands of flowers and trophies was this inscription: *"Lafayette in America – Where can one be better than in the bosom of his family?"*

Some former comrades-in-arms, seated at his sides, reclaimed the right to serve him, while reminding him merrily that they had won this right at Yorktown where he had not refused their services. The dinner ended with a large number of toasts. They drank *to France*, the friend of liberty in America; may she never become the friend of oppression in Europe! Then we left Salem to lodge in Newburyport. Although the weather continued to be dreadful, the General could never get the escort of cavalrymen of the Salem militia to desist from accompanying him; it galloped alongside his coach for nearly 7½ miles, swords in hand, at the risk of crashing down 20 times, so much had the roads deteriorated.

In spite of all the diligence that we could muster, it was very far into the night when we arrived at Newburyport. The flash of lights and of fires ignited in the streets and public places, the uninterrupted noise of the cannon and the bells, the shouts of the citizens, and the sight of a multitude of armed soldiers advancing rapidly to the sound of the drum, would have made us believe that we were entering a city taken by storm and delivered up to fires, if the words *Liberty*, *Fatherland*, *Washington*, *Lafayette*, which struck our ears ceaselessly, had not reassured us, while reminding us that we were attending a national and truly popular festival.

Despite the advanced hour of night, the General was obliged to devote a rather long time to welcoming the residents who rushed in a crowd to the door to greet him. We had gone down to Tracy's Inn, which had been prepared by the town to give us lodging. It is there that Washington stayed in 1789; the room which he stayed in had been preserved since that time with the greatest care; the furnishings had not been changed at all; and General Lafayette had the pleasure of resting in the same bed where, 35 years before, his paternal friend had rested. By the joy which shone in the eyes of our host, it was easy to divine the feelings which animated him, and how difficult it would be now to induce him to part with furnishings which had served both Washington and Lafayette.

We left Newburyport early in the morning, and toward the middle of the day we arrived in Portsmouth. Numerous infantry corps and nearly the entire population, led by their magistrates, had repaired to the entrance of the City to receive General Lafayette. A thousand children from different schools were arranged in double rows on his way, and although these poor children had for their entire headdress wreaths of flowers and rain was falling profusely, not one of them wanted to leave his post. The procession which had formed to accompany the General at his entry into the City was 2,000 long. After he traversed the principal streets, he came to a stop in Congress Street, where they bid us to enter Franklin Hall. The President of the City Council made the following speech before the citizens who were assembled there:

> General! The magistrates of Portsmouth have been charged by their fellow citizens to express to you the gratitude and joy which your arrival causes in them.
>
> Having enjoyed, as we do, the happiness which a free government creates, our gratitude comes naturally to those whose courage had obtained it for us. Those intrepid men among us who have, at the moment of danger, come to the defense of their country have, without a doubt, *rights* to our veneration; but it is clear, nonetheless, that in fighting for the liberty of

their country, they were working to assure their own happiness and the future of their children; the particular feeling of interest which motivated them does not at all diminish the value of their services, but the disinterested zeal which brought you from a foreign land to aid the inhabitants of this one stands out in remarkable relief. In us, the love of liberty was but a patriotic sentiment; in you, it was the result of a sentiment nobler still, the love of the human race.

After an absence of 40 years far from our country, in the midst of so many troubles and unrest, you have returned to us such as you left us, a firm and constant friend of liberal principles. Through the numerous events of your life, our hearts have followed you; in whatever situation you have been in, be it at the head of the National Guard, be it in the prison of Olmutz, be it in the midst of representatives of the Nation, you have always shown yourself to be the first friend of America, always worthy of our esteem.

Permit us then to receive you as the Nation's Guest and to render to you all the honors which it is in our power to bestow on you. They are the voluntary tribute of hearts burning with gratitude. We wish our children to understand that virtue alone has the right to such homage and that in the midst of a free people merit never stays without reward.

We pray that you receive our sincere wishes for your happiness and your health. Each day we direct our prayers to heaven that your noble example should encourage the wise men of all nations and support them in the struggle which they have taken on in favor of the freedom of the entire world.

In his response, General Lafayette expressed his joy to see happy America again, after so long an absence, and his appreciation for the reception which he had received. In concluding, he said, "I thank you, citizens, for having thought of me when I was in the midst of events whose memory you have wanted to save. The approbation of a free, virtuous and enlightened people is the most beautiful recompense that one can receive and one which, like true glory, is priceless. This recompense is sweeter still because it is accorded to an adopted son … ." Here general applause and unanimous cheering interrupted him and proved that this adoption was in all their hearts.

Following this, the General was presented to the Governor of the State of New Hampshire, Mr. Morril, who had come expressly to welcome him and who greeted him in the name of the State. After his presentation to the Governor, he was surrounded by some aged companions-in-arms among whom he recognized General Smith, who had served for three years under his command as captain of light infantry. While they expressed mutual and heartfelt satisfaction at meeting again, they were interrupted by another old soldier from the Revolution, who, weeping with emotion, had come to recount loudly how, during the war, *the Marquis* had rendered to him a great number of personal services. The General was very anxious to interrupt this recitation which caused him great embarrassment, but which excited the profound interest of his audience.

While we went to take possession of our lodgings, which had been prepared in the house of the last Governor of New Hampshire, Mr. Langdon, we encountered some Indians in the street; they were the first that I had seen. They piqued my curiosity to the point that I could not conceal it. As soon as the members of the committee who accompanied us left, I saw a dozen savages, inhabitants of the forests of Canada, arrive obligingly at nearly the same time as we arrived at our lodgings. I learned that they had come from beyond the Great Lakes to exchange some fur skins for some trifles and liquors. I swear that I found nothing about them that corresponded to the idea that I had formed about these children of nature. Their clothes had no other character than those of a pauper; crosses and rosary beads had replaced their beautiful feather headdresses, their fur skins and their weapons; no longer did their intoxicated faces have that expression of noble pride which, they say, so particularly distinguished the savage man; their manner appeared at first affectionate; but soon we recognized that they were only servile or selfish. They spoke to us about baptism and confession as their Manitou priests, doubtless, spoke to them; in a word, it appeared to me that these poor unfortunates had made only a change of superstitions, and that civilization had only brought them its vices, without compensatory benefits. Their appearance assured me that most of them had become idlers, drunkards and thieves, without losing any of their ignorance. An old man who appeared to be their chief, and who spoke a little French, informed us that his tribe was established in Canada. On the question which we put to him whether he was happy in the vicinity of the English, he responded that he loved the French very much; as soon as he was informed that we were French, he and his companions immediately shook our hands heartily. There were several women; some suckled their infants; they appeared to me to be very miserable and not at all pretty.

While we conversed with our civilized Indians, a new procession made ready to conduct General Lafayette to the Navy Yard; he proceeded there a little while after, but his son and I could not accompany him; wishing to take advantage of one occasion, sure and ready, to give news to our friends in France, we decided to stay at the lodgings to write letters. We felt, however, some regret about not having seen the Navy Yard, which they say is very beautiful and very extensive.

The rest of our day was occupied with a public dinner which all the authorities and a large number of citizens attended and also Mr. Salazar, the *chargé d'affaires* in the United States from the Republic of Colombia.[4] After the dinner, we went to a ball where more than 400 women were presented to General Lafayette. We left the ball at midnight and climbed into our carriage to return to Boston, where we awaited some companions for the trip to New York; but, before continuing our trip, I want to devote some pages to the History, the Constitution and the current condition of the State of New Hampshire, of which Portsmouth is the most important city by population, which is more than 7,000 people, and by its commerce, which is very extensive.

The State of New Hampshire is between 42° 42′ and 45° 14′ latitude north and between 4° 29′ and 6° 10′ longitude east of Washington; its area is about 9,280 square miles; its shape is that of a trapezium with its base in the middle; it is bounded on the North by lower Canada, on the South by Massachusetts, on the East by Maine and the ocean; and on the West by the Connecticut River, which separates it from the State of Vermont. Its coastline has about 18 miles of development and is in general sandy and slightly uneven. In the interior, one finds some considerable enough hills; the highest ones are the White Mountains. The most extensive bodies of water that one encounters there are Lakes Umbagog and Winnepesaukee and the Piscataqua and Merrimac Rivers. One can say that the soil of New Hampshire is of the earliest formation. It is generally fertile; however, the most productive parts are the banks of the rivers, which deposit by their flooding a very fertile silt. On the seashore, they reap a plentiful harvest of a grass which they call salt hay, which is very suitable for livestock. The most abundant mines are iron mines in the Districts of Franconia and Enfield. One finds also, they say, some native silver in small veins in the mountains of the West, but it is only a very small quantity and mined at too great expense. Black lead is very abundant in the District of Sutton and near Mount Monadnock.

The hot weather of summer is short, but extreme. As to the cold, it must be very severe since Lake Winnipesaukee, which is 24 miles long and in some places 12 miles wide, freezes three months a year, to the point that it

---

4. Mr. Salazar, whose conversation had revealed him to be a profoundly learned man who was entirely devoted to republican institutions, finished winning our hearts by making a toast to Mr. Destutt de Tracey and proclaiming the felicitous influence of his writings on the two hemispheres.

is able to support heavy carriages. Nonetheless, the climate there is very healthy, and examples of longevity are not rare. One often sees there people who live beyond 100 years.

New Hampshire was discovered in 1614 by Captain Smith, and the first settlements, composed of fishermen and planters, were made on the Piscataqua River in 1623. These settlements were united with the Government of Massachusetts in 1641. A dispute concerning rights on the lands purchased from the Indians led to the separation of the two provinces in 1692. In 1727, New Hampshire gave itself its first Constitution and determined its boundaries with Massachusetts. In 1765, the people repulsed the Stamp Act, and consequently engaged in the Revolutionary War, in which they conducted themselves with perseverance and vigor until its end. The State of New Hampshire was the ninth to vote for the new Federal Constitution of the United States, by the vote of its legislature, which carried it by a majority of 11, the number of voters being about 300. This event decided in favor of the establishment of the Federal Government. The new State Constitution was adopted in 1792; it was preceded by a Declaration of Rights, and it recognized three powers, *the Legislative, the Executive and the Judicial.*

The Legislative power resides in a Senate and House of Representatives which compose together the General Court or the General Assembly; and each branch exercises a veto on the other. Money bills originate in the House of Representatives, but they can be amended by the Senate, which rules on objections to passage.

The Senate is composed of 13 Senators elected each year by the citizens paying taxes. The requirements for candidacy are (1) one must be 30 years old; (2) one must possess property worth 200 pounds in the State; (3) one must have lived in the State for seven years before the election and be a resident of the District by which he has been chosen.

The House of Representatives is composed of deputies of the different towns, from each of which the number is proportionate to the population, at the rate of one Representative per each 150 taxpayers at least 21 years old, and a rate of two Representatives for 450, so that 300 more taxpayers are necessary for each new Representative.

The election is held by secret ballot, and none can be eligible if he does not possess an estate valued at 100 pounds in his District, of which half must be his personal property. It is also necessary that he live in the District at the time of his election, and in the State for two years. Each male inhabitant 21 years old, except paupers and those exempted from taxes at their own request, has the right to vote for the nomination of Senators and Representatives.

The Executive power is entrusted to a Governor and five Councillors. The Governor is chosen for one year, also by all the citizens 21 years old who pay some taxes, and if two persons have an equal number of votes, the choice is determined by a vote of the two Houses. To be elected Governor, it is necessary to be 30 years old, to possess property worth 500 pounds, of which half must be real estate situated inside the State. The Governor is commander-in-chief of the land and naval forces; with the advice and consent of the Council of the State, which he calls into session at his will, he names the Attorney General, and the other judicial officers. He has the right to pardon convicts, except those who have been judged before the Senate on an order of accusation of the House. He signs all the commissions, which are countersigned by his Secretary.

The Councilors are also chosen by all the taxpayers 21 years old, and they require of them the same qualifications as for Governor, with this difference, however, that at least 300 pounds of their property must be real estate. The State Secretary, the Treasurer and the General Manager are chosen by the Senators and Representatives. The County Treasurer and the Recorder of Deeds are named by the inhabitants of the different Districts.

The Representatives of Congress are chosen by the inhabitants gathered at town assemblies, and their votes are sent to the State Secretary who counts them before the General Court. It is the same way that they choose candidates for President and Vice President. The two Senators in the Congress are chosen by the General Court.

The Judicial power is composed of a Superior Court of four Judges who make two circuits of the counties annually; of a Lower Court with the same number of Judges in each county who sit four times a year; of a Court of General Session, of Justices of the Peace who sit at the same time; of a Court of Verification of Deeds, consisting of a single Judge, who sits every month in a different county; and of Courts of Justice.

The Judges are named by the Governor and the Council and stay in office up to the age of 70. If they are accused of state crimes, they can be prosecuted at the request of the Legislature.

The jury, composed of 12 men of property, whose decision renders judgment in all lawsuits, is chosen by the Municipal Council from persons who possess an estate of 50 pounds; the names of one-third of the members are put in one box, and two-thirds in another; they take from the first the jurors for the inferior court; this is done by the Town Clerk in public meeting.

The General Court is authorized to reform the Judicial system, according as it considers it appropriate or necessary for the public good; and to give to the Justices of the Peace jurisdiction in civil cases, when it does not concern real estate and the damages do not exceed four pounds, with a right of appeal to another court and trial by jury.

The Chief Justice receives $1,500 per year. Each Judge receives $1,200. The Sheriffs, like the Judges, cannot stay in office after their 70th year; nor can they take legal action or receive fees like lawyers or counsel of a private party, or commence a civil suit as long as they are in the exercise of their duties.

All the civil or military officers swear the following oath before entering into the exercise of their duties:

> I solemnly swear to maintain allegiance to the State of New Hampshire, to defend its Constitution, and to carry out with impartiality all the duties of my office, as Governor, Senator, etc., in the best manner possible, following the statutes, the regulations, the Constitution and the laws of the State of New Hampshire, so help me God.

If the officer is a Quaker, he adds to his oath: "I make this oath under the pains and penalties of perjury."

The financial organization is both economical and extensive. Each town names one or several Collectors to whom they remit the different schedules of taxes, with full powers to seize, if necessary, the property and person of delinquents. If someone refuses to produce a statement of his property which is subject to taxes, the Municipal Council is authorized to designate by its decision the sum which this individual must pay. County taxes are apportioned by Judges of the Court who sit four times a year, and the proportion which each town must pay is specified in the warrant of the County Treasurer.

Each year in April they make a new census of the property of taxpayers; all this property is taxed at a rate of 6% of its income, except fallow land and buildings, which pay only 1/2% of their current value. The mills and the ferryboats are taxed at 1/12th of their annual revenue; business capital is taxed according to its value, and money at interest is taxed at 3/4%.

The debts that the State had contracted in 1814, and which had mounted with interest to more than $30,000, have been discharged, and they have now considerable funds in the Bank of the United States.

The wisdom and the economy of the administration and the fairness of the Government have borne their fruits. The success of New Hampshire cannot be doubted; it is attested to by the spread of knowledge, by the richness of Commerce, by the prosperity of Agriculture, and by the rapid growth of the population. This increase, despite the constant emigration of the men of the North to the new regions of the South and especially the West, is, moreover, very remarkable. In 1755, the population was about 34,000; in 1790, it was 141,885; in 1800, it was 183,858; in 1810, it was 214,460; and today it has grown to 244,161. In this number, there are close to 800 free Colored persons; as to Slaves, I did not count any of them. Although they had no special law of the State against Slavery, the philanthropic spirit of the inhabitants, and certainly their well-understood self-interest, have made short work of this scandal; and one can say today that there are no Slaves any longer in New Hampshire and also that there are no Slaves any longer in the States that they sometimes call New England. This population of 244,161 furnishes 52,384 workers to Agriculture, 8,699 to Manufacturing and 1,068 to Commerce.

The State of New Hampshire can put close to 25,000 men under arms by taking only citizens between 16 and 45 years old. This armed force can be considerably augmented in case of need by men who are on the emergency list; this list is composed of men from 45 to 60 years old and all those who are exempted from ordinary service by regulations governing the formation of militias. The exemptions are the same as those of Massachusetts.

I have said that, in the State of New Hampshire, the spread of knowledge was great. The advantage of a good general education is due to the solicitude of the Government and the foresight of the Constitution, which stipulated to the Legislators and the Magistrates that they always consider as a sacred duty the superintendence of the interests of Letters and Sciences and of all the public schools; and that they encourage private schools and give rewards and privileges too for the advancement of Agriculture, the Arts, Sciences, Commerce, Manufacturing and the Natural History of the locality.

As in all the rest of the Union, the absolute liberty in matters of religion is declared by the Constitution as a natural and inalienable right; no one can be disturbed or impeded by reason of his religious opinions; the law does not recognize any dominant sect. All the ministers of the different congregations have an equal right to the protection of the Government, and they receive their salaries from their congregants, whose esteem they are obliged to try to obtain; and they obtain it only by giving an example of their virtues. Also the morals there are generally pure; common-law marriages and celibacy are valued little. It is rare in the towns to find a bachelor 30 years old. The girls marry early; it is not rare to see mother and daughter feeding their infants at the same time; one can easily find the grandfather, the father and the grandson working together in the fields.

There remain very many things to learn about the State of New Hampshire; but the General having promised to make a second visit next spring, I will take advantage of it to collect some information that I have not been able to obtain during such a short stay.

September 2 – Upon leaving the ball, we boarded the carriage to return to Boston, where we awaited our companions for the trip to New York. Having arrived at two o'clock, we set out again at four, making our way by Lexington, Lancaster, Worcester, Tolland and Hartford. In each of these places, General Lafayette received displays of affection from all the citizens, which touched him deeply, but to which he had hardly the time to reply, so swiftly did we travel. The first day in Bolton, we had stayed in the charming country house of Mr. Wilder, whose amiable hospitality will not be erased from our memory. The second day, we stayed at Stafford, after having attended the glittering festivities of Worcester, and on the 4th at ten o'clock in the morning, we arrived at Hartford, a pretty, very mercantile city, situated on the West Bank of the Connecticut, 40 miles from its source. Its population is 4,726, and it shares with New Haven the advantage of being the seat of the Government of Connecticut.

General Lafayette entered Hartford, preceded by an escort of numerous militiamen, and was welcomed by the entire population with the most animated demonstrations of veneration and love. The City Council came to meet him, and the Mayor addressed him. They led us afterwards to the State House, where he was received by Governor Wolcott who, in welcoming him in the name of the State, said:

> Dear General, I am very happy to be able to salute you again in this fortunate capital of Connecticut, where virtuous and enlightened people have already enjoyed, for a long time, the advantages of republican institutions that they have established under the smooth administration of magistrates chosen each year by their free vote.

The principles for which we have pleaded in our councils and fought for on the fields of battle are triumphant here, and we hope with the aid of heaven to transmit them in all their purity to our most distant future generations.

These principles are now prevalent and have been adopted over all of the part of our continent which extends from the Ocean to the great plains of Missouri and from the Lakes to the Gulf of Mexico; in these vast regions, our sons and daughters, sources of an immense future population, are already developing rapid progress in the Sciences, Religion, Industry and all the Arts that perpetuate and improve powerful nations. Each day the Humanities and Commerce increase our might and our resources. We have made alliance with all those superior souls who, from all the countries of the civilized world, have come here to enjoy this liberty of actions and opinions to which we are so accustomed that now we would not be able to live without it. In some parts to which you will proceed, you will be welcomed by patriots who have shared your glorious works, or by their children, who appreciate your services. You will encounter also very many of those gallant Frenchmen whom dismissals and banishments have sent here to seek a liberty that has been refused them in their own country; all agree to recognize in you the benefactor of the United States and humanity, and they spontaneously unite to bless you and call out to heaven that, after a long and happy life, you be accorded a glorious immortality.

After this oration, to which the General responded with fond effusiveness, there were numerous presentations of all the people whom they had been able to admit into the hall. It was difficult for the assembly to contain its emotion upon seeing old General Wadsworth arrive with the epaulettes which Lafayette had worn at the Battle of Brandywine, where he had been wounded, and the shoulder sash in which they had carried him off the field of battle still bore some traces of his blood. These objects had been given to General Swift after the peace, and his family had preserved them scrupulously in memory of the one who had worn them and of the cause which he had defended.

At the moment when we were leaving the State House, General Lafayette found himself in the midst of 800 public schoolchildren, who offered him a gold medal on which was inscribed: "The children of Hartford, to Lafayette, September 4, 1824."

After having traversed several streets strewn with flowers, we arrived at the institution for deaf mutes. About 60 young unfortunates arranged in a line awaited the coming of General Lafayette in that profound and eternal silence which the horrible whim of nature had inflicted on them. As they turned toward him, they pointed out a sign carrying these words with a hand-gesture toward the heart: *"That which the nation expresses, we feel!"* At their head was their instructor, Clerc, pupil of Abbé Sicard, and rival of Massieu. General Lafayette felt a keen pleasure in seeing that the love of liberty and of humanity had led this young Frenchman to this country where he was providing the most significant services.

When General Lafayette had reviewed the militias which had gathered under the orders of General Johnson and taken leave of the magistrates and leaders of Hartford, he was conducted aboard the steamship *Oliver Ellsworth*, by a detachment of 100 veterans of the Revolution, preceded by a musical band of the militia; after he had received the last farewell from his old companions-in-arms, the boat pushed free, and we commenced to descend the Connecticut River.

This river, which has its source between lower Canada and New Hampshire, a little below the 45th parallel latitude, sets the boundary between that State and Vermont and traverses Massachusetts and Connecticut, travelling through them from north to south; its course is about 300 miles, and, although often strewn with rocks, it is navigable for boats nearly up to its source, and large vessels can easily sail up the river for nearly 50 miles. In its course, it connects with a great number of small tributaries and it flows into Long Island Sound about 30 miles east of New Haven. They say that its banks are pleasant and fertile, but we were scarcely able to enjoy the sight of them.

A little after having left Hartford, our boat stopped opposite Middletown, a pretty little manufacturing town situated on the right bank. The noise of cannon and the cheering of numerous people who covered the riverside apprised General Lafayette with what impatience he had been awaited by the inhabitants of Middletown; he hastened to go ashore to express his gratitude to them, and it was only toward seven o'clock that he was able to return aboard *The Oliver Ellsworth*, so that soon the night enveloped us and hid our view of the pretty dwellings which adorn the entire course of the Connecticut; however, we could judge their number by that of the lights which appeared before us on the right and on the left, like a multitude of stars which shone in the darkness.

When daylight reappeared, we had left the Connecticut River, and we were sailing on Long Island Sound, commonly called the East River. To our left we had Long Island, and to our right New York State. In some parts where we looked, our gaze fell agreeably on elegant country homes, or on farms whose sight alone announced success and abundance. Although the sun was still quite near the horizon when I climbed on deck, I found a large number of ladies who, placed in the windows of their dwellings, already awaited the passage of the vessel which they knew was bringing General Lafayette back to New York. As our flag was recognized, it was greeted by the most touching cheering and by signs of the sweetest affection.

While I breathed the fresh air of the morning, always a little lively on the seashore, with pleasure and while my eyes contemplated with delight the delicious harmony of a beautiful nature and a rich and free industry, I was approached by one of our travelling companions, an old soldier of the Revolution, who came with us from Hartford and who, he said, had not been able to close his eyes the entire night, so much had he been excited by the joy of seeing his former General again. I asked him some details about the most remarkable dwelling-places which presented themselves to my gaze; and he gave them to me very obligingly and in a manner which made me believe that navigation of the Sound was familiar to him. On the question that I posed to him if he had visited Long Island sometime: "Oh, certainly yes," he said to me, "and it has been a long time since the first time! It was in 1776, and without the courage and ability of our worthy General Washington, it is probable that this first visit to Long Island would also have been my last and that my bones would now be resting there in peace. It would have been a shame, however, because I would not have enjoyed the happiness which I had yesterday to clasp the hand of the one who has done so much for the independence of my country. . . ." And I saw a tear of gratitude and emotion roll beneath the eyelid of the old patriot.

After some moments of silence, emboldened by his frank and cordial manner, I asked him what had taken place on his first visit with the memory of which so many other remembrances appeared to be associated. "Here are the facts," said he, while taking me by the arms and causing me to turn toward Long Island, which appeared to pass rapidly before our eyes, like a mobile panorama.

> In 1776, I was no longer a child, as you ought to presume in looking at my bald forehead and my white hair. I served in the Continental Army, and my regiment made up a part of the forces charged with defending Long Island.[5] On the 17th of August, the English and the Hessians, numbering about 24,000, protected by the artillery of their vessels, landed on the island. We had barely 10,000 combatants, and they were

5. *Teacher's Journal.*

positioned such that the major part could not take part in the battle. The fighting, however, was brisk and our resistance dogged, although the enemy had all the advantages of numbers, discipline and experience over us. The attack of the English was conducted with intelligence and bravery; but I daresay that, even if we were less skillful, our courage, on the other hand, earned us the respect of our adversaries. In short, we were surrounded before long, some of us were taken and the rest retreated, leaving in the hands of the enemy the victory and our two Generals, Sullivan and Stirling. We had lost 1,000 to 1,200 men, and the English perhaps more.

After this unfortunate engagement, we came to retrench in our lines in Brooklyn, where we were not at all safe. Fatigued and discouraged by our defeat, facing an enemy superior in force and emboldened by its success, knowing that a large fleet was preparing to cut off our retreat by entering the East River, we felt that we would only escape complete destruction by the protection of Providence and the wisdom of our General-in-chief.

Washington resolved to pull us out of this dangerous position. Taking advantage of the darkness of the night, he crossed the East River in person on August 29, and came to find us in our lines. His presence revived our hopes and our courage; we committed ourselves to his leadership with confidence, and our retreat was accomplished, a feat which alone would have sufficed to classify him among the best generals. It is true that, on this occasion, Providence also gave us vivid evidence of its protection. A thick fog enveloped Long Island the whole night, such that our movements were completely hidden from the enemy, although the atmosphere of the coast of New York was brilliantly bright. We passed so near the enemy that we heard clearly the sound of the workers who were preparing the attack for the morning. Before daybreak appeared, our 9,000 men with their belongings, their stores, their horses and their ammunition, had crossed the river in a spot which was more than a mile wide, without the loss of a single man. An hour after we had returned to New York, the fog lifted as if by magic and allowed us to see clearly the English entering our lines warily, where they were very surprised to find no one there any more.

During the narration of my old soldier, nearly all of our traveling companions had arrived on deck and were grouped around us, and soon the conversation became general. They spoke very much of Long Island, of the elegance and sumptuousness of its country homes, where the inhabitants of New York take pleasure in coming in search of rest and the fresh air of the sea during the great heat waves of summer. I learned that this island, formerly named Matawack[6] by the Indians, its ancient inhabitants, is 140 miles long and has a width which varies from 1 to 15 miles. It is the largest of the islands that one encounters from the Cape of Florida to Cape Sable. The coast, which is washed by the Atlantic Ocean, is flat, sandy and cut by several bays. The greater part of its surface is smooth. The soil is composed of a blackish, spongy dirt with a bed of sand that absorbs the rain and that is unfavorable for vegetation. Dr. Mitchell, translator of the work of Mr. Cuvier on the theory of the soil, has observed that a bed of sand of the sea extends the whole length of the island to a depth of 30-50 feet and that one finds there some quahog and oyster shells, and, in like manner, some pieces of wood hollowing out holes. A line of hills that traverses the island, from New Utrecht in the West up to the environs of Southold in the East, rises to Harbourg Hill more than 319 feet above sea level. In spite of the poor quality of the soil, one finds there the most beautiful nursery of fruit trees that there is in all America. It is cultivated by the careful attentions of Mr. Prince, a skilled horticulturist and nursery gardener, whose enlightened zeal renders great services to his country and who will be as a result – I have no doubt of it – extremely useful even to Europe, very many of whose erudite men already inquire into his writings.

It was about noon when we arrived in the Port of New York. General Lafayette hoped to return to the City without creating a stir; but the streamers and the flags which decorated *The Oliver Ellsworth* gave away his return, and the vessel *Franklin*, which was in our channel, saluted him with 13 blasts of its cannon. This greeting was a signal for all the citizens of New York, and when we approached Fulton Pier, we found the entire population, who welcomed him just as on the first day of his arrival and who accompanied him with cheering up to the City Hotel, where we found our lodgings again just as we had left them.

6. Warden, t. II.

Chapter VI

Festival Given by the Society of the Cincinnati – Origin and Status of This Society – Visit to the Public Institutions – Sword Given by the French of New York – Festival of Castle Garden.

Upon returning to New York, General Lafayette had learned that the members of the Society of the Cincinnati wanted to celebrate September 6, the anniversary of his birth, on the next day; and he received from them an invitation to dinner which he accepted with gratitude. Towards the fourth hour of the afternoon, we saw a long line of old men arrive marching two by two and holding each other by the arms in order to lend each other mutual support that the weight of years made necessary. They were preceded by a military band which was making vain efforts to regulate the pace of their unsteady footsteps. We descended at once into their midst; they took us into their ranks, attaching a medal of the order of the Cincinnati, which Washington had worn, on the lapel of General Lafayette, and we set out to go to the hotel where the dinner had been prepared.

A truly moving tableau was offered by these old warriors, the vestiges of the glorious War of Independence, conducting in their midst the companion of Washington, the adopted son of America. The crowd of people, who filled the streets which we crossed, evidenced the respect which the procession inspired in them by their serious and silent demeanor. The room prepared for the banquet was decorated with trophies of arms and with 60 banners bearing the names of the principal heroes who died for liberty during the Revolutionary War. The meal was enlivened by the open and heartfelt joy of the old soldiers who were pleased to recall the perils that they had shared.

I had the pleasure of being seated next to General Fish, who commanded a battalion of those intrepid militiamen at Yorktown who, under Lafayette's command, entered, weapons in hand, into the English entrenchments. He was kind enough to tell me the details of this glorious action, and even of the entire campaign. The vivaciousness of his narration made me forget his 70 years, and the interesting features of patriotism which he sprinkled into it interested me very much. "I well know," he said to me in concluding, "that the campaign of Virginia cannot be compared to your campaigns of Germany or Italy, no more than our strains and privations to your disaster at Moscow." – "And no more," I added, "than your results to ours; you have won happiness and liberty, and we, we have joined our shackles with those of all of Europe!" – This sad comment momentarily poisoned the happiness that I was enjoying at this banquet of patriotism and gratitude.

Towards the end of the meal, a suddenly raised curtain let us see at the far end of the room a large transparency representing Washington and Lafayette hand in hand before the altar of liberty, receiving a civic crown from the hands of America. The sight of this gave birth to new transports of joy among the guests, the expression of which was suspended only a moment by the loud voice of Colonel Swartwout, who suddenly began to read the order of the day of Yorktown, October 17, 1781: "Honor to the French division of Baron Viomesnil! Yesterday it stormed a fortification! Honor to the American division of General Lafayette! At the same time, it stormed another fortification; and tomorrow it will be first in the assault." Some prolonged *huzzahs* drowned out these words, and the room was shaken by a triple round of applause. But soon all were brought back to sentiments of a different nature by the emotional voice of General Lamb, who had them listen to a ballad, composed in 1792 during Lafayette's captivity in the dungeons of Austria, which was then very popular in America. I borrow the following translation of M.B. …

Close by his domestic hearth,
In spite of peace and comforts,
An old American soldier,
Expresses thus his griefs:
O you the pride of these shores,
Noble lover of liberty,
What is the price of your courage?
Chains and poverty!

Fortune, honor, sweet Fatherland,
Hope of a brilliant future,
Love of a cherished spouse,
Should have held you back, but no,
To fly to our defense,
Your noble heart left all.
But what was the reward for it?
Chains and poverty!

Companions, whom he led,
You saw that young hero,
As generous as intrepid,
Share your noble deeds.
His valor erased the outrage
Of the yoke brought by the English.
What is the price of this courage?
Chains and poverty!

As, long ago, a barbarian prince
Belisaire received irons,
And the proud conqueror of Bulgaria

> Filled the universe with his suffering.
> By similar injustices
> So Hannibal was persecuted,
> And obtained for his services,
> Chains and poverty!

Soon the advanced hour of the night and the need to put an end to the fatigue necessarily caused by emotions so profound as those that we had experienced during this family celebration forced us to depart. Having returned to the City Hotel, I remembered that often in Europe I had heard of the *Order of the Cincinnati*; I recalled even that I had heard some attack it violently as tending to destroy republican equality by creating privileges, and others cite it as justifying the existence of chivalric orders or privileges established by European monarchs. However, what I had seen and heard of the Society of the Cincinnati since my arrival in the United States did not reveal to me at all the existence of an order, created or tolerated by the laws, which was destructive of equality; but in order to clear up any doubts in this regard, on the next day I questioned one of our table companions of the night before who came to visit General Lafayette.

He responded by presenting to me a little brochure containing the origin and the rules of the *Society of the Cincinnati*. The reading of this brochure proved to me that ignorance or bad faith in Europe had misrepresented the character of this society which is no more a privileged order in the United States than is a *charitable association* in Paris or the *Biblical Society* in England. The Society of the Cincinnati is no other than a *free association* of former officers of the Revolutionary Army, who are united in the dual purpose of perpetuating the memory of their patriotic works and of coming to the aid of those among them whose age, infirmities and needs call out for help. As for the ribbon and the medal adopted by the Society, one must regard them as a decoration that its members wear in their meetings only, not as a decoration authorized or sanctioned by the Government. Additionally, in order to enlighten those who are seeking in good faith the truth on this point, I am going to present here the statutes and the regulations of the Society. They were proposed to the officers of the Army in 1783. The different regiments met to learn about them and named a council charged with examining them anew and debating them. On May 13th of this same year, 1783, there appeared the following declaration dated from the American Army camp on the banks of the Hudson.

> The representatives of the American Army being assembled to examine a plan which has been presented to them for the establishment of a society of which members must be officers, they have accepted it as written:

The will of the Supreme Governor of the universe, having determined the liberation of the Colonies of America from the domination of Great Britain, and having established them, after a bloody struggle of eight years, as free, independent and sovereign States, related by alliances, founded on reciprocity of advantages, with most of the princes and potentates of the world;

In order to perpetrate the memory of this prodigious event, as well as the mutual friendships which have been formed under the influence of the common danger, and often cemented by blood, the officers of the American Army, in a most solemn manner, join forces and constitute themselves in a *Society of Friends*, which will be perpetuated as much as possible, by the eldest sons of their children, or, in their absence, by the eldest collateral relatives who will be judged worthy of it;

The officers of the American Army, generally chosen by American citizens, having, like them, a great veneration for the character of the illustrious Lucius Quintus Cincinnatus, and being determined to follow his example by returning to their occupations after the war, believe that they can rightly take the appellation of Society of the Cincinnati.

The following principles will be unchanging and will form the bases of the Society of the Cincinnati:

To safeguard ceaselessly the preservation of the rights of man and the freedom for which they have fought and shed their blood, and without which there is no real happiness;

To augment with an indefatigable zeal and to cherish that union among the States and that national honor so indispensably necessary to the dignity and the future happiness of the American Empire;

To maintain that cordial affection which exists among the officers of the army and that spirit of fraternity and of kindness which should animate them in all things, and particularly when it is a question of aiding and protecting those of their colleagues and their families who are unfortunately in the circumstance of needing help.

The general society will be, for the ease of communications, divided into state societies, and those into as many districts as will be deemed necessary by the state society.

The societies of the districts will meet as often as the state society decides. The state societies will assemble every year, on July 4th, or more often if need be; and the general society, on the first Monday of May, annually, so long as it appears to be necessary, and, afterwards, at least once every three years.

At each meeting, the principles of the society will be examined anew, and better measures adopted to propagate them.

The state societies will be composed of all members residing in each respective State; and each member, moving from one State to another, will be considered as belonging to the society of the State in which he will then be domiciled.

Each state society will have a president, a vice president, a secretary, a treasurer and an assistant treasurer, all chosen annually by the majority of the voters in the state assembly.

Each state assembly will address annually, or more often if necessary, and circulate a letter to the other state assemblies, in which it will indicate everything which appears worthy of commenting on concerning the interests of the society or the general union of the states and make known the officers chosen for the current year. Copies of these letters will be transmitted regularly to the secretary general of the society who will register them in a book dedicated to this purpose.

Each state society will regulate all its special interests, and those of the district societies, while conforming to the principles of the Cincinnati; it will judge the qualifications of proposed new members, and it will be able to expel every member whose conduct is incompatible with honor or who, by his opposition to the general interests of the society, renders himself unworthy of being a part of it any longer.

With the purpose of creating funds sufficient to assist the unfortunates, each officer will deposit into the hands of the treasurer a month's salary. This money will establish forever the capital of the society; and the interest only will be used for aid.

Voluntary subscriptions may be completed in the district or state societies for the relief of unfortunate members or their widows and orphans; but they shall be used only by the state societies.

Every private donation, made by persons belonging to the society or not, will be deposited to the permanent capital of the society, and the interest on these donations alone will be used for aid.

The assembly of the general society will be composed of its officers and representatives of each state society; this delegation cannot be more than five members, and their expenses will be covered by their respective societies.

In the general assembly, the president, the vice president, the secretary, the treasurer and the vice treasurer will be elected to fulfill their duties until the next general assembly.

Every officer of the American Army, in active service as well as in retirement or dismissed from the service, who served in a campaign of the Revolutionary War has the right to become a member of the society. The eldest sons of those who died during the war have the same rights to be admitted into the society.

The foreign officers, who do not have a residence in any of the States of the Union, will be written on the rolls of the secretary general and will be considered as members of the society of the State in which they will be found.

As there are, and will always be at all times, men who in their respective States will attract attention by their ability and by their patriotism, and whose noble purposes embrace the same objects as the Cincinnati, it will be permitted to admit them as honorary members of the society, for life only, while taking care that their number, however, is never raised above one-fifth of the total of the officers or their descendants.

Each state society will be required to form a list of its members and, at the first annual assembly, the state secretary will draft on parchment two copies of the statutes of the society, and will present them to be signed by all the members. One of these copies will be transmitted to the secretary general to be preserved in the archives, and the other will stay in the hands of the state secretary. From these state lists, the secretary general will make a complete list of all the members of the society and will send a copy to each state secretary.

The society will have a decoration by which its members can be recognized; this will be a gold medal of a size appropriate to receive some insignias and will be suspended by a blue ribbon, bordered in white, as a sign of the alliance of France with America.

The society, deeply filled with gratitude for the generous assistance that America received from France and anxious to perpetuate the friendship which arose so happily between the officers of the allied forces during the war, determines that the general president will transmit, as soon as possible, a medal of the society to each of the officers named hereunder:

His excellency the Chevalier de Luzerne, minister plenipotentiary;

His excellency Mr. Gérard, last minister plenipotentiary;

Their excellencies the Count d'Estaing, - the Count de Grasse, - the Count de Barras, - the Chevalier Destouches, commanding admirals of the French Navy, and his excellency the Count de Rochambeau, Commander-in-chief, and the generals and colonels of his army.

The general president will announce to them at the same time that the society stands honored to count them among its members.

A copy of the formation and statutes of the aforementioned society will be sent to the most senior officer of each State, to be signed and approved by the officers of their respective States in the following manner:

We, the undersigned, officers of the American Army, declare that we are voluntarily members of the aforementioned society; and that we submit ourselves to the condition that it prescribes; this we undertake by solemn oath on the honor of one another.

Done in the encampments on the Hudson River in the year 1783.

The Society of the Cincinnati, as one sees by its statutes, possesses nothing alarming for equality, since it does not claim any privilege. However, from all parts of the American Union, there were raised against it accusatory voices who reproached the founders of the society for having desired, in the guise of beneficence and patriotic memories, to sow the seeds of a hereditary nobility. It is difficult to judge now if the founders, or at least some of them, were or were not apprehensive of having an ulterior motive in making this proposal, but it is certain that the articles of the regulations which provide for the son to succeed the father were very capable of giving offense to republicans as jealous of equality as the Americans. Each vigorously attacked the absurd principle of heredity, which found adversaries everywhere. Among the writings which appeared then on this matter, each urgently sought a letter of Franklin, which soon became public, although it was addressed to his daughter who had sent the papers which announced the formation of the Society of the Cincinnati to him in France. This letter, in which one finds all the zest and the originality of its author, contains arguments so conclusive and at the same time so pleasing against hereditary nobility that I cannot resist relating it here.

> Paris, January 26, 1784
> My dear child,
>
> The trouble you took to send me the newspapers is most pleasing to me. I have received, by Captain Barney, those which mention the Order of the Cincinnati. My opinion on this subject has little importance; I am astonished by one thing only: when the combined wisdom of our nation, in the act of confederation, manifested repugnance for establishing a nobility, how is it that, with the authorization of Congress or of a particular state, a certain number of individuals have the pretension to distinguish themselves, as well as their posterity, from their fellow citizens, and to found an order of hereditary knighthood, in direct opposition to the sentiment formally declared by their country?
>
> I speak as well of the several tendencies which have been introduced into the regulations of this order by its authors, who without doubt, will have been dazzled by that profusion of ribbons and crosses suspended in the buttonholes of foreign officers. Most probably, those who disapprove of their introduction will not have fought against it with enough energy, according to a principle similar to the one of your excellent mother on the subject of touchy people who demand even the most trivial

marks of respect. "*If trifles please them,*" she said, "*it would be cruelty to deny them to them.*" It is for these same reasons that, if they had consulted me, I would not have been opposed to the creation of ribbons and medals, but I would certainly have repulsed the idea of making these hereditary distinctions.

For one thing, the honor, for example, that our officers have so fairly acquired is personal in its nature and cannot be transmitted to others. Among the Chinese, the most ancient and wisest of peoples by their long experience, honor does not pass by *descending* but by *ascending*: When a man, as a reward for his valor or wisdom, may be promoted to rank of Mandarin, his father and mother would have the right, by this alone, to the marks of respect which are conferred on the Mandarin himself. It is thought that the good education and the good examples given by the parents to their son have made him capable of becoming useful to the state. This ascending honor is advantageous to society; it encourages the fathers and the mothers to take good care of the education of their children; but the *descending* honor, conferred on a posterity which will have done nothing to attain it, is not only absurd and unjust, but disadvantageous for even the children of the new noblemen.

They will become arrogant, they will scorn useful employment, they will fall into poverty, in a word, into the enslavement and baseness which accompany it. Such is the present state of what we call *nobility* in Europe. Or else, if in order to preserve the dignity of families, their entire fortune is provided to the eldest of the male heirs, they will see a new scourge appear for the industry and the improvement of the country, that odious mixture of arrogance, beggary, and sloth, which has already depopulated a part of Spain and rendered half of its lands uncultivated. The families will only stop from becoming extinct by a little encouragement granted to marriages and by a little care brought to agriculture.

I wish then that, in the Order of the Cincinnati (if they absolutely insist on it), the distinctive marks be granted to fathers and mothers of knights, more than to their descendants. I dare say that there would result from this both good examples and good effects. In this way, they would put into practice the fourth commandment of God, "*Honor thy father and mother*," whereas no divine precept commands us to honor our children. Certainly, there is no better way to render homage to the authors of our days than to carry out some actions the brilliancy of which reflects glory on them, and there is nothing more befitting than to show by a public act that it is the education or the good examples received of them to which we attribute all our merit.

As for the absurdity of the descendant as a celebrated person, one can not only show it as a simple thesis of philosophy but also demonstrate it mathematically. For example, the son of a man belongs only half to his family; he belongs for the other half to the family of his wife; if this same son marries, the grandson belongs to the grandfather no more than a quarter, and the great-grandson descends from him only an 8th; still some generations, and it will be no more than a 16th, a 32nd, a 64th, a 128th, a 256th, and so on; in nine generations that will have been born in 300 years (and this is not a very old nobility) our current Knights of the Cincinnati will be no more than a 512th in the being of their posterity. Supposing even that the present fidelity of American spouses be maintained intact for nine generations, this result is such a mere trifle that I do not see in it a motive sufficient for a reasonable man to brave the regrettable consequences of the jealousy, the envy, and the disaffection of his countrymen.

But let us leave off our calculations on this young noble, who must be only a 512th part of the current knight, and go back to his nine degrees of nobility. There has of necessity been a father and a mother, which makes four individuals; in going back in this way, one finds 8, 16, 32, 64, 128, 256, 512 persons who will have existed in succession, and combining for their share of the future knight. This progression is set up thus in numbers:

2
4
8
16
32
64
128
256
512
1,024

> Therefore, 1,024 individuals of both sexes in 300 years are necessary to make a knight. Let us suppose 1,000 knights: this works out to the necessary and successive concourse of 1,024,000 mothers and fathers, unless some of them might be seen as making more than one knight. Let us then subtract 24,000 individuals for this double employment, and let us consider if, after a reasonable estimate of fools, wretches and prostitutes who make up a part of this million ancestors, their posterity would be able to boast of taking its origin from the current knights of the Cincinnati. Future geneologists of these knights, while preparing the proofs of their descendancy in a direct line of so many generations (if we assume that honor is of a nature to be transmitted) will do nothing but prove the slight quotient of glory which belonged to each of them, since the very simple and clear calculations which I have just set out demonstrate that, in proportion to the antiquity of families, the entitlement to the celebrity of the ancestors will diminish, and that several generations more will reduce this honor to a little next to nothing.
>
> I hope, therefore, that our new order will renounce hereditary transmission and that it will be satisfied, like the Knights of the Garter, the Order of the Bath, of the Thistle, of Saint Louis, and the other European Orders, with the right to wear a medal for life, and that this honor will cease with the life of those who have earned it. It will not result, I hope, in anything bad. As for me, when I will enter into a company where faces new to me are found, I will acknowledge with pleasure, at this sign, the persons worthy of particular consideration. Unpretentious men will thus be exempted from seeking, in order to commend themselves to our interest, the occasion of recalling their services of the war of the continent, etc.…

Franklin's opinion and public opinion did not prevent the formation of the Society of the Cincinnati, but reduced it to its appropriate value, that is to say, that each grew accustomed to seeing in this body only a charitable association and were pleased to pay a tribute to it out of respect for the members who had acquired rights by their former services and by their personal character; but the principal of hereditary nobility was so discredited that today very few of the sons dare to succeed their fathers, and in some States they are not even admitted anymore.

The days which followed our return were in part devoted to visiting the public institutions and the forts which protect the Port and the harbor of New York. The most remarkable among them is Fort Lafayette, which is situated at the entrance of the harbor near the point of Long Island; its lights intersect with those of the fort constructed on Staten Island opposite it. The officers of the garrison, composed of a detachment of the regular army of the United States, gave the General a very cordial reception and showed us all the interesting details of the Fort, which has the immense advantage of being covered, and bomb-proof without being exposed to the inconveniences of cannon smoke, which finds free outlet by the corridors, which are not closed, into the interior of the court. The rain, which fell profusely, did not permit us to examine the other forts with as much attention.

Of all the public schools, the one which inspired in us the most lively interest was the *Free School of Young Africans*, founded and administered by the Society of the Emancipation of the Blacks. The General was accompanied in this school, as he had been in all the others, by a large number of ladies all of whom give assiduous attention to these kinds of institutions. There, they reminded him that he had been elected, unanimously, a member of the Society at the same time as Mr. Granville Sharp and Mr. Thomas Clarkson. This nomination suited his character and his well-known opinions on the Slavery of Blacks too well for him not to appear profoundly touched. Immediately after, a young Black child approached and said to him animatedly: "You see, General, hundreds of these poor children of the African race who appear before you; they share here, with White children, the benefits of education; like them, they are learning to cherish the memory of the services which you have rendered to America; and, more, they revere you as an ardent friend of the emancipation of our race and a worthy member of the Society to which we owe so much gratitude."

It would take a very long time, and it would be very difficult for me, to give the precise details of the charitable institutions that we visited in New York City. They are very numerous and, as each of them is the product of a particular association or a bequest, it would be necessary in order to make them well-understood to give a history of each of them. In general, one can say of all these institutions that they are under the protection and the influence of the authorities. Most of the administrative posts are filled without salary or honorariums by men who regard their nomination to these positions as honorable marks of the public's esteem and who fill them with a zeal and a probity which justifies it. There is ordinarily only paid work for the lower positions or if the duties require the sacrifice of all the time of the employee.

Most of these institutions are founded either by societies or bequests; they are maintained either by public subscriptions or by government subsidies. Thus, for example, in examining the account books of administration of the house of refuge for orphans, which was founded in 1806, one sees that this institution received, in the year 1822, $500 from the State Legislature, $287 as part of the funds allocated to public schools by the State, and $1,430 from private subscriptions. It also received $5,000 from a bequest made by Mr. Jacob Sherred, $25 in interest from a bequest made by Mrs. Mary Williams, $390 from anonymous gifts, $1,017 given by the Society of Magdalene, $19 from products made by the children, etc., and a multitude of individual gifts such as books, bound pennies, cloths, buttons, clothes, fruits, combs, etc. Whatever the nature or value of the gifts may be, they are received by the administration which records them scrupulously, as well as the name of the donors. It is with the aid of these gifts, wisely used, that the house had from 1806 to 1822 received and brought up 440 children, of which 243 are already placed in society in a manner useful for it and for them.

In the almshouse, there are more than 1,000 individuals of both sexes and of every age.

The main hospital of New York can hold nearly 2,000 sick. The insane persons, although under the same administration, are in a separate building.

In all these institutions, we were struck by the cleanliness of the rooms, the whiteness of the linen, the good quality of the food, and especially the affectionate and gentle manner of the employees towards those who are entrusted to them. One recognizes that the administrators are encouraged by something more precious than emoluments: public esteem.

The persons who accompanied us, and who appeared well-informed, assured us that in New York City there are more than 40 charitable and philanthropic societies, whose unremitting zeal contributes very much to the maintenance of all the institutions which we had visited and to the redress of personal misfortunes.

After having visited the Academy of the Arts, where there were a large number of plaster casts, prints and paintings given by Emperor Napoleon to the Academy, we went to the public library. It consists of more than 20,000 volumes. The choice of works in it has been managed tastefully, and all appeared to us to be in very good order. The public is admitted there every day, except Sunday; but no one can take out books with him, except shareholders, who number about 500.

During this second stay in New York, we also visited the two theaters several times; but it would be difficult for me to state my opinion of them, for each time that General Lafayette appeared in the hall, he became such an object of public attention, and the tumult caused by the public's manifestation of joy was so great, that it was impossible for the actors to continue their play; they were allowed to be heard only to chant some couplets in honor of the *Companion of Washington,* the *Captive of Olmutz* or the *Nation's Guest.* Some people of taste whom I questioned responded only that the repertoire of these theaters was composed ordinarily of English plays and that, in general, among the actors they could quote eminent subjects. The two halls are evidently too small for a large crowd, and their construction corresponds neither to the wealth nor to the beauty of New York City. To this the citizens say, with reason, that, having considered luxury and pleasure, it was necessary to attend to serviceable things and that they would be very humiliated if foreigners were impressed, not by the convenience and the beauty of their buildings of public use, but by the elegance of their theaters.[7]

On the 9th, we attended a spiritual concert given in St. Paul's Church, where the General heard upon entering the playing of that hymn, known under the name of *The Marseillaise,* which was composed, as one knows, for the Army of the Rhine by Bailly's nephew. The assembly there was noteworthy in the number and the elegance of the ladies. The different pieces that we heard were executed with a general effect which I had not found in the choruses and the orchestras that I had heard till then in the United States; for, it is necessary to acknowledge, music there is still in the infancy of the art. The causes for this are easy to find. For one thing, the English language is hardly musical; for another, the Americans have had up to the present little time to give to the cultivation of the arts of amusement. They still don't have schools of music. They have, indeed, some European artists who are trying to expand the interest in their art; but, in general, they have only found access to the very rich families who have given up lucrative occupations, and these families are as rare as the professors themselves.

Upon leaving St. Paul's Church, we went into the park facing the City Hall where the firemen were drawn up in battle array with their fire trucks. The General inspected them; after this, this militia of a new kind, but no less useful than that which is called to the defense of the territory, filed by with as much order as a division of artillery would have had. Thus, we saw pass before our eyes 46 fire trucks; each was hauled and escorted by a company of about 30 men commanded by a chief armed with a megaphone. On each truck was set a standard with the colors and the crests of the company. Many of these standards were imprinted with portraits of men whose names were dear

7. Since this time, the City has built a new theater which they say is as commodious as it is elegant.

to the people. We noticed everywhere the portrait of Washington and that of Lafayette. After all the fire trucks had filed by, we climbed to the balcony of City Hall where the General was addressed by the Commander-in-chief of the firemen and from which we saw the spectacle of the firemen's manuevers. They were all joined in a circle in the middle of which they had built a high pyramid with fire ladders and spears. On this pyramid they had placed a little house filled with combustible materials. They set it on fire and, when the signal was given, all the pumps worked at the same time, and struck so accurately that in less than two minutes the fire was extinguished. In meeting thus at the same point, all the jets of water formed a liquid dome dressed in the colors of a rainbow, to the most beautiful effect.

On the 10th, we were committed to dine at Colonel Fish's house; we were going to proceed there at four o'clock, when in leaving the hotel we found, arranged in battle array in front of the door, the 9th regiment of artillery which was coming to escort the General Lafayette up to his friend's house. At the moment when the General appeared, Colonel Muir, commander of this regiment, advanced toward him and offered him, in the name of his comrades, a richly decorated sword, all the parts of which had been executed in the shops of New York. In expressing to him his thanks, General Lafayette said to him: "It is with pleasure and gratitude that I receive this precious present from a corps of citizen-soldiers, each of whom well knows that the sword has been given to men to defend freedom where it exists and to conquer it where it has been destroyed by crowned and privileged usurpers." This response was drowned out by applause, and the General was led by the regiment and a large crowd of citizens to Colonel Fish's house. This day was ended by a beautiful fireworks display set off in honor of Lafayette in a public garden.

On the next day, the General attended, with his son, a Masonic festival of the Knights Templar, who affiliated them with their lodge, conferred on them the highest honors, and then presented them with richly worked medals. In the evening, we dined with the French residents of New York who had wanted to celebrate, with their compatriot, the 47th anniversary of the Battle of Brandywine. The dinner took place at Washington Hall; the patriotic and family festival was marked by a feature as successful as original. Very many Americans who attended were struck with astonishment; the table, extremely wide, offered a plan in relief of that great canal which, traversing New York State, joins Lake Erie to the Atlantic Ocean. This map, of a new kind, occupied a length of 70 feet on the table, where it was hollowed out in the depth of the wood and lined with lead. Extremely clear water filled the canal, which was bordered by the greenest grass representing meadows, in the middle of which rose representations of factories, trees and animals. Bridges, gracefully laid from one side to the other, masses of rocks under which the canal passed, and forests in which it was lost while meandering completed making a truly unique ensemble of this masterpiece of topography. Above the center of the table was an immense sun in a continuous state of rotation. Some allegorical pictures, full-length portraits of Washington and Lafayette, and trophies of the French and American flags completed the entirety of these delightful decorations. The banquet was presided over by Mr. Monneron. After the dinner, which was enlivened by fresh and cordial joyousness, they made a large number of toasts; they were all marked by that energetic patriotism which characterizes all that is said and done in a truly free country. I cannot resist the desire to relate some of them here.

By the stewards of the banquet: "*To the United States*, its national success is imperishable; it is founded on religion, on industry, on liberty." By the President, "To General Lafayette; we are proud that he is French!" And he added:

> Gentlemen! In the 14th century, the Lafayettes already improved the lot of those whom they called at that time *the vassals*. In the 15th century, field marshal Lafayette drove the enemy from French territory. In the 16th century, Miss Lafayette was the image of beauty, of virtue, of charity. In the 17th century, Madam Lafayette composed the works which will pass to the most distant posterity. In the 18th century, General Lafayette was born. He was born an enemy of tyranny, an impassioned lover of liberty. During his youth, he contributed to support and defend the birth of liberty in the United States. In a more advanced age, he appeared at the public rostrum: he spoke of liberty in Europe as he had known how to defend it in America. From this rostrum, he entered the ranks of the defenders of the Fatherland. I saw him in the perils of the Revolution; his genius and his composure never abandoned him. Quick to understand, eager to perform, he fought always for real liberty. I am an eyewitness and faithful historian. See these trophies, these flags, these standards, on all is written: *Liberty, Victory, Lafayette.*

To this toast, the General responded with this: "To the memory of the French who died for the cause of true liberty from 1789 to this day. Their spirits demand of us that so many sacrifices for the Fatherland not be wasted."

By Mr. Dias: "To the memory of Riego and to those other martyrs of liberty. Crime brings dishonor, not the scaffold."

By Mr. Chevrolat: "To France such that I would want it to be, without contrived conspiracies, without corrupting ministers, without mercenary accusers, without that slow oppression which silently undermines its energy and vigor."

Some stanzas to Lafayette, full of grace, harmony and patriotism, composed by Mr. Pillet and read by Mr. Chegaray, concluded by exciting the enthusiasm of the guests who parted company to shouts of "*Vive la liberté! Vive Lafayette!*"

For several weeks, New York City was engaged in preparations for a magnificent fete which was to surpass in taste and in brilliance everything which had been done for Lafayette up to then. They had chosen for the place of the gathering a circular fort about 600 feet in circumference, called *Castle Garden*, built formerly for the defense of New York on a breakwater in front of the Battery, and now dedicated to public festivals. A bridge 300 feet long joins this fort to the Battery. We had to leave New York on the 14th to take a trip on the Hudson, and the festival of Castle Garden took place on the 13th.

We went there in the evening, by the brightness of the lights. We found the bridge covered with luxurious carpets from one end to the other, and bounded at each side by a line of beautiful green trees. In the middle of the bridge stood a pyramid 75 feet high, illuminated by colored pieces of glass and topped by a brilliant star in the middle of which one read the name of Lafayette. Despite all the splendor that this entryway had, however, our astonishment and admiration increased more upon entering into the surrounding wall of the Fort. The hall, about 600 feet in circumference, around which extended a vast amphitheater, held nearly 6,000 people. The vault, supported at its center by a column 60 feet high, was formed of flags of all the nations, intermingled with elegance and symmetry. At the principal entrance was a triumphal arch of flowers and greenery, topped by a colossal statute of Washington resting on some cannon pieces. In the middle was raised the spirit of America carrying a shield with these words: "To the Nation's Guest." A pavilion lavishly decorated, and adorned with a bust of Hamilton, stood on a platform opposite the door. In the front were two cannon pieces taken from Yorktown. This pavilion was intended for Lafayette. Around the hall 13 columns carried arms of the first 13 States of the confederation. This circumference was lit up by more than 1,000 torches whose glare was reflected by a large number of stacks of arms.

As soon as the General appeared, the air around Lafayette was filled with *See the Conqueror Comes*; and a kind of shiver of admiration and respect accompanied him to his place. At the same instant, the curtains which surrounded and shaped the hall rolled up like sails and were raised as rapidly as a theater decoration, and the interior became visible to the eyes of the crowd which had come on boats around the breakwater to wait for this moment. The clear and brilliant moon lit up the harbor in which 1,000 boats and steamships crossed each other in all directions. Some moments after the General had taken his place below the lavish pavilion which had been prepared for him, a large transparency was suddenly uncovered opposite him, and offered him a faithful image of his home, La Grange, with its wide moats and its five Gothic towers, and this inscription below: "This is his home." General Lafayette was very moved by this considerate idea of his friends who, by the presence of this picture, wanted to give the character of a family festival to their fete. Several times during the night they tried to put together some dances, but each time that the General took a step to draw near, quadrilles erupted on his passageway and came to form a group around him.

The time appeared short to us in the midst of this delightful assembly, and we were very astonished to hear the signal of our departure at two o'clock. The steamship which was to conduct us to Albany had approached the breakwater in order to receive us on leaving the ball. We embarked with the committee which was charged with accompanying the General, and a large number of ladies and citizens who did not want to part with him; they received as many as the boat could carry. Captain Allyn, who was to leave for France on the next day, came on board to receive our embraces and our letters for our friends, and despite the darkness which had succeeded the brightness of the moon, we lifted anchor. Soon we had lost sight of *Castle Garden*, and instead of the joyous sounds of the music, we heard only the monotonous and rhythmic noise of our steam engine struggling against the swiftness of the waves of the Hudson.

Chapter VII

Sailing on the Hudson – Treason of Arnold – Military School of West Point – Newburgh – Poughkeepsie – Clermont – Catskill – Hudson – Albany – Troy – Return to New York.

The steamship *James Kent* on which we embarked had been prepared for this voyage with the most elaborate attentions by the committee charged by the City of New York to accompany General Lafayette; but they had not foreseen that so large a number of ladies would want to join them, and it happened that most of the men were obligated to sleep on deck, although *The James Kent* had more than 80 beds. As for us, we sought rest in vain in a very pretty room that we shared with General Lewis and Colonel Fish. The sound of cannon which at each moment announced that we were passing in front of a village and the shouts of our crew who were trying to pull us from the *Oyster Bed*, on which we had run aground during the darkness, prevented us from sleeping; and the first light of day invited us to climb on deck to enjoy the majestic views of the banks of the Hudson. Nothing is more imposing, in a word, as the sight of the high mountains, by turns wooded and rocky, which embanks the river in nearly its whole length. Upon entering for the first time in the *Pass of the Highlands*, one almost feels disposed to share the superstitious terror of the Indians, and one understands how the phantoms and their sinister groanings have for a long time exercised their sway even over the first Europeans who inhabited these places where nature displays itself only in bizarre forms and somber colors.

For the man who takes pleasure in the memory of the highway robberies of the Middle Ages and who loves to contemplate the ruins of the old castle-towers, the ancient refuge of the fierce feudal system, no doubt nothing is comparable to the banks of the Rhine; but, for the one who prefers nature still virgin and wild, nothing is more beautiful than the banks of the Hudson. This river has as its source the highest region between Lake Ontario and Lake Champlain and cuts the State of New York from the North to the South for 250 miles; it is navigable for boats of 80 tons up to Albany, 160 miles above its mouth, and ships ascend up to the town of Hudson, a distance of 132 miles from New York. It would be difficult, I believe, to estimate the number of boats of all sizes which engage in commerce between Albany and New York. The river is continually covered by them, and it is rare to sail a quarter of an hour without encountering a large number of boats, one following the other. The tide is felt some miles above Albany, where it is 12 hours later than at New York. The water is salty up to a distance of 50 miles above this latter city, where the ordinary rising is about a foot. At Pollepel

Island, to the north of the *Highlands*, it is about four feet, and at *Kinderhook*, situated 22 miles south of Albany, about three feet.[8]

In spite of the current and movement against the tide, we did six miles per hour. A group of former Revolutionary soldiers crowded around General Lafayette on the deck, and each of them was happy to recall to him the details of the events, the memory of which each point of the shore awakened in him. We had already passed in front of Tarrytown, and, at the site of this modest village, the old citizen-warriors had spoken respectfully of the names of *John Paulding*, *David Williams*, and *Isaac Van Vert*, who are immortalized as much by their noble disinterestness as by the service which they rendered to their country and to liberty in arresting Major Andre. *Stony Point* and *Fort Lafayette* where, by the judicious choice of a good position, Washington had been able to disrupt the communications of the English Army, were far behind us, and our Captain announced to us that soon we were going to see West Point when I noticed that suddenly the gaze of our traveling-companions was carried with sadness towards an isolated house which appeared not far from the riverbank to which the mountain slopes downward by the smoothest incline; soon, I heard uttered the word traitor and then the name of Arnold. This house, which seemed to awaken so the indignation of the travelers, was the one where, in a word, the infamous Arnold haggled over the price of the blood of his companions-in-arms and the enslavement of his Fatherland. The history of Arnold's treason contains a great lesson; it proves once again how important it is, in a well-organized state, to entrust employment only to men of well-known morality. In a captain, as in a magistrate, courage and ability, without probity, are no more than dangerous qualities of which one cannot attempt to take advantage without being exposed to serious harm.

Arnold was born in the State of Connecticut; but nature seemed to have denied him the virtues which characterize the inhabitants of this region so strongly. However, from the beginning, he embraced the sacred cause of his Fatherland with ardor; his military talents, his courage in combat, his resignation and his patience in the presence of exhaustion and hardship, and especially his brilliant services in the expedition to Canada, had acquired for him a great reputation in the Army and the confidence of Congress, which did not believe it to be an over-generous reward to elevate him to the rank of major general; he had been wounded at Quebec, and had not yet been entirely cured of his wounds, when in 1778, the enemy having evacuated Philadelphia, they entrusted the command of this City to him.

Unfortunately, to the courage that he had shown before the enemy, Arnold did not join that firmness of principles and rectitude of judgment that

8. Warden, *Statistics of the United States*.

alone could put him in a condition to resist the numerous seductions that necessarily surrounded him in the brilliant position in which he found himself; driven by pride and a ridiculous vanity, forgetting that he did not have the resources of a great personal fortune, he indulged in all the foolish expenses of a sumptuous table and of an expensive mode of living; he was not long in contracting debts very much greater than his revenues. In the hope of discharging them, he engaged in speculations whose workings should have alienated him and which had for him disastrous results. Impelled by the complaints of his creditors, he sought resources in the dishonesty of his administration, but the examination of his accounts by the commissioners of Congress substantiated a considerable deficit. Many citizens of Philadelphia complained of his numerous extortions; the Government of Pennsylvania accused him of even more serious deeds; finally, in June of 1778, Congress had him arrested and judged by a court-martial that found him culpable and sentenced him to be reprimanded by the General-in-chief; this sentence, approved by Congress, was executed at the beginning of 1779. Furious with seeing himself so battered at the same time by the law and by public opinion, Arnold flared up with bitter complaints against what he called the ingratitude of his fellow citizens and swore to avenge himself against them.

At that time they attached great importance to the fortress at West Point, for the preservation of which the American Army had for a long time maneuvered and often fought. They regarded this fortress as the key to communication between the States of the East and of the South; in short, its location on the summit of one of the highest mountains of the right bank of the Hudson, and its double line of batteries and of fortifications laid out by the most skillfull engineers made it an excellent defensive battle station; its occupation provided great influence on all of New York State. Arnold was not ignorant of this, and it is certain that he cast his glance on this important post in order to prepare his revenge. By means of intrigues and importuning, he obtained the command of West Point at the moment when he had just written to the English Colonel Robinson that he forswore his revolutionary principles, and that he eagerly desired to regain the esteem of his King by some dazzling proof of repentance. This letter began an active correspondence, which was conducted very much in secret, between Sir Henry Clinton and him. The principal object of this correspondence was the quest for a way to cause the Fortress of West Point to fall into the hands of the English as soon as possible.

In order to conduct this intrigue more securely, the English General chose one of his aides-de-camp, Major André, a young man as distinguished by his amiable qualities as by his military talents which had already assured him of a fine reputation among his companions-in-arms. A war-sloop named *The Vulture* ascended the Hudson with him up to King's Ferry, about 12 miles below West Point; from there, his communications with Arnold became more frequent and easier; but to better understand one another, an interview became indispensable, and the latter demanded it earnestly. André refused at first, whether he felt a secret repugnance to be in contact with a traitor, or, rather, it appeared unworthy to him for a loyal officer to penetrate the enemy lines under a name and a coat which did not belong to him; however, pressed by the desire to return the confidence of his general, he ended by agreeing to the rendezvous which had been appointed for the night, at the house of a certain Joshua Smith who had the reputation of being secretly in favor of the English party. Smith himself came to fetch Major André during the night of September 21, and led him to land with the aid of a longboat whose oarsmen were his own servants. André was welcomed by Arnold on the shore, and led to Smith's house where he stayed hidden up to the following night.

The conference having been concluded and the plans having been definitively fixed, André wanted to take advantage of the darkness to withdraw; but having arrived at the shore, he found that *The Vulture* had been compelled to move to a distance in order not to expose itself to the fire of a battery which was menacing it. The oarsmen who had brought him to land refused to bring him back to the sloop. He necessarily decided to return to New York by land; in order to hasten his progress, Smith furnished him a horse, and to vouch for him, Arnold delivered to him a passport under the name of James Anderson, assigned to the public service. This passport was useful for him to leave the lines of the American outposts successfully and to arrive at Crompound, where Smith, who had accompanied him, left him after having given him information to continue his route. He was approaching the English lines near Tarrytown when suddenly a militiaman who was patrolling between the two armies with two of his comrades sprang forward from behind a thicket and seized his horse by the bridle; at this sudden arrest, Major André lost his customary presence of mind, and instead of presenting the passport which he was bearing, asked the militiaman: "To which party do you belong?" – "To the party down there," answered the latter (that is how they designated the English Army which occupied New York). "And I also," Major André added imprudently; but hardly had he let out this fatal confession, than the arrival of the two other militiamen revealed to him his error and his danger.

He hoped to remedy the one and escape the other by offering his captors a purse full of gold and his very valuable watch, and he promised them, if they would let him go, the protection of the English Government and great riches. The more splendid his promises were, the more the three militiamen were persuaded that his arrest ought to be useful to the cause of independence, and rejected his offers with disdain, declaring to him that, although they might be very poor, all the gold in the world would not induce them to compromise their duties. At once they proceeded to a rigorous examination of the clothes of the unfortunate prisoner, in order to see if they could discover some document capable of enlightening them. Accurate plans of the approaches and the defenses of West Point, which they found in his boots, and several details written in Arnold's hand, confirmed their suspicions; they conducted him to Lieutenant Colonel Jameson who commanded the forward positions. André, doubtless intending to make known to Arnold that he must think of his own safety, demanded that they render an account at once of the arrest of *his officer Anderson on the road to New York*. On the receipt of this news, the traitor took flight, and went to seek reward for his infamy in the ranks of the British Army.

Major André declared himself an English officer as soon as he presumed that Arnold was safe. The nearly immediate return of General Washington hastened the convening of a court-martial presided over by General Greene, and on which Lafayette and Baron de Steuben sat. André appeared before this tribunal under the terrible accusation of espionage; his judges treated him with great deference and gentleness, and declared to him, from the opening of the proceedings, that he could consider himself excused by them from responding to every question which would offend his conscience; but the young unfortunate man, more jealous of his honor than his life, freely avowed his plans, and set forth his conduct frankly taking no other care than to exonerate those who had supported him in his undertaking. His candor and his courage moved his judges who could not entirely conceal their emotion while signing his sentence. As for André, he expected it and heard it resignedly. His last moments were worthy of his noble character. Here are details which Dr. Thacher, an eyewitness, gives.

> *October* 2, 1780 – Major André lives no more: I have just attended his execution. It was a scene of the most profound interest. During his imprisonment and his proceedings, he showed great nobility of character: they did not hear him offer the least complaint, and he appeared very sympathetic to all the displays of interest that they gave to him. He had left his mother and two sisters, whom he loved tenderly, in England; he spoke of them with compassion, and he wrote to Sir Henry Clinton to recommend them to his personal care.
>
> The watch officers, who stayed constantly with the prisoner, reported to us that, when they came in the morning to announce the hour of his execution, he did not allow

any emotion to appear. His calm and steady countenance contrasted greatly with the sorrow of those who surrounded him. Seeing his servant enter in tears: "Withdraw," he said to him, "and return only with the courage of a man." Every day General Washington sent him breakfast at his table; he received it on that day as usual and he ate it tranquilly; afterwards he shaved, made his toilet, and, after having put his hat on the table, he turned to the watch officers and said to them cheerfully: "Let's go, gentlemen, here I am ready to follow you." When the fatal hour sounded, a large detachment of troops took up arms. A huge crowd of people convened. All our officers were present, with the exception of General Washington and his staff. Sadness reigned in all the ranks, despair was on every face. Major André came from his prison to the place of execution between two noncommissioned officers who bore arms. The glances of the multitude fell with interest upon him. His face, full of dignity, showed his scorn for death; often a faint smile came to embellish his pleasing countenance, and he greeted all those whom he recognized in the crowd politely; they returned the greetings with a most affectionate earnestness.

He had expressed the desire to be shot, considering this form of death as more consonant with the military customs and opinions, and up to the last moment he had believed that this wish would be granted; but when he arrived opposite the gallows, he made an involuntary step back and stopped for some time. "What is the matter?," said an officer who was beside him. – "I am very prepared to die," he answered, "but this way is hateful to me…" While he waited at the foot of the gallows, I noticed a slight shudder in him; he supported his foot on a big stone, looked up for an instant, and made a movement of his throat as if he was gulping down something; but soon seeing that all the preparations had been completed, he sprang forward lightly into the cart, and raising his head proudly: "It will only be," he said, "a brief agony." Then, he took from his pocket a white handkerchief with which he blindfolded himself with a firmness which filled the crowd with admiration, and which made not only his servant who was standing near him but also all the spectators shed tears. When the rope was attached to the gallows, he removed his hat and passed the noose himself over his head, and he adjusted it to his neck without wanting to be helped by the executioner. He was in this state when Colonel Scammell approached him and informed him that, if he had something to say, he was permitted to speak. He then raised the handkerchief from over his eyes, and said: "I beg of you not to forget that I submitted to my fate as a courageous man." Then, the cart started off, left him suspended, and he expired almost immediately.

As he had said, he only felt a brief agony. He was dressed in his uniform and was buried at the foot of the gallows, and the place of his interment was consecrated by the tears of all those who witnessed his death. Thus, Major André died in the flower of his manhood, the most beautiful ornament and the honor of the English Army, the friend of Sir Henry Clinton. If the infamous Arnold was still capable of experiencing an honorable sentiment, he must have had his soul rent with shame and grief, upon learning of the tragic end of the unfortunate André. As for him, after having put the finishing touches on his dishonor, by serving in the ranks of enemies of his country, after the war he went to die in England under the weight of the scorn of those same people for whom he had dishonored himself.

Some time after Arnold had abandoned West Point, and when he had already had made himself conspicuous by the relentlessness with which he had rent the breast of his country by all the horrors of the war, they brought him an American grenadier who had just been made prisoner in a skirmish. The latter recognized him from having served under his command at West Point; Arnold questioned him on the impression that his flight had made on the garrison. The proud republican grenadier answered him with frankness, and did not at all try to conceal from him the general indignation. "Well! What would you have done if you had seized me?" – "We would have buried your leg shattered in front of Quebec respectfully, and we would have hooked your body to a gallows... ."

While the different groups that covered the deck were still cursing the memory of Arnold and expressing regret about the misfortune of Andre, the sound of cannon, repeated a thousand times by the numerous echoes of the Hudson, advised us that we were arriving at West Point. Our longboats put afloat carried us quickly to the shore. General Lafayette was received there by Major Thayer, the commander of the institution, and by Generals Brown and Scott, accompanied by their staffs. They had him climb into an uncovered carriage and they placed beside him the widow of Colonel Hamilton; and, followed by a long column of the ladies who had accompanied him, and by a large number of people who had assembled to greet him, he ascended slowly the steep road that leads to the Military School. During his ride, two cannon pieces placed on the top of a rock which stood above our heads rumbled ceaselessly. When we arrived on the plateau where the buildings of the institution sit, we found the young students in battle array. The General immediately passed by them in review and, afterwards, they maneuvered before him. After the maneuvers, they did him the honors of the fete that they had prepared for him with the most affectionate earnestness.

The location of West Point appeared to me very well-chosen for a military school; it is a very beautiful raised plateau on the right bank of the Hudson and is crowned by some other high mountains at the summit of which one still see the remains of the old Fort Putnam. The distance from the large cities, the silence of the forests, the appearance of nature, at the same time imposing and beautiful, all seem to invite meditation and study in this place.

The students are 200 in number. Vacant places are at the disposition of the President of the United States. To be admitted one must be at least 14 years old and at most 21; one must know how to read, write and compute numbers; and one must sign, with his parents or his guardian, a commitment to serve for five years, excepting one leave of absence before the expiration of this time. They teach there Natural and Experimental Philosophy, Mathematics, Chemistry and Mineralogy, Drawing and Military Construction, Strategy, Fencing and the French language. All the expenses of the institution are paid by the national treasury. Each student or *cadet* receives $16 per month, and two rations per day. Formed into companies, they perform all the duties as soldiers or noncommissioned officers and spend, each year, three months under the tent in order to learn the work of encampment; at the end of their course, they are commissioned for the different corps of the Army when there are vacant positions; but very many of them obtain permission to enter immediately into civilian life. The Government rarely refuses this right to those who claim it because its goal is less to have in this institution a nursery for soldiers than to form citizens capable of filling, in case of need, the primary positions in the militias which are improved in this manner every year by a good number of young, well-educated officers.

We had the pleasure of finding among the professors three of our compatriots, Messrs. Bérard, Du Commun and Gimbrede, who put great enthusiasm into answering our questions and who appeared to us to enjoy a great esteem among the leaders of the institution and the students.

At six o'clock, we descended to the riverbank in order to reembark. A large number of our companions on the voyage, feeling that it was not possible for them to stay any longer crammed together on *The James Kent*, left us to board another steamship which was returning to New York; and we continued our journey with our good and amiable members of the New York committee that was charged with accompanying the General.

At seven o'clock we arrived at Newburgh; we should have been able to disembark there at three o'clock, but our accident on the Oyster Bed had delayed us, and 30,000 people were waiting on the shore with the most animated impatience for the arrival of the Nation's Guest. The tables, they told us, had been set up since the morning: in a word, it was easy to comprehend this because here the reception was more tumultuous than I had yet seen anywhere else; but this same commotion of the people furnished us a fresh occasion to judge the authority of the magistrate over the people who, even in their moments of excitement, never lost any of that respect which citizens owe to laws to which they have freely consented.

After a rapid journey by torchlight across the streets of Newburgh, they conducted us in an uncovered carriage to the Orange Hotel, where the chief personages of the City offered us dinner. While we were at the table, a report spread in the City that the General was going to leave immediately; at this news, the entire population rushed in confusion under the windows of the hotel, and a thousand confused voices were raised to declare that it was horrible to tear away so abruptly from the citizens of Newburgh the friend whom they had desired to see for so long a time and so ardently; that the darkness which had covered his arrival had not permitted any person to see him; that they would be distressed not to be able to pay him homage with the preparations that they had made for his reception; and, finally, that they would not allow him to leave before the sun had illuminated his presence in the City and he had given his blessing to the children of Newburgh.

To the noise of these outcries was soon added that of the struggle which had just begun between the militiamen, who were defending the door of the hotel, and the crowd, who wanted to enter to reach General Lafayette. For some moments, the Mayor of the City who was at our table did not appear to be occupied very much by what was happening in the street; but after someone had come to forewarn him that the disorder could become serious and that the militiamen and the police officers were beginning to be worn out from resisting the multitude, he got up, took General Lafayette by the hand, and, preceded by two torches, led him onto a balcony that overlooked the street. At the sight of General Lafayette, shouts and applause arose from all sides, but with a gesture, the Mayor restored silence, then addressed the people. "Gentlemen," (for here the magistrates always use polite phrases in speaking to the people) "Gentlemen, do you want to distress the Nation's Guest?" – "No, No, No!" – "Do you want Lafayette to be deprived of his liberty in the country that owes its liberation to him?" – "No, No!" – "Well then, listen, therefore, to what I am going to say to you, and do not force me to invoke the law in order to restore order." – There was a profound silence – "Your friend is expected in Albany. He has pledged his word to be there tomorrow before day's end; he is already late because of an unforeseen accident that stopped him for three hours on his trip. If you keep him here until tomorrow, you deprive him of the pleasure of visiting all the other cities which also wait for him on his trip and you will make him miss all his engagements; do you want to cause him this trouble?" – "No, No, No!" And the air reverberated with applause and huzzahs. Then, General Lafayette himself addressed to the crowd some words of thanks which were received with great enthusiasm. However, the people, now silent, stayed still crowded together in the street but without obstructing the door of the hotel.

When the General descended, some citizens advanced and said that it rested with him to completely console the inhabitants of Newburgh, and that for this it would not cost him a quarter of an hour. "Our wives and our children have assembled near here, in a room that had been prepared to receive you; come for a moment to offer yourself to their eyes, and we will all be happy." It was impossible to resist so moving a request. We entered this room filled with women and girls prepared for a ball, who already no longer counted on seeing him, and his presence caused them a very pleasant surprise; in the outpouring of their joy, they all rushed towards him, and they covered him completely with the wreaths and flowers with which they had been adorned. Upon leaving this room, we found all the men arranged in a double row on the way which led to the riverbank, and the General could only arrive at *The James Kent* through the most affectionate and respectful expressions of all these good men who, in spite of his assurances, were still fearful that they had caused him trouble. He received the farewells of the Newburgh authorities on board; at the signal given by our captain we recommenced our voyage, despite the darkness which surrounded us.

The sun on its return found us abreast of Poughkeepsie; it was impossible for the General not to stop there. The wharfs and the shore were covered with militiamen, citizens and even a great number of ladies who had waited the whole night for the arrival of Lafayette.

Poughkeepsie is, like all the towns that border the Hudson, at once manufacturing and commercial; also its population is increasing rapidly. In 1820, it had 3,400 people; today the population has already risen to nearly 5,000.

It is at Poughkeepsie, in the home of George Clinton, that Washington, Hamilton, Chancellor Livingston and Mr. Jay were in the habit of meeting to discuss the Constitution that was accepted by the United States. This circumstance was eloquently reported to General Lafayette by Colonel Livingston who had been charged to speak in the name of the citizens.

In continuing our voyage, we visited the family of the late Governor Lewis, who inhabit a very pretty home on the left bank of the river, and at four o'clock we arrived at Clermont where we disembarked in front of the elegant dwelling of Mr. Robert Livingston. The fetes which had been prepared in this delightful place by the citizens who had flocked there from the surrounding districts and by the Livingston family detained us until the next morning.

Hardly had we left Clermont, when we saw the beautiful Catskill Mountain which, rising up some miles from the river, borders the horizon felicitously with its beautiful brown mass that spreads out in tiers at the center of which, bursting with whiteness, is the house of the *Garden of Pines*, situated 250 feet above the level of the Hudson. This house is an object of curiosity for the traveler, and a goal of walking for the inhabitants of the environs. The masses of citizens and militiamen, who covered a long jetty, which jutted out tapering into the river, apprised the General by their acclamations that the inhabitants of Catskill also expected a visit of the National Guest. We stayed in the midst of these people for several moments only, during which the General had the sweet satisfaction of conversing with some of his former Revolutionary companions, among which he recognized one named James Foster who was, in particular, attached to his service when he was wounded in the Battle of Brandywine.

To land at the little town of Hudson, we had only to cross the river a little obliquely, so to speak. At the Port, which was very commercial, General Lafayette was received by the authorities and by the entire population at the head of which they presented to him a detachment of about 80 soldiers of the Revolution; one of them left the ranks and showed him a sword that he had received from the General in Rhode Island. "After my death, it will change hands," he said, "but it will not change its point of destination: it will always serve in the defense of liberty."

Some triumphal arches had been built; a public banquet was prepared, and the ladies were dressed to dance, but it was necessary for us to renounce all these festivities in order to be able to arrive at Albany on the same day, where the General was awaited with impatience. The inhabitants of Hudson understood this situation perfectly and were kind enough to detain him for only a very short time.

The wealth of Hudson grows each day by its commerce and manufacturing; its population, which in 1820 wasn't quite 3,000 has risen now to more than 5,000. The Town is regular and well constructed; it rises in tiers about 100 feet above the level of the river. The largest vessels of commerce can easily land at its wharves; its environs are very irregular, of a pleasant look, and well-cultivated. Hudson was founded in 1784, and still contains very many descendants of the Dutch, who came to this country in 1636.

In spite of the strength of our steam engine, which allows us to ascend the river at a rate of more than six miles per hour, we only arrived at five o'clock in the evening level with Overslaugh, a little burg situated on the left bank of the river, a very short distance from Albany. Here, we had to abandon sailing because our boat took on too much water. We disembarked and found ourselves instantly placed in elegant carriages surrounded by an escort of dragoons, commanded by General Van Rensselaer and Colonel Cooper, and soon after we arrived at Greenbush, another village at the center of which we found a triumphal arch, where they offered us some refreshments, while members of the municipality gave speeches to the General. He answered them with that ease, that sense of saying the right thing, which, at least four or five times every day, astonishes those who hear him and engenders admiration of him.

It was only with the night that we arrived opposite Albany, on the banks of the river that we had to cross in order to enter into the City, which is situated on the right bank. A large moveable bridge called *Horseback* received, at one and the same time, our two carriages each harnessed to four horses, about 30 cavalrymen for our escort, as well as more than 150 pedestrians, and brought us easily on to the other bank which reverberated with the acclamations of the multitude and the uninterrupted sound of artillery. The scene in which we found ourselves situated there was grand and majestic; the darkness of the night rendered it still more imposing; but it was not without danger. Each cannon blast, by its noise and its sudden light, struck terror in the spirited horses that surrounded us and had no obstacle in front of them other than a rather light chain that would not have been able to prevent them from hurling themselves into the river, if they had not been restrained by some sturdy men. George Lafayette, in his fond solicitude for his father, had left the carriage and had imposed on himself the task of controlling the horses that were conducting the General.

At the moment when we made land, the cries of joy of the multitude redoubled. The escort and the carriage shot forward to the land with the speed of lightning, in the midst of a crowd so thick that it is difficult to conceive how, with so many people, whose enthusiasm in recognizing Lafayette thrust them up under the wheels of his carriage, none of them had been crushed. At the entrance to the outlying part of the City, the procession having formed in order, a troop of musicians began the march, and we went to the Capitol while traveling through streets brightened by innumerable lights and high pyramids of blazing wood. At the entrance to the street which led to the Capitol, a triumphal arch had been built surmounted by a large living eagle who, at the moment when the General passed, flapped his wings as if to pay homage to him.

At the Capitol, we went into the Senate Chamber; the galleries were filled with a large number of ladies; the municipal body was assembled there. The General was welcomed by the Mayor who gave a speech and expressed to him the gratitude of the United States, and especially that of the citizens of Albany, with eloquence – "Those who have shared with you the work of our Revolution and who are living still," he said, "greet you as a friend, as a brother. The generation that has risen since you have left these shores is animated by the same sentiments, and those who will be born in the centuries to come will celebrate in you the benefactor of America, the hero of liberty. In each of the hearts that beat around you, you have the place of friendship, and your eulogy is in every mouth...."

In his response, General Lafayette could not avoid expressing the astonishment that the numerous changes that had occurred in the look of all that now offered itself to his eyes caused in him. "It was only a half-century ago," he said, "that this City, already old it is true, but still very poor then, served me as headquarters on the frontiers of a vast wilderness; as commander of the Northern Department, I received there the renunciation of the Royal power, and the recognition of the more legitimate sovereignty of the people of the United States. Today, I find Albany a powerful and rich city, central seat of the Government of the State of New York, and the wilderness that surrounded it changed into fertile, well-cultivated plains; the present generation, rendered illustrious already by two glorious wars, and more still by its sincere attachment to institutions whose excellence assure to it an incontestable superiority over the arrogant power that wanted to arrogate to itself the right of control over it ...."

From the Senate Chamber, we passed into the rooms of Governor Yates, who, surrounded by his general staff, received the General with great cordialty and spoke to him in the name of the State.

On leaving the Governor's suite, they made the General proceed on to the principal balcony of the Capitol in order to present him to the assembled people. At the moment when he advanced between the two columns at the center of the balcony, an eagle descended and placed on his head a crown of laurels and immortelles. This scene was applauded vigorously by the numerous spectators.

Before we went to the hotel that had been prepared for us to lodge in, the General wanted to visit one of his former companions-in-arms, Mathew Gregory who, at Yorktown, had been one of the first in the assault of the entrenchments with Hamilton and him. There, we found a numerous gathering composed of Judges of the Supreme Court, members of the Bar, and principal officers of the State.

This day of emotion and fatigue, to which a less robust man than General Lafayette would certainly have succumbed, ended with a supper in which they drank to the *Nation's Guest, to Liberty* and *to the Sovereignty of the People*; and by a brilliant ball that we left at midnight in order to take a little rest.

Albany was founded in 1612 as a Dutch Colony and is, after Jamestown in Virginia, the oldest settlement in the United States. Situated on the right bank of the Hudson, 150 miles from New York, this City does not offer a pleasant sight; the terrain is especially uneven, its streets are, it is true, wide and well-aligned, but the architecture of the homes is in bad taste and recalls very much the old cities of Germany. With the exception of the Capitol, there is not a building that has a monumental appearance; this building produces a beautiful-enough effect by its location on a rise that ends a very beautiful street called *State Street*. This monument, which serves at the same time the Senate, the House of Representatives, the Courts of Justice, the Society of the Arts, that of Agriculture, etc., and which contains the Library, is constructed in granite taken from the banks of the Hudson, and the columns as well as all the exterior decorations are made of beautiful white marble taken from the quarries of Massachusetts. The principal façade is of Ionic architecture; most of the rooms are decorated and furnished with a luxury that one admires at first, but afterwards one cannot avoid blaming when one learns that it has thrown the municipal administration into debts that necessarily became a burden to the citizens. The total cost of construction rose to more than $120,000, of which at least $34,000 has been paid by the City.

The City Hall, the Academy, the Lancaster School, the Arsenal, the Prison and some of the monuments of public service are appropriately and commodiously constructed in brick.

The City is governed by a municipal body that is composed of a mayor, a recorder, ten aldermen, ten assistant aldermen, all named by the people. In order to simplify the administration and to facilitate the supervisory responsibility of the police, the City is divided into five sections or quarters. Some night guards are specifically charged with watching for the dangers of fire; an excellent organization of firemen assures prompt help in case of fire. These precautions are made necessary by the presence of numerous stores of oils and spirits, imprudently established in the middle of the City.

The police regulations are executed with a strictness that does not leave to any class of citizens the hope of transgressing them with impunity; among the thousand proofs that have been cited here is one that is very remarkable. The regulations expressly forbid horsemen to ride on the streets. Not long ago, the Mayor was at his country house, not far from the City; suddenly the sound of bells, and soon even the sight of flames apprised him that a fire had broken out. He threw himself on his horse, left and arrived in the City, which he traversed at a gallop up to the place of the fire; he dismounted and put himself immediately at the head of the firemen; in a short time, his example and sage counsel contributed to wiping out the danger, and he returned quietly to his home. The next day he received a summons to appear before the justice of the peace who sentenced him to *a fine* for having violated the regulations that forbid galloping in the streets. The Mayor did not think that his wrongful act was in any way justified by the reason which had made him commit it, and he submitted without grumbling to the sentence that he himself recognized to be fair. This submission to the law provided such a good example that, upon leaving the tribunal, he was welcomed by a large delegation of citizens who addressed to him their public gratitude for the eminent services which he had rendered the night before by courageously putting himself at risk to preserve the properties of his citizens.

The expenses of the City come to about $45,000 annually; its revenues this year (1824) are valued at more than $49,000, but its debt is more than $250,000. This debt, which necessarily depreciates the value of the property situated in Albany, was contracted by the extravagances of the former administrations: one has no doubt that this debt may soon be extinguished by a sinking fund of more than $100,000, and especially by the resources that the ever-growing prosperity of commerce offers daily.

As a commercial place, Albany is one of the most eminent cities of the Union. Since its origin, it has served as storehouse for all the products that arrive from the West. Now the ease of communication that has opened with Lake Erie, by the construction of a great canal for navigation, is going to increase its commercial preponderance even more.

Nearly 80 steamships navigate constantly between Albany and New York, and the number of sloops that navigate between these two cities is very much more considerable.

In 1820, the population of Albany was about 12,630; today it is about 16,000.

On the next day, September 18th, at eight o'clock in the morning, Mr. Clinton, with a great number of citizens, was already in General Lafayette's suite in order to offer to him, in the name of the Literary and Philosophical Society of New York, a diploma that made him a member of this Society. On this occasion, Mr. Clinton gave an eloquent speech which touched the General so much more because he found in the orator the son and the nephew of two very distinguished men with whom he was intimately linked during the War of Independence. During this brief ceremony, a large procession had formed in front of our hotel; and at nine o'clock we embarked, to the sound of cannon, on the canal that leads to Troy.

Five pretty galleys of those that regularly navigate the canal had been prepared for our trip; the first carried a troop of musicians; in the second was placed the General with Governor Yates, ex-Governors Clinton and Lewis, the Mayor and municipal council, and some of the principal citizens of Albany; in the last three followed the escort, commanded by Major Cole, which was composed of one artillery company and three infantry companies. We stopped for some moments en route to visit the arsenal of Gibbonsville, which belongs to the United States. This arsenal, one of the most considerable and best provisioned by the Union, was started in 1813 under the direction of Artillery Colonel Bomford, who was then attached to the War Department, and completed under the good offices of Major Dalliba, of the same branch who introduced there a system of administration remarkable for its order and economy. Upon his entrance into the yard of the arsenal, the General was received by the officers employed in this post and saluted by the fire of three cannon pieces seized at Yorktown. We noticed in the artillery park some French pieces given to the United States during the Revolutionary War, and all the field-equipment seized at Saratoga from General Burgoyne. We visited all the rooms containing arms; they are kept with a remarkable care and elegance;

we found there more than 30,000 rifles made after the best models of Europe, as well as a large number of very well-made pistols and swords. The ammunition warehouse also contained very considerable provisions.

It wasn't yet noon when we arrived at the point where the canal connects with the Hudson opposite Troy. At the sight of this City, which today contains nearly 8,000 inhabitants, and which by its commercial importance, holds the first rank after Albany in New York State, General Lafayette was astonished. "And what!," he shouted. "Is this City one which has just sprung from the ground by magic?" – "No," answered someone who was at his side, smiling, "but it was created and populated in a few years by industry protected by liberty." The General then recounted how when he passed the Hudson at this point in 1778 with a corps of troops under his command, there were then only two or three poor cottages in one of which he procured, with difficulty, a cup of milk and a piece of cornbread ... . While he was giving us these interesting details, our galley descended into the river, as 12 boats decked with flags ferried us in their tow.

On disembarking in the middle of a large population that lined the river bank, the General was welcomed by a committee charged with expressing to him the feelings of gratitude and attachment of the citizens. " Your indefatigable devotion to the cause of civil and religious liberty," the speaker said,

> Has made your name famous everywhere where the rights of man are respected and honored. The liberation of this country was an act worthy of the patriots by the advice and arms of whom it was accomplished. Their labors, their privations, their sacrifices, but more specifically still, your generous efforts have engraved in the heart of the citizens of these States a profound feeling of gratitude that increases each day with the development of a prosperity without parallel and the benefits of the most wise institutions.
>
> May you be able to enjoy for a long time among us the fruits of your glorious labors! These fruits you will contemplate in the form of our Government that guarantees order and liberty; in our system of jurisprudence, which assures at one and the same time public peace and private rights; in our public schools, which lavish on the poor as well as the rich the benefits of a good education; in the transformation of our immense wildernesses into fertile fields; in the birth, the growth, the multiplication of our cities, our towns and our villages; in the

creation of the numerous means of communication to facilitate our commercial relations; in the variety and the harmony of our different religious sects; finally, you will contemplate, moreover, the fruits of your labors and those of our patriots of the Revolution in the spirit of enterprise and industry of a frugal people, happy with its lot, obedient to its laws, at peace with itself and with the entire world, and raising its voice of thanks, first to God and then to their benefactors, at the head of which they place you, your virtues and your generous services.

Uninimous applause and shouts, repeated a thousand times, of *Welcome, Welcome Lafayette!* drowned out both the end of the speech and the General's response. Immediately, he was raised in the arms of the spectators and placed in an uncovered carriage, accompanied by old Colonel Lane, who fought with him at Brandywine, at Monmouth and at Yorktown. The procession, preceded by the members of the Masonic Lodge and followed by the numerous militia corps, went through all the streets of the City in the midst of cries of joy of this free and grateful people.

While we were having lunch in the house from the balcony of which we had seen all the militia of the City and those of the neighboring counties march by, the General received a message from the ladies of Troy who invited him to go to the girls' boarding school where they were assembled to welcome him; he went there readily. The avenues leading to this establishment, directed by Mrs. Willard, were decorated with branches of greenery and flowers and ended near the premises with a triumphal arch under which he was welcomed by a committee of five ladies, at the head of which was Mrs. Pawling. She in a few words expressed eloquently the patriotic sentiments of the ladies of Troy and their affectionate gratitude for the illustrious benefactor of their dear Fatherland. He was then led by this committee to the interior of this establishment, where no man entered with him; and some moments after, we heard the pure and angelic voices of the girls who repeated to him in chorus: *"In order to visit us, you have left your dear family in a faraway land; but do not grieve; aren't you here in your Fatherland? See how many girls of Columbia are proud and happy to greet you with the sweet name of father!"* Soon the General reappeared on the threshold; his face showed deep emotion; his eyes were full of tender tears. He slowly descended the steps, supported and surrounded by the principal ladies of the establishment; 200 girls clad in white followed him while raising towards the sky their harmonious voices of gratitude. They led him up to the outside gate, where they addressed touching farewells to him in the presence of several thousand spectators whom this scene held immersed in a religious silence.

General Lafayette did not want to leave Troy without making some private visits to persons of his intimate acquaintance, and particularly to Mrs. Taylor, with the family of whom he had been linked during the Revolutionary War. Mrs. Taylor is a young woman very distinguished by her spirit and by the knowledge that she acquired in the boarding school which we had just visited. At her house, we found a very attractive mineralogical collection, remarkable for its order and its richness. She offered the General, *as a souvenior of Troy*, a very beautiful herbarium containing more than 200 of the most remarkable plants from the surrounding areas collected, put in order and described by her.

After these visits, we left the City slowly in the midst of the people who blanketed the route that we had to traverse to arrive at the banks of the Hudson. Each one hurled himself toward the carriage of the General and wanted to clasp his hand. At every step, we saw fathers lifting their children above the crowd in order that they could see Lafayette better and ask for his blessing. At the moment when we were crossing the river, a triple *huzzah* and a salvo of artillery expressed the farewells and the last good wishes of the inhabitants of this wealthy and happy City.

The City of Troy is situated on the left bank of the Hudson six miles from Albany, a little above the point where the tide still can be felt, and in a rather wide plain, formed of alluvium and very fertile. In this spot, the river is still more than 800 feet wide. Sixty sloops, belonging to the citizens of the City, are continually employed in commerce, but this still does not prevent other boats from finding employment. The export of grains especially is very considerable. On all the streams that flow into the river and on the river itself are a large number of factories in full activity; they are particularly intended to grind, to saw, and to pour iron and lead. The most considerable of these mills is the one known as Adamsville. The principal building that houses the nailworks contains 24 machines appropriate for cutting and making the nailheads; they are all put in motion by an enormous cast-iron wheel, to which impulsive force is given by water current. They say that this factory works upon 1,000 tons of iron per year.

About two miles from Adamsville, one finds a beautiful cotton factory that has 1,700 spindles in action constantly, driven by 30 looms that the water puts in motion.

Alongside has been built a bleachery for cotton cloth where the bleaching takes place by some chemical processes at the rate of one or two pennies per yard.

On all sides, some tanneries, pottery works, paper mills, soap works and ship-building yards surround this City, which did not exist in 1787, which in 1801 was but a feeble village, which took the title of city only in 1816, and which in 1820 was ravaged by a fire from which the damages rose to more than $370,000 …! In the 60 days that followed this catastrophe, the insurance company faithfully fulfilled its obligations which raised up to $110,000, and in a short time the burnt-down buildings were rebuilt more fashionable, more commodious and more solid. Today, the City grows still on a regular plan; all the streets are wide, perfectly straight and provided with beautiful footpaths.

The inhabitants of Troy do not attract any less attention by their love of Letters and Sciences than by their industrial activity and skill. In their City, they have three periodical newspapers, four printing presses, five extensive libraries and a large number of public schools.

Troy possesses, moreover, still very many other sources of success and prosperity about which our too-short stay in this City did not allow me to obtain positive information; it appears that the work of canalization, to facilitate commerce, is worthy of particular attention; but perhaps I will have an occasion to come back to this subject because we must, they say, visit the longest part of the canals of the State of New York one day.

I observed with pleasure that the Colored population, which is not very numerous (around 300), freely joined its good wishes for the Nation's Guest with those of the White population. One counts now hardly 30 Slaves in the City and its dependencies. Three more years, and liberty will not have to blush any more in the presence of men of Color…!

Upon reentering Albany, where we returned by land, we visited Governor Yates and Mr. DeWitt Clinton, who was also Governor of New York State during 1817 and 1818. The latter, who has already had a long and brilliant political career, is called upon, if I am not mistaken, to play an important role in the affairs of his country. He had already been successively secretary of Governor George Clinton, his uncle; member of the legislative assembly of New York State; United States Senator; three times Mayor of New York; member of the Commission of Interior Navigation; President of the Canalization Council; Lieutenant Governor and finally Governor of the State; several charitable institutions owe him their existence; he is a member of nearly all the learned societies; and I will not be at all surprised if one day I shall hear his name proclaimed among those of the candidates to the Presidency of the United States. He is now 55 years old: it is difficult to have at the same time a more imposing stature and more noble character; everyone agrees in saying that his dominant passion is to contribute to the happiness of his fellow men. These are very great claims to esteem in a nation that knows so well how to reward those who have devoted themselves to its service.[9]

It was very late when we were able to leave Albany. We left the City as we had entered, by the brightness of the illuminations; and we rejoined our ship, *The James Kent*, at midnight, at the point where we had left it. A short time after, we started engines to descend the Hudson to New York, where we arrived on Monday, September 20, at dawn, after a sail of 26 hours, interrupted by some brief visits that we made again to Newburgh, West Point, etc.

9. Since this has been written, death has taken Mr. Clinton away from the affections of his family and the hopes of his fellow citizens.

Chapter VIII

New York.

Upon the return from our voyage on the Hudson, General Lafayette evinced the desire to renter the calm of private life in order to be able to devote some time to the sweet intimacy which a large number of his old friends clamored for. As a consequence, the public festivities were suspended, the citizens resumed their accustomed occupations, and I was able to examine more attentively the customs and the character of the people of this City, whom up to the present I had seen *only in festival attire.*

My first excursion was naturally to visit the whole length of *Broadway*, which they say is the bazaar of American Industry and which is also that of products of the entire world. Its length of about three miles, the width of its walkways solidly and neatly constructed in brick, the elegance of its homes, the wealth and variety of its stores and the always active crowd that enlivens it, make this street one of the most interesting promenades for the traveler who has the time to observe it. One thing alone mars it for my taste; it is that immense cemetery which borders one side of the street, and from which the passersby are separated only by an iron grill. This sight contrasts in a distressing way with the frolicsome joy of groups of girls who at every moment pass with a light step in front of this sad home of the dead. I am astonished that the wisdom of the corporation of New York, which has already done so much for the improvement and health of this City, has not yet thought to move this home of putrid emanations, which in certain seasons of the year can become so deadly to the whole population, further away.

Most of the other streets that join Broadway directly are also very neat and regular, but those that are situated in the vicinity of the wharves do not always offer an agreeable sight. One sees there a large number of wood houses, rather poorly built, which serve as a refuge for debauchery and habitual drunkenness. This latter vice visits great ravages here; it plunges a great number of its victims into prisons and hospitals; the greatest part of crimes or diseases have no other cause. The low price of spiritous liquors, which do not pay any sales tax, and perhaps also the excessive heat of the climate are the principal causes of this dismal passion. I have been assured that there are in New York City more than 3,000 cabarets in which sales are made of at least $3,000,000 in wine and hard liquors annually. This appears appalling to me with regard to the population.[10]

---

10. This prodigious consumption of liquors is explained easily by the presence of a large number of sailors whom the Port of New York welcomes every day.

Here prostitution is less common than one would suppose it to be in a city of extensive commerce, continually full of mariners and foreigners. One counts barely 3,000 public women, which is hardly 1/60th of the population. This proportion would be very low for Paris, and especially for London, where prostitutes ordinarily form 1/25th of the population. If one looks for the causes of this large difference, one finds them principally in the early and numerous marriages of the inhabitants of New York. Ordinarily, men marry here from 20 to 25 years old, and women from 16 to 20. Moreover, age of marriage is not determined by any law; and no law authorizes parents to oppose the marriage of their children anymore. The religious ceremony alone constitutes the act of marriage, and the difference in communions never prevents a minister of a sect from giving the nuptial blessing to those who come to ask it of him. Always sure of finding some means of subsistence for his companion and for himself, the young American is never stopped by considerations of fortune from determining his choice, which is always according to his heart. From this, there are fewer celibates in society and, consequently, fewer causes of corruption.

A third scourge, more terrible than drunkenness and prostitution, also exacts its ravages in the City of New York and brings harsh wounds to public morality every day. I want to speak of those bottomless pits that swallow up indiscriminately both the profits of the wealthy merchant and the savings of the poor worker, which present a danger to so many of the ancient, long-established virtues, and which, in exchange for the money entrusted to them, never return anything but disgrace and misery; in short, I want to speak of *lottery offices*.

The laws of the State of New York forbid the establishment of new lotteries, but the legislators believed that they should respect those already in existence because they were founded by virtue of privileges previous to the Constitution. Is it not a culpable deficiency, this respect for the bad law consecrated by time? Some people with whom I have spoken respond that the lotteries of New York did not have the immorality of others because their receipts, instead of going to the cash boxes of the Government, were used to support hospitals; nor are they a danger to the working classes because their high prices allow only the wealthy to have access to them. These arguments do not at all reconcile me to the lotteries.

Of all the cities of the United States, New York is certainly the one whose society ought to have lost its national character the most. The large number of foreigners who abound there without interruption would seem of necessity to have always been the driving cause of this. However, one finds in its physiognomy all the principal traits that maintain the national character. One of these traits is hospitality. A single letter of recommendation is sufficient here to give entrance into all the most distinguished societies; and, if their conduct and character respond honorably to the kindness that each is disposed to accord to them, it is easy for foreigners to draw pleasure and profit from it in a short time. Unfortunately, many of them show themselves to be unworthy of one received so kindly, and I have difficulty understanding how, after so many unhappy proofs, the inhabitants of New York expose themselves voluntarily still more to see their generous hospitality repaid by fraud, treachery and slander.

It is not at all rare to encounter here some Europeans who, questioned on the character of Americans, respond with insolence: "They are all selfish, corrupt and hypocritical." If, then, one proceeds to a careful examination of the conduct of any of these men who accuse with so much bitterness, one is very surprised to learn that he dares no longer to appear before such a person because he has been for such a long time his debtor, insolvent and in bad faith, that having been received first with trust into the bosom of such a family, he has been thereafter driven out of it for having tried to practice the most dastardly seduction there, and that he, finally, is now exposed to the contempt of public opinion which he had at first won over under the guise of virtues that he was incapable of really practicing. It would be easy for me, to justify my assertion, to name several of these men; but it would be very much more agreeable, if I were not afraid of offending their modesty, to name Messrs. P…, B…, M…, G…, etc., who by their intelligence have created an honorable existence and who, by the nobility of their character, have turned the French name away from the scorn into which so many adventurers have been able to plunge it.

Among so many calumnies spread by travelers, ignorant or in bad faith, there are however some troublesome truths that one cannot keep silent about without being remiss; thus I should not keep silent about the numerous bankruptcies which in New York, as in all the large commercial cities of the United States, bring to public morality wounds no less dangerous to the confidence and the security which, everywhere, commerce demands as indispensable foundations for its existence and prosperity. The man of bad faith is not impeded here in his commercial transactions by any coercive law. However, for some years the sound part, the honest part of commerce in New York, and it is the large majority, has raised its voice forcefully to call out before Congress for a law that insures to the creditors of a business in bankruptcy a legal right to share in the dividends which it abandons. It would prevent a merchant who finds himself embarrassed in his affairs from assigning in advance all that he possesses in payment to confidential friends who have lent him their names and their money to create the artificial credit with the aid of which he has caught the confidence of the public unawares. Congress has not been deaf to the demands of the Chamber of Commerce of New York and very many other cities; it has already inquired carefully into whether it was possible to make a law that curbs these abuses without, however, fettering the absolute freedom without which commerce cannot be conducted. The difficulties have appeared to the legislators to be large, but not insurmountable. One awaits very much their conscientious and enlightened zeal.

The women here follow the French fashions in their clothes, but are still entirely American in their customs; that is to say, they dedicate nearly their entire existence to the management of their household and the education of their children. In general, they live very secluded lives and, although most of them would be able to offer the resources of an agreeable and witty conversation, they occupy, however, only a small place in meetings, where young girls alone appear to have the right to hold sway. These latter, it is true, derive from their nature and education all the means to please. The unlimited freedom which they enjoy, without ever abusing it, gives to their manners a grace, a freedom and a modest abandon that one does not always find in our salons, where, under the name of reserve, they impose on our young girls so distressing an incapacity.

If American women are noteworthy for their strict fidelity to conjugal trust, the girls are not any less steadfast in their *engagements*. They have often pointed out to me in meetings several young people of 18 or 19 years, who for two or three years have been *engaged*, and whose future spouses were, one in Europe to study the Arts and Sciences, another in China for commercial affairs, and finally another dangerously occupied in whale-fishing in the most faraway seas. The girls so *engaged* hold a middle ground in society between their young companions who are still free and the women already married. They have already lost a little of the playful gaiety of the former, and taken on a tinge of the seriousness of the latter. The numerous suitors, designated here by name of *beaus*, who at first surrounded them in a crowd, and whom they welcomed before having made their choice, still display tender attentiveness towards them, but are now less fervent; and, if one of them, ill-informed, or swept along by some obstinate hopes, persists in offering his vows and his heart, this response, "*I am engaged,*" made with a gentle frankness and an indulgent smile soon destroys all his illusions, without however wounding his self-respect. – These kind of engagements which precede marriage are very common, not only in New York, but also in all the other States of the Union; and it is infinitely rare that they are not carried out with a scrupulous fidelity. Public opinion, which is very strict on this point, would not spare the one of the two parties who would have discarded the engagement without the consent of the other.

The people who believe that republican principles are incompatible with the possessions that wealth procures would find the luxury of New York excessive and would assume that a people who tread on fine English carpet, who pour the most refined wines of France in great waves into gold or crystal, and who hurry after pleasure in elegant chariots, cannot for long preserve their independence. These persons would have reason to be frightened of this if the luxury here were, like that of our princes and courtiers of Europe, born out of oppression and nourished by the sweat of the people; but they are reassured to think that here it is only the product of industry, the fertile and wealthy daughter of liberty.

Although New York may be a very extensive city containing a large population, and receiving annually into its bosom at least 30,000 foreigners, serious disturbances are unknown there; and the slightest offenses can only very rarely escape the surveillance of a police force which is not less astonishing by its activity as by the small clatter with which it proceeds. By the perfect order which rules the day and the night, it seems to be everywhere; however, one does not see it doing anything. The security that it guarantees to foreigners, as to citizens, is not as in Paris the result of the odious combination of murderous gendarmes with dirty and loathsome spies. The traveler is not obligated, upon entering an inn, to state his name, his occupation, his plans, in order to obtain the protection due to all; in a word, after having stayed in New York, one is forced to agree that its administration, like a good genie, makes its benign influence felt everywhere without showing any part of itself.

Europeans, who for so long a time have been accustomed to putting up with a man or several men, under the name of government, impeding the exercise of natural rights by other men under their administration at their whim, have difficulty conceiving how there can exist a nation in which all individuals, without exception, can travel, come and go in all directions, traverse great distances, enter all the cities and sleep peacefully in all the inns without being obligated to have on them that ridiculous and tyrannical permission of *the authority*, written on a scrap of paper, called a *passport*. This unlimited freedom to travel in all directions causes them astonishment that extends sometimes to incredulity. The following anecdote, which I guarantee actually happened, is a pleasant enough proof of this.

Banished in 1815 by the Restoration, General … had been forced to leave Paris precipitiously and had been seeking a place of refuge near a friend in Le Havre, from which he hoped to be able to pass without danger into a land less hostile than that of his Fatherland. Soon the occasion for this was offered to him. A captain of an American ship, moved by his sad situation, took him readily on board and brought him to the United States. At first, the joy of being beyond the fear of the danger that menaced him, which General … experienced, was the feeling that entirely absorbed him; he forgot that he was fleeing his country, his family, his friends perhaps forever; the vast ocean and the prospect of 30 days which separated him from New York gave him a security which was only disturbed by the sight of the new land to which he was coming to request shelter. He recalled with fright that the haste with which he had left Paris did not allow him to take any documents. Without authentic papers, *without passport*, what was going to become of him? Nonetheless, he disembarked; and the customs officer, who questioned him politely about the nature of the objects which his portmanteau contained, made him experience a feeling of dread that he had felt before only when Emperor Napoleon, his master, regarded him with a displeased look. But after some moments, the customs officer let him go without requesting his passport.

Doubtless it was inadvertence; but it was necessary to take advantage of it very quickly; and our general officer, lighter-hearted by half, quickly loaded his little baggage on the shoulder of a porter by whom he was led into one of the hotels of Broadway. There, a domestic servant received him and admitted him into a room which contained four or five beds on several of which were some belongings which indicated that they had already been taken possession of. He asked with anxiety if it was not possible to have a private room. There was still one which contained two beds; they gave that to him while promising him that he would not have a companion.

When he was alone, he breathed at last, and thanked his lucky star for having conducted him so successfully through so many dangers. The next steamer from Le Havre was to bring letters of credit to him; he would then be able to make himself known and obtain protection. It was only a matter, then, of avoiding arrest as an adventurer, a vagabond or a suspect, of passing 15 days in his retreat, and he was resigned to it. Already he had passed three long days in *solitary confinement* when, on the morning of the fourth, the owner of the hotel presented himself to him, and, with an air of politeness without urgency, of interest without curiosity, said to him: "Sir, I am not indiscreet by nature, and I do not have a practice of tormenting my guests with impertinent questions, but I am afraid that this strict retreat to which you appear to be condemned since your entry into my house might be caused by trouble or by some awkward embarrassment, and I come to offer you without ceremony my services which I urge you to accept." The simple and cordial tone in which these words were spoken encouraged the poor recluse. "You appear to me to be a good man," he said to his host, "and I want to put my trust in you. My situation is troublesome; you are going to be the judge of it." Then throwing a worried look around the room and lowering his voice, he said:

> I am a French officer, forced in consequence of great events that you are doubtless aware of, to leave my country. I come here to seek a refuge from banishment .... The Americans and their Government are hospitable, I know, but, in a word, here, like everywhere else, the police entrusted with watching over the safety of the citizens must require that foreigners make themselves known, and how can I do this, since I do not even have a passport? What papers would I rely on to obtain permission to reside in this city or to go to another? You are offering me your services, you say? Now then! May you be my bail for the police, may you make it so that I would be able to reside in this city without being disturbed, and my gratitude would have no bounds ....

By this speech, by the agitation which accompanied it, the American innkeeper believed that the French officer was crazy, and he would have persisted in this opinion, if the former had not finally explained to him the importance and the indispensable necessity of the passport for the European traveler. The innkeeper hurried to reassure him by telling him:

> The authority that governs us emanates from ourselves, and we have not been foolish enough to accord to it the absurd right to paralyze our most natural rights, like traveling, for example, in such or such a direction, and as far as we desire to. Foreigners who land on our soil, like us, are allowed to enjoy all rights, the exercise of which does not offend the rights of other men. Go then from Labrador to the Gulf of Mexico, from the Atlantic Ocean to Lake Huron, or live as a peaceful inhabitant of New York; and I will guarantee you the most perfect security, the most absolute freedom.

General ... had difficulty believing this assertion, but, however, experience wasn't long in convincing him of it, and in the first trips that he made, he was moved less by the beauty of nature and the appearance of a country entirely new for him, than by the blessing of not being obligated at the entrance of each city or at each relay station to show his passport to a gendarme.

The activity of the Port of New York presents one of the most animated and the most varied tableaus that one could imagine. It is rare that a half an hour passes without a ship leaving or landing on the shore. The wharves are continuously covered with numerous groups of travelers who are leaving or arriving; the variety of their dress and their languages proves that there are few parts of the globe with which the United States may not have relations. In the midst of this crowd which diverse feelings of astonishment or regret enliven, it is easy to recognize the Americans by the calm, I should say almost the indifference, with which they leave or see again their native land and the friends who accompany them to the ship or welcome them on the shore. Accustomed since childhood to compare the prodigious distances that separate the different points of the country that they inhabit, the American is less affected at the moment of undertaking a voyage from New York to China than is a burgher of Paris who makes ready to go to see the ocean at Dieppe.

One can develop an idea of the ease with which Americans travel outside of their homeland by having a look at the tables that present the number of passengers annually disembarking into the different ports of the Union; one will see that the citizens of the United States appear there in a huge proportion in relation to their population.

The following table, which contains the nationality of passengers who have disembarked in the Port of New York alone from March 1, 1818 to December 11, 1819, will also enable one to judge approximately the proportion in which each nation furnishes travelers to the United States:

American	16,628
English	7,629
Irish	6,067
Scottish	1,492
French	930
Belgian	590
German	499
Swiss	372
Spanish	217
Dutch	155
Italian	103
Danish	97
Portuguese	54
Prussian	48
Swede	28
African	5
Sardinian	3
Norwegian	3

Chapter IX

Departure from New York – Route from New York to Trenton – Battles of Trenton and Princeton – Visit to Joseph Bonaparte – State of New Jersey.

On September 23, we left New York for the third time. The utter silence that ruled among the crowd that filled the streets, the sadness stamped on all the faces, indicated that this third absence of Lafayette was to be of long duration. How this departure contrasted with our initial arrival! Today not a cry of joy, not an acclamation, but only that same silent look of the people and the militiamen who formed a double line from our hotel to the riverbank where the vessel waited for us! The General wanted to traverse the long distance that we had to travel on foot, and he sent back the carriages that they had prepared, but when he was on the doorstep, he was so surrounded and so crowded by all those who wanted to see him one more time that it was impossible for us for some time to disengage him to open up a passageway by which he could advance. At each step his walk was slowed by the most emotional farewells; at each step men hurled themselves in front of him, took his hand, shook it with fondness, and left him abruptly while diverting their faces in order to conceal the tears that they hadn't the strength to hold back.

Accompanied by a large delegation of the City, we boarded the steamship *James Kent*, which was to take us to the lands of Jersey, from which we were separated only by the North River which, in this spot, is of prodigious width. At the moment when we raised anchor, the cannon sounded, but how mournful its sounds appeared to us! They seemed to be in harmony with the farewells of the crowd that sighed sadly on the shore; we shared in this sadness, and perhaps we were going to surrender to our emotion, when suddenly a striking contrast came to change the nature of our feelings in spite of ourselves. On one bank we left behind a devastated family weeping for the departure of a father; on the right bank we heard shouts of joy of free men who were coming to welcome their liberator. Soon we were in their midst, and their open and cordial welcome alleviated a little of the grief of our departure.

Mr. Williamson, Governor of New Jersey, had assembled at Paulus Hook, where we landed, his entire general staff and a detachment of militias with whom he escorted the General during his entire route across the State of New Jersey. Our course was traced by Bergen, Newark, Elizabeth, Rahway, New Brunswick, Princeton and Trenton. In each of these towns, and in each of the villages that separated them, General Lafayette was welcomed in the midst of the most brilliant fetes, prepared by the same spirit of enthusiasm and gratitude, the expression of which he had received in all the other parts of New

England. At Bergen, a delegation of the Town presented to him in the name of the inhabitants a cane made of a branch of an apple tree under which he had had lunch with Washington, when he had traversed this town with him during the Revolutionary War. This apple tree was uprooted in 1821 by a horrible storm. These diverse circumstances were carved on the golden knob of the cane.

At Newark, a pretty little town on the Passaic, the Nation's Guest was greeted by the patriotic singing of numerous choruses of boys and girls. He slept at Elizabeth and, on the following day, he entered New Brunswick to the sound of bells and cannon. On the 25th, he stayed for a time at Princeton, where the President of the University, at the head of the professors, came to present to him a diploma as a member of the community which had been awarded on him unanimously under the Presidency of Dr. Witherspoon. On the same evening he arrived finally at Trenton where a large gathering of people awaited him, at the head of which the magistrates expressed the feelings of love and of gratitude toward him that were aroused in each citizen.

This entire route which we had traversed for these two days is commonly called the Garden of the United States. In a word, this name is admirably suited to this fertile part of the Jeseys, which numerous watercourses irrigate and which the most beautiful plantations which it would be possible to imagine adorn so gracefully. If, in this two-day trip, our eyes had been constantly pleased by the sight of beautiful nature, our imaginations had been not less agreeably occupied by the historical remembrances that at each step the land which we tread upon recalled to us. It was by this very route that Washington effectuated his beautiful retreat in 1776 after having been checked on the North River. It was at Trenton and at Princeton that, by a bold maneuver, he undertook the offensive that was to restore the confidence in his troops and to lead them to victory under his colors against his presumptuous adversaries.

The details of these glorious days could not fail to interest me keenly; also I listened to them avidly when I heard them recounted by some aged members of the Society of Cincinnatus with whom we dined the day of our arrival at Trenton. Here is how they reported the facts to which they had been witnesses.

> Washington, having learned that an advance corps of 1,500 Hessian and English cavalrymen under the command of Colonel Rahl had established a base at Trenton, formulated a plan to surprise him and to storm his position if it was possible. In order to effectuate the plan, he chose Christmas night, thinking rightly that discipline and vigilance would feel the

effects of the holiday a little. There weren't more than 3,000 men under his command; he took 2,400 of them, and divided them in two divisions, one under the command of General Greene, the other under the command of General Sullivan. With the aid of boats, he crossed the Delaware at their head in the middle of the night of December 25, in weather that was frightful due to rain and snow. Having disembarked on the Jersey shore, he directed one of his columns to the left in order to take the main road to Maidenhead and the other straight to Trenton, by following the length of the river. The march was so rapid and secretive that the two columns arrived at seven o'clock in the morning on the advanced posts, which were entirely surprised. From the first gunshots, the brigade took up arms, and some men tried to harness up the artillery that had been put in the church, but they were prevented by the speed with which the advance guard of the Americans arrived among them. The Hessians and the English, seeing themselves surrounded from all sides, soon gave up defending themselves. Colonel Rahl and some other officers having been seriously wounded during the first clash, the men surrendered unconditionally. This action, which won for the conquerors six cannon pieces, about 100 small arms, three war-flags, 1,200 prisoners, and very much equipment, cost them at most about ten men. General Washington decided that the Hessians would be sent to the interior of Pennslyvania and that they would be left with all their belongings. This generous treatment, which they were far from expecting, inspired in them a great veneration for the American general who, they said, *was a very good and very kind rebel.*

After this success, Washington withdrew behind the Delaware from which, after having received considerable reinforcements from the states of Maryland and Virginia, he returned anew to the Jerseys, and came to encamp at Trenton. At this news, Lord Cornwallis recognized that he had been mistaken when he had believed that the war was drawing to its end. He felt, indeed, that his adversary was not a man to abandon the fight as long as it was possible for him to fire one more shot; consequently, he resolved to press him vigorously. In spite of the rigors of the season, he assembled all his troops that had been dispersed in winter quarters and marched against him with considerable forces. At his approach, Washington withdrew behind Assunpink Creek, in such a manner that the Town of Trenton was between the two armies, which, during the first night, exchanged some cannon fire, after which they stopped for a time to watch each other. However, Cornwallis grew stronger everyday, and he was waiting only for the arrival of two brigades from Brunswick in order to attempt the passage of the Creek and to attack. Washington's situation was then very critical, supplies began to be short and all communication between the Jerseys and the States of the West were cut off; but he did not despair of the well-being of the blessed cause that he was defending.

On January 2, at one hour after midnight, he ordered that the fires be kept well-lit and that some soldiers be left to maintain them, while the army, marching by the right in order to later cut back to the left, passed behind the English Army, and proceeded inland into the Jerseys. The movement was dangerous, if it wasn't secret; for it was necessary to prolong it considerably on the right in order to cross Assunpink Creek more easily at its source, and to then fall upon Princeton. It was executed with some rare good fortune. About a mile from Princeton, Washington's advanced guard, upon entering a large road, found itself face to face with the English regiment of Colonel Mawhood, who, thinking he was completely secure, was marching without precautions towards Trenton. Soon the fight began. The American advance guard was at first repulsed by the rapid fire of the English. General Mercer, who commanded it, giving way to his impetuosity, wanted to renew the attack with bayonettes; but while springing over a trench, he fell in the midst of the English who massacred him ruthlessly at the moment when, believing himself a prisoner, he offered them his sword. The Americans, discouraged by the loss of their leader, withdrew into the woods, awaiting the bulk of the Army, which was not long in arriving.

The English corps continued its route towards Maidenhead so that General Washington, upon arriving at the place of the action, found only the 48th English regiment, which, at the sound of the first gunshots, had proceeded on the main road. He attacked it suddenly, dispersed it and took some prisoners. During this time, General Sullivan was advancing rapidly, leaving on his left the road to Princeton with

> the intent to go around this Town and to cut off all hope of retreat to Brunswick for the troops that occupied it. A forest through which he had to pass was occupied by 200 English whom he dislodged in an instant and whom he drove without respite to the great college of Princeton, in which they would have been able to establish a stubborn resistance, but for the fact that they did not consider occupying it, a circumstance which made it necessary for them to lay down their arms almost without a fight. Washington, at the head of his principal corps, dispersed or captured all those he found in front of him, reassembled his forces, and marched rapidly on Middlebrook. He would have wanted rather to push on up to Brunswick, which in the first moment he would have stormed without difficulty; but he had marched 30 miles in one day, and his troops were exhausted by fatigue. It was necessary for him to come to a stop. It would be difficult to portray the astonishment of Cornwallis when he heard of the audacious attack, 12 miles to his rear, of an enemy, which he believed was in his presence in the midst of the fires that still shone on the banks of Assunpink Creek. He withdrew towards Brunswick, and from that moment the Jerseys were free and Pennsylvania was heartened.

It was Saturday, September 25th when we arrived at Trenton. On the following day, Sunday, after a religious service that we heard in the Presbyterian Church, we boarded a carriage with the Governor and one of his aides-de-camp, and without escort or pomp, the General went to Bordentown, the residence of Joseph Bonaparte. The ex-King appeared very touched by the visit of the Nation's Guest, and received him with an expression of feeling and cordiality which proved to General Lafayette that time had not lessened the sentiments of affection which he had shown to him formerly. He kept us to dine with him, and we made the acquaintance of his family which, at this time, was composed of only his daughter and his son-in-law, the Prince of Canino, son of Lucien Bonaparte. Before dinner was served, Joseph drew General Lafayette into his office and kept him there for more than a full hour. We passed this time conversing with the Prince of Canino, whose manners are very affable and whose mind appeared to be very cultured. The study of the Sciences, and particularly that of Natural History, occupies, they say, a great part of his time; he has continued with remarkable talent Wilson's great work of ornithology, and has achieved a status equal to his.

After the dinner, at which Madam Canino did the honors with very great amiability, we found the gardens and the courtyards filled with inhabitants of the environs, who brought their children to be blessed by the patriarch of liberty. Joseph himself ordered that all the doors be opened, and in a moment, the rooms were invaded by a pressing crowd. It was a truly remarkable scene, the one which these good American rustics offered under the sumptuous paneled ceilings of Bordentown. Although their eyes might be unaccustomed to all the splendor of royal furnishings, they did not stop at all to look at the beautiful pictures of the Italian School or the French School, or at those exquisite bronze or marble statutes with which Joseph's rooms were decorated with an elegant profusion; it was Lafayette alone whom they wanted to see, and after having seen him, they left satisfied and as if incapable of being occupied from now on with something that could divert them from their good fortune. When the contented crowd had silently left the house, General Lafayette hastened to apologize to his host for having drawn such a large gathering of visitors to him; to this Joseph replied very amiably that he considered himself very happy that his neighbors had indeed wanted to join their respects to his own; "besides" he added, "I have been accustomed for a long time to see them as numerous in my house because every year on the Fourth of July we celebrate the anniversary of American independence together."

The time had passed rapidly during this visit, and the Governor of the State was obliged to remind the General that we had only the time necessary to return to Trenton before night; and soon we set out on our way. Joseph and his family wanted to accompany the General during a part of the route. We shared the carriages that had been prepared for us, and we traversed the immense and beautiful property, the peaceful possession of which appeared to me to be very preferable to Joseph's so-tumultuous possession of the Kingdom of Spain, rather slowly. When we had rejoined the main road, Joseph stopped the carriage and addressed himself playfully to General Lafayette: "Permit me," he said, "to stop at my borders, and to return you here to the tenderness of the Americans who claim the happy right to do you the honors of their country." He embraced the General tenderly, shook our hands affectionately, and moved off rapidly with his family.

During this entire visit, Joseph Bonaparte appeared to be a witty and amiable man. The beneficence that he practices around him, the generosity with which he greets strangers, and particularly the unfortunate French and, finally, the grace of his character have, they assure us, won over every heart to him. His fortune is considerable his family cherishes him; however, he does not seem happy. That is the result, I believe, of his not yet having forgotten the great misfortune he had in being King.

Upon our return to Trenton, we passed the evening with the Governor, his family and some of the principal citizens of the State. They conversed about many of the events of the American Revolution in which General Lafayette had taken the most prominent part. The memory of the sacrifices of all kinds made during this glorious epoch led the conversation naturally to the immense benefits that they had reaped from it in every part of the Union. One of the Governor's officers, a man with a cultivated mind and having remarkable knowledge, outlined for us rapidly the growth of prosperity in the State of New Jersey since it was rescued from the ridiculous and absurd Colonial system. This Province, whose first settlements were founded in 1628 by a Swedish company and which, after having passed successively into the hands of the Dutch and the English, changed rulers at least ten times in the space of 72 years, counted hardly 25,000 inhabitants a century after its formation and, at the very most, 100,000 at the moment when it was called upon to enjoy the benefits of independence, counts at least 280,000 today. Although the State of Jersey had been constantly a theater of the Revolutionary War and, consequently, its losses had been considerable, nonetheless, today its prosperity equals that of the most prosperous states. Protected by 40 years of peace and freedom, its industry has created for it a prolific source of wealth.

The Constitution of the State of Jersey was discussed and adopted by the Provincial Congress held at Burlington on July 2, 1776. This Constitution was preceded by a declaration in which the following principle was established.

> All constitutional authority, exercised up to this day by the Kings of Great Britain on the Colonies or on their other possessions, existed only by virtue of a contract consented to by the people in the common interest of the entire society. Protection and allegiance being, in the nature of things, reciprocal benefits which depend equally the one on the other, the contract is susceptible of being dissolved by the people when these advantages are withdrawn from or refused to it; and considering that George III has refused his protection to the good people of the Colonies; that he has tried by diverse acts to deliver them to the absolute power of Parliament, and that he has made war against them in the most cruel and outrageous manner for the sole reason that they wanted to maintain their just rights, all authority exercised in the name of the King of England is necessarily at its end.

The Constitution of New Jersey also established three powers, the legislative, the executive and the judiciary, but with this difference that in this State the governor is always a member of the legislative assembly and chancellor of the State. He is elected every year by the council and the general assembly. He has the right to grant pardons to convicts, even in the case of treason; he is commander-in-chief of the military forces; however, he has no influence on the nomination of captains and subordinate officers who are always elected by the companies in each county. It is only the generals and the staff officers who may be elected by the council and the assembly.

The military forces are composed of about 40,000 men of all branches. The regulations for the militias are very nearly the same as in the State of Massachusetts.

Chapter X

Entering Philadelphia – History of the Constitution and the State of Pennsylvania – Commerce, Agriculture, etc. – City of Philadelphia – Its Monuments, Its Public Institutions, Its Prisons, etc.

On Monday, September 27, we crossed the Delaware on a bridge about 900 feet long and entirely covered, so as to offer travelers a good shelter against bad weather. Pedestrians traverse it on a beautiful footpath. The road is divided in the middle, and carriages are obliged to take one side when going and the other side when returning in order to avoid accidents. It was constructed pursuant to the drawings of Mr. Burr, who placed the first stone in 1804. It was finished in 1812. Upon entering Pennsylvania soil, General Lafayette was welcomed by the Governor of the State at the head of his staff, and in the presence of the troops and citizens of Morrisville, assembled in great numbers. From Morrisville, we went to sleep at the Frankfort Arsenal, while passing by the charming little town of Bristol. We resumed our trip on the following morning in the midst of an escort more numerous than that of the day before; and, as we were approaching Philadelphia, the pedestrians, the horsemen and the carriages augmented the procession to such an extent that we advanced further only with the greatest difficulty. In a plain, a short distance from the City, were about 6,000 men of the voluntary militia in handsome uniforms and under arms, forming a square in the middle of which General Lafayette was received to the sound of cannon by the civil and military authorities.

After he had traversed the ranks of the militia on foot, and they had filed in front of him under the orders of General Cadwalader, we started marching with them in order to enter the City. Never was it more truthful to say that the entire population had come to meet General Lafayette. Only those inhabitants whom age or frailty prevented from going stayed in their houses. Stepped rows of seats had been built on each side of the streets to the height of the roof in order to hold the spectators. In the principal street of the suburb that we entered, all the different corps of trades were drawn up in battle array, as it were. At the head of each corps was a workroom composed of some workers executing works of their profession. On the side of each of these workrooms was a banner on which one saw the portraits of Washington and Lafayette, with this inscription: *To their wisdom and their courage we owe the free practice of our trade.* Among all these corps of artisans, one noticed especially that of the printers. Above a press, set up in the middle of the street, was this inscription: *Freedom of the press, the surest guaranty of the rights of man.* From this press poured forth profusely odes to Lafayette and patriotic songs which they threw into our carriage as we passed by, or they distributed to the people who followed. After the artisans were the public schools, teachers and students, all decorated with a *Welcome Lafayette* ribbon. A detachment of cavalry was at the head of the procession.

The Nation's Guest was in a magnificent barouche pulled by six horses; beside him they had seated the venerable Judge Peters, who was the Secretary and the moving spirit of the War Department during the Revolution; following came the Governor, the Mayor, the Municipal Council, the Judges in different carriages; finally, George Lafayette and his father's secretary in a carriage similar to the General's carriage, and behind us four huge chariots resembling tents in their form rolled sluggishly, each containing 40 old Revolutionary soldiers. One could not contemplate without emotion these veterans of liberty whose eyes half-extinguished by age still found tears to express their joy and unexpected good fortune which they savored in seeing their former companion-in-arms; their enfeebled and trembling voices came to life again while blending with the sound of the martial instruments that accompanied them, and found a new vigor in order to repeat their former chants of war, to bless the names of Washington and Lafayette, and to cry out, "Long live liberty!" A long infantry column brought up the rear. The procession, after having traversed all the principal streets and passed under 13 triumphal arches, stopped in front of the City Hall where we alighted. While we took some moments of rest there, the Deputies and the Senators of Pennsylvania, the Municipal Council, the Judiciary corps and the military authorities assembled in the great hall. Some moments after, at a signal given by 13 cannons, they brought us into this hall, and the General having been conducted to the foot of the statue of Washington, the Mayor gave a speech in which he said:

> Forty-eight years ago, in this City, in this very hall that one could justly call the cradle of independence, an assembly of such men as the world has seldom seen, eminent in virtue, in talent, and in patriotism, declared in the face of the world their determination to govern themselves by themselves; and to take for themselves and for their descendants a place among the nations. Very few of those who lived then are alive today; but in this number history will find, and we take pride in placing, General Lafayette, whose entire life has been dedicated to the maintenance of liberty and to the defense of the inalienable rights of man.
>
> General! Some of your compatriots who came to our aid are no longer alive; but this people remembers them, and future

> ages will consecrate their glory. Let us endeavor to forget for a moment those glorious shades in order to congratulate the hero whom we have the good fortune to welcome.

In listening to this speech, in recognizing this hall in which the Declaration of Independence was signed, the hall at the door of which he waited in 1777 with so much anxiety for permission to dedicate his good right arm and his fortune to a cause then nearly desperate, General Lafayette felt an emotion that he had difficulty containing and which manifested itself several times in his response. "My entrance into this great and splendid City," he said,

> The solemn and touching memories that accompany me here, and the affectionate reception which is given to me awaken in my heart the feelings that I experienced 50 years ago.
>
> It is here, in this sacred enclosure, that the independence of the United States was emphatically declared by a council of wise men. In anticipating that of all of America, it began for the civilized world a new era, that of a social order founded on the rights of man, an order of which the success and peace of your republic demonstrates the advantages every day. Here, Sir, was formed our brave and virtuous Revolutionary Army; here, inspired by Providence, came the fortunate idea to entrust command of it to our well-loved Washington, that warrior without blemish. But these memories and a throng of others are mixed with the profound regret for the loss of men, great and good, for whom we have to mourn. It is to their services, Sir, to your respect for their memory, to the friendship that binds me to them, that I must assign a large part of the honors that I have received here and elsewhere, honors well above my personal merit.
>
> It is also under the auspices of their venerated names, as much as by the impulse of my own sentiments, that I beg you, Mr. Mayor, and you, members of two councils and inhabitants of Philadelphia, to accept the tribute of my respect, my affection and my profound gratitude.

Afterwards, all the people were permitted to file before the Nation's Guest in order to shake his hand. This ceremony lasted several hours and offered the picture of the most perfect equality that it would be possible to imagine. Before generals marched working men with blackened hands, sinewy arms, sleeves rolled up; beside a magistrate was a farmer clad in simple cloth; the priest and the artist came holding each other by the hand, and some children, assured of seeing their rights and their frailty respected, marched boldly in front of soldiers and sailors. This variety of dress contrasted remarkably with the uniformity of countenances, all of which expressed the same sentiment of gratitude and admiration.

After this reception, the General was conducted to Washington Hall, in the midst of an ever-growing crowd; a splendid dinner was served, all the authorities attended, and numerous toasts were made. They drank to Greece reborn, to which they wished a Washington for chief and a Lafayette for friend.

In the evening, a population of 120,000, augmented by 40,000 outsiders flocking from different parts of the Union, walked in the gleam of the lighting and the bonfires, while chanting of the exploits of the champion of liberty; and the rejoicing of the people which, in Europe, though under the protection of the police, would have been marked by murder, thefts, and accidents of all kinds, passed here without the slightest disorder. The following morning, the Mayor came to visit General Lafayette. He held in his hands the reports which he had received from his police officers, and he showed them to us. "See," he said with an animated expression of satisfaction, "see how free men conduct themselves! More than 40,000 outsiders have come to take part in the festivities of the people under my administration; and I had not believed, however, that it was necessary to augment the number of my guards. Thus, there were only 116 without arms, and they have not had a single offense to quell in this night of joyous popular excitement! Here are their reports..., not a complaint..., not the slightest trouble...." And joy shone in the eyes of this virtuous administrator, all of whose success had its source in the prudence of his citizens. I thought that the Mayor of Philadelphia would have made a very bad police commissioner in Paris.

On the following days, the General received, in the Hall of the Declaration of Independence, the addresses of different corporations, or regularly constituted bodies such as the Clergy, the Philosophical Society, the Bible Society, the University, the Chamber of Commerce, the Bar, the school children, the light infantry of Washington, the Beneficent Association of Lafayette, the Revolutionary soldiers, the French residents of Philadelphia, etc. At each of these speeches, General Lafayette responded with an extemporaneous speech, so fluent, elegant and appropriate to the different circumstances that surrounded him or that the speaker called to mind, that the astonishment and admiration of the public increased by the minute.

The delegation of the Clergy offered a picture very interesting and very worthy of engaging the attention of a European. Led by Bishop White, who was Chaplain of the Congress during the Revolutionary War, it was composed of about 80 ministers, nearly all of different denominations, but all animated by the same spirit of tolerance and charity. The speaker always expressed himself in the name of the ministers of the *different communions of all denominations*, and rendered himself the faithful voice of their unanimous sentiments in saying: "All of us are delighted to owe to your efforts, in part, the good fortune of living under a government that accords equal protection to all religious congregations, whatever their denomination might be, while imposing on them no other obligation but to respect the peace and legal order of civil life." The General responded:

> The unanimous displays of affection and esteem with which I am honored by the worthy ministers of the different religious congregations of Philadelphia and the environs pierce my heart with feelings of the deepest gratitude, and furnish me fresh proof of the holy brotherhood which, on this favored land, joins together the ministers *of a Gospel of liberty and equality*. Republican principles, in a word, can never find a more powerful support than the one which ministers, who join the inestimable advantage of being freely chosen by their respective congregations to their eminent personal virtues, naturally lend to them. I beg of you, Gentlemen, to receive my respectful and affectionate thanks for your fine address, which is so much more touching for me since it is presented by an old and worthy friend, by the friend of Washington, whose patriotic prayers and blessings have been so often associated with the great events of the Revolution in this Hall of Congress.

The speech of Bishop White and the response of General Lafayette awakened in me, I confess, some very new ideas. I began to understand that, under a good government, religion and liberty, far from being incompatible, can lend each other mutual support and that in order to secure this happy alliance, unknown in Europe, one thing was necessary, that the government, renouncing the absurd and monstrous system of wanting to make of religion its instrument or its prop, leave to the citizens themselves the right to choose and to pay homage to those whom they wish to entrust the direction of their consciences.

I have said that the French residing in Philadelphia had come to express to General Lafayette their personal feelings of attachment and the pleasure that they experienced in seeing one of their compatriots enjoy such a brilliant triumph.

They had joined together under the Presidency of Mr. Du Ponceau, whom they charged with being their spokesman and who acquitted himself with warm-hearted eloquence that had its source in the belief in and the love of liberty.

Mr. Du Ponceau, whom we had the pleasure of hearing address General Lafayette again at the head of the Philosophical Society of which he is a member and of the Philadelphia Bar of which he is one of the principal ornaments, has lived in the United States since the Revolutionary War. He served with distinction in this war under the command of Baron de Steuben, whose aide-de-camp he was. As legal expert, man of letters and scholar, Mr. Du Ponceau has acquired in his adoptive country a brilliant reputation which the practice of all the virtues continues to enhance. During our stay in Philadelphia, we counted as happy those times which we passed in his always amicable, always instructive company.

We also found in Philadelphia another compatriot whom we had the great pleasure of holding in our arms: I want to speak of General Bernard, of that man, as modest as he is learned, whose talents and disinterested patriotism have been misunderstood by the French Government of 1815. General Bernard, who, as one knows, burst through the imperial Court of Bonaparte without losing any of his republicanism, which can be considered a phenomenon, has found here fit appreciators of his merit. Charged by the American Government with insuring the defense of the Union by a complete system of fortifications, and the prosperity of its commerce by the construction of canals and roads in an immense development, he will give us the satisfaction of seeing a French name associated nobly with all the beautiful enterprises of a great nation. One cannot know General Bernard without according to him a sincere feeling of esteem, admiration and friendship.

All the time that General Lafayette was able to steal from the attentiveness of his numerous friends and of the people of Philadelphia, was dedicated to visiting the institutions of the humanities and of public utility, which are very numerous in this vast City. But before detailing them or describing them, I want to cast a quick glance at the founding and the history of Pennsylvania.

It was in 1627 that a company of Swedes and Finlanders landed on the banks of the Delaware and lay the first foundations of this Colony, which later developed so rapidly under the agreeable and humane institutions of William Penn. The wisdom and moderation of the Swedes and their excellent administration ought to have assured them of peaceful possession of a soil which they had acquired with the freely given consent of the natural proprietors, the Indians; but 30 years had hardly passed when they were ousted by the Dutch, who themselves were not long in being ousted by the English, who were no less greedy but more skillful than they.

In 1681, Charles II, King of England, wanting to reward the services that Admiral Penn had rendered to the Crown, granted his son, William Penn, 20,000 acres of land on the banks of the Delaware. This grant was guaranteed by a charter that contained the following clause:

> The Colony will carry the name of Pennsylvania. William Penn, his successors and lieutenants, provided with the consent of the majority of free men, or by their freely assembled representatives, will make levies of monies for public purposes, will establish tribunals, will name judges, etc.... The laws will be devised with reason and so as not to be in opposition to those of England; the sovereign reserves the right to acquaint himself with private questions and judge them in case of appeal. In all cases where the positive law of the Province is silent, the laws of England will be followed. A duplicate of all the laws made in the Province will be placed every five years in the Privy Counsel; and if in six months after it will have received them, they are declared contrary to the royal prerogative or to the laws of England, they will be considered as invalid. The proprietors will be able to levy such taxes on merchandise as the assembly will determine; they will always have a deputy at the Court in London to respond to that which could be alleged against them; and in the case where they would be censured by the tribunals, and would not have satisfied the sentence within the course of a year, the Monarch will be able to take back the government until they have satisfied it, without that bearing any prejudice, nonetheless, to the private landowners or, in like manner, to all other inhabitants of the Province. They would be able to transfer their property. The property of lands already occupied by Christians must be preserved for them. The Monarch will not impose taxes or assessments on the aforesaid Colony without the consent of the proprietor or the assembly; or without an act of the government.

On July 11 of the year when this charter was granted to him, the proprietor and those who were to emigrate with him agreed:

> That having to distribute lands to the buyers, they would take that which would be necessary for roads; that all business

with the Indians would be conducted in the public market; that all disputes between the emigrants and the Indians would be judged by six emigrants and six Indians; that, on five acres, they would leave one of them forested in order to conserve the oaks and the white mulberries for the construction of ships; that no person would leave the Province without noticing it in the public market, three weeks beforehand.

At the end of that very year, the Colonists arrived in Pennsylvania, and lay the foundations of their settlement. Penn himself arrived at the beginning of the following year, and purchased from Lord Berkeley and the heir of George Carteret, for the sum of 4,000 pounds sterling, some parts of New Jersey, which he added to his property, and thus found himself the possessor of all the land contained between 40° and 43° latitude. He also bought some lands from the Indians for which he paid them with the greatest punctiliousness, thinking that the European title did not give him the right to ruthlessly deprive the uncivilized nations of their legitimate and natural possessions. Also, his spirit of justice and moderation did not take long in winning over the attachment of the Indians, who, at first hostile to all the White settlements, soon became his kindly and faithful allies. His reputation soon reached even to Europe, and inspired in a multitude of men, unhappy in their country, the desire to go to seek peace and liberty near him. The first Colonists who had arrived with him imitated his virtues, and the settlement prospered.

As early as 1682, William Penn convened a general assembly of inhabitants, and engaged them to attend with him to the drafting of a constitution, execution of which would be entrusted to a governor assisted by a provincial council, and by the inhabitants formed in a general assembly. The council was to be composed of 70 members chosen by the inhabitants, and presided over by the governor or his representative. This council was to be renewed annually by thirds. On this occasion, William Penn made a speech in which he set forth this proposition too misunderstood by the people and the governments of Europe:

> Whatever the form of a government may be, the people are always free when they are governed only by the laws, and they participate in the making of the laws; that this is the only way by which the people could be free; that, beyond these conditions, there is only tyranny, oligarchy and confusion; that the great purpose of all government is to cause its power to be respected by the people, and to protect the people from abuses of power; that, in this manner, the people are free while

obedient, and the magistrates honorable and honored by the justice of their administration and their submission to the law.

However, troubles arose; they were caused by the complaints of Lord Baltimore, the Governor of Maryland; and William Penn was obliged to go to England in order to vindicate his rights. During his absence, he entrusted the Government to five commissioners, who dissatisfied everybody by their abuses of authority. In these circumstances, King James having abdicated, his successor seized the Government of Pennsylvania; but three years later, that is to say in 1696, he returned it to its proprietor. In 1699, Penn returned to Pennsylvania, and resumed the management of its affairs; he then proposed a new constitution, which was adopted, and which was preserved up to the time of the Revolution. Soon afterwards, some new controversies called him back to England, where he died in 1718 from an attack of apoplexy. His death was a great misfortune, without a doubt, for the glory of the Colony that he had formed, but the Society of Friends, of which he was the head, proved itself a worthy heir of his virtues, and continued with its liberal policy to attract to its bosom all men to whom religious persecutions and the despotism of the Kings of Europe were repugnant.

From 1729 to 1754, the Colony received 35,517 refugees, most of them Irish and German. One then saw arise from the bosom of this new population all those different doctrines which divided consciences and split the Colony into Quakers, Episcopalians, Presbyterians, Catholics, Lutherans, Calvinists, Moravians, Covenanters, Methodists, Universalists, etc. Some of these sects, unfortunately, sank into that spirit of proselytism and intolerance of which they themselves had been victims in Europe, and one saw them sometimes persecute the Indians, their neighbors, in order to impose their beliefs on them. It was their fanaticism which, in 1763, under the abominable pretext of clearing the land of heathens, massacred ruthlessly the Conestoga people, who were living so peacefully and so trustfully under the treaty concluded with William Penn. This act of barbarism destroyed the good harmony which had reigned for nearly 60 years between the Indians and the Colonists, and stirred up wars which ended only in 1779 with the nearly complete destruction of the former, the sad remnants of whom were relegated to the banks of the Niagara.

From the death of Penn up to 1763, the good understanding between the Colony and the Mother Country did not appear to have undergone a change, but the Stamp Act found, in Pennsylvania, the same spirit of resistance as in New England, and in 1768 the Provincial Assembly protested energetically against the right which the Parliament in England wanted to arrogate to itself to tax the Colonies. In 1773, the tea imported by the English into the Port of Philadelphia was destroyed as it had been in Boston, and all of Pennsylvania responded with unanimous shouts of approval to Massachusetts' call for insurrection. Finally, it was in Philadelphia where, in 1776, 54 deputies of the 13 States, joined together under the Presidency of John Hancock, signed the immortal Declaration of Independence of the United States. Towards the end of the same year, the Convention of Pennsylvania assembled at Philadelphia and adopted and proclaimed a new constitution that was preceded by the Declaration of Rights and the following preamble:

> The objects of the institution and the maintenance of government ought to be to assure the existence of the political body of the state, to protect it, and to give to the individuals of which it is composed the power to enjoy their natural rights and other benefits that the author of all existence has heaped on men; and every time that these great objects of government are not fulfilled, the people have the right to change it by an act of their common will and to take measures that appear to them necessary to assure their security and happiness.
>
> Up to the present time, the inhabitants of this republic, being acknowledged subjects of the King of Great Britain, solely in consideration of the protection which they expected of him, and the aforesaid King having not only withdrawn this protection, but having begun and continued still, with a spirit of inexorable vengeance, to wage against them the most cruel and most unjust war, employing not only the troops of Great Britain but, moreover, foreign mercenaries, savages and slaves, in order to reach the objective which he has proposed and which he acknowledges of reducing them to a complete and shameful submission to the despotic domination of the British Parliament; having, moreover, practiced against the aforesaid inhabitants several other acts of tyranny that have been fully exposed in the declaration of the National Congress, all of which have broken and destroyed the bonds of subjection and fidelity towards the aforesaid King and his successors and caused all the powers and all the authorities derived from him in these Colonies to cease; as it is absolutely necessary, for the well-being and the security of the inhabitants of the aforesaid Colonies, that they should henceforth be free and independent states and as there exists in each part of them a form of government, just,

permanent and suitable, of which the authority of the people is the sole source and foundation, conformably to the views of the honorable American Congress, we the representatives of the free men of Pennsylvania, assembled specially and expressly for the purpose of forming a government, according to the principles set forth above; acknowledging the goodness of the Supreme Governor of the universe, he who alone knows to what degree of happiness on the earth the human race can reach in perfecting the art of government; acknowledging the supreme goodness that he has in permitting the people of this state to make by their own common consent without violence, and after having deliberated with mature consideration, the laws that they judge the most just and the best to govern their future society; fully convinced that it is our indispensable duty to establish the fundamental principles of government that are the most appropriate to procure the general happiness of the people of this state and their posterity, and to permit future improvements without partiality or bias for or against any particular class, sect or denomination of men, whoever they may be; by virtue of the authority that our constituents have vested in us, we order, declare and establish that the following *Declaration of Rights and Plan of Government* be the Constitution of the Republic, and that it remain there in force forever and without alteration, except in the articles that experience will demonstrate later on to require improvements, and which will be corrected or perfected by virtue of the aforesaid authority of the people, by a body of delegates, composed as this plan of government directs it, in order to obtain and assure in the most effective manner, the great object and the true purpose of all government, such that we have set forth above.

Declaration of Rights of the Inhabitants of the State of Pennsylvania.

Article 1. All men are born equally free and independent, and they have certain natural, essential and inalienable rights, among which one must count the right to enjoy life and liberty and to defend them; the right to acquire property, to possess it and to protect it; finally, the right to seek and to obtain their happiness and their security.

Article 2. All men have the natural and inalienable right to worship all-powerful God in the manner that is dictated to them by their conscience and their understanding. No man ought to be nor can he be legally constrained to adopt a particular form of religious worship, to establish or support a particular place of worship, or to hire ministers of religion against his will or without his own free consent; any man who recognizes the existence of God cannot be justly deprived of any civil right of a citizen, nor can he be attacked in any manner by reason of his opinions in the matter of religion, or of the particular forms of his worship; no person in the state can be, nor ought to be, clothed with, nor can he arrogate to himself the exercise of, any authority that could permit him to disturb or to obstruct the right of conscience in the free exercise of religious worship.

Article 3. The people of this state alone have the essential and exclusive right to govern themselves and to regulate their internal administration.

Article 4. All authority originally residing in the people, and, consequently, emanating from them, it follows that all officers of government invested with authority, be they legislative or executive, are their agents, their servants, and are at all times accountable to them.

Article 5. Government is or ought to be instituted for the common interest, for the protection and the security of the people, of the nation or of the community, and not for the profit and the private interest of a single man, a family or an assemblage of men who make up only one part of that community. The community has the incontestable, inalienable and indefeasible right to reform, change or abolish the government, in the manner that it judges the most suitable and proper to procure public happiness.

Article 6. In order to prevent those who are invested with the legislative or executive authority from becoming oppressors, the people have the right, at the times they judge to be appropriate, to cause the officials to return to private life, and to fill the vacant posts by certain and regular elections.

Article 7. All elections must be free, and all free men having the same sufficient, plain and common interest, and being attached to the community by the same bonds, all ought to have an equal right to elect the officers and to be elected to the different posts.

Article 8. Each member of society has the right to be protected by it in the enjoyment of his life, his liberty and his property; he is accordingly obligated to contribute for his part to the expenses of this protection, to give, when it is necessary, his personal service or an equivalent; but no part of a man's property can be justly taken away, or applied to public uses, without his own consent or that of his legitimate representatives. Any man who has scruples about bearing arms cannot justly be forced to do it, when he pays an equivalent; and, finally, the free men of this state cannot be compelled to obey laws other than those to which they have consented for the common good themselves or by their legitimate representatives.

Article 9. In all the prosecutions for crimes, a man has the right to be heard by himself or by his attorney, to demand the cause and the nature of the accusation that is brought against him, to be confronted by witnesses, to admit all the proofs which can be favorable to him, to demand a prompt and public investigation by an impartial jury of the locality, without the unanimous opinion of which he cannot be declared guilty. He cannot be forced to admit proofs against himself, and a man can be justly deprived of his liberty only by a judgment of his peers in accordance with the laws of the country.

Article 10. Every man has the right to be, in his person, his house, his papers and all his possessions, safe from all searches and seizures; consequently, every *warrant* is contrary to this right, if preliminary oaths or affirmations have not sufficiently established the basis for it, and if the order of requisition given by the *warrant* to an officer or messenger of the state to make searches in suspect places, to arrest one or more persons, or to seize their properties, is not accompanied by a specific designation or description of the person or the objects to be searched or seized. Finally a *warrant* must be issued only in prescribed cases and with the prescribed formalities.

Article 11. In controversies relative to property and in the proceedings between two or more private parties, the parties have the right to an investigation by jurymen, and this form of proceeding must be regarded as sacred.

Article 12. The people have the right and the freedom to speak, to write and to publish their opinions; consequently, freedom of the press must never be impeded.

Article 13. The people have the right to bear arms for their defense and for that of the state; and, as in times of peace standing armies are dangerous for liberty, one must not be maintained; and the military must always be held in strict subordination to the civil authority, and always be governed by it.

Article 14. Frequent recourse to the principles of the constitution, and a constant adherence to those of justice, moderation, temperance, industry and frugality are absolutely necessary to preserve the advantages of liberty and a free government. Consequently, the people must pay particular attention to all the different matters in the choice of its officers and representatives; and it has the right to require of its legislators and magistrates a strict and constant observance of these same principles in the making and the execution of the laws necessary for the good administration of the state.

Article 15. All men have a right to leave the state in which they live, in order to take up residence in another that wants to receive them, or to form a new state on vacant land or on land that they acquire, every time that they believe that they can by this secure happiness.

Article 16. The people have a right to assemble, to consult for the common good, to instruct their representatives, and to demand from the legislature, by way of addresses, petitions or remonstrances, the righting of wrongs that they believe have been done to them.

The Constitution that was adopted after this Declaration of Rights was revised in 1790. Now, as in all the other states, it establishes three powers: the legislative, the executive and the judicial.

The legislative power resides in a house of representatives and a senate. The representatives are chosen annually by the citizens. Their number varies by reason of the population, and must never be below 60 or above 100. The conditions for being a representative are the age of 21, the right of citizenship having been acquired for three years, three years' residence in the State before the time of the election, and one year in the town or district which elects, unless an absence is for public service.

Senators are elected every fourth year. Each year, the quarter that leaves is renewed by the election of others. The total number of senators can be neither less than a quarter nor more than a third of the representatives. To be a senator, it is necessary to have attained the age of 25, to be a citizen and inhabitant of the State for four years, and an inhabitant of the electoral county for the year which precedes the election.

Every free individual 21 years old, having lived in the State for two years before the election, and having paid some tax during this period of time, is a voter. The elections are conducted by a poll in each county. The members of the electoral bureau, on receiving the voter's ticket, are to verify his name and his right to vote in a manner such that no one would be able to vote twice or vote without the right to do so.

The executive power is entrusted to a governor who is elected by the citizens every three years: he must be 30 years old and have lived in the State seven years before his election; he cannot continue in his office more than nine years out of twelve. He commands all the armed forces of the State, so long as they are not called to the general service of the Union. He can summon the general assembly in extraordinary circumstances. He has the right to reject a law submitted for his approval, but it can nonetheless be approved afterwards, if after this opposition, it is adopted by two-thirds of the houses.

The judicial power is exercised by different courts of which the judges, named by the governor, can only be removed by the demand of two-thirds of the houses. These courts are: a supreme court, composed of a chief justice and four judges, a court of *oyer and terminer*, charged with civil and criminal cases; a court of common pleas; a court of errors and appeal; and, finally, quarter sessions of the peace for each county. This latter court is charged with judging only the less important thefts and frauds. This jurisdiction in the town belongs to the mayor's court, composed of the mayor, the clerk and one alderman.

Each public officer, upon entering upon his duties, is obliged to take an oath to the Constitution, but they do not require any profession of religious faith by him.

Since this Constitution was adopted, Pennsylvania has not stopped increasing in population, wealth and fortune. In 1790, it did not have 450,000 people; today it contains 1,500,000, of which 141,000 are constantly occupied in making its agriculture thrive, the prosperity of which can be compared to that of our most productive French departments. Especially since the property has been divided up more by the increase in the population, agriculture has made rapid progress. The ancient properties of 1000 to 1200 acres are today, for the most part, parceled out in farms of 80 to 100 acres, on each of which a comfortable house has risen with well-arranged farm sheds and outbuildings and lush orchards, which constantly furnish the great markets with the most beautiful fruits that one can see. Since the employment of gypsum as fertilizer, the land has increased very much in value; it would be, I believe, difficult to find land below $100 an acre around the large cities, and below six or seven dollars in the less inhabited parts of the State.

Most of the farmers are not only cultivators, they are tradesmen and manufacturers; they themselves make garments of wool that they wear, and they sell much brandy that they make with extracts of peaches, corn, rice, buckwheat and maple sugar; they also collect much cider, and for their private consumption they make wine with wild strawberries, raspberries, currants and cherries, but very little with grapes. The War of 1812, by paralyzing the external commerce of Pennsylvania, contributed very much to the development of its manufactures; they are now very numerous and very varied, and, according to the last estimates, it appears that they employ capital of more than $40,000,000 and at least 60,000 workmen.

Since the last war, commerce has resumed its former activity. However, exports are not in keeping with the industry of the State; they consist principally of corn, flour, steers, pigs, linseed, iron tools, planks, soap and candles. In 1820 they did not exceed $8,000,000. The coastwise trade is considerable, and about 30 vessels are customarily engaged in commerce with the Indies, China and the coast of the Northwest. In all, internal and external commerce occupies about 7,000 people.

Commerce, Agriculture and Industry not encountering any obstacle to their development, and not having any considerable burden to support, cannot fail to see their prosperity grow each year. Taxes are light, since never can any of them be raised to more than one percent of the value of property. Here is how they are assessed and levied. Every three years, at the time of the general election, *the people* choose assessors, who, after having made an appraisal in money of the value of taxable properties, send to the county commissioners the names of two respectable property owners of the district, one of whom is named receiver. The latter announces to the citizens the rate of the taxes and the day when their objections will be heard by the commissioners; the payments take place afterwards, and the money is turned over to the treasurer of the county, who is elected for three years by the county commissioners and who collects for his fees a percent of the funds that pass into his hands. Taxes are levied on land, houses, mills, factories, ground rents, livestock over four years old, on profitable trading commissions, and in general on all the positions with the exception of those of ministers of the Gospel and schoolteachers; finally on the licenses to keep taverns and on adults who do not practice any profession.

The excellent financial organization of the State and the strict management exercised in regards to all the expenses of government never requires extraordinary taxes. Moreover, this allows the administrators to assign rather considerable funds to the execution of the 17th article of the Constitution, which prescribes that the legislative power be engaged with all appropriate means to increase institutions of public education in order to provide free elementary education to indigent children and to contribute to the rapid development of the Arts and Sciences. Primary schools for the poor and academies for the study of literature and sciences are encouraged not only by the attentions of the legislature, but also by the sacrifices and the constant efforts of all the citizens who get up a subscription among themselves to create new ones, wheresoever the need for them is felt.

The civil laws of England are still for the most part in force in the State of Pennsylvania. Their preservation was one of the conditions stipulated in the grant which Charles II accorded to William Penn. They could have been changed entirely at the time of the Revolution since, then, the ties with England were broken; but time and custom had so sanctified them that they were preserved intact, and, even today, they have experienced still only rare and slight modifications. It could not be the same as to criminal laws. The penal code, often bloodthirsty, could not be suitable to the gentle and philanthropic *Society of Friends*; also, from the early days of the Colony, it was an object of attacks by Mr. Penn who sought to substitute for it a code more in conformity with the spirit of his sect, which stood up forcefully against the death penalty or which desired at least that it not be applied so easily and so frequently. However, Parliament was deaf to this cry of humanity and amended both Penn's code and the tolerant decrees of Calvert who had preceded him by nearly a half a century.

After the Revolution, Penn's disciples, always animated by his philanthropic spirit, raised anew their voices against the cruelty of the English penal code. This voice found an echo in the luminous and profound writings of Franklin, William Bradford, Caleb Lowndes and Dr. Rush, and soon the death penalty was applied only to murders and poisonings with premeditation. Imprisonment and hard labor in proportion to the strength of the convict replaced corporal punishments and the shameful branding that corrupted the soul while delivering the body to eternal scorn.

It was in 1793 that these fortunate changes were effected. During this time, numerous and effective reforms on the amelioration of the prisons, on the lot of the prisoners and especially on the philanthropic system of moral reformation of the prisoners, were produced in Philadelphia, and were soon imitated in the entire Union. It was not only the Governments of the States or the town corporate bodies that were occupied with this issue; but also a great number of charitable associations, among which the Quaker Society occupied the first rank and devoted itself to this great and good work. Among all the witnesses whom one could cite, I will restrict myself to one of the most respectable and effective philanthropists of Europe, Duke La Rochefoucauld-Liancourt, who, in an important and very instructive work for the time – his trip to the United States was in 1795, 1796 and 1797 – spoke with enthusiasm about prison reforms of the United States, and particularly of the state prison of Philadelphia, which was administered principally by the members of the Society of Friends. This word "state prison" has another signification in Europe; but here it signifies prisons constructed by the state legislatures for those condemned in the courts of justice. Every time in England, France, and other parts of Europe that they wanted to ameliorate the prisons, it was always those of the United States, and more especially still those of Philadelphia, that they took as models.

Nevertheless, the moral means of reform, so well detailed in the work of La Rochefoucauld-Liancourt and by some other travelers, did not for long satisfy the ardor for improvement that animated the directors of these institutions. On the other hand, it is probable that the prisons of Pennsylvania, upon receiving a large number of prisoners, among whom were a large number of emigrants from Europe and a great proportion of men who were less susceptible to reform, gave results less satisfactory than in the time described by Mr. Liancourt. They wanted to do still better and many respectable friends of humanity thought that solitary prison, leaving the prisoner to his reflections or to those that they suggested to him and separating him from other convicts, offered more of a chance for his conversion. Consequently, as no expense frightens Americans once they have become convinced of a great public utility, they built near Philadelphia, at considerable cost, an immense building with courtyards and cells where each prisoner can be confined apart, and where by the form of construction, the authorities can exercise easy and continual surveillance.

This magnificent building was in construction when General Lafayette, accompanied by a committee charged with paying the respects of the City to him, went to visit it and was welcomed by the worthy directors and administrators who explained to him the improvements obtained. Courage was necessary to dare to contradict men so virtuous, so experienced, so generous in intention as in the execution of their beneficent works. The candor and conviction of the General overcame his reluctance, and with all the consideration and all the respect that was due to them, and as his personal situation required still more, he pointed out to them that solitary imprisonment was a punishment that it was necessary to have experienced to judge well; and that the virtuous and enlightened Malesherbes, who during his ministry under the Old Regime had mitigated the lot of state prisoners, regarded solitary imprisonment as conducive to madness. The General observed that, during the five years of his captivity, he had passed one entire year in this manner and another part of this time in seeing a companion for only one hour a day, and he added while laughing that he had even proven that it was not a means of reformation, since they had put him there for having wanted to revolutionalize the people against despotism and aristocracy, he spent his solitude in dreaming of it, and he left no more improved in this regard. General Lafayette also made some observations on an over-assiduous surveillance such as the one, for example, to which he himself had been subjected during the first period of his captivity, when he was closely guarded continually by a noncommissioned officer, who was relieved, day and night, every two hours.

Mr. Adams, then Secretary of State, appeared to support these observations. They have since been the subject of a controversy in the public papers and pamphlets, where men of one or the other opinion, while rendering justice perfectly to their feelings and intentions, held different opinions. "I see," said General Lafayette,

> That in the States where the prisons are less crowded, in New Hampshire, for example, or in the State of Vermont, the administrators (in New Hampshire, it's the Senate), the legislators and the public find the method still good, and they obtain the reform of convicts that you complain of not obtaining any more in Pennsylvania and in the most populous States. Why shouldn't your beautiful institution be divided into several parts, of which each contains no more prisoners than there are in one prison of New Hampshire or Vermont? These divisions would provide a means of separation by offenses or of emulation for prisoners who conducted themselves well,

> and since, in your admirable and philanthropic generosity, you have incurred the expenses of a cell for each prisoner, enclose them apart at night instead of packing them into these vast dormitories, where it is very true that the prisoners corrupt each other reciprocally, much more than in the day and at work where they are watched by their guardians.

This discussion of opinions equally well-intentioned, and in which, one must agree, the directors and administrators have the advantage of experience, was not restricted to Pennsylvania or even to America. Several European philanthropists, who saw in the prisons of Pennsylvania a kind of perfection, have become alarmed and have regarded this acknowledgement of inadequacy, this need for change, as necessarily impeding the efforts of the friends of humanity in Europe. One of the most prominent men of England, the celebrated Mr. Roscoe, had already written some erroneous opinions, relying on what he believed had been expressed in a report on prisons to the New York Legislature. They responded that this point of view, or rather the expression of it, belonged to the reporter not to the legislature or to the public. Soon after, Mr. Roscoe entered into the discussion relative to the prison of Philadelphia. He published some pamphlets on this subject that did honor equally to his mind and his heart.

This is the current state of the question which the subject of this visit has prompted me to enlarge on. A numerous, enlightened and experienced portion of the citizens of Pennsylvania, particularly in Philadelphia, appeared disposed to try solitary prison, not as the exception but as the base of the penitentiary system; many other men of merit, whom I have seen and heard from the two coasts of the Atlantic, are of an opposite view; but it is already fortunate for a country that they are occupied with such interest and immediacy by questions of this kind. There is no doubt that the experiment will be conducted by people who are well-intentioned and disposed to modify their system if they see some drawbacks in it.

After having obtained reforms so wise and so generously devised, philanthropy, always active among Pennsylvanians, was occupied without respite with all that could contribute to repair or diminish the evils of mankind. The administration and the citizens competed zealously, as I understand it, in every part of the State to multiply hospitals, and charitable institutions endlessly. During 1774, a society dedicated to the abolition of the Slave Trade and the relief of free Blacks illegally held in Slavery was created and had Franklin for its first president.

The society to procure first aid for the drowned and for the suffocated was established in 1780. This society has propagated extensively the use of devices necessary for the drowned and has established prizes for those who have contributed, in whatever way it might be, to saving the life of their fellow men. Four charitable societies for women, having as a goal the relief of widows and orphans, were founded during the years 1793, 1802, 1809, and 1811. The Pennsylvanian Washington Charitable Society, founded in 1812, also merits being cited. It is composed of more than 3,000 members, each of whom turns two dollars into the treasury at the time of his admission and pays the same sum annually. These sums are dedicated to the relief of members of the society or their families.

One counts nearly 30 mutual benefit associations for the working classes, which are designated by the name of *Society of the Master Masons*; *Society of Carpenters*; *of Stone-cutters*; *Society of Printers*; *of Master Artisans*; *of Physicians*, etc. There are similar associations for foreigners and their descendants; among them one counts the *Beneficent Society for the French in Distress*, founded in 1805; the one for Germans was founded in 1801. A thing very worthy of notice is that, of the four great charitable institutions that exist in the City of Philadelphia, there isn't one that is not founded by or supported by donations or private subscriptions and administered by citizens who dedicate their time and their attentions without remuneration. These four institutions are: *Pennsylvania Hospital*; the *Hospital of the Church of Jesus Christ*; the *Philadelphia Dispensary*; and the *Home for the Aid of the Insane*.

Most of the travelers who have visited Philadelphia agree on this point, that the rigidity of the customs and the seriousness of the character of the Quakers, who are numerous in this City, have influenced society in general in a regrettable manner by imposing on it an air of coldness and monotony, which renders it unbearable for strangers. I can neither contradict these travelers nor side with their opinion; for how should I be able to make a judgment reasonably about a population that I have only seen during an outburst of enthusiasm and gratitude that dominated every heart and swept along the most serious men, the Quakers themselves, on the footsteps of him who was the object of it. It is difficult to believe, however, that society lacks charms and resources in a City where the Arts and the Sciences are cultivated with as much ardor and success. The educated men who belong to the Philosophical Society, to the Medical Society, to the Linnean Society, to the Academy of Natural Sciences, to the different societies of agriculture, etc; the vast public libraries, the magnificent museums, the numerous newspapers of all kinds, etc., must offer in this City food sufficient for the most active mind and can, in my opinion, compensate very amply for the absolute lack of all the frivolities to which we unfortunately attach so high a value in Europe.

One can affirm that Philadelphia is the most uniformly beautiful city not only of the United States but of the entire world. Its beautiful streets, all of which intersect at right angles, its broad, always clean walkways, the elegance of its houses built of brick and decorated with beautiful white marble, the lavishness and the good taste of its public monuments, offer at first glance a seductive sight, but one which can, in the course of time, tire the eye by its excessive uniformity. Its plan, which was drawn by Penn himself, extends from the right bank of the Delaware up to the left bank of the Schuykill. This area is about two miles long by a mile wide. Only two-thirds of this length is covered with buildings, but every day sees new houses rising, and I believe that a few years will suffice to fill the space that is still free between the Schuykill and the City.

Among the monuments of public utility that decorate this beautiful City, one cannot omit pointing out the *Old Bank of the United States*, which is the first building constructed in Philadelphia with columns and a portico. It was commenced in 1795 and completed in 1798. Its principal facade, all in white marble, resembles very much that of the Stock Exchange in Dublin, which they say served as a model for it. This edifice is today the home of the wealthy banker, Stephen Girard.

The New Bank of the United States, the work of the American architect Strickland, is generally considered to be the most beautiful piece of architecture of the Union. It offers, on a small scale, a rather exact image of the Temple of Minerva at Athens. Its entire construction is in beautiful marble mined from the quarries of Montgomery County in the State of Pennsylvania.

Perhaps, before ending this chapter, I ought to resume with the description of the brilliant and varied fetes that the inhabitants of Philadelphia offered to their National Guest during the eight days which he passed among them; but their simple enumeration would carry me very far beyond the circle in which I want to enclose the narrative of this trip or rather this triumph; and, in spite of all the pleasure that I would have had in speaking of the Masonic dinner, the City Ball, the visit of General Lafayette to the marine arsenal, the evening party given by General Cadwalader, etc., I find myself compelled to leave Philadelphia for Baltimore, where the Nation's Guest will be welcomed with the same transports of gratitude and affection.

Chapter XI

Trip from Philadelphia to Baltimore – American Aristocracy – Fort McHenry – Arrival in Baltimore – Description of Baltimore – Defense of the City in 1814.

On October 5, General Lafayette received the emotional farewells of the inhabitants of Philadelphia, and we embarked on the Delaware at eight o'clock in the evening in order to descend to Chester. We were accompanied by the Governor, the committee of arrangements, a battalion of volunteers and a large number of staff officers. We arrived at Chester at eleven o'clock at night, and we entered it by the gleam of the lights. The room in which the General was welcomed and given speeches reminded him of a very memorable time of his life. It was in this same room that he came to have the first dressing put on his wound after having been wounded at the Battle of Brandywine. Before dismounting from his horse, he had had the strength and the presence of mind to rally a part of the troops who were fleeing, and to place them in front of a bridge in order to stop the enemy, if it had thought of following up on its initial success. These different circumstances were recalled in a very touching manner by the orator charged with welcoming the General in the name of the inhabitants of this Town. After having had an excellent supper, prepared by the attentions of the women of Chester, we went to pass the rest of the night in the home of Colonel Anderson, an old companion-in-arms of General Lafayette.

On the following day, we pursued our route, and we arrived in good time at the frontier of the State of Delaware from which we had to cross the point which juts out between the States of Pennsylvania, Jersey and Maryland. There, we took leave of our Philadelphia companions, who left us only after having remitted us into the hands of the committee from Delaware, at the head of which General Lafayette received with great pleasure old Colonel McLane. He had commanded a company of partisans during the Virginia campaign with great courage, and today, in spite of his 80 years, came to present himself to the General on horseback, wearing the hat and the plume of the Revolution.

We arrived to dine at Wilmington. This pretty City, built equally distant from Brandywine and Christiana, is the largest of the State of Delaware. Although its population does not rise to quite 6,000, it is, however, the center of a considerable commerce facilitated by the means of navigation it has at its disposal. The proximity of Philadelphia and Baltimore provides great activity to its factories. Despite the entreaties of the inhabitants, the General was obliged to continue his trip in order to arrive on the same day at Frenchtown where we had to find a steamboat to take us to Baltimore. We were a little delayed in our progress by a stay of a few hours in Newcastle, where we attended the wedding of Victor Dupont with Miss Van Dyke. The wedding ceremony, which was conducted according to the rites of the Reformed Church, interested us deeply because of its character of moving simplicity. It took place in a drawing room in the presence of the families to be united and some invited friends. The Minister of the Gospel, having joined the two young people, addressed a short speech to them in which he explained to them clearly and without mysticism the duties that their new situation was going to impose on them in the social order, and spoke to them, as a husband and father of a family to whom the practice of them was long familiar, of the virtues that alone could contribute to their happiness. Finally, after having joined them in marriage, he ended with a touching prayer expressed in the English language, to which everyone could join from his heart, because everyone could understand it. In spite of the absence of costumes and decorations, this ceremony appeared to me as worthy and as imposing as Catholic marriages.

The night was very advanced when we arrived at Frenchtown where the steamboat, *The United States*, charged with conducting us to Baltimore, had already been waiting for a long time. A little before Frenchtown, on the Maryland border, General Lafayette had found a large delegation, and the aides-de-camp of the Governor of this State, who announced to him that they were assigned to accompany him to Fort McHenry, where the Governor himself had established his headquarters to receive him. In the middle of this delegation, the General recognized with great pleasure several of his old friends and especially two Frenchmen, Colonel Bentalou, a former officer of Pulaski's legion, and Mr. Dubois-Martin, a graybeard of 83 years, who had been charged in the past with preparing the ship on which Lafayette had escaped from Bordeaux in order to come to the United States. At the moment when we would have been embarking, they informed us that Mr. John Quincy Adams, the Secretary of State, had just arrived at Frenchtown, returning to Washington, and that he had readily accepted the invitation to join in the retinue of General Lafayette, for whom this was an additional pleasure, because Mr. Adams was an old and good acquaintance.

Very many travelers who have visited the United States, and who claim to know the customs of this country, have suggested that the Americans, despite their republican institutions, were essentially aristocratic in their practices. The following event will answer, I believe, this accusation decisively, and this event will not be an isolated one, nor will it be an exception, because I will have very many others similar to it to report.

On board the steamboat that was carrying us on the Chesapeake, they had prepared a room for General Lafayette and, as the committee of arrangements had the kindness to consider that those who had shared his fatigue ought also to share his rest, they had placed in this same room two other beds, one for his son and the other for his secretary. We were ignorant about how our traveling companions, who were numerous, were arranged to pass the night, when George Lafayette, while going to take some air on the deck, recognized that the room in which we had dined was suddenly transformed into a vast dormitory, the floor of which was covered with beds that the crowd was sharing unceremoniously. Among those who were getting ready to stretch out on a modest mattress, he noticed with astonishment Secretary of State Adams. He ran to him and begged him earnestly to change beds with him; the former refused declaring that he was very well and that he would be dreadfully sorry to separate the son from the father. I happened upon this debate, and I joined my entreaties to those of George Lafayette. I remarked to Mr. Adams that he did not have the same objections to make against my proposal, and I added that I hoped, indeed, that he would not condemn me to the sorrow of sleeping in a good bed, whereas I knew that a man of his character was stretched out on a hard one. He answered me with some obliging words but which constituted, however, a formal refusal. Finally, pressed by our combined entreaties, and by the name of General Lafayette which we invoked, he declared to us that even if he would be disposed to accept our offer, he would still be obliged to refuse it because above all he was obliged to respect the decisions of the committee of arrangements, and the committee had decided that no one would be admitted into the General's room, except his two companions of the trip.... George Lafayette ran immediately to a member of the committee and requested of him, in the name of his father, that Mr. Adams be admitted into the room in place of one of us. This latter stipulation did not appear admissible to the committee which, after a short deliberation, decided that a fourth bed would be set up in General Lafayette's room and that Mr. Adams would occupy it, not because he was Secretary of State, but because General Lafayette wanted to have him near to him by virtue of his being an old friend. Mr. Adams decided to leave the crowd to come to join us, only on the formal invitation of the committee. If aristocracy is in American mores, one must admit at least that the high officials of the Government enjoy its prerogatives but little.

During the entire night we had sailed in frightful weather; but, in the morning when we entered the beautiful Patapsco River, on the banks of which rises the wealthy City of Baltimore, the sun dispersed the clouds, and its first rays, gilding the vast horizon that unfolded before us, permitted our eyes to recognize already the steeples of the City, the forest of ships' masts that habitually filled the Port, and the bastions of Fort McHenry that defends the entrance to it. At nine o'clock, four steamships, *The Maryland*, *The Virginia*, *The Philadelphia* and *The Eagle*, covered with flags and streamers and loaded with a multitude of citizens who had come to greet their guest by saluting him with a triple welcome with which their grateful voices made the air resound, left the Port and came to form a line behind the *The United States*, which continued majestically its sail towards the riverbank. When we were only a short distance from it, several longboats presented themselves to effectuate our disembarking. The first to land on the bank carried General Lafayette, Secretary of State Adams, General Smith, Mr. Dubois-Martin, and Mr. Morris, president of the committee; it was commanded by Captain Gardner, and maneuvered by 12 of the most skillful boatswains in Baltimore. We shared the other longboats, and we came to disembark at the foot of Fort McHenry.

On the principal bastion of the Fort, they had hoisted the national flag that had flapped there during the last war; this flag, pierced by a thousand holes, still bears witness to the vain efforts of the English artillery. At the entrance to the Fort, General Lafayette was surrounded by a troop of men clad as simple citizens, for the most part disabled; this troop was the remnant of that which in 1814 proved so energetically to the English how much men who fight for liberty, their country and their family, are superior to mercenaries paid by kings to serve their passions. Fort McHenry defended by some citizen-heroes saw then, before its weakened walls, the failure of the arrogance and the exertions of an English fleet, which was obliged to withdraw sheepishly after a bombardment of more than 48 hours.

At the moment when General Lafayette entered the Fort, the cannon announced him to the citizens of Baltimore, who at this time were leaving in a crowd to come to meet him, and were covering that long peninsula that jutted out from the City to Fort McHenry between two bays that form the Patapsco River. On the raised platform of the Fort were joined a large number of former Revolutionary officers, magistrates, etc., and a detachment of infantry, which, in opening its ranks, allowed us to see, *Washington's tent* behind it. If, at this sight, General Lafayette felt very many different feelings awaken in him, his son was no less moved to see again the man who had the happy and noble idea of bringing it to add to the solemnity of this day. Mr. Custis, the author of this thoughtful act of attentiveness, was the adopted grandson of Washington; it was with him that George Lafayette passed two years of his youth under the hospitable roof of Mount Vernon, during the captivity of his father in the dungeons of Olmutz. The memory of their old brotherhood, and of the cruel loss of the one who had served as their father, made them feel a mixture of pleasure and grief that they could only express by the silence of their tears and of their embraces....

General Lafayette, after having tried to calm his initial feelings, advanced towards Washington's tent where he was welcomed by Governor Stevens who addressed to him the following speech:

> General, in welcoming you and congratulating you in the name of the inhabitants of the State of Maryland, I am fulfilling a task very dear to my heart, but I really fear that I will express only feebly the sentiments of the people whom I am proud and happy to represent on this occasion. It was under this tent, the object of our reverence, that you so often clasped the friendly hand of our illustrious Washington; often it also saw you contribute your advice towards his wise resolves, or share with him the fatigue and the frugality of the soldier. But it is useless to recall here the circumstances of your intimate relationship with this great man; they are always present in our memory, they fill every heart with the most animated gratitude for the generous companion of our fathers, the courageous and disinterested soldier of liberty. May this feeling of gratitude for the author of the benefits that we enjoy never be lessened in the heart of my fellow citizens!
>
> Ten years have hardly passed since, on this very soil, our courageous fellow-citizens proved that they knew how to defend that precious liberty won by you; ten centuries will have passed without yet erasing the memory of the glorious example that you gave to them.
>
> You are going to enter this City of Baltimore that you have already known at another time; its growth and its improvements will offer to you the symbol of our national prosperity under popular institutions and a truly representative government. The monuments that adorn this City will bear witness to you of the feelings that animate its inhabitants.
>
> The column we have raised to Washington's memory is a proof of the constancy of our affections for and gratitude to the heroes of the Revolution; on a column of a more recent date, you will find the evidences of our gratitude towards those who have devoted themselves to the cause of liberty.
>
> Welcome, three times welcome, General, to the land of Maryland! Nothing that we do will express in an energetically enough manner either the sentiments that we retain for your

> person and your principles, or the pleasure that we have in welcoming in you a father who, after a long absence, returns to the greetings of his family.

After this speech, to which General Lafayette responded with all the effusion of a grateful and profoundly moved heart, we entered the tent, under which was the aged Colonel Howard. He had rendered his youth illustrious in the *War of Independence*, crowned his old age with the laurels that he won in 1814 in the defense of Baltimore, and filled the interval between these two great epochs of his life with a continual devotion to the cause of liberty. This venerable patriot, at the head of members of the Society of the Cincinnati, also wanted to give a speech to the General and to express to him the feelings of all of his former companions-in-arms who could not contain the bursting out of their joy any longer and who vied with one another to rush into the arms of their former chief who, as they presented themselves to him, recognized nearly all of them and reminded them vivaciously of the times and the places where they had shared the same dangers and hardships.

Finally, we left Fort McHenry and the procession formed to enter Baltimore. General Lafayette began the trip in a carriage drawn by four horses: the vast stretch of terrain that we had to traverse was, to our left, filled by a line of militia on foot and on horse, which formed in columns behind us as we passed in front of them. To our right were all the people, having left Baltimore en masse. We arrived, thus, at the entrance to the City, where a triumphal arch borne on four beautiful Ionic columns had been built. Under this arch 24 girls clad in white, crowned with myrtle and armed with lances on each of which was written the name of one of the States of the Union, welcomed the Nation's Guest, placed wreaths around his neck and crowned him with laurels. At the same time, the sound of cannon mixed with the animated acclamations of the multitude. The procession continued its route, and after having passed under triumphal arches while traversing all the streets, stopped in front of City Hall, where in the principal hall, the General was addressed by the Mayor, who said to him:

> ...Here, there is no throne other than that of the august Monarch of the Universe, the only one before whom the citizens of this republic bow their heads. But we never lay our humble thanks at the feet of the All-Powerful for the benefits that he has assigned to this happy country without requesting his blessing for you, whom he has made the instrument with the aid of which he has overturned the tyranny that weighed upon our Fatherland. Our City, General, although it occupies

> only a very little space, can be considered as the symbol of this vast land that we occupy; it was hardly a village when you saw it 40 years ago; today, you are welcomed here by 65,000 people who live within its boundaries. General, such are the fruits that the tree of liberty bears! If it is agreeable to you, in the evening of your life, to recall that it was your blood that made this tree fertile, it is no less so for us, at this happy time, to be able to assure you that we will never forget it….

In his response, General Lafayette proved that he had not forgotten the zeal of the inhabitants of Baltimore for the cause of liberty.

> It was under the auspices of the patriotism of the Baltimoreans, it was with the support of the generosity of the merchants and the devotion of the women of this City, that at a difficult time when there wasn't a day to lose, I was able to begin in 1781 that campaign of which the happy issue has thrown so much luster on the services rendered to our cause. Mr. Mayor, today, I admire with pleasure your improvements, your prosperity, your national guard, your monuments..., and there remains nothing more for me to desire, since this morning under the tent of our fatherly and venerated chief, I have pressed the hands of some of those brave voluntary dragoons of Baltimore who made the Virginia Campaign with me....

After this response, and when they had presented to him all the members of the municipal council, we returned to the principal street of Baltimore, at the center of which a platform, covered and decorated with luxurious carpets, had been built to receive General Lafayette and those who were accompanying him. It was from there that we saw file the militias of Maryland, the martial appearance of which revealed the warlike character of the men of this beautiful country. This entire troop marched to the sound of a military band that played *The March of Lafayette*. Among the numerous corps who passed before our eyes, they pointed out to the General one that marched pressed close together under a tattered standard. This corps was that of Forsythe's cavalry, and this standard was the one under which Pulaski died before Savannah.

Pulaski,[11] after having fought for a long time and vainly for the freedom of Poland, his Fatherland, only abandoned it when the cause of independence was altogether hopeless, and in order to find places where he was able to shed his blood for the principles that he had defended up to then.

---

11. *American Biography.*

Virginia and Maryland were completely devastated by the war when, in 1778, he organized a legion in Baltimore. The arts were not cultivated, and all activity of the citizens was directed towards the war; it was difficult to procure for the new legion a glossy flag: they were therefore obliged to have recourse to simpler colors. A piece of crimson silk, obtained with great difficulty, was embroidered by the Moravian nuns of Bethlehem, Pennsylvania. On one side were the letters U. S. (*United States*), and the words *Unita virtus fortior*; on the other was a sky illuminated by 13 stars, with this legend: *Non alius regret*. Such was the flag of Pulaski, which always led the warriors whom it served to rally on to the road to glory.

In 1778 the lieutenant colonel of this legion fell on the English bayonettes at Egg Harbor in New Jersey; in 1779 the colonel, who had already commanded a regiment of Hussars in the armies of Frederic the Great, was hacked up by sword thrusts in front of Charleston. On October 9th of the same year, General Pulaski, who had given his name to the legion, was mortally wounded by grape-shot at the siege of Savannah. In 1780 the major was cut down by sword at Mark's Corner. Colonel Bentalou was then the most senior surviving officer; he took command of the legion, and, at the end of the war, he inherited its flag, which he carefully preserved. Since the Revolution, it had not been unfurled, but he thought that the arrival of Lafayette was an occasion glorious enough to restore it to the light. After the ceremony he deposited it in the Museum, to which he had made a gift of it, and where it was received into the hands of the women of Baltimore.

After the review, they led us to our headquarters in an elegant hotel maintained by Mr. Barney, brother of the intrepid Commodore Barney wounded fighting gloriously at the head of his marines at the Battle of Bladensburg in 1814. In the evening the municipal authorities, the senators and the members of the legislative assembly of Maryland, and the Governor and his staff came to dine with the General. At the end of the meal, the table-companions exchanged numerous toasts that, for the most part, contained the expression of their attachment to the person and the principles of Lafayette, or sometimes, according to American custom, the expression of the opinion of their political party. Mr. Adams, still moved by the touching scenes he had witnessed in the morning at Fort McHenry, gave the following toast which was received in the midst of unanimous applause: "To the tears of glory, gratitude and joy under Washington's tent."

Each moment of our stay at Baltimore was marked by the most brilliant fetes, the most delicate attentiveness. It is difficult to do justice to the elegance and the refinements of the inhabitants of this City, in which one finds the agreeable conjunction of American freedom and French grace. The ball given by the City was all that one could have in the most perfect of its kind. It had been prepared in the theatre, and arranged with inimitable taste. All the boxes were filled by the ladies, and no one occupied the stage. We were ushered to the stage, accompanied only by some members of the committee; at the moment when the General appeared, an invisible band announced him by playing *The March of Lafayette*. The illuminating gas leaking abundantly from the numerous ducts and diffusing suddenly cascades of dazzling light into the hall unveiled to our astonished eyes the most ravishing tableau that I had ever seen. The brilliancy of a flowerbed covered with the most beautiful flowers would have paled beside that with which this crowd of pretty women glistened as they were waving their handkerchiefs, throwing flowers, and expressing with gentle tears the happiness they felt in seeing their cherished Guest of the Nation. Instantly, they abandoned their places, hurled themselves to the middle of the hall, and surrounded the General, who stayed for some time incapable of expressing his gratitude to them, so much was he moved. Finally, the dance began, and gave us the opportunity to admire in more detail the charms and beauty of the women of Maryland.

We stayed only five days in Baltimore, but General Lafayette's time was so skillfully divided that he was able to respond to nearly all the invitations which were given to him. He attended in succession the fete of the Freemasons, and the one of the members of the Society of the Cincinnati, etc. Each day he received numerous delegations of a large number of towns, who requested earnestly that he endeavor to visit them. He traveled through the diverse public institutions of Baltimore, and, on Sunday, attended the divine service celebrated by the Bishop. The Mass was admirably chanted by the ladies and maidens of Baltimore, under the direction of Mr. Gilles, an excellent teacher, who for some years has spread the taste for good music and trained a large number of distinguished students in this City. On the same day, the officer corps of the militias was presented by General Harper who, on this occasion, delivered a speech of which the following passage seemed altogether notable. "This freely given homage of our hearts," he said,

> Lacking in flattery or ambition, is so much more precious to you since you well know that it is the testimony of a nation in favor of those principles of government for which you have shed your blood in this hemisphere, and suffered so much in the other. This testimony will perhaps not be useless to the sacred cause that you have embraced. At a time when Europe is divided into two parties, of which the one strives to perpetuate absolute power, and the other fights courageously for equality of rights and for constitutional government, it will be, we hope, of

> great encouragement for the friends of the good cause to learn that here there is no division, and that the American Nation is unanimous in its feeling of attachment to liberty.

General Lafayette responded to the speaker by assuring him that he shared his views, his wishes and his hopes.

The evidences of affection, public or private, with which the citizens of Baltimore showered their guest, are too numerous for me to attempt to report them all; however, I cannot refrain from citing only the following circumstance. The night before our departure, we had passed the evening at General Smith's house; we returned on foot accompanied by only two or three people. In spite of the brilliancy of the lights that lit up our way on the footpaths of the wide street, we were hoping to be able to pass unnoticed across the crowd which was numerous, but the figure of General Lafayette and his gait betrayed us: he was recognized by some pedestrians and, his name flying from mouth to mouth, the crowd instantly beset our way. However, we were approaching our abode and we were already congratulating ourselves for not having been too delayed, when George Lafayette, feeling himself held back by his coat, turned around and saw a young girl, beautiful as the day, her hands folded, crying out in the most moving tone of voice: "Ah! I beg of you, let me only touch his clothes, and you will have made me happy...." General Lafayette heard her, walked towards her and held out a hand which she seized and kissed with rapture, after which she ran away while hiding her tears and her blush in her handkerchief....An act like this, especially when it is not at all isolated, says more about him than the most skillful historian.

The following days we visited the City of Baltimore in nearly all its particulars. It appeared to me to be one of the prettiest cities of the Union. Although its streets were all very wide and evenly plotted out, it did not, however, have the monotony of Philadelphia. The ground on which it is situated has an undulating movement that gives to each quarter a varied character. From several elevated points of the City, the eye can take in not only the entirety of the buildings but also a part of the Port, the gleaming waters of the Chesapeake and the dark forests extending far away, which appear to have been placed there like natural shadows to bring out more strongly the magic tableau of a city of 65,000 created in the period of less than a half-century. The inhabitants of Baltimore appear in general to have a pronounced taste for the fine arts. I have already said that it was to a Frenchman that they owed their superior distinction in music over all the other cities of the Union; it is also to a Frenchman that they owe the development of the beauty of their architecture. Most of their public monuments have been constructed pursuant to the plans of Mr. Godefroy, who has for a long time lived among them. The Unitarian Church is a masterpiece of elegance and simplicity. The monument raised in memory of the citizens who died in defending Baltimore during the last war is of a severe style and beautiful execution. The column erected in honor of Washington rather resembles, by its elevation and its form, our column in the Place de la Vendôme in Paris. It is made of white marble. Its location on a little hill causes it to be seen from nearly every point of the City, and even from a rather great distance on the Bay.

The Port is secure and convenient; however, it happens sometimes that during the harsh winters it is obstructed by ice. Although nearly 200 miles distant from the sea, it is well-frequented. The large number of navigable rivers pouring into the Chesapeake make Baltimore the center of a very active interior commerce. Nevertheless, they have noticed for some years a diminution, perceptible enough, in the commercial activity of Baltimore. The causes of it are explained in different ways; but they believe that it will disappear soon or at least that it will stop being as influential when the beautiful project of establishing a railroad, which will open up and facilitate new connections with the Ohio, will have been completed.

Baltimore appears to me to be one of the cities in which a stay ought to offer the most pleasure. Its inhabitants, although committed with ardor to all kinds of industry, are not however strangers to studies that shape good taste and increase the domain of the spirit. One finds several learned societies there: one of them, under the name of the *Newtonian Society of Maryland*, founded in 1818, encourages the study of Natural History fervently. The *Economic Association* was founded in 1819 with the goal of encouraging manufacturing and domestic economy. The agricultural society isn't less noteworthy than the others in the services it renders and the merits of the men who compose it. Before our departure, all three of us had the honor of being named honorary members of this society. The anatomy collections of Messrs. Chiappi and Gibson, the museum of natural history, the painting gallery of Mr. Peale, and the mineralogy collection of Mr. Gilmor are beautiful amateur collections. The library of the City is composed of about 14,000 volumes, and is entirely at the disposal of the public. What ends up adding a great attraction to the advantages the City of Baltimore contains is the proximity of Washington, seat of the Central Government, which is only 37 miles away, and which, during the sessions of the Congress, offers a great appeal to people who want to follow the political debates to good purpose. However, in Baltimore, as in all of New England, Sunday is a little dreary with the austere religious practices, but there is absolute freedom of worship. At least 12 sects share the City, the most numerous one is that of the Catholics; and, although it has the force of numbers, it is nonetheless as agreeable, as tolerant, as charitable as the others, because it well knows that it wouldn't find any support from the authorities, if it wanted to intrigue and dominate as in some parts of Europe.

This City, so beautiful and so interesting, was, however, 45 years ago, only an assemblage of some homes rather badly built; in 1790, its population rose suddenly to 13,503 inhabitants. A new census found 26,514 there in 1800; 35,583 in 1810; 65,738 in 1820; and today (1824) they count more than 65,000, of which at least 50,000 belong to the White population and 11,000 to the free Colored population; 4,000 others have the misfortune of being Slaves. Happily, the number of the latter diminishes each day. The progress of philanthropy and of well-understood interest, although slow, is, however, continuous; and the friends of humanity would have the right to expect that in a few years the inhabitants of Baltimore will end by ridding themselves of this scourge of Slavery which one could call disgraceful, if one did not know of the obstacles they have had to surmount, at present, to their repudiating the horrible heritage that England has bequeathed to the United States, as if to punish them for having broken their Colonial yoke.

Wealth and the Arts, in being introduced into the bosom of the Baltimorean population, have not brought with them the indolence and corruption that some men claim to be their inseparable companions. The defense of Baltimore during the last war suffices to prove that its inhabitants are still, as in the days of their glorious Revolution, passionate lovers of liberty and courageous defenders of their independence. Their campaign of 1814 earned them too much honor and pleaded too successfully in favor of the system of militias in a defensive war for me not to retrace it here. I borrow details of it from the skillful historian of the last war, Mr. Brackenridge.

> When they learned that Baltimore was menaced by the English, all the inhabitants of the City without distinction of sex, age or rank, set to work; and, under the direction of General Smith, dug out a wide ditch and built an entrenchment to cover the northeast part, the only point where the City could be attacked from the land. The arrival of a large number of militias from Virginia and Pennsylvania, and still more, that of Commodore Rodgers at the head of his brave sailors, redoubled the zeal of the inhabitants of Baltimore. Rodgers occupied the fortifications constructed on the hill dominating the City; General Winder had command of the line infantry and of a brigade of Virginians; the militia and volunteers of Baltimore were placed under the command of General Striker;

finally they entrusted the high command of all the forces to General Smith, an officer of the greatest merit, whose services dated from the Revolutionary War.

The approaches to the City from the water side were defended by Fort McHenry, of which Major Armistead had command. The garrison of this Fort was composed of about 60 artillerymen and two companies of Coast Guard under the command of Captains Bunbury and Addison: they added to these three companies of volunteers, of which one, commanded by Nicholson, the Chief Justice of Baltimore, had volunteered for this arduous and dangerous service. They sent a detachment of sailors under Lieutenant Redman into the Fort; finally General Winder detached from his division 600 line soldiers, who, under the command of Lieutenant Colonel Stewart, camped outside the fortifications so that there were 1,000 men charged especially with the defense of this important position.

Two fortifications were constructed on the Patapsco, to the right of Fort McHenry, to prevent the enemy from landing behind the City; they were manned by some detachments of sailors; one of them, which they named Fort Covington, was entrusted to Lieutenant Newcomb, and the other, called the City Battery, to Lieutenant Webster.

It was of the highest importance for the safety of Baltimore that, in case the enemy attacked by land and water at the same time, it was driven back simultaneously from both sides. If the English Navy succeeded in reducing Fort McHenry to silence, there would be nothing any more to prevent it from coming to destroy the City from top to bottom. If, on the contrary, it was the attack from land that succeeded, from that time forward the Fort would not be of any help and would not even be defensible. It was, therefore, the defense of the Fort, as well as the defense of the entrenchments that covered the City, that the inhabitants were to provide for. The inhabitants were more especially disposed to do so besides on account of the devastating orders of Admiral Cochrane, and the horrors committed at Washington and Alexandria, and as they knew well that Baltimore was the point on which the English desired to satisfy their vengeance the most, by reason of the numerous patriotic efforts that the City had not ceased making during the entire war for the support of the national cause.

It would be impossible to form an accurate idea of the state of anxiety into which were plunged 50,000 people, of all ages, of all sexes, as they awaited the terrible crisis on which the salvation or the ruin of their City must depend; an anxiety so much greater as, even in the case of a successful resistance, each family had still to tremble about the fate, the life of a parent, of a friend; for, from the adolescent to the old man, every one who could man a gun was found in the ranks of the army. The committee of safety, composed of men advanced in years and of citizens who had the most influence (among them was found the respected Colonel Howard, one of the heroes of the Revolution) put the greatest activity into the defense preparations, and neglected nothing it could do to prevent or diminish the dangers of all kinds which menaced the City.

After the English army had reembarked, Admiral Cochrane descended the Patuxent and, after having gone up the Chesapeake, on the morning of September 11, he appeared at the mouth of the Patapsco, which was only about 14 miles from Baltimore, having with him 50 sails, as many warships as transports. On the following day 6,000 troops, the elite of the army that had served in Spain under Wellington, disembarked, commanded by General Ross, and immediately took the road to the City.

General Striker had demanded for the brigade which he commanded, composed entirely of Baltimore's militia, the honor of engaging the enemy first. This just demand having been accepted, he had set out en route on September 11 to proceed to Northpoint, having with him 3,000 effective forces; in this number were contained 150 cavalry, commanded by Lieutenant Colonel Biais, and more than 75 cannoniers who had with them six quarter-pieces and were under the command of Colonel Montgomery, Attorney General of the State of Maryland. Some light troops of Stansbury's brigade and volunteers of Pennsylvania went to take their posts at the mouth of Bear Creek, in order to cooperate with General Striker and to oppose any landing that the enemy should attempt at this spot.

Striker arrived at six o'clock in the evening at a chapel situated near the source of Bear Creek, about seven miles from the City. The entire troop stopped there for the night, with the exception of the cavalry, which pushed up to the Gorsuch farm, three miles further on, and some sharp-shooters who took their posts two miles in front of the camp.

On the next day, September 12, at seven o'clock in the morning, they knew from the mounted sentries that the enemy had landed on the near side of the Patapsco River. Immediately General Striker advanced up to Longlog Road; there, he stopped and arranged his troops in the following manner: The 5th Regiment was placed at the left side of the main road, whose right side rested against one of the branches of Bear Creek; from the other side of the main road, the 27th was arranged in battle formation so as to form a straight line with the 5th; the artillery was placed between these two regiments; the 39th and the 59th Regiments were formed 900 feet behind the first line; finally, the 3rd Regiment stayed a half a mile farther back in order to serve as a reserve corps, and betake itself everywhere it would be needed. The General, after this judicious disposition of his troops, resolved to wait for the enemy where he was and took care to forewarn the two regiments that formed the first line that, in case they would be forced to beat a retreat, they were to pass in the space between the 59th and the 39th regiments and go to regroup on the right and left of the reserve corps.

The General was not long in learning that the English were advancing rapidly by following the main road and, at the moment when he expected that their approach was going to be announced to him by the muskets of the sharpshooters whom he had placed in front for this action, this corps came precipitously back to the brigade, deceived by a false alarm and believing that the enemy had landed on Back River with the intention of crossing it. A part of the general plan having been lost in this manner, he placed the sharpshooters to the right of the first line.

The sentries having a short time later brought the news that an advance party of the enemy was already at Gorsuch Farm and did not at all appear to be on its guard, several officers offered to go to dislodge it. In a word, the companies of Captain Levering and Howard, and about 60 sharpshooters commanded by Major Heath, set out immediately on march, supported by the cavalry and a small cannon piece, in order to go to punish the insolence of these enemy marauders. This small force had gone hardly half a mile when it encountered the English Army; a rather brisk engagement began at once; Major Heath had his horse cut down under him, and several Americans were killed or wounded, but not without revenge, for the Commander-in-chief of the English force, General Ross, himself, received a fatal blow. It appeared that this officer had advanced imprudently to reconnoiter the American position, and that he was killed by one of the men of Howard's company. After Ross's death, Colonel Brook, who succeeded him in command, continued his march ahead, so that the American detachment was forced to turn back. When it had rejoined General Striker, the latter, thinking reasonably that the men who composed it were too fatigued to take part in the action which was to take place, gave them the order to withdraw to the reserve corps, an order which Captain Howard, son of the brave veteran of whom we have spoken above, requested permission not to obey, wanting to share all the dangers of his compatriots.

At two-thirty the enemy began to launch some incendiary rockets which fortunately produced little effect. Captain Montgomery immediately put into action all his artillery, and the English countered with a piece of six and a howitzer directed principally against the center and the left of the Americans. The fire became very brisk from one side to the other, but Striker caused his fire to stop, wanting that they shoot only when the enemy would be in the range of grapeshot; and, realizing that all the efforts of the English were directed against his left wing, he made the 27th Regiment fall back until it was in line with the 39th, and caused two cannon pieces to be advanced on this side. In order to render this important point stronger, he ordered Coloney Amey of the 59th Regiment to come and to draw it up at a right angle to the left side of the line, while pressing its extreme right up to the 39th Regiment. This movement was executed badly, and occasioned some confusion in this part: but, nonetheless, order was not long in being restored, thanks to the help of

Major Stevenson, the General's aide-de-camp, and brigade Majors Calhoun and Fraily.

Hardly had these arrangements been concluded when the enemy deployed its right column, and proceeded briskly against the 27th and 39th Regiments. The 59th, which was to support them, after having fired some rifle shots and being seized by panic, fled in such disorder that it was impossible to rally it and it swept along the second battalion of the 39th in its flight. Nonetheless, the impact of the English was received by the remaining troops with the greatest fearlessness, and they did not lose an inch of terrain. The firing then became general from one end of the line to the other. The American artillery, operated with the greatest dispatch, crushed the left column of the enemy; this column having already experienced an enormous loss, tried to take cover behind the buildings in woods; but these buildings, which Captain Sadler, who had recently occupied them, had set on fire, were not long in becoming engulfed in flames. At ten minutes after three, the English charged impetuously against the 5th and 27th Regiments; this charge had no effect; the Americans held well, although they had to deal with forces four times their size; for it is important to call attention to the fact that, with the flight of the 59th and part of the 39th, General Striker had no more than 1,400 men to oppose the entire English Army. The combat lasted until a quarter of four without the Americans having experienced the least disadvantage; but General Striker, realizing that the enemy with its numerical superiority was making ready to change its position, believed that it was necessary to retreat in good order to his reserve corps which had not yet engaged. Having joined with this corps, he formed anew his battle line, and waited for a while for that which the enemy commander was going to do; but the latter not appearing to want to renew the fight, Striker began to march, and returned to take a position on the left about one-half mile from the entrenchments which were guarding Baltimore. He was joined a little afterwards in this place by General Winder, who first had been stationed in the western part of the City, but had afterwards received the order to come to line up to the left of Striker with the Virginia Brigade and a company of dragoons.

The entire Baltimore Brigade, with the exception of the 59th and the second battalion of the 39th, which had been swept away by a burst of terror so pardonable to new troops who had never seen firing, was worthy of the greatest praise; experienced soldiers would not have been able to do better than these citizens assembled in haste; their losses climbed to 163 men, as many killed as wounded, about one-eighth of the troops who were engaged. Sergeant Major James Lowry Donaldson, of the 27th, a very distinguished jurist, was killed at the hottest part of the conflict; Majors Heath and Moore, as well as several other officers, were wounded. The English acknowledged a loss nearly double that of the Americans, and in their official report, they estimated the number of those who had opposed them at 6,000 men, to such a degree was the resistance they met unyielding and worthy of citizens fighting for their most cherished interests. General Striker took pleasure in rendering homage to all the officers who had supported him so bravely. He designated by name those who had been particularly distinguished, and he paid a special tribute of praise to Captain Montgomery who, with the feeble artillery that he commanded, had known how to continuously hold the entire English Army in check.

The news of the resistance that the English had experienced and of the death of General Ross inspired the most animated ardor among the troops charged with the defense of the entrenchments: they returned cheerfully to the different posts assigned to them, and prepared to receive bravely those who would be coming to attack them.

On the following morning, the English Army appeared two miles away, and was able to take a view of the whole of the American lines; it made diverse maneuvers in the morning that seemed to indicate that it wanted to begin the attack on the right, by approaching from the Hartford and York roads; but Generals Winder and Striker, while following all the movements of the enemy, forced it to abandon its first plan, and to concentrate all its forces at about one mile from the middle of the entrenchments. All appeared to indicate that the attack would have taken place the same evening, and, consequently, General Smith gave the order to Winder's and Striker's brigades to take a position on the right of the English in order to attack them in the rear if they tried to scale the lines, or in order to disturb them in their retreat if on the following morning they believed it necessary to take this latter course of action.

While these operations were taking place, the English fleet did not stay inactive; immediately after it had effectuated the landing of the troops, it made ready to bombard Fort McHenry; and on September 13 at daybreak, 16 ships presented themselves two miles from the Fort. Major Armistead distributed all his people in the different batteries, and the line infantry that had been detached from the Winder Brigade stayed in the outer trench in order to repulse any landing attempted by the enemy. Five galleys with bombs began to draw to about two miles distant from the Fort. It was observed that they carried their bombs, moistened them, and fired them continually and, even more terrible, that considering their distance, no cannon of the Fort could counter them.

The situation of the American garrison, forced to accept enemy fire in complete inaction, was horrible. A large number of bombs burst on the Fort; a piece of 24 of the southwest bastion was smashed to pieces, and the breaking of its gun carriage killed the lieutenant commanding at this point and wounded several gunners. However, in this cruel position, not a man wavered and all stayed at the posts which had been assigned to them. The ships having drawn a little nearer, all the batteries of the Fort immediately fired so intensely that they lost no time in going to take their former position, from which they continued the bombardment during the entire day of the 13th and the night of the 13th to the 14th.

Baltimore, thus attacked by land and sea, was plunged into a gloomy silence. The women and the disabled, who alone had stayed in the interior of the City, consumed by worry for themselves and even more for their friends and parents who were engaged with the enemy, did not take, as one could well imagine, any rest during this terrible night. They vainly tried to cover over their fright when towards midnight they heard the sound of frightful cannon fire which seemed to come from a place nearer than the Fort. Each believed that the enemy had won the victory and that all hope of resistance was lost; however, they were not long in being reassured upon learning that the enemy, which had tried to effectuate a landing between the Fort and the City, had been repulsed with losses by Lieutenants Webster and Newcomb, who commanded the battery of the City and Fort Covington. The following morning the English stopped their fire, after having hurled more than 1,500 bombs, which for the most part exploded in the air and covered Fort McHenry with their fragments. Nevertheless, only four men were killed and 24 wounded; and the interior structures of the Fort were all more or less undamaged. Among the wounded was Lieutenant Russell, a distinguished attorney from Baltimore: he had received his wound at the beginning of the action; but in spite of the pain it caused him, he did not want to quit his post and stayed there until the cessation of fire, thus giving the most noble example to his brothers-in-arms.

On the night of the 13th to the 14th, Admiral Cochrane held a conference with the Commander of the land forces, and both having judged it impossible to seize Baltimore, they decided to abandon their enterprise. However, they still continued the bombardment in order to deceive the Americans; and, during this time, the troops began their retreat, which was favored by an excessively dark night and by a pelting rain, so that one could not have any knowledge of this backward movement from the American lines. About 10,000 men were drawn up the length of the entrenchments, and it is likely that, if the attack had taken place, they would have made the enemy regret its audaciousness; but their courage was not put to the proof; at sunrise, all the English had disappeared. General Winder began immediately to pursue them, and he picked up a good number of stragglers, but the other American troops who had passed three days and three nights under arms in a continual rain, were too exhausted by fatigue to be able to follow the English Army which, as a consequence, effectuated its reembarkation without any obstacle. The following day the entire fleet of Admiral Cochrane descended the Chesapeake, and left the shores that it had proposed to destroy.

MONROE

Chapter XII

Farewells of the Inhabitants of Baltimore to Lafayette – Trip from Baltimore to Washington – Entrance into This City – Visit to the President – Description of Washington – Jesuits.

Our departure from Baltimore had all the luster of our entrance into this City, but it was not enlivened as the latter was by the noisy shouts of public joy. All the troops were assembled between the City and Fort McHenry, in order to carry out some grand maneuvers in the presence of General Lafayette, after which they offered us a farewell dinner under an immense tent, in which we discovered nearly every part illustrated by American valor during the War of 1814. During the meal, which Generals Smith, Harper and Striker, and Colonels Howard, Carroll and Bentalou, and some other veterans of liberty attended, they made a large number of patriotic toasts, one among others to General Smith, in which they paid him the tribute of praise and gratitude that his wonderful conduct as Commander-in-chief of the Maryland troops during the last war merited. The modesty with which the old warrior received this expression of esteem from his fellow-citizens proved to us how much liberty and good institutions inspire generous sentiments in men who enjoy them. He rose hastily, and, in a short speech full of the warmth of his soul, he reproached his friends for concentrating their gratitude on him alone, while so many brave men had more right to it than himself. "My arrangements and my orders would have been ineffectual," he cried out, "if I had not had free men for soldiers, and if I had not been so skillfully seconded by my worthy friend, General Striker... . O my fellow citizens stop, stop praising only me!...You would not want a republican to save for himself the honor of a victory which is common to us all... ."

At the end of the meal, a young officer requested permission to sing some verses composed by him. They were filled with those generous sentiments that the magical names of liberty, Washington and Lafayette naturally give birth to among Americans. He sang them with stirring expression; but when he came to the end and pronounced the name of the one whom he was singing of, his emotion betrayed his voice; he could not finish, and rushing headlong to the hand of Lafayette, covered it with his tears, and took flight to escape the accolades that his heart and spirit deserved.

The sun in approaching the horizon warned us that we had no more time to lose if we wanted to take advantage of the light to begin our trip. At once we left the table to go to our carriages, which awaited us some distance in the plain; but the crowd which surrounded them was so numerous that soon, in spite of the troubles of the people who were conducting us, the three of us were separated; the General and his son were, so to speak, carried in triumph on the arms of the citizens; and it was a long time before I could join them.

I have already stated that the day was very advanced when we separated ourselves from the citizens of Baltimore. The night overtook us on our way and made the trip very arduous for our escort, which had been constantly on foot since morning. This consideration, coupled with the desire that they had that General Lafayette enter Washington only during the day, caused the committee of arrangements to propose to him that he stop to sleep en route. The General accepted, and, soon after, we arrived in front of an inn where they invited him to alight. But as we were going to set foot on the ground, we heard a great tumult of jumbled voices that uttered the name of *Waterloo* with anger. At the same moment, an officer of the escort appeared at the carriage door and informed the General that the inn before which we stood bore the name *Waterloo* and asked him if he was agreeable to lodging there. The General answered that he would willingly go farther if he was not afraid of causing too much fatigue to the horsemen; but the latter asserted that they preferred to ride the horses to death rather than to permit him to stay any longer in a house whose name could recall regrettable memories to a Frenchman, and we immediately resumed our trip. Our militiamen, raging against the innkeeper, wanted first to set out to overturn his sign, and they would have done it if their leader had not prevented them by reminding them of the sacred right of property.

We slept two or three miles further on in an excellent inn where they told us how an old *Tory*, living in this country, and still very transfixed with this infatuation for the English, had rented this house to a poor innkeeper on the condition that he give it the name *Waterloo*. "But," added the one who gave us these details, "everyone mocks him, and no one wants to enter this inn; he is obligated to indemnify the innkeeper, but he is rich and obstinately sticks to this."

On the following day, October 12th, during the morning, Captain Sprigg appeared at the head of his fine company of cavalry, arranged in battle array and ready to escort General Lafayette up to Washington. Captain Sprigg was not long ago Governor of the State of Maryland, which he administered for several years in a manner to gain for himself the esteem and affection of all his fellow citizens. On leaving his government to return to private life, he believed that there remained for him still some duties to fulfill to his Fatherland. He organized a voluntary company of cavalry nearly entirely at his own expense and gave it a brave Polish officer, Colonel Lehmanowsky, who had fought in the ranks of the French Army for 20 years, as an instructor; and, overlooking his previous high position, he did not believe that it detracted from the dignity of an ex-governor to wear the modest uniform of captain. One could not refrain from a feeling of profound respect in seeing this patriotic soldier, surrounded by his cavalry, nearly all of whom are farmers of the county which he inhabits, busying themselves with military instruction, improvement of their organization, and especially development of their patriotic sentiments that his words and his example strengthen more every day. Captain Sprigg is also a father of an affectionate family, an active farmer and an enlightened man. At each step in this fortunate country, one finds similar characters.

Soon we encountered the municipal officers of Washington, the militias and the people who came to meet General Lafayette; then we left our carriages to pass into uncovered carriages, and a short time later we entered the Capital of the United States.

We had already been in the enclosure of the City for a half an hour, however, before our glances had encountered a single dwelling. Drawn on a gigantic scale, the plan of Washington cannot be filled out for a century. Only the space separating the Capitol Building from the President's House is inhabited, and this space has already formed a medium-sized town. Our movement, since entering the City up to the Capitol, was marked by cannon fire, and often slowed by the crowd that pressed around the procession. After having passed under a triumphal arch, we entered the Capitol Building, where General Lafayette was awaited by all the administrative authorities of the City. They led him on to an exterior balcony where the Mayor, in the presence of all the people assembled on the square, gave a speech to him in the name of the City. Upon leaving the Capitol, the procession set out again and led us slowly across the City up to the President's House; the route was lined by young people from the schools and by numerous militia corps. On this ride, we passed under the windows of some ambassadors of the Holy Alliance, for whom, doubtless, a triumph so beautiful, so pure and so simple, was a phenomenon they did not comprehend.

We arrived in front of the President's House: it is a very simple house, but in very good taste. It is constructed out of rather hard, white stone; it has only one story, and it comes to an end in an Italian-style platform. This first story is raised a little above the ground, and one arrives in it by an elegant colonnade; the courtyard in front of the house is formed by a beautiful iron grill with three gates of which the entrance is defended by neither guards, ushers, nor insolent valets. The crowd that accompanied the procession stopped in front of the grill, and we entered the palace accompanied only by the municipal authorities. A single servant opened the principal door, and we were then introduced into the reception room.

It is quite large, of elliptical shape, ornate and hung with tapestry with a very remarkable sumptuousness and severity of taste. The President, seated at the end of the large diameter of the room in an armchair, which was distinguishable from the other seats neither by its shape nor by its height, had with him the four State Secretaries; to his right and to his left were arranged in a semicircle the General officers of the Army and the Navy, some senators, and all the administrative leaders of the Government. All were clad, like the President, in a simple blue coat without braids, without embroidery, without decorations, without all those childish ornaments for which so many fools cool their heels in the antechambers of the palaces of Europe.

At the moment General Lafayette entered, all those assembled rose; the President went hurriedly to meet him, embraced him with all the affection of a brother, came next to us, took us by the hands with gentle affection, and presented all three of us individually to each person in the room beginning with the ministers. After this introduction, the circle broke up, groups were formed, and private conversations commenced on different points. During this time, the President, having joined the three of us near him, addressed the General in these words:

> You have learned by my last letter how much I want to have you in my house, you and your two traveling companions, during your stay in this City; but I am obliged to give up this pleasure. The people of Washington lay claim to you; they say that you are the Nation's Guest and that nobody other than themselves has the right to house you. I have yielded to the voices of the people, and the municipality has prepared a townhouse for you and has put a carriage at your disposal, in order to provide for all your needs. You must accept, but I hope that this will not prevent you from considering my house as yours. Your places will always be set at my table, and, every time that you have no engagements with the citizens, I want you to dine nowhere else but at my house. As for this evening, I know that the municipality expects you at a public banquet; tomorrow you will attend with it a grand dinner that I am giving for the principal officers of the Government, but once these ceremonies have concluded, I will do everything that I can to see to it that you will be as often as possible in my household....

This invitation was so urgently made and so cordial that the General did not hesitate to accept it, and added our thanks to his.

On the following day, in fact, we came to dine at the President's House; we found the ministers and the municipal, judicial and military authorities already assembled there. Before placing us at the table, Mr. Monroe introduced us to his wife, his two daughters and his sons-in-laws. We found in this entire family the same cordiality, the same simplicity as in the supreme leader of the Nation. Mrs. Monroe, although having passed the age of 50, can still be cited as a remarkably beautiful woman. Her amiability hardly permits one to notice the slight influence that time has had on her visage.

In the President's seating us at the table, I noticed that one place alone was designated; it was the one for General Lafayette, whom the President sat to his right. The other guests took their places at random, but all with a remarkable modesty; each seemed to do his utmost to make one forget about his high rank. Chance placed me between the Secretary of the Navy, Mr. Southard, and the Major General of Engineers, Mr. Macomb. The latter spoke the French language with great fluency. He was kind enough during dinner to answer all my questions, and I asked him very many of them, for all that I was witnessing appeared to me very strange, or at least very different from that which is in Europe. "You see here," he said to me,

> Nearly all the principal leaders of our Government, that is to say the *foremost servants of the people*. They are not very numerous and, consequently, easier to watch over. The people are only served better, and it costs them very little, for, of all these servants, there isn't a single one who would dream of enriching himself; their salaries are generally too small to stimulate greed; one could even rest assured that most of them, forced to neglect their personal affairs for public ones, will leave the administration less wealthy than they were upon joining it; but sufficient compensation awaits them on their return to their hearths; it is the esteem and the gratitude of their fellow citizens, if they have fulfilled their mandate faithfully....

I would have really wanted to have some details about most of these men whom the people call their servants, but the conversation became general and we were soon obliged to give up our private conversation. "On your return from Yorktown, you will probably spend some time here," said General Macomb; "then you will be able to study at your convenience the public character and the domestic customs of our men of state. The study of this can be of great interest to a European, and if I can make it easier for you by some explanations you will require, I will give them to you with pleasure." I eagerly accepted General Macomb's offer, and I promised myself to profit well from his good counsel.

The following three days, which we passed in Washington, were used by the General to visit Georgetown, which is separated from the Capital of the United States only by a small stream, and which also gave him a brilliant reception; to receive a large number of citizens each day; and to spend some time with the family of his paternal friend, Washington. For me, I took advantage of these three days to visit the City and its monuments, and to gather some notes on the District of Columbia.

Some time after liberty, commerce and industry had effaced the bloody traces of the Revolutionary War and rendered calm the great American family of the United States, Congress thought with reason that each State, in particular, having need of its entire independence, none of them could accommodate for a very long time the presence of the Central Government, which itself needed to locate itself so as to avoid every influence of locality. As a consequence, it acquired a small portion of land on the borders of Maryland and Virginia, and established the seat of its operations there in 1800. This portion of land, which is ten square miles and which the Potomac River traverses, was named the District of Columbia and was placed under the direct administration of Congress. The two largest quarters of the District of Columbia are Georgetown and Alexandria, both older than the forming of the District. The first is very prettily situated on the slope of a hill between the Potomac and Rock Creek; its population is about 7,000; it contains a foundry for cannons of which I will have an occasion to speak later; but its commerce, although active enough, is rather less extensive than that of Alexandria, situated seven miles lower on the right bank of the Potomac. The population of the latter is 8,000, and its exports, which consist principally of flour, raise nearly $900,000 annually.

As to the City of Washington, it is, as I have already said, formed on so large a scale that its 13,000 inhabitants gave it the look of a town. Without its public monuments, one would take it for a newborn colony, striving to clear land for cultivation. In some of its quarters, more than 20 minutes are required to go from one dwelling to another, and, on the way, it is not rare to encounter a plough laboriously turning up a field which probably will still produce crops instead of monuments for half a century. The projected streets are all wide, straight and parallel to each other. But one of the greatest mistakes that has been made is not to have preserved on each side a line of trees that would have marked the directions better and would have offered cover against the heat of the sun.

The most beautiful monument of Washington City is without any doubt the Capitol. It contains two halls, spacious and very well laid out for the meetings of the House of Representatives and the Senate, another for the sessions of the Supreme Court of the United States, and a national library. The Capitol was burned in 1814 by the English, who conducted themselves like Vandals when they took Washington; but today it has left behind its cinders, and is more spacious and more sumptuous. They were still working on it when I visited it.

The naval arsenal, which is situated not far from the Capitol, is one of the most beautiful and magnificent establishments of its kind. All the woodwork and ironwork is carried out there by steam-powered machines. I saw several large frigates under construction there. The weapons rooms appeared to me to be plentifully supplied. They pointed out to me guns intended for the defense of entrenchments; they are composed of several guns bound in clusters above a single support which can shoot 50 shots in succession without being reloaded. Commodore Tingey, who commands this arsenal, and who did the honors of it with a kindness that one does not know how to commend too much, had promised to allow me to try one of these guns, but, the time having been short, I was not able to judge their usefulness, which some American officers praised very much. In the middle of the principal courtyard stands a memorial column built in honor of the American sailors killed before Algiers in 1804.

Constructed out of white marble, and encircled by allegorical figures, it was executed with great skill. But, in 1814, the English, basely jealous of all foreign glory, tried to destroy it; it still bears numerous marks of sword cuts with which they had struck it in their brutal fury. The Americans have not removed any of them, and have hardly raised their voice against this act of vandalism; but they have engraved on the base of the monument, in large characters, this stern phrase: *Mutilated by the English in 1814*.

After the Capitol, the most noteworthy monument is the President's House. The four large buildings that surround it, and which serve in the administration of the four ministries, are commodious, spacious, and solidly built, but have nothing remarkable in their construction. The City Hall is not completed, it is even so little advanced that one cannot judge the effect that it will produce as a monument. As for the theater, it is a small shack in which three or four hundred spectators cannot venture without confronting the danger of being crushed.

Columbian College, founded a short time ago, contains as yet only a very small number of students. The choice of director and of professors presages a brilliant future for it; but it has a formidable rivalry in the proximity of Georgetown College. This institution, which we visited the day after our arrival in Washington, and in which General Lafayette was greeted with great displays of gratitude and patriotism, is directed by the Jesuits. When I saw the Reverends in the dress of the Order, I could not at first refrain from a distressing feeling. All the misdeeds with which they reproach the Society of the Jesuits in Europe presented themselves en masse to my startled imagination, and I lamented the blindness of the Americans who entrusted the education of their children to a sect so inimical to every liberty.

Upon returning to Washington, I could not avoid communicating my thoughts and fears to Mr. Cambreling, a young representative of the State of New York with whom I was passing the evening. He listened to me at first with a smile, but, when he heard me express the wish that all Jesuits should have been driven out of public education in every country, he shook his head with a look of disapproval. "This action," he said, "will never be taken by us; at least I hope it won't be; it would be, in my opinion, contrary to the spirit of freedom that animates us; it would be unjust with regards to the Jesuits, about whom we have had nothing to complain, and besides I do not know of any power in our society that would entitle us to prescribe this measure." – "It is possible that you have not had cause to complain about the Jesuits because here they are still not very numerous, and they have not yet attained power, but patience.... See what has happened in Europe and tremble!" – "That which has happened in Europe can never take place among us; inasmuch as we will be wise enough not to change our institutions; inasmuch as we will have *neither king, nor state religion, nor monopoly,* we will not have to dread either intrigues or the influence of any *association* – "Here, close by the government, near which the Jesuits are intriguing?" – "But among us the government is the people. Now, I understand indeed that the Jesuits in Europe by force of intrigues have the ear of a king and have filled his mind with religious terrors, with the aid of which they have torn from him riches, honors, power, etc.; but, sincerely, do you believe that, despite the trickery and shrewdness you assume for them, your Jesuits would ever succeed in persuading an entire nation, free and enlightened to despoil itself for them, to surrender itself to them hands and feet bound? Never! Besides, what would be the voice that they would raise to make themselves heard and to persuade?" – "Public Education." – "But in order that public education be for them an effective means of action, it would be necessary for it to be their monopoly; now, thanks to the wisdom of our institutions, we have no monopolies of any kind; we do not groan as you do under the leaden yoke of a privileged university. Among us, each father of the family is the sole judge of the manner by which it suits him to raise and educate his children, and, from this, there is competition among all who want to devote themselves to the practice of public education, competition maintained only by a sincere attachment to our institutions, a deep respect for the laws which are our handiwork, and the practice of all the virtues which make a good citizen. The Jesuits themselves are required to fulfill these conditions in order to gain the confidence of the public and they have gained it: to the extent that they shall earn it, I do not see by what right one would come to deprive them of the exercise of a right which is common to all; and if one day they will render themselves unworthy of it, public opinion will mete out justice to them...." – "Well! My God," I cried out, "with us also public opinion should be able to mete out justice, but public opinion can drive them neither from the university, the councils of the prince, the wealthy institutions they have founded, nor from the occupations they have invaded." – "Well then!" replied my young representative coldly, "*Don't have any of that,* and your Jesuits then will be no more dangerous than ours."

TOMBEAU DE WASHINGTON

à Mount-Vernon (Virginie).

Chapter XIII

Departure for Yorktown – Washington's Tomb – Celebration of the Anniversary of the Taking of Yorktown – Details of the Siege of This Town in 1781.

The militias of Virginia had for a long time evidenced to General Lafayette their desire to celebrate with him the anniversary day of the taking of Yorktown, on the very terrain that had seen the accomplishment of this great event that, in ending the Revolutionary War, assured forever the independence of the United States. In order to accept this honorable invitation, the General left Washington on the 16th of October, crossed the Potomac on a bridge more than a mile long, and was welcomed on the Virginia side by a corps of troops under the command of General Jones. His ride up to Alexandria and his entrance in this Town were marked by the continuous sound of the artillery placed on his route and by the acclamations of the people who accompanied it. We dined and slept in Alexandria. It was at the moment when we were going to sit down at the table with all the magistrates and a large number of citizens that the Secretary of State, Mr. Adams, informed us of the death of the King of France, Louis XVIII.

On the 17th, we embarked on the steamship, *The Petersburg*, which had on board the Minister of War, Mr. Calhoun, Generals Macomb and Jones, and a large number of other officers as well as very many citizens. After sailing for two hours, the cannon of Fort Washington informed us that we were approaching the final resting place of the eldest son of American liberty: at this sad signal, to which the band accompanying us responded with doleful tones, we climbed up on the bridge, and the land of Mount Vernon offered itself to our gazes. At this sight an involuntary and spontaneous movement caused us to kneel down. Some longboats facilitated our landing and soon we tread upon the soil Washington had so often tread upon; a carriage received General Lafayette, and the other travelers ascended silently the steep footpath that leads to the solitary dwelling of Mount Vernon. In returning under this hospitable roof that had served as a refuge for him when the *crimes of the terror* snatched him violently from his Fatherland and his family, George Lafayette felt his heart break in finding the one whose paternal cares had assuaged his misfortune no longer there, the one whose example and wise lessons had inspired in his young mind those generous sentiments that today make him an example for good citizens, the model for fathers and husbands, the most devoted son, the most reliable friend; and his father recollected with emotion all that which the companion of his glorious works recalled to his mind.

Three descendants of Washington came to take the General, his son and me to the tomb of their uncle; our numerous companions of the trip went into the house, and, some minutes later, the cannon of the Fort boomed anew, announcing to the whole country that Lafayette was rendering homage to the ashes of Washington. Simple and modest as he who rests there after his death was during his life, the tomb of the citizen-hero is hardly noticed across the black cypress trees surrounding it. A hillock, raised a little and covered with grass, a door made of wood without inscriptions, some wreaths already dry and others still green, indicate to the traveler who visits these premises the place where the one whose powerful arms broke the chains of his Fatherland rests in peace. At our approach, the door was opened, General Lafayette descended alone at first into the burial vault, and some minutes later reappeared on the threshold, his face inundated with tears; he took his son and me by the hand, made us enter with him, and with the motion of his hand pointed out to us the coffin of his fatherly friend; he rests beside the woman who was his companion during his life and whom death now joins to him forever. We bowed down together in front of the coffin near to which we respectfully brought our lips; in getting up, we threw ourselves into the arms of General Lafayette, and we mixed our tears with his sorrows....

Upon leaving the burial vault we found the three descendants of Washington praying fervently for their uncle and mixing into their prayers the name of Lafayette. One of them, Mr. Custis, offered the General a golden ring containing some hair of the great man, and took us down the road to the house where our traveling companions awaited us. An hour was devoted to visiting the house and the gardens, which are now the property of a nephew of Washington who carries his name, and fills one of the highest places in the American judiciary. He wanted to change nothing about the property that was left to him by his uncle, in the memory of whom he renders the most respectful and fond devotion. George Lafayette assured him that all in this house was still such as he had left it 28 years ago. He found, in the place where Washington had fastened it himself, the principal key to the Bastille that Lafayette had sent to him at the time of the destruction of this monument to despotism. The shipping ticket is still carefully preserved with the key.

The location of Mount Vernon on the right bank of the Potomac is very picturesque and overlooks the course of this majestic river in the distance. The house, small and very simple, is surrounded by beautiful woods. The tomb is 200 paces from the house.

After some moments of rest, we took the footpath that descends to the river bank; our walk was in silence; each of us carried in his hand a branch of cypress cut from above Washington's tomb. We resembled a grieving family who was coming from putting a cherished father who had recently died in the ground. Already we were on board, already the rapid waves had carried us far, however, no one had broken the silence of his meditation.... Finally, Mount Vernon disappeared behind the winding and high banks of the river, everyone drew near, formed a group on the stern of the ship, and listened attentively to Lafayette speak of Washington into the evening.

A little after our departure from Mount Vernon, we encountered the steamship, *The Potomac*, which was carrying on board a company of volunteers from Fredericksburg, commanded by Captain Crutchfield, and a large number of passengers who came before the General. The two boats, after having exchanged greetings, sailed together during the entire night, and arrived on the following day at the mouth of the York River where they found five other ships, with which they sailed up the river to the town of Yorktown. We stopped for a moment opposite the point marked for our landing, and, at a signal given by the artillery stationed on the river bank, we landed with the aid of longboats commanded by the brave Captain Elliot, the same man who contributed so strongly to the destruction of the English Navy on Lake Erie on September 10, 1813.

The General was greeted on land by the committee of Yorktown, by the Governor of Virginia and his Council, by the Chief Justice of the United States, John Marshall, and by a large number of Army officers. The higher banks of the river were filled with a crowd of ladies who had come from very far, and its waters offered a view altogether picturesque in the number, variety and the arrangement of the ships with which they were covered. After having responded to the speeches of Mr. Leigh, President of the committee, and of the Governor of the State of Virginia, General Lafayette was led to the headquarters which they had prepared for him in the midst of the acclamations of the people. His headquarters were established in the very same house which Cornwallis had inhabited during the siege of the Town, 43 years before.

Yorktown, which has never recovered from the disasters of the Revolutionary War because its dangerous location could not attract new inhabitants, appeared to us, by its current condition, very appropriate to mark the fete that we were to attend on the morrow. Some houses in ruin, blackened by fires, or riddled with bullets; the land covered with remnants of arms, bomb blasts and overturned gun carriages; tents grouped together or dispersed, according to the nature of the terrain; small squads of soldiers placed at different points; all, in a word, offered to us the image of a camp set up in haste around a village taken and occupied after an unrelenting struggle. The manner in which we were lodged added more to the illusion of this tableau: a single bed had been prepared and was offered to General Lafayette, and all those who accompanied him, officers, generals, Governor, even ministers, took their places pell-mell on some mattresses or straw in unfurnished, half-covered rooms. During the night, 60 officers, formed in a voluntary company, stood guard at the headquarters, around which they bivouacked.

On the 19th, as soon as the day appeared, the booming cannon in the plain broke our sleep and made all the troops that surrounded us take arms. General Lafayette, accompanied by the arrangements committee, went under Washington's tent, which had traveled with us and which was set up some distance from the headquarters. There he received the different officer corps of the regiments surrounding us. During this presentation, we witnessed the most moving scenes. Two old Revolutionary soldiers fell down in a faint while squeezing the hand of their former general. But that which especially attracted the attention of the spectators was the appearance of Colonel Lewis, who presented himself in the dress of a highland Virginian, and requested permission to speak to Lafayette in the name of the citizens of his district. "General," he said,

> The children of the mountains join wholeheartedly with their brothers of the plains to celebrate your return to this country; they rejoice that you have been given the opportunity to appreciate, after an absence of 40 years, the happy results of *self-government*, founded on the natural rights of man, rights which you so nobly have contributed to being recognized. When, in your youth, you came voluntarily across the frothy mountains of the deep Ocean to fight and spill your blood for the independence of America, you were doubtless far from foreseeing such fortunate results. Then we were only a weak little tribe with regard to military resources in the eyes of the universe, but already there burned in our hearts the sacred love of liberty! We dared to fight, and thanks to Lafayette, and his generous nation, we conquered!...
>
> Now, see!... We are 10,000,000 inhabitants, we have cut down those immense forests that contained in their bosom the savage man and ferocious beast, and in their place we cultivate fertile fields, we raise villages that soon are changed into wealthy cities. Our commercial flag floats on all the seas, and our navy, now triumphant, plows the vast Ocean! Such is the influence of a free government founded on wise, humane laws,

> which are executed in good faith! However, a sad thought comes to disturb the happiness which we are enjoying in seeing you again. We dread your return to Europe; the despots of that hemisphere are jealous of your always growing glory, sustained by virtues which they are incapable of practicing, and their easily offended politics can yet shut you up inside the walls of their dungeons. So stay with us, Lafayette, stay with us! In each of our homes, you will find a domestic hearth; in each of our hearts, you will find a friend. Our filial love will delight your last years, and, when it please the powerful God of nature to call you back into his bosom, you shall present yourself to him, crowned with the benedictions of a free and powerful nation, and we will respectfully place your ashes beside those of your immortal adoptive father, and we will water your tomb with tears of gratitude.
>
> What I have said, it is in the name of the Children of the Mountains.

As soon as Colonel Lewis had completed this speech, which was warmly applauded by the audience, the General took his hands fondly into his own, thanked him affectionately and prayed that he express all his gratitude to the Children of the Mountains of Virginia. He quickly recapitulated their good deeds and numerous services they had rendered to him during the Revolution.

At eleven o'clock, all the troops approached the headquarters, near which they formed in columns, and some moments later they began to march in order to conduct General Lafayette under a triumphal arch they had built on the same location of the English fortification that he had taken possession of in the past, at the head of the American troops that he commanded during the siege of Yorktown. His march took place through a double line of ladies whose animated joy and elegant dress contrasted conspicuously with the trappings of war that surrounded us. He was welcomed under the triumphal arch by General Taylor, who, after the different corps had occupied the places assigned to them, and silence was established in the midst of the crowd surrounding him, took the floor and in an eloquent speech, rapidly developed the themes of enthusiasm and gratitude which the Americans felt for Lafayette. "Here, around us," he said,

> Everything speaks to us of the past and awakens our memories. These plains, on which the plow of peace has not yet effaced the traces of the works of war, these ramparts half

knocked over, this village in ruins in the middle of which one still recognizes the pits hollowed out by bombs, reminds us how long, cruel and uncertain was this struggle, on the outcome of which the emancipation of our Fatherland depended.

There, on this little rise, the last scene of this bloody drama ended in the taking of an entire army, and our liberty was assured forever. In the presence of such memories, how do we contain our gratitude for the hero whose courage assured us the benefits of liberty.

The soil we tread upon was then a fortification occupied by the enemy, and our vivid imagination recalls to us at once the young chief whose valor rendered us masters of it! Can we then be here without reminding ourselves also that, rising above those preconceptions which mastered every mind, even the most generous, he knew how to discern, in the initial resistance of an obscure and faraway colony, the movement of such moral force that it was destined to give a new direction and a new character to political institutions and to ameliorate the lot of the human race? Can we forget that, deaf to the seductions of power, ambition and pleasures, he came then to offer to us with a noble prodigality, his sword, his fortune and the influence of his noble example?

And, when, in the old warrior who presents himself to us today, we recognize that young leader, with what vividness does our memory retrace for us the events of his life! With what happiness do we see that his entire life has realized the promises of his youth! In the political assemblies as in the camps, in the palaces of kings, as in their dungeons, we find him always animated by the same spirit, the same courage! At one time curbing the abuse of liberty of the popular spirit, at another time opposing the excesses of power, but marching always with a firm step toward the objective of the efforts of his whole life, the moral and political betterment of the entire world.

General! In the most beautiful days of antiquity, it was neither the lure of gold nor ambition for power that aroused men to generous enterprises; a simple oak or laurel branch was the reward for true merit or brilliant services; in order to earn it, the statesman devoted himself with ardor to extended

> thought; the warrior gave generously of his blood, and the orator made heard his most sublime tones. This reward was coveted by all, but virtue alone won it. However, it was feared sometimes that it was conferred too lightly as a result of the enthusiasm of the citizens for recent success.
>
> Here we will not have to fear this drawback; time, which sometimes dulls the brilliance of an ordinary virtue, has made yours more brilliant; after half a century has passed, your triumph is proclaimed by the sons of those who witnessed your exploits.
>
> Be pleased, then, General, to accept this simple, but expressive offering of their gratitude and admiration; permit one of their leaders to place on your brow the sole crown that you will not disdain wearing, the emblem of civic virtues and martial valor. You will not be offended, General, if we have mixed into this crown some cypress branches; they are the expression of our recognition of and regrets for those courageous men who had the glory of sharing your dangers, but who were not to have the good fortune to be present at your triumph; your heart should have been roused with anger against us if, on an occasion so solemn, in the midst of the acclamations of joy which your presence arouses, we had forgotten them.

Here, the speaker advanced towards General Lafayette, placed the crown on his head, and cried out forcefully so as to be heard by all the assembly: "In the presence of the citizens, defenders of Virginia, and on this fortification, scene of his valor, I offer to Lafayette this wreathed crown for a twofold triumph; in combat, he was a hero, and, in civil life, the benefactor of the world!"

General Lafayette was profoundly moved, and his emotion was augmented more by the enthusiasm with which these last words of the orator were received by the multitude. However, always dominated by that modesty which is so strong a characteristic of his, he hastened to snatch the crown from above his head, and turning towards Colonel Fish, one of the officers who had valiantly seconded him in the attack on the fortification: "Look here," he said, "this crown belongs to you also; guard it like a deposit for which we are obligated to account to all our comrades"; then, addressing General Taylor, he directed these thanks to him. "I am happy," he said,

> To receive such honorable evidences of the friendship of my old companions-in-arms in these places where American and

French arms were so gloriously joined in a holy alliance in favor of the independence of America, and the sacred principle of the sovereignty of the people. I am also happy to be greeted in this manner on the very place where my light infantry comrades acquired one of their most honorable rights to the love and the esteem of their fellow-citizens.

He ended by paying a tribute of gratitude to the officers who had directed the attack on the fortification, and among them he named Hamilton, Gimat, Laurens, and Fish, and said that it was in their name, in the name of the light infantry, and only in common with them that he accepted the crown that they had just offered him.

After this ceremony, all the troops filed in front of him, and we returned to the Town, where we passed the rest of the day in the midst of all kinds of rejoicing. A piquant-enough circumstance came to add to the interest of this patriotic and military festival: I have already said that General Lafayette had, in arriving at Yorktown, established his headquarters in the same house where Cornwallis had had his headquarters 43 years before; in examining the cellars in order to properly store the refreshments and the food, some servants discovered a large box in an obscure corner; its weight and its old appearance piqued their curiosity. They opened it and to their great astonishment found it filled with candles, blackened by the passage of time. The inscription they read on the lid of the box apprised them that it was part of Cornwallis' provisions during the siege; soon they made known this discovery in the house; from there it spread rapidly into the camp; in a short time all the candles were brought up, lit and placed in a circle around the camp, where the ladies came to dance the entire evening with the militiamen. A ball in Yorktown in 1824, in the gleam of Cornwallis' candles, appeared such an amusing thing to all our old Revolutionary soldiers that, in spite of their advanced age and the fatigue of the day, most of them did not want to retire until after the candles were entirely consumed.

Although more than half the night had passed when we were permitted to take some rest, nonetheless, the desire to traverse and visit the terrain on which American independence was assured by a brilliant victory with more attention did not permit me to stay in the arms of sleep for long. When I awoke daylight had barely appeared and when I arrived at the ruins of the old surrounding wall of the Town, the first rays of the sun still in the horizon revealed to me the temporary camp of the militia already abandoned. I saw a part of the troops divided in ships being readied to leave the shore, while the diminishing noise of the drum behind the forest which began a little distance from the

Town indicated to me the route the detachments, which were regaining their hearths by land, had taken. Although all around me then offered the exact and piquant tableau of a war scene, my attention was not, however, diverted for a long time from my principal goal. I soon prepared to explore the surrounding wall of the Town, the exterior construction works, and the positions of the two armies from which the *Holy Alliance* had made the independence of a young nation and the rights of man triumph on the American continent.

In spite of the creation of some gardens, and the vain efforts of the plow to fertilize the soil, which offers nearly everywhere only sterile sand in some places, I succeeded easily enough in finding the outline of the wall of the Town. The outline described an arc of which the chord was formed by the York River, which in this spot was very wide and navigable even for frigates, but I had very great difficulty in recognizing the outer works. However, with the aid of a map of the siege, I was pursuing my research when I noticed a man seated at the foot of a little pyramidal monument, who appeared to be immersed in deep thought. On this pyramid were engraved in large characters the names of *Rochambeau*, *Viomesnil*, *Lauzun*, *Saint-Simon*, *Dumas,*[12] in a word, all the principal officers of the French corps who had fought and conquered at Yorktown. While I was reading and rereading with a sweet satisfaction these glorious names that will remind the most distant posterity of the honorable part France took in the struggle of American liberty against English tyranny, the old man got up, I greeted him, and soon we entered into a conversation on the objects that surrounded us and which appeared to interest the two of us equally.

He told me that he had served under the command of Lafayette in the Virginia Campaign and the siege of Yorktown; that, having retired for 40 years in a small farm only a few miles distant from here, he had not yet passed an anniversary of the taking of Yorktown without coming to these places to pay his tribute of sorrows to his old companions and of gratitude to the French Nation. "Since," he said,

> You appear to have so keen an interest in the details of this event, in which I had the good fortune to take an active role, let us ascend together to the part of the fort that has remained standing in the midst of so many ruins; from there, we will be able to take in with a glance the plan of operations, and I will be able to make myself better understood.

---

12. The latter is the same man who today holds an honorable place in the ranks of the constitutional opposition. The career of Mathieu Dumas has not ceased, for a single instant, to be in harmony with his glorious debut.

After the old soldier had looked around us as if to gather his memories, he made me sit down next to him; we turned our backs to the Town, and the plain which the besieging army occupied stretched out before us. "You know," he said to me,

> How Cornwallis, after a campaign of six months, was led by the youthful Lafayette from place to place across Virginia to be trapped in Yorktown, from which he could only leave by laying down his arms. Therefore, I will start my narrative from the time when Lafayette, in establishing himself at Williamsburg, rendered Cornwallis powerless to escape him.
>
> In the first days of September, Cornwallis had tried to reconnoiter our position; but considering that it would be impossible for him to overrun it, and knowing that all retreat was foreclosed to him by the French fleet commanded by Mr. de Grasse, he resigned himself to run the risks of a siege, and began to fortify himself to the best of his ability. Each of us thought that, taking advantage of the enthusiasm which our latest successes aroused in our ranks, Lafayette would not give his adversary the time to get his bearings, and would lead us on the field to a final victory; but the youthful General made proof on this occasion of a moderation, perhaps more admirable than his courage and his skill. Neither the entreaties of his officers who pressed him not to let the occasion of collecting new laurels in bringing the final blow to the English Army escape, nor the offers of Admiral de Grasse who, by Mr. Saint-Simon, proposed to him the support of his garrisons and even of a party of sailors from his 38 ships to second his efforts, could induce him to undertake anything before the arrival of the allied army commanded by Washington and Rochambeau. "When it is a matter of such great importance," he said to them, "I will never prefer the satisfaction of my own pride to the certainty of a shared success"; and he waited up to the end with a patience that would have astonished even an old captain.
>
> On the 13th, Washington and Rochambeau arrived at our camp and went on the 17th aboard *The City of Paris* in order to plan with Mr. de Grasse the means to join the French Fleet in the success of the enterprise. All the combined forces were united on the 26th, and on the 28th we marched on Yorktown

to encircle it; this was done without the loss of a single life. The French corps, commanded by Rochambeau, occupied the space between the high water of the river and a marsh which is nearly facing us, but which you cannot see because it is screened by some woods and some ravines from the shelter of which one could, without risk, restrain the enemy at pistol-range from their works. The grenadiers and the riflemen of the advance guard of this army were commanded by Viomesnil. On the next day, the American Army passed this same marsh and established its left flank there and went to base its right flank at the foot of the York River. The encirclement of the place was thus complete, and tightened as closely as possible. Lauzun's Legion, a cavalry corps, and a half a brigade of American militia went to take their position on the other bank of the river, at Gloucester, where they could only establish themselves after having dislodged Tarleton, who was found there with 400 horsemen and 200 infantrymen.

During the night of the 29th to the 30th, the enemy, fearing to be confronted with a surprise attack in the very extended position it had fortified, took the course of abandoning its camp on *Pigeon Hill*, which you see there in front of us, and retaining only the two fortifications outside the main part of the place. The day of the 30th was used to lodge us in the works abandoned by the enemy, which put us within reach of confining the enemy in a less extended circle and gave us the greatest advantages. From the time we cut open a trench, a noble competition established itself between our brave allies and us. Although quite young as soldiers, and without experience of the operations of a siege, we had, however, the satisfaction of earning the praise of the French who agreed that, by our zeal and our intelligence, we deserved being associated with experienced troops.

Messrs. Duportail and Querenet managed the works at the head of the engineers; d'Aboville commanded the French artillery, and General Knox the American artillery. In spite of enemy fire, the trenching proceeded rapidly; as early as the 9th, three batteries were already operative on this spot. General Washington himself fired the first cannon, and, at this signal, we began a furious cannonade to which the enemy responded with the greatest vigor. On the 10th, some red-hot cannon balls, fired from a French battery and directed at a small English squadron stationed on the river, set fire to a vessel of 44 cannons and to two other smaller boats. This fire, which began in the evening and continued very far into the night, offered to the eyes of the besiegers and the besieged a terrible and magical spectacle. The consuming flames hurled themselves in high columns along the masts and spread a lugubrious brightness on all our batteries, which seemed to lend us their lights only to facilitate the means of our destroying each other. This combat of the night ended only when the fire, lacking nourishment, returned us to the darkness.

On the 14th, the English no longer possessed exterior works except two large fortifications; one on the site where Lafayette received the civic crown yesterday was, as you see it, situated here to our left near the foot of the river. The other was very much more to the right, precisely where that pyramid stands at the foot of which we met. At that time Washington resolved to seize them, and the entire day of the 14th and a part of the 15th were employed battering them with cannon fire in order to destroy the abattis which protected the approaches and to facilitate the attack by storming the fortifications. During the entire time that this cannonade lasted, Washington and Rochambeau, on foot, went around with their staff officers, stood as near as possible to the enemy entrenchments to judge better the effects of our batteries, and made themselves admired by the entire army for their cold courage. In order to calm the impatient ardor of Viomesnil, who claimed that they were burning powder uselessly and that the moment to deliver the assault was already favorable, Rochambeau descended alone into the ravine separating him from the enemy, climbed calmly on the opposite side up to the pistol-range of the English batteries, and returned afterwards to assure Viomesnil coldly that the abattis were not yet shattered enough, and that it was necessary to wait at least until the parapet was a little more leveled, *in order that his grenadiers would be exposed for a shorter time.*

Finally, the enemy fire began to slacken, and Washington judged the time favorable to deliver the assault. Lafayette, at the head of the American light infantry, was charged with the attack of the fortification on the left of the besieged forces, and Viomesnil, at the head of the French grenadiers, with that on the right. Lafayette thought with reason that in order to storm the entrenchments defended by experienced soldiers with young troops, it was necessary to count only on the audaciousness and the speed of the attack. Consequently he ordered the men of his division to unload their firearms, formed it in a column, and led it himself, sword in hand and at a run, across the abattis; and in spite of the enemy fire, penetrated into the fortification of which he made himself master in a few minutes. This brilliant success cost him only a few men. He sent his aide-de-camp Barber to Viomesnil at once in order to inform him that he was in his fortification and to ask him where he was. The aide-de-camp found the French general at the head of his column of grenadiers waiting patiently, weapons in hand and under terrible fire of the enemy, for his pioneers to have methodically prepared for him a path across the abattis. "Tell Lafayette," answered Viomesnil, "that I am not yet into mine, but that I will be there in five minutes." As a matter of fact, five minutes later his troop entered the English entrenchments, drums beating and in as good order as in a parade. In this action, the discipline, the courage and the composure of the French grenadiers shone in all their brilliance, but it cost them a considerable number of killed and wounded. As soon as we were masters of the two fortifications, we established good quarters there that were tied to the second parallel, and we built new batteries which accomplished the encirclement of Cornwallis' Army and enabled us to fight indirectly along the entire interior of the place at a shooting range that could only be deadly to that army.

During the night of the 15th and 16th, the enemy made a sally of 600 elite troops commanded by Abercrombie. They met resistance at all our fortifications, but they succeeded in tricking the French posts of the second parallel by presenting themselves as American, and, with the aid of this ruse, arrived at a battery at which they spiked four cannons; immediately the Chevalier de Chastellux arrived with his reserve and forced the English into a precipitous retreat. Thanks to the work of General d'Aboville, commander of the French artillery, the four badly spiked pieces were capable of firing six hours later.

It appeared that this sally had as its principal object the concealment of the retreat of Cornwallis and his army. Indeed, we learned a little after that the English General had resolved to leave behind his sick and his equipment in this place, to cross the river during the night, to attack the troops that occupied Gloucester without warning, and after having crushed them, to clear a way by land to New York; this project was bold and worthy of a man like Cornwallis. Already his boats were readied, already even a part of his troops were landed on the opposite bank, when a violent storm arose suddenly and rendered it absolutely impossible for him to continue his operation. He considered himself very fortunate to have been able to return his troops into the place from where they came before the daylight had come to reveal his secret; he recognized from that time that there was no more hope of safety for him, and on the 17th he requested to hold a parley.

The negotiations lasted until the 19th; they were conducted by the American Colonel Laurens, whose father was a captive in England, and by the Viscount de Noailles. The surrender declared that Cornwallis and his Army would be prisoners of war, that the troops would march gun on shoulder, flags covered, drums beating an English or German march, and that they would come to lay down their arms on the slopes in the presence of the allied armies. This surrender was ratified by the Commanders-in-chief, and at noon detachments of allied troops occupied the principal positions. When the English left the Town to file before us, we were arranged in two lines, the Americans to the right of the road and the French to the left; at the end of these two lines were all our general officers; in the middle of them, one recognized easily our well-loved Washington by his height and by his beautiful battle-horse which he controlled with inimitable grace. At the moment when the head of the English column appeared, all our glances searched for Cornwallis, but detained by an illness, he was represented by General O'Hara. The latter, whether by error, or by calculation, came to present his sword to General Rochambeau, who with a signal pointed out General Washington to him, while saying "that the French Army was only auxiliary, it was from the American General that he must receive commands." O'Hara appeared angered and advanced towards Washington who received him with a noble generosity. It was evident to us that the English, in their misfortune, were particularly driven to despair by being obligated to lay down their arms before the Americans; for their officers and soldiers put on a show of turning their heads towards the French line. Lafayette noticed this, and avenged it in a very pleasant manner; he ordered the band of his light infantry to play the melody of *Yankee Doodle*, a melody which the English had applied to a song they had composed to ridicule us at the beginning of the war, and which they had never failed to sing in front of the prisoners that they had made of us. They were so thin-skinned at this pleasantry that many of them smashed their arms in anger while laying them down on the slopes.

Cornwallis himself shared with his soldiers this weakness of pride which made them redden to be vanquished by those whom they stubbornly considered always rather like rebels than citizens armed for the defense of their rights. On the day following the surrender, finding himself in the midst of the allied generals who had come to visit him, he sought, in speaking to Lafayette, to always separate his glory from that of the Americans: "I decided more willingly to surrender," he said in addressing our young general, "since I knew that beside the Americans were the French, whose character assured me of a humane and honorable treatment for my army" – "And what!" Lafayette answered him sharply, "has your Lordship then so quickly forgotten that *we Americans*, we know also how to be humane towards captive armies." This response, which alluded to the taking of Burgoyne's Army by the Americans some time before, prevented Cornwallis from returning to this subject.

"You see," said the old soldier whom I had not dared to interrupt a single time during his account, with so much interest was I listening,

You see that Lafayette was for us on all occasions a good and ardent friend, he was not content with serving our cause with his counsel, and with his sword in battle, but he defended, moreover, our character and reputation when they were attacked unjustly, while identifying himself with us and making himself jointly responsible for all our actions, so to speak. Besides, the English, who affected so much scorn for us, should have spoken less often of *humanity*, since they offended against this virtue with the most horrible actions every day. We will never forget that during the Virginia Campaign, so glorious for

> our arms and so fortunate for our independence, conflagration, pillage and murder accompanied them across our towns and villages. Often they coldly massacred prisoners after combat, and finally during the siege of Yorktown, giving up hope of conquering us by force of arms, they tried to infect us by sending into our midst more than 100 unfortunate Negroes who had caught smallpox and whom our compassion took in at the foot of their ramparts. But why dwell so long on the crimes of a tyranny that we have destroyed and that a half century of success and liberty ought to have blotted out of our memory? Haven't I besides a sweeter task to fulfill in telling you of the rights that the French army and its virtuous chief have acquired to American gratitude?

He then recounted to me with feeling a host of characteristics that prove, indeed, that never was an army better disciplined, nor did it understand better the duties of an ally as this little French Army. I should add that this evidence of an old American soldier speaking in my presence, so to speak, of the facts that he cited was not the only such evidence that I received during our long trip; everywhere, even in the least hamlets once occupied by the French Army, I heard people commend its strict discipline, its profound respect for property, its patience under hardships, its courage in combat, its moderation in victory; and, I confess, this praise of the noble conduct of my fellow citizens made my heart throb with sweet emotion every time.

Why then does the French Restoration of 1815 which, in order to fasten its colors to glorious memories, or to make the people forget the prodigious warriors of the tricolor cockade, invoke nonstop the plume of Henri IV, that shone only in civil wars, or the flags of Louis XIV, which witnessed only victories too dearly paid for and devastating retreats? Why not claim as a legitimate heritage a part of the glory of the War of American Independence? Is it not so that the grenadiers of Rochambeau marched under the *white flag* in the taking of Yorktown? Is it not the case that our navy immortalized itself while assuring the freedom of a young nation by the rout of the English fleets under the colors of *legitimacy*? Or, indeed, would they repudiate this glory only because it was acquired to the benefit of freedom? I do not know. But what is certain is that while we were celebrating the anniversary of the taking of Yorktown, the French squadron, commanded by Admiral..., which found itself in the Bay of Hampton Roads and could hear the acclamations of American gratitude for the services of France, stayed coldly uninvolved with a festival that it should have considered a family festival for the two nations. Moreover, we knew that this indifference or this repugnance that one cannot explain was shared neither by the crew nor by the majority of the officers. Among the latter, some managed to leave their ship secretly, and, concealed under civilian dress, attended incognito this patriotic scene, in which the Americans would have hastened to place them in the first row if they had been allowed to appear in their uniforms and under their colors.

When I returned to headquarters, I found our traveling companions very occupied with this question, and several of them stated that the French Admiral had conducted himself in this manner by reason of instructions that had been given to him by a higher authority.

Chapter XIV

Route from Yorktown to Richmond by Williamsburg and Norfolk – History of Virginia – Some Considerations on Slavery of the Blacks.

The acclamations of gratitude and the tumult of arms, which had momentarily disturbed the habitual calm of Yorktown, had already ceased when, on the morning of the 20th, we began to proceed to Williamsburg, former capital of the State of Virginia, today a second-rate town, which has preserved hardly anything any more of its bygone importance. Its college, founded under the reign of William and Mary and bearing their names, was still celebrated for its excellent curriculum for half a century, but it seems to have shared the sad fate of the town to which it belongs. Williamsburg is situated in a plain between the *York River* and the *James River*. Two creeks that flow into these large rivers draw near to one another, a little before the town, and create a narrow causeway, as it were, on which General Lafayette had established that excellent position which Cornwallis put to the test without success when he wanted to try to get out of the trap his young adversary had made him fall into. Although the population of Williamsburg can be scarcely more than 1,400 or 1,500, the General was welcomed with great emotion, and had the pleasure to embrace a rather large number of old friends with whom he passed the day. On the second day following, we went to embark at Jamestown in order to go to Norfolk. Our sail on the *James River* was very interesting for the General and for some of his old traveling companions, who, at each point on the river, saw a page of the history of their glorious Virginia Campaign.

It was nearly five o'clock when we arrived in the huge Hampton harbor; the sun already hurled its rays obliquely on the *Fort Oldpoint-Comfort*, which appeared to us from afar to rest on the smooth surface of the sea. Beyond we noticed several vessels whose majestic sides were raised like high defensive walls; they were the ships of the French squadron. Some cannon blasts that we heard towards the south, and the columns of smoke rising toward us from that direction indicated the position of Norfolk. It is situated on flat and marshy terrain at the entrance to the Elizabeth River and appears above the surface of the waters only when one is very near to it. Our ship soon touched the piers of the Town, and upon his landing, General Lafayette was saluted by the sound of artillery from the two forts that defended the entrance to the river and from ships in the Port.

I will not undertake to describe the festivities prepared by the inhabitants of Norfolk to receive the Nation's Guest; they were, as everywhere, stamped strongly with a patriotic character and the gratitude of the people. The young girl, who under the emblem of the spirit of Norfolk, received General Lafayette under a triumphal arch and expressed to him the feelings of the citizens, deserves, however, particular remembrance; her beauty, her eloquence, and the modest assurance with which she carried out her mission made so profound an impression on all the spectators that doubtless time will not erase it.

Of all the towns which we have visited up to now, Norfolk is the one that offers the least agreeable appearance; the houses are generally badly constructed; the streets are narrow and poorly aligned. By reason of the marshes surrounding it, the air there is unhealthy and illnesses are common during autumn. Its population has not quite risen to 4,000. However, its commerce is very active with the States of the North, with Europe, and especially, with the West Indies; its Port, which because of its depth can receive the largest vessels and because of its area can hold at least 300 of them, is the single good port of Virginia and North Carolina; so that it is through Norfolk that all the imports and exports of these two States are made. The exports consist principally of corn, wheat, flour, maize, wood of all kinds, meat and salted fish, iron, lead, tobacco, tar and turpentine.

One finds at Norfolk a rather large number of French families having emigrated from Saint-Domingue. These families first chose this refuge because it was nearest to them, and afterwards they undertook to settle there because of the Slavery of the Blacks that allowed them to keep and employ the unfortunate Negroes they had been able to bring along in their flight. It is a sad and revolting spectacle that some of these refugee settlers, who can find no other means of contending with their troubles than by sacrificing their unfortunate Slaves to hard labor of which they gather the receipts, offer still today. Very many Slaves who work in the Port are Slaves hired out in this manner to tradesmen who board them and pay them 75 *cents* per day, which they faithfully pay each day to their indolent masters.

On the next day, we visited Portsmouth, a very small town situated exactly opposite it, on the left bank of the *James River*, which contains a beautiful ship-building establishment. There we saw a superb vessel of 74 called *The North Carolina*, which had been only afloat for a few days. On returning to Norfolk, we were welcomed with great pomp by the Freemasons, who had the kindness to admit all three of us as honorary members of their lodge. In the evening, there was a very brilliant ball to which the citizens of Norfolk hoped to see the officers of the French squadron come, but it appeared that the same reasons that had prevented them from appearing at the Yorktown festivities also deprived them of the pleasure of coming to dance with the ladies of Norfolk; for we did not see a single one of them, at least in uniform. Upon leaving the ball, that is to say at eleven o'clock, we retook our place on the steamship which immediately began to go up the Elizabeth River again to take us to Richmond, capital of Virginia, from which we were still 100 miles distant. They waited for the Nation's Guest with so much more impatience there as this City contains, in comparison to its population, the greatest number of witnesses of his efforts to the benefit of American independence. It is at Richmond, as a matter of fact, and around its walls that the multiple actions between Lafayette and the traitor Arnold, supported by General Phillips, took place.

All business was suspended in order to welcome Lafayette, and despite an extremely inconvenient rain that fell abundantly and even kept us on board for some time longer, the eager crowd proceeded up to Osborn, where he was to disembark, to meet him. The official entrance could only take place on the following morning. Forty soldiers who had fought in the Revolutionary War were presented to him immediately after his arrival, and among these several had served under his command in Virginia. It was with a feeling of emotion that they saw their former general again, and he, also full of emotion, astonished them by recognizing them and by calling by their names those soldiers who more particularly had shared his works and his dangers.

On the following day, the bad weather having ceased, the festivals resumed their course with a new splendor. It was at the Capitol, modeled on *La Maison Carrée* of Nimes, and situated on the most elevated part of the City, that the General was greeted and addressed by Chief Justice Mr. Marshall, in the presence of the civil and military authorities and a great gathering of citizens. Among the citizens we had the pleasure of finding some French, and particularly Mr. Chevalié, who for nearly 30 years has lived in Virginia where he has not stopped enjoying the friendship and the esteem of his adoptive fellow-citizens. In spite of the multiplicity of festivities in the middle of which we were as if swept along during our stay in Richmond, we were able, however, to spend some time in the private company of the most distinguished men of the City; it was in the always instructive conversations with them that I collected the details which I wanted on the history, the Constitution and the customs of Virginia which I am going to relate here.

That part of the American continent called Virginia, which was one of the oldest English Colonies of the Western Hemisphere and which now forms one of the largest States of the great republican family of the United States, was discovered, according to the English, by John Cabot and by Verrazano, according to the French. Verrazano took possession of it in the name of Francis I. But whoever should be the fortunate seafarer who landed first on this fertile land, it is nonetheless true that its first settlements date only from 1587, the time at which Walter Raleigh took possession of it in the name of a company of English merchants. This feeble colony was composed of only 500 individuals in 1605, yet it was not long in being reduced to about 60 by hardships of all kinds and by the repeated attacks of the Indians. It is probable that these weak remnants would have been destroyed entirely before long if a new expedition, composed of three ships commanded by Captain Newport, had not come to bring them aid in men, arms and provisions. It was then that Jamestown was founded and that its feeble ramparts offered to the Colonists a refuge against the arrows of the Indians.

But new trials were reserved for the Colonists. To war and to famine was soon joined dissension, and the Colony would have doubtless been destroyed if the influence of a single capable man to save it had not finally prevailed. Captain Smith soon became the soul of the Colony by his courage and his skill. He successfully waged war against tribes that refused to negotiate, and he contracted alliances of friendship with others, which soon brought plenty to the Colony. It was already flourishing and beginning to forget its initial misfortunes when Captain Smith was taken prisoner by some enemy Indians who would have surely put him to death if the young Pocahontas, daughter of Powhatan, Chief of the tribe, had not by her entreaties and her tears obtained his reprieve at the moment when the funeral pyre was being lit for his torture.

Restored to freedom, after some time Captain Smith hurried to return to Jamestown, where he found the Colony reduced again to the most miserable condition. Only 38 persons had survived, and they were making ready to entrust their existence that they had put in jeopardy by their lack of foresight and their presumptuousness to a frail longboat. Captain Smith still had enough influence on them to hold them back; his actions created some new resources for them, and new reinforcements were brought to them by Newport. The Colony began again to prosper, but a new incident soon plunged it again into straitened circumstances and was on the brink of destroying it forever. They believed that they could explore for gold in a stream with a sandbank above the village, and the insane desire to amass it led them to abandon the only work by which they could hope for a successful existence. The famine began again to decimate the Colonists, who were again obligated to have recourse to the one whose prudence had saved them so many times.

Smith, opportunely making use of the fear he had struck in some tribes and the friendship he had inspired in others, obtained aid from the Indians that brought plenty back to Jamestown. He then undertook to reconnoiter the country at great distances to determine its resources. To this end, he embarked in a fragile dinghy and, in the midst of all kinds of dangers, explored most of the great watercourses that flowed into the Chesapeake, and reported on them, and on all the territory that actually composes Virginia, with details so precise they still serve today as a foundation for the works of the best geographers. In a word, Smith's genius saved the Colony, and it continued to extend its boundaries up to 1610, a time when a deadly accident prevented him from continuing his works. On returning from an expedition, his powder-box caught fire, and the explosion afflicted him with cruel wounds. His friends pressed him to return to England; he acceded to their solicitations, and six months later, the 500 Colonists that he had left behind well-armed, well-provisioned and beginning to enjoy their herds and harvests, were already reduced to 60 individuals, more like apparitions than men.

Such was the fate of the Colony but for the arrival of three ships and a large number of new immigrants brought by Lord Delaware. This unexpected reinforcement lifted the courage of the Colonists, and the wise administration of Thomas Dale soon gave unforeseen growth to the Colony. It was then that Mr. Rolfe, one of the Colonists, married Princess Pocahontas, the same one who had saved Smith's life. This alliance had immense advantages for the Colonists because Powhatan, as well as all the tribes obedient to him, undertook to support the English in all their wars and to furnish provisions to them. How much is it to be regretted that the example of Mr. Rolfe was not followed by his companions! It would have been very easy for them to assure their prosperity by such alliances, and they would have spared humanity from very much blood and from very many tears!

After this marriage, the Colonists devoted themselves in peace to the cultivation of tobacco, which brought them a great deal of money, and they assumed nearly all the expenses of the Indians, their allies, who proved to be faithful observers of the treaty, although it was very hard on them. Sir Thomas Dale took advantage of this prosperity to perfect the administrative system; but, unfortunately, he had as a successor in 1617 Captain Argall, whose haughty and tyrannical temper was on the point of provoking the greatest disorders, when the Colony again experienced changes of fortune. Recalled by the company, he was replaced by George Hardy who, in order to decide on the ways of correcting the mistakes of his predecessor, convened a general assembly of the inhabitants of Virginia.

From this time dates the introduction of the representative system in this Colony, which was not long in experiencing felicitous results. The company in London gave its assent to this new form of government and fixed the basis for it in a charter that it granted on July 24, 1621. This charter declares:

> That in Virginia there should be in the future a legislative body which should be called *General Assembly*, consisting of a governor, twelve councilors, and representatives of the people; that the councilors and the representatives should make the laws, and that the government should have the power to approve them or reject them; that the laws should not be effective until after they are ratified by the company; and that as soon as the government of the Colony should be formed and be well-established, the orders of the company should not be effective any more in the Colony without the consent of the General Assembly.

The company, however, did reserve the right to name and to dismiss as it pleased the governor and the councilors. In spite of this reservation, the Constitution of Virginia was henceforth settled; and its inhabitants, although they were servants of an association, suddenly found themselves changed into free men and citizens. At the same time, the company sent to Virginia 160 young girls, poor but of irreproachable conduct; they were welcomed eagerly and married to the young Colonists who paid the expenses of their crossing, 120 pounds of tobacco for each girl.

The rights of the company in London, already weakened by the concessions made to the Colonists, were soon repudiated by King James I; and, three years after, Virginia passed under the direct rule of the English Government. Meanwhile the population of Virginia, confined at first in the vicinity of Jamestown, now expanded little by little into a vast country by following the great rivers that flow into the Chesapeake. However, while increasing their forces, the Colonists became less prudent day by day with regard to the nations of the land, on whom they carelessly bestowed all kinds of humiliations. Powhatan was dead, and the tribes whom he had governed had chosen in his place a warrior with a great reputation, who came from the banks of the Gulf of Mexico.

Opechancanough, as this new chief was named, had an abiding hatred for Europeans because he foresaw how they would be deadly to his nation; he had no difficulty in making his compatriots share his hatred and his fears, and he caused them to enter into a vast conspiracy against the common enemy. The secret was scrupulously kept for four years and was revealed only at the moment of its implementation by an Indian whom the English had baptized.

In spite of the treachery, the plot was partially executed, and 400 Colonists fell under the tomahawk of the Indians. The reprisals were harsh and were suspended only by a treaty that concealed the most heinous purpose. The Indians, full of confidence in the protestations of their enemies, devoted themselves, without suspicion, to the work of the harvest, when the English fell upon them without warning and slaughtered them horribly. The feeble remnants of the tribes who escaped this massacre were not long in perishing miserably in the forests and disappeared forever.

The Colonists, henceforth sole masters of this immense country, were able to extend it easily, but even this advantage did not fail to be deadly to them, and they would have certainly succumbed to the horrors of famine if there had not taken place a new reinforcement of Colonists and supplies to replace those destroyed by the Indians. This time aid did not come from the company because it had been dissolved by King James. This assault of the Crown against a company which had spent more than three million for the establishment of the Colony and which, despite its mistakes deserved gratitude for this astonishing performance, at first distressed the Colonists, but nonetheless turned out really to their benefit. They were able to defend themselves against the encroachments of the Royal Government; and they obtained confirmation of all the rights that they had won before the extinguishment of the company.

Up to 1651, the Colony was peaceful and prosperous. The troubles that arose in England with the violent death of Charles I disturbed it only very little, and resulted in a treaty in which Cromwell recognized, in a specific article, that Virginia was exempt from taxes, fees and imposts of all kinds; that England could not, without the consent of the General Assembly, burden it with any charge to construct their forts or castles, nor, finally, to keep standing armies there. But from 1652 the Colonists began to feel the effects of the strict views of the English Republic with regard to the commerce of the Colonies. During the ten years of Cromwell's reign, their discontent grew to the point that when Governor Matthews, named by the usurper, died, the inhabitants of the Colony, taking advantage of this sort of interregnum, overthrew the Republican authorities and proclaimed Charles II, who was still a refugee in Holland, King. Thus he found himself *King of Virginia* before being certain of regaining the throne of England. The death of Cromwell, which took place this same year of 1660, saved the Colony from the danger to which its imprudent attachment to the cause of the Stuarts had inevitably exposed it.

The Virginians were not long in repenting of their devotion to the new King, whose ingratitude was more noxious to them than Cromwell's tyranny. Far from abolishing the restrictions that already impeded the commerce of

Virginia, Charles II augmented them, to the contrary, and perpetuated them by the *Navigation Act.* The reestablishment of the Gallican Church, with all its intolerance; the violent revocation of all the acts that could perpetuate the memory of the Revolution; the plundering of property in order to compensate the agents of the Restoration; the continual lowering of the value of tobacco; all, in a word, combined to embitter the Colonists, and to dispose them to a popular uprising; the occasion which was to provoke it was not long in presenting itself, and civil war burst out in the Colony. A squadron sent by Charles II to the aid of Governor Berkeley arrived at the time when Bacon, leader of the insurgents who were already masters of Jamestown, had just died: no one showed the talents necessary to achieve what this bold and skillful leader had undertaken, and the insurgents accepted the amnesty which Berkeley offered them; but this attempted insurrection only embittered Charles II, whose despotism soon knew no bounds. It came to the point of prohibiting them by law from complaining about or speaking ill of the administration of the Governor, under pain of the most severe punishments, and several insurrections were forcibly suppressed.

Nevertheless, in spite of the violence and the injustices of the parent state, commerce resumed some activity, and the population, finding some new resources in its industry every day, grew rapidly. In 1688, they counted already more than 40,000. But in feeling their strength increase, the Colonists also felt their hatred for the Royal Authority grow; and when the first cries for independence were uttered by the Colonies of the North, Virginia responded by raising the standard of insurrection. During the month of June 1776, the representatives of the people, assembled and numbering 112, at the Capitol in Williamsburg, drafted and signed the Declaration that burst forever the bonds of tyranny which up to then had attached the Colony to the Motherland. This Declaration, in establishing in a clear and precise manner the rights of each member of society, sanctified the principle of the *Sovereignty of the People*, and rejected as a monstrosity the principle of *Heredity* in the exercise of power. It was soon followed by the publication of the Constitution that emerged triumphant from the Revolutionary War. In 1785, the assembly passed the act revising the laws and establishing religious liberty; finally in 1788, Virginia completed her revolution, and affirmed its independence by adopting the Constitution of the United States.

The State of Virginia, on account of the antiquity of its founding, its size, the fertility of its soil, and the mildness of its climate, should be the most wealthy and the most populous state of the American federation. Nonetheless it has no more than 1,600,000 inhabitants, dispersed over an area of 40,960,000 acres. That is to say that in proportion to its area it has only half the population of the State of New York, which is its contemporary, and hardly more than the population of Ohio, whose existence as a state and whose constitution is only about 20 years old. This difference that at every turn is revealed to the attentive by the distance between its towns, the weakness of its villages, the concentration of property, and the poverty of its culture, will disappear only when Virginia, understanding better its true interests, and putting them in harmony with the principles of liberty and equality so clearly established in its Declaration of Rights, and so vigorously defended by its arms, will have finally abolished Slavery of the Blacks.

When one has examined with care the truly noble and liberal institutions of the United States, understood well their working, and admired their fortunate effects, the soul suddenly runs cold, and the imagination is startled in learning that, in some places of this vast republic, the horrible principle of Slavery reigns yet with all its sad and monstrous consequences. One then asks himself with astonishment whence comes this contradiction between sublime theories and a practice so disgraceful for humanity! This question which long has been for the philanthropists and politicians of two hemispheres a subject of always very animated, but less often good-faith discussions, will not be long in being resolved, we hope, by reason of the well-understood interest of those whom it touches the closest. While waiting, I will venture here some observations, not with the pretension to end the discussion, but in hopes of restoring to their truthful condition some facts which have been misrepresented either by ignorance, by passion, or by the bad faith of some authors.

We are no longer, happily, in any part of the civilized world, to debate the justice or injustice of the principle of Slavery of the Blacks: today, every man whose mind is sound agrees that this principle is a monstrosity, and it is indeed wrong to presume that there are in the United States more than elsewhere individuals insane enough to attempt to defend it, whether by their writings or by their discourse. For me, who has traversed the 24 states of the Union in the course of more than a year, and has had the occasion to listen to very long and lively discussions on this subject every day, I profess to having encountered only one person defending this principle seriously; he was a young man whose rather poorly organized mind was filled with confused and fairly ridiculous ideas on Roman history, and he was completely ignorant of the history of his country. "The greatness of the Romans," he said to me in response to my expression of chagrin in seeing Slavery sadly coupled with American freedom,

> The greatness of the Romans rested on Slavery. If, like those masters of the world, we want to preserve in our character that austere dignity conducive to virtue, we must not occupy

> ourselves with details that are suited only to narrow the mind. How to succeed in studying thoroughly the science of government, for example, if we are obliged to devote our time to the administration of our properties, the cultivation of our lands, and to the management of our factories? How to preserve a noble self-respect in dealing with our equals, if we shall not acquire first the practice of command by making our Slaves obedient to us?

This entire lengthy tirade recited with emphasis appeared only ridiculous to me, and I did not think it fitting to respond to it. It is however often on similar, isolated occurrences that some writers have relied to declare that Americans of the United States are stubborn partisans of Slavery.

For every man of good faith, here, I believe, are the most essential points for the discussion of Slavery in the United States.

1. Did the Americans adopt Slavery willingly?

2. Since they won their independence, have they demonstrated by their acts their aversion to Slavery?

3. Today, do they understand well all the danger of the situation in which Slavery places them, and are they conscientiously doing all that it is possible to do to eradicate the evil?

4. What should be the most effective means to attain the freedom of the Blacks as soon as possible?

If these four questions were examined with impartiality, it is probable that they would renounce those violent declamations that wound without instructing and that offer to those against whom they are directed no means of redressing the wrongs of which they are accused. I shall not indulge in an elaborate examination of these questions that beg for a scope larger than the one that I can accord to them here: I will only touch on them lightly so to speak. But every time in the course of my trip that the opportunity presents itself, I will accurately report the facts to which I was a witness. I hope these will be, more than all the discussions, suitable for making known the state of Slavery and the progress that the public mind appears to be making on this subject every day.

This crime, by which a man, misusing his strength and his understanding, subjects to his whims or to the satisfaction of his needs another man less educated than he and reduces him to the condition of Slavery, was perpetrated in Virginia in 1620. It had as perpetrators the misery of the Colonists whose wearied and ill-fed bodies could no longer make the soil productive and the avarice of the Dutch who delivered to them, like beasts of burden, some unfortunate Negroes whom they had stolen in the sands of Africa in order to sell them later. The English, no less eager for silver than the Dutch, soon turned to this abuse of power, which fosters idleness, as a source of wealth, and they hastened to exploit it to their profit, and from that time their vessels poured out thousands of Slaves annually on the American continent. Nonetheless the sentiments of humanity that famine had for some time stifled in the hearts of the Virginian Colonists revived with the return of fortune and plenty. In about the year 1680, the General Assembly of Virginia requested of the parent state that it finally put an end to this commerce in human flesh, infamous and unnecessary in the future, since now the population was numerous enough and active enough to cultivate a land that required only the lightest work to reward the tiller richly. Other Colonies repeated this cry of justice and philanthropy, but the parent country was callous and responded only by this atrocious resolution of Parliament: *The importation of Slaves in America is too lucrative for the Colonies to be able to insist that England renounce it forever*. This response was accompanied by threats to which it was necessary to succumb since they were in no condition to resist them. Nonetheless, the General Assembly renewed several times its demand, which had the different result of obtaining an act by which the importation of Slaves to Virginia was hit with a rather large tax in 1699. While this was not a remedy for the evil, it was at least a palliative.

This state of affairs lasted so long as the Colonies were under the yoke of England; when they broke it, and when they had assured their independence, their different governments turned their attention to Slavery, and inquired into the means to make it disappear. But this hideous evil had thrown down roots so deep that it had, so to speak, passed into the customs of the citizens. Consequently, the remedy was difficult and could not obtain immediate results any more. For all that, those who had undertaken to triumph over it did not lose courage; their writings and their speeches rekindled all the spirits, and Virginia again had the honor of providing a great example by prohibiting first the importation of Blacks into its territory. This example soon was followed by nearly all the other States, and some went further; several, like Pennsylvania, declared all the children of Color who were born after the promulgation of the law free. Others, like New York State, declared that after a certain time no one could possess Slaves. Congress, following the general movement of minds, did what no European power had yet dared to do: it prohibited the Slave Trade, which it likened to piracy, while imposing the penalty of death on it. Finally of the 13 original States, eight proclaimed the freedom of Blacks by acts of their particular legislatures; only the most southern States, in which the Black population had grown with such rapidity that in some places it was quadruple the White population, in which it inspired dread, lagged behind.

Today, the Confederation is composed of 24 States: 13 of them have abolished Slavery by law, the 11 others are still sullied by it; among the latter five are the old States; the others were formed by breaking those up or out of the Louisiana Territory after they purchased it from the French. In this latter part of the United States, the prejudices against the Black color still holds, it must be confessed, a blindfold over the eyes of a great number of Slave-owners. Accustomed as they are from their earliest infancy to seeing in the African race only an inferior species incapable of ever acquiring the qualities suitable for a free citizen, they do not try to give their Slaves that education without which it is very true that liberty would be, in their hands, only a weapon detrimental to society and to themselves; and they believe that they have done enough for humanity in ameliorating the horrors of Slavery by good treatment. But, in their blindness, they forget that in a social state the right of citizenship cannot be denied to a class of men without putting them, so to speak, in a state of war in regards to those who enjoy it. If the oppressed are of sufficient number to demand the reason of this denial, the presumption is that they will not always peacefully put up with such an injustice, at least that they will not be crushed under the weight of tyranny.

This terrible truth, repeated for a long time in every part of the Union by the voice of philanthropy and by that of religion, which although less powerful in the South than in the North, exercises nonetheless very great influence there, is beginning meanwhile to affect minds in the Slave States. Every day sees the number of men who desire to and who are seeking the means to rid their country of this horrible plague grow. Of all the means offered to date, none has produced very effective results yet; and it is true that all present great difficulties in their execution; for although certain European philanthropists, who would perhaps themselves be very embarrassed if they were in the place of a Carolinian or Georgian planter, speak of it, one cannot consider the immediate and general liberation of the Slaves without exposing to greater misfortunes not only the Whites, but also the Blacks, who, by reason of their excessive ignorance, would see in freedom only the right to do nothing and to indulge in every excess. I dare to state that for at least four-fifths of the Slaves of the United States immediate freedom would be only a sentence to die of hunger, after having destroyed everything around them. Therefore, I believe that in such circumstances not to give men the exercise of their rights immediately is neither to violate these rights, nor to continue to protect the violators of them; it is only to put into the manner of destroying the evil that prudence which is necessary for the justice that one wants to render to these men to become more certainly a means of happiness for them. Here prudence requires that emancipation be gradual. It remains, therefore, to examine whether in the United States the Slave-owners are indeed doing what it is necessary to do in order to bring about this gradual emancipation surely and rapidly.

Among those who desire to deliver their country from the disgrace and the debasement of Slavery, all do not think alike about the measures that it is necessary to take relative to the lot of the Slaves. Some people had proposed first that, in order to indemnify the masters for the loss of their Slaves, they sell them to the English or French Colonies of the Antilles. This inhumane idea was repulsed with horror by most of the planters who declared that they could never be persuaded to send men whom they had made accustomed to a regime of gentleness to be destroyed under the cruel lash of the Colonists of Guadeloupe or Martinique. Some others had the idea of dedicating a portion of the vast territory that extends to the foot of the Rocky Mountains to the establishment of a Colony into which they would have been able to send all the young Negroes 20 years old, and the young Negresses 18 years old, after having given them, at public expense, a primary education and having provided them with all the objects necessary to their settlement. This Colony would have been able, afterwards, to govern itself and to become a powerful ally of the United States; but when this proposal was made, the prosperity of the United States was not yet great enough so that they could find the funds necessary for such an undertaking, and, let us say it, the public mind was, perhaps, not yet advanced enough to appreciate the importance of it.

For some years this idea has been taken up again, modified and finally put into execution by a society formed in 1818 under the Presidency of Mr. Bushrod Washington. This society, which now counts in its bosom all the most distinguished men of the different States and of which General Lafayette has just been named Vice President for life, has succeeded in founding, under the protection of the American Government, a Colony on the coast of Africa, which will probably soon attain the dual goals of serving as a refuge for the Blacks of the United States and of being at the same time a center of knowledge and industry for Africa from which one day the civilization of this part of the world will spring.

However, whatever the efforts and the success of this philanthropic society for colonization of Black men of the United States may be, one cannot reasonably expect it to bring about the abolition of Slavery by itself. If the

Slave-owners do not hasten to educate the children of their Blacks in order to prepare them for freedom; if the assemblies of the Southern States do not set a time more or less distant by which these States will not be able to possess Slaves any more, this part of the Union will be perhaps exposed, still for a long time, to the deserved reproach of outraging the sacred principle contained in the first article of the Declaration of Rights: *that all men are born equally free and independent*. However, everything leads one to believe that the time has arrived where gradual abolition of Slavery is going to proceed rapidly. The consciousness of *personal interest well-understood*, understood better now by the Southern proprietors, is beginning to make them realize that, in a few years, their products will have trouble withstanding competition with those of Mexico and of South America, if they do not renounce their ruinous system of agriculture soon. Already very many of them do not fear to attack overtly the unfortunate prejudices of their fellow citizens, while declaring that they would be very much happier and very much wealthier if the Black population were reduced enough so that they could, without danger, have workers of that color by the day and thus to replace this ruinous crowd of children and the old, whom they are obliged to support in idleness, by competition of free labor.

So then, according to the opinion of the men most disposed to the abolition of Slavery, the greatest obstacle to emancipation, be it general or gradual, is too large a population of Blacks; therefore, the diminution of this population is necessary first to attack Slavery, and the system of colonization was then wisely devised since it has as its object offering the dispersal of the overabundance of this population. The emancipation of the Republic of Haiti adds, moreover, to the facilities offered for this outflow to the African Colony of *Liberia*. But, unless one should want to compromise the security and the prosperity of the Colony of *Liberia* and of the Republic of Haiti, it is necessary to send to one or the other of these places only immigrants whose customs and intelligence could contribute to the success of these new societies. Now, it is unfortunately only too true that nearly the totality of the Blacks of the United States is still too degraded by ignorance and Slavery to furnish today good citizens for emigration.

It is, therefore, to enlighten and shape the young generations of the African race that all the efforts of the friends of humanity and of that genuine liberty that does not admit of the ridiculous distinction between men based on the difference in color of their skin must strive. One will reach this noble goal only by establishing, multiplying and encouraging everywhere free schools for children of color of both sexes. It is in vain for some men blinded by their prejudices to write that one must give up hope of improving the African race and that this race is only an intermediate stage between man and beast in the ladder of creatures. Already, numerous facts answer this absurd assertion; and, besides, couldn't one ask of these men so proud of the whiteness of their skin, who judge the Negroes only on what they are and not on what they could be, couldn't one ask them if they, indeed, know what their descendants would be after some generations if Slavery suddenly passed from the Negroes to the Whites? But why be afraid of this resistance of prejudice that seems to weaken each day and whose impending extinction is foreshadowed by the humanity with which, in general, all the planters believe themselves obliged to treat their Slaves today!

Some acts, which I will have occasion to cite, will succeed in proving, I hope, that relative to Slavery the public mind of the United States is now on a good course, that it is necessary only that it be encouraged more, and that some good advice on the means to make use of it would be rather more useful than attacks that are too violent and often unjust by their exaggeration.

I will end these observations by remarking that the State of Virginia, in a population of 1,065,366 persons, counts 462,281 persons of color, of whom 37,113 are free. This latter number never appears to increase very much because it is the one that especially provides individuals to the colonization of *Liberia* and to the emigration to Haiti and because in general the uneven life of the free Negroes in the cities is harmful to their reproducing.

JEFFERSON.

Chapter XV

Masonic Fete – Voyage to Petersburg – Visit to Mr. Jefferson – His House, His Farm, His Slaves – Montpelier – Mr. Madison – Religious Freedom – Return to Washington by Orange Courthouse and Fredericksburg.

Among the magnificent fetes the citizens of Richmond offered their National Guest, the description of which I am forced to forego, there is one, however, about which I cannot dispense with speaking because it is appropriate to give an idea of what a certain institution is in the United States. The Inquisition has so many times lit its funeral pyres in the persecution of this institution in Spain and in Italy, and some European Governments permit it even today only with repugnance. I want to speak of the institution of Freemasonry.

On Saturday, October 30, after having been introduced with the customary ceremonies into the Masonic Temple where all the members of the different lodges of Richmond were gathered together, we left in a great procession in order to take us to the fraternal banquet that had been prepared in a hotel at the other end of the City. The procession, composed of more than 300 persons, was formed in this manner. At the head, a detachment of *brothers* armed with swords opened the march. After this detachment was a troop of musicians playing American and French national tunes among which was *The Marseillaise*. Behind the band were two long rows of brothers of the lower ranks, and between these two rows were all the great dignitaries of the society, carrying in their midst a Bible placed on an elegant cushion of velvet embroidered with gold and surrounded by Masonic symbols. Among these great dignitaries, the Governor of Virginia, the great Chief Justice of the United States, and very many officers of the State appeared in the first rows.

All the brothers were clad with the insignia of their rank, and their variety offered a truly original tableau. All the streets that we traversed were filled with a large crowd of spectators who, by their attitude and their silence, expressed all the respect that this ceremony inspired in them. Before taking our place at the table that had been prepared for us in a lavishly decorated hall, a Protestant minister belonging to the Masonic Order addressed a speech to us in which he reminded us that true Masonry rested on *truth, equality, and charity*; that to fulfill our duties as a Mason was nothing other than to discharge those duties that we have to fulfill to God and to men. He concluded his speech by blessing our meal, which we began with very great seriousness but which ended with bursts of that true joy, so often spiritual, which particularly distinguishes the inhabitants of Virginia. Before we retired, a large number of patriotic toasts were given by the guests. The one given by General Lafayette was received with enthusiasm; it was worded as follows:

> Liberty, equality, philanthropy, true Masonic symbols: may the practice of these principles always deserve the esteem of our friends and the censure of the enemies of the human race!

Afterwards, we took the route to the Temple with the same ceremonies and in the same order as in coming from it to the hotel, and we went to conclude the evening in the company of numerous men who joined us at our residence. There, I found in the crowd that filled the rooms a large number of *our brothers*, and, naturally, the conversation turned to the day's festivities. One of them having asked me what I thought of it, I was unable to prevent myself from telling him that I believed that a like ceremony would appear very extraordinary in France, and that I doubted very much that a Masonic procession could traverse the Parisian streets without arousing merriment and silly jokes of the people. "But, nonetheless, you also have processions in France," he said to me, "because I recall having seen several during the trip that I made to your country two or three years ago, and I did not notice that they were treated with ridicule by the people…." "Oh, but that is very different," I exclaimed, "those processions that you have seen in France are those of the Catholic Church; they have another purpose and other forms than your Freemason procession." – "It is very different, you say," replied *my brother* (whom I then recalled having seen in the ceremony wearing the insignias of the highest ranks) seriously, "Let us see, therefore, the differences. For me, I confess to you, I find in them, to the contrary, be it said without offending you, only some resemblances. If it is the aprons and the ornaments of our brothers that you find too ridiculous to be shown in public, I will say to you that I find the caps and the vestments of your priests no less bizarre. If we carry at the head of our processions some relics, don't the Catholic priests all carry them? And do you believe that the Bible, which contains the word of God, deserves less to appear at the head of a procession than a cross of silver or even of gold? Like those of the Catholics, our processions march to the sound of music and the singing of the initiates, and here the advantage of the comparison is, I believe, in our favor, first, because our music without being less solemn, is, however, less monotonous, and because our songs being in the national language can be understood by the multitude. Finally, my brother," he added while squeezing my hand, "if from the comparison of the external forms I pass to the comparison of the moral purpose, I am happy to think that there is still no difference. We propose, as you know, in our association to improve the human race by enlightening it, and to relieve the unfortunate by sharing our wealth with them. What more noble purpose do the Catholics seek to attain by the practice of their religious rituals? And if we march with them towards this common goal, why should we appear more ridiculous to the eyes of the multitude?"

As he was a stranger and a Freemason, it was not proper to push the discussion further, and I kept silent, from which my interlocutor probably concluded that I was siding with his opinion. Some moments later, he resumed the conversation on the same subject and told me why Freemasonry enjoyed such great favor in the United States: "My compatriots are, as you know," he said, "great travelers, especially by sea; consequently, they often run the risk of falling into the hands of the pirates who invest the regions of the West Indies that we visit very much. These pirates, who plunder and hang everyone without distinguishing their religious beliefs, have a particular respect for the Freemasons whom they treat nearly always as brothers. I would be able to show you, without leaving Richmond, a large number of individuals who owe the saving of their life and their fortune only to a Masonic sign made at the right moment under the scimitar of pirates." – I understood then the veneration and the zeal of Americans for Freemasonry.

General Lafayette intended to leave Richmond to go to visit his good, old friend ex-President Jefferson, but a pressing invitation that he received from the citizens of Petersburg brought about a slight change in his plans. He resolved to yield first to this invitation and to return afterwards to Richmond to take the road to Monticello. We had to travel the sandy and wooded route from Richmond to Petersburg, which is only about 25 miles, for nearly six hours. On the way the horsemen of the escort showed us in a clearing an old wooden church which served as headquarters to Lafayette when, during the war in Virginia, he maneuvered on this terrain in order to try to prevent Cornwallis from joining with General Phillips. Upon our approaching closer to the Town, General Lafayette recognized the position from which he had attacked with cannon fire and burned Petersburg, in order to dislodge the English who had entered it by a march so swift that he had not been able to prevent them. The details of this part of the Virginia Campaign, so interesting with regard to strategy, are briefly, but very clearly, reported in the excellent work of Mr. Marshall, entitled: *Life of General Washington*.

The 24 hours that the General was able to spend in the midst of the citizens of Petersburg were marked by pleasures of all kinds. In traversing the streets, the inhabitants pointed out to him with very much laughter how much the Town had advanced from being burned by him in 1781. "See," they said to him, "at that time, we would have been able to welcome you only in poor wooden houses; today there are large, well-built brick houses and we can offer you all the comforts of life."

Petersburg presents, in a word, an agreeable appearance that announces the affluence of the inhabitants. It is a pretty little town of about 7,000 people, built on the southeast bank of the Appomattox River, which is navigable from this point up to its mouth in the James River for ships of 60 tons. All the products of the South of Virginia, and most of those of North Carolina have, so to speak, no other outlet than Petersburg; also the commerce of this place is especially considerable in tobacco and in flour, which is in large part manufactured by the numerous mills situated near the Town, below the waterfalls of the Appomattox.

After having returned to Richmond to take 48 hours' rest, we set out for Monticello, which is 80 miles distant from it. The voluntary cavalrymen of Richmond and a delegation of the committee of arrangements accompanied us. We slept the first night at Milton, a small village located halfway, where a large number of farmers from the environs assembled to provide a patriotic banquet to General Lafayette. The following morning, at the moment when we were going to climb into the carriage, I was seized by a horrible vomiting of bile and I was unable to leave my room. They believed, and I myself believed at the time, that I was threatened by a bilious fever, a malady very common in Virginia at this time of year, which is often fatal. However, a cup of tea and two hours' sleep restored my strength enough for me to be able to climb into a carriage and to continue the trip. In spite of my protestations, George Lafayette had left the retinue of his father in order to stay with me. This evidence of friendship, and the affectionate care that he gave me, provided a benefit to me that I will never forget, which contributed greatly, I believe, to gaining my recovery. We traveled briskly enough to arrive at Monticello only a little time after the General. We found Mr. Jefferson still moved by the pleasure of having been able to hold his old friend in his arms; he welcomed us in the midst of his large family with a charm that dissipated in an instant the timidity that at first I could not fend off in approaching a man who has done so much for other men.

When one recalls how Jefferson's life was occupied with and useful to his fellow men, one feels himself possessed with a holy veneration for him; but when one has lived for several days near him, very soon to this feeling is added that of trust and affection. It is difficult, I believe, to find a man whose conversation might be more agreeable and more instructive at the same time. Endowed with a memory that readily carries him back into the midst of the events of his life, familiar with nearly all the Arts and Sciences, his conversation can easily satisfy all the needs of a mind desirous of improvement.

Born at Shadwell in Albemarle County, Virginia, on April 2, 1743, Thomas Jefferson was educated at the College of Williamsburg, and he dedicated the first years of his youth to the study of law. The considerable fortune that his father, Peter Jefferson, one of the earliest Colonists, had left him put him in an advantageous situation; and more still the grandeur of his mind and his character soon called him to the Legislature of Virginia, which in 1774 sent him as its representative to the Continental Congress. He was not long in making an excellent reputation for himself in the bosom of this august assembly which, in 1776, adopted his draft of the *Declaration of Independence*, a composition not less remarkable for the depth of its thoughts as for the clarity, dignity and the energy of its style, which sufficed to render its author illustrious forever; but Jefferson could not stop after so glorious a debut in his political career. He was to pursue it in its entirety at the same pace, and also to find the means of paying his tribute to the Sciences and the Arts which he never neglected.

By turns Legislator, Governor of Virginia, Representative, Minister Plenipotentiary, Secretary of State, Vice President of the United States, he passed by all the high public positions in nearly a quarter of a century before arriving at the First Magistracy of the Republic. His appointment, which took place in 1801, in opposition to John Adams was regarded as a triumph of the Democratic Party over the Federalist Party. Then, as at all times, the defeated party vented its despair by great shouts, secret agitations, and incendiary pamphlets. The newspapers which were its voice railed immoderately against the new President and all the men who were helping to abolish wasteful positions, to introduce strict economy in all branches of the administration, to reduce the army to no more than was necessary and, finally, to give to the Constitution that straightforward interpretation that suits so well the simplicity of its conception. But Jefferson scorned these unavailing clamors and did not continue any less the work of reform and improvement that he had undertaken. In vain, some friends, in their mistaken zeal, came to advise him to have recourse to a law repressive of the abuses of the Press; he repulsed their dangerous advice: "I am very fortunate," he responded, "on account of this continuous censure that the newspapers carry on against my administration; for among all violent words dictated by passion, one truth can be found, and I will take advantage of it. Besides," he added, "a government whose actions are performed in broad daylight, whose members live in the midst of their fellow citizens, to whom all their words are addressed, and in front of the eyes of whom all their actions are carried out, has nothing to fear but its ill deeds."

Sublime and severe lesson that the European Governments ought to have taken advantage of!

So much wisdom and steadiness could not remain without reward in the midst of a nation with good sense. Jefferson was reelected President with a near unanimity of votes in 1805. Among the remarkable deeds which make his administration conspicuous, the Louisiana Purchase in 1803 was not one of the least advantageous to the United States.

Finally, in 1809, he returned to private life and came to seek rest in his place of retirement, Monticello. There at the summit of a mountain that dominates a fertile and pleasant valley in the distance, in a house simple, but in good taste, built under his direction and, so to speak, with his own hands, in the midst of his children and grandchildren, whose idol he is, he still dedicates all his time and all his faculties to the betterment, to the happiness of his fellow men. By his attentions, *Charlottesville* has seen a university rise up in its bosom, now richly endowed, and already containing a large number of students. Some years more, and this institution will be for the States of the South and the West what Cambridge is for the States of the North, a fertile source of enlightenment from which the young will come to draw the knowledge and the principles that make good citizens. The retirement home of Mr. Jefferson enjoys a great reputation for hospitality in all of Virginia; I noticed, as a matter of fact, that it was constantly open, not only to a large number of visitors from the surrounding area, but also to all foreign travelers who were led there by the very natural curiosity or desire to see *The Sage of Monticello* and to converse with him.

I have already said that he had been the architect and, so to speak, the builder of his residence. It has the shape of an irregular octagon, with porticos to the east and to the west and peristyles to the north and in the middle. Its size, including peristyles and porticos, is about 110 feet by 90. The exterior, in the Doric order, is surmounted by balustrades; the interior of the home is decorated in different architectural styles; the entrance hall is after the Ionic, the dining room decorated in Doric, the drawing room in Corinthian, and the dome in Attic. The rooms are decorated with different forms of these orders in their true proportions according to Palladio. Everywhere, in this delightful home, one finds proof of the good taste of the proprietor and of his well-informed love for the arts. His drawing room is decorated by a collection of paintings, in which one notices with pleasure an Ascension of *Poussin*, a Holy Family by *Raphael*, a Flagellation of Christ by *Rubens*, and the Cruxification by *Guido*. In the dining room, he has four handsome busts of Washington, Franklin, Lafayette and Paul Jones; there are also other fine pieces of sculpture in different parts of the house. The library, without being extensive, is of an excellent selection; but what especially excites the curiosity of visitors is the splendid museum which is at the entrance to the house. It contains, in offensive and defensive arms, in clothing, ornaments, and tools of the different uncivilized tribes of North America, the most varied and complete collection that may ever have been made. Mr. Trist, the son-in-law of Mrs. Randolph, Mr. Jefferson's daughter, a young man as amiable as he is learned, was kind enough to point out to me among the arms those that belonged to Tecumseh; they were not at all remarkable, either in their form or material, but one cannot avoid considering them with interest when one is acquainted with the history of the extraordinary man to whom they belonged.

They know that Tecumseh, born in the midst of the Chippewa Indians, on the Canadian border, was chief of his nation and that his courage and his genius had acquired for him immense influence on all the neighboring nations. This child of nature had been marked by his mother with the seal of greatness. In a perfectly modeled body, with the most imposing appearance, he contained the soul of a hero, and one can declare that if chance had caused him to be born in the midst of the shining lights of civilization, his immense intelligence would have placed him among the foremost men of his century. For a long time, he entertained in secret the hope of putting up an insurmountable barrier against the always growing power of the Whites. To this end, he had, for several years, traveled to nearly all the Indian tribes, in order to invite them to join a league which he wanted to form. His persuasive, inspiring eloquence had assured him of numerous partisans; already he believed that he could glimpse in the near enough future the time in which he could raise the *Tomahawk* which was to regenerate his brothers against the Whites, when suddenly war broke out between the United States and England.

Tecumseh contemplated this event with joy, for according to him it was to be favorable to his plans, since it was going to hasten the destruction of his enemies by their own hands. He resolved at first to remain an inactive spectator, but soon changed his mind. To contribute first towards the destruction of the strongest in order to have afterwards only to strike against the weakest appeared to him as the wisest policy; and he yielded willingly to the solicitations of the English who sought his alliance by every possible means. He was then 40 years old: since his childhood he had taken part in all the actions against the Whites, and still no one could reproach him for one of those cruel acts so common to his compatriots in the intoxication of victory. He had repugnance for spilling blood after combat, and one saw him often defend his prisoners against the fury of his own warriors. With so noble a character, he was soon to be ashamed of the atrocious conduct of his allies who incited the Indians, whom they had gotten drunk in a dastardly manner, to massacre their wounded prisoners. He showed the utter disdain that they had inspired in him when he refused with a noble pride both the rank of brigadier general and a silk sash that General Proctor offered him in the name of the King of England, as reward for his courage in the battles of Brownstown and Magagua; but always preoccupied by his great plans, he believed that he should persist in his alliance with the English until the Americans, whom he regarded as more dangerous enemies, were destroyed.

At the sound of his formidable voice, new tribes came to line up under his command, and it was at the head of the elite of his warriors that he came to the banks of the Thames River to lend, for the last time, the force of his arms to his allies in the battle that they had joined with General Harrison. From the beginning of the action Tecumseh had thrown himself furiously in the midst of the battalions that were opposed to him and had at first unsettled them by the boldness of his attack; but these battalions soon regained their poise and the combat became horrific. The Indians, aroused by the example of their valiant chief, renewed without cease their attacks, which the Americans repulsed with an equal fearlessness. In the middle of the fray, Colonel Johnson advanced nearly alone towards a dense group of Indians who were rallying to the cry of Tecumseh. The vividness of his uniform and the whiteness of his horse made him noticeable, and he became the target of all the blows. In a moment, he was thrown down riddled with wounds. At that time, Tecumseh arrived near him and lifted his tomahawk to put him to death; but struck, whether by his fearlessness or his sad situation, he hesitated an instant, and this instant was fatal to him, it was that of his death.... Colonel Johnson, gathering the strength left to him and recognizing the full extent of the danger he was facing, grasped a pistol in his belt and shot it nearly point-blank into the chest of Tecumseh, who fell dead at his side.... So perished this extraordinary man on whom rested all the hopes of so many nations which declined each day, and whose civilizations will soon have been destroyed up to the very traces of their past existence. The body of Tecumseh was discovered among the dead after the battle. The Americans recognized him by his imposing appearance and, to pay homage to his courage, which they had so often experienced, they buried him with all military honors.

The land that surrounds Mr. Jefferson's home and that constitutes his property is several thousand acres in area, but only 1,200 to 1,400 acres are cleared; the rest is still covered by forests. The principal products are cereals and tobacco. The fields seemed to me to be cared for well enough in general, but, if I judge by some observations I have made, farming must be very costly and consequently must leave very little profit to the owner. Like all the farmers in Virginia, Mr. Jefferson derives profit from his land with Slave-labor; that is to say, he needs about 50 Negroes to work the land, and he must feed, house and clothe 100 of them; for if from 100 Slaves one deducts the old, the children, the feeble women and the ill, one will surely find that there remain hardly 50 individuals capable of working; moreover, one must add that 50 active individuals do not do the work that 30 free men paid by the day would do; and that is easily understood. The free worker, paid by the day, knows that, if he does not bring all his strength and all his intelligence to his work, the one who pays him will stop employing him in order to hire another more industrious worker, and that he will be reduced to poverty. The Slave worker, to the contrary, knows that, whether his work is poor or valuable, his lot will always be the same; he is not ignorant of the fact that, in order to conserve the investment which the individual represents, his master will always be forced to feed him, lodge him, clothe him, care for his health and protect him. Also, without worries as without hopes for the future, the Slave worker can have, ought to have, but one desire, namely that of rest. What does it matter to him, indeed, that the prosperity of his master grows or diminishes! Aren't the results always the same for him? Is it not always the case in Slavery?

From these considerations, one can boldly conclude that 30 free workers, paid by the day, would do the work of 100 Slaves whom a landowner is obliged to feed and clothe during the entire year in order to have 50 workers. Suppose that the upkeep of each Slave costs the master only one franc per day, and that the salary of the free worker costs him three, there would be a difference of 10% per day, in favor of farming by free hands. This difference does not appear, at first, very great, but if afterwards one takes account of the enormous capital of at least 50,000 francs that the purchase of 100 Slaves must cost; if one also takes into account the 52 Sundays and the holidays that one does not pay free workers for, during which the Slaves nonetheless eat, although they do not work, one would see how this difference becomes very large, and one would have difficulty understanding how an owner-farmer (apart from feelings of humanity, and consulting only his personal interest) does not make more efforts to replace Slave farming with free farming.

The good appearance and the cheerfulness of the Negroes of Monticello attest, if it is necessary, to the humanity of their master, if such a noble character had need of attestation. All those whom I conversed with assured me that they were perfectly happy, that they had not submitted to any bad treatment, that their work was very pleasant, and that they farmed the land of Monticello with so much more pleasure since they were nearly certain of not being torn away to be transported elsewhere so long as Mr. Jefferson was living. This conversation proved to me that, whatever the owners say about it, there would be an infallible means of awakening the love of work among the Slaves and of winning their affection; this would be to make them attached to the soil, to accustom them to consider themselves as being an inalienable part of the property to which they belong, to give them the assurance that they will enjoy the improvements or embellishments that they create by the sweat of their brow. When they know that the land that saw them born must nourish them up to the end of their days, they would attach themselves to it and take pleasure in rendering it more productive. The masters themselves would gain the affection of some beings whom they would no longer be accustomed to consider as beasts of burden to be gotten rid of when they do not have the ability to drive them. Forced to keep them, they would take more care in their moral and physical improvement. Then those horrible sales would cease. They break the ties of nature or affection without pity, snatch a child from his mother, separate the husband from his wife, the brother from his sister, the unfortunate from the friends who are joined to him by the same shackles.

The objections against general and immediate emancipation are unanswerable; the objections against gradual emancipation are subject to debate; but the objections against changing Slavery into serfdom, as I have just pointed out, appear to me to be very easy to refute. The Government of the United States has given a magnificent lesson to the entire world by stigmatizing and punishing the Slave Trade as a capital crime. Virginia has acquired important rights to the gratitude of the friends of humanity by opposing from its infancy, so to speak, the importation of Slaves to its territory; but there remain still more palm-branches to collect in this road to justice and humanity; the next to be assigned will belong, I believe, to the State that is the first to replace its Slaves with *serfs*.

Before leaving Mr. Jefferson, we went with him to visit the University at Charlottesville; he drove us there in a very elegant carriage, made by his Negroes on his residence; it appeared to me very well-built, and I found that there was in its perfection a powerful argument against those who claim that the intelligence of the Negroes could never rise to the height of the mechanical arts.

At Charlottesville, all had been prepared by the citizens and the students of the University, joined together in order to welcome General Lafayette in a worthy manner. The sight of the Nation's Guest, seated at a patriotic banquet between Jefferson and Madison, aroused among the guests an enthusiasm that was expressed in spurts crackling with sincerity and spirit. Mr. Madison, who had arrived the same day at Charlottesville to be present at this reunion, distinguished himself to all by the originality of his mind and the subtlety of his allusions. Before leaving the table, he asked to make a toast, and it concluded: *"To liberty: she has virtue for a guest and gratitude for a feast.*" His thought was easily understood by the guests and applauded rapturously.

After the meal, we visited the institution. It is composed of two parallel lines of little buildings, each one offering in its construction a different kind of architecture. Between these two lines, at their end, rises another building constructed on the plan of the *Parthenon of Athens*, reduced to one-fifth of its original dimensions, containing a library and an immense circular hall intended for general meetings. All the diverse construction had been managed by Mr. Jefferson himself, who took pleasure in spending several hours each day, sometimes in the midst of the workers, sometimes in the midst of the students and professors, all of whom felt all the better for his wise counsel.

Before we took leave of the youth of Charlottesville and of the respected professors, Mr. Spottswood led us into a small room where he showed us a rattlesnake that wandered freely on the floor. They had captured it some days before in order to offer it to George Lafayette who had evidenced the desire to have one of them. We contemplated with pleasure this dangerous reptile, whose piercing look, supple movements, pale gray body, broken up by wide black bands and noisy tail, would have doubtless inspired a sentiment of another kind, if we had not known that they had rendered his rage impotent by tearing out the grooved tooth with the aid of which this animal introduces death so subtly into the veins of the victim which he can reach. The poison secreted by the rattlesnake is, they say, so violent that it often produces death in less than a half hour. For a long time, they doubted the possibility of providing an effective remedy to the bite of this reptile, perhaps some persons even doubt this still; however, Doctor Thacher claims positively, in his excellent military journal of 1776, that the use of olive oil and mercury succeeded perfectly in the following case.

On arriving at Ticonderoga, an American soldier had the affrontery to want to catch a rattlesnake by seizing it by the tail. The snake turned and bit him in the hand. In less than half an hour, his arm and shoulder swelled to more than double their natural size; and his skin took a shade of yellow to dark orange. Soon all of the same side of his body experienced the same condition, and his stomach felt the effects of violent urges to vomit. However, several hours passed without death supervening; then Dr. Thacher, and two of his doctor friends, resolved to make the patient swallow a large quantity of olive oil, at often repeated doses, and to rub down the affected parts with a mercurial salve at the same time. After two hours, the remedy operated in an efficacious manner. The alarming symptoms disappeared, the swelling diminished, and, after 48 hours, the return of the patient's health was complete.

The Indians claim to have a remedy for rattlesnake bites; they maintain that, by immediately applying the well-mashed pulp of a kind of tuber rather similar to a small potato on the wound, they paralyze the action of the venom completely and avoid all its consequences. I give this only as a popular opinion that merits serious examination, which I have not had the occasion to give it during the too-rapid course of our trip.

Despite all the happiness that General Lafayette enjoyed near his old friend Mr. Jefferson, it was necessary to leave him, for other attachments and other engagements called him again to very many parts of this vast republic, of which we had yet visited only a small part, although, since our landing, we had traveled constantly at a rate of nearly 40 miles per day. Upon leaving Monticello, we went to Montpelier, the charming residence of the ex-President of the United States, Mr. Madison. There, we found, with some nuances, nearly the same customs, the same virtues as at Monticello.

The career of Mr. Madison had an astonishing similarity to that of Mr. Jefferson with whom he was always linked by the most fond friendship. Like his illustrious friend, Mr. Madison devoted himself at an early age to the study of law and was called, still young, by his fellow citizens to defend their most cherished interests in the legislative assemblies. Like him, he shone by his talents of oratory and by the boldness of his ideas in that assembly that immortalized itself in declaring an *independent country*. Like him, he was called twice by the people to the First Magistracy of the Republic, and during a part of his administration he had to withstand a foreign war that ended gloriously; like him, finally, in leaving the House of the President of the United States, he went in retirement to make his field productive and to cultivate Letters with which he had never broken all connection despite the numerous political positions of his so active life.

Mr. Madison is now 74 years old, but his well-preserved body contains a mind still young and full of a sweet sensibility that he was not afraid to let us see in its entirety when he expressed to General Lafayette the pleasure which he had in having him in his home. Although the habits of reflection and work should have made him develop on his visage the appearance of great severity, nonetheless, all the impressions of his heart paint themselves rapidly on his features, and his conversation is ordinarily animated by a sweet cheerfulness. Mrs. Madison also contributes very much, by the grace of her mind and the charm of her character, to making more precious still the open hospitality with which strangers are received at Montpelier.

I will not give any details about the cultivation of the property of Mr. Madison; it is all that it can be in the hands of a man remarkable for his good taste and his spirit of order, but who can employ only Slaves who, whatever may be their gratitude for the good treatment of their master, must always prefer their present rest to the enlargement of his wealth.

The four days that we spent at Mr. Madison's were agreeably occupied with walks on his beautiful property, and more agreeably still in conversations in the evening on all the great American interests that one knows are so dear to General Lafayette. The society that was then habitually assembled at Montpelier was composed nearly entirely of landowners of the vicinity, who, in general, appeared to me at least as well-versed in understanding all the great political questions of their country, as in understanding those of agriculture. General Lafayette, who, while understanding very fully the troublesome position of the Slave-owners in the United States, and not being able to disregard most of the obstacles that stand in the way of a more speedy emancipation of the Blacks, nevertheless, never missed the occasion to defend the rights that *all men without exception* have to liberty, and to raise in the midst of Mr. Madison's friends the question of Slavery. It was taken up and discussed by them frankly in a manner to confirm in me the opinion that I had already formed of the honorable sentiments of the majority of Virginians on this deplorable matter. It seems to me that now, in Virginia, Slavery cannot continue to exist anymore for a long time, for its principle is condemned by all enlightened men, and, when public opinion condemns a principle, its consequences do not have a very long time to stand.

After the question of Corporal Slavery of the United States, they discussed the no less important question of *Spiritual Slavery* to which some peoples of Europe are condemned by the *dominant religions*, by the *State religions*. Mr. Madison's friends expressed satisfaction that this slavery at least was not known in their dear Fatherland. They went into some details which apprised me that they would not be men to be satisfied with what we in Europe invoke ceaselessly as a blessing; I want to speak of religious *tolerance*. "Tolerance," one of them said to us,

> Is without doubt preferable to persecution; but it would be intolerable in a free country, because it indicates an insulting arrogance. In order to give a religion the right to tolerate, and to make the others submit to the shame of being *tolerated*, it is necessary first to prove that the tolerant religion is the only good one, whereas the *tolerated* ones are bad. But how to obtain this proof, since each believes that its own religion is the best? The word tolerance is, therefore, an insult, and can only be reasonably replaced by the word *freedom*. This religious freedom we now have it to the full extent of its

meaning, and we can be sure that of our 24 States, there isn't one of them where it would not be understood better than in any part of Europe. For all that, we also have had our times of *tolerance*, I would say even our times of *intolerance*; before our glorious revolution, for example, we wailed still under the laws by virtue of which, for certain degrees of heresy, a father could be deprived of the right to raise his own children, every individual could lose the rights of a citizen and a part of the protection of the laws, and some could even be burned.... Today, what a happy difference! Thanks to our new laws, worthy of the wise immortals who were called upon to draft them, no individual can be compelled any longer to observe any religious sect, to frequent any place, to support any minister of whatever religion it may be, or be coerced, restrained, disturbed, or oppressed in his person or his property; and, finally, one cannot persecute him in any manner on the subject of his religious opinions; but all men have the freedom *to profess and to sustain by argument* their opinions on religious matters, and these opinions cannot lessen, enlarge or affect anything with regard to their civil rights.

As they well realized, I had paid scrupulous attention to this so-interesting conversation; one of our speakers who had seen this took me aside while Mrs. Madison prepared the tea, and said to me:

Since you take such an avid interest in all that is connected with the creation of our institutions, I want to inform you of a fact of which my friend has not at all spoken, in the fear, no doubt, of offending the modesty of the master of the house. – Perhaps you know that, before the Revolution, the Anglican religion was dominant in this State; its ministers, unhappy with the equality that the law of 1776 established among the different religions, unhappier still with the law of 1779 that deprived them of the salaries that they had received up to then from the Government, declared that they could not be satisfied with voluntary contributions, and during the session of 1784 to 1785, presented to the General Assembly a petition seeking to obtain *the support of the ministers of the Gospel* by the Government. This petition, supported by the skills of the most popular men of the House, appeared to have joined together the majority of the votes. In order to paralyze its success, some members demanded and obtained the referral of the petition to the following session in order that its printed language be submitted to the judgment of the public. During this time, Colonel G. Mason and Colonel G. Nicholas beseeched Mr. Madison to draft a refutation of the petition. This refutation, distributed widely to the people, had such success that soon it was covered by a prodigious number of signatures of men of all the sects or communions, and at the next session the petition was forcefully rejected. You will, I have no doubt, be pleased by a reading of this document which, I tell you, contains all that one can say of the most forceful and the wisest arguments in favor of religious freedom; I can send it to you tomorrow, for I still possess several copies of it.

Since Mr. Madison's *Declaration of Religious Freedom*, which responded to this request, there has been no national religion in the United States; the expenses of a sect are furnished by voluntary contributions. This state of affairs contrasts noticeably with the politics of the European nations; and nonetheless, religion is not at all neglected among us. It is true that the population of the countryside does not possess a large number of places where it would be able to celebrate its worship; but one must not forget that this population is widely distributed in small portions in new territory; and, moreover, that Europe owes the great magnificence of its churches, not to the religious zeal of an enlightened century, but, to the superstition and the bigotry of centuries of ignorance. One will notice, besides, that in the large cities of Europe, where the excess of population is no longer in harmony with the original foundations of the church, the places where worship is celebrated are not very much greater in number in proportion to those of the United States. In 1817, Boston, whose population was 40,000, had 23 churches; New York, whose population was about 120,000, had 53; Philadelphia, which contained 100,000, had 48; Cincinnati, in the State of Ohio, peopled by 8,000 inhabitants, although it counted hardly seven years since its founding, had five temples, and they were building two others. It is only between the large cities of America and Europe that the comparison can be made; and if support of the churches is regarded as undeniable proof of zeal for religion, one will observe that they build new churches in Europe by means of forced contributions, while in America they are built by means of voluntary contributions.

The following morning, before leaving Montpelier, I received, indeed, the document in question and I examined it hastily: I did not find it at all beneath the eulogy that they had given to it. The principles it contains are so simple, so reasonable, so eloquently established and defended that it seems to me difficult to be able to say anything more on this subject. The publication of such a document being capable, in my opinion, of producing only good results in all times and places, I believe that I must provide here a translation as faithful as the difference of the spirit of the two languages permits.

To the General Assembly of the State of Virginia; Memorial and Remonstrances.

We, the undersigned, citizens of the Republic of Virginia, having taken into consideration a bill printed by order of the General Assembly in its last session, having as a title: *"Bill for setting the salary of the ministers of the Christian Religion,"* persuaded that this bill, protected by the force of law, can become a source of abuse in the hands of the authority, we believe that we are obligated, as faithful members of a free state, to vote against this bill and to justify our vote as follows:

We vote against the bill.

Because: we regard it as an incontestable truth that our religion or the form of worship that we render to our Creator, as well as our outward practices, can be determined only by reason and conviction and not by force or violence. It is a right for each man to practice his religion according to his conscience. This right is natural and inalienable. It is inalienable because, the opinion of men being formed only by the evidence created by their own mind, they cannot obey the precepts of another man. It is a duty of each man to render homage to the Creator, but only an homage which he himself judges worthy of Him. This duty precedes, in order of time, the rights of the social body; it must be considered as relating to the Governor of the Universe. If a member of a social body in entering into a lesser association ought not to stray from his duties towards a general authority, with greater reason ought a man who becomes a member of a social body not forget the respect and fidelity that he owes to the Sovereign of the Universe. We affirm, consequently, that the rights of man in religious matters cannot be restrained by the institution of a social body in any way, and that religion does not fall within the competence of its authority in any way. It is true that, in the case where a question divides the society, there is no other principle to decide it than the will of the majority; but it is also true that the majority cannot injure the rights of the minority.

Because: if religion does not fall within the competence of the social body, it is still even less subject to the authority of the legislative body. The latter is only the creature and the deputy manager of the former; its jurisdiction is derivative and limited; if it is limited with regard to the other bodies of the same degree, it must be limited all the more with regard to its constituents. The preservation of a free government does not require only that the demarcations and the limits that determine the prerogatives of each department of the authority be invariably maintained, but also that it not be allowed that any of them cross the great barrier which protects the rights of the people. Legislators who do not respect this guaranty abuse the authority that is confided in them and become tyrants; and the people who endure these abuses are no longer governed by laws made by them, nor by an authority established by them, but become slaves.

Because: it is proper to take alarm at the first attack directed against our liberty. We believe that this far-sighted solicitude is one of the foremost duties of good citizens, and one of the most noble traits characteristic of our Revolution. The free men of America did not wait for the power of a usurper to be strengthened by its exercise, and for the issue to become complicated by precedents. In the principle itself they saw the consequences, and they hastened to avoid the consequences by destroying the principle. We consider this too good a lesson to want to forget it soon. Who does not see that the same authority that can favor Christianity to the exclusion of all other religions could also favor with the same ease a particular sect of Christianity to the exclusion of all other sects? And that the same authority which, today, can force a citizen to pay *only three cents* for the support of any institution could soon force him also to contribute a large part of his fortune to the support of all institutions and in all possible cases.

Because: this bill violates the equality that ought to be the basis of each law, and which becomes more indispensable as it is more liable to be destroyed by the validity or the influence of the law. *If all men are, by their nature, equally free and independent,*[13] one must also regard all men as entering into society on equal conditions, as giving up and regaining an equal portion of their rights. And above all, they must be regarded as having *an equal claim to the free exercise of religion, by listening only to the voice of their conscience.*[14] When we ourselves are assured of the freedom to embrace, profess and observe the religion that we believe to be of divine origin, we cannot refuse an equal liberty to those whose soul is not yet open to the conviction that has struck us. If someone abuses this liberty, it is an offense towards God and not towards men; it is thus to God alone and not to men that he must render an account. This bill violates equality by levying taxes on some and creating exemptions for others. Are the Quakers and the Menonites then the only ones who are regarded as too useless and blameworthy for the authorities to support their religion? Are the others then the only ones to the piety of which one could entrust the care of public worship? Must these sects be endowed, to the prejudice of all the others, with extraordinary privileges that would make proselytes right in the bosom of the other sects?

Because: the bill permits a civil magistrate to constitute himself a competent judge of a true religion, or to use religion as an instrument of civil authority. The first fact is an arrogant claim twisted out of the contradictory opinions of legislators of all times and all places. The second is an impious overturning of the means of security.

Because: the program proposed by the bill is unnecessary for the support of the Christian religion; to say that it is necessary is to contradict even the history of this religion, each page of

13. Declaration of Rights, Article 1.
14. Declaration of Rights, Article 16.

which denies the authority of the powers of this world. It is also to contradict the facts, since it is well-recognized that this religion has existed and prospered for a long time, not only with the support of human laws but also in spite of these laws; and not only during the period of miraculous assistance, but even a long time after it was abandoned to its own strength and to the ordinary cares of Providence. To speak of laws in order to sustain a religion is to weaken in those who profess this religion a pious confidence in its innate excellence, and in the protection of its Author; it is to nourish in those who still reject it the suspicion that its friends know its falsity all too well to dare to abandon it to its own strength.

Because: experience has proven that ecclesiastical establishments, far from preserving the purity and efficacy of religion, have had a contrary influence. For nearly 15 centuries, they tried the legal establishment of Christianity: what were the fruits of these endeavors? On all sides more or less arrogance and indolence in the clergy; ignorance and servitude in the laity; bigotry, superstition and persecution in both. Ask the priests what was the most beautiful time of Christianity. All, of whatever sect they may be, will tell you that it was the one that preceded the time of its incorporation by the civil polity. Now, propose to bring Christianity back to its original state, in which the priests would have to expect a salary only from the gratitude of their flocks; immediately they will predict their ruin. In which case should we therefore believe their testimony? Is it when they speak for or against their personal interest?

Because: if religion does not fall within the competence of the civil authority, how can they say that its legal establishment is necessary to this authority? What influence, in fact, have the ecclesiastical establishments had up to now on civil society? One has seen them sometimes erect a spiritual tyranny on the ruins of the civil authority; one has seen them often support political tyranny, but one has never seen them defend the freedoms of the people. Legislators who desire to destroy public freedoms are able to find support in the institution of the priesthood, but a just government, instituted to protect and perpetuate freedom, doesn't need such help. A good government will be made even better by protecting each citizen in the exercise of his religion, as it protects him in his person and his property, by respecting the rights of each sect, and by not permitting any sect to injure the rights of any other sect.

Because: the proposed action is far from that generous policy which, offering a refuge to the persecuted and the oppressed of each nation and each religion, promised new glory to our country, and an increase in the number of citizens. But what sad portent of a sudden degeneration does this bill offer us! Instead of perpetuating a refuge to the persecuted, it is itself a signal of persecution. It pushes every citizen whose religious opinions do not conform to those of the legislative authority out of the ranks of equality; whatever the difference should appear from the Inquisition in form, it only differs from it, nevertheless, by degree. The one is the first step, the other the last on the road to intolerance. The courageous man who groans under this scourge, in other countries far from us, must regard this bill as a signal placed on our shores in order to advise him that from now on he must seek under another sky that liberty and philanthropy that could have previously offered him an assured haven with us against persecution.

Because: it also has a tendency to exile our citizens. Their number will diminish every day by virtue of the advantage that other locations will offer them. To add new incentives to their emigration by destroying the freedom that they now enjoy would be to give an example of folly equal to that which dishonored and depopulated some flourishing kingdoms.

Because: it tends to destroy that moderation and harmony which the prohibition that our laws make of meddling in religious discussions has established among the different sects. Torrents of blood have been spilled in the Old World by efforts of the secular arm to extinguish all religious discussions, while making all differences in religious opinions disappear. Time has in fact shown the true remedy. Everywhere they have tried it, the relaxing of a strict and rigorous policy has by itself alleviated the evil. America has proven that freedom without restrictions has, if not destroyed entirely, at least effectively combatted its influence on the prosperity of the state. If, in spite of the happy experiences of the past, we begin today to contract the limits of religious liberty, I would no longer know by what harsh-enough name to stigmatize our folly. Take advantage, at least, of the lessons that the first effects of the projected innovation give us. The appearance of the bill has changed that forbearance, that love and that Christian charity, which reigned among us just a few days ago, into animosities and jealousies that will not soon be quelled. What will we have to dread if this enemy of public tranquility comes armed with the force of the law?

Because: attempts to enforce, by the sanction of the laws, acts obnoxious to such a large number of citizens tend to weaken the laws in general and to loosen the societal bonds. If it is difficult to make a law respected that is not considered generally to be necessary or useful, how much does the difficulty increase when the law is recognized to be improper or dangerous! And then how fatal can the proof of the powerlessness of the government in the exercise of its general authority be!

Because: a measure of such great importance ought not to be adopted without acquiring proof that it is demanded by the majority of citizens. But, to date, no satisfactory method has yet been proposed to learn the voice of the majority and its influence in this case. – The citizens of each county are invited, it is true, to express their opinion relative to the adoption of the bill at the next session of the assembly. Our hope is that, after a serious examination, none of the former will adopt the dangerous principles of the bill. If the outcome betrays us, this confidence would still remain to us, that a sincere appeal made to the latter would bring about the rejection of this law, which is inimical to our liberties.

Because, finally: the equal right of each citizen *to the free exercise of his religion, according to the voice of his conscience,* is tied by the same act to all our other rights. It is a natural right the importance of which we are sensible of. If we consult the declaration of these rights, which belong to the good people of Virginia as the fundamental bases of their government, we find it specified there and enlarged on with solemnity. Now either we must recognize that the legislature has as a boundary of its authority only its will, and, in the full extent of this authority, it can destroy our fundamental rights;

or rather it is obligated to respect this sacred right: either it can alter freedom of the press, abolish the jury, appropriate to itself the executive and judicial powers, deprive us of the right to vote, and, finally, set itself up as an independent and hereditary assembly; or, rather, it does not have the authority sufficient to elevate the proposed bill into law.

We, the undersigned, declare that the General Assembly of this State does not have this authority, and in order that no effort be omitted by us against so dangerous a usurpation, we oppose this remonstrance to it. May the Supreme Legislator of the Universe enlighten those to whom it is addressed. May He, with one hand, divert them from any resolution capable of injuring His holy prerogatives, and of disappointing the trust that we have placed in them; and, with the other, lead them to measures worthy of His blessing, capable of augmenting their own glory, and strengthening the freedoms, the prosperity and the happiness of the Republic.

(A multitude of signatures followed.)

On November 19, we left Montpelier to go to Fredericksburg by passing through Orange Courthouse. A large escort, under the command of Captain Masson, had arrived in the morning to wait for General Lafayette, and Mr. Madison wanted to accompany him. Upon arriving at Orange Courthouse, we found the entire population drawn up in two lines between which the General passed in order to arrive near Colonel Barbour, ex-Governor of the State of Virginia, who had been charged by his fellow citizens to address the Nation's Guest. While traversing these two lines, the General received expressions of regret from some old Revolutionary soldiers whom age and distance had prevented from joining their companions-in-arms for the celebration of the anniversary of Yorktown. He consoled them by displays of friendship and of remembrance to which they appeared extremely responsive. After Colonel Barbour's speech, Miss Derby presented him a bouquet of flowers in the name of her young companions, to which she joined an affectionate and loving speech. Afterwards, we stayed for the time necessary to attend a banquet presided over by Colonel Barbour where, according to custom, 13 toasts were proclaimed during the dessert. These 13 official toasts were followed by a large number of private toasts that expressed all the feelings of patriotism and gratitude aroused by the day's festivities. After the meal, we separated from Mr. Madison who, despite his 74 years, mounted his horse nimbly and returned alone through the woods to his peaceful abode. As for us, we continued our trip in the midst of the escort that had accompanied the General in the morning, and which had been increased considerably by a large number of citizens who wanted, by following him, to prolong the pleasure that they had in being with him.

After traveling for some time, we encountered on the route a multitude of people, pressing around a triumphal arch built at the intersection of the road and a narrow footpath that one could hardly make out through the thickness of the woods. We soon learned that the path, which girls were sprinkling with flowers and the crowd was examining with a touching interest, was the road which Lafayette had opened on June 15, 1781 in order to proceed by a rapid and stealthy march from the banks of the Rapidan to the banks of Mechunk Creek, where Cornwallis was very surprised to find him in battle array when he believed he could seize the supplies of all the Southern States stored at Albemarle without resistance. This latest proof of the honorable remembrance that the Americans retained for all of his actions touched General Lafayette deeply; he was moved nearly to tears when he found himself covered with flowers by the girls and, in descending from the carriage, when he found himself surrounded and hugged tenderly by all the citizens who were waiting for him beneath the triumphal arch.

He conversed with them for a long time and recounted to the young people how much these places reminded him of the debt that he owed to their fathers. “It is even here,” he told them, “at the moment when I was carrying out a movement by this footpath that could have been so fatal to me if it was not crowned with success, that they abandoned their harvests to join my little army, and, during this entire campaign, the distance from their families, the hardships of all kinds, the ruinous abandonment of the cultivation of their land, and the difficulty of having rations did not prevent them from remaining with the army well beyond what one had the right to require of them.” – But what General Lafayette did not tell them, because modesty prevented him from speaking of it, is the skill with which he uplifted the courage of the most downhearted men in this very circumstance, nor did he tell them that he knew how to keep those with him who were the most disposed to withdraw.

The militiamen having been retained very much beyond their time by delay of those who were to replace them, and complaining of it more and more every day, the General agreed that their discontent was just; he expressed to them how sensitive he was to the considerable injury that must be resulting to them from the fact that they were staying so long far from their homes, and especially to the unexpected, inconvenient delay that he had not been able to foresee before departing; he added that he could not imagine the cause of it.

He apologized to them for having kept them beyond their time; he declared to them that he did not have the will to keep them any more, and concluded by according to all of them permission to go; he informed them, moreover, that, for himself, he could not abandon the position that had been entrusted to him and that he would remain with the small number of regular troops that he had. He knew the character of the men he was commanding perfectly, and, by this means, he obtained the results that he was anticipating; for, after the speech, he would have had very great difficulty in making a single one of them leave without giving him a certificate stating that he had been ordered to go. "Who is the wretched man," they said to each other, "who could even think of abandoning the Marquis?"

This is how the Americans called Lafayette during the entire time of the war. This manner of referring to him had become such a habit that it was still in use in all the United States when we arrived in New York. For several days, the newspapers giving accounts of his movements and the festivities that were given him did not use any other appellation in speaking of him, and they only stopped using it when they learned that the General had consistently refused to resume this title since his renunciation of it in the bosom of the National Assembly. But his contemporaries had very great difficulty ridding themselves of an old habit, which had not been without some charm for them because it carried them back to the time of their youth. I recall that in Philadelphia an old lady, who had known him very well during the Revolution, and who probably pictured him still such as she had seen him then, rushed headlong towards him in the crowd shouting: "Let me pass, let me pass so that I can see again this good young Marquis!"

It was only at sunset that we arrived, on November 20, at Fredericksburg where the General was welcomed by the young children formed in a battalion under the name of Lafayette's Cadets. The night was already dark and the Town resplendent with lights when we arrived at the place where the Mayor gave his welcoming address. A splendid meal and a ball, at which all the ladies of Fredericksburg sparkled, concluded this day of traveling. The next day, Sunday, we attended a divine service in the Episcopal Church with the Freemasons who had led us there with great pomp. The minister who officiated was a member of the lodge. On Monday we spent a part of the day with the family of Captain Lewis, nephew of General Washington, and in the evening, we left for Washington City, accompanied for several miles by the people of Fredericksburg. On the line of Strafford County, of which we traversed only the tip, the militia rushed before the General in order to escort him to the Potomac where we waited for the ship that would take us to Washington after a night of favorable sailing.

Couché fils sc.

MADISSON.

END OF FIRST VOLUME

VOLUME TWO

G.al WASHINGTON.

Chapter I

Festival of the Farmers of Maryland – Indian Delegation Presented to General Lafayette – Message of the President of the United States – Extraordinary Honors Rendered to the Nation's Guest – National Reward Offered by Congress.

On arriving at Washington, we went to dine at the President's House, and after 24 hours of rest, we left for Baltimore, where we were invited, as members of the Agricultural Society, to be present at the annual festival of the farmers of Maryland. This festival has as its purpose the distribution of rewards and incentives to all those who, in the course of the year, have made progress in agriculture or in the arts of domestic economy. The different products are submitted, without the name of the producer, to the examination of a jury, on the report of which the prizes are distributed by the Agricultural Society. The exposition appeared to us to be rich in products of all kinds. A great number of horses, cows, and sheep, noteworthy by their fine form, proved to us how much care the farmers of Maryland bring to perfecting the breeds. Some models of agricultural implements; linen, hemp, cotton, and wool cloths; wines, grains, arranged so they could be examined by everyone; all attested to the spirit of research and improvement of the industrial class of this wealthy State.

General Harper opened the meeting with a very instructive speech on the current state of the progress of agriculture in Maryland, and General Lafayette was charged with distributing the prizes to those who had won them. After the prizes were handed out, all the farmers were formed in two rows by Mr. Skinner, Secretary of the Society, and General Lafayette passed in front of them while shaking the hand of each of them. After this ceremony they cheerfully took a seat at the table where they drank many toasts to him: *To the Nation's Guest*; *to the farmer of La Grange*, etc. The General responded to all these compliments by making the following toast: *"To the seed of American liberty transplanted on other shores. Stifled to the present time, but not destroyed by evil European weeds, may it be able to germinate and rise anew, more vigorous, more pure and cover the soil of the two hemispheres!"*

Before leaving Baltimore, we visited several farms of the surrounding area in each of which Lafayette carefully took notes on the different improvements that appeared to him to be of useful application for his farm at La Grange. He especially admired the beautiful steam boiler[1] of the President of the Society with the aid of which one could feed the numerous herds more

1. Since our return to France, the General has received from Mr. Morris, a citizen of Baltimore, a similar boiler and has put it into operation on his farm.

economically and more abundantly. Mr. Patterson offered him a young bull and two heifers of an elegant form that was extremely rare. They are of a race which has been created, they say, in England in the county of Devonshire. He also received from several other farmers some wild turkeys suitable to increase the race of European turkeys; some pigs of extraordinary size and shape, etc.; in a word, each one wanted to offer some products to the farmer of La Grange, and he accepted with all the more thanks, since he saw in each of these presents a means of being useful to contemporary French Agriculture.

Upon our return to Washington, we found the City very much more animated than before our departure. The number of foreigners and citizens from all parts of the Union, who assembled there at the time of the opening of the Congress, had flocked there at this time in very much greater numbers still, drawn by the desire to be there at the same time as the Nation's Guest, and in order to witness the installation of the new President whom the people had elected this year. The ambassadors of the European powers, the representatives of the new States of South America had come to resume their posts which they had left during the summer months; even some delegations of Indians had come from the depths of the most distant forests to set forth the needs of their brothers. These delegations came to visit General Lafayette the day after our return. They were presented to him by Major Pitchlynn, their interpreter. At their head were two chiefs whom we had seen sitting one day at Mr. Jefferson's table during our stay at Monticello. I recognized them by their ears which were cut in long thongs, decorated with long strips of lead. One of them, named *Mushalatubee*, addressed the General in the Indian language, and said to him:

> You are one of our fathers. You fought at the side of Washington. We clasp your hand here as that of a friend and a father. We have always marched in the pure path of peace, and it is this path that we have followed to come to see you. We present to you pure hands that have never been stained by American blood. We live far from here in a country where the burning sun hurls its rays on us perpendicularly. We have had as neighbors the French, the Spanish and the English; but now our only neighbors are the Americans, in the midst of whom we live as friends and as brothers.

Then *Pushamata*, the foremost of their chiefs, spoke in his turn and expressed himself in these words:

> There have been 50 snows since you drew your sword as Washington's companion: with him you fought the enemies

> of America. In mixing your blood generously with the blood of your enemies, you have proven your devotion to the cause that you were defending. After having ended this war, you returned to your Fatherland, and now you come to revisit this land where you are honored and blessed by the gratitude of a numerous and powerful people. You see everywhere the children of those whose liberty you defended crowd around you and clasp your hands with a filial affection. We have heard recounted all these things in the depths of our most faraway shelters, and our hearts have been consumed by the desire to see you. We have come, we have clasped your hand and we are satisfied. It is the first time that we see you and probably the last. We will no longer meet. The land will separate us forever....

In uttering these last words, the old Indian had something solemn in his countenance and his voice. He seemed perturbed by sad premonitions. We learned of his death a few days later; it took place before he could set out to return to the midst of his people. Sensing that his end was coming, he called his traveling companions, asked them to lift him up and to dress him in his most beautiful vestments and requested that they bring him his arms so that his death would be that of a man. He evidenced the desire that at his interment the Americans should render to him military honors and that they should shoot the cannon over his tomb. They promised him this: then he began to converse with his friends, and expired gently in the middle of the conversation. He was very old and he belonged to the tribe of the Choctaws as did some of those who came to visit the General. The others were of the Chickasaw tribe.

On returning to Washington, the General had found messages from all the States of the South and the West by which they expressed to him the desire and the hope that the people of these parts of the Union had of receiving a visit from him. The representatives of these different States, who had arrived to sit in Congress, came to see him each day and spoke to him enthusiastically of the preparations which their citizens were already making to receive the Nation's Guest in a dignified manner. He felt, indeed, that it would be difficult, not to say impossible, for him to refuse requests expressed to him in so touching and honorable a manner. Hence, he came to a decision to accept all these invitations, but it was decided that, in view of the too-advanced time of the season, he would recommence his traveling only at the end of winter, a part of which he would devote to rest in Washington, where he would be able to follow the debates of Congress. But as the debates were not to open for a few days, he resolved to take advantage of the time which remained to him to visit all the members of General Washington's family who were in the environs of the Capital.

First, he went to the home of one of Washington's nieces, Mrs. Lewis, who lives in Woodlawn. This lady had been brought up at Mount Vernon with George Lafayette, and time had not destroyed the fraternal friendship which had been established between her and him. She received us with great affection, as did her husband and family. We stayed for four days at Woodlawn, surrounded by the most affectionate solicitudes. We left Woodlawn laden with small presents that were of great value to us, because nearly all of them consisted of objects that had belonged to the hero of liberty, the immortal Washington.

As Woodlawn is only a portion of the old property of Mount Vernon, we had only a walk to go to have dinner with Judge Bushrod Washington. Afterwards, we returned to Arlington, to the house of Mr. Custis, of whom I have already had occasion to speak. His house, built on scaled-down plans of the Temple of Theseus, stands on one of the most beautiful sites that one could imagine. From the portico, the eye can embrace, at the same time, the majestic course of the Potomac, the commercial activity of Georgetown, the rising City of Washington, and, in the distance, the vast horizon below which are the fertile fields of Maryland. If Mr. Custis employed only a dozen well-paid free workers, instead of a large number of indolent Slaves who ate up his produce and left his roads in bad repair, I am sure that he would not have been long in tripling his revenues and in having one of the most charming properties, not only in the District of Columbia, but also in all of Virginia.

While the General was visiting his friends, Congress opened its session, on December 6, according to custom. On the 7th, at noon, the Houses had received the message of the President, and, at our return to Washington on the 8th, we could read this political document, always so noteworthy in the United States. The President's message was still more interesting this year because it was the last great act of the administration of an honorable man and because its influence perhaps saved the Republics of South America, I do not say from the intrigues, but at least from the attacks of Europe. I urge those who want to learn how, in a legitimate government, the head of state, freely chosen by the people, renders an accounting to his citizens of the sacred mission which they have entrusted to him, to read Mr. Monroe's message of December 6, 1824. They will see there with what candor this wise magistrate gives to Congress the details of all the acts of his administration; with what simplicity he speaks of his agreements with all the Kings of Europe; with what frankness he lays out the needs, the resources, in a word, the condition of the state; but also with what courage, what dignity, he declares to the entire world that the Republic, faithful to its commitments, will regard all attacks directed against its allies as a personal offense, and will always repulse with all its power the unjust principle of foreign intervention in the affairs of a nation!

One will perhaps be grateful to me for reporting here the part of the message relative to the Republics of South America. Here is how Mr. Monroe expresses himself:

> With regard to the struggle in which our neighbors are now engaged, it is evident that the Spanish power does not make itself felt anymore, so to speak. These new States have completed the work of their independence recognized by the United States, and maintained it without too much foreign opposition. The troubles that were manifested in some parts of these vast States originated from internal causes that had their source in the character of their first governments, and which are not yet entirely eliminated. But it is manifest that these causes are growing weaker each day, and that these new Republics will soon be strengthened by governments elected and representative, similar to ours in all their parts. We ardently pray that these Republics continue to march on this road, because we have the deep-seated conviction that it must lead them to success; but, despite our prayers, we did not believe that we ought to offer our intervention because we think that each people has alone the right to give itself the government that it believes to be best suited to its interests. They have, moreover, our example before their eyes, and they alone are competent judges of our efforts, of our success, and of what is best-suited to their needs; we leave them to their own inspirations with the hope that the other powers will follow the same policy as we.
>
> We have made known to the entire world the profound interest that we take in the independence of these new States, the alacrity with which we have recognized their independence, and especially our desire that they be free in the choice of their government. Separated, as we are, from Europe by the vast ocean, we cannot have any interest in the wars that occur between the European Governments or in the causes that produce them. That the balance of power, in its continual oscillations, leans in favor of the one or the other matters little to us: it suffices to us to preserve with the one and the others amicable relations that would protect their interests and ours. But with regard to our neighbors of the South, our situation is different. We cannot allow European Governments to intervene in their affairs, especially those which regard the choice of their government, and we would be obligated to

> consider every intervention of this kind as an aggression that would be personal to us. It is satisfying to know that some of the Powers with whom we are in relations of friendship, and to whom we have explained our intentions on this subject, have appeared to be disposed to approve of them.[2]

The President also rendered an account of the reasons for the visit of General Lafayette to the United States and of the circumstances which had attended it. "In conformity with a resolution of Congress taken in the last session," he said,

> General Lafayette had been invited to visit the United States, and had received notice that a ship of the State would proceed to the French port that he would want to designate in order to conduct him to that part of America where he judged it convenient to land. His modesty led him to refuse this offer; but he answered that for a long time he had intended to visit the Union, and that certainly he would carry it out in the course of the year. Last August, he arrived at New York where he was received with displays of affection and gratitude to which the importance of his services and the sacrifices which he made for us give him so great a claim. A unanimous feeling with regard to him has manifested itself in all parts of America, and he has received invitations from all the States which truly want him to visit them. Everywhere he has appeared, the population of the surrounding area has joined to welcome and honor him. Everywhere he awakens the most lively interest in calling attention to the surviving heroes of our Revolution, who shared with him its labors and its dangers, and whom time has spared up to the present.
>
> Undoubtedly, a spectacle more worthy of interest could never be shown to mankind, because it would be impossible that an equal concurrence of feelings and circumstances so remarkable would be reproduced. It was quite natural to expect this feeling from those who fought with him for the same cause; but his presence has moved all classes of citizens, even the youngest ones. In a word, is there an individual in the Union whose family has not taken part in the War of Independence?

2. Did Mr. Canning forget this part of the message of the President of the United States, or did he think that it was unknown to Europe, when he boasted two years later, of having put the Republics of South America on the list of nations by recognizing their independence first?

> Is there a child who has not heard the story? Hasn't the entire Nation, for 40 years, appreciated the outcome every day! We fought for our public and individual freedom, and our efforts were crowned with success. The presence of the one who, guided by such noble ideas, took so active a part in our cause, could not fail to produce a profound impression on individuals of all ages. It was natural that we would take the most lively interest in his future well-being, as we do. His rights to our gratitude are well known.
>
> For these reasons, I invite the Congress to take into consideration the services which he has rendered, the sacrifices that he has made, the losses that he has experienced, and to vote a grant in his favor which responds in a manner worthy of the character and the grandeur of the American people.

After this message was read, the Houses, according to custom, immediately named committees to engage in the work relative to each article of the message. The one which was charged with that which related to the General was invited to present its conclusions with the shortest delay.

But other committees had already been named to occupy themselves with the official reception for the General in the bosom of the Congress; and, on December 8, these committees having been joined together, Mr. Barbour made known to the House of Representatives the result of their judgment. They were of the opinion that, in order to prevent the difficulties that would have possibly arisen in the ceremonies to follow, each House should engage separately in the reception for the Nation's Guest. The Senate deliberated afterwards on the manner in which General Lafayette would be welcomed into its bosom, and the committee was authorized to continue to be the intermediary between the Senate and him for the entire session.

On the 9th, Mr. Mitchell, in the name of the same committees, proposed to the House of Representatives the following resolutions, which were adopted unanimously.

> General Lafayette will be congratulated publicly by the House for acceding to the wishes of Congress which called him to the United States; assurances will be given to him of the gratitude and the profound respect that the chamber maintains for the eminent services that he rendered during the Revolution, and

> of the pleasure that it feels in seeing him again, on the scene of his exploits after so long an absence. To this end, General Lafayette will be invited by a delegation to proceed into the bosom of the chamber, next Friday at one o'clock. He will be introduced by the committee, welcomed by the members, standing and bareheaded, and addressed by the Speaker.

When these resolutions of the committee became known to the public, the militias wanted to take up arms to give all the brilliance of military pomp to the entrance of the Nation's Guest to Congress; but General Lafayette, having learned of their intention, hastened to offer his thanks, while telling them that "he did not believe that it was fitting in the circumstances that he should be surrounded by a display of arms." The militias, always eager to do what would be most agreeable to him, renounced their plan at once and, at 12:30, we climbed into carriages with the Senate committee to proceed to the Capitol building.

At precisely one o'clock, the doors to the Senate opened, and General Lafayette was introduced into the bosom of the assembly by Mr. Barbour, president of the committee. On arriving at the center of the hall, Mr. Barbour said in a loud voice: *"We present General Lafayette to the Senate of the United States."* The Senators, standing bareheaded, received this announcement in the deepest silence. Afterwards, the committee led the General to a seat placed to the right of the President of the Senate, Mr. Gaillard. Immediately, the motion was made to suspend the session so that each Senator could come individually to show his respect for the General. This motion having passed, the Senators left their seats in succession and came to clasp his hand warmly. The session was then dissolved.

On the following day, the General was led again to the Capitol building by a delegation of 24 members of the House of Representatives. The cortege was composed of a dozen carriages, but without escort, without pomp and without decorations. Our trip across the City was slow and silent. At the sight of the first carriage, which carried the General, the citizens stopped, took off their hats, but they did not cheer. This silence, this simplicity had something solemn about it. While waiting for the session to be commenced, they led us into the conference room. Since the morning, the public galleries had been filled with a crowd. The benches were occupied by the foreign diplomatic corps and by the most distinguished people of the City. By reason of the great multitude of spectators, the part of the hall that the Representatives did not occupy had been given over to the ladies invited to the session for this time only.

When the Representatives had taken their place, Mr. Condict mounted to the rostrum and proposed that the Senate be invited to the session; another member, Mr. Poinsett, responded that, the House not being in the actual exercise of its functions, this invitation was perhaps unnecessary; but this motion passed by a large majority. The President, or rather the Speaker, because that is what one calls the one who directs and sums up the debates of the House, then asked the members who were sitting on the right side to pass to the left side to cede their places to the Senators. The doors were opened and the Senators came to take their places. Some moments after, two members of the House called "Mr. George Lafayette and Mr. Levasseur," and led us within the assembly, where they had us take our places on the cabinet-ministers' bench. Then, when a signal was given, the doors were opened, and General Lafayette appeared between Mr. Mitchell and Mr. Livingston, followed by the entire committee that had escorted him. At this sight, the whole assembly rose, took off their hats and remained silent. When the General arrived at the center of the hall, the Speaker, Mr. Clay, took the floor, and said to him:

> The House of Representatives of the United States, actuated by its own feelings and spokesman for those of the Nation, could not impose on me a duty more satisfying to fulfill than that of offering you its hearty congratulations on your recent arrival in this country. I am complying with the wishes of Congress by giving you the assurance of the high degree of satisfaction which your presence in the first theater of your glory inspires. Among the members who make up this body, there are found only a few men who have taken part with you in our Revolutionary War; but all have learned, from unbiased history or from reliable traditions, of the perils, the suffering, the sacrifices to which you voluntarily submitted, and the conspicuous services which you rendered to a faraway people, nearly unknown, and still in its infancy, in America and in Europe. All feel and recognize the extent of the obligations you have imposed on the Nation. But, however interesting and important the relations which you have at all times entered into with our States may be, they alone do not explain the respect and admiration of this chamber. The constant steadfastness of your character, your imperturbable devotion to liberty based on legal order, during every vicissitude of a long and perilous life, lay claim to our profound admiration. During the recent convulsions that have agitated Europe, in the middle as well as after the cessation of political

thunderstorms, the people of the United States have always seen you faithful to your principles, standing head held high amidst all dangers, encouraging the friends of liberty with that voice that is so well known to it, and a faithful and fearless champion of liberty, ready to spill the last drop of your blood for it, which you have already so nobly and so generously spilled here for the same holy cause.

Often we have formed the vain desire that Providence should permit the patriot to visit his country after his death, to contemplate there the changes to which time has given birth. Today, the American patriot of times passed would see forests cultivated, towns founded, mountains leveled, canals opened, great roads built, great progress made in the Arts, the Sciences and in the increase of the population.

General, your current visit provides the happy accomplishment of this wish. You are here in the midst of posterity. Everywhere you must be struck by the physical and moral change which has taken place since you left us; this City itself, which bears a name that is dear to you and dear to us, was recently built in the bosom of the forest that covered its soil. But there is one point on which we do not find any change. It is the feeling of our constant devotion to freedom, of our living and profound gratitude for the friend whom you have lost, the father of the country, for you, General, and for your illustrious companions in the theatre of the war and in its councils, as well as for the numerous benefits which we enjoy, and for the very right which I am exercising at this moment in addressing myself to you. This sentiment, so dear today to more than 10,000,000 people, will be transmitted without being weakened to the most distant posterity, reaching from age to age to the innumerable generations that are destined to people this continent.

The profound emotion that had swept over the Speaker, and which had visibly shaken him during his speech, passed rapidly into the hearts of all the audience, and each one waited with a kindly anxiety the response that he presumed had been written by the General for so solemn an occasion. But how agreeably surprised they were when they saw him advance several steps towards the Speaker, cast some looks of emotion and gratitude on the assembly, and then, after some moments of reflection, speak distinctly, even to the most distant galleries, the following extemporaneous speech with his sonorous voice:

> Mr. President and gentlemen of the House of Representatives. When the people of the United States and its honorable representatives in Congress have deigned to choose, in my person, an American veteran to bear witness to their esteem for our joint works and to their attachment to the principles for which we have had the honor to fight and to spill our blood, I am happy and proud to share these extraordinary honors with my dear companions-in-arms and in revolution. Nonetheless, it would be ungrateful and insincere of me if I did not acknowledge the individual part you are according to me in these marks of goodwill, to which my heart responds with emotions too profound for me to be able to express them.
>
> My obligations to the United States, Sir, surpass greatly the services that I have been able to render to them. They date from the period when I had the good fortune to be adopted by America as one of its young soldiers, as a well-loved son. During nearly half a century, I have continued to receive constant proofs of their affection and of their trust; and, at present, Sir, thanks to the precious invitation that I received from Congress, I find myself welcomed by a series of emotional receptions of which a single hour would do more than compensate for the works and the sufferings of an entire life.
>
> The approbation of the American people for my conduct in the vicissitudes of the European Revolution is the greatest thing that I could receive. To be sure, I can stand fast with head held high, when in their name and by you, Mr. President, it is solemnly declared that on each occasion I have stayed faithful to American principles of liberty, equality and true social order to which I have been devoted since my youth and which, till my last breath, will be a sacred duty to me.
>
> You have, indeed, alluded to the particular good fortune of my situation, when, after so long an absence, it has been reserved to me to see the immense progress, the admirable communications, the prodigious creations of which we find an example in this City, whose very name is a venerable palladium; in a word, to see all the grandeur, all the prosperity of these fortunate United States

which, at the same time that they offer a noble guarantee to the full complement of American independence, spread the light of a very superior political civilization on all parts of the world.

What surer gauge can one give of the national perseverance in the love of liberty than the very benefits that are certainly the result of a virtuous resistance to oppression, of institutions founded on the rights of man and on the republican principle of a government of the people by themselves?

No, Mr. President, posterity has not yet begun for me, since, in the sons of my old companions and friends, I find again the same public sentiments, and, permit me to add, the same feelings for me that I had the good fortune to be acquainted with in their fathers.

Sir, I was permitted, 40 years ago, before a committee of a Congress of 13 United States, to express the ardent best wishes of an American heart. Today, I have the honor, and I feel the delightful pleasure of congratulating the representatives of the Union, so greatly augmented, on a realization of those wishes, very much more than all human expectations and on the nearly infinite prospect that we can surely foresee. Permit me, Mr. President, to add to the expression of these sentiments the tribute of my profound gratitude, of my loving devotion and my deepest respect.

I will not undertake to describe here the profound impression that the response of the General produced on all the spectators and the entirety of this scene so simple and yet so majestic. Perhaps, I would not be understood by everybody. For me, I confess, I could not avoid comparing this moving tableau of national recognition crowning civic virtues with the pompous ceremonies in the midst of which the Kings of Europe appear surrounded only by a burst of royal purple and by arms, and these latter appeared to me no more than brilliant representations of the stage, which one could perhaps take pleasure in beholding, if one did not know how onerous they ordinarily were to the people.

After the honors, unknown up to then, that Congress had just given to General Lafayette, it seemed that all expressions of national gratitude had been exhausted. However, Congress, attentive to the words of the President's message, and especially to the expression of public opinion that manifested itself in the newspapers and in private letters addressed from all parts of the

Union to the representatives every day, believed that there remained to it still something to do, and it hastened to name a committee charged with finding the ways to make acceptable to the General a grant worthy of the Nation that wanted to offer it to him. This committee made a report on December 20 in which, after having recalled the services that Lafayette had rendered to the American Nation, and the sacrifices he had made for the establishment of its independence, it proposed that they offer him as compensation and as a gesture of gratitude, a sum of $200,000 (about 1,000,000 francs), and the ownership of 24,000 acres of land chosen in the most fertile part of the United States.

This proposition was readily received by the Senate, and they believed that it would pass without discussion immediately but, at the moment when they were going to send it to the House of Representatives, a Senator took the floor and said that he had no objections to make, either against the sum that they wanted to vote or as to the services for which they proposed it; that he was second to none in gratitude to and in friendship for General Lafayette, whose virtues and sacrifices he believed one would never know how to reward too much; but he believed that, in this circumstance, the method adopted was defective; that, charged as Congress was with administering the revenues of the people, he did not believe that Congress was permitted to dispose of them other than for public service; that he believed that each State individually demanded with reason the right to give expression to its gratitude to Lafayette; finally, that he was voting against taking this proposition into consideration in order to avoid establishing a precedent the consequences of which could be disastrous afterwards.

The eloquence of Mr. Hayne triumphed easily over this opposition, born of a conscience excessively scrupulous in matters of finances, and the bill having been read a third time, the assembly voted on the entire project, which was adopted nearly unanimously. Only seven votes were cast against it, and it was universally recognized that even those who voted against the bill were counted among the friends and the warmest partisans of the General. Reasons of public order, and with some, the custom of deciding against every extraordinary measure of finance, had alone determined their opposition.

The proposal was not received with less alacrity and goodwill in the House of Representatives. As soon as the committee presented its report there, all other discussion was put aside, and the bill was deliberated on. The discussion that was engaged in was, like the one that had taken place in the Senate, without dispute on the rights of the General to national gratitude, and was concerned with the legality of the means employed.

After its third reading, the bill was adopted by a majority that counted barely a few votes in opposition. Here is the form in which it was promulgated by the Government.

> *Act Concerning General Lafayette.*
>
> Article 1. Enacted by the Senate and the House of Representatives of the United States, assembled in Congress, that in consideration of the service and the sacrifices of General Lafayette during the Revolutionary War, the Secretary of the public treasury is and remains authorized by these presents to pay him the sum of 200,000 dollars, taken out of funds to which there has not yet been given any intended purpose.
>
> Article 2. Enacted, moreover, that there be granted to the said General Lafayette, for his enjoyment of it, to him and his heirs, a piece of land that will be allotted to him, by the authority of the President on lands of the United States not yet granted.

While these discussions were taking place in the Congress, General Lafayette, who did not know that they were occupying themselves entirely with him, was at Annapolis where the Legislature of the State of Maryland had summoned him. It was only the day after his return to Washington that the two committees of the Senate and the House of Representatives imparted to him the resolution of Congress. Mr. Smith undertook to speak, and, while presenting him the decree, said to him:

> General, the Senate and the House of Representatives have instructed us to make known to you the adoption of an act that concerns you and of which we are delivering to you a copy. You will see that the two houses of Congress, in appreciation for the great sacrifices that your ardent devotion to the cause of American freedom has cost you, believed that they ought to reimburse you for a part of the expenses that you have incurred. The noble principles that characterize you will not permit you to object that the Nation discharges its obligations to you in this way. We have been chosen to express to you the hope of the two houses that you will not refuse their request and that, indeed, you will be willing, in accepting the gift that is made to you, to add this proof of your regard to all those which you have already given to the American Nation. For the Nation's part, the feelings that it has vowed to you will last so long as

> it knows how to appreciate the freedom that it enjoys. Deign to receive this special expression of the pleasure that we have at being the instruments of this communication.

General Lafayette felt great embarrassment upon learning of the munificence of the Congress towards him. He, first, wanted to refuse because he thought that the evidences of affection and gratitude of the people that he had received since his arrival in the United States were a beautiful and honorable enough reward for his services, and he never desired any other. But, nonetheless, he felt, by the manner by which this offer was being made to him, that he could not refuse it without putting himself at risk of offending the American Nation and its representatives, and he decided to accept it at once. "Gentlemen," he responded to the members of the committee,

> The huge and unexpected gift that the Congress, after so many other displays of good will, has truly wanted to make to me, requires the deepest gratitude of an old American soldier and an adoptive son of the United States, two titles more dear to my heart than all the treasures of the world.
>
> However proud as I am of all the displays of affection that the people of the United States and their representatives in Congress have given me, the magnitude of this last kindness has awakened in the midst of my gratitude, some feelings of hesitation from which I am unable to defend myself. But at this time, the gracious resolution of the two houses does not permit me to feel any other sentiment than that of the gratitude of which I pray that you are indeed willing to be the spokesmen. Deign also, Gentlemen, to offer the homage of my profound respect to the Congress and to receive yourselves the assurance of my personal thanks.

The news of this Act of Congress soon reached into all parts of the Union by way of the newspapers, and a unanimous cry of approval was raised on all sides. Some States even went so far as to express a willingness to add more to what Congress had done. So, for example, Virginia, New York and Maryland were already preparing to vote new sums to give to the Nation's Guest. It took all the General's forceful moderating influence to curb this excess of gratitude that would have ended by putting at his disposal all the funds of the United States, for, once the States engaged in this contest of generosity, it was difficult to foresee where it would stop.

Meanwhile, the newspapers, voices of public opinion, while applauding all that Congress had done, attacked the small number of members who had voted against the national gift in the Senate and the House of Representatives with an intensity that pained General Lafayette. These attacks were, in effect, more especially unjust since, as I believe I have already said, most of the opponents were personal friends of the General, and entirely devoted to his interests; but, in voting, not against the proposal, but against its form, they had remained faithful to the principle that they had followed constantly of never granting funds for expenditures other than those recognized as indispensable to the public service. Some of them believed that they ought to explain this themselves to the General: "Not only do we share the gratitude and admiration of our fellow citizens for the services that you have rendered to us," they said to him, "but we also think that the Nation would never be able to discharge its obligations to you, and yet we are 26 who have voted against the proposal of Congress...." – "Well," the General answered them, while cordially clasping their hands, "I can assure you that if I had had the honor to be your colleague, we would have been 27, not only because I share the opinion that determined your vote, but also because I think that the American Nation has done far too much for me." This response was not long in being reported by all the newspapers, and only added, as one could well imagine, to the popularity of the one who had made it.

I have already said that, during the deliberations of Congress, the General had proceeded to Maryland at the invitation of its legislature, which had also wanted to accord to him the honors of a reception in public session. We had left Washington on December 16, accompanied by Dr. Kent, Mr. Mitchell, some representatives of the State of Maryland, and a detachment of cavalry of the voluntary militia. On the route, we had visited the family and the beautiful farm of Captain Sprigg, ex-Governor of Maryland, and we had arrived at Annapolis in the afternoon. The representatives of the City had proceeded before the General, at a rather large distance from it; and despite the frightful weather, the troops had advanced up to Miller's Hill. Another corps of militia had come from Nottingham, situated 30 miles from Annapolis. The thunderstorm had retarded its arrival, but did not reduce the zeal of the citizens. At Carol's Lane, two miles from the City, the General, in spite of the remonstrances that were made to him, wanted to descend from the carriage, and, head uncovered, he came to thank the militiamen for the affection that they had demonstrated to him. "They have exposed themselves to the rigors of the weather for me, and I do not want to delay expressing my thanks to them," he said. At the border of the district, there took place an interesting encounter between him and soldiers of the Revolutionary Army, several of whom had aided in carrying him from the field at the Battle of Brandywine, when he was wounded there.

His entrance to the City was announced by 24 cannon shots and the national flag, which they hoisted over the State House. They led him into the hall of the legislature, which persons of distinction and soldiers of the War of Independence filled, and had him take a seat where he listened to the speech given by the Mayor, in the name of the City. In his response he recalled that Annapolis had been the theater of events to be remembered forever in the annals of the United States; that it was inside of these walls that Washington lay down the power entrusted to him by the Nation; that the inhabitants of this City had always been worthy by their patriotism of being witnesses or protagonists of this majestic scene.

The following day, Friday, December 17, the militias of the county, the voluntary battalion of Annapolis and the artillery of the United States executed extensive maneuvers before the General with very much cohesion and precision.

The following Monday, he received from the Legislature of the State honors absolutely like those which had been bestowed some days before by the Congress. The day concluded with a public dinner that all the Senators and all the Representatives attended and a ball given by the Mayor of the City.

Annapolis is a city of 2,500 people, built very nicely on the Severn River, which flows into Chesapeake Bay. It is the seat of government of the State of Maryland, but will never become an important place, at least on account of its commerce, which is entirely absorbed by the Port of Baltimore, which is very near.

To return to Washington, we traveled by Frederickstown, where the General was welcomed eagerly by the population and by a large number of his old companions-in-arms among whom he recognized Colonel McPherson, at whose house we took lodging. At a public banquet that was offered to him by the City, the table was illuminated by a candelabrum holding a large number of candles whose base was an enormous bomb fragment carried away from the siege of Yorktown.

Frederickstown is, immediately after Baltimore, the most notable city of Maryland. It is situated in the middle of a fertile plain on the western bank of the little Monococy River. Its population, which is barely 3,000, is in large part engaged in manufacturing.

Chapter II

Election of the President – Public Character of the President – Ministers and Public Officials – Congress – The Great Public Dinner of the First of January.

When we disembarked in New York in the month of August, the people of the United States were at that time when they are occupied with the choice of a new political leader. This choice is renewed every four years. It is always accompanied by a great popular excitement, and that is understandable because it interests all the citizens equally. Nevertheless, this excitement does not bring any disorder in its train. Since the establishment of the Constitution, the Nation has proceeded nine times in the election of its President, and none of these elections has been disturbed by a serious occurrence. The newspapers, it is true, as organs of the parties who descend into the electoral arena, become at that time arsenals in which one finds weapons of all forms and of all characters, and they all conduct themselves at times in a very discourteous manner; but the exaggeration, the violence of the newspapers stays in the newspapers and never drags the masses beyond the limits of the law.

The election of 1824, like the nine elections preceding it, thwarted the perceptions of European politicians who, with an assurance that only ignorance or bad faith can give, forecast that finally the Constitution of the United States was going to undergo a test that it was impossible to withstand, and that from the bosom of the turbulent American democracy, civil war and the overthrow of the established order was going to ensue. These predictions were based on the fact that the Nation, which until the present time had been able to limit its choice to a small number of men to whom the affections of all were attached by the memories of the Revolution, found itself obliged today to start a new category due to the depletion of these men and, consequently, to open the door to the ambitions of all. To what point were these calculations based on reason? We are going to see by an examination of what happened.

But before giving an account of the manner in which this tenth election of the President occurred, on the dissentions of which the enemies of the legitimate rights of the people in Europe rested all their hopes, it will be necessary, I believe, to point out here briefly the procedure according to which the law requires this election to be made. The Federal Constitution invests in the President of the United States the executive power. The duration of his office is four years. The law does not determine the number of times that he can be reelected, but the example given by Washington, and followed scrupulously by his successors, has the force of law today, and no one up to the present has pursued the possibilities of a third election. Each State names individually, in the way indicated in its constitution, as many Electors as it has Senators and Representatives together in Congress; but no Senator, Representative, or employee of the Government, can be chosen to be an elector.

The Electors join together in their respective States, and choose, by means of a ballot, two persons of which at least one must not be a citizen of the said State. They make a list of all these persons so named and of the number of votes each has obtained. The Electors sign and certify this list which is transmitted to the Senate President, who, in the presence of the Senate and the Representatives together, counts the votes. The one who has the greatest number of votes is named President, if this number constitutes a majority of the Electors. If the votes are divided in such a way that no one has the necessary majority, then the House is called upon to choose itself, by way of a ballot, among the three persons who collected the greatest number of votes. In this choice, the votes are counted by State, the delegation of each State having only one vote at that time. The majority necessary in this case is to be two-thirds of the States.

Congress determines the time of the elections, which must be the same in every State.

Some men, who enjoy a great reputation for talent and patriotism in the eyes of the Nation, have expressed for a long time the wish to see this Article of the Constitution, which authorizes each State individually to determine the method for the choice of Electors, changed. They wanted to see all the States divided into electoral districts, each of which would choose one Elector, by the vote of the people who would thus attain, everywhere equally and without intrigues of party, the exercise of one of their most precious rights, the choice of the First Magistrate. The same men would also require that the Electors invested with the powers and the trust of the people would never be forced to abandon to any organized authority the right to decide a question of which the solution belongs only to themselves. These wishes appear to me to be wise, and will end up, I believe, by being fulfilled; but my intention not being to engage in a critical examination of a Constitution that I consider very superior to all those of Europe, without excepting that of England, I will pass at once to the recitation of the actions that preceded and accompanied the election I witnessed.

The powers conferred on Mr. Monroe were to expire on March 4, 1825. The Congress, before ending its session, had appointed November 19, 1824 as the time on which the electoral process would commence; but, from the beginning of this same year, the American people, always passionate, always active when it is a question of their political interests, were in all parts of the territory already divided into an infinite number of factions formed, whether it be by interests of locality, by feelings of affection, or by influences of party, in order to be active for a long time in advance of the choice of the First Magistrate of the Republic. From the bosom of these factions, still uncertain in their wishes, sprang a multitude of candidates whose pretensions or hopes were often destroyed on the same evening of the day that saw them born. Nevertheless, the citizens, at first divided, but communicating easily among themselves by way of the thousands of newspapers and pamphlets that the press generated at every moment in these circumstances with a prodigious abundance, were not long in grouping themselves in more distinct, more compact aggregations, and soon, in a word, formed no more than four large parties all raising the banner of patriotism, but writing upon it the name of the different candidate for which each announced that it was ready to fight.

The names thus proclaimed were those of John Quincy Adams, William Crawford, Henry Clay and Andrew Jackson, all four equally worthy of commendation by virtue of their talents, their patriotism and the great services rendered to the State. I will not retrace here their political careers, and I will not undertake to depict their private characters; very many others have already done so before me; I will say only that at the moment when the voice of the people designated them as candidates for the Presidency, Mr. Adams, son of Washington's successor, was Minister of Internal and External Affairs; Mr. Crawford, Minister of Finance; Mr. Clay, Speaker or President of the House of Representatives; and General Jackson, Senator in Congress for the State of Tennessee. The old parties of Federalists and Democrats, existing, so to speak, in name only, do not appear to have had any role in this choice which one can only attribute to general esteem shared with the sense of locality; that is at least what the composition of the four parties seemed to indicate. Indeed, one saw all of New England, which one knows is almost always unanimous in its resolves, group itself around Mr. Adams, who was thus supported by the seven States of *Maine*, *New Hampshire*, *Massachusetts*, *Rhode Island*, *Connecticut*, *Vermont* and *New York*. Mr. Crawford was supported by the three States of *Delaware*, *Virginia* and *Georgia*; and Mr. Clay by the three States of *Kentucky*, *Ohio* and *Missouri*. But General Jackson had for himself the imposing body of nine States, *New Jersey*, *Pennsylvania*, *South Carolina*, *North Carolina*, *Tennessee*, *Mississippi*, *Indiana*, *Illinois*, and *Alabama*. The States of *Maryland* and *Louisiana* divided their votes among three candidates.

As soon as these parties, so formed, had raised their particular colors, the war of newspapers and pamphlets began among them with a violence that one could not conceive of in Europe. It seemed that freedom of the press celebrated a period of unrestrained revelry. Accusations of all kinds were directed with an equal vehemence by each party, not only against the opposing candidates, but also against their partisans. The defense was no more temperate than the attack. The long columns of several hundred daily newspapers, all filled with electoral discussions, seemed to announce that the people in their entirety had only a single thought any more, a single occupation, the choice of their President. Nevertheless, through this conflict of all the passions, expressed with a licentious freedom, often appeared some more serious writings, more moderate, more conscientiously devoted to the search for the truth and the demonstration of the true public interest; and these readily received writings alone left durable marks, and proved by their favorable influence this truth, that unlimited freedom of the press carries in itself the most effective remedy to the evils that it can sometimes engender.

By the heat of the discussion, spirits had already arrived at a high degree of emotion when General Lafayette arrived on the American shore. Then, as if by magic, the electoral zeal was suddenly paralyzed. The newspapers, which the day before were fighting furiously to clear the path to the Presidency for their candidate of choice, immediately closed their long columns to the passionate discussions of the parties, in order to open them only to the unanimous expression of joy and national gratitude. In the public banquets, instead of the caustic toast inspired by the desire to attack a dreaded adversary with ridicule, they only toasted the health of the Nation's Guest, around whom all the parties gathered and embraced. In a word, for nearly two months, all the hostilities as well as all the emotions excited by this election which, they say, were to have delivered the country to the most terrible convulsions, were forgotten, and one could only think any more of Lafayette and the heroes of the Revolution.

Nevertheless, the approach of the time fixed for electoral contest soon reawakened all the desires, all the fears, all the hopes and returned to journalism all its violence, all its exaggerations. As early as the first days of October, some States proceeded to the choice of their electors. They were all finished towards the first days of November. The newspapers, in giving the details of these first elections, pointed out by the results that all the parties had remained faithful to their banners, and from that point, one could foresee that the question would not be decided by the Electors; because, they, faithful to their mandate, could only maintain by their vote the equilibrium of fortunes established by their mandates. Consequently, it was to the House of Representatives that the right to give the Nation its First Magistrate was going to belong; and, at once, all the passions from all parts of the Union were called to this assembly. Enticements and threats were not at all spared; and in the midst of the shouts of the parties, one heard sinister cries of *election by armed force, civil war*! "Jackson, the glorious Jackson, who, by his courage saved the Fatherland before the walls of New Orleans," some militia officers of York, Pennsylvania shouted violently, after General Lafayette had left the hall of the banquet that they had offered to him,

> The immortal Jackson is the chosen candidate of the people! Our representatives in Congress cannot, without betraying us, choose another for President! If trickery and corruption make the pretensions of Adams prevail, well then, our bayonettes will do justice! We will go to the Capitol! We will proclaim there, we will cause to triumph there, Jackson's rights by the force of arms, and the militias of Pennsylvania will teach the entire union that they have not at all lost their old energy for the defense of that which they believe to be just!

And these threats were followed by unanimous applause. Then, I confess, my heart sank. "And what," I said to myself, "will the duration of this Government so wise, the only one on earth that may be on all points in harmony with the interests of society, with the dignity of man, be ever so short?..."

Meanwhile, in Washington, all was calm. The President prepared his message. Mr. Adams and Mr. Crawford, despite their rivalry, were not less united in the accomplishment of the duties that their ministerial functions made common to them. General Jackson took his place in the Senate with his customary zeal. Mr. Clay fulfilled his functions as Speaker of the House of Representatives with the same impartiality; and Congress, unconcerned, disdaining the threats, repulsing the intrigues, opened its session and began its work by an act that earned it the approval of the Nation when it was known. Finally, the day fixed for the casting of the votes of the Electors arrived, and only then did the population of Washington and the outsiders who were joined there display all the interest that they were taking in the choice of the First Magistrate of the Republic.

From the morning of February 9, the long avenue that leads to the Capitol was covered with a large crowd. The House of Representatives had opened its session at an earlier hour than usual, and at ten o'clock the public galleries and the surrounding halls were already filled with a large gathering of ladies, citizens and foreigners of distinction. All those who had not been able to penetrate the interior of the Capitol anxiously waited outside for the result of this procedure which, in a few moments, was going to confirm so many fears, crown so many hopes. In spite of the diverse passions that agitated this crowd, the most perfect calm presided at this assembly; and, moreover, it was not compelled by the agents of the police; the sanctuary of the Nation's representation was not polluted by the presence of armed force; but respect for the law, more powerful than all the passions, sufficed to maintain order.

At eleven o'clock, the Speaker of the House opened the session. Two hundred and fifteen representatives were present; only one, kept in his home by a serious illness, was absent. The legislative business began as usual and lasted until noon, the hour at which the Senate, preceded by its sergeant of arms and led by its President, presented itself to the assembly and took the seats that had been reserved to it. The President of the Senate, situated to the left of the Speaker of the House, handed over to a committee the sealed votes that he had received from the different States. This committee, gathered at a table opposite the two leaders, began, in the middle of the most profound silence, to verify the votes. This operation lasted for nearly three hours without any who might be in the assembly giving the least sign of impatience. Finally, one of the members of the committee got up and proclaimed in a loud and intelligible voice the following result: John Quincy Adams, candidate for President, has obtained 84 votes divided thus: *Maine*, 9; *New Hampshire* 8; *Massachusetts* 15; *Rhode Island* 4; *Connecticut* 8; *Vermont* 7; *New York*, 26; *Delaware,* 1; *Maryland* 3; *Louisiana*, 2; *Illinois,* 1. William Henry Crawford, second candidate, has obtained 41 votes divided thus: *New York* 5; *Delaware* 2; *Maryland,* 1; *Virginia,* 24; *Georgia,* 9. Andrew Jackson, third candidate, has obtained 99 votes divided thus: *New York* 1; *New Jersey* 8; *Pennsylvania* 28; *Maryland* 7, *North Carolina*, 15; *South Carolina,* 11; *Tennessee,* 11; *Louisiana,* 3; *Mississippi,* 3; *Indiana,* 5; *Illinois,* 2; *Alabama,* 5. Henry Clay, fourth candidate, has obtained 37 votes divided thus: *New York,* 4; *Kentucky* 14; *Ohio* 16; *Mississippi* 3.

After the proclamation of this counting of votes, the President of the Senate took the floor, and declared that, none of the candidates having obtained the majority required by law to be President, the House was called upon to choose itself, in the form prescribed by the Constitution, between Mssrs. Adams, Jackson and Crawford, who were the three candidates accumulating the greatest number of votes. He added after that, among the candidates for Vice President, Mr. Calhoun was elected Vice President, having obtained 182 votes. Then he withdrew with the Senate in order to allow the Representatives to proceed with the election which was their duty.

This result had been nearly predicted, and consequently produced in the assembly and even in the public galleries only a very minor sensation. But when, on the invitation of the Speaker of the House, the delegates of the different States took a poll among themselves to determine the collective vote of each State and when afterwards these votes were delivered into the hands of the committee charged with counting them, the close attention manifested by the numerous spectators was represented by such varied characteristics that it would be impossible to describe it.

Finally, after some moments of the most silent waiting, the committee announced to the Speaker of the House that, after scrupulous scrutiny of the votes, it was acknowledged that John Quincy Adams of the State of Massachusetts had obtained 13 votes; that Andrew Jackson of the State of Tennessee had obtained 7 votes; and that William H. Crawford, of the State of Georgia, had obtained 4. Immediately, the Speaker of the House took the floor and declared that John Quincy Adams, having obtained the majority of the total number of votes, was lawfully elected President of the United States, to enter in office on the date of March 4, 1825, and, immediately after, he adjourned the House.

No one had expected to see this contest concluded by a single ballot. This prompt result threw all the spectators into such astonishment that at first they remained immobile and silent; but moments after a low murmuring was heard in the galleries, in the midst of which suddenly some applause burst out, which the Speaker of the House immediately repressed by ordering that the galleries be evacuated at once; and that took place without the slightest opposition.

The results of this election, so long and so ardently debated in the entire Union, certainly must not have satisfied all persons present, and yet during the exiting from the Capitol, one did not hear any recrimination, any complaint. The winners themselves observed the greatest dignity, and did not at all offend the ears of their adversaries by ill-considered expressions of the joy that they must have felt in their triumph.

On the following morning, a committee of the House of Representatives made the official communication to President Monroe of the selection of his successor. The same committee also presented itself at Mr. Adams' house, and announced to him that the House, in conformity with the procedures prescribed by the Constitution, had chosen him to fill the office of President of the United States for four years. Mr. Adams received this communication with a modesty and a simplicity that is represented admirably in all the words of his response to the committee. "Gentlemen," he said,

> On receiving this honorable expression of the representatives of the people and of the States of the Union, I am deeply affected by the circumstances in the midst of which it has

been given to me. Up to the present, all my predecessors in this noble office, to which the favor of the House summons me, have been honored by the majority of the votes in the primary electoral colleges; my lot has required that, because of the divisions of opinion of my compatriots, I have been placed in loyal competition with three of my fellow citizens, who rightly enjoy public approval to a very high degree, and whose character, talents and services have no more sincere and respectful admirer than I. The names of two of them have been presented along with mine to the decision of the House of Representatives in conformity with the demand of the Constitution. Their names have always been intimately associated with our national glory, and one of them has obtained, I must acknowledge it, a greater number of popular votes than I.

In this state of affairs, if, in refusing to accept the power that is conferred on me, I could furnish to the people the immediate means of expressing again its wishes in a more unanimous manner, I would not hesitate a single instant to do it and to call once more upon its sovereign will; but the Constitution does not itself state that the novel question which a refusal would raise would be decided in this manner. Thus, I will stay in the post that has just been assigned to me in the name of the country by constitutional means. Intimidated by the greatness of the task that has been imposed on me, but encouraged by the hope that the generous support that our fellow citizens have always accorded me in the course of my life, entirely devoted to their service, will not be withdrawn from me, I will deliver myself with confidence to the wisdom of the legislative advisers who must direct me in the path of my duties, and I will pray especially for the protection of the One who holds our life in His hands and who is the source of all our success.

Gentlemen, I beg you to make known to the House my profound gratitude for the confidence it has bestowed on me, and receive yourselves my thanks for the kindly manner in which you have communicated its decision to me.

It would be rather interesting, it seems to me, to compare the style of a citizen of the United States arriving, by the will of the people, to the supreme magistracy with that of a European king at the moment of his succession to the throne by divine right. Perhaps this comparison would not be without profit for the nations that made it.

On the same day, there was a large evening party at President Monroe's house. I had already attended this kind of gathering, which is very noteworthy by the numerous and varied company that one encounters there, the agreeable freedom which reigns there, and the amiable simplicity with which Mrs. Monroe and her daughters do the honors. But this time the crowd there was so large that one could hardly take a step. The desire to see the newly elected President and his rivals whom one presumed were to be found there, and who as a matter of fact came, with the exception of Mr. Crawford who was still detained at home by his illness, had attracted all the inhabitants of Washington City.

After having greeted Mr. and Mrs. Monroe, whom I had much difficulty reaching, I searched eagerly for Mr. Adams and the other candidates; it seemed to me that their situation vis-à-vis one another must be embarrassing, and I was curious to see how they would manage it. Upon entering a side room, I noticed Mr. Adams: he was alone in the middle of a large circle that had formed around him. His demeanor was simple and modest, as was his custom throughout his life. At each moment, some people left the crowd and came to offer him their congratulations which he received without embarrassment, and to which he responded by clasping their hands cordially. Some distance away, in the midst of a group of ladies, was Mrs. Adams. She appeared to me to be beaming with contentment; but it was easy to recognize in her features that she was affected more by the personal triumph of her husband than by the advantages or the amenities that could result for her.

While I was scrutinizing this interesting tableau attentively, there was a tumultuous movement at the door of the room, and a murmur of satisfaction was uttered in the entire assembly; I soon recognized the cause of it upon seeing General Jackson appear. Everyone rushed headlong on his passage; each wanted to clasp his hand and to pay him their compliments. To all these displays of interest, he responded with an abandon full of cordiality. My attentive glances were carried alternatively to Mr. Adams and to General Jackson; I was curious to see how these two men, who were rivals the preceding day, would approach each other. My wait was not long. When they noticed each other, they dashed towards each other, clasped hands and held them tightly for a long time. The congratulations offered by General Jackson were frank and sincere. Mr. Adams appeared profoundly moved by it, and the numerous witnesses could not restrain from expressing their satisfaction. Mr. Clay arrived a moment later, and the same scene recurred. Perhaps this one produced less of an effect than the first because Mr. Clay, having had less chance of success, was supposed to have to make less of an effort to resign himself; but it did not serve any less to prove to me how wise a people is who have such men as these to choose from. The generosity of character that General Jackson had just shown reassured me entirely about the threats of the militias of Pennsylvania.

Just at the moment when my thoughts were turning to this subject, I encountered in the crowd two officers with whom I had dined at York, and whom I had noticed especially for their emotional excitement. "Well," I said to them, "the great question is decided, and in a manner contrary to your wishes. What are you going to do? Will you soon begin the siege of the Capital?" – They began to laugh. "You recall our threats then," one of them said to me.

> We were, indeed, very busy shouting; but our adversaries did not take account of it, and they were right; they have judged us better than we would have wanted them to. Now that the law has spoken, we have only to obey it. We will second Adams with the same zeal as if we had supported him; but at the same time, we will shine a light on his administration, and according to whether it will be good or bad, we will defend it or attack it. Four years are passed very soon. And the consequences of a bad election are very easy to repair. –

"Yes," I said to him, "easier than the consequences of legitimacy or heredity." – They left me while laughing, and on the following day, no one spoke of the election any more.

In considering with what ardor and what passion the parties contest the Presidency for a man of their choice, one would be tempted to believe that the President of the United States can be an inexhaustible source of advantages of all kinds for his friends or his partisans, and that his power is such that he can dispense favors, jobs, riches at will. In order to erase this error, it will suffice for me to cite the article of the Constitution that sets forth the powers of the head of the government, and one will agree that it leaves in this hands fewer means of corruption than what the puniest prefect has with us.

> No individual other than a citizen born in the United States, or being a citizen at the time of the adoption of this Constitution, can be eligible to the office of President. No person will be eligible to this office who has not attained the age of 35 years and who has not resided in the United States for 14 years. In case the President may be deprived of his office, in

case of death, resignation, or incapacity to fulfill the powers and duties of this position, it will be entrusted to the Vice President, and Congress can by law provide in the case of dismissal, death, resignation, or incapacity of both the President and the Vice President and order what public officer will fill the Presidency in such case until the cause of the incapacity no longer exists, or until a new President is elected.

The President will receive compensation for his services at fixed intervals that will not be increased or diminished during the period for which he will have been elected, and during that same time, he will not be able to receive any other remuneration from the United States or any one of them.

Before his entrance into office, he will take the following oath: I solemnly swear that I will fulfill faithfully the office of President of the United States and that I will use all my efforts to preserve, protect and defend the Constitution of the United States.

The President will be commander-in-chief of the armies and the navies of the United States and of the militia of the different States when they will be in the service of the United States. He can demand the written opinion of the principal officer in each of the executive departments on every subject relating to the duties imposed on him; and he will have the power to grant a reduction of the sentence and even a pardon for offenses against the United States, except in the case of those charged by the House of Representatives.

He will have the power, by and with the consent of the Senate, to make treaties, provided that two-thirds of the Senators present approve; and he will nominate, by and with the consent of the Senate, and will appoint ambassadors, other public ministers and consuls, judges of the highest courts, and other employees of the United States whose nominations will not have been provided for in any other manner in this Constitution, or which will be determined by law. But Congress can by law assign the nominations of those subordinate employees to the President alone, to courts of law or to department heads.

> The President will have the power to fill all vacant positions during the interval between sessions of the Senate, granting appointments that will expire at the end of the next session.
>
> From time to time, the President will provide Congress information on the state of the Union, and he will recommend to its consideration such measures that he will judge to be suitable. He can, on extraordinary occasions, convene the two houses or one of them, and, in case they might be divided on the time of their adjournment, he can adjourn them at such time that will appear appropriate to him. He will receive ambassadors and other public ministers. He will see to it that the laws may be faithfully executed, and he will give all employees of the United States their commissions.
>
> The President can be removed, if, following an accusation, he is convicted of treason, squandering the public treasury or other crimes and misconduct.

One sees that the Constitution, in determining in a precise manner the prerogatives and the powers of the First Magistrate, has had in mind more the happiness and interests of the Nation than the satisfaction of an individual and his family. Also, the President is found in a situation such that, whatever his personal character might be, it is impossible for him to make a serious attack on liberty, on rights, on the honor of his fellow citizens. He does not have, like some kings of the Old Continent, several millions of revenues and immense properties. The law only accords to him a salary of 130,000 francs; but it is not on the sumptuousness of his apparel, on the brilliance of his numerous guards, or on the number of his courtiers that the majesty of his person rests.

Not being able to entrench himself behind the responsibility of his ministers or to cover himself with the infallibility of his character or the inviolability of his person, which the constitutional act does not guarantee, the President of the United States himself is truly obliged to consider carefully and personally all the acts of executive power that rest only with him; and the citizens are so persuaded that the functions of the head of state can be well-fulfilled only by work every moment of every day that they would be very astonished, and perhaps even very unhappy, if, now and then, the newspapers announced that the President worked on such day for two or even three hours with such minister.

Finally, in order to give a fair idea of that simplicity to which the President of the United States is reduced by the structure, others would say the parsimony, of the Constitution, I believe that I can do no better than to report the following anecdote which I borrow from the witty author of *Voyage to the United States in 1818*.[3]

> Bleeker Olsen, minister of Denmark to the United States under the Presidency of Mr. Jefferson, having learned on his arrival in Washington that the President was ready to receive company every day at two o'clock, presented himself at this hour to pay his respects to the chief of the American Nation. Mr. Jefferson received him with so much politeness and cordiality, and entered into so animated a conversation with him, that an hour had elapsed before the foreigner noticed that his visit had been extraordinarily prolonged. At last, the discussion began to languish, and the foreign diplomat waited for them to dismiss him, as the President, as one could presume, desired that he terminate his visit; but the simplicity of the *arrival* had not been sufficient to make a European minister understand that of the *departure*. The representative of the King of Denmark stayed rooted to his seat, waiting for the signal for his retreat. He waited in vain for this signal; the President did not give it. Persuaded that he was unwelcome, feeling himself more and more ill at ease, desiring to leave and nonetheless fearing to commit, by leaving, a greater offense against decorum, the poor minister stayed seated, counting the minutes. Finally the dinner hour arrived and Mr. Jefferson crowned his confusion by begging him to stay and to share a family meal. Bleeker Olsen arose, mumbled an excuse and escaped from the room.
>
> From the President's House, the disconcerted minister rushed to the house of an American acquaintance, who held a position in the Government and with whom he had already conversed about the national institutions. He recounted to him his adventure, and following this he took part in a discussion on this subject. "How," he said to the American, "should I have withdrawn without their dismissing me? Do you not then have any etiquette for this? Do you not recognize any distinction of rank or position? How do you exist as a nation? What means do you take to preserve to your constituted authorities the respect necessary to give them influence and to obtain strength in the Government? Perhaps you have some other formalities that I do not know; explain them to me; teach me the rules that I must observe in my relations with your President."

3. *Voyage to the United States*, by Miss Wright, translated by Mr. Parisot in 1822.

They then told Bleeker Olsen that he had left the formalities of etiquette in the Courts of the sovereigns of Europe and that the only privilege the President of the United States enjoyed in his relations with his fellow citizens was to receive visits without returning them, a custom founded on the simple reason that, if he returned a visit, it would be necessary that he visit everyone; and this, because of too large a quantity of people who came to visit him and because of his numerous duties, was absolutely impossible.

The same minister, dining several days later with Mr. Jefferson, did not fail to apologize for the length of his last visit, and, after having explained the cause of it, attested to the surprise that customs so new to a European caused in him. "I know," he added, "that it is not for a foreigner to criticize the customs of a country that he visits; I am equally persuaded that the current President can put himself above all formality; but the interest that I take in your country will serve as an excuse if I find fault with a simplicity of manners that can be good for a Jefferson; but that would be perhaps dangerous for his successors. There are some general rules that one ought to abide by, because they were made for all times and for all men. Believe me, Sir, or, rather, believe the experience of the centuries that justify me in affirming that the rules of etiquette cannot be violated with impunity, and that, in order to assure the stability of governments, their leaders must be surrounded with a splendor and a pomp made to command the obedience of the multitude."

"I do not pretend," answered Mr. Jefferson, "to contest the correctness of your observation in relation to kings; but, as for me, Sir, I am not a king. Permit me to tell you an anecdote that will explain the difference. You know the passion of the King of Naples for the hunt. It happened that, on a superb day to take this pleasure, his majesty was obligated to hold a great reception. The introductions were more numerous than the King himself had expected and threatened, by their interminable duration, to deprive him of his favorite amusement. Finally, he lost patience, and turned towards the famous Caraccioli, who was then Minister of Foreign Affairs. 'Marquis,' he said to him, 'how these formalities are annoying!' – 'Your Majesty,' answered Caraccioli with a profound reverence, 'your Majesty forgets that your royal personage itself is a *formality.*'"

"I do not know," the person from whom I heard this anecdote said to me, "if Bleeker Olsen felt at that moment the arrow that the President had shot at him; but he stayed in our country, and before he left it, appeared to have understood that our Government does not need to be propped up by artificial means; that it does not have at its head an irresponsible being created by a superstitious fiction, a *formality*, but one accountable for all his actions, who has duties numerous and important to fulfill, and whose place in the public esteem is marked by the manner in which he fulfills these duties, and not by vain pomp and by the frivolous rules of etiquette."

If the difference that exists between the President of the United States and the Kings of Europe is great, the one that exists between the ministers of this Republic and our ministers is no less prominent. A minister of the United States has a salary of only 30,000 francs, no mansion, no furniture, no lifestyle paid by the Nation; no sentries at his door; no servants in ridiculous costumes to introduce him when he goes out; outside of his ministry, no privilege, but also no responsibility for his acts before the people. Chosen by the President, he is, so to speak, only his instrument and devotes all his time to him. As he does not have at his command an army of directors general, division chiefs, employees of all classes at high wages, he is obligated to put his own hands to work and truly earn his salary, which is too modest, it is true, to enable him to give sumptuous dinners often to the members of Congress, but which is sufficient, for all that, to a prudent and conscientious man who understands well that it is only by his activity and probity, and not by intrigues and corruption, that he will accomplish the duties that are imposed on him and that he will live up to the trust with which he has been honored.

The habits of the American ministers are so simple and so little different from those of their fellow citizens that nothing, absolutely nothing, in their outward appearance could make them recognized in public. During the initial time of our stay in Washington, when we wanted to return the visits to them that they had the kindness to make to us, we needed to ask several times not where their mansion was, for the people did not understand us, but where their dwelling was, although we were already on the street where they lived. Sometimes, when we knocked on the door of their home, it was they themselves who opened it for us; often we encountered them, portfolio under their arm, returning on foot from their ministry to their home where a modest family meal awaited them. All that, without a doubt, appeared very *bourgeois* to us; but in the United States, where the people value good administration more than the luxury of their administrators, they find all that to be natural, and I believe that they are right.

This extreme simplicity of the ministers extends also to all the other public officials, and in it lies the secret of this system of government that we admire so much and which we will probably never attain.

A Senate and a House of Representatives form the legislative power of the United States, a power that derives directly from the people, and that counterbalances the strength of the executive power to such a degree that, if it happened that the Nation, in a moment of error, accorded the Presidency to an unsuited or ill-intentioned man, the troublesome influence of this man would be very nearly paralyzed by that of the Congress.

The Congress has the power:

To establish and to provide for the collection of taxes, duties, imposts and excises; to pay the public debts and to provide for the common defense and general welfare of the United States. But the duties, imposts and excises established must be the same for all the States of the Union;

To print money on the credit of the United States;

To regulate commerce with foreign nations, between the different States and with the Indian tribes;

To establish a general rule for naturalizations; and general laws on bankruptcies in the United States;

To mint money, to regulate its value compared to that of foreign monies, and to fix the standard of weights and measures;

To assure the punishment of counterfeiters of currency and public documents;

To establish post offices and postal routes;

To encourage the progress of the sciences and useful arts, while ensuring for limited times to authors and inventors the exclusive right to their writings and their inventions;

To establish courts subordinate to the Supreme Court; to define and punish piracies and felonies committed on the high seas, and offenses against the laws of nations;

To declare war; to grant letters of marque and reprisals, and to make rules concerning captives on land and at sea;

To raise and maintain armies, but funds for this purpose can be voted for no more than two years;

To create and maintain a maritime force;

To establish the rules for the administration and organization of land and sea forces;

To provide for the calling of the militia to execute the laws of the Union to put down insurrections and to repel invasions;

To provide for the organization, arming and discipline of the militia; and

To provide for that part of the militia necessary for the service of the United States, while leaving to the respective States the nomination of officers and the establishment of discipline prescribed by Congress.

All the bills establishing taxes must be debated first in the House of Representatives; but the Senate can concur with amendments as with other bills. Every bill that has received the approval of the Senate and the House of Representatives is presented to the President of the United States before becoming law; if he approves it, he affixes his signature on it, otherwise, he sends it back with his observations to the chamber in which it was proposed; it records at full length the objections in its journal, and discusses the bill anew. If, after this second discussion, two-thirds of the chamber declares itself for passing the bill, it is sent back, with the objections of the President, to the other chamber which also discusses it; and if the same majority approves it, it becomes law; but, in this case, the votes of the chamber must be decided by *yes* or by *no*, and the names of the persons voting for and against must be written in the journal of each respective chamber. If, at the end of ten days (not including Sundays), the President does not send back a bill submitted to him, it has the force of law as if it had been approved by this magistrate, unless in the meantime Congress prevents the return by adjourning.

It is on the first Monday of December every year that the Congress convenes. The duration of its session varies depending on the importance of its work, but rarely extends beyond the month of May. From the middle of November, one sees the Senators and Representatives sent by each State of the Union arrive in Washington City. Among those are very many who have had to travel about 500 miles across uninhabited forests and difficult roads in order to come to fulfill their mandates. On arriving, they lodge simply and economically in an inn, where they often find a bed only in a common room with four or five of their colleagues. The table is also common among all those who live in the same inn. It is there where, after a frugal meal, they ordinarily conduct interesting conversations in which they discuss in advance, and with cordiality, most of the questions that are to be debated during the session.

The first Monday of December having arrived, the session opens and from the first meeting the work begins, because each one is already at his post. The presiding officer of the chamber, charged with managing and summarizing the discussions, occupies a raised rostrum, in front of which the representatives are seated, two by two at small tables conveniently arranged in a semi-circular enclosure, surrounded by large galleries full of a numerous public. After the reading of the message of the President of the United States, and the formation of 23 committees charged with examining the different questions that must be submitted for discussion, the debates open. They do not resemble in the least those that take place in our Chamber of Deputies. They are calm and serious. One never hears long written speeches, laboriously developed in the cabinet, and passing by all objections, delivered there.

Each member speaks from his place, and the discussion never has any other character than that of a lively conversation between people who have a high opinion of each other and who desire total freedom of opinion for others as much as for themselves. When a member speaks, if he allows himself to be carried away by the ardor of a long improvisation, one recognizes easily, by the manner with which he expresses himself, that he is animated more by the desire to convince the others or to clarify himself, than by being preoccupied with the manner in which his oratory will be judged in any drawing room or by any coterie. But, whatever the effect that he produces on his audience may be, he is certain not to be interrupted either by vile shouting or by applause the inappropriateness of which offends the dignity of the assembly. Order in the chamber, skillfully instituted by the presiding officer, does not need the intervention of armed and ridiculously dressed bailiffs in order to be maintained. A lone man, called sergeant-at-arms, stands guard at the door of the hall so that the public does not enter in the midst of the representatives; and two young boys, seated at the foot of the presiding officer's rostrum, are busy noiselessly and inconspicuously distributing letters, bulletins and reports addressed to the members of the assembly.

It is in this manner that each day, during a session of several months, is conscientiously employed by the representatives of the Nation in discussing the most cherished interests of the people. As soon as the session closes, each deputy returns to his constituents, and, if he has fulfilled his mandate well, finds in the reception that they give him the sweetest reward that he could aspire to.

Carried away by the desire to recount here, as it appeared to me, the character of the principal powers of the American Government, I notice that I have neglected a flock of interesting details concerning our stay in Washington; perhaps I will have the occasion to take them up again later; but, in the meantime, I will not end this chapter without speaking of the fete given by Congress on January 1. This day had been appointed by the two Houses for a grand gathering at a banquet offered to General Lafayette. The representatives of the people wanted to display American hospitality in this manner, by seating the Nation's Guest at a table where the entire official family attended in person. Mr. Gaillard, temporary President of the Senate, and Mr. Clay, Speaker of the House of Representatives, presided over the meal. Mr. Gaillard had General Lafayette on his left and, on his right, President Monroe, who departing this time, doubtless because of General Lafayette, from the rule that he had made never to attend any public fete, had nonetheless accepted the invitation; Mr. Clay had likewise at his sides ministers of the United States. Among those invited were General Dearborn, Minister of the United States to the Court of Portugal; Generals Scott, Macomb, Jessup and our dear compatriot Bernard, beside whom I had the honor of being placed; Commodores Bainbridge, Tingey, Stewart and Morris, as well as several public officers of very high rank. Among the guests, General Lafayette had the pleasure of finding some of his old companions-in-arms. Captain Allyn, of *The Cadmus,* having recently arrived from France[4], had also repaired to the place of the invitation which he had received. The hall was decorated with the greatest brilliancy, and the guests were animated by a spirit of harmony that showed clearly enough that they considered this ceremony like a family festival.

It is in such gatherings that one can study the public spirit of a people, especially when their representatives, freely chosen, and not having any reason to flatter the Government or to conceal their thoughts, give free flight to all their feelings. There is especially in a full-bodied meal a certain enthusiasm that tends to show in a more conspicuous light that part of the character of the guests which, on every other occasion, would not have been manifested in as perceptible a manner. The political opinion of the legislators of the Union

---

4. It was at this time that Captain Allyn brought the beautiful full-length portrait of Lafayette, painted by Mr. Scheffer and offered by this young artist to Congress, which accepted the honor and placed it in the Capitol rotunda, where it gives proof of the well-earned reputation of its painter.

was thus to be expressed in this circumstance with more force, with more abandon than it had been in solemn sessions where the seriousness of the protocol tends to paralyze their effusiveness. It is in the toasts and in the vows that accompany them that one finds this opinion in its entirety. Some recall principles; others their application as it is understood by Americans. Here, it is "*To the people, source of all powers; to public opinion and to freedom of the press, blazing sword which guards the approaches to the tree of liberty,*" that they make their toasts and give their vows. There, it is "*To Greece reborn and revived in Athens and in Sparta; to the Republics of South America, to which the example of the Union paves the way for similar successes.*"

The health of Mr. Monroe having been proposed for a toast, everyone rose spontaneously, and one could observe that the tributes were given less to the chief of the Republic, than to the venerable patriot whose many services commended him to the love of Americans. He declared his thanks with a voice touched with emotion that moved the guests, all the more as the words seemed to be the farewells of the President, after a magistracy of eight years. Then they drank the following toast in honor of General Lafayette: "*To the great apostle of liberty, whom the persecutions of tyranny did not destroy, whom love of riches did not influence, whom popular applause could not lead astray. He was always the same, in the chains of Olmutz, in his different works, at the pinnacle of power and glory.*" At this toast, the General rose and said:

> Words to render all my respect and all my gratitude for the kindnesses which you are bestowing on me fail me; but I hope that you will do justice to the ardor of my feelings for America. Permit me to respond to the toast that has just been made with this: *To the perpetual union among the United States. It has saved us in stormy times, one day it will save the world.*

Making allusion to the current situation of the General, Mr. Gaillard, President of the Senate, proposed a toast in his turn and accompanied it with these words: "*May the very generous defender of the rights of man obtain the greatest recompense that it may be given to a man to receive: the admiration, the gratitude and the affection of all mankind.*"

Immediately after, and as if the thing had been a continuation of what had just been said, Mr. Clay, Speaker of the House of Representatives, rose and laid claim to the attention as well as the benevolence of the assembly; then, in an eloquent and short speech, he turned the attention of the guests to the Republics of South America which, without the support of any nation, without help, without the self-sacrifice or the example of a Lafayette, moved only by consciousness of their rights, and protected by their mountains, are fighting to win their freedom. He bemoaned the fact that the principles of political order had given the Union the painful duty of remaining a spectator to their efforts. He expressed pity for Spain, so unfortunate in the midst of its errors, nourishing the dream of the conquest of its colonies; he portrayed it as impotent for its projects, and deplored a neutrality that repelled the community of principled people.... Here, the Speaker, overcome by his own impatience, interrupted himself and proposed a toast to the health of *the liberator Bolivar, the Washington of South America.*

In a rather remarkable parallel of events, while they were associating the name of Bolivar to the festivities they were conducting in Washington in this manner, the name of Lafayette was also honored publicly in Caracas.

This toast ended the meal, and the moving and patriotic scenes that had taken place during its continuance. Each of the guests expressed regret that all Americans had not been able to have a place there.

GEORGES WASHINGTON

à la grande nation des États-unis d'Amérique.

Chapter III

Departure from Washington – American Opinions – Sea Lion – Family of Free Negroes – Raleigh – Fayetteville – North Carolina.

Since the first days of February, General Lafayette had received such pressing invitations from all the States of the South and of the West of the Union that he was no longer allowed to hesitate anymore on the course that he had to take; and, from that time, we busied ourselves actively with both the itinerary of our journey and the means to surmount the difficulties that everyone assured us would be very great on a trip of this nature and this length. We had, as a matter of fact, a distance of more than 3,000 miles to travel in less than four months in order to be present in Boston on June 17, where the General had been enlisted to attend the celebration of the anniversary of Bunker Hill; and a part of the country that we had to traverse was barely inhabited or had only difficult and poorly laid out roadways. But thanks to the experience of General Bernard, to the knowledge of the Director General of the Post Office (McLean) and the advice of the representatives who were in Washington, George Lafayette succeeded in laying out an itinerary so well-calculated that his father did not have to fear omitting any of the important points of the different States that we had to visit on his trip, although most of these points were to be found several miles to the right or the left of our principal route; and his time was so rigorously accounted for that, barring illness or serious mishaps, we ought to arrive in Boston on the promised day.

We did not neglect any of the proper precautions to enable us to overcome the obstacles that everyone warned us about on this additional trip. The General's friends could not contemplate the hardships and the dangers to which, they said, he was going to be exposed without a feeling of fright. Madam Eliza Custis of the Washington family hastened to offer him her commodious and smooth-running carriage. We bought some good saddle horses to replace the carriage on very bad roads; we reduced our baggage as much as possible, and on February 23, at nine o'clock in the evening, we embarked on the Potomac which we descended up to its mouth in Chesapeake Bay. From there we reached Norfolk, where we disembarked early in the morning on the 25th after two nights and a day of favorable sailing. We left on the same day to dine at Suffolk, a very small town, where the General was awaited with all the bustling zeal and the benevolence that he had encountered at every turn up to then. Our trip, favored by a beautiful road and fine weather, was very speedy.

Some miles from Norfolk, we were obliged to stop for a while on the road at an inn that was isolated and of rather spare appearance in order to refresh our horses. We had remained in our carriage when the innkeeper presented himself at the door, asked to see the General, and begged him earnestly to descend for a moment and enter his house. "If you might have only five minutes to give to me," he said, "do not refuse them, because it would be five minutes of happiness for me." The General gave in to his entreaty, and we followed him into a lower room the plainness of which bordered on poverty but which was remarkably neat. *Welcome Lafayette* was blackened with charcoal on the white wall and was ringed by some fir branches collected at the entrance to the nearby forest. Near the hearth, where resinous wood crackled, was a little table covered with a neat tablecloth that was laden with flasks of brandy and whisky; alongside a plate covered with glasses was another plate filled with slices of bread carefully arranged. These modest refreshments were offered to us with a kindness and a cordiality that increased their value very much.

While we were having them, the innkeeper had disappeared; he returned a moment after accompanied by his wife who was carrying a young boy of three to four years, whose fresh and firm cheeks bore witness to the tender cares of which he is the object. The father first presented his wife to us, then took the child in his arms, and, after having made him put one of his little hands in the General's hand, made him repeat expressively the following words: *"General Lafayette, I thank you for the freedom that you have won for my father, my mother, for me and for my country...."* While the child spoke, his father and his mother fixed their fond looks on the General; their hearts were in agreement with the words of the child; and the tears that escaped from their eyelids against their will demonstrated how vivid and profound their gratitude was. If I can judge by what I myself felt at the sight of this tableau, so simple yet so sublime, General Lafayette must have found this moment one of the sweetest of his life. He was unable to conceal his emotion; he embraced the child tenderly, and escaped into his carriage, where the blessings of this family, which was free and so worthy of being free, accompanied him.

On the same day, a little before our arrival at Suffolk, some Negroes stopped us and begged us to enter their cabin, situated at the side of the road, in order for them to show us a very extraordinary animal, which they told us was a sea lion. It was about seven feet long and was clad with a rough skin of tawny color speckled with black; the thickness of its body, near the shoulders, was a little like that of a calf, and diminished considerably until the posterior extremity terminated in wide fins; its small head, round and slightly flattened, resembled that of a tiger a little; its mouth was furnished with teeth long, strong and sharp; its limbs, excessively short, had the shape of a hand; its digits were joined together by a membrane capable of great expansion, and were armed with very strong and very sharp claws. The Negroes told us that, while walking on the banks of the *Elisabeth River* at low tide, they noticed this animal on the sand, where it appeared to have been left by the waves: when it saw the men, it walked towards them, but without hostile intentions. Nevertheless, the Negroes first took flight; it followed them for a long time, but very slowly, as it is easy to conceive, in examining the small length of its limbs, which appeared to have been made for swimming rather than walking. After having gone about 100 steps in his flight, one of the Negroes, who was armed with a rifle, turned around and fired at the animal, who received the shot in the side and expired almost immediately.

Some compliments on their courage and some coins made these poor Negroes, whom we left to visit a neighboring dwelling that they said belonged to a large family of free Blacks, very happy. The house was very well maintained as much in the interior as the exterior. I was struck by the orderliness and the cleanliness of the household, as well as by the good appearance of the inhabitants, who appeared to me to be in a state of affluence and well-being very superior to that of most of our European peasants. One of our traveling companions, a citizen of Norfolk, assured us that this family had more than doubled the value of their property in several years, by its intelligence and its activity. I urge those who still persist in believing that Negroes are incapable of providing for their needs in the state of freedom to visit this family, which besides is not the only family that one could cite in Virginia.

After having stopped for a time in the midst of the citizens of Suffolk, we continued our route to Murfreesborough, where we were to sleep. Our late arrival there had the air of a nocturnal military rout. The bad condition and the length of the road had exhausted our horses, and we believed for a while that we would be obliged to sleep at the foot of the hill on which this town is situated. An enormous woodpile lit on a neighboring mountain whose flames illuminated our difficulties; the lights of Murfreesborough, which presented the image of a town delivered up to flames; the noise of the cannon that resounded to our right and which had the effect of a battery that had attacked us on our flank; the shouts of our escort; the whiplashes and the curses of our coachmen, none of all that spurred on our horses who, planted in the mud up to the knees, seemed to have taken root there, and refused to make the least effort to pull us out of this unfortunate situation in which they had left us for nearly an hour. Finally, we arrived, and we were very amply compensated by the cordial hospitality of the inhabitants of Murfreesborough, who spared nothing to prove to General Lafayette that the citizens of North Carolina were no less sincerely attached to him than those of the other States.

From Murfreesborough, we went to Halifax on the following day, where we crossed the *Roanoke* with the aid of a ferry boat, to the sound of the artillery of the militia who were waiting for General Lafayette on other bank. Halifax was once Cornwallis' headquarters during the North Carolina campaign. It was there that this English leader made the decision, which proved so disastrous to him, to enter Virginia. We only slept in Halifax, and we proceeded in two days by frightful roads to Raleigh, a pretty little town situated to the west of the Neuse River, which is the seat of the government of North Carolina. The population of Raleigh is about 2,700, of which nearly 1,500 individuals appeared to be of the Colored race, free or enslaved. One of the most precious monuments of this Town is the superb statue of Washington; executed in marble by Canova; it is maintained with the utmost care in one of the halls of the Capitol.

The Governor of the State, the officers of the Government, the militias, and, finally, the entire population had consulted together and agreed on how to receive and celebrate the arrival of the Nation's Guest in a worthy manner; the enthusiasm had been such that, despite the bad weather, a company of voluntary dragoons had traveled nearly 125 miles to attend this family festival. The good men who composed it had solicited and obtained permission to serve as guards to Lafayette on that day; and they had based their pretensions on that fact that the County of Mecklenburg, to which they belonged, was the first of the State to proclaim independence at the time of the Revolution. *"When it is a question of serving liberty or Lafayette,"* they told us, *"we must always be first."* Governor Burton was attentive in affording the honors of his residence to the Nation's Guest in a manner worthy of him.

The night before our arrival in Raleigh was nearly marked by a very unfortunate event. In one of the carriages that were following us were Mr. Daniel, general of the militia, and a young staff officer; their horses bolted and the coachman, being unable to control them anymore, collided roughly with a tree trunk that was obstructing the road. The violence of the impact tossed the two travelers and the coachman a distance from the carriage, but the most badly injured was poor General Daniel, who remained nearly unconscious on the spot. Our ride was suspended at once, and General Lafayette, who was already far in front at the head of the procession, hastily returned in order to see for himself the nature of this accident. General Daniel was already beginning to recover his senses when the ill-considered zeal of his friend, General Williams, almost rendered his condition more fatal than even his fall. The latter wanted imperiously to bleed him on the spot. He was already holding in his hand the fatal lancet and was going to proceed to the operation, when George Lafayette entreated him insistently to do nothing, while drawing his attention to the fact that we had just eaten, and that a bleeding immediately after a meal could have grave consequences. After having given General Daniel the principal attentions that his situation required, we transported him to the house of a wealthy farmer whom we had visited in the morning some miles from there, and the next day our injured man joined us in Raleigh, entirely recovered from his fall, and tenderly expressing gratitude to George Lafayette for having saved him from the lancet of his friend.

At first I had been very surprised at seeing General Williams pull a lancet from his pocket determined to bleed his friend; but one of our traveling companions told me that in the States of the South and the West, and more especially in those of which the population is very dispersed, the art of bleeding is common to nearly all the large landowners. The difficulty in finding a surgeon at the time of an accident often imposes on them the necessity to do the bleeding themselves, and they sometimes do it so extensively that the most fearless phlebotomists of the French School would be frightened by it.

On March 4, we arrived in the pretty little City of Fayetteville, situated on the western bank of the *Cape Fear* River. The weather was dreadful, the rain fell in torrents, and yet, several miles before the City, the road was covered with men and children on horseback, and militiamen on foot; in the City the streets were covered with a crowd of ladies dressed in all their finery, who were rushing incautiously across the rivulets to approach the General's carriage, so seized by the pleasure of gazing on him that they didn't appear to notice the deluge that seemed destined to engulf them. This enthusiasm is more easily understood when one considers that it was manifested by the inhabitants of a city founded 40 years ago to perpetuate the memory of the services rendered by the very person whom they were honoring on this day.

They conducted General Lafayette onto a raised platform facing City Hall where he was welcomed and addressed in the name of the City Council by Chief Justice Toomer. In his speech, the orator recapitulated enthusiastically the obligations that America had to Lafayette, recalled the persecutions to which he was exposed in France and in Austria for being faithful to the principles of liberty and the rights of man that he had been the first to proclaim in Europe, and ended by setting up forcefully a comparison between the young Republics of the United States and the old Monarchies of the old European continent. "Here," he cried,

> The shadows of error have been dissipated before the lights of truth. The doctrines of divine right and passive obedience are considered to be only memories of barbaric times. Our political

> institutions are founded on the sovereignty of the people, who are the source of all powers. The jargon of legitimacy is not understood among us. The only holy alliance that we recognize is that of religion and virtue, of liberty and knowledge. The sunshine of liberty extends the sphere of its creative influence each day; South America is regenerated, and its shackles are broken. The thrones of Europe, which have no support other than the force of bayonettes, are shaken up to their foundations, and the genius of our country will soon be able to celebrate the spirit of universal liberation.

After General Lafayette had expressed his gratitude for the reception that the citizens of Fayetteville were affording him, and his sympathy for the opinions of the speaker, they led us to the residence of Mr. Duncan MacRae, where our lodgings had been prepared, in a manner at the same time elegant and comfortable, by the attentions of Madam MacRae. The General was received there by the committee charged with providing for all his needs. "Here, you are in your city," said the president of this committee, "you are in your house, in the midst of your children. All is at your disposal." Each moment of our too-short stay in Fayetteville was filled by festivals of gratitude and friendship. Despite the bad weather that did not cease from vexing us, the voluntary companies of militia, which had been joined together to render military honors to the last surviving major general of the Army of the Revolution, did not want to leave the small camp that they had established facing the balcony of the house from which the General could easily observe their maneuvers. They were found still under arms on the following morning at the time of our departure, and we passed before their battlefront in order to leave the City. It was then that General Lafayette, wanting to prove his gratitude to all of them, walked up to them and clasped the hand of each officer and each soldier affectionately while traversing every row. This conduct excited the enthusiasm of the spectators to such a high degree that a large part of the population, wanting to prolong the pleasure of seeing him, accompanied him very far on the road and left him only when the sun was very near the horizon.

The commerce of Fayetteville is very prosperous and can only increase more because of its vicinity to the Cape Fear River, which is navigable to the sea. The products of the surrounding areas consist principally of tobacco and grain; its population is nearly 4,000, and it increases with a very remarkable rapidity; unfortunately, nearly one-third of this population is composed of Slaves and grows in the same proportion as the free population, a circumstance that probably will be adverse to the complete development of its resources for some time yet. What I say of Fayetteville can be applied to the entire State of North Carolina which has more than 200,000 Slaves out of a population of 640,000.

The climate of North Carolina is, they say, salubrious and very favorable to all kinds of farming; nevertheless, the part that we traversed did not present an agreeable appearance to us: many pine forests often inundated by the brooks that watered them; much sand; few cultivated lands; and those lands that are cultivated produce only rice and indigo. They assure us that, in the hilly part of the State, wheat, rye, barley, oats, maize, tobacco, hemp and cotton are harvested in abundance. This last article is obtained, ready for manufacturing, at a rate of 150 pounds per Slave.

It is also in the most elevated part of the lands that they find native gold in rather large quantities. They obtain it solely by straining the dirt; its purity is quite remarkable. They have collected there 23 karats fine, which is of a quality superior to the American and English coins made of this metal. The grains are of different sizes; the largest that has been found of late weighs nearly five pounds. In 1810, the mint of the United States received 1,341 ounces from there, the value of which was $24,689. In Montgomery County, very many people are occupied with searching for this metal. Everyone obtains permission to search for it on the condition that he remit half of what he finds to the owner of the land.

In spite of all its sources of wealth, North Carolina appears to me to be one of the least advanced States of all those we have visited up to now. The principal cause of it must be attributed to Slavery. Its Constitution, although in general copied from those of the other States, differs from them nonetheless in some particulars, and preserves some traces of aristocracy. Thus, for example, in order to be elected senator, it is necessary for one to be the owner of 300 acres of land; to be a representative, one must possess 100 acres; finally, no one can be governor if he is not a freeholder of property producing $1,000. All the while proclaiming religious liberty, the Constitution of North Carolina nonetheless has the misfortune of having preserved a troublesome distinction between denominations; thus, every man who denies the truth of the Protestant Religion cannot pretend to any public office.[5] I know well that in a country where the Government is not involved with the support of the clergy of any denomination, the disadvantage of this distinction is less important; but it is nonetheless a serious attack against the equality established and recognized by the law. A more serious fault of this Government is to have neglected for too

5. See Article 32 of the Constitution of North Carolina. Article 31 excludes from the Senate, from the House of Representatives and the State Council all members of the clergy, without distinction as to beliefs or sects, so long as they are exercising their pastoral functions.

long a time the means of propagating primary education. It is only since 1808 that the legislative body has decreed the establishment of public schools and provided for the expenses necessary to make them prosper. Despite the faults that I have just pointed out, one cannot deny that the inhabitants of North Carolina are, by their patriotism, worthy of being a part of the great federative family of the United States. In order to prove this, it is sufficient to cite one fact: during the Revolutionary War, the enemy could never procure a pilot on its coasts. I should add that it was to the militias of this State to whom the brilliant successes of the Battles of Briar Creek in 1779, of Waxhaws in 1780, and of Guilford in 1781 were owed.

Chapter IV

Entrance into South Carolina – Route from Cheraw to Camden – Monument Erected to Baron de Kalb – Road from Camden to Charleston – Colonel Huger – History, Institutions and Customs of South Carolina.

Twenty-four hours after our departure from Fayetteville, in the middle of a pine forest, we encountered the delegation of the State of South Carolina that had been sent to meet General Lafayette. This meeting took place on the borders of the two States. Our kind and amiable traveling companions from North Carolina entrusted us to the care of their neighbors while giving us vivid evidence of regret for a separation that pained us as much as it did them, and we continued our route with new carriages and a new escort of new friends up to Cheraw, a pretty little town which, three years ago, had hardly four houses, and which today counts more than 1,500 inhabitants.

The road that we had to travel on the following day was long and difficult; often it was even almost impassable; in certain spots we found it entirely blocked by overflowing rivers; in others, we could advance across marshland only by rolling slowly on an inadequate causeway formed by tree trunks rather badly arranged one next to the other. Consequently, we traveled so slowly that night overtook us on the road and it soon became so dark that many horsemen of the escort lost the course of the road in a spot where it was barely outlined in the sand, and lost their way in the forest. The carriages of the procession began to lose their proper separation, and towards ten o'clock, George Lafayette and I noticed that the carriage in which we were riding was very far behind all the others. Some moments later, we felt ourselves shaken violently and we heard a loud crash. Our carriage shaft had broken, and we were left in the middle of a bog. Our position was rather disagreeable, and we would have had some difficulty pulling ourselves out of it without the aid of two dragoons who had not abandoned us and who insisted, despite our protests, that we mount their horses. We arrived in a few minutes in view of the encampment that surrounded the house which was to serve as our refuge, and in which the General had already been established for nearly an hour. This house was altogether isolated in the middle of the forest. We were very well-received there. They offered us an excellent supper and some rather good beds, in which we would have probably slept very well if the trumpet had not been sounded during the whole night to reassemble our lost horsemen.

At our rising, my eyes were struck by a spectacle altogether new to me. We were in the middle of what they call in America a *New Settlement*, that is to say the clearing of land or the building of a new habitation in the middle of the woods. The house in which we had passed the night was the sole dwelling, and it was not yet entirely completed; alongside it, the framing of other buildings, intended, no doubt, to serve as barns and stables, was beginning to be raised. Half-cut tree trunks gathered together in great numbers indicated the landowner's intention to undertake still other buildings soon; and already, the forest was almost entirely cut down within a rather large radius. There remained standing only some trees of prodigious height, not only deprived of their branches, but also sometimes despoiled of their bark, and blackened along their entire length by the action of the flames with the aid of which they had destroyed the weaker trees around them. It is difficult to imagine something more saddening than a scene such as this.

"It is nevertheless in this manner," said one of our traveling companions to me "that all our little towns that you find so joyful, so attractive, begin. Cheraw, where you slept yesterday, and which pleased you so much, resembled this one only a few years ago, and perhaps you will find here another Cheraw if you come back in four or five years. See," he continued while drawing me towards that part of the forest which the blade and the fire had respected,

> See with what care and what skill the founder of this future city has laid the foundations of a fortune that he hopes to enjoy before a little time has passed. Here is a space of several acres surrounded by a rude fence, in which his cows, his horses and his pigs are enclosed. These animals, raised and substantially free, and easily finding plentiful nourishment, are going to multiply to infinity soon, and assure him a part of his subsistence. Next year, that portion of land that has just been cleared will probably bear a rich crop of maize or rice; but the landowner, while awaiting the moment when he will be able to harvest his food, procures it for himself by trading. He pays for it in turpentine that he collects from those enormous pines that surround him; a little cut made in the tree trunk gives an outlet to the liquid, which they receive in a vase. Three thousand trees furnish 75 barrels of turpentine annually; but it is not only trees endowed with a vigorous growth of vegetation that supply his needs; he also makes those that time has destroyed contribute to them. From dead trees he extracts tar that he obtains by burning the wood on a grill below which is a vase that receives the boiling liquid; and sometimes from herbs and sometimes from plants, which he removes from the driveways of his house, he extracts a large quantity of potash with which he augments his wealth even more. Each year is

> going to see an increase in the land around him which is put into production, and soon other *Settlers,* encouraged by his success, will come to gather together around him and to help him to create the new town in which he will be permitted to aspire to the public offices that his fellow citizens will entrust to his talent and his public-spiritedness....

While we were thus occupied in having a quick look at the current resources of our host and his future fortunes, General Lafayette had completed his preparations to depart, and, at the signal given by the trumpets, we resumed our journey across the sands and the pines to repair to Camden where we were to lodge. During the night, the weather had changed, and a clear sky favored our ride; although we might be still in the month of March, we felt the heat of the sun keenly, and all around us had the appearance of an already-advanced Spring. Upon approaching Camden, where one sees a large number of perfectly cultivated gardens, we were very astonished to find all the trees in flower and the air scented with the perfume of plants as in France in the month of June.

Camden is not a large town; it contains at the very most 1,200 inhabitants; nonetheless, we found there a numerous population gathered together from more then 80 miles around to welcome General Lafayette, and to be present at the laying of the first stone of a funeral monument that they were to construct to the memory of Baron de Kalb. General Lafayette was received a little before the Town, near the former quarters of Cornwallis, by all the citizens in arms, and was conducted with great ceremony and in the midst of groups of young girls, to the lodging that had been prepared, where he was addressed by young Colonel Nixon with a warmth of feeling it would be impossible for me to recount here. The attentive crowd applauded rapturously when the speaker said to the General that his visit to the United States had added a new page to history, and that the luster of the triumphs of Greece and Rome paled before the harmonious unanimity of this popular acclaim.

On the following morning, a long procession, formed principally of Freemasons, and followed by the civil authorities and delegations of the different institutions of South Carolina, came to take the General from his lodging, and conducted him, accompanied by religious music, towards the spot where the funeral ceremony was to take place. There they inaugurated the monument to be erected by the generous inhabitants of South Carolina to that unfortunate hero. An inscription in a noble but unpretentious style recalls the patriotism, the services and the glorious death of de Kalb.

One knows that de Kalb was German and that, after having served a long time in France, he came to America, like Lafayette and Pulaski, to offer his services to liberty. He was second in command of the army of General Gates in the unfortunate Battle of Camden, where the Americans were completely defeated. He had performed some prodigious feats of valor at the head of troops from Maryland and Delaware, when at the conclusion of the action his 11th wound killed him and deprived the American cause of one of its most skillful and devoted defenders.

After his remains, which had been preserved with care, were deposited in the monument, and were received with military honors, the stone that was to cover them was set by General Lafayette; on it one read:

THIS STONE
HAS BEEN PLACED OVER
THE REMAINS
OF
BARON DE KALB
BY
GENERAL LAFAYETTE
1825

The hand of the General, placed on the stone, followed it as it descended slowly, and the crowd contemplated with religious silence the old French warrior, after nearly half a century, giving the last rights to the German warrior, on a land that spilled the blood of each of them and that their arms combined to free. What glorious and painful memories this scene must have awakened in Lafayette's mind! Alas! In his long triumph, how many tombs to be visited, from the one to which he descended at Mount Vernon to the one that will soon be raised at Bunker Hill!

The ceremony ended with a speech by the General in which he paid his tribute of esteem to his former companion-in-arms. The General praised de Kalb's civic virtues, his military talent and his indomitable courage in defense of the cause of liberty.

We left Camden on the 11th to travel to Columbia, the seat of government of South Carolina. This city is pleasantly situated on a healthy and fertile plain on the shore of the Congaree River. We found all the streets by which the procession that was conducting the General was to pass, ornamented with banners and triumphal arches. On one of these, three very beautiful girls held up flags on which the names of Lafayette, de Kalb and Pulaski were written in gold letters. Under a tree, situated near the house that we were to occupy, the General stopped and was addressed by the Mayor of the City, a young man very distinguished in his talents, who, during our stay in Columbia, was most amiably and tenderly attentive to us. Governor Manning also addressed the General in the presence of the people in the place where the Congress of Carolina meets. The evening, as well as the following day, were dedicated to public rejoicing.

On the first evening, after having traversed the streets that were brightened by glittering illuminations, we went to visit the academy that was directed by the celebrated Dr. Cooper. We had the pleasure of conversing with the professors, all of whom were of the first rank. We found three of them who expressed themselves in French with great aptitude. They informed us that they had resided in Paris for a long time, where they boasted of having acquired the knowledge and the insight which they are now charged with communicating to their young fellow-citizens. On the following day, several corps of militia, among which we noticed the company of young students of the academy, under the name of Lafayette Guards, came to execute maneuvers under the General's windows. Following that, we spent the day in the company of some of Lafayette's former companions-in-arms, who were pleased to recall to him the days when they had fought and suffered with him for the independence of their country. In the evening, at the ball, which was very noteworthy for the beauty of the women who graced it, and for the good taste that had governed the arrangements, we made the acquaintance of a young lady who aroused in us a lively interest; she was the spouse of one of the three professors about whom I have just spoken.

Born in Paris, she had been transplanted only three months ago on this new land, in the midst of customs that must have seemed to her entirely foreign at first, and with which she nonetheless appeared to be already in perfect harmony. She was presented to the General who received her with great warmth. Towards the end of the evening, her French and American feelings, magnified greatly by the displays of friendship and admiration which she saw being lavished on Lafayette, burst out in a rapture that she could contain no longer. "My God!" she cried out suddenly, "How happy I am today and proud to be French, to be of the same native land as General Lafayette!" Then after having rushed towards the General and having kissed his hands, she turned towards me vivaciously: "I beg of you, tell the General's family how happy we would be to receive them here as we have received him! And tell them also that, for myself in particular, I have for the children of La Grange the friendship of a compatriot, and, for Lafayette, the gratitude of an American." This scene was deeply felt by everyone, and the General thanked the young lady with all the effusiveness of a heart strongly moved.

On the 14th of March, we left to go to lodge some miles from Charleston where the General was to make his entrance on the 15th. An escort of voluntary horsemen from Columbia was in battle array in front of our door at the time of our departure and was readying to accompany the General to Charlestown; but he thanked them, and insisted that they not proceed far from the City because the road that we had to travel during the day was long and difficult, and because the sky was threatening us again with a downpour.

As a matter of fact, it was only with much difficulty and very late that we arrived at our destination. The night and the rain overtook us in the middle of a thick forest through which it was difficult to recognize the narrow and tortuous road. Towards nine o'clock at night, the carriage in which I was riding broke down; that of the General, which was riding ahead with the Governor and some staff officers, continued on its route without noticing this accident; but George Lafayette's carriage, which in this instance was behind us, found the road obstructed; its horses were frightened and rushed headlong through the trees where the carriage came to a stop and was obstructed. George Lafayette and his traveling companions, Colonel Preston and the Mayor of Columbia, immediately got out, succeeded by the strength of their arms to push their carriage ahead of mine and offered me a place beside them in order to continue the trip, while some servants went on horseback, they said, to try to obtain light and the help necessary to repair the broken carriage. I accepted their offer; but I was hardly alongside of them when, darkness baffling the skill of Colonel Preston who had wanted to assume the reins of the horses, we found ourselves again in the thickest part of the forest, and in such a predicament that we would have surely overturned if we had tried to take one step more. Consequently, it was necessary for us to wait under the weight of a battering rain for nearly one hour for the return of the servants who finally came with large resin torches. They helped us out of our embarrassed state, and at eleven o'clock at night we arrived, very wet and very fatigued, at Mr. Izard's house, where we found the General and his traveling companions who had already arrived some time ago. The hospitable table of Mr. Izard and his friendly welcome and that of his family made us immediately forget our misadventure, which we were the first to laugh about during dessert.

So as not to keep the citizens of Charleston who had made immense preparations to receive the Nation's Guest waiting, we took to the road early in the morning. At the moment when we were going to take leave of the Izard family, we saw arriving from the City an escort of voluntary cavalry with whom we left at once. As we advanced towards Charleston, the monotony of the fir forest disappeared. Our eyes then feasted pleasantly on a host of shrubs, verdant and elegantly shaped, among which stood majestically some beautiful magnolias. The entrance to the City appeared to us like a delightful garden. The cold of the night had condensed the fragrances of the orange, the peach, and the almond trees covered with flowers, and the air was scented. We stopped for a time to change carriages and to allow the procession the time to form, and, at the signal of the cannon, we entered Charleston.

The inhabitants of Charleston, as citizens of the City which received the young Lafayette on his first arrival on American soil in 1777, were anxious to prove that nowhere else had they preserved the memory of his devotion to the cause of liberty more than among them; thus, the reception that they gave him could be compared both for the brilliance of the decorations, and for the enthusiasm of the people, to all the most beautiful ones that we had seen in the principal cities of the United States. Militias from the farthest points of the State had arrived to join the Charleston militia. Some voluntary cavalrymen had traveled, they said, up to 50 miles per day in order to be present at the post to which their patriotic gratitude appointed them.

Among the diverse corps which left the City to meet the General was one that most especially caught our eyes; its uniforms were absolutely like the one that the Parisian National Guard wore at the time of our glorious Revolution. The language in which the men who made up this corps uttered their *huzzah* when the General passed before them apprised us of the fact that they were French, and we experienced a very sweet emotion in hearing some compatriots add their voices to those of liberty and gratitude.

The French Company took its place in the procession when we entered the City, and, with a notable sense of delicacy, the Americans yielded to them the place of honor near the General. The procession was soon enlarged by a great number of detachments, composed of clergy, the Society of the Cincinnati, veterans of the Revolutionary Army, students of different faculties, officers of the Navy and the Army of the United States, judges of different courts, children of free schools, benevolent societies, German, French, Jewish and Spanish, the Association of Artisans, etc. All of these detachments were distinguished by the form, color and the slogans of their banners, and the rest of the population, following on horseback or on foot, filled the air with shouts of *Welcome Lafayette,* with which the sound of artillery from the ships that filled the Port and of all the bells were mixed for more than two hours without stopping. But of all these demonstrations of popular affection, what moved the General most was the touching and generous idea of the citizens of Charleston to have him share the honors of his triumph with his brave and excellent friend, Colonel Huger.

It is well-known that during his captivity in the fortress of Olmutz General Lafayette was almost rescued by the dedication of two men whom the same generosity of feelings had joined for this dangerous undertaking. These men were Bollman, a German doctor, and the young Huger, an American. Huger was the son of a descendant of a French family proscribed by the revocation of the Edict of Nantes. Lafayette had been received in his house when he disembarked for the first time in Charleston. A series of unfortunate incidents made this generous attempt miscarry, and it just missed costing them their lives and earned Lafayette some fresh hardships imposed by his jailers. Upon leaving the dungeons of Austria, the young Huger returned to his country, where he found his reward in public esteem for the noble enterprise and for the dangers that he had risked. Now father of a family, farmer and Colonel of a militia, he lives retired and generally loved on a beautiful property some miles from Charleston. On disembarking in New York, General Lafayette had already had the satisfaction of pressing him to his grateful heart. When we entered Charleston, his fellow-citizens insisted that Huger take his place beside the Nation's Guest in his triumphal carriage, where he shared with him the public's felicitations and approbation. At the banquet, at the theatre, at the ball, everywhere in fact, Huger's name was inscribed beside the name of Lafayette, to whom the inhabitants of Charleston did not believe they could express their gratitude better than by demonstrating equally deep gratitude to the one who had not been afraid to risk his life to set him free in the past.

After the procession had traversed every part of the City, it stopped at City Hall where the Mayor, at the head of the municipal corps and in the presence of the people, gave the following speech to General Lafayette.

> General, it is a very pleasant duty for me, as the First Magistrate of this City, to express to you the joy and the emotions which your presence among us inspires. In order to pay to your virtues the tribute of our gratitude, we will not employ the bombastic and servile style of the Courts, but rather the language of republican sincerity. We would be angered if the world could suppose that it is to the man ennobled by hereditary titles that our homages are addressed. Like you, we think that blood does not give any right to preeminence; also, like you, we honor only that nobility which no sovereign of the earth can confer; the nobility of virtue.
>
> We admire in you the man whose purity of private life is intimately bound to all the other qualities that distinguish the soldier-patriot. We salute in you the illustrious defender

> of the rights of man, the enemy of factions, and the hero of freedom…; titles that make you dear to all virtuous and free men, from all parts of the world, but which attach to you more intimately and affectionately still the citizens of these States, which, each day, experience the benefits of *Self-Government* on the individual happiness of the people, and on the growing glory of the Nation. We recognize in you the ardent friend of our menaced infancy, our disinterested benefactor, the leader of our Revolutionary warriors, and the well-loved companion of our Washington.
>
> Such are your claims to our gratitude; you have sealed them with your blood; they are engraved in every American heart, and nothing can make us forget them so long as our Republic stands.

The applause of the public ratified the words of the speaker and blanketed the response of the General, who had recalled, with an eloquence imprinted with the gratitude of his heart, the early obligations that he had to the citizens of Charleston, the noble devotion of the ladies of this patriotic City, and the courage of the Carolinians during the entire Revolutionary War.

Colonel Drayton also addressed the General in the name of the Society of the Cincinnati, after which we were conducted to the sumptuous lodgings they had prepared for us, where, during the entire next day, the General received visits from all the corporate groups of the City. The company of French riflemen that we had noticed on entering the City presented itself first; its military band, which marched ahead, saluted the General with two patriotic tunes, *Yankee Doodle* and *The Marseillaise*. Then, Mr. Labatut and one of his comrades addressed the one to whom they came to render homage; after which the company filed before him, while mixing displays of the most tender affection with the military honors that they were rendering to him. When the General complimented the officers on the handsomeness of their bearing and the good taste of their uniform, "we could not choose a more honorable one," they responded. "Lafayette and our fathers wore it in the glorious days of the liberation of our country, and it continuously reminds us that the primary obligations of an armed citizenry are to the maintenance of public order and the defense of the rights of man." We spent some delightful moments devoted to memories of the Fatherland in the midst of these brave men. All spoke of her with fondness and enthusiasm, all made ardent prayers for her happiness…. Among them were some refugees!

Shortly after the French Company withdrew, there arrived all the members of the Clergy, joined under the leadership of Reverend Doctor Furman, whom they had chosen for their spokesman. One saw among them Episcopalians, Presbyterians, Jews, Roman Catholics, and German and French Protestants. Upon seeing their touching association and the displays of benevolence that they made to each other, one could have believed that they all belonged to the same communion. I will not report here the long and eloquent speech of Dr. Furman; but I can assure you that, like the speech of Bishop White of Philadelphia, it confirmed what I have already said about the liberal spirit of a clergy who, without support from a government that seems to ignore its existence, feels the need to gain public esteem by the practice of the true virtues.

I forego the recitation of the fetes, balls, fireworks, and banquets which we attended during our stay in Charleston because it would be necessary to repeat nearly everything which I have already said for so many other large cities; but while I leave the General in the midst of his former companions-in-arms, at the head of which he found again the respected General Pinckney, conversing with each other about the glorious memories of their youth, I am going to endeavor to sketch quickly the history and the customs of South Carolina.

This part of the North Amcrican Continent was explored for the first time in 1512 by Juan Ponce de Léon, Spanish Governor of Puerto Rico. Struck by the beauty of the vegetation and by the agreeable look of the countryside, he gave it the pretty name of Florida; but finding neither gold nor silver mines, he gave up the plan to found a settlement there. For a long time the Kings of France, England and Spain coveted this country, but it was only in 1562 that France decided to enforce its claims. At the urging of Admiral de Coligny, who wanted to establish a refuge for Protestants there, a naval officer named Jean Ribaut, born in Dieppe, was sent with two vessels and some landing troops to reconnoiter the coast and to found a colony. Jean Ribaut landed at the mouth of a river, below 30 degrees latitude, and established possession by the erection of a stone column on which he engraved the arms of France. After some travels on the coast, during which he established relations of friendship with the natives of the land, he arrived at the mouth of the Albemarle River, where he formed his first settlement, which he called Carolina in honor of Charles IX. He protected it by a small earthen fort, the defense of which he entrusted to about 40 men whom he left behind under the command of one of his officers, named Albert, and returned to France. This leader, very strict in the exercise of the discipline that he had established, was soon massacred by his soldiers. The latter, desirous of seeing their native land again, soon embarked and made sail for France; but hardly had they lost sight of the coasts that they were leaving, when a dead calm kept them at sea for so long that their provisions had been long since exhausted and they had already begun to devour one another when they were met and aided by an English vessel that brought them to England, where Queen Elizabeth required them to relate the account of their horrible adventure.

Two years later, a new expedition left under the command of René de Laudonnière in order to reestablish and protect the Colony; but whether it was fate, or incompetency on the part of the leader, the expedition had only unfortunate results. The complaints of the Colonists against Laudonnière arrived in France, and the Government decided to send Ribaut to take charge of the affairs of the Colony. He was surprised, at the mouth of the May River, by a Spanish squadron of six ships, which attacked him vigorously, and from which he escaped only by entering the river. Determined to offer a vigorous resistance to the Spanish, Ribaut landed his men, entrenched them carefully, went to look for Laudonnière's best troops, which he had left in Fort Carolina with all the individuals who were unable to bear arms, and reembarked in order to search for the enemy; but, assailed during the night by a horrible storm, his ships broke up on the rocks.

It was only with difficulty that he and his soldiers gained the shore in order to surrender to the Spanish, who massacred them in a cowardly manner and without pity. The sick, the women and the children who had stayed in the Fort experienced the same fate. It was only Laudonnière and some of his men who escaped, and, as if by a miracle, later found the means of returning to France, where they reported the unfortunate death of their companions. The French Court displayed only indifference to this horrible event; but the public did not conceal its indignation, and some powerful men demanded vengeance. One of them named Dominique de Gourges, a gentleman from Gascogne, resolved to be the avenger of his compatriots; he outfitted three ships at his own expense; took on board 200 soldiers and 80 sailors, and arrived at the mouth of the May River, where he presented himself under the Spanish flag; landed with the aid of this ruse without being recognized, he marched rapidly on Fort Carolina, then seized it, as well as two others, aided by the natives of the land, put the Spanish garrisons to the sword, razed the fortifications to the ground, and returned triumphant to France carrying arms and plunder. This bold enterprise struck terror in the Spanish, and made them forever disgusted with Carolina, which up to the reign of Charles II of England, remained abandoned by all the European nations.

It was then that the English Government, under the pretext of protecting some families who had escaped the tomahawk of the Indians of

Virginia, and who had settled at the mouth of the May River, seized the entire country between the 31st and the 36th parallel latitude, and granted it to eight gentlemen of the Court, the King reserving to himself homage and fidelity, *as a Fief of the Royal Castle of Greenwich*, and also reserving to himself a quarter of the gold or silver that would be found within the borders of this territory. The celebrated Locke was entrusted with drafting a constitution for the new Colony. By this Constitution, a kind of permanent royalty was practiced by the eldest of the settlers, and was supported by an aristocracy in which one found an outlandish collection of lords, barons, counts and chiefs, whose powers and pretensions, ceaselessly running into each other, were soon dominated by the tyranny of the Palatine, which was the name given to the head of state, whose foremost claim to power was his age. This Constitution, the inferior conception of a great genius, was destroyed in 1720.

Shortly afterwards, the Colony saw its population grow rapidly with the political and religious persecutions that were then ravaging Europe. It received, at almost the same time, English Royalists, Parliamentarians, and Nonconformists. France sent the elite of its citizens banned by the revocation of the Edict of Nantes to it. The mountains of Scotland saw their inhabitants leave to request asylum there in 1730; and in 1745 it was enriched by Swiss and German refugees. From that time, Carolina had the sense of its strength, and resisted the abuses of powcr of thc English Government; it refused to pay taxes imposed without its consent, and it gave its support to the resolutions of the Colonial Congress, which its delegates attended in 1765. Nevertheless, when the issue of breaking the bonds that united Carolina to the Mother Country arose in 1775, there was a division of opinion among the Colonists, and one rather considerable part took arms in favor of the English Government.

Civil war was about to break out, when a very extraordinary circumstance led to a reconciliation of the parties. The same day when hostilities began in Lexington, Massachusetts, dispatches from England arrived in Charleston. The Revolutionary committee seized the mailbag, which contained letters addressed to the Governors of Virginia, the two Carolinas, Georgia and Eastern Florida by which they were ordered to use force of arms to reduce the Colonies to obedience; at about the same time, they received from Savannah information about an Act of Parliament that authorized the Governors to place the Colonists outside the law and the protection of the King and to confiscate their property. These diverse documents, published by the committee, reunited all the citizens in the same feeling of indignation, and the assembly that was called together afterwards posed this question: *Do we want to die enslaved or live free?* The response could not have been in doubt. All swore to defend their rights and to rush into arms. Some imprudent

Tories, who tried to hold the country with the help of the Indians whom they had taken in their pay, were soon annihilated by patriotic militias, who after a long and difficult struggle against the English troops from Savannah, finally assured the independence of Carolina by the celebrated victory they achieved at Eutaw Springs in 1781.

It was in the middle of the troubles of the War, in 1778, that Carolina was given its first Constitution. It was very much in conformity with the principles of the Revolution; but perhaps it felt the effects of the haste with which it had been drafted. It was revised, modified and adopted in its current form at Columbia on June 3, 1790. Such as it is now, it would appear to be very democratic in Europe; but compared to the Constitution of Pennsylvania, for example, and to some other States of the Union, it is quite aristocratic. The conditions for eligibility imposed on the governor, the senators and the members of the house of representatives reduce those eligible to a small number. The senators, elected for four years, in the number of 43, must be at least 30 years old, must have resided in the State for five years before the election, and must possess an estate of 300 pounds sterling, free of debts; if the candidate does not live in the district where he is elected, his estate must be 1,000 pounds sterling.

The representatives, who number 124, are elected for two years. They must also be White, free, at least 21 years old, and must possess an estate of 150 pounds sterling, or a plantation of 500 acres of land and *ten Blacks*. If the candidate does not reside in the district where he is elected, the value of his estate must be 500 pounds sterling. He must be a citizen of the State and must have lived there for three years before the election.

One can see that the two houses of the senate and of the representatives are composed only of a portion of the most wealthy propertied men. It is from this legislative power, as it may be a little aristocratic, that the executive power derives; for it is by a joint session of the two houses that the governor, in whom the executive power resides, is named. The conditions of eligibility for governor are very high and restrict the choice of the houses to a rather narrow circle. Every candidate for this magistracy must be 30 years old, and a citizen of the State, having resided there for ten years before his election, and must possess *in his own right an estate of 1,500 pounds sterling*. The powers of the governor last only two years.

The most troublesome condition that one encounters in the Constitution is the one that imposes on legislators the obligation to possess Slaves. I know very well that it will necessarily disappear before the abolition of Slavery; but doesn't it seem to have been put in the Constitution as an obstacle itself to delay abolition? And wouldn't the abrogation of this article be a salutary step in favor of emancipation?

As in all the States of the Union, organized religion is not in any way supported by the Government, which only guarantees to the diverse communions the free exercise of their religious practices, as long as this exercise does not consist of licentious acts or of practices incompatible with the peace and the security of the State. Ministers of religion are not eligible for the positions of governor, lieutenant governor, or member of the assembly as long as they continue in the exercise of their pastoral functions. The communions are numerous and varied, as one could see by the composition of the religious groups that came to congratulate General Lafayette.

One has perhaps noticed that it is only in speaking of the communions of South Carolina that I have named the Jews; it is, in fact, in this State alone, as it were, that they are of a large enough number to be noticed: one counts about 1,200 of them in the State. The City of Charleston alone contains nearly 500 of them who, during the last war, distinguished themselves by their courage and their patriotism, by furnishing a corps of 60 volunteers for the defense of the country. The rest of the United States contains barely 5,000 Israelites, most of English or German origin. Those of South Carolina are more particularly of French and Portuguese origin. The Synagogue of Charleston was built in 1794. Before this time, the Jewish Congregation of this City had only a very small building in which to practice its worship. According to the description of Charleston by Dr. Theact, the Israelites began to meet in a religious society in about 1750; as soon as ten persons had joined together (that is the number required by the law of the Hebrews for the exercise of publish worship), they procured a suitable place for their purposes. The present building is elegant and spacious. The society that constructed it is called *Kalh Kadosh Beth Eloëm*, which is to say: religious society of the house of God. *Kalh* or *Society* is the name of the entire Hebrew Congregation. The present number of member-subscribers is about 70, which entails more than 300 individuals having the right to enjoy the use of the Synagogue, as well as the benefits that this right carries with it. The Reform Society consists of 50 members, which with their families make more than 200 dissenters.

South Carolina is located between the 32nd and 33rd parallels latitude; its area is about 29,000 square miles; its soil is very varied. From the shores of the Atlantic to 80 miles into the interior of the land, the country is a vast plain rising imperceptibly to about 200 feet above sea-level; and its surface is divided into pine forests that grow in a light sand of little value, immense marshes that render the air unwholesome in autumn, savannas that produce only grass, and highlands, which are adapted for the cultivation of cotton. Rice is grown successfully near the rivers whose overflow increases the fertility of their shores. Beyond this plain, the country is mountainous, productive, and healthier than the lower part, where the humidity of the winters and the changeableness of the temperature in every season renders illnesses very common.

The population of this State is 502,741 inhabitants, whom one can divide in three classifications: 237,460 free Whites, 6,806 free Colored persons, and 258,475 Slaves. One sees that the number of Slaves surpasses by very much that of free Whites; thus this State began to feel the effects of the disadvantages of Slavery to such a degree that its fear led it to adopt safety measures that offended humanity and property rights at the same time. By one recent law, every traveller who enters into Carolina with a Colored servant finds himself instantly deprived of his servant, who is put in prison and only released when he leaves the State. How is this measure useful? It is a question that I would be very embarrassed to answer. It is, they say, to avoid dangerous contact between the Slaves of this State and the free Black foreigners who would not fail to speak to them of liberty….

This state of affairs relative to Slavery in South Carolina is so much more distressing since it contrasts conspicuously with the character of the inhabitants of this State. The Carolinians are particularly distinguished by the culture of their mind, the elegance of their manners, their politeness and their hospitality towards strangers. This latter virtue is so common in South Carolina that one finds there very few inns outside of the large cities. Travelers can boldly present themselves at the home of every farmer whom they find on their route and are assured of being well-received there. The disposition to help the indigent is so great in Charleston that, besides a large number of private associations, there are five public benevolent societies there whose revenues, already very considerable, are increased more every day by the generosity of the citizens.

The three days that General Lafayette spent in Charleston were marked by fetes whose brilliance and good taste enraptured him; but, of all the refined attentions that they lavished on him, the one that moved him most was the gift which the City gave him of a beautiful portrait of his friend Colonel Huger. This beautiful miniature, of just large enough dimensions, joined the merit of the most perfect resemblance with an admirable execution; it recalls very much the manner of our celebrated Isabey, and would not be disavowed by him. It is painted by Mr. Fraser of Charleston, who already enjoys a great reputation in the United States, but who seems to have surpassed it in this work. The frame of solid gold is made that much more valuable by the elegance and the delicacy of the work as by the richness of the material. It came from the shops of two Philadelphia artists, and would have done honor to our most skilled French jewelers.

The Governor offered the General a very beautiful map of South Carolina, enclosed in a handsome silver case, in the name of the State. Very many other persons also came to offer him attractive mementos that he accepted with gratitude; and, on March 17, he left Charleston taking with him the regrets of his friends and the blessings of the people.

Chapter V

Fort Moultrie – Edisto Island – Alligators – Savannah – Funeral Monuments – Augusta – State of Georgia.

The roads of South Carolina being generally very bad, the Charleston committee resolved to conduct the General by sea to Savannah, where he had been expected for a long time. We embarked on March 17 on board an excellent steamship, prepared and well-provisioned for us by the attentions of the committee, and we took our leave of the inhabitants of Charleston who, lined up on the wharf and pressed together in a crowd on boats, responded to the farewells of their guest with their cheers. Before losing sight of Charleston, we headed towards Sullivan Island, on which stands Fort Moultrie, which saluted General Lafayette with all its artillery. This Fort, which commands the passage through which ships must enter the Port of Charleston, was defended with exceptional courage by the Carolina militia on June 28, 1776 against English forces who were very much greater in number and superior in experience. The militia were commanded by General Moultrie who, during the entire Revolutionary War, maintained his noble reputation for valor and skill that the defense of this important position had won for him.

We continued sailing after this, entering between the continent and the bordering islands, the chain of which extends as far as Savannah. We went ashore at one of them, named Edisto, where General Lafayette was awaited; but as it was impossible for him to stay there more than two or three hours, the inhabitants, who were assembled at the house of one of the principal landowners, decided to offer him all the fetes that they had prepared to last several days immediately. We had all at the same time the speeches, the public dinner, the ball and even the baptism of a charming little infant to whom they gave the name Lafayette; then we crossed the island in a carriage rapidly in order to rejoin our steamship, which was waiting for us on the high sea. On this short ride, what we saw of the island appeared to us to be charming; the vegetation struck us especially by the variety of its produce; the bushes, both sweet-smelling and elegantly shaped, are pleasantly mingled with larger forest trees; and in the dunes that run along the bank of the seacoast, we saw beautiful palm trees that give to the little dwellings they shade an altogether picturesque look. This island, which lies at the mouth of the river of the same name, 40 miles southwest of Charleston, is 12 miles long and 5 miles wide. It has been inhabited, they say, since 1700.

During the rest of our sail to Savannah, we skirted the islands of Hunting, Beaufort, Port Republican, Hilton Head, etc., and often by such narrow passages that the sides of our ship nearly touched the land on each side, and it had rather the look of rolling on the grasslands that surrounded it than that of gliding on the water which disappeared beneath it. It was nearly midnight when we passed in front of Beaufort, and everyone on board was sleeping; but we were soon awakened by the shouts of the citizens who had waited up to then on the bank, and General Lafayette, having gotten up, gave in to their entreaty that he spend some moments among them.

In the morning at sunrise, as we approached the mouth of the Savannah River, we began to see some alligators stretched out on the bank or swimming around our ship. Our captain killed one of them with a rifle shot, and sent a longboat to retrieve it. It was about eight feet long, and they assured us that it was to be considered only medium-sized; there are those that obtain the size of 12 feet, sometimes, they say, even 15 or 18 feet. The size of their body is then equal to that of a horse. Having reached this degree of growth, the alligator is a dangerous animal because of its prodigious strength and its agility in water. Its shape is a little like that of the lizard; it differs from it only in its wedge-shaped tail, flattened on its sides, which, from the abdomen to its extremity, diminishes imperceptibly. As with the rest of the body, it is covered with scaly material, impenetrable by all arms, even by a musket ball. It is vulnerable only near the neck and behind the front members which have exactly the shape of a man's arms. The head of an alligator of the largest size is about three feet; the opening of his jaw is of the same dimension; its eyes are very small, sunk in his head and covered; its nostrils are wide and so spread out at the top that, when it swims, its head resembles a wide, floating beam at the surface of the water. Its upper jaw is movable alone, it opens nearly perpendicularly, and forms a right angle with its lower jaw. On each side of the upper jaw, immediately below the nostrils, are two long and strong teeth, slightly pointed and cone-shaped. They have the whiteness and polish of ivory, and are always exposed, and this gives the animal a frightening look. In the lower jaw, just opposite these two teeth, are two holes adapted to receive them. When the alligator strikes one jaw against the other it produces a noise absolutely like that which one obtains by striking a plank violently against the ground: this noise is heard at a rather great distance. This animal destroys very many aquatic birds, has a decided taste for dogmeat, and even willingly attacks a man when it believes that it can surprise him.

When on the morning of the 19th we arrived in sight of Savannah, we noticed on the shore the entire population and the militia assembled together, who had been waiting for several hours. Soon we heard the majestic welcome of the artillery and the shouts of the people. We responded to them by the cannon-fire of our ship, and by the patriotic tunes that our band caused to echo from the shore. To this initial feeling of pleasure that the greeting of the citizens of Savannah made us experience, a feeling of painful regrets suddenly succeeded: it was necessary for us to separate from our traveling companions from South Carolina. Among them was the Governor of that State, several staff-officers and some members of the committee that had received us in Charleston. The Governor, faithful to the laws which prevented him from leaving the borders of the State, resisted all requests that were made to him to disembark, and said his farewells to the General with the emotion of a son separating from a father whom he is to see no more. Some moments later, we were in Georgia at the entrance to Savannah, where the General was welcomed and addressed by Governor Troup, in the midst of a fervent crowd. The carriage and the triumphal arches, the acclamations of the people, the wreaths and flowers thrown by the ladies, the sound of bells and cannon, all, in a word, demonstrated to Lafayette that, although he had changed States, he was nonetheless always in the midst of the same friendly and grateful people.

A commodious lodging had been prepared in the elegant house of Mrs. Maxwell; they conducted General Lafayette there in a large procession. After he had had some moments of rest, the Mayor and the Municipal Council of the City came to congratulate him, and the day concluded with a public dinner, which the civil and military authorities of the State and of Savannah, the Clergy and a large number of citizens attended. After the customary 13 toasts, the table companions made a large number of voluntary toasts, all strongly impressed with that patriotic and republican character which always distinguishes American gatherings: General Lafayette responded to the toast which was made to him by the following: "*To the City of Savannah*: may its young prosperity prove more and more to the Old World the superiority of republican institutions and of government of the people, by themselves." A hymn to liberty, sung to the tune of *The Marseillaise*, ended the banquet and we returned to our headquarters in the gleam of the lights with which the entire City shone.

Early on the following day, Sunday, the General received a visit from the French and the descendants of the French residing in Savannah. Their leader was Mr. Petit de Villers who spoke in their name and who, in a speech replete with the expression of the feelings of his compatriots for Lafayette, depicted warmly the benefits of American hospitality toward the exiled French whom despotism of all kinds forced to request asylum in the United States successively. In his response, General Lafayette said to them:

> It is with deep feeling that, in the midst of the kindnesses which have been heaped upon me, I find myself welcomed by those of my French compatriots and their descendants who, in

this happy American land, have found a refuge against very diverse persecutions, all of which are condemned by the true spirit of liberty. The moving details of the benevolence of which they have been the object, so well expressed by you, Sir, are doubly dear to my heart. I like to think that admiration for the institutions to which the United States owes its great prosperity cannot be a vain sentiment and that other peoples would prefer to exercise all their rights cheaply, rather than to pay very dearly for oppression, vexatious interferences, and obstacles of all kinds.

After the visit of the French, there followed those of the officers of different societies; the Clergy came next, at their head was Reverend Carter who, in complimenting the General, congratulated him especially for the fact that his efforts in favor of American independence had also resulted in the establishment of religious freedom. "Here," he said, "each man renders to God the homage that his conscience inspires in him; in our happy City the priests of all the different communions live together like brothers, give each other proofs of their reciprocal esteem and affection every day, and each of them gives thanks to God, our common Father, for the religious liberty which we enjoy. But, General, whatever the difference of our opinions may be on some points of theology, be assured that we are sincerely and cordially united in the prayers that we address to the Eternal One for your prosperity in this world and for your happiness for eternity."

To his thanks, the General joined the expression of satisfaction that he felt in seeing America give so beautiful an example of true religious freedom to the old Europe which only understands still a very limited tolerance. "In religious societies as in political societies," he added, "I am persuaded that election by the people is the best guarantee of mutual confidence."

For a long time, the citizens of Savannah had intended to pay a tribute of gratitude to the memory of General Greene, considered, with reason, as the hero of the Revolutionary struggle of the South, and to General Pulaski, that brave Pole, who, despairing of the cause of liberty in his Fatherland, sacrificed his life to American independence. They thought that General Lafayette's presence would add to the solemnity of the ceremony, and they resolved to take advantage of his stay in Savannah to request that he lay the foundation stone of the funeral monuments that they wanted to erect. Consequently, all being arranged, they proposed it to him, and he accepted with so much more alacrity since he was very pleased to find the occasion to display publicly his esteem for the character of General Greene whom he had been particularly fond of.

The ceremony was strongly impressed with that character born of a blending of exalted religious and patriotic ideas that especially distinguishes all the actions of the American people. In conformity with the resolution taken in the assembly of citizens, presided over by Colonel John Shellman, the Masonic Society, which was charged with all the details relative to the construction of the two monuments, formed a large procession at nine o'clock in the morning of March 21 and proceeded to the sound of music to seek out General Lafayette at his lodgings. The Grand Priest, the King and the other officers of the Royal Chapter of Georgia were clad in their most handsome costumes and their most handsome Masonic jewels. In front of them an elegant embroidered banner was carried. When they began to march with the General, the procession, augmented by militia and citizens, was formed in the following order:

The troops of the United States; - Generals and their staff-officers; - citizens and foreigners; - the committee charged with looking after Lafayette; - the judges and the sheriffs; - the ministers of the clergy, not initiated in Masonry; - the Mayor and the Municipal Council; - the Governor and his retinue; - the committee in charge of the monuments; - the Grand Guardian, sword in hand - the Lodge of Hope; - the Lodge of the Union; - the Lodge of Solomon; - the Chapter of Georgia; - the members of the Grand Lodge; - a master Mason carrying a golden vase full of corn; - two Masters carrying silver vases containing wine and oil; - the principal architect carrying the bevel square, the plumb-bob and the level; - the secretary and the treasurer; - a large candle carried by a Master; - the Holy Bible, the bevel square and the compass carried by another Master accompanied by two servants; - two large candles carried by Masters; - the Grand Chaplain; - ministers of the clergy initiated in Masonry; - two Grand Guardians ; - Deputy Grand Masters; - a Master of the most ancient lodge, carrying the Masonic constitutions; - the Grand Deacons armed with black sticks; - the Grand Master with the General and his retinue; - finally the Grand Sword-bearer; unsheathed sword in hand.

Upon arriving at the site intended for the monument to General Greene, the troops formed in battle array to the right and to the left in order to receive the procession in their midst. The schoolchildren, dressed uniformly and carrying baskets full of flowers that they scattered in the path of General Lafayette, were already gathered there. The people, arranged in a crowd behind them, seemed positioned there to protect their fragility, and to present them to the Nation's Guest. After the most profound silence was established in the middle of the attentive throng, the Masons and the monument committee came to draw up to the west of the foundations for the monument, and the other parts of the procession took their places to the east. They then had General Lafayette advance near the place that had been prepared to receive the cornerstone. He was surrounded by the Grand Master, the Grand Guardians, the Chaplain, the High Priest, the King and the Secretary of the Georgia Chapter, the Governor, Colonel Huger, George Lafayette, etc. A national tune, played by a troop of musicians, gave notice that the ceremony was going to begin. Then the President of the monument committee began to speak in these terms:

> Citizens: the solemn ceremony that gathers us together has for its purpose the placing of the cornerstones of monuments that the gratitude of a people is going to raise to the glory, the virtues and the sacrifices of two illustrious soldiers of our Revolutionary War.
>
> To build monuments to perpetuate the memory of famous men was a custom of all the ages and of all peoples. The humble tombs of the moderns and the gigantic pyramids of the ancients offer us proof of this.
>
> As a symbol of recognition, these monuments certify the justice of these peoples; but it is especially in the vigorous encouragement that they give to the accomplishment of generous acts that their wisdom is shown. They invite the youth to contemplate the lofty deeds that their inscriptions recall and inspire in them that dynamic emulation which is the source of moral virtues and national glory.
>
> Among the Greeks, who understood so well the glory and the rewards accorded to patriotism and valor, the destruction of a statue was a horrible sacrilege, even when the merit of the one to whom it had been built was questionable. How much more sacred must be then the marks of gratitude and admiration voted by the unanimous opinions of an entire people to those men whose reputation is left more brilliant still by the test of time, and built on a foundation made secure by the hand of their most noble compatriots and companions-in-arms in the struggle and the triumph of freedom. Yes, fellow citizens, they will be doubly sacred, these displays of our gratitude, since the hand that is going to help us to build them was one of the first to seize the sword to defend the rights of man, and to assure a glorious peace to our country.
>
> The names of 300 Spartans who fell to the Thermopylae were known by all the children of Sparta. American youth will

recall not only the names, but even more the character and the exploits of each Revolutionary patriot. When they read on this monument the name Greene, they will feel a noble pride in recounting the dangers and the triumphs, the disinterestedness and the valor of this defender of our glorious cause. May our children invoke no more the powerful names of Greece and Rome, but may their youthful ambition come to be invigorated by those beams of the glory of our compatriots that reflect their brilliance on ourselves, and which imbue us with a most invigorating warmth! May the citizens of Savannah recall forever with pride that in their midst repose the ashes of this intrepid war leader! May they be faithful guardians of these precious relics of our most glorious days!

General Lafayette, in the name of and in the presence of my fellow citizens, I ask your cooperation in the accomplishment of the sacred duties that we are going to fulfill in laying the foundations of this monument dedicated to the memory of Major General Greene. In the name of liberty, I ask you to join with us in dedicating to posterity this memorial to the virtues and the talents that graced the life and sanctify the remains of one of your most noble associates in the cause of our independence. In the name of our common Fatherland, I invite you, as a Revolutionary soldier, shining with a glory unique in your rank and in your renown, to endorse, by laying this cornerstone, the reputation of a patriotic hero whose name is inscribed beside yours in the most brilliant pages of our history, and whose tomb will be doubly hallowed both by the one who will have laid its foundation and by the one whose memory it will call to mind.

Most respectable Grand Master, conformably to the wishes of my fellow citizens and in the name of the monument committee, I pray that you solemnize the laying of the cornerstone of the monument that we are going to construct to the memory of General Greene according to the rites of the ancient fraternity to which you belong.

After the speaker had made this last invitation, General Lafayette indicated that he wanted to speak, and soon the silence and the attentiveness redoubled in the midst of the crowd, and each person, turning his gaze towards him, prepared to receive his words; he advanced a little, and in a solemn voice, said:

> The great and good man to whose memory today we pay a tribute of respect, affection and profound regret, acquired in our Revolutionary War a glory so pure and so true that even now the name of Greene alone reminds us of all the virtues, all the talents that can render illustrious the patriot, the statesman and the military leader; nevertheless, it lies with me, his brother-in-arms, and I am proud to be able to say it, his most sincere friend, to declare here to you, Sir, his brave compatriot and companion-in-arms, that the kindness of his heart was equal to the force of his noble, strong and enlightened mind. The trust and the friendship that he secured was one of the great proofs of the excellent judgment that characterized our paternal chief. By the love of the State of Georgia towards him, the Army itself is honored; and, as for me, I present myself before you, before the new generations, as a representative of this Army and of the deceased or absent friends of General Greene, to applaud the honors rendered to his memory, and to thank you for the displays of sympathy that you accord to me in this moving and melancholy solemnity and for the part that you want me to take in it.

When the former comrade of Greene had stopped speaking, a brother of the Lodge of Solomon, arrayed with Masonic emblems, left the crowd, and joining his voice to the grave sounds of the music, sang the following hymn:

> Author of light, source of love, from the height of your celestial throne, look upon us, and lend us the support of your power to raise a monument to glorious deeds!
>
> A monument to the heroes who exist no more, to the heroes who have shone brilliantly in our battles, may your spirit animate us with the breath of freedom, and may you lead us to victory!
>
> Let the marble return to dust in the ground, let the children of liberty be cut off by death, but let fame proclaim the name of the patriot until the moment when the trumpet of the Archangel shall sound!
>
> Hear our prayers, God of our fathers, their children invoke your blessed help! Protect our rights, keep us free, great God! And all of us shall sing to your glory!

This last stanza was repeated in chorus by the assembled crowd, and the prayer of the people rose to heaven with the solemn sound of reverberating cannon.

During this time, the cornerstone had been readied, and before it was laid, the Master Chaplain, Mr. Carter, pronounced the following prayer in a loud voice:

> All-powerful God, most glorious Architect of the universe, dispenser of wisdom and Father of all the mercies, give us the help that we humbly request of you for the accomplishment of this solemn ceremony! May this monument, which is going to be built in memory of virtue, be the shame of the wicked and the pride of the good! May these homages, which we render to those who already are no more upon this earth, remind us that we ourselves are like strangers there and like transients; that marble monuments themselves turn into dust under the assaults of time; and that our names can only escape oblivion by their inscription in the sacred book of eternal life!
>
> May your blessings descend especially on our illustrious brother by the hands of whom these foundations are going to be laid; may his name, which is inscribed in our hearts by gratitude, be also, by your mercifulness, written in the book of salvation! Finally, if, in your profound wisdom, you decide that we are not to see him again on earth after this day, allow us at least to be united with him in that happy and glorious fatherland, where they have no need to build monuments, where they think no more of engraving epitaphs.

After this prayer, which was listened to in scrupulous silence, the Grand Master ordered the secretary of the monument committee to prepare the different objects that were going to be placed under the foundations as mementos of the time. These objects were several medals struck in the likeness of the Nation's Guest, of Washington, of General Greene, of Franklin; coins struck in the United States at different times, as well as paper money of the State of Georgia; some engravings, among which were portraits of General Charles Pinckney and Dr. Kollock, and all the details relative to the ceremony. Finally, there was a medal on which were written these words: "The cornerstone of this monument to the memory of Major General Nathaniel Greene was laid by General Lafayette, at the request of the citizens of Savannah, on March 21, 1825, A.D...."

The stone was then lowered to the bottom of the excavation to the sound of funereal music. The principal architect presented the bevel square, the plumb-bob and the level to the Grand Master, who laid them on the stone while uttering sacred words. Then the gold and silver vases were brought on the platform, where, having been passed by the hands of the Grand Master and the Grand Guardians, they were presented to the General who, according to custom, spilled the corn, the wine and the oil that they contained on the stone, while pronouncing the following invocation:

> May the infinite kindness of the Author of nature grant to the inhabitants of this City all that which can contribute to happiness, to affluence and to the pleasures of this life; may He assist us in the erection and completion of this monument; may He protect the workers against all accidents; may He preserve their works from destruction, and grant to us all an ample provision of the corn of sustenance, the wine of refreshment, and the oil of pleasure.

The General then descended to the stone and struck it with three strikes of the mallet; all the brothers came in succession to fulfill their duties, and the High Priest of the Royal Chapter of Georgia, censer in hand, came to bless the cornerstone. When all these ceremonies were concluded, the Grand Master returned all the objects that were to be used in the completion of the monument to the principal architect, and addressed him in these words:

> Brother architect, you are charged with the direction and supervision of the workers who are going to construct the centotaph built in the memory of a soldier of our Revolution, in memory of the immortal Greene; you have seen the cornerstone of this monument laid by the hand of the one who was his intimate friend and comrade-in-arms; by the one who was the vigorous champion of freedom in the two hemispheres; by the one whom we call with pride our compatriot; by General Lafayette; in returning to you all that is necessary for the accomplishment of this glorious task, I enjoin you, in the name of the ties that bind a Mason to his comrades, to discharge your duty in a manner to do honor to your workers and yourself.

The stone was then sealed to the sound of the band, which played a national tune. The ceremony was terminated by a triple salvo fired by troops of the United States.

This imposing and solemn spectacle was observed for its entire duration by the numerous spectators in a scrupulous silence that indicated their profound veneration for the dead man whom they were honoring and the living hero who was associating himself with them in this moving and melancholy rite.

The procession then began to march in the same order as before, and proceeded to Chippewa Place, where the same ceremony was repeated for the laying of the cornerstone of the monument to be built to Pulaski.

Before returning to his lodgings, General Lafayette went to the home of Brigadier General Harden to attend the presentation of a flag embroidered by Mrs. Harden, and presented by her to the first regiment of the Georgia militia. On this most lavishly fashioned flag was the portrait of General Lafayette, and several inscriptions recalling different glorious epochs of the Revolution. The officers and soldiers burst out with equal enthusiasm upon receiving it, and swore that, under these colors, presented by the beautiful woman and consecrated by Lafayette, they were assured of always conquering the enemies of freedom and of their Fatherland.

Some hours later, in spite of the lively entreaties of the citizens, especially the ladies, who had prepared a ball for the same night, the General, pressed by time and by his numerous engagements, was obliged to leave Savannah, and we boarded *The Alatamaha* with the Governor of Georgia, his staff and the committee of arrangements, in order to proceed to Augusta, which is situated on the Savannah River, 180 miles from its mouth.

We had found in Savannah a young man whose name and fortunes were well suited to inspire in us a lively interest; he was Achille Murat, son of Joachim Murat, ex-King of Naples. At the first report of General Lafayette's arrival in Georgia, he had left Florida, where he was a planter, precipitously, and he had come to add his homage and his congratulations to those of the Americans whom he now regards as his compatriots. Two days spent with him gave us a fondness for his character and his mind that those who will be in a position to know him will not be able, I believe, to refuse him. Barely 24 years old, he had enough strength of mind to know how to extract great advantages from an event that very many others in his place would have regarded as an irreparable misfortune. Deprived of the hope of wearing a crown that his birth promised to him, he brought the meagre remains of his royal fortune to the United States, and, wise enough to appreciate the benefits of liberty that were enjoyed there, became a naturalized citizen of the United States. Far from imitating so many fallen kings who never knew how to console themselves for the loss of their past power, Achille Murat became a farmer, kept his name without any title, and, by his straightforward and altogether republican manners, promptly gained the affection of all those who came to know him. He has a cultivated mind and a heart full of the most noble and generous impulses. He preserves a profound and melancholy veneration for the memory of his father. George Lafayette having cited in conversation characteristics of the brilliant and chivalrous gallantry that Joachin Murat so emimently possessed, Achille Murat appeared quite moved by this, and, some time later, finding himself alone with me, he said with emotion: "George has made me feel a very great happiness, he has spoken well of my father…."

The conversation having fallen on European politics, he expressed himself very frankly on the Holy Alliance, and, in general, on all kinds of despotism. I could not prevent myself from telling him, in jest, that it was a very extraordinary thing to hear such a discourse from the mouth of a hereditary prince. "Hereditary prince!" he replied animatedly, "I have found the means to be better than that; I am a free man!" One thing, nevertheless, pained and astonished me; it is that Achille Murat, free in the choice of his residence in the United States, has come to establish himself precisely in the country that is afflicted by Slavery. This choice appears to me to be reasonable only for the man who has decided to work with all his power towards gradual emancipation of the Blacks, and to give to his neighbors the example of justice and humanity by preparing his Slaves for freedom; but I believe that this noble project has not entered into the plans of our young republican who, to judge by some features of his conversation, appeared only too disposed to adopt the principles of some of his new fellow citizens on the Slavery of the Blacks. Is it then necessary that the original sin of royalty always betrays itself by some small manifestation!

Savannah is the largest city of the State of Georgia. It is situated on the right bank of the river of the same name, about 17 miles from its mouth. All its streets are wide and straight, intersect each other at a right angle, and are planted on each side with a line of very gracious trees called the *Pride of India*, for which the inhabitants of the States of the South have a marked predilection. Although built 40 feet above the level of the river, the location of Savannah is unhealthy; yellow fever rarely lets an autumn pass without exerting its cruel ravages there. Nonetheless, commerce is very active; its port, which can receive ships drawing 14 feet of water, sees more than six million dollars worth of cotton leave annually. Its population is about 7,523 inhabitants divided in this manner: 3,557 Whites, 582 free Colored persons, and 3,075 Slaves. The number of persons employed in manufacturing is approximately equal to that of persons occupied with commerce, which is about 600.

On leaving Savannah, we sailed first for more than 60 miles between some low marshlands, from which a large number of streams emanated, and on which grew the most profuse and varied sylvan vegetation that it may be possible to imagine. Among the tallest trees, one notices four or five kinds of pine, nine kinds of oak, some tulip trees, some poplars, some plane trees, some sassafras, etc., below which grow more than 40 kinds of bushes, of which the shape, the flower, the foliage, and the fragrance produce the delights of our most brilliant flowerbeds. Beyond this plain, the ground rises rapidly about 200 feet above sea level, and offers at intervals some beautiful plateaus on which are found some lush cotton plantations.

As we were approaching Augusta, two steamships, filled with a large number of citizens of this City, came in front of our ship and saluted General Lafayette with a triple acclamation, and with the sound of artillery which they had on board. We answered them with the patriotic song, *Yankee Doodle*, and by three cannon blasts. They joined with us and we went up the river together while forcing the steam to compete in speed. There was something frightening in this contest; the three roaring ships seemed to fly in the midst of black swirls of smoke which concealed us from each other's sight. Victory stayed with *The Alatamaha*, which caused a rather animated joy in our brave captain, who appeared to me to be a man to blow up his ship rather than allow himself to be defeated on such an occasion.

The General, forced to adhere rigorously to the calculations of his itinerary, had resolved at first to spend only a day in Augusta; but it was impossible for him to resist the lively entreaties of the inhabitants who begged him to stay two days, so that a large part of the preparations that they had made for him would not have been in vain. He yielded, and the fetes that they gave to him were so multifarious that, for the first time since the beginning of this prodigious trip, he felt a fatigue, which caused us a moment of anxiety.

Among the citizens who received the General on his landing on the shore of Augusta we found one of our companions of the voyage on *The Cadmus*, Mr. King, a young lawyer very respected by his fellow citizens. This meeting was not only very agreeable for us, but also very useful; as we moved away from the Savannah River, our communications with the Atlantic were going to become more difficult; it was therefore very important for us to leave our dispatches in Augusta, so that our friends in Europe would have our news one more time before we had set out into the interior lands, and Mr. King was kind enough to undertake to send them, as well as some belongings that we removed from our baggage in order to ease the burden on us, because they forewarned us that we were going to traverse the worst roads that we had yet encountered since our departure from Washington.

The day after our arrival, they invited the General to go to visit, on the other side of the Savannah River, a kind of prodigy which proved to what point good institutions are favorable to the growth of population, to the development of industry, and to the happiness of men. It is a village called Hamburg, composed of about 100 homes, built at the same time by a single owner, and entirely inhabited in less than two months by an active and industrious population. This village has not been in existence for two years, and already its port is filled with ships, its wharfs covered with merchandise, and its inhabitants assured of an always increasing prosperity. Hamburg, located on the right bank of the Savannah, belongs to South Carolina.

On the 25th, we left Augusta, which is a well-constructed city, containing more than 4,000 inhabitants, in order to repair to Milledgeville, while passing Warrenton and Sparta. The General was very fondly received in each of these little towns; but everywhere we found only roads in bad condition and so broken up that we were obliged to travel part of the way on horseback. Fortunately, the carriage that carried the General resisted all the perilous situations, or it would necessarily have broken down 20 times. On the first day the shaking was so violent that the General vomited, which initially alarmed us very much, but which stopped entirely after a good night spent at Warrenton.

We arrived on March 28 on the banks of the little Oconee River, near which is found Milledgeville, the capital of Georgia. This town, which by the dispersion of its homes and the multitude and the extent of its beautiful gardens resembles more a beautiful village than a city, contains a population of 2,500, in the midst of which General Lafayette was welcomed as a father and a friend. The citizens, led by their magistrates, came to welcome him on the banks of the river, and the aides-de-camp of the Governor led him ceremoniously to the house of the chief of state, who had claimed the honor of lodging him. The day was passed in the midst of honors and pleasures of all kinds. After the official presentation in the State House, where the General was addressed by an American citizen of French descent, Mr. Jaillet, Mayor of Milledgeville; after the visit that we made to the lodge of our brothers in Masonry and the review of all the militia of the county, we dined at the house of Governor Troup, who had gathered all the public officials and principal citizens, with whom we repaired in the evening to the State House, where the ladies of the Town had prepared a ball for General Lafayette. But at this ball there was neither the possibility or the will for anyone to dance. Each person anxious to talk to or listen to the Nation's Guest kept near him and eagerly seized the occasion to display his gratitude and affection to him. Moved nearly to tears by the kindnesses with which they surrounded him, the General forgot completely that Georgia was a recent acquaintance of his. He also forgot,

I believe, that we had to leave early in the morning on the next day and that some hours of rest would be very necessary for him, because he passed a large part of the night conversing with his new friends.

Before undertaking the account of the continuation of our trip, which took us from the bosom of the most advanced civilization to the midst of the still-savage tribes of primitive children of America, I am going to record here some observations on the State of Georgia.

This State, located between the 30th and the 35th degrees latitude north and the 3rd and 9th degrees longitude west of Washington, is bound in the North by the State of Tennessee, in the Northeast by South Carolina, in the Southeast by the Atlantic Ocean, in the South by Florida, and in the West by the State of Alabama. Its area is 58,200 square miles, and its population is 340,989 inhabitants, of which nearly 150,000 are Slaves, a truly appalling proportion, which must necessarily lead Georgia into an embarrassing situation one day, if its government does not take measures to diminish it. Here, as in all the Slave States, Blacks are a kind of asset that they sell like all other properties, and which they can inherit; but their introduction into the State as an object of commerce is strictly prohibited; after the current legislation, a person who brings a Slave into the State and either sells or puts him up for sale in the course of the year which follows his introduction, is subjected to a fine of $1,000 and imprisonment of five years in state prison.

The prejudices against the Colored race are still very strong among Georgians, and I have not noticed them make great efforts in favor of the abolition of Slavery; the laws even place impediments on gradual emancipation, for an owner cannot free his Slave without authorization of the legislature. The ancient Black Code introduced by the English, and which was a code of blood, has fallen into disuse, and has been replaced by some laws protective of Slaves. Thus, for example, whoever now intentionally deprives a Slave of life or limb is condemned to the same penalty as if the crime has been committed against a White, except in case of insurrection; but they feel that this law, applied by judges who are Slaveholders themselves, and under the sway of the same prejudices as their fellow citizens, must often be only illusory; and also one can say truthfully that if the Slaves of Georgia do not perish under the lash of their masters, as too often happens in the French Colonies, it is only due to the naturally gentle and humane temperaments of Georgians, and not to the effectiveness of the laws, which allow that a Slave *can die accidentally in receiving moderate punishment* without the one who inflicted it being culpable of murder.

Georgia was, they say, the one of the former Colonies in which the Revolution had the least support. The Royal party retained great influence for a long time, and, augmented by a large English corps under the orders of Colonel Campbell, maintained the Royal Government until the end of the war; also, the Patriots had to suffer more there than everywhere else.

It was only in 1798 that the Constitution, which had been adopted in 1785 and amended in 1789, was definitively put in force by a general assembly of representatives. This Constitution is very nearly identical to that of South Carolina.

If Georgia is not yet one of the most wealthy States of the Union in the abundance and variety of its products, the cause of it must be attributed only to the influence of Slavery. There cannot not be a land more favored by nature than this country, and one could easily extract from it all the products of the most opposite of climates. The seashores and the adjacent islands produce up to 600 pounds of cotton per acre, for which the average price is 30 cents a pound, and the same ground can provide four crops without fertilizing. Sugar can be grown on the land with equal success. The white mulberries grow there in such great quantity that Georgia could easily free the United States from the annual tribute of several millions that they pay to Europe, if the cultivation of silk were entrusted to skillful and interested arms, that is to say free arms. Tea grows uncultivated in the environs of Savannah; in some choice spots, indigo provides three crops a year; in the interior, the land produces wheat and maize in abundance; finally, vegetables and fruits of all kinds grow there with a rare ease. But in order to make the source of so many riches frutiful, there would be needed a level of activity and industry rarely possessed by men accustomed to entrusting the care of their existence to the dedication of unfortunates who are brutalized by Slavery.

I urge persons who would want to get a fair idea of the resources that Georgia offers, and of the great things which this State is destined to achieve, if, finally yielding to the voice of humanity and interest, it abolishes Slavery, I urge them, I say, to read the excellent work of Captain McCall, published in 1811 and bearing the title, *History of Georgia.*

Chapter VI

Departure from Milledgeville – Macon – Indian Agency – Meeting the Indians During a Thunderstorm – Hamley – Tribe of McIntosh – Uchee Creek – Big Warrior – Captain Lewis – Line Creek – Montgomery – Farewell to McIntosh – Cahawba – State of Alabama – Mobile.

On March 29, after having left the citizens of Milledgeville and having expressed our gratitude to the committee of arrangements and to the authorities of the Town and the State for the kindnesses which they had heaped upon us, we set out en route with aides-de-camp of Governor Troup. He had arranged everything in advance with skillful foresight so that the General would feel only the least possible inconvenience that we were going inevitably to encounter in a trip across a country without roads, without towns, and nearly without inhabitants; for, in order to arrive into the State of Alabama, we had to traverse that vast territory separating it from Georgia, which is inhabited by the Creek Nation, a small tribe that civilization has afflicted with some of its vices without being able yet to rescue it from the habits of a nomadic and savage life.

On the first day, after some hours of traveling, we arrived in Macon, where the General was welcomed eagerly by the citizens and a large number of ladies, whose elegance and excellent manners contrasted singularly with the look of the country that we had just traveled through. Macon, a pretty little town, somewhat populated today, did not exist 18 months ago; it emerged as if by magic from the middle of the forests. It is a civilized place, lost in the still immense domain of the first children of America. Several miles from there we are in the midst of virgin forests: the tops of these old trees, which seem to be as old as the world, swing above our heads; the wind drives them with that sound, in turn low and intense, that Mr. de Chateaubriand calls the voice of the wilderness. The road that we were following was a kind of trench or ditch at the bottom of which the General's carriage had great difficulty rolling, and often ran the risk of being smashed; we followed him on horseback, and in that manner we arrived in the evening at the Indian Agency.

The Indian Agency is an isolated building in the middle of the forests; it was constructed last year to be used at conferences between the Indian chiefs and envoys of the United States. It is there that the treaty was agreed to after which the Indian tribes, still residing on the left bank of the Mississippi, consented to withdraw to the right bank, on condition of receiving a rather considerable sum of money. The year 1827 is assigned as the time for the evacuation; and it is not without pain that the Indians see the arrival of the end of their ancient estates; they are leaving with sorrow the vicinity of civilized men whom they nevertheless detest; they accuse their chiefs of having betrayed them in making this surrender, and we are assured that it has already cost the life of Chief McIntosh, one of the signers of the treaty.

We passed the night at the Indian Agency; we had been expected there the evening before by about 100 Indians, for the name of General Lafayette has survived among them by tradition for 50 years; but the delays that we had experienced en route having exhausted their patience, they had gone to prepare a reception for us elsewhere. For the second day, we had 32 miles to travel by a road less and less passable. A storm the like of which they do not see in Europe, which nonetheless I do not want to pause to describe, thereupon came to assail us and scattered us for several hours. Most fortunately, we came upon a shelter: it was a cabin built by an American, not far from the road. Some Indian hunters, doubtless accustomed to seeking refuge there, were drying their clothes around a large fire where we took our places without being recognized or drawing great attention. To the contrary, my attention was very keenly excited by this encounter, the first that I had had of this kind. I had heard so much spoken of the customs of these men of nature, and, like all who live in a civilized country, I had formed such singular ideas of them that the least of their gestures, the tiniest piece of their clothing and their armor was nearly as great a cause of astonishment for me as was, in turn, the fact that the Indians appeared to experience nothing at all upon seeing us. As much as sign language allowed me, I asked them a host of questions to which they responded in pantomime, at the same time expressive and laconic. People had extolled the impassiveness of the Indians as a natural trait and as peculiarly developed in them by education. I wanted to try some experiments in this regard, not knowing how they would take them; I challenged one of them by some hostile demonstrations; but my anger, although feigned rather well, did not appear to move him any more than the tricks of a child would have done. He continued the conversation without looking at me and without his face expressing either fear or disdain.

After several attempts of this kind, always received with that imperturbable calm, I returned to displays of benevolence; I offered the Indians a glass of brandy; this yielded better results. They drained it. I showed them some coins in my hand, and they seized them unceremoniously. I soon left them; and it appeared to me that we parted very good friends. The end of the storm having allowed us to gather together and set out on our route, we arrived at a resting place better than that of the night before. It was a group of cabins constructed with tree trunks stacked up and covered with bark. The host was an American whom reversals of fortune had forced to take refuge in this place, where he did a rather lucrative trade between the fur skins furnished by the Indians and the commodities taken from the civilized country. His small farm consisted of some rather well-cultivated acres, a well-stocked farmyard, and the dwelling I have described.

On our arrival, we found seated in front of his door two Indians, one young, the other a mature man, and both of whom were of a remarkable stature and beauty. They were clad in a short coat, made of light, fringed material, pressed to the body by a belt embroidered with little beads of a thousand colors. They wore shawls of bright color rolled very elegantly around their heads; their boots made of buckskin covered their legs to above the knee. They got up at the approach of the General and greeted him; the younger one, to our great astonishment, complimented him in very good English. We soon came to know that he had spent his youth in a college in the United States, but that he had escaped several years ago with the help of a benefactor to return among his brothers, life among whom he preferred to that among civilized men. The General asked him many questions about the life of the Indian people. He answered them with a great deal of sense and precision. When he was asked about the late treaty with the United States, his countenance became somber; he stomped on the ground with his foot, and, bringing his hand to the handle of his knife, he murmured the name McIntosh, in a manner to make us tremble at the dangers to that Indian chief; and, as we appeared to be astonished, he exclaimed, "McIntosh has sold the land of his fathers, he has sacrificed all of us for his greed. The treaty that he has concluded for us; it is impossible for us to break it, the coward!!!" He stopped at this violent exclamation, and a little afterwards calmly commenced another subject of conversation.

When he saw us a little rested, Hamley (that was the name of the young Indian), invited us to visit his dwelling, which we noticed on the slope of a hill a little distance away. Two of the Governor's aides-de-camp and I accepted the invitation, and we followed the two Indians. On the way, they showed us a fenced-in enclosure filled with stags, doe and roe deer, which they called their preserve and which, in effect, provided for their needs when the hunt was unsuccessful. Hamley's cabin adjoined this enclosure. We entered. There was a large fire in the hearth, the day was on its decline, and the spacious dwelling was lit up by flames of pinewood. The furnishings were composed of two beds, a table, some coarse chairs; some wicker-baskets, firearms, and bows and arrows were attached to the wall, as well as a violin. The arrangement of all indicated the presence of a half-civilized man. Hamley's companion pulled off the violin, and wielding the bow with more vigor than lightness, played some fragments of Indian tunes, which suddenly put Hamley in a mood to dance; but, whether he was being courteous, or whether he desired to give rise to a comparison that was to his advantage, he begged us to dance first in the style of our countries. The serious Americans who accompanied me refrained from it. Younger or less reserved than they, I did not make him beg me more, and I danced some steps of our ponderous French dances. Hamley did not ask for more. I saw him suddenly throw off what might encumber him, seize a large cape and leap triumphant into the middle of the room, as if to say: this scene is mine. I withdrew in order to allow him free rein. His first movements, slow and passionate, became more animated by degrees; his dancing, incomparably more daring and more expressive than that of our opera dancers, was soon no more than a whirlwind that the eye could barely follow. In the intervals when he caught his breath, his steps were softly cadenced, his head gently inclined, and, following the graceful movements of his most supple body, his eyes shone with an emotion that gave a crimson tinge to the copper color of his complexion. The cries that he let out on leaving this reverie to recommence his spirited rushing movements had an effect on us which was most unexpected and difficult to describe.

Two Indian women, whom I learned afterwards were Hamley's, approached the dwelling while it resounded with Hamley's raptures and our applause; but they did not enter, and I barely caught sight of them. They had the beauty of the women of this race; their clothing was composed of a long white tunic and a scarlet shawl thrown over their shoulders; their long hair, black as ebony, floated freely. They wore on their necks a necklace with four or five rows of beads, set in the enormous silver pendants which are the principal ornament of Indian women. I believed, by their reserve, that Hamley had prevented them from approaching us, and I didn't even question him about them. There were also some Negroes in the cabin of the young Indian; but they did not appear to be in the status of Slaves in his house: they were some fugitives to whom he had given asylum, who paid for his hospitality with their work.

I would have gladly been Hamley's hunting companion and table companion for several days, but it was necessary to continue our trip. We withdrew, and on the following day, March 31, we set out on our way. As we went deep into this country of forests, the Indian land seemed to obliterate in us the kind of prejudice that leads civilized men to want to impose their state of society on nations not at all removed from the primitive life, and to consider the invasion of the places on which this supposed barbarism reigns as a noble and legitimate conquest. To the Americans' credit, it is necessary to say that it is not by extermination or by war but by treaties, where their intellectual superiority exerts in truth another kind of violence, by which they pursue their system of aggrandizement against the Indian tribes of the West and the North. Among these men civilization is not tainted by crimes like that of Great Britain against the Indians of the Orient; but while rendering this justice to them, one cannot be prevented from taking an interest in the fate of the dispossessed Indians. Thus, in encountering at each turn the bark hut of the Creek hunter, still inhabited in the security and simple virtues of a benighted age, we were unable to contemplate without sadness the fact that soon it would be torn down and replaced by the farm of an American farmer.

It was on the banks of the Chatahouchee River that, for the first time, we saw Indians gathered together as a group to welcome the General. A large number of women and young boys peered through the foliage on the opposite bank, and, on seeing us, cried out as a sign of joy. Some warriors descended the slope of a hill a little distance away, and rushed to a part of the riverbank near a ferry boat from which we were to disembark. The variety and the singular sumptuousness of their costumes presented the most picturesque view.

George Lafayette jumped to land first, and in a moment was surrounded by men, women and children, who became excited, jumped and danced around him, touched his hands and his clothes with an air of surprise and rapture that caused him nearly as much embarrassment as emotion. Suddenly, as if they wanted to give to their joy a more serious and more solemn expression, they drew back, and the men lined up abreast in front of us. The one who appeared to be the chief of the tribe gave the signal of a kind of greeting with a piercing and long-prolonged cry that was repeated by the entire throng; then they rushed again towards the ferryboat.

At the moment when the General was going to disembark, some of the strongest of them took hold of a little cabriolet that we had with us and had the General climb into it, not wanting, they said, their father to set foot on wet soil. The General was carried in this manner in a palanquin up to a certain distance from the riverbank. Then, the one whom I had already noticed to be the chief of the tribe approached him and said to him in English that all his brothers were happy to be visited by him who, in his affection for the inhabitants of America, had never made distinctions by blood or color; that he was the father dear to all the races of men who inhabited the continent. After the chief had spoken, the other Indians all came to place their right forearms on the forearm of the General in succession, in the Indian manner, as a sign of friendship. They did not want to abandon the cabriolet; and, pulling it themselves, in this manner and by small steps they ascended the hill, from which we had seen them descend, and on which one of their largest hamlets was located.

While we were walking, I approached the Indian chief; I thought that, since he spoke English, he had been brought up like Hamley in the United

States, and that was what he told me. He was about 28 years old, of medium height; but the beauty of his frame was perfect, his face was noble, his expression sad. When he wasn't speaking, he fixed his large black eyes, covered by thick eyebrows, on the ground. When he told me that he was the eldest son of McIntosh, I could not recall without pain the curse against this chief of the Creeks that I had heard the night before. This was without a doubt what gave the air of despondency and meditation to the young man; but from what I could gather from his conversation, I had a still better explanation: his intelligence had been developed only at the expense of his happiness. He appreciated the true position of his Nation; he saw that it was weakened, and foresaw its impending destruction; he sensed how inferior it was to those that surrounded it; he recognized that it was impossible to hold on to the nomadic life of the men of his race. The vicinity of civilized men had caused them not to make any progress and had introduced among them vices that were foreign to them: he appeared to hope that the treaty, which removed them to a country entirely uninhabited, would reinvigorate the ancient organization of the tribes, or at least guarantee their preservation in the condition in which they are today.

In the meantime, we arrived at the top of the hill; there we saw helmets and swords gleaming; cavalrymen were arranged in battle array along the road. They weren't Indians, but civilized men sent by the State of Alabama to meet the General. The peculiar triumphal march to which he had been obliged to be a party then ceased. The Indians watched the American escort place itself around the General jealously; but we were approaching their village: they ran in order to precede us there. Upon our arrival, we found them gathered together, their clothes cast aside, prepared to present the spectacle of their war games to us.

We arrived on a vast field around which about 100 Indian huts had been built, crowned by the verdure of dense thickets; one could make out a house larger than the others: it was that of the American agent; he kept an inn at the same time, and his wife ran a school in which they sought to teach the children of the Indians. All the men were gathered in the field, deprived of part of their clothes, faces painted with a bizarre assortment of colors, some of them wearing feathers in their hair as a mark of distinction. They announced to us that they were going to *contest the field* in honor of their White Father. And, indeed, we saw them separate into two troops, form two camps at the extremities of the field, name two chiefs, and challenge each other to a kind of combat. The cry which was uttered by each of the two troops, and which they told us was the war cry of the Indian tribes, is perhaps the strangest inflexion of the human voice that may be possible, and the effect that it produces on the warriors, young and old, is still more extraordinary. The games began. They explained to us that it was a matter for the two parties to throw a ball, similar to those of our schoolboys, beyond a marked goal, and that victory would go to that of the two troops that reached this goal seven times. We saw, in a word, the combatants, each armed with two long racquets, hurl themselves in front of the light projectile, jump over one another in order to reach it, seize it in the air with extraordinary skill, and send it beyond the goal. When the ball was lost by a player, it rolled onto the grass; then all heads were lowered, they collided with each other, and often it was only after a long struggle that one of the players succeeded in picking it up again. In the midst of one of these long combats, while all the players, backs bent, crowded in a circle around the ball, one Indian detached himself from the group, went far away, returned running, sprang forward, and after having turned several somersaults, landed on the sturdy shoulders of the other players, without making them give way, leapt in the middle of the circle, seized the ball, and hurled it beyond the goal for the seventh time. This player was McIntosh. Victory went to the camp of which he was chief; he came to receive our congratulations in the midst of the acclamations of a part of the Indian women, while the spouses of the vanquished seemed to address words of consolation to them.

After this entertainment which gave him much amusement, the General went to visit the interior of some Indian dwellings and the Indian school. As we prepared to set out again on our route, we saw the young McIntosh reappear, clad in the European style. He asked the General's permission to accompany him up to Montgomery, where he had to bring his ten-year old brother in order to entrust him to a citizen of the State of Alabama, who had generously offered to take charge of his education. The General gave his consent, and all together we left for Uchee Creek, an American inn, situated on the shores of the stream which bears this name. We arrived early at this way-station, and were able to visit the surroundings, which were delightful. Accompanied by McIntosh, I soon become acquainted with the Indians of this region. We found some who were practicing shooting with a bow there. I desired to try my strength in doing as they did; in like manner, McIntosh armed himself with a bow: he had the arm and the sight of William Tell. Some of the proofs of skill that he gave, if reported, would hardly be believed. I admired especially the skill with which, while lying nearly flat on his stomach, he launched an arrow that, striking the ground some paces from there, rose again by a slight ricochet, and flew a prodigious distance. It is a means that the Indians used to project their arrows far against the enemy without being seen. I tried in vain this peculiar shot: each time my arrow, instead of ricocheting, went deep into the ground.

We were returning to Uchee Creek, when we made the acquaintance of an Indian chief who was proceeding to this inn. He was on horseback with a woman riding behind him on the horse. At some distance from the house, the Indian dismounted and went to greet the General and to make some purchases. During this time, his woman stayed to watch the horse, brought it to him when he departed, held the bridle and stirrup for him, and afterwards jumped up behind him. I asked my traveling companions if this woman was the Indian's spouse, and if this was the condition of the women of this Nation. They answered that, in general, they were kept close by their husbands in this kind of domestic arrangement; that in the farming country, it was they who cultivated, labored, sowed, and harvested; that with Indian hunters the women carried the game, the household articles, the camping implements, and traveled considerable distances burdened in this manner; and that the cares of motherhood hardly excused them from these laborious tasks. Nevertheless, in the walks that I took afterwards in the vicinity of Uchee Creek, the lot of women did not appear to me as bad as this account made it out to be. I saw the women drawn up in a circle in front of almost all the dwellings, busy weaving baskets or mats, and amusing themselves with the games and bodily exercises which the young men engaged in before their eyes; and I did not notice any sign of harshness on the part of the men or of servile dependency on the part of the women. I had been so well received in all the Indian huts neighboring Uchee Creek – the whole region watered by the stream was so beautiful besides – that it seems to me still that it was one of the most delightful sojourns that I have experienced.

From Uchee Creek to the cabin of Big Warrior, which is the nearest stopping place, is a day's march; we made it there across a country peopled by Indians. We encountered them assembled several times on our route and were helped by them to escape uninjured from this passage, which was dangerous because thunderstorms had encumbered the road and swelled the streams. In one of these circumstances, the General received a very moving token of the veneration that these simple men had for him. One of the streams that we had to cross was overflowing an uncovered wooden bridge at this time, and the carriage of the General was required to pass on this bridge. Imagine our astonishment, on arriving at the bank, to find about 20 Indians there who, holding each other by the hand and having water up to the chest, marked out the course of the bridge with a double line! We were very happy for this assistance, and the Indians, for their sole reward, wanted only the favor of clasping the hand of the General, whom they called their White Father, the envoy of the Great Spirit, the great French Warrior who had come formerly to deliver them from the tyranny of the English. McIntosh, who translated their speech, also expressed to them the General's and our good wishes.

The hamlet of Big Warrior is so named because of the extraordinary courage and tall stature of the Indian who was chief of it. We arrived there too late; the chief had been dead for some time; the council of elders was going to assemble to give him a successor, and they designated one of his sons, notable for the same bodily strength, as the one who ought to be chosen. The son spoke with George Lafayette very much; he expressed himself in English, and we were astonished by the singular indifference with which he spoke about the death of his father. But, in this regard, the Indians do not have the same idea of what we call mourning and sorrow; to them, death does not appear to be an evil, either for the one who leaves life behind, or for those from whom he is separated. Big Warrior's son appeared sorry only because the death of his father, having occurred only a short time ago, did not permit him to dispose of his inheritance and to present to the General one of the headdresses of this celebrated chief.

We spent only one night with Big Warrior's family; on the following day, we arrived at Line Creek, that is to say, the border of the Indian country. We were greeted there by an American who had married the daughter of a Creek chief and adopted the life of the Indians, Captain Lewis, a former officer of the Army of the United States; his dwelling was comfortable and elegantly furnished for an Indian cabin. Captain Lewis, who is a man distinguished by his knowledge and character, appeared to us to wield great influence on the Indians; he had gathered a large number of them on horseback and armed for war in order to form an escort for the General. One of the neighboring chiefs arrived at the head of a delegation to address the General; his speech, which appeared well prepared, was quite long and was translated for us by an interpreter; he began with great praise of the skill and courage that the General had formerly shown against the English; the most brilliant circumstances of this war were recalled and recounted with a language whose pomp did not lack a certain poetry. The Indian chief concluded approximately in these words:

> Father, they will speak for a long time among us about how you returned to visit our forests and our cabins, you whom the Great Spirit had sent in days of old from the other coast of the great lake in order to chase out the enemies of men, the English, with their blood-red coats. The youngest among us will tell their grandchildren that they have touched your hand and seen your face; perhaps they will see you again yet because you are the favorite of the Great Spirit and you do not grow old; you would still be able to defend us if we were ever menaced.

The General responded with the aid of an interpreter to the farewells of the Indians; he gave them advice to be prudent and temperate; he recommended that they live always as good neighbors with the Americans and regard them as their friends and brothers; he told them that he would also be thinking of them always, and would say prayers for the welfare of their homes and the glory of their warriors. We were directed then towards the stream which separates Creek country from the State of Alabama. The Indian cavalry of Captain Lewis, mounting small horses light and lively as deer, some armed with bow and arrows, others with tomahawks or battle-axes, followed us in a long unordered line, the end of which was lost in the thickness of the forest. Having arrived at the bank of the stream, they turned the bridle and disappeared while uttering loud shouts; some of the chiefs directed to us a last farewell, and we bid adieu to Indian country.

We spent the night on the shores of Line Creek in a little village of the same name, nearly completely occupied by men whom the love of gain has brought from the most faraway places of the globe to the middle of these wildernesses in order to exploit to their profit the simplicity and especially the current needs of the unfortunates who inhabit them. These greedy men, who unscrupulously poison the tribes with hard liquors, and who ruin them afterwards with bad-faith transactions, are the most cruel and dangerous enemies of the Indians, whom they nonetheless accuse of being thieving, lazy, drunkard and vindictive. If the limits within which I had already proposed to confine my narrative had not already been exceeded against my will, I would be able to prove easily how these vices for which they reproach the children of the forests are only the result of their proximity to civilization, and how the Whites often surpass them in bad faith and in cruelty. I will be satisfied with citing here two events taken from the midst of more than a thousand, all of which are to the dishonor of those men so proud of the Whiteness of their skin, who call themselves *civilized.*

Not long ago, a trader, an inhabitant of the State of Alabama, passed among the Creeks in order to do business there; having met one of the chiefs of the Nation, he entered into negotiations with him for some fur skins, but as the conditions that he proposed were all to the disadvantage of the Indian, in order to resolve the negotiation more easily, he made him drunk with brandy; after the negotiation was concluded, they set out together to proceed to a neighboring village; on the way, the Indian reflected on what he had just done and realized that he had been tricked. He wanted to explain his position to the trader, but the discussion soon turned into a violent quarrel following which the Indian struck a tomahawk blow to his adversary and stretched him dead at his feet. Twenty-four hours later, on the initial complaint brought by the Whites, the murderer was arrested by his own people who, after having assembled their great council, declared him guilty of cowardly assassination for having struck to death a White who was without arms and defenseless; then they led him on the banks of Line Creek, where they had invited the Whites to join them to witness the justice which they were going to hand out, and they shot him in their presence.

On the same evening of our arrival at Line Creek, I went into a shop to make some purchases; while I was asking for what I needed, an Indian presented himself and asked for some whiskey of the value of a 12-cent piece which he offered; the master of the house took the piece and told him to wait a moment because the gathering of those who were buying was considerable; the Indian waited patiently for a quarter of an hour after which he demanded his whiskey; the merchant appeared to be astonished and told him that if he wanted whisky he would have to give money first. "I gave you 12 cents only a moment ago," the Indian said to him. The unfortunate man had no sooner uttered these words when the merchant rushed forward violently, seized him by the ears, and, with the help of one of his assistants, threw him brutally out the door while treating him as a thief. I had seen him give the 12 cents,[6] and I was convinced of the good faith of the one and the knavery of the other; I felt myself moved by anger, and despite the delicacy of the situation, I would have advanced in order to intervene against this abuse of force; but all had passed so quickly that I barely had time to speak. I went out to see what the Indian was going to do; I found him some steps from the house, where he had stopped absorbed in some melancholy thoughts; a moment later, he crossed his arms on his chest and began to walk with large steps towards the land of his brothers; having arrived at the edge of the stream, he passed it without hesitating and without appearing to notice that the water was rising above the knees; having arrived at the other side, he stopped, turned around, and, raising his eyes to the sky at the same time as he stretched his menacing fist towards the land of the Whites, he uttered some Indian words forcefully. Ah! Without a doubt at this moment he called down the vengeance of heaven on his oppressors; this vengeance was clearly due him, and yet his prayer was in vain.... Poor Indians! They plunder you, they beat you, they poison you or excite your passions with hard liquor, and then they call you savages!... Washington said: "Any time that I have been called upon to judge a dispute between an Indian and a White, I have always had proof that the White had committed the first wrongs." Washington spoke truly.

The conduct of the American Government in regard to the Indian tribes is very different from that of the men[7] of whom I have just spoken. Not only does it protect them against particular acts of mistreatment, and sees to it that the treaties which the neighboring States make with them are not disadvantageous and are executed in good faith, but, moreover, it sees to their needs with an entirely paternal solicitude. It is not rare to see Congress vote funds and provisions for the tribes whom a bad harvest or a great calamity exposes to famine.

6. The cent is worth a sou. One hundred are necessary for a dollar.

7. I have noticed that the majority of these men are composed of nearly all the nationalities of Europe, but the Irish predominate.

We left Line Creek on April 3, and on the same day General Lafayette was welcomed in Montgomery by the inhabitants of this village and by the Governor of the State of Alabama, who had come from Cahawba to meet Lafayette with his entire general staff, and a large number of citizens who had left their dwellings from the most distant points in order to join him. We spent the following day at Montgomery, and we left it only on the night of the 4th to the 5th after a ball at which we had the pleasure of seeing Chilli McIntosh dance with some very pretty women who certainly did not suspect that they were dancing with a savage. The farewells which McIntosh gave to the General were very sad. He appeared overwhelmed by melancholy premonitions. After having left the General and his son, he encountered me in the courtyard where I was walking; he stopped me, made me put my right forearm on his, and raising his left hand toward the sky: "Farewell," he said to me, "accompany our father always and watch over him. I pray the Great Spirit to also watch over him and to make him arrive soon without mishaps in the midst of his children who are in France. His children are our brothers; he is our father. I hope that he will not forget us…." His voice was moved; his face somber, and the moonbeams, which fell obliquely on his copper-colored visage, gave to his farewells a solemnity by which I was profoundly affected. I wanted to respond to him, but he left me abruptly and disappeared.

At two o'clock in the morning, we embarked on the Alabama River, on board the steamship *The Anderson*, which had been lavishly and comfortably prepared for the General, and filled with a troop of musicians, sent to meet him by the City of New Orleans. All the ladies of Montgomery accompanied us up to the river bank, where we took leave of them, and soon the cannon announced our departure, which was illuminated by enormous bonfires on the river bank. Our voyage up to the Tombigbee River was delightful. It is difficult to imagine anything more romantic than the elevated, rocky and often wooded shores of the Alabama. During the three days that we traversed them, the echoes repeated the patriotic tunes that our Louisiana musicians played. We stopped a day at Cahawba, where the government officials of the State of Alabama had, in concert with the citizens, prepared for the General some fetes as noteworthy in their elegance and good taste, as they were touching in their cordiality and the feelings of which they were the expression. Among the guests with whom we took our places at the public banquet, we found some compatriots whom political events had driven out of France. They told us how they had been part of the unfortunate Colony of Champ d'Asile. Now they live in a little town that they have founded in the State of Alabama, to which they have given the name Gallipolis. All led me to presume that they are not very prosperous. I believe that their European prejudices and their inexperience in commerce or agriculture will prevent them from being formidable competitors of the Americans for a long time yet.

Cahawba, seat of the Government of the State of Alabama, is a newly born town whose population is still very small, but whose beautiful location, at the confluence of the Cahawba and the Alabama Rivers, seems to promise rapid growth.

The State of Alabama, which formerly like Mississippi was only a section of Georgia, to which its history as a Colony is intimately linked, received a territorial Governor from Congress in 1817, and it was only in 1819 that it was admitted into the federation as an independent State. The Act of Congress that gave political existence to Alabama reserved a part of the public lands for the establishment and the support of public schools. The same act also prescribed the setting aside of five percent of the sales of these same lands for the construction of the roads and canals necessary to the State.

The Constitution adopted by the citizens of Alabama established three powers: legislative, executive, and judicial. Instructed by the experience of their neighbors, they have recognized the uncontestable superiority of democratic principles over all others, and have adopted them with all their consequences. Every citizen, regardless of wealth, is eligible for the offices of senator, representative and even of governor. The qualification of citizenship of the United States, two years of residency in the State, and being 27 years old are the only conditions required by law. Senators are chosen for three years, and are reelected in thirds each year; the representatives are elected every year; the governor is elected for two years and can stay in power no more than four out of six years. Every citizen 21 years old and having resided in the State a year has the right to vote. The judges are chosen by the legislative assembly and can only be cashiered by a public trial. With institutions that give to each citizen so direct a role in the administration of public affairs, it is impossible for the State not to prosper; also, its population and its wealth have been increased prodigiously for its recent formation as a state. This growth would certainly have been still more rapid if Alabama had not kept the fatal principle of Slavery of the Blacks which Georgia, its mother State, bequeathed to it. The population of this State was only 10,000 in 1810, already grew to 67,000 in 1817, and today is nearly 128,000. Of this total, one counts nearly 40,000 Slaves. In this estimate of population, I do not include the Indian tribes of the Choctaws, the Cherokees and the Chickasaws who reside in the east and the west of this State.

From Cahawba, we sailed downriver to Claiborne, a small fort that is also on the shores of the Alabama River. Detained by the entreaties of the inhabitants, the General spent several hours there in the midst of the most moving displays of affection. Mr. Dellet, who had been charged by the citizens with expressing their sentiments to him, acquitted himself with an eloquence that one is very astonished to encounter in places which, but a short time ago, resounded only with the wild cry of the Indian hunter.

A little below Claiborne, I saw that the banks of the river were noticeably lower. When we had passed the mouth of the Tombigbee, we found ourselves in the midst of low, marshy meadows but of a very fertile appearance. Finally, on April 7, we arrived in the Bay of Mobile, at the far end of which the town of the same name is located.

The journey that we had just made in three days, which is more than 300 miles on account of the winding of the river, formerly took a month or six weeks of navigation for loaded boats ascending the river and half that much for boats descending. One sees what a prodigious revolution the application of steam power to navigation must have brought about in the commercial and industrial relations of this country.

The Town of Mobile, which is the oldest settlement of the State of Alabama, is situated very advantageously for commerce, in a beautiful plain, about 20 feet above the ordinary level of the water. This Town stagnated for a long time, as much under the despotism of the Spanish Inquisition as under the maladministration of the French Government. Often, it was ravaged by yellow fever. Today, all its wounds are closed; some years of liberty have made a prosperous town of it. When the Americans took possession of it, it contained barely 200 homes; today its population is more than 1,800. Formerly, it exported barely 400 bales of cotton; this year it exported more than 16,000 bales.

The arrival of the steamship *The Anderson* in the Bay was announced by artillery fire from Fort Condé, and, when we landed at the wharf at Mobile, the General found the committee of the Town and the entire population gathered to receive him. They soon conducted him to the center of the Town, under a triumphal arch, the four corners of which were ornamented with the flags of Mexico, the Republics of South America and of Greece. In the center was the flag of the United States. It was there that he was addressed by Mr. Garrow in the name of the Town, in the presence of the municipal officials. Afterwards he was led into an immense hall constructed expressly for his reception. There he found all the ladies to whom he was presented by the Governor; then Mr. Webb addressed him in the name of the State. In his speech, the orator accurately traced the picture of the sad situation into which despotism and ignorance had formerly plunged the Town of Mobile and the rich land that surrounds it; he then depicted the rapid and always growing progress that liberty and republican institutions had made in the Arts, in Industry and in

Commerce which, today, makes these same places a wealthy and happy country; he attributed this fortunate change to the glorious and triumphant efforts of the Revolutionary patriots whose courage and resolve had been sustained by the noble example of Lafayette; and he ended by expressing regret that the same efforts of French patriots should not have obtained results as satisfactory for their country.

In expressing his thanks to the speaker, the General said:

During my happy voyage across the young State of Alabama, I had until now been delightfully affected by the miracles of recent creations and rapid improvements; but here, Sir, I find yet new subjects for mutual congratulations. When I left American shores, this part of the continent was only a poor French Colony; today, it has become a worthy member of that powerful confederation that has achieved the highest point of political civilization and of domestic happiness that one has ever known on this earth.

I will not follow you, Sir, in this series of flattering memories that you have wanted to recall. Nevertheless, permit me to observe that if the sentiments that impelled our friends in Europe and myself to affirm on the ruins of the Bastille the principles of national sovereignty recently proclaimed; to swear on the altar of the Champ de Mars the oath that an armed Nation gave to constitutional laws derived from the people; afterwards, to defend these laws against intrigues, errors and anarchy and, in a more recent time, the catastrophe of Waterloo; to attempt to put back into the hands of the people those powers that we intended to cast against all the members of a coalition inimical to French liberty and the rights of humanity: if all these sentiments, I say, have not been rewarded by all the wished-for success, nevertheless, we have made some progress towards the emancipation of Europe, and the seed of American principles has not been altogether lost. I cite as witness to this heroic Greece, as to which I join cordially with the sentiments that you have so felicitously expressed, thinking that all the friends of liberal ideas ought to give assistance to it.

I thank you, Sir, for your affectionate sympathy for the emotions I have felt on this happy American visit, where all that I see, all that I feel, attaches me more and more to the admirable Federal Constitution, whose preservation, as well as the most intimate union among the States, is necessary not only for their security and their prosperity, but also for the security and the prosperity of the entire world.

Permit me to renew here the homage of my intense gratitude and my respectful attachment.

Hoping that the General would be able to spend several days in their midst, the inhabitants of Mobile had made immense preparations for the fetes that they counted on offering him; but most were in vain. Pressed for time, he had to give in to the solicitations of the New Orleans delegation who urged him to leave the following morning. However, he accepted the public dinner, the ball, and the Masonic ceremony; after which, he went on board the ship that was to transport him to take some hours of rest, which a day filled with so many sweet emotions had made so very necessary for him.

Chapter VII

Departure from Mobile – Gulf of Mexico – Passage of the Balize – Landing at the Battle Lines of New Orleans – Entrance of General Lafayette into the City – Fetes and Public Ceremonies – Battle of New Orleans

The ship aboard which we retired upon leaving the ball was *The Natchez*, an excellent and beautiful steamship, sent by the City of New Orleans to transport the General from Mobile to the banks of the Mississippi. Mr. Davis, an experienced Captain, commanded it, and he brought the Louisiana delegation at the head of which was Mr. Duplantier, an old friend and companion-in-arms of the General. At daybreak, the cannon was heard; and at this signal we raised anchor. Having climbed onto the deck, the General received the farewells of the citizens who pressed in a crowd on the shore and showed their regrets by their expressive gestures and gloomy silence. After a half hour of sailing, the Town of Mobile slipped away from our glances beyond the horizon which grew larger around us, and soon even the smoke of the cannon, turned white by the rays of the rising sun, did not rise high enough any longer so that we could still see it. At last the return of the night found us sailing in the open sea in the Gulf of Mexico.

In order to go to New Orleans, we had to choose between two routes: either to pass behind the Dauphin, Horn, Dog, Ship and Cat Islands, traverse Lake Borgne and Lake Ponchartrain and land some miles to the rear of the City; or advance very boldly across the Gulf up to the mouth of the Mississippi, pass the Balize and go up the river. Full of confidence in the soundness of his ship, our Captain decided on the latter route, which was not altogether without danger, but which would make us 24 hours earlier. We were not long in regretting his decision. Suddenly the sea became furiously agitated. Then the movements of the ship became so disagreeable that we were obliged to go to bed in order to escape the seasickness which overpowered nearly all of us. During the night the wind became still greater and the waves became so strong that some of them, hurling themselves through the ports, inundated our room and our beds. The noise of the wind, the waves, the steam engine and the creaking of the ship combined in such a way that we appeared destined to be engulfed from one moment to the next.

At daybreak I climbed on deck, where I discovered the most imposing and terrifying sight; we were arriving at the Balize. One cannot resist a certain emotion at the sight of this superb river whose rapid coursing and prodigious width betoken a conqueror rather than a tributary of the Ocean. Its waves, driving back the waters of the sea to a great distance, pile up thousands of tree trunks of prodigious size on the muddy islands at its mouth which divide the river into five branches. The tree trunks, having survived for some centuries near the frozen pole, have come to die under the devouring, burning skies of Mexico and to nourish, by their remains, a new vegetation. Enormous alligators, looking askance and with a ponderous gait on floating tree trunks, threaten the navigator and seem to want to contest the entrance to the river. For a long time after we were on the Mississippi, we believed that we were on a new sea, so separated from each other were its shores and so prideful were its waves. It was not until after some hours of sailing that its bed contracted, allowing us to see its muddy banks, that its flow lost a little of its violence.

In the morning we passed by Fort Plaquemine, which saluted our colors with 13 cannon blasts, and night overtook us still sailing before we were able to see the walls of New Orleans. It is nearly 60 miles above the Balize that one begins to find some variety in the vegetation that adorns the riverbank. Up to there one sees only cypress trees covered with gloomy *Tillandsia* which the natives call *Spanish Moss*. This parasitic plant, which forms a long and thick drapery on trees which grow in marshes, has a more especially lugubrious look about it, as one ordinarily encounters it in climates where yellow fever reigns. It is, they say, the resource for animals who seek a refuge in the woods during winter. The inhabitants of Louisiana use it to stuff mattresses and seat cushions; to this end they beat it after having washed it in an alkaline solution; then, when it is dry, it has the appearance of long black thread. It is of such durability that it is considered indestructible. They use it also in construction by mixing it with mud or hard soil.

Towards midnight I went up on deck for a moment; the night was dark, the sky covered with thick clouds, and the air filled with muffled roaring. Then the batteries of New Orleans fired 100 cannon blasts in order to announce that the day of the arrival of the Nation's Guest was beginning.

At daybreak we awoke near the famous lines where 12,000 elite English troops were crushed by several hundred men, half of whom were carrying arms for the first time. To shouts of *Vive la liberte! Vive l'ami de l'Amerique! Vive Lafayette!,* which astonished us by being spoken in French, we went up on the deck. How astonished we were to see the riverbank covered with French uniforms! For a moment we believed ourselves transported to the bosom of our Fatherland, liberated again, and our hearts beat with joy. General Lafayette disembarked to the sound of artillery and to the cheering of a considerable throng who, despite the inclement weather of the day and the distance from the City, filled the embankment. He was received by a large escort of cavalry, and by the 12 marshals who had been named to lead the procession. Leaning on the arm of his former companion-in-arms, Mr. Duplantier, and on that of General Villeré, he proceeded to Montgomery House, which served as headquarters to Jackson on the day on which he covered himself with glory by his noble defense of the lines. The Governor of the State was waiting for him there, and he greeted the General by speaking to him in this manner in the name of the people of Louisiana:

> General, today Louisiana enjoys the good fortune of receiving on its soil the one whom an entire people with a unanimous voice has saluted with the glorious title of the Guest of the Nation; the one who, fighting for the cause of liberty and of humanity, spilled his blood for it a long time before it appeared as a new star in the federal constellation.
>
> General, Louisiana did not share the perils and the glory of the War of Independence, but it recognizes and appreciates, as much as its sisters of the Union, the services that have marked your career in that memorable struggle. Its inhabitants are as attached to the principles of the Revolution as their brothers in the Union, and as determined to preserve unsullied the benefits acquired by their ancestors. It is not by empty declamations that they manifest love of country; they invoke the testimony of the land on which we tread. It is here that, with their brothers-in-arms, led by the fearless Jackson, they vanquished an enemy proud in its discipline and its number, and raised an imperishable monument to American valor. The annals of peoples do not offer a victory won in circumstances as appropriate as this one to call brilliant, and to render it glorious. By this victory, our soil was liberated from a foreign invasion, and it is to it that we owe those trophies worthy of arresting the gaze of the warrior who hoisted the American flag on the redoubts of Yorktown. Patriotic warrior, I salute you; welcome to this land consecrated by the death of patriots.
>
> In the same way as all the people of the United States, we rejoice in seeing the one who was the friend of our infant Nation come in his old age to look upon its maturity, and to rest his eyes on the edifice that he helped to build. You have seen with pleasure the progress made in the space of half a century by the States that were the immediate theater of the Revolutionary War. It remains for you to look upon scenes

no less worthy of your thoughts. Louisiana will offer you a delightful and comforting spectacle which none of the other States has been able to afford to you; here you will acquire the sweet conviction that your generous efforts for the cause of liberty have not been unfruitful for all those who pride themselves for having a common origin with you. This State founded by the French, in which the largest part of the inhabitants are their descendants, enjoys completely, as a member of the American confederation, that liberty for which you fought and spilled your blood. The moderate and wise use to which the French have known how to put this freedom here responds triumphantly to those who have proclaimed them unworthy of it, and who have slandered you for having worked to obtain for them the greatest of benefits. On the lands watered by this superb river and the rivers which carry their tribute to it, where 50 years ago civilization had not yet marked its luminous path, you will find States spontaneously formed, strong in resources and in all the vigor of youth. There, where the Indian roamed in vast wildernesses, you will find fields covered with abundant harvests, flourishing towns, active commerce, and a population free, enterprising, and cultivating everywhere with success the arts that enoble man and make social life attractive. In calculating only the present sum of happiness, you will be gratified; but, in turning your glance into the future, with what delights will you see in prospect the always-increasing prosperity of the future times! Rapid in its course, civil and religious liberty will march on without ever stopping; its inexhaustible energy will multiply its new creations everywhere, new states will follow one another, and millions of free men, hidden in the future, will bless the illustrious philanthropists whose virtues have raised the glorious edifice of American freedom with the same fervor and the same enthusiasm that animates us today.

As First Magistrate and speaking in the name of all Louisianans, I repeat it to you, welcome to this land discovered by your forefathers.

The Governor's speech, depicting former Frenchmen enjoying a freedom that one still considers problematical in France, made a profound impression on the General, and he responded in this manner:

When I see myself on this majestic river, within the borders of this Republic from which I received so honorable and affectionate an invitation, feelings of American and French patriotism are joined in my heart, just as they are mingled in this fortunate Union, which has made Louisiana a member of the Great American Confederation established for the happiness of several million living beings, for that of so many other millions yet to be born, and as an example for the human race. But I feel an emotion still more passionate in receiving on this celebrated soil, in the name of the people of this State, by the voice of their First Magistrate, so affectionate a welcome. It is here, Gentlemen, that under the leadership of General Jackson, after a vigorous attack against the enemy that had just invaded this territory, the blood of the sons of my revolutionary contemporaries was mixed with that of the children of Louisiana on that memorable day when a victory, incomparable if one considers the circumstances of it, ended a war just in principle and conducted brilliantly in all respects in so glorious a manner.

You want then, Sir, to congratulate me on the gratification that the marvels I have witnessed have already made me feel, and on that which those marvels which remain for me to see are preparing for me, a gratification so much more delightful for an American veteran since we find in these marvels irresistible arguments in favor of principles for which we have raised the standard of independence and liberty.

I thank you especially for the kind and generous observation that you have made that in this State one can be persuaded of the aptitude of a population of the French to use the benefits of a free government wisely, and I may be permitted to add that one finds here, consequently, proof of the part that despots and European aristocrats have had in the deplorable excesses that have retarded up to now the establishment of liberty in France.

After this response, everyone who had been able to enter the house was presented to the General in turn. There was present a large number of veterans of the Revolution, among others Colonel Bruian-Bruin, who served at the siege of Quebec, where brave General Montgomery perished, Judge Gerrard, who fought at Yorktown, and Colonel Grenier, who after having served gloriously in the three revolutions of America, France and Colombia, retained the courage and the passion of youth at 70 years. A large number of ladies had come to meet the General, and through Mr. Marigny they expressed their feelings to him, and congratulated him on his arrival in Louisiana.

After all the presentations were concluded, the procession formed, and, despite the rain which was falling profusely, we set out towards the City. We advanced slowly because of the crowd that blanketed the main road and the embankment at the approaches to the City. When we arrived at the City limits, we encountered troops drawn up in two lines in the middle of which we passed to the sound of martial music. In spite of the bad condition of the road, the General wanted to traverse these two lines on foot, and only reascended his carriage after having extended his gratitude to the officers who were on his way. The procession resumed its route and was augmented by the troops which fell in with it, and the more it advanced, the more the crowd grew despite the continuing bad weather. Nonetheless, such a great concourse, the sight of a triple row of boats decked with flags which bordered the riverbank, the sound of artillery from the land and from the sea, the ringing of bells and the prolonged cheering of an immense population, produced a sensation difficult to define; finally, in the midst of displays of such warm affection, traversing the waves of people eager to look upon him, the General arrived at the entrance to the great plaza, and was conducted by the committee of arrangements under a triumphal arch of an altogether monumental style and of exquisite taste.

This monument, 68 feet high, 40 of which were below the crown of the arch, and a total of 58 feet wide, 20 feet of which consisted of an open arcade, and 25 feet deep, rested on a footing simulating Sera-Veza marble; the base, forming a pedestal in green, Italian marble, was adorned with colossal statues of Justice and of Liberty. This allegorical base supported an arcade of the Doric Order, accompanied by four coupled columns on each face. The curves of this arch were composed of 24 stones each decorated with a star of gilded bronze, joined together by a projecting stone on which the word *Constitution* was engraved, representing in this manner the 24 States of the Union joined by a single bond. On the pediment simulating yellow Veronese marble were displayed two figures of Fame blowing a trumpet held in one hand and holding in the other a laurel with banners, bearing on one side the name of Washington and on the other the name of Lafayette; the national eagle in relief surmounted the whole. The upper pedestal supported a vertical section of seven feet, on which was written, on one side in English and on the other in French: "A Grateful republic has dedicated this monument to Lafayette." At the top of the monument was constructed a group representing Wisdom resting her hand on the bust of the immortal Franklin, and the four corners were adorned with lavish national trophies, decorated with bundles of wood and standards. The names of the members of Congress who signed the Declaration of Independence and those of the officers who distinguished themselves during the Revolutionary War decorated different parts of the triumphal arch. The beautiful work, designed by Mr. Pilié and constructed by Mr. Fogliardi, offered a remarkable totality, and the reliefs were of the most beautiful effect.

It was under this monument that the General was greeted by the municipal corps at the head of which was the Mayor, Mr. Roffignac, who addressed him in the name of the citizens of Orleans. “Within these walls, founded by our common ancestors,” he said,

> Everything, General, must be a source of emotions for you. In the too-short stay that you propose to make here, you will notice, doubtless, the effects produced by our wise institutions. They are the results of that glorious independence for which you fought, and of that exalted constitution in the establishment of which you cooperated. Thus, let us join our thanks to that which the American people address to you; they are heard from Maine to the banks of the Sabine River and will be the consolation and the glory of your life.

In expressing his thanks to Mr. Roffignac, the General did not allow the occasion escape to pay his tribute of esteem to the memory of the father of this honorable magistrate. “On my entrance into this capital,” he said, “I am filled with gratitude for the greeting that I am receiving from the people of New Orleans, and from its worthy Mayor, whose name recalls to a contemporary of his father all the memories of his sincerity and his bravery.” Mr. Roffignac appeared extremely moved by this homage rendered by Lafayette to the noble character of his father, and some teardrops escaping from his eyes demonstrated the fullness of his gratitude.

Upon leaving the triumphal arch, the General was led, always in the midst of the acclamations of the crowd who pressed upon his passage, to the Palace of Justice, where he was addressed by Mr. Prieur in the name of the City Council; from there we proceeded to the hotel of the municipality where our lodgings had been prepared, and which the people of New Orleans already called only by the name *Lafayette House.* After having taken some moments of rest there, the General went to take his place on the balcony to see all the troops that had taken up arms for his reception march by. All the corps that passed before our eyes were noteworthy for the elegance of their uniform and the strictness of their bearing. The grenadiers, the gunners, the dragoons, the Frankish, the light infantrymen, the Union Guards, the riflemen, the New Orleans Guards, the Lafayette Guards, in turn attracted the attention of the General. But when, following some *Riflemen*, whose name recalled so many memories of their fearlessness, he noticed a line of a hundred *Choctaws* marching according to Indian custom in single file, he was very moved to see that with a delicate attentiveness they had sought to inform him that his name was known by the warriors of the most remote Indian Nations, and that the authorities had admitted into the ranks of militias these brave Indians who had been auxiliaries of the Americans in the *Seminole* Wars and who, for nearly a month, had transported their encampments near to the City, in order to see the *Great Warrior*, the *Brother of the Great Father, Washington.*

On the following day, the General received a visit from the Vice President of the House of Representatives, and from members of the Legislature who were then in the Capital of the State; and immediately after, the Bar of New Orleans was presented to him, led by Mr. Derbigny, who had been chosen as speaker. In a speech full of noble thoughts and pronounced with a touching eloquence, Mr. Derbigny commended, with as much proportion as refinement, that rectitude of judgment, that firmness of character that always guided the steps of Lafayette into the path of justice during the political storms, at an equal distance from the excesses of all the parties. Then, in speaking of the great and useful lesson that his triumph in the United States was giving to the universe, he added:

> The present generation congratulates itself in having to contemplate a spectacle so moving, so sublime. One sees from time to time pomp-filled ceremonies when the powerful of the earth display themselves to the eyes of a dazzled multitude; never yet had they seen, never perhaps will they see again, an entire people of free men rise in a body spontaneously to bring the homage of their gratitude and their affection to the feet of an individual without power. Enjoy their recognition; it is a worthy reward for your virtues. May it always serve as encouragement to all the honorable hearts which aspire to imitate you! And may it bring despair and shame to arrogant and egotistical men who make use of power only for the enslavement of the human race!

In his response the General carefully avoided alluding to the eulogies that had been addressed to him, and occupied himself only with the general interests of Louisiana and the particular deeds of those who were complimenting him; he congratulated the citizens on the fact that, after having been subjected to the criminal laws of France and subsequently of Spain, they had ameliorated these laws successively, and were going still to perfect that part of their code in a manner that could serve as a model for the rest of the United States, whose criminal laws are already so superior to those of all other peoples.

Pressed insistently to visit the English theater and the French theater on the same evening, the General allowed it to be decided by lot to which of the two he was going first; chance favored the English theater. He proceeded there towards seven o'clock, and he was welcomed with an enthusiasm that one cannot describe; they presented an appropriate piece, whose merit neither he nor the people could appreciate, because attention was borne only to the Hero of Yorktown, who made them forget for a moment the Prisoner of Olmutz whom the actors were playing; he went afterwards to the French theater where they were counting on the moment of his arrival impatiently; when he appeared, the most animated applause, the repeated cries of *Vive Lafayette!* interrupted the production; everyone rose; they seemed to see Themistocles entering the Olympic Games; finally, calm being restored a little, the General took his place in the box of honor that had been prepared for him, and saw with pleasure the last act of the charming comedy, the *L'École des Vieillards*, which appeared to me to be as much to the taste of our former compatriots, the Americans of Louisiana, as to the inhabitants of Paris. Before retiring, the General listened to a cantata played in his honor, all of the allusions of which were grasped with a kind of exhilaration.

In the course of Tuesday morning, a delegation of resident and refugee Spaniards presented themselves to compliment the General, and especially to express to him their gratitude for the manner in which he had opposed the invasion of Spain and the ruin of the liberal constitution in the French Chamber of Deputies. The spokesman of the delegation spoke to him in this manner:

> General, the resident Spaniards and those who have been exiled, united on the soil of the United States, join their good wishes and have the honor, by their spokesman, to address to you their sincere congratulations on your arrival in these States, whose fruitful liberty is due in part to your sacrifices and your steadfast resolution; these same Spaniards express satisfaction with the happy occasion which procures for them, in the midst of patriotic memories for some and distressing anxieties for others, the sight of a hero, whose conduct, words and actions vindicate their liberal opinions, and the extreme course that they have taken to withdraw from a government that pursues them, condemns them and delivers them up to

> the hazardous fortunes of expatriation. Your esteem for the brave and unfortunate Riego; the tribute that on all occasions it pleases you to pay to the memory of this unfortunate victim sacrificed to the security of a suspicious and cruel Court; the homage by which you honor the ashes of this virtuous patriot, are all at the same time the most felicitous encouragement and the most glorious reward for those who dedicate themselves to the defense of the sacred cause of liberty. Some Spaniards who have admired his virtues and shared his opinions, today unfortunate and nomadic, come before you, General, with a clear conscience; and, if they dare to salute you, it is because they are not culpable; they are unfortunate; but if their sacrifice could assure the prosperity of their country, they would gladly offer their life to it; and under the sword they would invoke you, General, and those who, like Lafayette, are not opposed to the age, to knowledge and to liberty, the impediments to despotism, tyranny, and the destructive Inquisition. General, accept the affectionate homage of our admiration for you, and may the unfortunate Spanish refugees obtain from you a glance as consolation for them and for all those who flee the devastating scourge of tyranny; this glance, General, will be evidence of your protection, proof of their vindication, and hope for a more happy future for their Fatherland and a more certain future for its glory.

The General, whose principles had induced him to vigorously oppose a measure disproved of by France, a measure that had produced results so distressful for all of Spain, a measure some of whose courageous victims he had before his eyes, was profoundly affected by the expressions of gratitude that had just been spoken in regards to him, and he responded in these terms to Mr. Campe, President of the delegation:

> I am equally touched and flattered, Sir, by the testimonies of esteem and confidence with which I see myself honored here by the former children of Spain, today citizens of this State, and to whom are joined the Spanish patriots recently banished by the terrorism of a government, the usurper of their legitimate rights.
>
> While I congratulate those among you, Gentlemen, who have the honor of being members of the great American Federation, let us all together enjoy the concept that the cause of liberty will end up by triumphing everywhere over hostile

alliances and fallacious intrigues; already your beautiful language, the language of Padilla, has become, over an immense area of this hemisphere, a language of independence and republicanism; already, at two different times, in the country of the illustrious, preeminent Riego, it has made heard the most eloquent and most generous sounds in the bosom of the Cortes, and whatever may have been the temporary success of a war detested, I like to think, by the French people, and of a deceitful influence about which the Spanish patriots have nothing more to learn, liberty will return soon to enlighten and to make fruitful this most interesting part of Europe; only then will the shades of Riego, his young and unfortunate wife, and so many other victims of superstition and tyranny be appeased. In the meantime, Gentlemen, I am very cognizant of the value that the exiled Spaniards, among whom I have the honor to count several personal friends, want to put on my high esteem for them, and I beg all of you to accept my heartfelt and respectful thanks.

This was not the first time that General Lafayette paid his tribute of esteem, admiration and regret to the unfortunate Riego; already, on more than one occasion, he had expressed his opinion openly about the unfortunate death of this generous martyr to liberty, and the entire American Nation had shared the sympathy of the veteran of the French Revolution for the constant and the courageous defender of the Revolution of the Peninsula.

On the ensuing days very many other delegations followed each other to General Lafayette to offer him the expression of their attachment and devotion to his principles; among these delegations were staff-officers and militiamen, the Medical Society, the Clergy, and free men of Color, who in 1815 contributed with exceptional courage to the defense of the City. Our last two evenings were filled, one by a public ball and the other by a Masonic dinner party. I will not undertake the description of these fetes, which, by the beauty, elegance and amiability of the ladies of New Orleans, by the enthusiasm and the open cordiality of the citizens, the fervent concerns and the delicate attentions of the magistrates and the lavishness and profusion of the particulars, equaled all that we had seen of the most beautiful of their kind.

However, in the midst of the happiness that the Louisianans made him enjoy, the General experienced a moment of disquiet and sadness. Ominous rumors reached him. They told him of a very animated discussion that had been held between the general staff and the officers of the militia on the subject of certain prerogatives of the legion, challenged by one party and upheld by the other with equal ardor, and the consequences of which could lead to bloody results after the departure of the one whose presence imposed, even on the most hot-headed ones, a discretion demanded by the duties of hospitality. In so serious a circumstance, the General did not hesitate to use all his influence to bring together citizens whom a moment of error or a false point of honor had divided temporarily; consequently, he invited all the officers of the different corps to repair to his home. When they were joined there, he said to them, "Gentlemen":

> You sense, I believe, the motive which has induced me to invite you to assemble around me. I am ignorant of nothing that has happened, and I foresee the consequences too clearly! But here, Gentlemen, it is not only your business, it is mine which is involved; and I would never be consoled for having been the cause, however innocent, of the misfortunes which could result from a point of honor insufficiently moderated; for, I cannot conceal the fact that, absent my arrival, absent the visit with which you have consequently honored me, no dispute would have taken place. If, then, I had been able to foresee such trouble, I swear to you that, despite the zealous desire that I had of seeing a country which has been dear to me for very many years, despite the length and the fatigues of a trip undertaken to respond to the urgent invitation of Louisianans, I would have written from Mobile to excuse myself, and I would have preferred the bitterness of regret to that of causing the least trouble. Consider also the injurious rumors that the ill-intentioned are going to spread. It will not be a simple dispute about the allocation of ranks. It will be for all of Europe dissension among the elements of the population; and I will have to suffer the pain of having sown the seeds of discord where I had found at first only peace and harmony. Will I be, then, less happy in Louisiana than in another state where I have extinguished hatreds that lasted for more than 20 years, and will I find less respect among those whom I consider in part as my compatriots than among citizens in regards to which I haven't any other bonds than those of their confidence and their own goodwill?
>
> It is not incumbent upon me to interfere in the purely parliamentary question that concerns the prerogatives of the legion, and the powers of the chiefs of the militia; but since you are

> willing to rank me among the old soldiers who have garnered some glory in the War of Independence, you should be willing also to grant me, indeed, some understanding of a point of honor. Promise me, then, that, after those who shall believe they have some cause for self-reproach will have taken the first step, the others will take the second.

Immediately one of the superior officers, having moved forward, said to him with a noble candor: “General, I remit my honor into your hands; I subscribe in advance to what you will do.” The eldest of the complaining officers said to him: “Consequently, General, I entrust my honor and that of my comrades who will not disavow me to you as well.” The General took the hand of each of these worthy men, and, having joined them in his own, he had the pleasure of seeing all those, who a moment before had renounced the sweet title of brother-in-arms, rush into each other’s arms. This touching scene had several witnesses who soon spread word of the details of it. And the news was received with a kind of rapture since it was that of a sincere reconciliation as to all that Louisiana cherishes and reveres.

General Lafayette had planned to visit the battlefield of January 8; but the continued bad weather and the necessity to respond in two or three days to so many expressions of interest made it necessary for him to renounce this plan. A colonel of the general staff, witnessing the consternation that this sacrifice caused to me, was kind enough to propose that I go alone with him while the General made some private visits. I accepted eagerly, and we left at once in a carriage that he sent for. On the way he informed me that he was born in France; that, situated by the chance of his birth in the privileged portion of society, since infancy his mind had been filled with the aristocratic privileges of his caste and that, although still very young at the time of the French Revolution, he had believed that it was his duty to defend the privileges of some against the natural and sacred rights of all, and that he had joined the Vendéans. “Then,” he said to me,

> I believed in the legitimacy of absolute monarchy, and in the heredity of virtue as well as the rights of the nobility with all the fervor of ignorance; and at first, I fought for them with all the courage, all the devotion of a fanatic; but the campaign had barely ended when reason bursting the bonds with which my education had shrouded it taught me that, instead of fighting, as I had thought, for justice and truth, I had become only the instrument of some men who had decided to sacrifice all, even their Fatherland, to their private interests, and at once I

sheathed my sword, which I ought never to have drawn for a cause so unjust, so absurd. At that time, I was about to return to France, and make honorable amends for my errors by devoting myself to the principles and the country whose ruin I had at first so foolishly longed for; but when I learned that the French Revolutionaries, forgetting both their point of departure and the goal that they at first wanted to attain, had allowed themselves to be dominated and led astray by some ferocious men who outraged liberty every day by the crimes that they committed in its name, and that they would allow me to live among them only insomuch as I consented to absolve my original sin, that is to say the chance of my birth, in the blood of the most virtuous patriots, terror-stricken and horrified, I withdrew, and I went to look in a foreign land for the liberty and equality that my country had enjoyed for only a moment, at the time when I was incapable of appreciating all their value.

I traveled for a long time to the different States of Europe without finding there what I was looking for. Everywhere, I found the criminal alliance of royalty, nobility and the clergy against the happiness and the interests of the people. Disgusted forever by such a state of affairs, I proceeded to North America, and I wanted to see if its institutions, which I had heard about, would respond to my desires and to my hopes; they surpassed them. I settled with pleasure in the midst of a people fortunate enough and wise enough to recognize no laws other than those that they provide for themselves. Do not believe, however, that I have become entirely indifferent to the destiny of my first Fatherland; no, I have not been able to forget entirely, and it is not without a sweet feeling of national pride that I have often heard speak, on the banks of the Hudson or the Potomac, of the glory of its arms; but even this glory has not been able to give me the desire to return to its bosom, because I knew that each of its victories cost it the sacrifice of one of its liberties. When Louisiana became a member of the great republican family of the United States, I came to reside there in order to experience the happiness of seeing free Frenchmen and to hear them talk of freedom in my native language. I was living in New Orleans for a short time when, in 1815, the constant enemies of freedom of other peoples in two hemispheres presented themselves before this City in order to conquer it. I rushed immediately to arms, joyful to find the occasion to prove my gratitude to my new country, and my sincere attachment to the principles which govern it; and today I am proud to be able to say that my presence on the battlefield which we are going to visit was not altogether useless.

My companion had barely finished these words when our carriage stopped, and we got out at the point of the river where the extreme right of the line of defense stood. Before traversing the site, the Colonel was kind enough to explain to me the operations that preceded and led to the battle of January 8. I understood by these details how difficult it must have been for General Jackson to oppose, with the handful of men that he had at his disposal, the disembarking and the rapid progress of an army of 15,000 men, that is to say, four times his army. The position selected by the American General to await reinforcements and to finally stop so formidable an enemy appeared to me very well-chosen. He built his entrenchments about five miles in front of the City, along an old canal whose left side disappeared in the thickness of a very marshy forest, and whose right side rested upon the river. The whole length of this line was about 4800 feet; but the 1800 feet of the left being inaccessible, the enemy was reduced to attacking on a front of about 3000 feet, and to advancing, entirely unprotected, over a perfectly level plain.

However, whether it was for lack of time or thoughtlessness, General Jackson committed two serious errors; the first was to build his entrenchments on a straight line and perpendicular to the river, so that at that same time he deprived himself of fire from the back, he exposed himself, if the English, more fortunate or more skillful, would have gone up the river in some vessels as far as the entrenchments; he exposed himself, I say, to having the entire line raked by enemy artillery; the other mistake was having set up his second line at such a great a distance from the first that if the one were forced, it would never have had the time to reach the other, and its troops would have been cut down in the interval. These two errors would have sufficed, as it is easy to imagine, to compromise the safety of an army more numerous and more disciplined than General Jackson's army; but the destiny of American freedom prevailed, or rather the supernatural courage of citizens who fought on that day to maintain their independence and the safety of their families, and the inflexible steadfastness of Jackson himself covered those errors, which would have destroyed a less patriotic army, with the laurels of the most brilliant victory.

I will not report here all the details which were given to me with as much clarity as precision on all the operations that preceded that glorious day; I refer those who want to study them to the excellent memoir of Mr. Lacarrière-Latour, and to the no-less distinguished writings of Messrs.

Brackenridge and McAfee; but I cannot resist the desire to recall here some of the brilliant deeds that saved Louisiana and immortalized its defenders.

Despite all his efforts, General Jackson had been able to gather only 3,200 men and 14 pieces of artillery of different calibers for the defense of his entrenchments. Pressed by time, he had been forced to complete the upper part of his parapets with bales of cotton that he had had brought from the City. He had been in this position for 24 hours, and he was expecting to be attacked at any moment when on January 8 at daybreak he saw the English Army, 12,000 men strong, advance towards him in three columns, of which the most formidable threatened the part of the left flank occupied by the militias of Tennessee and Kentucky. In addition to his arms, each soldier carried fascines or scaling ladders and marched in the deepest silence. The Americans allowed them to advance up to within half-range of the cannon, and then opened a terrible fire of artillery on them to which the English responded by a triple cheer and the dispatch of some Congreve rockets and, indeed, by hurrying their march and closing their ranks as the cannonballs decimated them. This coolness and this determination, which seemed like it ought to assure them a prompt victory, did not last long. At the moment they arrived within gunshot range, the men of Tennessee and Kentucky commenced musket fire on them which in an instant dispersed their columns and forced them to seek shelter precipitously behind some thickets that covered their right. Truly, never was infantry fire more sustained and more deadly than that of these fearless American militias. The men, placed six deep, loaded the arms quickly and passed them to the front row, which was composed of able marksmen, each of whose shots brought certain death to the enemy.

While the English officers, with a courage worthy of a better cause and a more fortunate fate, tried to rally their scattered soldiers to lead them to a new attack, an American gunner from the battery commanded by Lieutenant Spotts noticed in the field a group of anxious, excited officers carrying someone in their midst with difficulty. "It is perhaps the commander-in-chief only wounded," he shouted, "he must not escape us!" And immediately, he aimed in that direction; the shot having been fired, Pakenham, the English commander, was cut in two in the arms of his friends. At once, the desire for vengeance rallied the English; officers and soldiers rushed together in a new column that Keane and Gibbs, Pakenham's successors, drew up to the attack furiously. But the fire of the Americans redoubled with intensity and accuracy; Keane and Gibbs fell in turn, the one mortally, the other seriously wounded; and the column, struck down again, disappeared and left only some debris in the field.

While in the center of the line of battle, the citizen-soldiers crushed their adversaries in this manner without losing a single man, fortune seemed to want to test those on the right with a reversal. Twelve hundred English, led by an audacious chief, had advanced rapidly along the river and had unexpectedly fallen upon a small redoubt defended by a company of riflemen and a company of the 7th Regiment. Surprised at this point, the Americans retired at first in some disorder. General Jackson, with a vigilant eye that nothing escaped at this decisive moment, noticed from afar an English officer mounting the entrenchments, brandishing a menacing sword in one hand and assisting his soldiers to scale the ramparts with the other. Jackson ran immediately towards the spot, met the fugitives on his route, stopped them, and in a terrible voice demanded of their chief who gave him the order to retreat. "The enemy has breached the entrenchments," answered a captain. "Well then," resumed Jackson harshly, "go and let your bayonettes make them quit them…." And this order was executed immediately. In an instant, the English, who believed themselves conquerors at first, fell under the blows of the Americans. Among the dead was the intrepid Colonel Regnier, an old French emigrant who had passed into the service of England, the very one whom they had seen standing boldly on the entrenchments, helping and encouraging his soldiers to scale them. After the battle, several American soldiers claimed the honor of having killed him. But none could prove his claim like two of Captain Beale's voluntary riflemen. The one said: "If my rifle has not tricked my eye, this man must be shot in the head." – "If my bullet did not miscarry en route," said the other, "he must have taken it in the heart." They examined the body of Colonel Regnier carefully and found the heart and the brow each pierced by a bullet.

This battle, which decided the fate of New Orleans and perhaps even that of Louisiana, lasted only three hours, and cost the Americans only seven men killed and six wounded, while the English left nearly 3,000 men and 14 pieces of cannon on the battlefield. General Lambert, the sole English General still able to command, ordered a retreat and rushed to seek his safety and that of the remnant of his army on the fleet commanded by Admiral Cochrane, who the evening before had said with his accustomed boasting that, if he was charged with the attack of the American lines, he would storm them in less than a half hour with 2,000 sailors, sabres in hand.

It is in this manner that a little army, composed of citizens levied in haste, and commanded by a general whose military career was hardly begun, saw fall before its patriotic efforts this English Army which passed for one of the most courageous and experienced of Europe and prided itself for having finally expelled the French from Spain.

When I returned to the City, I found General Lafayette surrounded and beset by a large number of ladies and citizens of all ranks who, knowing that he had to leave on the next day, came sadly to take leave of him, and to clasp his hand one more time. In the crowd, I noticed some clergymen, and among the latter I found a Capuchin whose dress, new for me, had already attracted my attention the day of our arrival. What I heard said about him interested me very much, and perhaps you will be grateful if I relate it here.

Father Antonio (that is what they call him) is a venerable Spanish Capuchin of the order of Saint Francis, who has lived in Louisiana for many years. Animated by an ardent and sincere piety, Father Antonio prays silently for all the world without requesting prayers of anyone. Situated in the midst of a population of different sects, he does not believe himself obliged to disturb others' consciences by seeking to recruit in the name of his God. Sometimes, like a Capuchin, Father Antonio begs, but it is always when he has a good deed to do and when his feeble income, exhausted by his constant charity, does not permit him to do it himself. Every year when, on the return of autumn, yellow fever, spreading its deadly hand on New Orleans, causes the frightened wealthy to flee into their resplendent country estates to seek refuge against disease and death, then Father Antonio's virtue is displayed in all its brilliance, in all its strength. In these days of terror and of bereavement, how many unfortunates abandoned by their friends, even by their parents, have owed their health and their life to his dedication, his caring and his piety! Of all those whom he has saved (and there are very many of them) there is not a single one who could say: "Before bestowing his attentions on me, he asked what religion I belonged to…." Liberty and charity, that is the entire morality of Father Antonio, and so he is not liked by the Bishop.

When he came to see the General, he was clad, according to the dress of his Order, in a long brown robe clasped on the waist by a coarse rope. When he saw the General, he threw himself into his arms while shouting: "Oh my son, I have found grace before the Lord since he has allowed me to see and hear the most worthy apostle of liberty before my death." He then conversed with him for some time with the most tender affection, complimented him on the glorious and well-merited reception that the Americans were giving him, and withdrew modestly into a corner of the room, far from the crowd. I took advantage of this moment to approach him and to greet him. How moved I was by his conversation! What gentleness! What modesty! And, at the same time, what warmth of spirit!... Each time that he spoke of liberty his eyes shined with a divine fire, and his gaze fell on the one whom he called his hero, on Lafayette…. "How fortunate he is," he said to me:

> How pure is the source of his glory! With what delights must he contemplate the result of his work and the 12,000,000 men free and happy because of him! Oh! Certainly, this man is cherished by God.... He has done so much good for other men!

He came yet again to see us on the morning of our departure. When the public had left the rooms, and when he found the General alone, he ran to him, and pressed him rapturously in his arms: "Farewell, my son!" he cried,

> Farewell, well-loved General! Farewell! May the Lord walk before you, and, after your glorious trip, may he lead you to the bosom of your well-loved family to enjoy there in peace the memory of your good deeds and of the friendship of the American Nation.... Oh my son, perhaps some new works are still in store for you!... Perhaps the Lord will reserve you yet for the liberation of other nations.... So, my son, consider poor Spain.... Do not abandon my dear country, my unhappy country....

And tears, escaping from his eyes, moistened his long beard, white with age; sighs stifling his voice, the venerable old man placed his brow on General Lafayette's shoulder, and stayed for some moments in this position, always murmuring: "My son, my dear son, do something for my unfortunate Fatherland!..." It was not without deep feeling that the General tore himself away from this pious patriot, who before withdrawing, also gave his benediction to George Lafayette.

Nevertheless, the 15th being set as the day of departure, the rooms of the General's apartment were filled early in the morning with an even larger crowd than that of the day before. He found there a large number of ladies and especially children whom their fathers brought there, they said, so that they could gaze on the features of the benefactor of the country, the friend of the great Washington. The General left on foot from *his house*, which was surrounded by the entire population. Cries of *Vive Lafayette!* greeted him as he passed. On crossing the parade grounds, on which several companies of the legion and line troops lined the streets, he displayed his gratitude to all the officers whom he encountered there; he again expressed to the captain of the gunners, Mr. Gally, to what extent he appreciated the merit of the excellent corps that he commanded; and, as he had learned that this officer was traveling shortly to France, he beseeched him in the most pressing manner to be kind enough to bring news of him to his family at La Grange.

He mounted the carriage at the end of the parade grounds to travel to the wharf, where the steamship that was to conduct him to Baton Rouge was waiting for him. The levee was covered with an innumerable population. The balconies, the rooftops, all the boats and all the steamships that were found within range of the place of his embarkation were overloaded with people; and when he went on board, a prolonged cheer greeted him, but it was the sole cheer, and more than 10,000 people stayed absorbed in a profound silence until *The Natchez* was out of sight. A single cannon was heard at intervals, and gave to this separation a kind of solemnity, the impression of which was profound and general.

The Governor and his staff, the Mayor and the municipal corps, the committee of arrangements, to which we had so many and such great obligations, embarked with us in order to prolong for some time the pleasure that they had in being with the General; but, two miles from there, most were obliged to leave us. It was not without genuine sorrow that we were separating from these worthy magistrates of the people, whom we had known for only a few days, it is true, but nonetheless had known enough to appreciate very much.

Chapter VIII

History and Constitution of Louisiana – Baton Rouge – Natchez – State of Mississippi – Sailing to St. Louis – Reception of General Lafayette in That City.

For a long time the French had vast and prosperous settlements in Canada, and nonetheless they did not yet suspect the existence of the Mississippi River, when some of their traders learned from the Indians with whom they dealt that there was a *Great River* that flowed into the Gulf of Mexico to the west of their land. It was during the year 1660 that this happened. Three years later, Frontenac, Governor of Canada, desirous of confirming the truth of this assertion, sent a Jesuit missionary, Father Marquette, at the head of a small detachment to explore this country. The Jesuit sailed up the Fox River towards its source; from there he traversed the Wisconsin, which he descended up to its mouth in the Mississippi, and he found that the Indians had spoken the truth.

Twenty years later, Count Robert de La Salle not only verified the existence of this river, but also confirmed that it offered an easy passage to the Ocean; he descended it from the Illinois River to the Gulf of Mexico, while Father Hennepin, a Franciscan, ascended it up to the Falls of Saint Anthony, 750 miles above this river. Count Robert took possession of the entire course of the river and the surrounding country in the name of his master the King of France, and built forts in order to assure peaceful enjoyment of the land to the Colonists whom he hoped to see arrive soon in large numbers because the soil appeared to him to be fertile. But it was only in 1699, however, that the first Colony was founded at Biloxi by an officer with a great reputation in the French Navy. Lemoine d'Iberville is the name of the officer who first entered the Mississippi by sea, and then ascended the river up to Natchez, which he chose for the capital of Louisiana, and which he named Rosalie, in honor of the wife of Chancellor Pontchartrain.

In order to populate this new capital, they sent some girls from France with some well-chosen soldiers whom they excused from military service and gave to them as husbands. They granted to each Colonist some acres of land, a cow, a calf, a rooster and some hens, a gun, a half-pound of powder and two pounds of lead which were delivered to them each month as provisions for three years. Then the missionaries arrived who, instead of making the land productive by the labor of their arms, or developing the industry of the settlers by their counsel and their wisdom, began to preach to the Indians of the vicinity in order to convert them to the Catholic religion. Soon these missions bore fruit, that is to say the Indians pretended to believe in the new truths that they were teaching them, and became hypocrites in order to obtain brandy. This liquor, which was the first reward of their conversion, exacerbated all the passions for which they already had the unfortunate predisposition, and from that moment they became dangerous and cruel enemies of the Colony, instead of good and useful neighbors, which they would have been without a doubt if the Colonists had sought their alliance openly without being concerned with the manner by which they worshipped God. Nonetheless, after several years, the cordiality and the sweetness of the French character counterbalanced the baleful influence of the missionaries, and nearly all the savage Nations, except the Chickasaws, made an alliance with the Colonists and rendered them great services.

Bienville, brother of Iberville, and then Governor of Louisiana, devoting himself to his passion for exploration, explored the greater part of the tributaries of the Mississippi, and lay the foundations of some new settlements on their banks; but, then, none of them succeeded. The number of Colonists had considerably diminished when in 1712 Antoine Crozat, who had amassed a fortune of 40,000,000 francs by his trade in the Indies, bought the concession for all of Louisiana, with the exclusive right to trade there for 16 years. Included in his letters patent were all the rivers that flowed into the Mississippi and all the lands, coasts and islands situated on the Gulf of Mexico between Carolina to the east and Mexico to the west. But Crozat was not long in recognizing how exaggerated were the hopes that he had placed on this country, and he hastened to renounce the grant that had been made to him, in order to obtain another of 25 years in favor of the Commercial Company of Mississippi, of which the famous Law was the founder. But this commercial company was hardly more successful than Crozat; instead of attracting farmers who would have made it prosper to the bosom of the Colony, it received only adventurers greedy for riches attracted by the would-be gold and silver mines, with which they had said that the country was plentiful, and who, disappointed in their hopes, did not delay returning to Europe. Despite the efforts of the Government initiated by the commercial company, the proprietors were soon reduced to being scattered, and to establishing military posts where they remained until help and reinforcements were sent to them. The first expedition that arrived then was composed of criminals and women of ill repute sent by the French Government. The commercial company was angered with reason, and declared that it would not allow the Colony to be so morally and physically poisoned again in the future.

In 1718, New Orleans, composed of some cabins built by traders from the Illinois and named in this manner in honor of the Duke of Orleans, the Regent, passed under the jurisdiction of the Governor General, Mr. de Bienville, and received a rather large number of new Colonists. Two villages were established in its vicinity by Germans, under the leadership of a Swedish Captain, Arensbourg, who had fought in 1709 alongside Charles XII in the battle of Pultowa. The Colony then began to truly prosper. Also from 1723 one saw arrive from far and wide hosts of Capuchins, missionaries, Jesuits and pious Ursulines. These latter were at least good for something. They were entrusted with the education of orphaned girls and with the superintendence of the military hospital, in consideration of an annual allowance of 50 crowns. Intolerance, inseparable companion of all privileges, and especially religious privileges, began to be felt in the Colony as soon as the Capuchins, the Jesuits, etc., had appeared there. A royal edict of 1724 expelled the Jews from the Colony as declared enemies of Christianity and they were ordered to disappear in three months' time under pains of prison and confiscation of their property. It is in this manner that Royalty and the Church conspired then, as before and since, to dry up the most abundant sources of public prosperity.

In 1729 the intrigues of England, which provoked Indian tribes against the Colony, also struck a baneful blow to its development. The war, waged then by General Perrier de Salvert, ended successfully enough; nonetheless, it was only due to the affection of some Indian women for some French officers that the garrison was not completely massacred one night, and this would have caused the total ruination of the Colony. These last hostilities, and the despicable intrigues of the parent state, made the Colonists lose time and the fruit of their labors; and the company, disgusted and cheated in its hope for gain, abandoned this country which in 1731 reverted to the King's domain, and was not administered any better. In 1759 its financial affairs were in such disorder that the treasury was indebted for more than 7,000,000 francs, because the French Government had spent about double that which the Colony had returned to it for different services to Louisiana. At the end of a badly conceived, badly fought, and badly concluded war in 1763, Louis XV had just lost Canada, and Louisiana was also going to be taken away; but his ministers, in agreement with Madam Pompadour, the King's official mistress, received 15,000,000 francs from the Court of Madrid; and this Colony was ceded secretly to Spain, and with such haste that the Governor of Louisiana had not yet been able to receive his instructions when the Spanish warships arrived at the mouth of the Mississippi with the leaders assigned to take possession of this immense country. The Governor and the inhabitants of Louisiana refused to recognize Spanish authority, and the commissioners were obliged to return to Europe. Three or four years passed in negotiations with the Colonists who persisted in staying under French dominion.

Finally, in 1769, an angry Spain dispatched General O'Reilly with considerable forces; having arrived before New Orleans, O'Reilly displayed the most conciliatory disposition; his proclamations spoke only of forgetting the past, and were a complete success. The unrest of the people subsided, and the Louisianans resigned themselves; as a sign of reconciliation, O'Reilly gave a banquet on board his fleet, to which he invited the leaders of the Colony, the magistrates and the principal inhabitants. These confidently accepted the invitation; but at the moment when they were going to leave the table, O'Reilly had them seized by his soldiers and shot. One of them, Mr. Villeré, had been spared, and embarked aboard a frigate to be transported to the prisons of Navarre. His wife and children, having learned of the fate that threatened him, wanted to go to beg for mercy or at least to receive his farewells; they were already near the frigate from which he held out his arms towards them, when the unfortunate man fell before their eyes, pierced by bayonette thrusts of the assassins whom the traitor O'Reilly had entrusted to guard him.

After this horrible execution, the Spanish, with 4,000 troops of the line and a considerable train of artillery, entered New Orleans, whose inhabitants were dumbstruck. The English Protestants and the small number of Jews who had escaped the effect of the Royal Edict of 1724 were soon banished by the new power; all commerce of the Colony was prohibited except with Spain and its possessions; a military court was established, and its iniquitous judgments struck down all the French officers who had remained; five of them were shot and seven others were thrown into the dungeons of Havana for ten years; finally, during an entire year, the infamous O'Reilly gorged himself on blood and riches, and departed, taking with him the scorn and hatred of the entire population. His successors in the Government had very much to do to make amends for his crimes, and one owes them the justice of saying that they succeeded rather very well at this. During 33 years of Spanish domination, the Colony was very calm and rather prosperous. To this day, the memory of Dom Unsaga, Dom Martin Navarro, and Dom Galvez is preserved in a respectful manner.

During all these changes that occurred in the situation of Louisiana, its borders had never been determined in a very precise manner. In 1795, the United States Government made a treaty with Spain by virtue of which the borderlines were mapped out, and free navigation of the Mississippi was assured to the contracting parties. But soon, despite this treaty, the Spanish shipowners and the crews of warships were guilty of plundering the commerce of the United States; freedom of navigation on the Mississippi and the right to disembark in New Orleans were denied to Americans. Immediately, President Adams took steps to obtain justice. Twelve regiments were raised, and an expedition was prepared on the Ohio River to descend to Louisiana; but some intervening changes in American politics made them abandon this plan for the moment, and the regiments were disbanded. The following year, Mr. Jefferson, then President, demanded again that Spain execute the terms of the treaty. That power, feeling its weakness and fearing that it would be compelled to give up the Colony, secretly sold the Colony to the French Republic on March 21, 1801.

Upon learning of this cession, the American Government was justly alarmed; it foresaw that French administration and intelligence, placed on a soil so fertile in riches and resources, would be a rivalry more formidable for it than that of the Spanish and that the new neighbors would be able to close to it the navigation of the Mississippi and monopolize the commerce of the Gulf of Mexico and the Antilles; and it immediately conceived a plan to oppose by force the occupation of Louisiana by France, by joining with England against it. But this project was reversed by the Treaty of Amiens. Peace having been made with England, France no longer feared any obstacles to its projects, and an expedition was readied by it to go to occupy Louisiana and to strengthen its tottering rule in St. Domingo at one and the same time.

At once the American Government resorted to negotiations, and proposed to buy Louisiana. Events followed each other with such speed that the situation of France had changed once again when these proposals arrived. Threatened with a new war with England, wearied by the struggle to prevent St. Domingo from falling, burdened with a rather considerable debt to the United States, the First Consul believed that the sale of Louisiana was a good transaction, the opportunity for which would extricate him from more than one difficulty, and he sold the Colony. The United States agreed to pay France $15,000,000 on the condition that $3,750,000 of this sum would be held back for the benefit of American merchants, whose claims against the French Government were based on illegal seizures of which they had been victims. This treaty, signed in Paris on April 30, 1803 by Messrs. Livingston and Monroe for the United States and Mr. Barbé-Marbois for France, was ratified in the month of October, and the transfer of the Colony to the American Commissioners took place on December 20 of the same year.

All the interested parties to this transaction had the right to congratulate themselves on its conclusion. France gave up the troubles of a faraway dominion which had been for it more onerous than profitable, received 60,000,000 francs which it needed to make war, and, without disbursing a cent, relieved itself of a sum of nearly 20,0000,000 francs owed to American merchants. The United States affirmed its independence while giving itself new borders more secure than the old ones; it assured itself of commercial predominance in the Gulf of Mexico and in the Antilles; and increased a hundredfold the value of the products of the States to the west of the Alleghenies, by the free navigation of the Mississippi. Finally Louisiana itself, in entering into the great federal family, received an honorable and independent existence as a body politic, and would see its industry and its prosperity freed from the vexatious interference of a capricious master.

Louisiana was immediately established as a territorial government by the United States Congress which gave it Mr. Claiborne as Governor. And in 1811 it was admitted as a member of the Union and allowed to give itself a government and institutions of its choice. The representatives of the people, freely elected and meeting at New Orleans, drafted and signed a constitution that was then submitted to the United States Congress which approved it. This Constitution was more or less copied from those of the other States. Only the people of Louisiana believed that they ought to take the most precautions possible against corruption and abuses of power. Thus, for example, it was decided that every person convicted of having given or offered presents to public officials would be declared ineligible to serve as governor, senator or representative.

The general principles of the Constitution were established in this manner:

A sum of money can leave the treasury only for the intended purpose designated by law. – The funds for the support of the army must not be appropriated for a term of longer than one year, and a regular account of receipts and expenses must be published every year. – Judgment by jurors must be with the shortest delay possible. – There must be freedom of the accused with bail, except in capital crimes. – A law will never have retroactive effect. – No law can destroy private agreements. – Each citizen can write and print his thoughts on every subject, on responsibility however for abuses of this freedom. – Free emigration from the State is authorized. – All laws contrary to the Constitution are null and void. – The Constitution is capable of revision following the prescribed method.

If I believed that it was necessary to find new proofs of the superiority of the independent government over the Colonial regime, whether the latter arose from a monarchy or a republic, it would suffice for me to point to Louisiana, at first a Colony for nearly a century, and not advancing beyond infancy; continually taken and retaken, at one time by the Spanish at another time by the French, and always incapable of resisting the one or the other; costing its parent state $187,000 per year; and finally, after the numerous emigrations from Europe, offering only a feeble population of about 40,000, spread over a vast territory of fallow land. I would then point to this same Louisiana, after 20 years of an independent and republican government, having more than tripled its population; defeating under the walls of its wealthy capital an army composed of the elite troops of England; receiving annually in its ports more than 400 ships charged with exchanging its valuable products with those of all parts of the globe, and offering, in all its towns, all the resources, all the enjoyments which can contribute to a happy life and which are ordinarily the product of a civilization of long standing.

The State of Louisiana, enclosed in its new borders, is located between 29 degrees and 33 degrees latitude and between 12 and 17 degrees longitude. It is bounded to the north by the territory of Arkansas; to the east by Mississippi, to the south by the Gulf of Mexico; and to the west by the Mexican province of Texas. Its area is 48,000 square miles, divided into 26 parishes or counties; its population is about 153,500 inhabitants, among which one counts, unfortunately, nearly 70,000 Slaves. The capital of this State is New Orleans, a city admirably situated with regards to commerce, regularly laid out, ornamented with beautiful buildings and containing a population of 28,000. The greatest disadvantage of New Orleans is that of being located on alluvial ground often flooded by the overflowing waters of the Mississippi; this is probably the principal cause of yellow fever which is prevalent there every autumn. The impossibility of finding a single stone in all this alluvial soil is the reason that, even at present, they have not been able to pave the streets of the City, and, in the rainy season, it is very difficult to proceed on foot; the footpaths that are built along the houses scarcely save pedestrians from the mud, and do not prevent carriages from sinking sometimes up to their axles. The administration has at long last taken the step of causing the delivery of stones suitable for paving from the upper part of the Mississippi, which the vessels take along as ballast. This method is time-consuming and expensive, but it is the only practical one.

Most of the travelers who have visited New Orleans claim that the customs of this City feel very many effects of the presence of numerous Colonists who emigrated from St. Domingo. These people have the reputation of loving pleasure nearly up to license, and of being harsh towards their Slaves. The love of gambling and of dueling, which often ensues, causes, they say, very many disturbances among them. To confirm or disprove this judgment by my own opinion would be a culpable pretension on my part. My rather short stay in this City did not allow me to study the character of the society, and I have been struck only by the spirit of patriotism, liberty and hospitality that has been expressed enthusiastically in General Lafayette's presence.

Twenty-four hours after having left New Orleans, we arrived at Duncan Point where the citizens of Baton Rouge, a city situated eight miles above, had sent a delegation ahead to General Lafayette to request that he stop for a while in their midst. The General accepted the invitation gratefully, and two hours later we disembarked at the base of the amphitheater on which the City of Baton Rouge sits. The beach was covered with citizens at the head of whom marched the municipal corps, and the first regiment of the Union had come to arrange itself in battle array under the very star-spangled standard that, a short time ago, had been planted on the ruins of Spanish despotism by the inhabitants of these parishes in contempt of the greatest dangers. Accompanied by the people and their magistrates, the General went into a hall that had been prepared to receive him, and in which he found the busts of Washington and Jackson crowned with laurels and flowers. There he received offerings of affection from all the citizens, and he went with them to the fort where the garrison, which had been waiting for him, gave him a 24-gun salute and marched before him. Afterwards, we entered the principal part of the building to visit the interior of the barracks; but how astonished we were on entering the first room to find, instead of beds, arms, and military equipment, a numerous assembly of ladies brilliant in their beauty and their attire who encircled the General and offered him refreshments and flowers! The General was very moved by this pleasant surprise, and passed some time with great pleasure in the middle of this enchanting garrison. On our return to the City, we found a large number of citizens who had gathered to offer the General a public banquet at which sincere American cordiality, joined with French charm, presided.

It was almost night when we reboarded *The Natchez* to continue our journey. On leaving Baton Rouge, we were sorry to separate again from some of the people who had come with us from New Orleans, among others, Mr. Duplantier senior, whose active and tender friendship, as well as that of his son, had been of great service to General Lafayette.

Baton Rouge is located on the left bank of the river, 137 miles above New Orleans. In this passage, navigation of the Mississippi is very interesting. For some miles on leaving New Orleans, the eye settles on riverbanks enriched by beautiful cotton and sugar plantations, and beautified by groves of orange trees, in the middle of which the dwellings of the planters rise up in bursts of white. Little by little the gardens, the homes become rarer. But up to Baton Rouge one continues to see beautiful, well-cultivated lands. These plantations unfold the length of the river and extend sometimes nearly one mile behind it up to thick forests that serve as their boundaries. The soil is formed entirely of fertile sediment deposited by past inundations of the Mississippi, which is now contained in its bed by artificial dikes. A special law imposes a duty on each riverbank landowner to maintain with care the portion of the dike which is constructed in front of his property; also, one sees Slaves everywhere continuously occupied in driving posts, interweaving tree branches, and piling up soil where the river threatens to force a passageway; in spite of all these precautions, sometimes the river hurls itself forward over the obstacles that they oppose it with and spreads devastation and death with its flooding on the dwellings it traverses. A year does not pass without some landowners having the sorrow of seeing the fruit of long and hard work taken away from them in a few minutes. All the lands that border the Mississippi from its mouth to 600 miles above it are subject to floods. Nevertheless, upon leaving Baton Rouge, the left bank appears to rise far enough above the level of the water to be safe from these disasters.

From Baton Rouge to Natchez, there are 260 miles, which we traveled in 30 hours of felicitous sailing. On this journey, we encountered a large number of boats of all shapes and sizes, filled with all kinds of products from the furthest parts of the Union. But the ones that attracted most of our attention were those large square-shaped ships without masts, without sails, without oars, descending the river at the mercy of the current, and resembling large boxes more than boats. They call them *barges*. They are ordinarily manned by Kentuckians who travel in this way to sell their grain, their poultry and their livestock in New Orleans, and who, after having received the sales price, also sell the planks of their barges, which would not be able to ascend the river, and return to their homes on foot across the States of Mississippi, Alabama and Tennessee. They say that each summer more than 1,500 individuals travel the 1,700 miles by water in this manner in their barges, and nearly 1,100 make their return on foot.

On Monday April 18, some cannon blasts that we heard in the distance at daybreak announced that we were approaching a city; some moments later, the first rays of the sun gilding the top of the banks of the Mississippi which, in this spot, rise to 150 feet above the surface of the water, allowed us to see the rooftops of Natchez. Our steamship stopped a little before arriving opposite the City, and we disembarked at Bacon's Beach where the General was awaited by the citizens with a four-horse carriage and an escort of voluntary cavalry and infantry. We would have been able to disembark a little higher up and arrive at the City by a more direct route; but the members of the committee of arrangements were clever enough to conduct us by a circuitous route, along which all the beauties of the country unfolded before our eyes. As we advanced, the procession was augmented by citizens on horseback, militia on foot, ladies in carriages, and nearly the entire population, which came in a crowd to receive their dear and long-awaited guest. Two speeches were made to the General, one at the entrance to the City by the president of the committee of arrangements, the other by the Mayor, on one of the most elevated points of the banks of the Mississippi in view of the City and the river, the source of its prosperity. At the moment when the General concluded his response, a man left the crowd precipitously, approached the carriage while waving his hat in the air, and cried out: "Honor to the Commander of the Parisian National Guard! I was under your command in '91, my General; I was a part of the batallion of the Filles Saint-Thomas. I still love liberty as I loved it then: *Vive Lafayette!...*" The General was pleasantly surprised to find on such distant shores one of his former citizen-soldiers who reminded him in so moving a manner of the happy time when he could reasonably believe in the happiness and liberty of his Fatherland. The General held out his hand affectionately and expressed to him the pleasure that he felt in meeting him in a free and hospitable land.

At the moment when we were going to enter the hotel that we were to stay in, we saw a long column of children of both sexes coming towards us; they were led by Colonel Marshall who asked the General for them and in their name for permission to shake his hand. The General readily consented to this desire of the children of Natchez; and they marched in good order before him, each successively placing one of his little hands in the hands of the one who had fought for the liberty of their fathers. The parents, witnessing this scene, contemplated it in silence and with emotion. When this scene was finished, I heard them congratulate one another on the fortunate influence that this day would have on the future of their children. "When they are grown," they said, "and when upon examining the pages of the history of their country, they will find the name of Lafayette intimately connected to all the events that have brought about the liberation of their fathers, they will recall the grace of his manners and the sweetness of his voice when he greeted them in their childhood, and they will feel their love of a liberty won by such a man increase...."

The inhabitants of Natchez did not leave anything undone to make the 24 hours their guest passed among them delightful. The public banquet concluded with toasts that they made *to the Nation's Guest; to the victory of Yorktown; to France, fighter for the freedom of the New World; to the victory of New Orleans*; finally, *to all the memories of American glory and patriotism.* It was only after the ball which ended at dawn that the General could think of reembarking. The ladies employed all their charm and grace in order to keep him for the longest possible time; but we counted our minutes, and at six o'clock in the morning we were already aboard our ship.

At the moment when the General was going to leave the shore, an old Revolutionary soldier presented himself to him while displaying his breast covered with scars. "These wounds are my pride," he said; "I received them at your side while fighting for the independence of my country,…your blood flowed the same day, my General;…it was at the Battle of Brandywine, which just missed being deadly for us." — "Indeed, it was a rough day," answered the General; "but let us agree that we have been well rewarded for it since." — "Oh! It is very true," replied the old soldier; "today, for example, aren't we happy beyond all our desires;…you receive the blessings of 10,000,000 free men, and I shake the hand of my brave General! Doesn't virtue always have its reward!..."

Everyone applauded the enthusiasm and the sincerity of the old soldier, and the General pressed him heartily in his arms.

On leaving Natchez, we separated from the excellent Mr. Johnson, Governor of Louisiana, who had not wanted to leave the General so long as he had been within the boundaries of his State. He remitted us to the care of the State of Mississippi, and left us to Mr. Prieur, recorder of the City Council of New Orleans, Mr. Caire, his private secretary, and Mssrs. Morse and Ducros, his two aides-de-camp, to do us the honors of Louisiana up to St. Louis. In taking leave of the Governor, General Lafayette expressed to him the most sincere affection, and charged him to convey in his name all the gratitude he felt for the reception, so full of cordiality, that had been given to him in Louisiana.

Natchez was formerly the capital of the State of Mississippi, but has ceased being the capital because its location is not central enough. Its population is nearly 3,000, and its port is a place of rest and provisioning for all the ships that sail between New Orleans and the States of the West, and this gives it a great deal of activity. This City was founded in 1717 by some French soldiers and laborers who had been in the garrison of *Fort Rosalie* and who, finding the terrain beautiful, settled there after having obtained their discharge from service; most of them bought their plots of land from the Indians of this canton who lived at some distance from the river, where they had five villages very near to one another. The one that they called the *Great Village*, where the principal chief of this nation lived, was built along a little river called the *White River*. It is to the west of this village that some Frenchmen, led by Hubert and Lepage, had built *Fort Rosalie*.

When one has seen the environs of Natchez, one easily understands how the first Colonists renounced their native land to establish themselves in these still wild places. It is difficult to encounter a more fertile soil, a more vigorous growth of vegetation, more agreeable and more varied undulations of the terrain; the valleys offer fertile pastures, the hills are crowned with sassafras, catalpa, tulip trees and superb, large-flowering magnolias, the top of which rise to more than 100 feet high and the large, white flowers of which scent the air deliciously. Nevertheless, one cannot avoid a distressing feeling in thinking that these meadows so green, these groves so fresh, and this nature so vigorous and gay are sometimes visited and saddened by yellow fever.

Natchez is the only city of the State of Mississippi that we visited; moreover, I will only say a few things about this State; I shall recount only that for a long time, like Alabama, it was part of the State of Georgia, from which it was separated in 1800; that it was in 1817 that it took its place as an independent body politic in the Union, and that it gave itself a constitution. The fertility of its soil and the ease of passage for its products have especially contributed to the increase of its population; in 1800 it had only 6,850; today it counts 76,000. If one did not include nearly 30,000 Slaves in this number, its prosperity would be greater still. Nonetheless, one finds very many considerable fortunes in this State; it is not rare to meet landowners who have 30,000 or 40,000 francs in revenue; the principal products are cotton and corn.

The State of Mississippi is located between 30 and 35 degrees latitude north, and between 11 and 14 degrees longitude west of Washington City; its area is 45,350 square miles; it is bounded to the north by the State of Tennessee, to the east by the State of Alabama, to the south by the State of Louisiana and the Gulf of Mexico, and to the west by the State of Louisiana and the territory of Arkansas. Although the population there may be still very dispersed, the land is nonetheless rather high-priced; on the banks of the river, land is worth from 50 to 60 dollars an acre; land is a little less expensive as one goes farther away from the means of transport.

On withdrawing from Natchez, we parted from the civilized world, so to speak. From this City to St. Louis, we did not encounter a cluster of houses that deserved to be called a town or even a village; the banks of the Mississippi are lower again, and offer now only lands flooded and covered with thick forests impenetrable to the rays of the sun; the swarms of mosquitoes emanating from there, which hurl themselves in thick clouds on travelers, render sailing nearly intolerable, especially at night, if one has not taken the precaution of providing oneself with mosquito-nets. The only habitations one encounters in spots elevated a little above the water level of the river are rude cabins inhabited temporarily by hardy speculators of the North, who always abandon the *good* for the hope of the *better*, retreat ceaselessly from civilization, and go to seek their fortune in the wildernesses. The dangers of navigation grow with the monotony of the shore; at each step, one encounters monuments of recent disasters. Here it is a whirlwind that has traversed the river and which, in its devastating course, has on each bank uprooted and taken down thousands of trees, which by their prodigious height were the pride of the forest, as if they were feeble reeds. There, our Captain points out to us a *snag* or a *sawyer*, the slanted point of which has pierced a boat that the waves have immediately engulfed; further on, some woodcutters, while delivering the wood we needed, told us about the explosion of a steam engine which caused the death of more than 40 passengers; and we were not long in seeing for ourselves the shore covered with travelers who were waiting impatiently for their ship, which had been pierced by a *snag,* to be repaired to brave the danger from which they had just barely escaped.

These *snags* and *sawyers*, so feared by the navigator, are very numerous the entire length of the river. The former are trees, dragged along by the great flows of water, which, after having floated for some time, are implanted by their lower extremity in the riverbed, and present their top above or below the surface of the water, according to their length, but always inclined in the direction of the current. The *sawyers* differ from *snags* only in that they are less securely fixed in the riverbed, and the current impresses on them a continual vibration that causes them, in turn, to conceal and then raise their tops above the surface of the waters. Since their position changes often, they are very difficult to avoid; and if ships ascending the river have the misfortune of running into them, their destruction is nearly certain because they are pierced in such a way that the water, entering through an opening, sinks them, sometimes in a few minutes.

But one has little disposition to worry about all these dangers when one has, as we did, on board a good ship skillfully steered, all the delicacies of life, and the inexhaustible resources that the society of good and amiable fellow-travelers offers. To the New Orleans committee were added two citizens of Natchez as representatives of the State of Mississippi to General Lafayette. We are indebted to the attentions and the cheerfulness of both parties for not having known a single instant of boredom or worry during the long voyage.

After having sailed for five days by the State of Louisiana, the territory of Arkansas and a part of the State of Missouri to our left and the States of Mississippi, Tennessee and Kentucky to our right, we arrived at the mouth of the Ohio without making any stops other than those necessary to take on wood that we needed to fuel the furnace of our steam engine. This wood was sometimes delivered to us by woodsmen who inhabit the banks of the river and who live only off the products of the boundless forests surrounding them. Often we obtained our own supplies in the absence of the woodcutters. In this case, our Captain, after having had his crew take the quantity of wood that was necessary for him, left in exchange a note that he nailed to a tree and on which he inscribed the number of cords of wood that he had taken, the name of his ship, the place of his residence, the date of his passage, and his signature. This method of commerce with the woodsmen of the Mississippi is very common, and I have heard it said that no example of bad faith on the part of the purchasers has ever been offered. They have always shown themselves to be very scrupulous in the payment of their bills, which are often only presented to them some months later at Natchez or New Orleans.

Having arrived at the mouth of the Ohio, we had traveled 450 miles from the town of Natchez. Our pilot then declared to us that the upper part of the Mississippi was too little known for him to risk leading us in the midst of the dangers that one encounters there at every step of the way. Consequently, our good Captain Davis caused us to enter the Ohio to go four miles from its mouth to take on another pilot, whom, fortunately, we found immediately. On going there we encountered a steamboat whose narrow shape and unsteady sailing made us assume that, intended for navigating small streams, it had found itself on the agitated waves of a large river only by an extraordinary circumstance. This steamboat was *The Mechanic*, carrying the delegation of Tennessee, sent ahead of General Lafayette to conduct him up the Cumberland to Nashville, where he had been expected for a long time and where the plan of his trip to St. Louis was not yet known. After a brief conference with the delegates from Tennessee, who strenuously insisted that the General proceed immediately on board their ship, it was resolved that we would continue our voyage to St. Louis on *The Natchez*, that a part of the Tennessee delegation would come with us, and that the other part would remain on board *The Mechanic*, which would remain stationed at the mouth of the Ohio until our return. These arrangements having been made to the satisfaction of everyone, we left this beautiful river to reenter the Great River. We noticed with astonishment that, at the confluence of these two masses of water, the current appeared to be suspended for some miles, a fact that seemed to indicate an equality of volume and force in the two rivers at this spot.

As one leaves the mouth of the Ohio, the appearance of the banks of the Mississippi changes completely. The shores are higher and also offer a greater number of dwelling-places. At intervals one finds traces of the old French settlements, and pretty, well-timbered islands present themselves from time to time to the eyes of the sailor, like beautiful bouquets of greenery, and break the monotony of the river. At first, one encounters the Island of Birds, made delightful by its blooms, then those of the Two Sisters and the Dog's Tooth. Finally, there is English Island, which recalls the first settlement made by the English in the middle of these wildernesses in 1765, which was almost immediately destroyed by the Indians, who saw with regret their old friends, the French, dispossessed by traders whom they did not like. Forty miles from the confluence stand, nearly opposite each other, Cape Girardeau and Cape Lacroix, each named in this manner by the French whom Frontenac, Governor of Canada, sent to confirm the statement of the Indians who said to him that from *the northern border ran a great river which neither went towards the place where the Great Spirit rises, nor towards the place where it falls*. There is now on Cape Girardeau a small town, recently founded, which already has begun to prosper. A little further upriver on the eastern bank, one sees the ruins of old fortifications, which present themselves in an altogether picturesque manner. These are the remains of Fort Chartres, constructed at great expense in 1753 by the French for the defense of the upper Mississippi, and now abandoned by the Americans as entirely useless.

Several hours after having passed by Fort Chartres, while we were walking on the deck of our ship, our Captain pointed out to us a flock of young Louisiana geese, led by their mother and the father. The elegant shape, and the so well-delineated plumage of these beautiful birds, made me want to lay hands on the entire family. Immediately, I sprang into the longboat with two sailors whom the Captain had assigned to me, and I wended my way toward the goose family while trying to confine it between us and the riverbank. The parents, frightened, made their escape to the shore while uttering loud cries; but the little ones, too weak still to fly or to clear the steepness of the banks, soon fell, in large part into our hands, and we carried five back, which our Captain was kind enough to keep, while promising us to raise them with care and bring them to New Orleans, from which Mr. Caire undertook to send them to La Grange, in order to populate the General's farm.[8]

As I was returning from this little expedition, I noticed in the middle of the river another very tempting quarry; it was a superb stag swimming with as much calmness and skill as if he were in his natural element. When he heard our shouts mixing with the noise of our steam engine, he put his long, branching antlers on his back, plunged into the water to escape from our sight, and rapidly went far away from us by hurling himself into the strongest currents. When he felt protected from our pursuit, he reappeared on the water, set his antlers upright again proudly, and continued his trip tranquilly. It is not rare, our traveling companions tell us, to see many of these animals passing in this way from one shore of the river to the other and visiting the fertile islands that adorn its course.

---

8. These geese, as well as some Mexican hoccos given by Mr. Duplantier, some wild turkeys given by Mr. Thousand of Baltimore, some Devonshire cows given by Mr. Patterson, some partridges of a species unique to America given by Mr. Skinner, etc., today adorn La Grange where General Lafayette does his utmost to preserve and multiply their species.

A hundred miles from the Ohio, the banks of the Mississippi suddenly take on an imposing look: they rise precipitously to more than 80 or 100 feet above the water level. The riverbanks are made of very hard granite. Throughout their entire height, they are impressed with deep, horizontal furrows that appear to have been hollowed out by the friction of the water when the river flowed to the different heights that they mark. Some of these furrows are nearly a foot deep: they are spaced unequally to each other, and they indicate the successive lowering of the waters. At the current level of the river, the furrow is barely outlined. How much time then has been necessary for the formation of each furrow by the sole action of the water on so hard a stone? The solution of this single question would perhaps greatly disturb the calculations of the makers of systems that pretend to determine the time of the formation of our globe.

Some distance further up the river, the steep rocks leave a rather large gap with the shoreline where Herculaneum stands. The location of this village is altogether romantic; the towers, built on the rock that crowns it unevenly, give it a fantastic character, and pique the curiosity of travelers. From the height of these towers, which jut out precipitously from the hewn stone, they throw molten lead, which cools down by rolling in the air, becomes round, and fall as lead shot into vast containers of water placed below. The large or small holes of the iron sieve through which the lead passes when they pour it while boiling hot form the different calibers that they desire to have to use them in hunting. Lead mines which are found in abundance on the banks of the Merrimac River, which flows into the Mississippi ten miles from this spot, have given birth to these establishments whose prosperity grows every day.

On the 28th, at the end of the day, we arrived at a rather poor village that the French founded formerly under the sad name of *Vide-Poche*, and which today is known better by the name of Carondelet. Although we were no more than six or seven miles from St. Louis, as we could not arrive there by daylight, the members of the different committees who accompanied the General resolved to pass the night at anchor on the river, and to wait until the next day to arrive in this City. As soon as the inhabitants of Carondelet had knowledge of the presence of General Lafayette in their vicinity, they rushed in a crowd aboard the boat in order to greet him. They are nearly all French. For a long time the settlement consisted of about 60 homes at most, and promised but little growth. Little-suited for commerce, the people were engaged only in agriculture, yet only in a manner to provide just the necessities of life. Most came from Canada, and settled on a portion of land along the Mississippi without learning whom these lands belonged to. They cultivated these lands, some for 10 years, others for 20, and none among them thought of assuring themselves of the ownership of the little farm that he had created by the sweat of his brow. Today, as the United States Government sells much of the lands that it possesses in these regions, these unfortunates run the risk at every moment of seeing themselves dispossessed by purchasers who will come to claim their rights. They spoke of their concerns to the General, who promised them that he would make their situation known to the Federal Government and that he would take an interest in their fate. These good people, in the simplicity of their gratitude, offered him, whom they already regarded as their protector, all that they thought would please him; one brought him some tame geese of the Mississippi, another a young doe which he had raised; still another, some petrifications and shells he believed to be valuable. The General saw that if he refused their gifts he would wound their feelings; thus, he hastened to accept them and arranged afterwards that they receive tokens of his gratitude.

On April 29, in the morning, we saw arrive aboard our ship Governor Clark of Missouri, Governor Coles of Illinois, and Colonel Benton, all three of whom came to accompany the General up to St. Louis. Some moments later, a steamship, *The Plough Boy*, filled with a large number of citizens, drew up alongside *The Natchez*, and the Nation's Guest was saluted by a triple cheer that made the forests of Missouri echo with *Welcome Lafayette*. Then we raised anchor, and at nine o'clock we noticed a considerable assemblage of structures, of rather whimsical architecture, rising in the middle of beautiful clusters of greenery and cheerful gardens, overlooking the river's course in the distance. It was the City of St. Louis; its name, and the language of a part of its inhabitants, soon recalled to us its origin. But if we were struck by the diversity of the languages in which they greeted General Lafayette, we were no less struck by the uniformity of the sentiments that they displayed towards him. The riverbank was covered by the entire population who answered by their shouts of joy the clamorous greeting of the artillery of our two ships. At the moment when the General set foot on land, Dr. Lane, Mayor of the City, presented himself to him at the head of the municipal corps and greeted him in these words:

> Welcome, Lafayette, to the distant regions of our immense republic. Few men among us have had the good fortune to look upon your venerable face; but your heroic acts are engraved in our memory and in our hearts in indelible strokes. Your sacrifices in the service of the cause of our Fatherland during the weakness of its infancy without coveting any reward other than the one that a generous soul finds in the accomplishment of a good deed; your devotion to the defense

> of the rights of our Nation, and your hospitality towards those of our compatriots who went to France during this stormy time; your voluntary renunciation of your hereditary privileges; your constancy in the defense of the rights of man, good order and rational liberty; in a word, the steadfastedness and purity of your long life in so many difficult circumstances are known to us completely. And we will explain to our descendants that magical effect which your presence exercises on our citizens, who rapturously experience a feeling of gratitude and veneration towards you which perhaps can be equaled, but never surpassed.
>
> In offering to you and your family the cordial hospitality of our City, we take pleasure in hoping that the sight of some of your former companions-in-arms, and especially the enjoyment of contemplating in your old age the rapid propagation of those principles of government to the establishment of which you had contributed so successfully and directly in your youth, will cause you to settle among us.

At the moment the General pronounced the last words of his response to the Mayor, an elegant carriage drawn by four horses approached the riverbank and received him to take him to the City, through all the ways of which we traveled in the midst of the acclamations of the people. He was accompanied by Auguste Chouteau, the venerable old man by whom St. Louis was founded by Mr. Hempstead, a former Revolutionary soldier, and by the Mayor. These gentlemen led him to the house of Mr. Chouteau's son, which had been prepared to receive him, and which stood open to every citizen indiscriminately who wanted to visit with the National Guest. Among the visitors, the General found with pleasure Mr. Hamilton, son of General Alexander Hamilton, former aide-de-camp of Washington, whom General Lafayette had loved so much, and an old French sergeant of Rochambeau's army, named Bellissime. The later could not contain the expression of joy that he felt in seeing a compatriot honored in this way by the American Nation.

The inhabitants of St. Louis knew that General Lafayette could only pass a few hours among them, and they put to good use the little time that he could spare by having him see everything of interest that their City or its environs contained. While the dinner was being prepared at Pierre Chouteau's house, we left in a carriage to visit, on the banks of the river, traces of ancient Indian monuments that some travelers say are tombs and others consider to be ancient fortifications or places of assembly for the celebration of religious rites. Unfortunately, all these opinions are equally subject to debate because these monuments have not preserved distinctive-enough characteristics for one to be able to draw reasonable conclusions. Those that are close to St. Louis are nothing but high ground covered with turf whose ordinary shape is a rectangle. Their common height is barely eight feet, but must have been very much more considerable before the soil had settled over the centuries. Their sides all are on an incline, and the average length of their base is 80 to 100 feet, their width varies from 30 to 60 feet; what leads me to believe that these earthen monuments were never used to establish fortifications is that none of these masses is surrounded by ditches and that they are located too near to one another. These *mounds* (this is how the Americans call all these monuments) are not only common in the vicinity of St. Louis, but also in the entire State of Missouri, in that of Indiana, and on the banks of the Ohio, where one encounters, they say, much more interesting ruins of the greatest antiquity. This seems to indicate that this world, which we call *new,* was the seat of a civilization perhaps much earlier than that of Europe.[9]

From the *mounds* of St. Louis to the confluence of the Missouri and the Mississippi would have been only a three- or four-hour trip; but the General's time was calculated to such a degree that we were obliged to forego the pleasure that viewing the junction of these two rivers, which have their origins in the midst of regions in which nature alone still holds unrivaled sway, would have procured for us; and we returned to the City to visit the collection of Indian curiosities of Governor Clark. This collection is the most complete and the most varied that it may be possible to find. We visited it with much more interest since it was shown to us by its creator, Mr. Clark, who himself collected all the objects of which it is composed in the faraway regions that he traversed with Captain Lewis.

One finds there all the clothing, arms, fishing, hunting and military implements in use among the diverse tribes that dwell towards the sources of the Missouri and the Mississippi. Among the objects that commonly serve as dress for Indian hunters, collars made of claws of a prodigious size caught our attention. These claws come, said Mr. Clark, from the most frightening of the animals of the American continent, the grizzly bears of the Missouri, whose ferocious intelligence increases the terror which their size and their prodigious strength inspire. The bears of this species join together, 10 or 12 in number, sometimes more, to hunt and share their prey in common. Man is their game of choice, and when they fall upon his tracks, they hunt him down with *barks* like our hounds chasing a rabbit, and it is difficult for a man to escape the

---

9. On this subject, see the very interesting work of Mr. Warden entitled: *Researches on the Antiquities of North America.*

persistence of their pursuit. This animal is altogether unknown in Europe, even in the most magnificent menageries. The Collection of Natural History of London possesses only one claw, which they consider a great rarity.[10]

Mr. Clark visited some Indian tribes near the sources of the Missouri and the Mississippi which, until he did, had never seen a White man, and among which he had nonetheless found traces of ancient connections with peoples more civilized than themselves. Thus, for example, he brought back a whip that the horsemen of these tribes use to ride their horses, and its knots, the arrangement of which is very complicated, are arranged exactly like the knots of the *Knot* of the Cossacks. He presented an article of clothing of a chief of these tribes to General Lafayette, and this garment has a striking resemblance to a Russian frock coat. It is made of buffalo skin so well-prepared that it has all the suppleness of a skin dressed by the most skilled tanner. From these facts and some others, Mr. Clark and Captain Lewis, his traveling-companion, concluded that there existed in the past near the pole a connecting route between Asia and America. In 1814 these two intrepid travelers published an interesting account of the trip which they made in 1804, 1805 and 1806, by order of the American Government, to explore the sources of the Missouri and the course of the Columbia River up to the Pacific Ocean.

We would have willingly stayed still much longer in Governor Clark's museum to listen to the learned particulars that he had the kindness to give us about his prodigious travels; but they advised us that the dinner hour was approaching, and we withdrew to proceed to Pierre Chouteau's house. On the way we visited attentively the part of the City that we had not yet seen. We were amazed at the whimsical construction of some homes that appeared to us to be the oldest ones built. They were generally composed of a single story, surrounded by a balcony covered by a large, projecting roof. Someone pointed out that formerly the ground floor was not inhabited, and that the staircase that led to the higher floor was movable and could be removed at will. This precaution was inspired in past times by the need of the first inhabitants of St. Louis to obtain shelter from nocturnal and unexpected attacks of the Indians who looked upon the permanent settlement of Whites in their midst with anxiety. When St. Louis, a weak village, passed under Spanish dominion, the Indians of the environs were still so numerous and so enterprising that the inhabitants could hardly resist them and hardly dared to travel any more. They report that, in 1794, an Indian military chief, with a part of his Nation, entered St. Louis and addressed these words to the Spanish Lieutenant Governor from whom he had demanded an interview:

---

10. Since his return to France, General Lafayette has received a young Missouri Bear which was sent to him by Governor Clark. He has presented it to the professors of the Botanical Garden, who have had it placed in the menagerie where the public can now see it.

> We have come to offer you peace. We have warred against you for many moons, and what has resulted? Nothing. Our warriors have used all their means to fight yours, but you do not want to, you do not dare to, measure your strength with us! You are a pack of old women! What can one do with such people, if not make peace, since they do not want to fight? Thus, I come to offer it to you, to bury the hatchet, to lighten the chain and to open communication with you again.

Since that time the Indian tribes have become considerably weakened and, in large part, they have moved to distant places; that part that stays in the vicinity of St. Louis displays an altogether peaceful disposition towards the inhabitants with whom they do a considerable trade in furskins. Besides, today, the population of St. Louis is numerous enough to have nothing to fear from such neighbors any more. It is about 6,000 and will probably double in a few years because this City appears to be called to a brilliant future in these vast regions, in the midst of which civilization, led by American liberty and industry, advances with giant strides.

St. Louis is already the great warehouse for all the commerce of the regions to the west of the Mississippi. Its location nearly at the junction of four or five large rivers, whose branches border all the most distant extremities of the Union, renders communication easy and speedy with all the places that can supply the necessities or luxuries to its fortunate inhabitants. How astonished is the mind when one considers that such prosperity is the work of only a few years, and that the founder of such a thriving city still lives today and has enjoyed for a long time the results that he had not only not hoped for but which he even would have refused to believe, if they had predicted them to his young and ardent imagination when, for the first time, he landed on the deserted shores of the Mississippi. This enterprising man who with his own hatchet cut down the first tree of the ancient forest where the City of St. Louis is located; who already accustomed to the difficult work of clearing land, built with his hands the first house around which, in so short a time, the buildings of a prosperous city were to be grouped; who, by his courage and his conciliatory spirit, at first repressed the fury of the Indians and later won their goodwill; this fortunate man is Auguste Chouteau.

I have already named him as one of those who was charged by the inhabitants of St. Louis to show the Guest of the American Nation around their City. It was at the house of his son, Pierre Chouteau, that we took our places at the banquet of republican gratitude. It was a very interesting thing to see seated at the same table the founder of a great city, one of the principal defenders of the independence of a great nation and the representatives of four young republics, already made prosperous by their industry, made powerful by liberty and made happy by their wise institutions. As one could imagine, the conversation was animated and most interesting; they questioned Auguste Chouteau very much about the adventurous undertakings of his youth. They asked the friend, the companion-in-arms of Washington, about some details of the glorious and decisive Virginia Campaign; and they listened with pleasure to the delegations of Louisiana, Mississippi, Tennessee and Missouri paint the picture of the prosperity of their respective lands. What moved General Lafayette perhaps most in this gathering was the unanimity of sentiments among the table-companions who, although not all speaking the same language, were nonetheless in so much agreement about the excellence of the republican institutions under which they deemed themselves fortunate to live.

Before leaving the banquet to proceed to the ball that the ladies had prepared, they exchanged toasts, all of which bore the imprint of the fortunate harmony that reigned between the old French population and the new American population. Mr. Delassus, formerly Lieutenant Governor of Louisiana, drank: "*To the United States and to France*! May these two countries again produce a Washington and a Lafayette for the liberation of the rest of the world!"

Governor Coles toasted: "*To France*, made dear to our hearts by so many memories, but especially for having given birth to our Lafayette."

General Lafayette ended by toasting the health of the venerable patriarch who in 1763 founded the City of St. Louis; and, immediately after, we left the table to go to the ball, where we found the most brilliant and most numerous company which was ever assembled, they say, on the western shore of the Mississippi. The lustre of the decorations of the hall and the elegance of the ladies who filled it made us forget entirely that we were at the entrance to a wilderness that the Indians themselves considered to be insufficient to their simple needs, since they only lived there periodically. We participated in the pleasures of the evening up to nearly midnight, the hour at which we returned on board *The Natchez*, in order to take a little rest while awaiting the return of daylight that was to illuminate our departure. At the moment when we were going to set sail, several citizens of St. Louis offered us some objects of interest, such as bows, arrows, peace pipes, and clothing of the Indians of the Missouri; we accepted with gratitude these tokens of goodwill that we have saved as sweet souvenirs of the happy times spent so far from our country.

Chapter IX

Changes Occurring in the Navigation of the Mississippi Since the Use of Steam Power – Arrival at Kaskaskia – The Canadians and the Indians – Remarkable Meeting with an Indian Girl Brought up Among the Whites and Returned to the Uncivilized Life – Indian Ballad – State of Illinois – Departure from Kaskaskia – Separation of General Lafayette and the Louisiana Delegation.

Governor Coles, who had sailed with us, requested of General Lafayette and obtained his assent that he would not leave from the shores of the Mississippi without visiting the State of Illinois in front of which we would pass while descending the river. It was decided that we would stop at Kaskaskia, a large village of that State, and, although we were nearly 24 miles from it, we arrived there a little after noon, so successful and rapid had our sail been. Since the fortunate application of steam to navigation, the changes occurring in the relations among the riverside towns of the Mississippi have been prodigious. Formerly the trip from New Orleans to St. Louis required three to four months of the most difficult work that one could imagine. The motion of the oar not always sufficing to conquer the resistance of the river's current, the crew were often obliged to cause the boat to be towed by some men who, with the aid of a small skiff, went in front of the boat from time to time in order to use one of the trees of the riverbank as a point of support. This procedure, slow and difficult, and the hardships and the bad diet that were the result, caused diseases in the crews of the boats to which a third of the men customarily succumbed. Today this same trip, which is nearly 1,250 miles, is made in ten days without hardship, without privations, between a good bed and a good table, and often in very good company; the return is usually made in five days; so that New Orleans and St. Louis, which are separated by such a great distance, are nonetheless now accustomed to be considered as two neighboring cities, whose inhabitants know each other better and make reciprocal visits more often than those of Paris and Bordeaux are able to do.

General Lafayette was not expected in Kaskaskia, and nothing had been prepared for this unforeseen visit. While we were disembarking, someone ran to the village, which is located about a half a mile from the shore, and soon returned with a carriage for the General who, a moment later, saw himself surrounded by a large number of citizens who rushed up to welcome him. In the procession that formed to accompany him, one saw neither military trappings nor the brilliant triumphs that they had bestowed on him in the prosperous cities, but the tones of joy and of republican gratitude that struck his ears must have been very sweet to his heart, since they proved that the love and veneration of the people for their founders had also been perpetuated everywhere where American freedom had spread.

We followed the General on foot, and we arrived at nearly the same time as he did at the house of General Edgar, a venerable soldier of the Revolution, who welcomed him with affectionate enthusiasm and who ordered that all his doors remain open so that all the citizens could enjoy with him the pleasure of clasping the hand of the adopted son of America. After they had allowed a few moments to the rather tumultuous explosion of feelings that the presence of the General inspired in the citizens, Governor Coles raised his voice and requested silence of the citizens, which they accorded to him with an alacrity and a respect that proved to me that his authority rested, not only on the law, but also on the general affection for him. He then advanced towards Lafayette, around whom the circle of spectators had grown a little, and addressed him with an emotional speech in which he depicted for him the raptures that his presence caused among the population of the State of Illinois and the auspicious influence that the memory of his visit would engender later in the young witnesses of the enthusiasm of their fathers today for one of the most valiant founders of their freedom. "Love of liberty," he said,

> Which is the sentiment characteristic of the Americans, does not exercise more sway over our hearts than our enthusiastic devotion to and our veneration for the heroes and the sages of our Revolution. We glory in their actions, we consecrate their memory, we venerate their names, we are devoted to their principles, and we are firmly resolved never to renounce the rights and the freedoms won by their virtue, their valor and their wisdom.... Animated by these sentiments and in the presence of one of the most virtuous, most disinterested and most heroic champions of our rights and of our independence, in the presence of one of the fathers of our republic, of an apostle of liberty, a benefactor of the human race, our emotion does not allow us to express the nature and the force of the feelings which stir in us any further....

Here, indeed, Governor Coles' voice faltered noticeably, and he was obliged to break off in order to collect his thoughts. During this moment of utter silence, I glanced at the gathering in the midst of which I found myself, and I was struck with astonishment in noticing the variety and the strangeness of its makeup. Alongside men whom the dignity of their bearing and the patriotic excitement of their expression made easily recognizable as Americans, were other men whose coarser clothes, the liveliness and the intensity of their movements, the expansive joy of their faces, recalled very much the natives of my country; behind those near the door and on the veranda that surrounded the house, some large reddish figures, semi-nude, leaning on a bow or a long rifle, remained outside motionless and impassive; they were some of the Indians from the surrounding area.

After a pause of several seconds, the Governor resumed his speech, which he ended by presenting faithfully and with great eloquence the list of benefits that America had received from its freedom and of the fortunate influence that its republican institutions would exert on the rest of the world one day. When the speaker had concluded, a faint murmur of approval arose in the assembly and was prolonged until they noticed that General Lafayette was going to respond; then an attentive silence resumed, and each person, desirous of hearing him, drew nearer to him and contracted the circle around him. Then he took the floor and said:

> It is with deep pleasure, Sir, that I find myself in the State of Illinois, and that I see myself welcomed, in the name of the people, by the respected Governor whose sentiments in regards to me, expressed with so much kindness, fill me with gratitude, while his patriotic hopes, his liberal pronouncements, inspire in me the greatest sympathy and the highest respect. A sacred promise, well-known by all the citizens of the United States, obliges me to shorten my visit to the western part of the Union, but I take inexpressible satisfaction in having seen for myself the growth of the prosperity and of the importance of this young State, such as they are, trebly guaranteed by its republican institutions, by all of its local advantages, and by its generous resolve to cultivate these blessings according to the purest principles of American freedom. To these cordial congratulations, I add my thanks for the honor that you have done me by associating my name to those of my well-loved and venerated friends. Accept, I beg of you, for the citizens of the State of Illinois, for the representatives in the two houses, as well as for their First Magistrate, the expression of my gratitude for the affectionate invitation that they had addressed to me, for the reception that was given to me today in the patriotic town of Kaskaskia. I join to this all good wishes of my devotion and my respect.

After these reciprocal felicitations, another no-less interesting scene ensued. Some former Revolutionary soldiers left the crowd and came to shake the hand of their former general; while he was conversing with them and listening to them cite with emotion the names of those of their old companions-in-arms who also fought at Brandywine and at Yorktown, but to whom the enjoyment of the fruits of their labors had not been given, nor the ability to add their voices today to that of a grateful country, those men whom I had noticed to have some relation to our French countrymen, in dress and in manners, came and went vivaciously into all parts of the room where they sometimes formed small groups in the midst of which one heard the most open and the most animated expressions of joy burst out in the French language.

Having been introduced to one of these groups by a member of the committee of Kaskaskia, I was received at first with great goodwill, and soon I was overwhelmed with a multitude of different questions when they learned that I was French and that I was accompanying General Lafayette. “What! You also come from the great France? Will you give us some news of this beautiful, dear country? Are they happy there, are they free as we are here? Ah! What a pleasure to see some good Frenchmen from the great France!” And the questions succeeded one another so rapidly that I did not know which one to listen to any more. I was not long in realizing that these good people had as much ignorance about the affairs that concerned their Motherland as enthusiasm for it. They knew of France only what tradition had preserved among them of the reign of Louis XIV; and they had no idea of the convulsions which have rent the country of their fathers for 40 years. “Haven’t you had,” said one of them who had just asked me a host of questions about General Lafayette that an American child of ten would not have asked, “haven’t you had, in addition, another famous general, called Napoleon, who has made very many glorious wars for you?” I think that, if Napoleon had heard a similar question asked, his vanity would have suffered somewhat. He who believed that he had filled the universe with his name, because he had overturned some ancient thrones in Europe and destroyed freedom in France, nonetheless was hardly known on the banks of the Mississippi! At 5,000 miles, at most, from the scene of his glory, they spoke his name only while expressing doubt! In truth, there is something there to discourage the most burning passion for fame….

I did my best to answer the questions of my Canadian, and to make him, as well as those who surrounded him, understand who this *famous General Napoleon* was. At the recitation of his exploits they first clasped each others’ hands and drew themselves up with an air of superiority, while saying: “That is how it is among our brave French…. It is only among them that one can find a man like that!” But when I told them how the famous general had made himself Consul; how he had made himself Emperor; how he had destroyed our freedoms and crippled the exercise of our rights in succession;

how finally he himself was felled while leaving us, after 20 years of war, nearly at the point from which we had left at the beginning of our Revolution, they all became sad as if they were going to weep, and exclaimed:

> And you have suffered all that! How, in beautiful France, in great France, is one not free like in the State of Illinois! Good God, is it possible! What, you cannot write freely all that you think? You cannot go everywhere without a passport! It isn't you who name the mayors of the towns and villages? It isn't you who choose the governors or the prefects in your departments or your provinces? You do not have the right to elect your representatives to the National Assembly? None of you are called to the election of the head of the Government, and yet you all pay such heavy taxes! Well, good God, our good Frenchmen of the great France are then more to be pitied than the Negro Slaves of Louisiana whom they say, for all that, are very unfortunate! Because, in a word, if the latter do not practice any of the rights that all of us practice here, at least they don't give money to anyone and have masters who feed them….

During all these exclamations, I did not know what to say anymore. My face turned red, and I confess that my national pride suffered singularly in hearing some ignorant Canadians express sentiments of pity for my compatriots; and to make a comparison to their disadvantage between the wretched Slaves and them, but these sentiments were too well-established for me to be able to complain of them, and I kept silent. I only promised myself to be more discreet in the future and not to speak with so much abandon in front of free men about the political condition of my country.

While I was conversing with the Canadians, the crowd, motivated by a sense of delicacy and kindly attentiveness, withdrew imperceptively to allow General Lafayette the time to take some moments of rest while waiting for the hour of the banquet that the citizens were preparing in haste. Desirous of profiting from the short time that we were to stay at Kaskaskia, I went along with George Lafayette to explore the environs of the village, or to converse with some inhabitants, and we left the General with our other traveling companions and some former Revolutionary soldiers at General Edgar's house. Having arrived at the public square, we found nearly all the citizens walking together and conversing joyously about the event of the day. We found in their groups the same variety of countenances as that which had struck us so greatly in the reception hall; while George was collecting from an American some details on the origin and current situation of Kaskaskia, I approached a small circle of Indians in the middle of which stood a man of great height and strange appearance. His face, without being copper-colored like that of the Indians, was nonetheless very tanned. His short clothes, his wide waistband from which a powder horn hung, his long leather gaiters extending above his knees, all his attire, in a word, gave proof of a hunter of the forests. He was leaning on a long carbine, and appeared to inspire by his speaking a lively interest in those who were listening to him. When he saw me, he came towards me without haste, but with a marked goodwill. He held out his hand; I gave him mine which he clasped cordially. I experienced a moment's hesitation before speaking to him, not knowing if he understood English or French; but he spoke to me first himself in the latter language, and I soon found myself very much at ease with him.

He informed me that he was of mixed blood, that his mother was of the Kickapoo tribe and his father was a White man having come from Canada and speaking the French language. He customarily lived among the Indians of the vicinity, who have very much affection and great respect for him, because, despite the 50 years and the wear and tear that was beginning to turn his hair white, he is still their equal in running, in hunting, in all the bodily exercises, and he often serves them as an intermediary with the Whites, whose language he understands perfectly, although his usual language is that of the Indians. Those who surrounded him were not all similarly clad or painted. It was also easy to discern some differences in their features and in their manners. I concluded from this that they were not all from the same tribe. The tall hunter confirmed this opinion of mine while telling me that at this time there were three or four camps of Indians around Kaskaskia, having come to sell their fur skins, the product of their great winter hunt. He named for me the different tribes which occupied these camps, but their names were so unusual, or so badly pronounced, that I could not understand them; indeed I heard only that of *Miami* which, repeated two or three times, made a small man, who up to then had held himself motionless before me, wrapped in a wool blanket, rouse himself; his face, debased by intemperance, was painted red, blue and yellow. At this name Miami, he raised his head, assumed a ridiculous air of dignity, and said to me: "I was to be chief of the Miami Nation. My grandfather was chief, my father was chief; but the Miami have decided, unjustly, that I would not succeed my father, and today, instead of having a large quantity of furs to sell, I have nothing: I will leave Kaskaskia without being able to take away arms, munitions or tobacco…." While he spoke in this manner, a man painted like him, but of very tall stature and athletic form, was regarding him with a contemptuous look. He said to him, while striking him lightly on the shoulder:

> How dare you complain of the justice of the Miamis? Your grandfather was our chief, you say? Your father was our chief also? But have you then forgotten that your grandfather was the bravest of our warriors, and that the wisdom of your father in our councils was listened to like the voice of the Great Spirit! But you, by what right would you be a commander of men? Weak as an old woman, you haven't even the courage to hunt to satisfy your needs, and you would surrender us to the Whites for a bottle of fire-water….

A scornful gesture concluded this harsh invective, which the tall hunter immediately translated for me in French; and the fallen prince, leaning sadly on a little bow, like those with which Indian children practice, kept his silence. His fate appeared to me to be truly worthy of pity; but, nonetheless, I could not refrain from a feeling of esteem for the Miami Nation, which does not believe that *legitimacy* in a prince could take the place of all the virtues.

I was still in the midst of the Indians, questioning the tall hunter on the state and the strength of their tribes, which civilization is rapidly decimating, when I saw arriving the secretary of the Governor of Louisiana, Mr. Caire, who came to propose that I go with him to visit an Indian encampment whose location they had pointed out to him a very little distance from the village. I accepted, and we left immediately so as to be able to return for the dinner hour. On leaving Kaskaskia we first passed the river of the same name over a wooden bridge, solidly built and very well-maintained. Afterwards we walked about 20 minutes in a plain up to the entrance of a forest which we went into by a narrow footpath marked out along a stream. As we advanced, the ground rose more steeply to our right and to our left, and soon we found ourselves in a kind of gorge formed by a succession of little hills covered with very thick woods. After a good quarter of an hour walk, we arrived at a barrier, which we scaled and behind which two horses passed, attracting our attention by the sound of the bells that they wore on their necks. A little further along the gorge grew larger and formed a delightful little valley, in the middle of which some huts made of bark stood in a semicircle; it was the Indian camp that we were looking for.

All the doors of the huts were turned towards the inside of the circle, and the floor of the huts, raised about three feet off the ground, was slightly inclined, like the planking of a camp-bed. With the exception of a very old woman, occupied with cooking some maize on a fire in the open air, we found no one else in the camp. Whether she harbored ill will or she understood neither French or English, this woman did not answer any of our questions and observed us, with the greatest indifference, look at and even touch all the objects in the huts which piqued our curiosity the most. All was arranged with sufficient order, and it was easy to recognize the place which the women occupied by the little toilet utensils such as mirrors, combs, pouches of paints to color the face, etc., that we noticed there. After a rather detailed examination of the entire little camp, we were going to withdraw when my attention was arrested by the sight of a kind of very small mill wheel, on the bank of the stream that traversed the camp, that appeared to have been thrown on the shores by the swift current. I picked it up and put it back where I believed it had been originally placed by some children on two stones that were raised a little above the water; and the current, striking its wings lightly, made it turn rapidly. This childish act, which probably would have left my memory and which I would not be talking about now if, on that very evening, it had not put me in a rather extraordinary position vis-à-vis the Indians, aroused the attention of the old woman very greatly who, by her gestures, expressed lively satisfaction to us.

On returning to Kaskaskia we found, at that place, Mr. de Syon, a very amiable young Frenchman of great intelligence who, on the invitation of General Lafayette, had left Washington with us to visit the States of the South and the West. Like us he had just made an excursion into the environs, and appeared to be very joyful at the discovery that he had made; he had met in the middle of the forest at the head of a band of Indians a young, rather pretty woman, who spoke French very well and who expressed herself with a grace that he still appeared to be amazed at. She had asked him if it was true that Lafayette was in Kaskaskia, and, on his affirmative response, she had evinced a great desire to see him. "I always carry on my person," she said to Mr. de Syon, "a relic that is very precious to me; I should like to show it to him; it would prove to him that his name is no less venerated in the midst of our tribes than among the American Whites for whom he fought…." And, in so speaking, she pulled from her bosom a small letter case that enclosed a letter wrapped carefully in several pieces of paper. "It is from Lafayette," she said, "he wrote it to my father a long time ago, and my father, while dying, left it to me as the most precious thing that he possessed…." At the sight of this letter, Mr. de Syon had proposed to this young Indian woman that she follow him to Kaskaskia, while assuring her that General Lafayette would feel very great pleasure in seeing her; but this proposal appeared to embarrass her, and under various pretexts, poorly enough chosen, she refused to come there. "Nonetheless," she added, "if you will have something to tell me this evening, you will find me in my camp which is very near the village; everyone will show you the route because I am very well known in Kaskaskia: my name is *Mary*."

Mr. de Syon's narration piqued my curiosity deeply, and I would have willingly left at once with him in search of Mary; but at that moment a member of the committee of Kaskaskia came to notify us that they were going to sit down to dinner; and, indeed, we saw General Lafayette leaving General Edgar's house, in the midst of a procession of numerous citizens, and traversing the square to proceed to Colonel Sweet's house where the meal had been prepared. We joined the procession and took our places at the banquet where the General found himself seated under a vault made of flowers prepared by the ladies of Kaskaskia with so much skill and taste that it produced the effect of a rainbow by the mixing of the most vivid colors.

I had spoken to General Lafayette about the encounter with the young Indian girl; and since he displayed a desire to see her, I left the table with Mr. de Syon at the time when the table-companions were beginning to exchange patriotic toasts, and we sought a guide to lead us to Mary's camp. Chance served us wonderfully since we spoke to an Indian of the same tribe that we wanted to visit. Led by him, we passed over the Kaskaskia bridge, and soon, in spite of the darkness that was beginning to envelop us, I recognized the footpath and the brook that I had followed in the morning with Mr. Caire. At the moment when we were going to climb over the barrier that crossed the road, we were stopped by the frightening howls of two enormous dogs who leapt forward to defend the passage and who would have probably have ill-treated us if the voice of our guide, which they doubtless recognized, had not suddenly calmed them. We arrived without other obstacles in the middle of the camp, which was illuminated by an enormous fire, around which about a dozen Indians, crouching on their heels, were conversing while preparing their supper; they welcomed us cordially, and, as soon as they were informed about the reason for our visit, one of them conducted us to the hut belonging to Mary, whom we found asleep on a bison skin. At the voice of Mr. de Syon, which she recognized, she sprang up from the ground, and listened attentively to the invitation which we gave her on behalf of General Lafayette to come to Kaskaskia; she appeared to be very flattered by it; but she told us that, before deciding whether to follow us, she wanted to speak to her husband.

While she consulted with him, I heard a shrill cry uttered; I turned around, and I saw near me the old woman whom I had found alone in the camp in the morning; she had just recognized me in the gleam of the fireplace flame, and had just pointed me out to her companions who, immediately quitting their work, hurled themselves into a circle around me and began to dance with great displays of joy and gratitude. Their bronze and nearly naked bodies, their outlandishly painted faces, their expressive pantomime, the reflection of the flames that painted all the surrounding objects reddish, all gave to this scene a look that had something infernal about it; and, for a minute, I believed myself to be in the midst of demons. Witnessing my embarrassment, Mary put an end to it by ordering the dancing to stop, then gave me an explanation of the *honors* that they had rendered to me. "When we want to learn if an enterprise that we are considering will be successful," she said,

> We place in the flow of a stream a small wheel resting lightly on two stones; if the wheel turns for three days without being knocked over, the omen is favorable, but if the current sweeps it along and throws it on the shore, it is certain proof that our projects are not approved by the Great Spirit, unless a stranger comes to raise the little wheel before the end of the third day. You are the stranger who has restored our manitou and our hopes, and it is for this reason that you have been celebrated among us.

In pronouncing these words, Mary allowed an ironic smile, which made me doubt her belief in the "manitou," to play on her lips. "You do not appear very convinced," I said to her, "of the efficacy of the service that I have rendered in raising up your manitou?" She silently shook her head, then raising her eyes towards the sky, she said: "they have taught me to place my trust higher; … all my hopes rest on the god whom they have taught me about, the god of the Christians…." — I had, at first, been very astonished in hearing an Indian woman speak French so well, and I was no less astonished in learning that she was Christian; Mary noticed it and, in order to end my astonishment, she began to tell me her history, while her husband and the warriors who were to accompany her to Kaskaskia hastily had their supper, which consisted of maize cooked in milk.

She told me that her father, who was chief of one of the Nations that lived on the shores of the Great Lakes of the North, had once fought with about 100 of his men under the command of Lafayette, when Lafayette commanded an army on the frontiers of the North; that he had won great glory, and earned the friendship of the Americans; a long time after, that is to say about 20 years, for reasons unknown to Mary, he had left the banks of the Great Lakes with some of his warriors, his wife and his daughter; and, after having traveled for a very long time, he had come to settle on the banks of the Illinois River. "I was very young then," Mary told me,

> But I have, nonetheless, still not forgotten the horrible suffering that we endured during this trip, which was made in the middle of a harsh winter, across a country peopled by

Nations whom we did not know; our sufferings were such that my poor mother, who had nearly always carried me on her shoulders, already very loaded down with baggage, died from them some days after our arrival. My father placed me in the care of another woman who had also emigrated with us and occupied himself with the means to assure us peaceful possession of the lands on which we had just settled, by making an alliance with our new neighbors; the Kickapoos were the ones who welcomed us best; and we soon considered ourselves as making up a part of their Nation. In the following year, my father was chosen by them, with some of their own, to go to settle some interests of the Nation with the agent of the United States Government residing here at Kaskaskia; he wanted me to make the trip; although the Kickapoos had shown themselves to be very generous and hospitable to him, nonetheless, he feared that war would break out in his absence, because he already knew of all the schemes of the English to incite the Indians against the Americans; it was this same concern that committed him to accede to the request that the American agent made of him to leave me in his family to be raised with his daughter who had just been born; my father had very great respect for the Whites of this great Nation for which he had fought in the past; he had never had to complain about them, and the one who offered to take care of me inspired in him great trust by the sincerity of his manner, and, especially, by the honesty with which he treated Indian affairs; hence, he left me and returned to the shores of the Illinois, promising to come to see me every year after the great winter hunts; he came as a matter of fact several times afterwards; and I, despite the tedium that the sedentary life caused me, grew up for all that. I responded to the attentions of my benefactor and his wife; I was affectionate to their daughter who grew up with me and the verities of the Christian religion easily replaced in my mind the superstitions of my fathers, which I had barely learned; nevertheless, I confess, despite the influence of civilization and religion on my young being, the impressions of my childhood were not entirely eradicated in me; if the enjoyment of a walk led me into the thickets of the forest, I breathed more easily, and I was obliged to do violence to my feelings in order to return to the house; when in the evening, seated in the fresh air at the entrance to my adoptive father's dwelling, I heard in the distance, in the silence of the night, the sound of the booming voice of the Indians who were assembling to return to their camp, I felt myself tremble, and my weak voice imitated that wild cry with an ease that frightened my young companion; and, when by chance some warriors came to consult my benefactor about their treaties, or some hunters came to offer him a part of the takings of their hunt, I was always the first to run ahead to greet them; I displayed to them my joy in every way imaginable, and I was unable to prevent myself from admiring and desiring their simple ornaments which appeared to me very preferable to the brilliant jewelry of the Whites.

Meanwhile, for five years, my father did not appear at the time of the return from the winter hunts; but a warrior, whom I had often seen with him, came to find me one evening at the entrance to the forest, where I was seated, and said to me: "Mary, your father is old and weak, he has not been able to follow us up to this place; but he wanted to see you once more before he dies, and he has charged me to bring you to him." While saying these words, he took me by the hand forcefully, and dragged me away with him. I had not yet had time to answer him, or even to make a decision, when we were already very far away, and I saw well that he did not leave me with any other choice but to follow him. We walked nearly the entire night, and, at dawn, we arrived at a hut made of bark built in the middle of a small valley. There, I found my father seated on some bison skins, his eyes turned towards the place where the sun rises. His face was painted as if for a day of combat. His tomahawk, whose handle was decorated with several scalps, was beside him; he was calm and silent, like an Indian who was waiting for death. When he saw me, he pulled from within an otter-skin pouch a paper rolled up carefully in a very dry skin, and he handed it to me while enjoining me to preserve it as a precious thing. "I wanted to see you one more time before dying," he said to me, "and to deliver this paper to you, which is the most powerful manitou that you could use with the Whites to interest them in your favor, for all those to whom I have shown it have given me special displays of affection. I received it from a great French warrior whom the English feared as much as the Americans loved him and with whom I fought in my youth…." After these words, my father was silent, and, on the next day, he ceased to live. *Sciakape,* that is the name of the warrior who had come to fetch me, covered

> my father's body with tree branches, and brought me back to the place where he had taken hold of me….

At this point, Mary suspended her tale and presented me with a letter a little darkened by time, but rather well-preserved. "Look," she said to me smiling, "you will see that I have faithfully fulfilled my father's wishes; I have taken great care of his manitou…." I opened the letter, and I recognized the signature of General Lafayette. It was dated from the headquarters at Albany, June 1778, after the campaign of the North, and addressed to Panisciowa, Indian chief of one of the Six Nations, to thank him for the courageous manner with which he had served the American cause.

"Well," Mary said to me, "now that you know me enough to be able to introduce me to Lafayette, do you want us to go to him so that I can also clasp the hand of him whom my father revered as a courageous warrior and friend of our Nations?" – "Willingly," I answered; "but it seems to me that you have promised to inform us how, after having tasted for some time the pleasures of civilization, you returned to the hard and uncivilized life of the Indians?" At this question, Mary lowered her eyes and appeared troubled. Nonetheless, after a slight hesitation, she resumed in a lower voice.

> After the death of my father, Sciakape returned often to see me. Soon we became fond of one another; he had no difficulty in persuading me to follow him to the middle of the forests where I became his wife. This decision distressed my benefactors very much at first, but when they saw that I was happy, they forgave me; and every year, during the entire time that our camp is established near Kaskaskia, I rarely spend a day without going to see them; if you want, we can pay them a visit, for their house is almost on our way, and you will see by the reception that they give to me that they have retained their regard and their affection for me.

Mary spoke these last words with a kind of pride, which proved to us that she was afraid that we had formed a bad opinion of her in relation to her flight with Sciakope from the home of her benefactors. We accepted her proposal, and she gave the signal for our departure. At her call, her husband and eight warriors presented themselves to escort us; Mr. de Syon offered her his arm, and we set out on our way.

We were all very well-received by the Menard family; but Mary especially received the most tender displays of affection from all the people of the house. Mr. Menard (that is the name of Mary's adoptive father) was in Kaskaskia in his capacity as a member of the committee charged with receiving General Lafayette, and Mrs. Menard asked us if we would undertake to conduct her daughter to the ball to which an illness prevented her from going herself. We accepted with pleasure; and while Mary helped Miss Menard to finish dressing, we took our places around a large hearth in the kitchen; hardly had we sat down, when I saw moving in the corner of the fireplace a black mass of which, at first, I had great difficulty in recognizing the nature and shape; but finally, after a careful examination, I recognized that it was an old Negro, stooped over by age. His face was so wrinkled and deformed by time that it was impossible to distinguish a single feature of it, and I only guessed the location of his mouth by the small cloud of tobacco smoke that came out of it from time to time. This man appeared to be paying great attention to the conversation that had commenced between us and a young man of the Menard family, and, when he heard that we were traveling with General Lafayette and that we had come from St. Louis, he asked if we had found a large number of French there; I responded that we had seen some French there, and, among others, the founder of the City, Mr. Chouteau. "What?" he cried out in a loud voice which did not appear to belong to so broken a body. "What! You have found *Little Chouteau*? Oh! I know him well, I do, Little Chouteau; we traveled together a great deal on the Mississippi, and at a time in which very few Whites had penetrated up to there." — "But do you know," I said, "that the one you call Little Chouteau is very old, that he is certainly more than 90 years old." — "Oh! I know it well, but what does that matter, it does not prevent me from having known him as a child." — "But how old are you then? —

> Upon my faith, I do not know anything of it, because they never taught me how to count. All that I know is that I left New Orleans with my master, who took part in an expedition sent by the Company for Navigation of the Mississippi, under the command of young Chouteau, in order to construct a fort up the river. Young Chouteau was barely 16 years old; but he was chief of the expedition because his father was, they said, one of the wealthiest shareholders of the company. After having rowed for a long time against the current and experienced great hardships, we finally arrived not very far from here, where we began to build Fort Chartres. Oh! My God! I seem to be there now; I see from here the large stones that we carried, the large vaults that we constructed. Each one of us said: "Here is a fort which will last more than all of us, and more than our children." I also believed this very much, and, nonetheless, I have seen the last of it; for it is now

> in ruins, and I still live. Do you know, Sir, how many years ago we built Fort Chartres? —

"But at least 80 years ago, if I am not mistaken," — "Well then count, and you will know my age very nearly. I was at least 30 years old at that time, for Little Chouteau appeared to me to be a child; I had already served three masters, and I had already suffered greatly…." — "By this account, you would be 110 years old, Father Francis" — "My word, I believe that I am at least that old, for I have worked and suffered a long time…." — "What!" said the young man who was seated near interrupting him, "Do you suffer now, Father Francis? —"Oh! Pardon me, Sir, I do not speak of the time that I have lived in this house. Since I belonged to Mr. Menard, it is all different; now I am happy. Instead of serving others, everyone serves me. Mr. Menard doesn't even want to permit me to go to look for a piece of wood for the fire, he says that I am too old for that. But I must also tell everything, Mr. Menard is not a master for me, he is a man…; he is a friend…."

This homage of the old Slave rendered to the humanity of his master gave us a high opinion of the character of Mr. Menard. While we were still listening to old Francis, Mary and Miss Menard came themselves to notify us that they were ready and asked us if we wanted to set out on our route immediately because it was beginning to get late. We took leave of Mrs. Menard, and we met up with our Indian escorts again who had waited patiently for us at the door and who resumed their positions around us, some distance ahead, behind, and on our sides, in order to guide and protect our march, as if we had crossed into enemy territory. The night was very dark, but the temperature was very mild, and the air was studded with phosphorescent flies that shined around us like sparks of fire. Mr. de Syon led Miss Menard, and I gave my arm to Mary who, despite the darkness, marched with an assurance and a casualness that only life in the forests can produce. The fireflies occupied my attention and interested me greatly because, although they were not the first that I had seen, I had not yet ever seen so large a number of them. I asked Mary if these insects, which, by their fantastic look, as it were, are so suited for astounding the imagination, had never given rise to popular beliefs or stories among the Indians. "Not among the Nations of these lands where we are familiar with their large number every year," she said,

> But I have heard it said among some Nations of the North where these flies are rarer that they commonly believe that these are the souls of friends whom death has taken away from us, who have come to console us or to demand of us the fulfillment of some promise. I even know several bal-

> lads on this subject, and one among them which appears to have been produced a long time ago among a nation that lived a little more to the north of us and which no longer exists. It is by songs that the great events and popular traditions are ordinarily preserved among us, and this ballad that I have often heard sung by the young girls of our tribe leaves no doubt about the belief of some Indians relative to fireflies.

I requested Mary to sing this ballad to me, and she did at once and with much grace. Although I understood none of the words, which were in the Indian language, nonetheless I found a great harmony in the arrangement of the words; and in the extremely simple music in which they were sung, I found an expression of profound sadness. When Mary had finished her ballad, I asked her if she could translate it into French for me, so that I could understand the meaning. "With difficulty," she said, "because I have always experienced great obstacles in rendering exactly the words of us Indians into French, when I serve as an interpreter for them to the Whites; but I will try." And she translated approximately like this:

> The harsh season of the hunts had passed. Antakaya, the most handsome, the most skillful, the bravest of the Cherokee warriors, had returned to the shores of the Arolachy where he was awaited by Manahella, the young virgin promised to his love and his courage.
>
> The first day of the moon of flowers was to illuminate their union. Already, the two families, gathered around the same fire, had given their consent; already the young boys and girls had prepared and decorated the new cabin which was to receive the happy couple; when at sunrise a terrible cry, a cry of war uttered by the sentry who always kept watch at the top of the hill, summoned the old men to a council, and the warriors to arms.
>
> Some Whites had appeared on the frontier. Murder and robbery accompanied them. The fertilizing sun had not yet gone to the middle of its journey, and already Antakaya had left at the head of the warriors to repulse robbery, murder and the Whites.
>
> "Go," said Manahella to him while trying to conceal her grief, "go to fight the cruel Whites, and I will pray that the Great Spirit wraps you in a cloud as proof against their blows....

I will ask him to bring you back to the shores of the Arolachy, to be loved by Manahella…."

"I will come back," Antakaya had responded, "I will come back…. My arrows will not have missed their mark, my tomahawk will be reddened by the blood of the Whites; I will bring back their scalps to decorate the door of the cabin; then I will be worthy of Manahella, then we will adore each other in peace, then we will be happy."

The first day of the moon of flowers had shone, already very many others had followed without them hearing news of Antakaya and the warriors. Stooping on the banks of the Arolachy every evening, the sad Manahalla built some small pyramids of polished stones to the evil spirits in order to weaken their anger and prevent them from being opposed to her beloved, but the evil spirits were inflexible, and their violent breath overturned the little pyramids.

On the last night of the moon of flowers, Manahella met a pale and bleeding warrior on the banks of the river. "Die, poor ivy!" he said to Manahella; "die!; the most beautiful oak of our forests, that superb oak in the shade of which you counted on enjoying rest and happiness, has fallen! He has fallen under the redoubled hatchet-blows of the Whites. In his fall he has crushed those who were striking him, but he has fallen! Die, poor ivy, die! because the oak which was to serve as your support has fallen!..." Two days after, Manahella died.

Antakaya, whose courage had been cheated by fate, had fallen covered with wounds into the hands of the Whites, who had taken him very far away. But, finally, he had escaped and, after having wandered through the forests, he came back to mourn his defeat and to plan his vengeance beside Manahella….When he arrived, she was no more…. Driven by the most violent despair, on that evening he ran to the banks of the Arolachy, called Manahella, but only his echo answered the accents of his grief.

"Oh Manahella!" he cried out, "if my arrows have missed their mark, if my tomahawk has not drained the blood of the Whites, if I have not brought back their scalps to decorate the door of your cabin, forgive me…. It is not the fault of my courage, the evil spirits have fought against me…. And yet I have not uttered a complaint, nor even sighed, when the iron of my enemies has torn my breast; I have not lowered myself to ask them for my life! They spared it in spite of me, and I was consoled only by the hope of being able to avenge myself one day, and to offer you a great number of their scalps. Oh, Manahella! Come only to tell me that you forgive me, and that you allow me to follow you into the empire of the Great Spirit."

At that very moment a vivid light, pure and airy appeared to the eyes of the unfortunate Antakaya. He saw in it the soul of his beloved, and he set out to follow it through the valley the whole night long, begging it to stop and to forgive him. At daybreak, he found himself on the shores of a large lake; the light had disappeared, he believed that it had passed over the lake. Immediately, in spite of his weakness and fatigue, he made a boat out of a tree trunk that he hollowed out, and he made an oar out of a branch. At day's end his work was complete. With the darkness the delusive fly returned; during the entire night Antakaya pursued his delusion on the trembling surface of the water. But it disappeared before sunrise, and with it the faint breath of the hopes and of the life of Antakaya vanished.

Mary had just finished her ballad, and I was expressing my thanks to her when we arrived at the bridge to Kaskaskia. There Skiakape gathered the escort, spoke a few words to his wife, and let us enter the village alone. We approached Mr. Morrison's house where the ball that General Lafayette was attending was being held. Then, I sensed that Mary was trembling. Her distress was so great that she could not conceal it from me. I asked her what was the cause of it. "If you want to spare me from great embarrassment," she said, "you will not lead me into the midst of the ladies of Kaskaskia. Today, they are doubtless in their most brilliant dresses, and the coarseness of my clothes will inspire in them scorn or pity for me, and each of these two sentiments will pain me equally. Besides, I know that they condemn me for having renounced the life of the Whites, and I will feel ill at ease in their presence."

I promised to do what she desired, and she was reassured. Having arrived at Mr. Morrison's house, I had her enter a lower room, and I went up to the ballroom to inform General Lafayette that the young Indian woman was waiting for him below. He hurried to descend, and several members of the committee came down with him. He saw and listened to Mary with pleasure, and could not conceal his emotion in recognizing his letter, and in seeing with what holy veneration it had been preserved during nearly half a century in the midst of a savage Nation to which he had not even supposed that his name had ever reached. For her part, the daughter of Panisciowa expressed intensely the happiness that she enjoyed in seeing the man at whose side her father, she said, had had the honor of fighting for *the good American cause.*

After a half an hour of conversation in which the General took pleasure in relating the displays of loyal and courageous conduct of some Indian Nations towards the Americans during the Revolutionary War, Mary evinced the desire to withdraw, and I accompanied her up to the bridge where I remitted her to the care of Sciakape and his escort and took leave of her.

At midnight the General received the farewells of the ladies and citizens of Kaskaskia, who were gathered at Mr. Morrison's house, and we returned on board our ship to continue our voyage to the mouth of the Ohio immediately. Governor Coles wanted very much to have us traverse that part of the State of Illinois comprised within the angle that the two great rivers form — we would then have rejoined our steamboat at Shawneetown, where we would have been able to visit the salt mines which they say are very beautiful; but, aside from the fact that this would have taken the General more time than he could dedicate to this visit, this route did not accord with the plan that he had of ascending the Cumberland River in order to go to Nashville, where the representatives of Tennessee were charged with conducting him. Mr. Coles embarked with us to accompany the General as far as the State of Tennessee, and we felt a true pleasure in it for he is a man both pleasant to deal with and having rare merit.

Everyone is in agreement that he fulfills his duties as Governor with as much philanthropy as justice. He owes his elevation to the office of Governor to his opinions about the abolition of Slavery of the Blacks. He was at first a landowner in Virginia where, according to the custom of this region, he had his lands farmed by Negro Slaves. After having openly expressed his aversion for this kind of farming for a long time, he thought that it was his duty to put into practice the principles that he had first professed, and he desired to give freedom to all his Negroes; but, having recognized that their emancipation, pure and simple, in Virginia would be more harmful than useful to them, he brought them with him into the State of Illinois, where he not only gave them freedom, but he also set them up at his own expense in such a manner that they would be able to procure a happy existence by their own labor. This act of justice and humanity diminished his fortune considerably, but did not cause him any regrets. In this period, some men, misled by ancient prejudices, tried to have the article of the Constitution of the State of Illinois that abolished Slavery reformed; Mr. Coles fought these men with all the ardor of his philanthropic soul and with all the superiority of an enlightened mind. In this honorable struggle, he was supported by the people of the State of Illinois; justice and humanity triumphed, and soon afterwards Mr. Coles was elected Governor by a huge majority. This was a very honorable reward for him, and to it is added today another which must be very sweet for him; his emancipated Negroes have succeeded completely and offer an unanswerable argument to the adversaries of emancipation.

Some hours after our departure from Kaskaskia, we were at the mouth of the Ohio, which we ascended up to the mouth of the Cumberland River, where we arrived before night. The steamship *The Mechanic* was waiting to conduct us to Nashville. When it was necessary to leave *The Natchez* and our traveling companions from the State of Louisiana, we felt a heart-pang as if we were leaving our home and our family. This sentiment is easily understood when one considers that we had spent almost a month and traveled 1,800 miles aboard this ship in the midst of an amiable, witty, considerate company of which each member had become a true friend for us. For their part, Messrs. Morse, Ducros, Prieur and Caire displayed to us regrets no less sincere. In spite of their long absence from New Orleans, they would have, nonetheless, willingly prolonged their mission, they said, in order to spend some more time with their dear Lafayette; and our excellent Captain Davis expressed his deepest regrets that a boat other than his was going to be charged with transporting the Nation's Guest; but on the other hand, the representatives of Tennessee were not disposed to cede to others the right to do the honors of their State, and, even if they had been willing to accept the services of Captain Davis, they would have been forced to renounce them because *The Natchez* would not have been able to navigate on the too-shallow waters of the Cumberland. Thus, it was necessary for us to take our leave of the Louisiana committee and that of the State of Mississippi, a parting that we also regretted very much, and to pass aboard *The Mechanic* where we were welcomed and treated in a manner to make us predict that we would soon experience a new sorrow in being separated from our new traveling companions.

Gal. JACKSON.

Chapter X

Cumberland River – Arrival at Nashville – Militias of Tennessee – General Jackson's House – Shipwreck on the Ohio – Louisville – Route from Louisville to Cincinnati by Land – State of Kentucky – Anecdote.

It was May 2 at eight o'clock in the evening when we entered the Cumberland River where, despite the darkness, we sailed the entire night. This river, which is one of the largest tributaries of the Ohio, takes its source to the west of the Cumberland Mountains, waters the State of Kentucky by its two branches, and the State of Tennessee by its central channel which forms a large arc; it is navigable during a flow of 400 miles; in the daylight we were able to judge the richness of the country that it traverses by the large number of ships loaded with all kinds of products that we encountered. Since, from its mouth in the Ohio to the environs of Nashville, the shores of the Cumberland are flat, wooded and sometimes marshy, one does not encounter any town right on the banks in this entire part of the river; all the settlements are at some distance inland, and we could not visit them; but many of their inhabitants came with the help of longboats to greet the General aboard *The Mechanic*, and this often slowed our trip because it was necessary for us to stop at every moment to receive visitors and to allow visitors to depart.

On Wednesday May 4 at daybreak, we noticed that the banks of the river rose perceptively above our heads, and presented some favorable and safe locations for towns and villages; at eight o'clock we still did not observe any dwellings, but, nonetheless, we already heard in the distance the sound of bells ringing which announced to us the proximity of a population and preparations for a solemn ceremony; some moments later we saw the tips of some structures on the horizon and, on a plain nearer to us, a multitudinous throng of men, women and children who seemed to be expecting the arrival of something extraordinary with animated anxiety; finally, when our boat was near enough to the crowd to be recognized, a cry of joy arose from the shore, and the air resounded 1,000 times with *Welcome Lafayette*; it was the greeting of the inhabitants of Nashville for the Nation's Guest. This greeting was prolonged and without interruption until we had arrived beyond the City at the landing place where the General was welcomed by the illustrious Jackson who boarded a carriage with him to conduct him to Nashville; several cavalry corps preceded them; and the procession which formed behind them was composed of all our traveling companions to whom a multitude of citizens who had rushed from the environs came to be added; we entered the City by a wide avenue bordered by militias distinguished by the brilliance of their uniforms and by their fine appearance under arms; it was easy to recognize by their martial air that they counted in their ranks a large number of those citizen-soldiers before whom the English retreated beneath the walls of New Orleans. To enter the City, the procession passed under a triumphal arch, at the summit of which were written these words repeated ceaselessly by the crowd: *Welcome Lafayette, friend of the United States!* And above it flew the American flag attached to a pole topped by a liberty cap.

After having traveled over the principal streets, we arrived on the public square, which was decorated by a thousand banners hung from the windows and also by a triumphal arch, under which was a raised platform where the Governor of the State was waiting to address the National Guest. His speech was not only moving in the sentiments of affection and gratitude with which it was strongly imprinted, but also was very noteworthy in the richness and fidelity of the picture that it presented of the current situation of the State of Tennessee, and of the rapidity of its growth under the influence of freedom and of the wise laws that governed it. General Lafayette responded to him with that heartfelt emotion and felicitous choice of expression which so often during his long trip aroused the astonishment and admiration of those who heard him. Then, from the two sides of the triumphal arch, came 40 Revolutionary officers or soldiers, most worn out by age, some mutilated by the war, and despite that, nearly all having come from the most distant parts of the State to be present at the triumph of their former General; they advanced towards him in the midst of the acclamations of the people, and they surrounded him with their displays of affection and their patriotic memories; among them was one especially remarkable for his great age and for the acuteness of the expression of his joy; he threw himself into the arms of the General and, while weeping, exclaimed: "I have had two beautiful days in my life, the one when I disembarked with you in Charlestown in 1777, and this one; now that I have seen you again, I have nothing more to wish for, I have lived enough…." And the emotion of this old man was communicated to the entire crowd which stayed silent for some time. In spite of his infirmities, they said that he had traveled more than 125 miles to procure this moment of happiness. We learned later that his name was Hagy, that he was born in Germany, and that he had come on the same ship as General Lafayette to America where he had fought the entire Revolutionary War under his command.

After having dedicated some time to the endearments of his former companions-in-arms, General Lafayette remounted the carriage with the Governor, and proceeded to the pretty residence of Doctor McNairy who had prepared lodgings for us at his house and who, with his whole family, welcomed us with the most amiable hospitality. The General was received at the door by the municipal corps and the Mayor, who addressed a speech to him in the name of the inhabitants of Nashville. After having congratulated him for his successful arrival in the City and having eloquently retraced the forms of the displays of recognition that America had given him, he added:

> Here, we can neither show you battlefields nor converse with you about victories in which you played so glorious a part during our Revolutionary War; too far removed from the place of these great scenes, this City, now the capital of a new, independent State which did not then exist, and which, nonetheless, is already the eighth largest in the Union by population, this City, I say, has emerged only a short time ago from the bosom of the wilderness, and yet you are greeted here by a rather good number of those veterans who fought at your side for the conquest of the rights which they now enjoy, and their numerous descendants throng in front of you in order to express their gratitude to you. These generations will undoubtedly pass away soon; but the memory of this day will be transmitted to the generations that follow, and it is with rapture that the children who today have left their school-benches to come to greet you will recount one day to their children that they have had the good fortune to gaze upon the friend and benefactor of their country, the noble Lafayette….

The General thanked him by replying:

> My trip across the States of the South and the West, of which you were kind enough to speak with a moving solicitude, has been for me a continual source of the most happy and grateful emotions; I have experienced them in the spectacle of the benefits of those republican institutions of which a patriotism, no less republican, is the safeguard; I have found them in the stupendous results of national independence, of government of the people by themselves, and of the most liberal sentiments; I have found them in all the displays of affection for me that can elevate the most and delight the human heart, and in all the attentions that can make a trip rapid, easy and agreeable. Such has been my happy march up to this capital where, today, the people of Nashville, its worthy magistrates, and you, Mr. Mayor, deign to welcome me in a most honorable and loving manner.
>
> While, with such special kindness towards me, you want to recall those bygone times of which it is true that your City,

> which was not yet born, cannot show any trace on its beautiful hills, we have the pleasure of seeing in its bosom very many old soldiers of the war for independence and freedom, as well as their numerous and courageous posterity; I have seen the latest theater of the glory of these brave descendants whom I have had to honor to salute, when after having paid homage to the tombs of Greene, de Kalb, and Pulaski, I visited the battle lines of New Orleans where you have fought so nobly under the command of your illustrious compatriot. I pray you, Mr. Mayor and gentlemen of the corporate body, to accept for the citizens of Nashville and for yourselves the tribute of my respectful and affectionate gratitude.

Then, the people shouted three cheers and withdrew silently to allow their guest to take a little rest before dinner; but the General took advantage of this time to pay a visit to Mrs. Jackson, whom he learned was in town, and to Mrs. Littlefield, the daughter of his old companion-in-arms and friend General Greene.

At four o'clock, a new procession came to conduct us to the public banquet presided over by General Jackson at which more than 200 citizens took their places. In the number of guests was a venerable old man named Timothy Demundrune who was the first White man who came to settle in Tennessee. In accordance with the American custom, the meal concluded with the candid and emphatic expressions of the opinion of each table-companion about the every-day acts of the administration and the public character of the magistrates or the candidates for the different offices; among these numerous toasts, I will cite the three following ones, which appeared to me to be particularly suited to make known the predominant sentiments of the people of the State of Tennessee:

> *To the present century*: it favors the reign of liberal principles. Kings are forced to unite against freedom, and despotism is on the defensive.
>
> *To France*: republican or monarchical, in its glory or in its reversal of fortune, it will always have rights to our gratitude.
>
> *To Lafayette*: tyrants have oppressed him, but free men honor him.

To this last toast, the General rose, expressed his thanks and asked permission to make the following toast:

> *To the State of Tennessee and to its capital, the City of Nashville*: may our heritage of revolutionary glory be united

> forever with the brilliant laurels of the last war, in order to form one of the perpetual bonds between every part of the American confederation.

The presiding officer of the banquet then gave the signal for departure, and we proceeded to the Masonic Lodge where 300 brothers in the most brilliant costumes received us with the most fond cordiality. We passed a veritable family evening with them. The eloquent speaker, Mr. William Hunt, delivered an excellent speech which, in the Masonic form, presented a tableau of the most noble precepts of patriotism and philosophy, and the meeting concluded with an elegant meal, at the end of which the General proposed a toast that was received with the most lively enthusiasm; it was to the memory of our illustrious brother Riego, martyr of liberty! On withdrawing to proceed to our headquarters at the house of Dr. McNairy, we found the City lit up with brilliant illuminations, and a large number of homes decorated with transparencies representing General Lafayette with different emblems, all very ingenious.

On the next morning as soon as we had arisen, we proceeded to the south of the City where we found all the militias of the neighboring counties gathered together in a camp that they had been occupying for several days while waiting for the arrival of General Lafayette; some of the corps that we saw under arms had traveled, they told us, more than 50 miles to come to add to the solemnity of the reception to be given to the Nation's Guest by their presence. After having observed them conduct maneuvers before him, the General traversed their ranks to show them his admiration for their excellent deportment, and expressed to them his gratitude for the proofs of affection that they had come to give to him. During this time George Lafayette and I conversed with a staff-officer who was kind enough to give us some details about the organization of military forces of the State of Tennessee. "They are composed," he told us,

> Of 30,000 infantry troops which, considered as light infantry, can be, I believe, boldly put up against the best regular troops of Europe with success. We young people, accustomed from an early time to the hardships and the rigors of the hunt, acquired such skill that it became proverbial among our neighbors, and I do not think that the English will soon forget the proofs that they had of it before the battle lines of New Orleans. I could also invoke the testimony of our brave General Jackson who, during the latter campaign, received from his soldiers, nearly every morning, a dozen thrushes killed by bullets with such care that all those that were hit outside the

head were considered unworthy of being offered to him. To this exceptional skill of our citizen-soldiers, add their temperance, their toughness of character, and, above all, their love of their country and its institutions, and you will agree that a regular army would very soon have to repent of its contempt for such a militia. As for military discipline, I know that your European prejudices regard it as inapplicable to corps that are not permanent and not salaried; however, see what passes before your eyes and you will, perhaps, change your opinion. Here are voluntary companies who, under the leadership of officers of their choosing, have left their daily occupations and have traversed rather great distances to come to pay homage to Lafayette. For the more than 15 days that some of them have camped near our City, not a single disorder has drawn attention to their presence; but if the least complaint against them had reached our magistrates, the civil tribunals would soon have rendered justice in regards to it.

One will find, perhaps, in our staff-officer's manner of expressing himself, a great deal of national vanity; nonetheless, I am persuaded that this sentiment did not at all enter into his discourse. He praised the military virtues of his fellow-citizens by conviction as he would have praised, in foreigners, other virtues that he believed they had. I have often noticed that, in general, Americans have little understanding of that species of hypocrisy that we call modesty, with which we believe that we are always obligated to envelop ourselves when we speak of ourselves and of the good qualities that we possess. They believe, and I am of their opinion, that true modesty consists less in deprecating ourselves than in not speaking with exaggeration or unnecessarily of our own merits.

A frugal repast, prepared and served by the military under the tent, concluded this visit to the camp of the Tennessee militias, after which we returned to the City where we visited the academy for young ladies of Nashville and Cumberland College. In each of these institutions, the General was received like a well-loved father by his children; and he departed from them with the sweet and comforting certainty that the careful and excellent manner with which they propagated learning and the love of freedom there could only increase the glory and perpetuate the happiness of his adoptive Fatherland. The committee of instruction of Cumberland College paid homage to him, as well as to General Jackson who accompanied him, with a resolution of the board of trustees, by which two new chairs, under the names of Lafayette and Jackson, for the teaching of Languages and Philosophy, were going to be established by means of a voluntary subscription already filled by the citizens of the State of Tennessee. Both of them accepted this honor readily; and affixed their signatures below the resolution before leaving this institution, which, although founded a short time before, already offers, nonetheless, very satisfactory results.

At one o'clock in the afternoon, we embarked with a large group to go to dine at General Jackson's residence, situated some miles up the river. We found there very many ladies and farmers of the environs whom Mrs. Jackson had invited to come to take part in the fete that she had prepared for General Lafayette. The first thing that struck me upon arriving at General Jackson's house was the simplicity of his residence. Still a little influenced by my European customs, I asked myself if this could really be the home of the most popular man in the United States, of the man whom the country proclaims as one of its most illustrious defenders, of him, finally, who, by the will of the people, had been on the verge of arriving at the supreme magistracy….

One of our traveling companions, a citizen of Nashville, witnessing my astonishment, asked me naively if, in France, our public men, that is to say the servants of the people, had a custom of living very differently from that of the other citizens? — "Certainly," I said to him,

> Thus, for example, most of our generals, all our ministers, and even a large number of our subordinate administrators, would believe themselves dishonored, and would not venture to receive a person at their houses if they only owned a house like that of Jackson; and the modest homes of your illustrious revolutionaries, Washington, John Adams, Jefferson, etc., would only inspire in them scorn and distaste. They must have, first, a large and vast edifice called a hotel in town, in which ten large families could easily reside, but which they fill with a throng of outlandishly, ridiculously dressed servants who, for the most part, have no other employment than that of insulting the honest citizens who come on foot to visit their master. Secondly, they must have in the country another large edifice, which they call a chateau, and in which they amass luxurious furniture, decorations, food and dress, in short, all the luxuries suitable for making them forget the country. Then, they must have, in order to go from one of these residences to the other, a large number of carriages, a large number of horses, a large number of domestic servants….

"Very well," interrupted my Tennessean, while shaking his head with an appearance of doubt; "but who then furnishes to these officials of the state all the money that such luxury must consume? And how is the business of the people carried on?" — "If you question them, they will tell you that it is the King who pays them, although, in fact, I could assure you that it is the Nation which, for them, is overburdened by taxes; and, as for the people's business, it is conducted after a fashion, but more often badly than well." — "But why do you permit this state of affairs?" — "Because we cannot prevent it." —

> What! You cannot prevent it? A nation so great, so enlightened as the French Nation cannot prevent its officials, its magistrates, its servants, in a word, from flaunting, at its expense, a scandalous, immoral luxury, and from conducting the business of the people badly! Whereas we, who count hardly a few days among the nations, enjoy the immense advantage of having for magistrates only simple, upright, hard-working men, who are more jealous of our esteem than eager for riches! Come, come, let me believe that what you have just told me is only a joke, and that you wanted, for a moment, to make fun of the simplicity of a poor Tennessean who has never visited Europe…. But, be assured that, however ignorant we may be here about what happens on the other side of the ocean, nonetheless, it is not easy to believe in things that run so strongly counter to good sense and the dignity of man….

No matter what I did and said, I could never make this citizen of Nashville understand that I was speaking in earnest, and I was forced to let him believe that we were not governed worse in France than in the United States.

General Jackson showed us in the greatest detail his garden and his farm, which appeared to us cultivated very knowledgeably. We noticed everywhere the greatest order, the most perfect cleanliness, and we would have been able to believe ourselves at the home of one of the wealthiest and most capable farmers of Germany if, at each step, our eyes had not been afflicted by the sad spectacle of Slavery. Everyone told us that General Jackson's Slaves were treated with the greatest humanity; and several people assured us even that it would not be astonishing if, before long, their master, who already had so many claims to the gratitude of his fellow-citizens, undertook to augment them still more by giving the example of gradual emancipation to Tennessee. This would be so much more easily done in this State since they count no more than 79,000 Slaves in a total population of 423,000, and since public opinion would be more favorable there than elsewhere to the abolition of Slavery.

Upon returning to the house, some friends of General Jackson, who probably had not seen him for a long time, beseeched him to show them the honorary arms that he had received after the last war; he yielded very graciously to their request and had a sabre, a sword and a pair of pistols brought to the table. The sword had been presented to him by Congress, and the sabre, I believe, by the army corps that fought under his command at New Orleans. These two weapons, of American manufacture, are remarkable in the finish of their workmanship, and still more so in the honorable inscriptions with which they are covered. But it was particularly to the pistols that General Jackson wanted to draw our attention. He presented them to General Lafayette and asked him if he recognized them. After several minutes of careful examination, the latter answered that, indeed, he recognized them as being those that he had presented in 1778 to his paternal friend Washington, and that he felt true satisfaction in finding them in the hands of a man so worthy of such a legacy. At these words, the face of *Old Hickory*[11] was covered by a modest blush, and his eye gleamed as on a day of a victory. "Yes, I believe that I am worthy of them," he shouted, while pressing to his breast his pistols and Lafayette's hands at the same time; "if not for what I have done but at least for what I desire to do for my country…." All those present applauded this noble self-confidence of the patriotic hero, and were convinced that the arms of Washington could not be in better hands than Jackson's.

After the dinner we took leave of General Jackson's family, and we returned to Nashville to attend a public ball, which was very brilliant, following which we reembarked on *The Mechanic* to continue our trip. Governor Carroll of Tennessee and two of his aides-de-camp embarked with us. We descended the Cumberland River rapidly, and on May 7 we returned to the waters of the Ohio, otherwise called La Belle Rivière; for this is how the first Frenchmen who discovered its shores named this majestic watercourse which, for 1,100 miles, waters the most pleasing and the most fertile country that it is possible to encounter. The Ohio originates at the junction of the Monongahela and the Allegheny in Pittsburgh, and flows into the Mississippi at 37 degrees of latitude. Its current is ordinarily one and a half miles per hour; but when the waters are high, it often equals that of the Mississippi, whose average speed is four miles per hour. The water of the Ohio has, say the Americans, a great *prolific* quality, and when you ask them on what this opinion is based, they point out to you with pride the numerous dwellings that have multiplied boundlessly on its banks, and the large number of children who emerge each morning, a little basket of provisions

11. Nickname that the soldiers had given to Jackson during the last campaign, doubtless to allude to the vigor with which he endured the hardships of war. The *Hickory* is one of the most vigorous and durable trees in the forests of North America.

in their arms, to join together and pass the day at school, and who return in the evening beneath the paternal roof singing of the benefits of freedom.

On the 8th at daybreak we arrived abreast of Shawneetown, where we disembarked with Governor Coles and the other members of the committee of the State of Illinois who to our great regret were unable to accompany us any longer. General Lafayette accepted the dinner which was offered by the inhabitants of this Town. We continued our sailing while quickening the pace of our little ship with all the power of its steam engine. Despite the departure of Governor Coles and his companions, we were still very numerous on board. All the beds of the great cabin, numbering more than 20, were occupied by the delegations of Missouri, Tennessee, Kentucky and by some other people who had asked to accompany General Lafayette up to Louisville. The general, his son, Mr. de Syon and the author of this journal shared what they call *the ladies cabin*, situated in the stern of the ship, which one reaches only by descending about ten steps.

During the entire day of the 8th, we had worked a great deal. The General had answered a large number of letters that were directed to him every day from all parts of the Union, and had dictated to me some notes for the manager of the work of the farm at La Grange, to whom he pointed out the changes or the improvements that he wanted made in the farm before his return to France. A bit fatigued by this work, he had gone to bed early and was already asleep when at ten o'clock, George Lafayette descended from the deck where he had gone to take a walk, and expressed to us his astonishment that in a night so dark our Captain did not stop his ship, or at least slow its pace. We found his observation quite correct, but accustomed as we were for some months to not stopping before any obstacle and to traveling all the time, we soon spoke of other things; and George did not delay going to bed and falling asleep with the deepest feeling of security. I stayed up to converse with Mr. de Syon and to write some notes. With the exception of our pilot and of two crewmen, everyone slept around us and at eleven o'clock; the utter silence that reigned on board was disturbed only by the muffled wailing of the steam engine and the rustling of the waves against the sides of our ship.

Midnight had sounded, and sleep began to invite us to repose when suddenly our ship experienced a horrible jolt and stopped short. At this extraordinary impact, the General awakened with a start, his son leapt from his bed half-dressed, and I ran to inquire on deck. There, I found two of our traveling-companions whom anxiety had doubtless brought there first, but who were already returning while telling me that we had probably hit a sand bar and that it could not be dangerous. Not very confident of this opinion, I entered the great cabin; all the passengers were in a state of animated excitement, but nonetheless still in doubt about the nature of the incident, very many of them had not even left their bed. Determined not to redescend without learning positively what was happening, I seized a light and ran to the front of the ship; the Captain arrived there at the same time as I did, and we opened the hold together; it was already half-filled with water that was rushing in a torrent through a wide opening…. "A snag! A snag!" he shouted, "quick, Lafayette!… my boat!... Bring Lafayette to my boat!" His cry of distress had resounded in the large passenger cabin where all mouths repeated it with terror; but it had not yet reached our cabin where I found the General who, nonetheless, on the advice of his son, had provisionally begun to be dressed by his faithful Bastien. "What news?" he asked me on seeing me return; "that we are sinking, my General, and that if we want to get out of trouble, we don't have a moment to lose…." And, immediately, I began to collect all my papers which I threw pell-mell into my letter-case; George Lafayette for his part hurriedly collected some objects that he believed were the most necessary for his father, and we entreated him to follow us; but, not having gotten completely dressed yet, he urged us to leave before him to provide a means of safety…. "What!" shouted his son, "do you think that in such a circumstance we could leave you for a single second!" And at once each of us seized him by one hand, and we dragged him towards the door. He followed us while smiling at our petulance and went up with us; but, hardly was he in the middle of the staircase, when he noticed that he had forgotten on his night-table his snuff-box, decorated with the portrait of Washington and wanted to go to get it; I returned to the far end of the cabin, found the snuff-box and brought it to him.

At that moment, the rocking of the ship was so strong and so irregular, the tumult above our heads was increasing in such a frightening manner that I believed that we would not have time to get out before being engulfed. Finally, we arrived on deck where all the passengers were pushing and shoving in confusion; some carrying their trunks, others looking for a longboat, and all calling for Lafayette. He was already in their midst, and no one recognized him, so dark was the night; the ship leaned so strongly to the starboard side that it was only with difficulty that we could stand upright on the deck. The Captain, helped by two sailors, had brought his longboat to this side, and I heard his reverberating voice calling out, "Lafayette, Lafayette!" but we were unable to reach him so great was the confusion that reigned around us. Meanwhile, the ship leaned over more and more; each moment the danger increased; we felt that it was time to make one last effort, and we penetrated to the middle of the crowd where I shouted: "Here is General Lafayette!" This shout produced the effect that I expected. The most profound silence superseded the tumult; a free passageway opened before us, and all those who were ready to leap into the boat stopped spontaneously, not wanting to think of their safety before that of Lafayette was assured.

The difficulty now was to persuade the General to leave before all his traveling companions and nearly alone, because the longboat could only hold a very small number of people; but he was forced to yield to the will of all, energetically expressed by each; the irregular shaking of the ship and the rocking of the longboat, which was more than four feet below our deck, made the passage from the one to the other very difficult, especially in the darkness of the night. The most agile young man would not have hazarded a leap because, in the darkness, he would have run the risk of hurling himself into the water; thus it was necessary to take the greatest precautions for the General. I descended first into the longboat, and while the Captain kept it as close as possible to the ship, two people lowered him down by holding him under his shoulders, and I received him in my arms; but his weight, added to mine on the same side of the boat, just missed capsizing it, and, losing my balance, I would have probably fallen into the water with the General if Mr. Thibodaux, formerly President of the Louisiana Senate, had not been alongside of me to lend me his support, which saved both of us. As soon as we were assured that the General was well settled on a bench of the longboat, we moved far away from the ship as quickly as possible in order to remove from the other passengers the means of coming to overload our feeble boat. Although the greatest difficulties were then overcome, all danger was still not yet averted. We had to reach land successfully; but at what distance from the land were we? Towards which shore ought we to steer ourselves? This is what the darkness did not allow us to judge rightly. Our Captain, an able man, decided quickly. Holding the rudder with a firm hand, he steered us towards the left bank, while ordering his two sailors to row gently. In less than three minutes, we landed successfully on a shore covered with a thick woods.

Upon disembarking, our first concern was to count and recognize each other; we were nine, the Captain and his two sailors, General Lafayette, Mr. Thibodaux, Dr. Shelby, carrying in his arms a young child of seven, daughter of a Presbyterian minister, her father and I. It was only then that the General realized that his son had not been with him in the longboat, and immediately his habitual calm in the presence of danger abandoned him. Anxiety taking possession of him, he surrendered to the most animated excitement; he began to call "George!, George!" with all his strength; but his voice was drowned out by the shouts that arose from the ship, and by the horrible sound which the steam made in escaping from the engine, and he received no response. In vain, to reassure him, I reminded him that his son was a good swimmer, that it was without a doubt voluntarily that he stayed on board, and that, with his sang-froid, he would know well how to escape danger; nothing of all I said could calm him, and he kept running along the riverbank calling "George!"

Then, I jumped into the longboat with the Captain to go to those who needed help. The ship was still afloat, although nearly on its side; the Captain went on board, and I received in his place about ten people who rushed headlong into the boat, and whom I brought to land without having been able to speak to George Lafayette, Mr. de Syon or Bastien. I did not dare to give an account of this first attempt to the General, and I was readying to make a second trip when a frightful crash and piercing cries of despair gave notice that the ship was sinking. At the same time, I heard the water being struck in several directions by the efforts of those who were saving themselves by swimming. Mr. Thibodaux, who had advanced into the water to better determine what was happening and to be more ready to give aid to those who needed it, noticed a man who, exhausted by fatigue, was drowning only a few paces from shore in a spot where there wasn't three feet of water; he pulled him in so easily that a child would have been able to render this service, and he stretched him out on the grass. But the unfortunate man was so confused by fear that he did not stop making the movements of a swimmer on the ground, and would perhaps have killed himself in this manner by his vain efforts if Mr. Thibodaux had not finally succeeded in reassuring him. At each moment other people arrived by swimming. I always hoped to recognize George in one of these groups, and the General asked everybody for his son but in vain; then, I myself began to fear for him.

Meanwhile, a new expedition, which reached us by the longboat, informed us that the ship was not entirely submerged, that it had run aground on the starboard side, but that its gangways on the port side remained above water, and that a large number of passengers had taken refuge there. Thinking that it was urgent to bring help to those who remained in this emergency, I again boarded the longboat, and, with the help of a sailor, I steered it towards the ship. I arrived on board at the prow. I called George with all my might; but no response. Then, I proceeded the length of the ship to go to the stern; in my passage I heard above my head a voice that shouted to me: "Is that you, Mr. Levasseur?" I listened and looked carefully; it was our poor Bastien holding himself with difficulty on the roof of the upper cabin, of which the incline had become very steep with the overturning of the ship. As soon as I was near him, he allowed himself to slide down and, fortunately, fell into the longboat. Having arrived at the stern, I called George again; he responded at once. His voice appeared to me to be perfectly calm. "Are you safe?" I shouted to him. "I could not be better," he answered gaily…. This reply occasioned in me great relief for my fears were truly beginning to become grave. At the same time Mr. Walsh of Missouri, who was beside George, passed to me all that they had been able to save of our belongings: a small suitcase of George's, a nightbag of his father's, my private letter-case that I had thrown on the deck when I had wanted to help the General climb down, and about 60 of the 200 letters that we had prepared for the mail the preceding days; all the others were lost. I immediately came back to land with Bastien and two other people that I had received in the longboat, and I hurried to reassure the General about the fate of his son.

As I had just assured myself personally that the ship, having found a point of support, could not sink any more, and that, consequently, there wasn't any more danger for those who had stayed on board, I thought that I could dispense with making new trips, and that I could occupy myself a little with the General, for whom we established a good temporary camp near a large fire of dry branches. In the middle of this work, George Lafayette and Mr. de Syon arrived with the last passengers. We then learned that at the moment of the shipwreck, George, seeing that I was in the longboat to look after his father, returned to our cabin, all parts of which water was penetrating, and had made Mr. de Syon and Bastien, who were imprudently trying to save their possessions, leave it; then, yielding ground only as the water forced him, he was constantly occupied with the care of those who were around him. He once found himself up to his waist in water. Nonetheless, his calm and his presence of mind served to reassure some people who, without him, perhaps would have been terrified and exposed to greater dangers. Finally, they told us, he would only leave the ship when he was certain that those who stayed there were professional sailors and could do without him. "George Lafayette," the Captain said to me, "must have been shipwrecked often; because he conducted himself tonight like a man who was accustomed to it."

From other reports, it appeared that, almost immediately after the General's departure, water entered our cabin with a violence that would not have allowed us to go out if we had stayed a few moments longer.

When we were well-assured that no one had perished, we started several large fires to dry us and to light up our position. The General slept some moments on a mattress that they had found floating and which was nearly dry on one side. As for all of us, we awaited daylight while cutting some wood to keep our fires burning. A rather heavy rain came to add to our discomfort, but fortunately did not last for a long time.

At daybreak, we again began the trips on board the ship to try to save some of the baggage and to obtain some food. The Captain, Governor Carroll of Tennessee, and a young Virginian, Mr. Crawford, directed these searches with great dispatch. It was a very singular thing, and at the same time very moving, to see a governor of a State, that is to say a first magistrate of a republic, without stockings, without shoes and without a hat, carry out the difficult trade of a sailor as if it had been his own, and do that very much more in the interest of others than in his own, for he had had nearly nothing to lose in the shipwreck. These different searches yielded us a trunk belonging to the General in which were the most valuable of his papers, and a very small part of the baggage of some other passengers. They also brought back a leg of smoked venison, some biscuits, a case of Bordeaux wine and a keg of Madeira. It was with these provisions that the roughly 50 men that we consisted of restored their strength which had been exhausted by a night of work and worry.

On its return, the day illuminated a rather interesting tableau. The riverbank was covered with debris of all kinds, in the middle of which each of us searched anxiously to see if he recognized any part of his property; some were enumerating their losses sadly, others could not prevent themselves from laughing at their lack of clothing or the clothing that they found themselves in; this latter attitude ended up by dominating the others, and soon jokes, circulating around the fires of our camp, cheered up even the most mournful faces, and transformed our shipwreck almost into a pleasure party.

At nine o'clock we urged the General to cross the river to go into a house that we noticed on the other shore, to take cover from a thunderstorm that threatened us. Mr. Thibodaux and Bastien accompanied him. Hardly had he departed when one of our troop, who was on watch on the shore, signaled to us a steamship that was descending the river; a moment later they pointed out a second one. This double news filled us with joy and hope. Soon, these two ships arrived opposite us and stopped there. One of them, a vessel of great size and remarkable elegance, was *The Paragon*; it was coming from Louisville and going to New Orleans to bring a large cargo of spirits and tobacco. By a stroke of luck very fortunate for us, one of our companions of misfortune, Mr. Neilson, was one of the owners of this ship; he hastened to put the ship at the disposal of the committee of Tennessee for the General's transportation, taking generously as his responsibility the chance of another misfortune and the loss of insurance.

Immediately abandoning our camp, our whole troop boarded *The Paragon*. Before leaving our Captain of *The Mechanic*, who stayed with his crew to try to save some of the remains, we offered him our services which he emphatically refused, while ensuring us that he had enough people for this work. But the poor man was very sorrowful; it was not, nonetheless, the loss of the ship, nor that of $1,200 that he had on board, nor even the fear of finding himself unemployed which tormented him most; his despair was from having shipwrecked the Nation's Guest.... "Never," he said, "will my compatriots forgive me for the dangers to which Lafayette was exposed on this night!" To try to calm him down, we drafted and all of us signed a declaration in which we affirmed that the shipwreck of *The Mechanic* was not to be attributed either to the lack of skill or imprudence of Captain Hall whose courage and disinterestedness had been experienced during the occurrence by all the passengers. This declaration, which was very sincere on the part of all the signers, appeared to give him great pleasure, but did not completely console him.

At the moment when *The Paragon* set out, I went with George Lafayette to go for his father. After half an hour of rowing, we rejoined our new ship, which in two days and without incident, conducted us to Louisville where we stayed for 24 hours. It was 125 miles from this City near the mouth of Deer Creek that we had been shipwrecked.

The fetes offered to the General at Louisville were marred by horrible weather; but the public expressions of feeling were no less moving for him. The idea of the dangers that he had just faced aroused in all hearts a tender solicitude that each one came to display to him with that simplicity and truth of expression that are peculiar only to free men. In the midst of the rapture that the coming of Lafayette excited, the citizens of Louisville did not forget the noble unselfishness of Mr. Neilson, to whom they gave great displays of gratitude. His name was proclaimed with that of the General in the toasts that they made at the conclusion of the public banquet. The shipping insurance company declared that *The Paragon* would remain insured without new charges, and the City offered him a magnificent piece of table silver, on which were engraved the thanks of the Tennesseans and the Kentuckians, for the generous manner in which he had risked a large part of his fortune so that the Nation's Guest should experience neither delay nor inconveniences in his journey.

On the day after his arrival at Louisville, in spite of the bad weather, the General crossed the Ohio in order to accept the invitation that was made to him by the citizens of Jeffersonville in the State of Indiana. He stayed there for several hours, and returned in the evening to Louisville to attend a dinner, a ball, and different entertainments that had been prepared for him; and on Wednesday morning, May 12, after having presented a stand of colors to a corps of voluntary cavalry which had been formed expressly some days before in order to escort him on his arrival, he began his trip to Cincinnati by land by passing across the State of Kentucky whose principal cities, such as Frankfort, Lexington, etc., he wanted to visit. Governor Carroll who, after having fulfilled his mission, by remitting the National Guest to the cares of the Kentucky committee, wanted to return to his State with his staff, nonetheless yielded to the pressing invitations that the committee made to him to accompany Lafayette further. The day of our departure all the militias were under arms. We found that by their fine comportment, their arms and their uniforms, they resembled greatly those of Tennessee with whom they are united by a feeling of fraternity to which the events of the last war have given a new force.

At the end of our first day of travel, we arrived at Shelbyville, a large and wealthy village situated in the middle of the most fertile and variegated country; on the next day at four o'clock in the afternoon, the General made his entrance into Frankfort, seat of government of the State of Kentucky. The fetes given on this occasion by the inhabitants of Frankfort, whom those of the neighboring counties joined, had a great splendor and were strongly imprinted with that ardent and patriotic character which generally distinguishes all the States of the Union, but which among Kentuckians is expressed perhaps even more with that vigor of a young people passionate for liberty and for its institutions. Some passages of the speech of greetings addressed to the General by Governor Desha who, in this circumstance, was only the spokesman of the citizenry, will serve better than all that I could say to describe the public mind of Kentucky.

After having traversed the principal streets of Frankfort, we came to the center of the City, and we stopped opposite a triumphal arch under which the Governor was waiting for the Nation's Guest; a cannon blast, fired from a nearby hill that dominated all the surrounding area, had suspended the cheers of the people; then the Governor advanced and in the midst of the utter silence of the attentive crowd spoke in this manner:

> General Lafayette, welcome! It is in the name of the citizens of Kentucky that I welcome you in the seat of government of this State; your presence among them occasions the most keen delight and, for want of the grandeur with which you have been surrounded in other States older than ours, they offer you what must always please the warrior and the philanthropist, the sincere homage of their hearts.
>
> We sincerely regret that the inexorable law of nature has accorded the enjoyment of this happy day to only so small a number of those who have had the honor of supporting you in the conquest that you have made for us of the greatest of possessions, liberty and independence; but perhaps you will feel some pleasure in seeing in their place the fearless children of the West who, while you were fighting on the shores of the Atlantic, lay in the middle of the forests of the wilderness, the foundations of a new State that later was joined with the original 13 States, which carried all the burdens of the revolutionary struggle.

We also know, General, how to appreciate that distinterestedness and pure love of the human race that brought you, on emerging from childhood, to leave the Old World where the greatest honors were reserved to you, where wealth and success were assured to you, and where almost everything, except liberty, flourished, to come to this side of the Ocean, through all the dangers and to lend your support to a still-infant people who were fighting against tyranny and oppression.

The reasons that induced our fathers to take to arms in favor of the Revolution are well known to us; it was neither the miserable three pennies per pound, nor the tax on tea that led them to revolt against the odious power of Great Britain; no, rather it was in order to procure the enjoyment of *self-government*; it was in order to have a free set of laws; it was for the establishment of equal rights; it was so that their children could one day stand upright and hold their heads up as men; in a word, it was in order to be free and independent that our Revolutionary heroes determined to brave the difficulties, the hazards, the perils of so unequal a struggle. In similar circumstances, we would think and act as they did, or we would be unworthy of the noble heritage that they have bequeathed to us; but, thanks to God, the same principles that animated them then are still alive in the hearts of the American people; and in no part, I tell you with pride, does the flame of liberty burn more brilliantly than in the midst of the sons of Kentucky.

We welcome you, General, as a champion of freedom; we honor you as a monument of our glorious Revolution, and we glory in being able to express to you our admiration for your character and our gratitude for the important services that you have rendered to the American people. In spite of that impudent saying of tyrants and of aristocrats, *that republics are always ungrateful*, we hope that ingratitude will never be a cause to reproach the American republic. A free people is essentially just, General; it knows how to appreciate the services that one renders to it, and it always rewards them in the most honorable manner.

General, on your arrival you have seen joy shine on every face; permit me now to offer to you the prayers of the citizens

> of Kentucky. May your days be numerous, General, and as happy as your career has been honorable; and, when you depart this terrestrial globe, may you be found again with our well-loved Washington in the abode of eternal bliss! Such is the sincere and ardent prayer of a grateful people.

This speech was drowned out by the applause of the multitude, and everywhere I heard it affirmed around me that it was impossible to render more truthfully the feelings of the citizens of Kentucky. Nonetheless, despite the transports of public joy, despite all the interest that he himself took in the homage rendered to the Nation's Guest, Governor Desha wore a haggard visage in the midst of the crowd, as if his heart had fallen prey to burning afflictions. I questioned a man alongside of whom I found myself on this subject. "Hey, what!" he answered me, "do you not know the horrible situation of this unfortunate father? Do you not know that, in a few hours, he will be called upon to decide himself the fate of a son whom the law will have perhaps condemned to death as an assassin?" These words numbed me with horror, and I begged the man who had just uttered them to explain himself further. "Some time ago," he said to me,

> A man of the surrounding area was found assassinated on a major road; the suspicions of the law immediately were focused on Governor's Desha's son whom reasons of jealousy, they say, would have driven to commit this crime; today, he is in prison under the burden of this capital charge; he will be called before his judges forthwith; and he will probably be condemned to death because, unfortunately, the proofs that on all sides were raised against him appear too obvious; now you should know that in our State of Kentucky the Governor has the right to remit the penalty of death, except in the case of treason against the State. Will Mr. Desha make use of this right to save the life of his criminal son, or rather will he allow a free course to the execution of the law that must avenge an outraged society? Between the feelings of a father and the duties of a magistrate, the alternatives are cruel, and, whatever side he takes, his heart will have to suffer equally; because, if he is able to snatch his son from death, he cannot shield him from infamy. We all sympathize with the grief of this unfortunate father; but at the same time we think that the only course that he has to take is to tender his resignation as Governor before the end of the trial, and thus to avoid

> deciding between human nature and justice. All his friends counsel this course, and we hope that he will take it."[12]

This narrative aroused my interest in Governor Desha greatly and concentrated my attention on him; if I had been struck at first by the melancholy of his face, I was no less struck afterwards by the courage with which he appeared to me to endure his misfortune; with a noble confidence, he raised his venerable head high among his fellow citizens, and seemed to say. *The offenses are personal; and, besides, up to the moment when the judges declare him guilty, an accused is innocent.*

After having passed several hours in receiving visits and displays of friendship from the entire population, the General went to be seated at a public banquet prepared on the public square before the Capitol building. The table, shaped in a semicircle, bore 800 places so that the detachments of militias who had come from Louisville to escort General Lafayette could take their places at the banquet where were found assembled a large number of officers of Tennessee and of Kentucky, who had distinguished themselves especially during the last war, such as General Adair, Colonel McAfee, etc.

In spite of his desire not to offend the customs accepted in the United States, the General was nonetheless obliged to travel on Sunday because his traveling days were strictly counted up to Boston, where he had to be present on June 17. Thus, we left Frankfort on Saturday, May 14, and we traveled nearly without stopping up to Lexington which we entered on Monday towards the middle of the day. On the way we had visited the pretty little town of Versailles where we stopped for some time to attend a public dinner offered by the citizens of the Town and those of the surrounding country who were gathered there, and we had come to sleep three miles from Lexington, where on Monday morning numerous militia corps, led by a delegation from Lafayette County, came to fetch the General. The procession was formed on a rise from which one could see the City of Lexington and the fertile fields surrounding it. We set out at eight o'clock. Rain fell copiously, and the sky, covered with thick clouds, portended a dreary day; but at the moment when we were about to enter the City, a cannon blast, fired from a neighboring hill, announced the arrival of the procession, and at this signal the rain stopped as if by magic, the clouds dissipated, and cascades of light falling from the sky revealed to us the surrounding country covered with numerous people anxiously waiting for the arrival of the National Guest. This scene, almost magical,

12. The newspapers have since informed us that Desha's son has been convicted of his crime and condemned to death, and that his father, exercising his right as Governor to grant a pardon, has spared him.

increased the enthusiasm of the multitude whose joyful cheering blended with the continuous rumbling of artillery that thundered around us.

The fetes of Lexington were extraordinarily splendid; but, of all the proofs of the public's happiness that caught the attention of the General, the one that moved him most profoundly was the picture of the development and the rapid progress of education among all classes of the people. Indeed, isn't it as admirable as it is astonishing to find in the middle of a country, which only 40 years ago was covered with immense forests inhabited only by uncivilized men, an elegant city of 6,000 people, containing two institutions of pubic education which, by the number of their students and the variety and depth of the knowledge that they teach there, can vie with the most well-known colleges or universities of the principal cities of Europe. First, we visited the college of young men directed by President Holley, who welcomed the General at the door of the institution and addressed a speech of greetings to him in which, after having eloquently described what Lafayette had done in his youth for the liberation of North America, he expressed regret that his efforts had not had the same success for the rebirth of France.... Afterwards, directing his thoughts towards a more comforting subject, he presented him a picture of American prosperity and of the felicitous influence that his visit was going to have on the young generations witnessing his triumph.

The General answered these different points of President Holley's speech by saying:

> After having enjoyed with the most lively feeling the affectionate manner by which I have been welcomed since my arrival in this State by the people of Kentucky, by its First Magistrate, and again on this happy day by the citizens of this City and this county, I feel at this moment profound gratitude for the honor I now receive from the university of the State and its respected President.
>
> It would be impossible for me to express with as much eloquence as you have done, Sir, the patriotic and enlightened observations, the happy predictions of the future that we have just heard; but I join in them with the most heartfelt sympathy; never more heartfelt, Sir, than when you spoke of the *constitutional union* among the different States of the confederation, a union so necessary, not only to the States that compose it, but to the well-being of all of humanity; the Union was the final recommendation of our great and good Washington in his farewell to the American people.

To your interesting remarks on the progress of knowledge in the States of the West, I shall add that already the western stars of the American constellation have shone with the greatest brilliance in the national councils. South America and Mexico will never forget that the first voice that made itself heard in Congress for recognition of their independence was *a Kentuckian voice*; just as they can never forget that it is to the wise and vigorous declarations of the Government of the United States that they owe the disappointment of certain hostile schemes against their independence, and their most speedy recognition by the European powers.

I will not enlarge on your allusions to the different parts of the history of France; too much time would be necessary to explicate them here. I restrict myself to thanking you, Sir, for having recalled that day when the Parisian National Guard had at the same time a double honor; on the one hand, in suppressing a counter-revolutionary attack against the sovereignty of the people; and, on the other, in thwarting, in large measure, the seditious and horrible attempt that, on that day, threatened to defile the cause of freedom.

Permit me also, Sir, to acknowledge the displays of esteem and friendship that you have kindly wanted to accord to me, and to offer you, as well as the University of Kentucky, the expression of my respectful gratitude.

Afterwards, the General took his place in an immense hall prepared for the exercises of the young people; and there, in the presence of the public, he was addressed in Latin, English and in French by three students whose essays, as elegantly written as well-delivered, merited the approval of the audience. He answered each of the young orators in a manner to prove to them that the three languages in which they had spoken to him were equally familiar to him, and that his heart was profoundly moved by the expression of their youthful patriotism.

He was no less satisfied to pay a visit to the young women's Academy, directed by Mr. Dunham and founded under the name of *Lafayette Academy*; 150 students greeted him with the harmonious sound of a patriotic song composed by Mrs. Holley and accompanied on the piano by Miss Hammond; thereafter, several girls congratulated him, some in prose, others in verse of their own composing. The speech of Miss MacIntosh and the beautiful ode of Miss Nephew produced an especially great impression on the assembly and made even eyes least accustomed to tears weep with emotion.

To so many and so moving proofs of esteem and veneration for his character, General Lafayette experienced a flood of feelings that it was impossible for him to fully express. Surrounded, pressed, caressed by these affectionate and innocent creatures, he abandoned himself to those sweet emotions to which, in spite of his age, his heart had not become a stranger. He could not tire of repeating how fortunate he considered himself for having been able to fight in his youth for a people whose every generation displayed to him such kindness; and the thorough command that the youngest children appeared to him to have of all of the deeds of his life filled him with the most lively gratitude. Finally, he tore himself away from this scene too full of emotion to be borne for a long time, while assuring the proprietor of the Academy that he was proud of the honor of seeing his name attached to an institution so honorable in its goal and so happy in its results.

In the midst of the fetes of all kinds with which they surrounded him and the description of which would be very much too long, General Lafayette did not forget what he owed to the memory and to the former friendship of his old comrades; having learned that the widow of General Scott lived in Lexington, he had himself driven to her home in order to present his respects to her. This visit was profoundly moving not only to Mrs. Scott and her family, but also to all those who had known General Scott, whose noble character and patriotic conduct during the Revolutionary War will always be cited with pride by his fellow citizens.

General Lafayette did not forget, moreover, a friendship which, although more recent, was no less sincere. After this visit he had himself driven a mile from Lexington to Ashland and the charming country home where Mr. Clay's family resided; the honorable Secretary of State was absent, but Mrs. Clay and the children performed all the honors of the house in his name with the most kind cordiality. This visit of the General was very pleasing to the citizens of Lexington, a fact that proved to me that the popularity of Mr. Clay, which rested on his talents and his genuine services, had not been diminished among his fellow citizens by the immoderate and perhaps even unthinking attacks directed against him by some partisan newspapers at the time of the presidential election.

After 48 hours of uninterrupted fetes, we departed Lexington where we left Governor Carroll and nearly all our traveling companions from Tennessee, Louisville, Frankfort, etc., accompanied only by a detachment of voluntary cavalry from Georgetown; we turned sharply to the left, and in 36 hours we reached that point of the Ohio where the beautiful City of Cincinnati, in which General Lafayette was awaited with the most lively impatience, stands. This trip by land from Louisville to Cincinnati gained us the advantage of viewing the marvels of creation brought about by freedom in a country that civilization has hardly snatched from the wilds of nature.

In 1775 Kentucky was known only by the reports of some fearless hunters who had dared to go to settle in the midst of the fierce tribes that inhabited this country; its name alone, formed by the Indian word *Kentucke*, which means *River of Blood*, recalled incessantly to frightened Whites the numerous murders committed against the first of them who had tried to enter there and seemingly should have prevented them from ever settling there; nonetheless, the courage, the actions, the perseverance of a Carolinian named Boone succeeded, after some rather fruitless attempts, in founding a considerable enough settlement there so as to be able to resist the repeated attacks of the Indians; soon afterwards the Revolutionary War, which won freedom and independence for the English Colonies, having ended, and the activity of the inhabitants of the Northern States driving them further towards new enterprises every day, they saw a flood of their emigrants carried towards Kentucky; and, as early as 1790, the population of this country had already risen to nearly 74,000. Up to this time Kentucky had been considered as a part of Virginia; but then, with the consent of that State, it detached itself from it and formed its own State, which was admitted into the Union in the year 1792; its population today is 560,000 people. The Indians, either destroyed or pushed into distant regions by civilization, have left a clear field to the industry of the Whites; in place of the old forests that served as home to them, there have arisen populous towns, abundant harvests, active and prosperous factories; in a word, Kentucky, despite its sinister name, has become a hospitable land, and is now one of the most brilliant stars of the new constellation of the West. We know how the courage of the inhabitants of Kentucky was illustrated during the last war and in what manner they have expressed their patriotic feelings in Lafayette's presence. Nonetheless, I will recount the following occurrence, which will serve, perhaps, to prove how deep the hatred of despotism is in all the classes of this fortunate people.

On a fine day during our journey, I had walked up a rather steep road, which was marked out on a hillside at the top of which I had stopped near an isolated cottage to wait there for the carriages that were coming slowly behind me, and that were still very far away, because I had walked rather quickly. A man who was smoking his cigar at the door of this cottage invited me to enter his home in order to rest there. I accepted gratefully this polite invitation.

The difficulty with which I expressed my thanks in English revealed me as a foreigner and earned me a host of questions on the place from which I was coming, where I was going, and the reasons for my trip. As these questions appeared to me to be dictated rather by a feeling of kindness than by an indiscreet curiosity, I hastened to answer them with all possible politeness. "Well then," shouted my host very joyfully, "since you have the good fortune to live near Lafayette, you will not refuse to drink a glass of whiskey with me to his health…." And at once the liquor and cigars having been offered, we began to discuss what interested my Kentucky host the most – the *National Guest.*

After having exhausted all the questions on this subject, he spoke to me about my country and the extraordinary man who had impressed on it 15 years of glory and despotism. He appeared to me to be enthusiastic about the military glory of Napoleon and profoundly afflicted by his miserable end. "Why," he said to me, "was he foolish enough to entrust himself in his misfortune to his most cruel enemy, the English Government, whose treachery he had so often experienced? Why did he not come rather to seek asylum in our hospitable land? He would have found admirers here, and, what is better, some sincere friends in the midst of which, free and without anxieties, he would have enjoyed the memory of his great deeds in peace."— "I believe," I said to him, "that you know little of the character of Napoleon; his soul was not made for sweet and peaceful enjoyments; new nourishment for the prodigious activity of his genius was a constant necessity for him, and who knows whether, seduced by ambitious new dreams at the sight of the resources that a young nation offers, he would not have attempted to substitute his will for your wise institutions as he did with us." — "We would have considered such an attempt as an act of madness," answered my host while smiling disdainfully; "but if, against all probabilities, we would have submitted a single moment to his liberty-destroying ascendancy, his success itself would have been fatal to him…. See this rifle," he added, while extending his finger towards a weapon placed in the corner of the room, "with it, I never miss a pheasant in our forests at a hundred paces;... a tyrant is bigger than a pheasant, and there isn't a Kentuckian who is not as patriotic and skillful as I am."

Chapter XI

Arrival at Cincinnati – Fetes Offered by this City – The Swiss of Vevay – State of Ohio – The Vinton Family – Route from Wheeling to Uniontown – Speech of Mr. Gallatin – New Geneva – Arrival at Braddock's Field – General Washington's First Feat of Arms – Pittsburgh.

On May 19 at ten o'clock in the morning we arrived on the left bank of the Ohio. The first object that attracted my attention on the other bank, nearly opposite us, was the beautiful City of Cincinnati, spreading itself out majestically on a vast amphitheater at the foot of which the river flowed peacefully at a width of more than half a mile. Several boats carrying a delegation of the City of Cincinnati and some staff-officers had waited since morning for the arrival of General Lafayette. We boarded the most elegant of the boats with our traveling companions from Frankfort, and we crossed the river rapidly. We disembarked to the sound of 13 cannon shots and of *Welcome Lafayette* repeated by thousands of voices who greeted America's Guest. In the presence of the people gathered on the riverbank and of several regiments of militia in battle array, Governor Morrow welcomed him in the name of the State and, having made a place alongside him in a carriage, conducted him to his hotel in the midst of displays of public enthusiasm that no words can depict.

It was General Harrison, whose name is so gloriously connected with the principal events of the last war, who received General Lafayette at his headquarters and who addressed him in the name of the State of Ohio. In a speech filled with sentiments of affection for and gratitude to him to whom it was addressed, General Harrison painted a picture of the prodigious growth and prosperity of which the State of Ohio and the City of Cincinnati presented the most wonderful example. "Here," the speaker cried,

> Here, General, there is nothing forced, nothing artificial in the happiness and prosperity which greet your eyes. This prosperous City in the middle of which we are happy to receive you was not built as an arrogant capital on the icy shores of the Neva River at the command of a despot directing millions of enslaved arms at his will. It was built by the hands of free men; it is today the natural and central market of a skillfully cultivated country; the throng which fills its streets in order to press around you is only a portion of the 700,000 inhabitants of this State who everyday address thanksgiving to the God of the Christians for the benefits which they enjoy; the

youth, who form at this moment your guard of honor, is only a small detachment from the 100,000 free men, armed for the defense of our rights, whose courage forms the sole rampart of our State. It is of their own free will that they are gathered together today to offer the expression of their gratitude to the benefactor of their country.

Happy Warrior! How different must your pleasures be from those of the over-vaunted conquerors from the lofty days of Rome who climbed to the Capitol surrounded by miserable captives and rich spoils of an unjust war! Here, your triumph does not cause a single painful emotion to the millions of spectators who enjoy it. Your victories do not draw a sigh from any man except tyrants whose oppressive power is weakened by them!

Happy mortal! The influence of your example will extend beyond the tomb. Your renown, associated with that of Washington, will teach future Caesars that the path of duty is the sole road to true glory and that the character of a warrior cannot be honorable if it differs from the character of a citizen!

Glory to the companion of Washington! To the friend of Franklin, Adams and Jefferson! To the devoted champion of liberty! Glory to Lafayette!

At these final words of the speaker, the crowd that filled the rooms pressed enthusiastically around General Lafayette, and each of them argued for the privilege of being individually introduced to him. There were present very many Revolutionary soldiers who were not the least ardent to claim the right to clasp the hand of their former comrade. There was also there a citizen of Cincinnati the name and the sight of whom excited in the General's heart some very sweet emotions; he was Mr. Morgan Neville, son of Major Neville, his former aide-de-camp and friend, and grandson, on his mother's side, of the celebrated Morgan, who made for himself so great a reputation for his skill and bravery at the head of a corps of partisans during the War of Independence. After some moments granted to official presentations and reciprocal congratulations, the General addressed his thanks to Mr. Harrison, and we proceeded with a large procession to the Freemason hall where several lodges were gathered to greet the Nation's Guest and to offer him fraternal felicitations on his arrival in the State of Ohio.

A public dinner and fireworks exploding above the most elevated part of the City ended this day, which was only the prelude to the more brilliant fetes that the inhabitants of Cincinnati had prepared for the next day.

The first honors that the General received at sunrise were those of the young boys and girls of the free schools. Joined together, 600 in number, and led by their teachers, these children were lined up on the principal street and made the air resound with *Welcome Lafayette*. When the General appeared before them, their young hands threw flowers under his footsteps, and Dr. Ruter, having advanced towards him, addressed him with this speech in their name:

> General Lafayette, the return to the bosom of our republic by one of its principal founders, after an absence of nearly half a century, gives rise to an association of ideas and emotions in our mind which is difficult to describe; when this part of the United States was still a wilderness without inhabitants to appreciate your works, you came to our shores to fight and to spill your blood for the defense of our national rights. Success crowned your efforts, you left behind America in peace, and you returned triumphant to your native land. Since then, many years have elapsed; revolutions have shaken Europe; some thrones have risen; others have disappeared. By the grace of Divine Providence, you have seen the storm pass, and you have escaped danger. And now in the brilliant evening of your life, returning to the theater of that memorable revolution in which you played so glorious a part, you contemplate the happy results in the innumerable benefits that the American people enjoy. On this liberated land, from east to west, under the roofs of surviving patriots, as over the tombs of our heroes cut down by death, freedom reigns! During your absence the wilderness has changed into a fertile land, populated by numerous inhabitants living in the midst of abundance, practicing religious freedom and cultivating the Arts and Sciences with success. Those of our citizens who first came to the West to settle this country brought with them the principles that you have defended so steadfastly, and they have transmitted them to their children. Our new generations know and cherish our political institutions; they have learned of your history in studying that of the Nation, and they will transmit to posterity the grateful memory of what you endured for the sacred cause of liberty.

> General, the people of the West thank God for having brought you to their shores and welcome you as their benefactor, as their friend, as the friend and companion of General Washington. All our hearts are given over to you, but perhaps none with more sincerity than those of this youth of our schools, in the name of whom I am happy to welcome you to the City of Cincinnati.

The General was very moved by the sentiments contained in this speech and wished to express his gratitude to Dr. Ruter; but, at that moment, the children surrounded him excitedly, held their youthful arms towards him and made the air resound with cries of joy. He received their caresses and their embraces with the tenderness of a father who is returning to his family after a long absence. Nonetheless, having obtained a moment of silence, he addressed the following response to Dr. Ruter:

> In the midst of the universal and so affectionate welcome that I am receiving from the State of Ohio in this wonderful City of Cincinnati, I want particularly to make note of the bustling zeal and the warmth of feelings which animate these young souls in favor of an old American soldier; it is sweet for me to acknowledge not only fresh displays of personal affection of parents and teachers but also the most satisfying proof of a precocious attachment to the principles for which their fathers fought and spilled their blood. Here, the eyes of young citizens are opened from their birth to see public prosperity and domestic felicity which are the very happy lot of the land of America. Here liberty and equality of rights surround them on every occasion at each stage of their tender years; and, when they will be capable of comparing their country with the parts of the world where aristocracy and despotism still exercise their baleful sway, they will learn more and more to love their republican institutions and to pride themselves in having the beautiful title of *American Citizen*. It is in this manner that in reflecting on the everyday effects of the War of Independence, on the source to which they owe their institutions, and their very own origins, they will be more and more disposed to maintain the feelings of a mutual affection among the diverse parts of the confederation. I pray you, Sir, to accept my deeply felt thanks for your kind address; I also offer the expression of my gratitude to the worthy instructors and directors, as well as to my young friends in your so very interesting public schools and boarding schools for each of the sexes.

While this ceremony was taking place, the militias were taking up their arms; at eleven o'clock they appeared in battle array on the public square; at their head shone the handsome companies commanded by Captains Harrison, Emerson and Avery; the General reviewed them; a moment later the artisans arrived formed in a long procession in the midst of which the banners of the different trades waved; the boat in which Lafayette had crossed the Ohio the night before followed behind, mounted on four wheels, with its oars trimmed and a flag waving in the air; a detachment of Revolutionary soldiers marched around it; they invited us to take our place in the middle of this procession, with which we made several turns in the City in order to arrive on a vast square near the House of Justice; there, the General climbed onto a raised platform, decorated with greenery; the people pressed around him; and the harmonies of an excellent orchestra having fixed the attention of the multitude, Mr. Lee sang a martial ode to the tune of *The Marseillaise*; the last verses of each stanza of which were repeated enthusiastically by the spectators. A speech on the solemnity of the day was to follow the patriotic songs; then we saw the orator who was to give the speech rise; he advanced towards the silenced crowd before which he held himself motionless for some time, his glance lowered, his hand pressed on his breast, as if he were overcome by the greatness of the subject that he was going to discuss; finally, his sonorous voice, although slightly touched by emotion, made itself heard, and the entire assembly was captivated by his eloquence. The benefits and advantages of freedom, the generous efforts of Lafayette for its establishment in the two hemispheres and the picture of present and future prosperity of the United States were the text of Mr. Benham's speech. He took such a hold of the imagination of his audience that, even when he had stopped speaking, the attentive crowd remained silent for some time as if to continue to listen to him.

The eloquence of the people is one of the distinctive characteristics of the Americans of the United States; the ability to speak well in public is given there to all citizens by the universality and the excellence of education; and this faculty is developed there to a high degree by the nature of the institutions that call each citizen to exercise that power in the discussion of public affairs. In each town, in each village, the number of individuals capable of speaking before a multitudinous assembly is truly stupendous, and it is not rare to encounter among them men who, although born into humble circumstances, have rightly acquired a great reputation for eloquence; one could cite at the head of these Messrs. Clay and Webster whose parents were, I believe, farmers, and who today would appear superior beside our most distinguished European orators.

After Mr. Benham's speech the people dispersed, and the fetes were suspended until the hour of the public dinner in order to afford the General some moments of rest. Hardly had we returned to Mr. Febiger's hospitable house where we were lodged, when I saw 30 to 40 men arrive who entered into the drawing room and who asked to speak to Lafayette. "We are citizens of Vevay," an old man who was at their head and for whom all the others appeared to have great deference, said to me in French:

> They led us to hope that the friend of America and of freedom would come to visit our little Town and that we would have the pleasure to show him our vines and to have him drink our local wine; but his passage across Kentucky has deprived us of this good fortune; nonetheless, not wanting to give up the happiness of seeing the man whose name was dear to us even before we had come to this country, we decided to come here to greet him.

I immediately advised the General who, being unable to come down at the time, sent his son to urge the visitors to wait for a moment. The latter gave George Lafayette a very warm welcome; and, after having repeated to him approximately what they had just said to me, they told us that they were all Swiss, for the most part from the canton of Vaud; that persecution by the local authorities, the need to ameliorate their condition and love of liberty had persuaded them to leave their homeland in order to come to live in the New World; that they had established a town in the State of Indiana on the banks of the Ohio about 50 miles from Cincinnati to which they had given the name of Vevay; and that there, in the number of about 130 families, they lived principally on the yield of their vines, the products of which they had introduced successfully into this part of the United States. While we were listening to these details, the General arrived; immediately the Swiss of Vevay having arranged themselves in a semicircle in order to welcome him, the eldest of them, whom I had heard called by the name *Father Dufour*, advanced towards him and said:

> General, you see in front of you men who, disgusted by the tyranny and the misery which reigned in the old Europe, left their native land to come to seek in this hospitable land the free exercise of their rights and their industry; our quests have not been in vain; we have become American citizens and we are happy.
>
> Formerly, General, in our beautiful country of Switzerland, some courageous men planted a liberty tree in the shade of which they hoped that their descendants would enjoy happiness; but, soon after, this tree was so overloaded with aristocratic grafts that it could bear only evil fruit any more, and

> even its shade became noxious; then we recalled that you also had helped to plant a liberty tree in another hemisphere; some truthful reports apprised us that on this tree the aristocratic grafts could not take hold, and that its vast branches offered a secure shelter against despotism. We came to look for this tree, General, and we found here the happiness for which we pay you homage today.

After these words of Father Dufour, all the inhabitants of Vevay hurled themselves in the General's arms and embraced him tenderly. They had brought some of their local wine; they offered it to us and we drank with them to the prosperity of their new Fatherland and to the regeneration of their old one.

The wine of Vevay, one must confess, is not an exquisite wine; yet, it is agreeable enough to drink, and it is, in my opinion, the best of the wines produced in the United States. Although vines grow naturally in the forests of North America, it is difficult, however, to cultivate them, and up to the present time, it is only with great trouble that they have succeeded in rendering them productive; the abrupt changes in temperature cause the vines to have diseases that manifest themselves by a multitude of little black spots on their leaves, and the coldness of the autumn nights often hinders the perfect maturity of the fruit. Yet, they have succeeded in acclimating some European plants which thrive rather well in the hands of the vine-growers of Vevay and which give promise of great products in the future.

While proceeding to the banquet, as we traversed the public square we saw some gunners lined up at their pieces of artillery; their uniform, elegant and austere, was that of French gunners; they told us that it was the artillery company of Vevay. It was as a matter of fact almost entirely composed of Swiss, among whom a large number had served in the artillery of the French army; their maneuvers that we witnessed were executed with a precision and speed which was altogether remarkable.

At the ball that followed the banquet, the citizens of Cincinnati displayed all the good taste and the elegance that ordinarily characterizes a city prosperous, rich in resources and long-molded by civilization; but what charmed the General the most was the kind attentions by which he was surrounded. More than 500 people enlivened this patriotic evening party at which there were in attendance Messrs. Morrow, Governor of Ohio; Desha, Governor of Kentucky; Duval, Governor of the Floridas; Scott, General of the Army of the United States, and a large number of other personages distinguished by their rank and their character.

At midnight, at the signal given by the artillery company of Vevay, we took leave of the citizens of Cincinnati, and we boarded *The Herald* in order to continue our trip. The General was unable to tear himself away from his circle of friends, and did not stop showing his admiration for the prosperity of Cincinnati and the State of Ohio, which he called the eighth wonder of the world. Indeed, one could not refrain from a feeling of astonishment at the site of the prodigious creations of liberty and industry of which this State offers so many examples. The population growth alone is a marvel. In 1790 there were only 3,000 people, and today there are nearly 800,000. In 1820, one counted only 9,642 inhabitants in the City of Cincinnati which now contains 15,000.

The State of Ohio is agricultural and manufacturing at the same time. Its fertile soil produces all kinds of grains and a large variety of fruits in abundance. In the southern part they grow a little cotton, but the north is remarkable in the richness of its pasture-land. Agriculture occupies, they say, the hands of 112,000 individuals, and manufacturing occupies nearly 19,000 annually. In the past year manufacturing produced wool, cotton and linen, leather, iron, nails and maple sugar worth nearly $2,000,000 in value. All these products, as well as those of agriculture, appear destined to increase considerably each year, and the surplus of interior consumption will always find an easy market because the State of Ohio is admirably situated for exporting its commerce. For nearly 400 miles the beautiful river that waters its southern and southeastern borders is navigable for rather large ships. Its northern borders are washed by the waters of Lake Erie for 75 miles, and a canal traversing the entire interior will soon join these two points so that the State of Ohio will be found on this great line of interior navigation that connects New York to New Orleans, while passing beyond the Allegheny Mountains.

To all these natural sources of prosperity is added still another benefit that the State of Ohio owes to the fortunate circumstances of the establishment of its Constitution. Slavery and involuntary servitude are abolished there. A Slave becomes free when he touches the happy soil of Ohio, and if he does not yet enjoy the right to vote there and some other political rights, he ought not to accuse the prejudice of the legislators but the sad state of ignorance in which his unfortunate race still wallows.

It was May 22 at midnight that we embarked aboard *The Herald* which was to take us up to Wheeling, a little town of Virginia, situated on the banks of the Ohio, nearly on the border of Pennsylvania. Although we had more than 300 miles to travel to arrive there, we nevertheless disembarked there on the 24th before the end of the day; it is true that during this voyage we stopped only for the time necessary to take on wood and to visit some settlements on the banks of the river such as Portsmouth, Gallipolis, Marietta, etc., which, for the most part, were founded by the French but whose population is today entirely American, at least with very few exceptions. It was in one of these little towns, at Gallipolis I believe, that we visited the family of a representative to Congress from Ohio, Mr. Vinton, one of the members of the small minority who voted against the national reward offered to Lafayette in the House of Representatives. Mr. Vinton had not yet returned from Washington City; but his family welcomed the General in his name with all kinds of displays of affection and veneration, and Mrs. Vinton only left him when he reboarded *The Herald* where she was kind enough to accompany him on foot with all her relatives. This kindness of the Vinton family moved the General very much, and proved to him once again that the members of the feeble opposition who had voted against the proposition of December 20th were nonetheless his sincere friends; and that, if they had risked their popularity among their constituents in such a circumstance, it was, as I have already said above, only out of motives of public order, and because of their constant resolve to declare against every extraordinary financial measure.

From Wheeling we proceeded into Pennsylvania by way of Washington, Brownsville, Uniontown, etc., On this route the General again found the Virginian and the Pennsylvanian populations in the same frame of mind as the preceding year, that is to say, everywhere the people proceeded in a crowd on his way and paid him the greatest honors. The little town of Washington, capital of the county of the same name, distinguished itself with the brilliance of its fetes; at Brownsville we crossed the Monongahela in a boat carrying 24 girls clad in white, who came to welcome the General and who crowned him with flowers at the moment when he touched the territory of the Town. At Uniontown, seat of Lafayette County, he was welcomed with a simplicity and a cordiality well-suited to recall the character of the founders of Pennsylvania. To address their National Guest the inhabitants of Uniontown employed as spokesman one of his eldest and best friends, Mr. Gallatin, whom Europe knows by his diplomatic works and whom the American leaders have always counted among their most capable defenders. Placed on a raised platform in the center of the Town, Mr. Gallatin addressed the following speech to him in the name of the people who surrounded him and listened in silence:

> General Lafayette, the citizens of this County desire at this time when you have arrived in their midst to show to you their joy, their love, their gratitude. These sentiments you have heard repeated to you in a thousand places and by thousands of voices; and what speech could be as eloquent as that of this multitude who on all sides hurl themselves on your

path to welcome you? Accept these sincere and spontaneous outpourings of the affection of a free people at once imbued by respect for your character and gratitude for your services.

Is it necessary to speak of those services? They are engraved in the hearts of all Americans. Who among them can have forgotten that, in the flower of his youth, General Lafayette abandoned for the American cause the advantages of his birth and his rank, the pleasures, the splendor of a brilliant Court and, what was the most precious to him, the pleasures of domestic happiness and conjugal love? Who does not remember that he came to help America at the most critical time of the struggle for independence; that he fought and spilled his blood for her; that he gained the friendship, the confidence of Washington, the love of all those who fought with him or who drew near him; that he played a large part in the last decisive triumph of *Yorktown*? But his services were not restricted to fighting on the battlefield. While he endured the hardships and braved the dangers of all the campaigns, nearly every winter he crossed the ocean to encourage our friends and to obtain aid from our illustrious and unfortunate ally and impaired his private fortune to supply our needs, without receiving any compensation from the United States; all these services were rendered with perfect disinterestedness.

The name that this County bears was one of the first tokens of public gratitude. While it reminds us of your virtues and our obligations everlastingly, it seems to give us the right to take special interest regarding you. Let this be my excuse if, at the risk of wounding your modesty, I keep you some moments longer than it is customary to do for ordinary welcomes.

At the time of the first Assembly of Notables, it was on your motion that the report of one of the committees demanded the restoration of the civil rights of French Protestants; and that decree which, after this demand, was rendered in their favor, preceded the French Revolution by a year.

At the time of this latter event, although you belonged to a distinguished family in the privileged class, you immediately made your appearance as one of the most zealous and most skillful defenders of the people. The part that you played in all the controversial questions at this time is known to all the world; but, by a mistaken opinion rather widely circulated (by means of lies and calumnies which party spirit has propagated), many people are led to believe that France garnered no other results from its revolution, only misery and carnage, and that, in the wake of the bloody scenes that the violence of the parties produced, no material benefit was obtained for the Nation. Yet, if we would consider carefully the magnitude of the obstacles that it was necessary to surmount and if we compare what France was at the time of our revolution with its current state, we would be less astonished that it has not effectuated greater changes, and we would be less distressed that such changes as it has effectuated have been bought at such great cost.

A *penal code*, still imperfect in its details but in the nature of its punishments as lenient as ours, has been substituted for the bloody rules of a barbarous century. A uniform *civil code* has replaced customs both superannuated and contradictory. The establishment of the *jury* in criminal cases; *public proceedings at law* in all cases; the adoption of the principle of *representative government* and the *annual vote on taxes*; *personal freedom* more respected; *freedom of the press* enhanced; *freedom of conscience* established; the *abolition of privileges* of individuals, classes, corporations, provinces; and a nation of vassals freed from all feudal obligation: all these subjects comprise a multitude of improvements, a radical change in the internal politics of France, more considerable than it has ever carried out in so short a period of time; for nearly all, if not all, of these benefits were procured in the first three years of the Revolution during that short period, during which alone you exercised an influence, a powerful influence, on the public affairs of France.

No, Sir, you have not lived in vain any more for France than for America. The foundation is laid, and *the life of nations is not measured by years but by generations*. It is not our part to judge the improvements that France needs, those which are suitable to its present condition. We can only ask heaven that she be able to acquire them not by violence but by gentle persuasion; that they be the result of mutual confidence happily reestablished, and not the result of new convulsions and sanguinary conflicts!

It did not depend upon you that such should have been the early, the immediate termination of the French Revolution. Taught, permit me to use the expression, taught in the school of a rational liberty under the illustrious founders of this republic, you were not a more energetic defender of the cause of freedom in the bosom of the Assembly than you were zealous in the command of the National Guard to preserve order, repress excess, prevent crimes and avoid the spilling of blood. You were always the sanctuary for, often the protector of, the innocent and the unfortunate, and when your efforts proved to be unavailing to defend them or to make them respected, it is because the obstacle was beyond all human power.

When the constitution that you and your enlightened colleagues had judged to be the most appropriate to assure the liberties and to procure the success of France; when this constitution that you had sworn to support and that foreign forces threatened in vain was attacked internally by madmen, you foresaw with a prophetic mind the disasters that were to follow. Faithful to your oaths, faithful to the people, indifferent to conventions, totally neglectful of all personal considerations, you entered the breach and, in that memorable circumstance, you sacrificed your popularity to the cause of the people, you to whom the approval and the love of the people have always seemed the sole reward of this world worthy of being sought after.

The aftermath is well known; for having tried to save the Fatherland, you were banished, dispossessed of the heritage of your fathers as an enemy of the people. It was not in a foreign land that you could expect recompense for your services in the cause of French liberty: the banished patriot found as refuge only a prison; locked up for some years, chains could bind your limbs; your soul was never laid low; it conserved all its energy and lived free.

Your banishment was the signal for all the evils which came to desolate your country. I will not enlarge on these deplorable scenes. Liberty abandons a land defiled by crimes committed in its sacred name; for, if the first of its benefits must be won by courage, virtue and wisdom alone can preserve it.

When, several years later, you had returned to your Fatherland, you found it in the hands of that extraordinary man to whom it was given to hold sway over the fate of the French and of Europe for a time. France was plunged into an ocean of glory; but it was no longer free. You rejoiced in the success achieved against its foreign enemies; you admired all that was great, approved all that was good; but you refused to share the honors, the high positions, the favors of the new Government. The right of suffrage was restricted to a small number of electors named by the executive power; the legislature was mute; individual freedom not assured; that of the press destroyed; all the powers concentrated in a single man. You withdrew into an honorable retirement, surrounded by a cherished family; and, for nearly 14 years, you were the model of all the private virtues as you had been of all the civic virtues. The benefits of ambition had never been the object of your desires. In the simplicity of your heart, you would not imagine that you were making a sacrifice; but it remained more difficult to practice your principles.

Your only son, the worthy heir of your name and your virtues, he whom we rejoice in seeing beside you, fought under the standards of the Emperor (they were those of France). He could only follow your example; thus he distinguished himself in a noteworthy manner; rapid promotion appeared destined to await him; a glorious career and honors seemed open before him; he bore your name. This career was suddenly halted; these brilliant prospects were closed forever; and you, the most loving of fathers, you made the highest sacrifice rather than give the potent approbation of your name to the system destructive of that cause to which your name was devoted.

Nonetheless, the colossus fell; while his sycophants betrayed him or abandoned him, you who had resisted him when he was at the summit of his power, you recalled then only that you owed to his initial victories your deliverance from the prison of *Olmutz*, and you were one of the first to propose the means of his salvation that some were then seeking to procure for him, and which, perhaps, without extraordinary blindness on his part, and the shameful treachery of false friends, might have been able to save him from the sad fate which awaited him.

When, afterwards, the free votes of your fellow citizens recalled you to the theater of public affairs, no one doubted the role that you were destined to fill. Vulgar minds can remember old persecutions, or even the indifference of which they had been the object. But, as long as your heart continued to beat, you appeared always as the defender of the rights of the people. However age could calm your ardor, discouragement dim your hopes; but when the veteran of the cause of liberty in two hemispheres, after having fought, spilled his blood, suffered the shackles of banishment for this sacred cause, appeared again to defend it, it was with a new vigor, with the utmost energy and the purity, the freshness of youth.

Such is the exquisite story of a life dedicated exclusively to the service of humanity, which during 50 years of activity, has not been tainted by any vice, disfigured by any act of inconstancy.... After so many labors, arduous experiences, unjust persecutions, personal tribulations, it has pleased the Divine Providence to accord to you, at the end of your days, the sweetest reward for your soul.

You left America, Sir, as it was commencing its new life, suffering still from all the evils that had accompanied the revolutionary struggle, without commerce, without wealth, without credit, without having yet experienced the impact of a central government. After a time of 40 years, it has been given to you to visit its shores. You find it already in the full strength of its maturity, maintaining a distinguished rank among the nations, the refuge of the oppressed of all countries as well as of all parties; having attained a degree of prosperity during so short a period for which one sees no example in the annals of the world. Its villages have become populous cities; its vessels blanket the seas; new States have arisen as if by magic in the middle of wildernesses; its progress in Manufacturing and the Arts, and, a little later, in the Sciences, and in Literature, has advanced at a pace equal to those of its territorial growth and its trebled population. We had been threatened with the certain dissolution of the Union, and 13 States were seen to relinquish voluntarily a portion of their sovereignty, in order to invest in the Central Government the powers necessary to the common defense; an act of wisdom and patriotism novel in the history of peoples.

The tranquility of a long peace has not weakened the Americans. The present generation has shown itself worthy of the one that preceded it, your companions-in-arms. On leaving here, you are going to Bunker Hill in order to erect a monument on the very land where the English learned, for the first time, what resistance they were to expect from a people who wanted to be free, and you arrive here from New Orleans, theater of that extraordinary and total victory that has not been surpassed in this century of military marvels. It was achieved against enemies superior in number by a band of citizen-soldiers whom a hero, having come out of their ranks, led, and by the work of the people. At the same time, a Pennsylvania farmer maintained the honor of American arms on our northern border, and our intrepid navy, despite a still very great inferiority of forces, showed the world that the queen of the seas is not invincible even in her element.

But what especially produces in you the highest satisfaction is the thought that this prosperity, this success which we enjoy, is the result of our free institutions; these have made unassailable the indefeasible rights of man, assured to each individual freedom of conscience, that of speaking or publishing his opinions, and the unrestricted exercise of his personal abilities; they have limited the acts of government to its legitimate objects, the protection of private property from passion and greed, that of the confederation against foreign aggression. The different branches of government have been invested only with the power necessary to attain their objects. Here we truly have the rule of law. Representative government is established in its most simple form, founded on universal suffrage and frequent elections. The result of this system is displayed to the inspection of the world; none of the ill consequences that they supposed to be inseparable from popular government has occurred.

Religion has preserved its beneficial influence in the midst of universal freedom of conscience and worship, although the tie between church and state has been completely dissolved. Public tranquility has not been affected, although individual liberty is so respected in practice and by right that *habeas corpus* has not been suspended a single time. Far from weakening government, unlimited freedom of the press has neither diminished its strength one moment, nor hindered its advance. Universal suffrage has been borne out by generally popular choices; frequent and multitudinous elections have never been accompanied by the slightest upheaval; and, even when the highest offices were in question, although they were pursued with the vigor which befits free men, whose spirits the publications of the press inflamed continuously, the constitutional decision was received with immediate obedience.

Here, all powers emanate from the people, and everything has reference to the people. We acknowledge with pride that our representatives have never abused the portion of the authority that was entrusted to them. In our foreign relations, while the Government has shown itself prepared to stand up for our rights, what nation could believe itself abused by the United States? And in our internal affairs, while the laws have been executed with impartiality, can one cite, in a period of 40 years, a single citizen persecuted or oppressed?

The complete success of this great trial, attempted in this country on the largest scale, this living proof that men can govern themselves, the magnificent example given by the United States, has not been lost on the rest of the world. Events that we could foresee, but that we believed were to belong to posterity, have taken place in our time.

One year before the day when you landed on this soil to join the American standard, there did not exist on this vast continent a single man (if he was not an uncivilized Indian) who did not acknowledge the supremacy of a European power; and, at present, in a period shorter than the short duration of the active life of a man, there does not exist, from Cape Horn to the origins of the Mississippi, a single province that has not shaken off the foreign yoke. History preserves the memory of the immense sacrifices, the acts of heroism and dedication, the unalterable perseverance that have produced such great results. Our Government, faithful to its principles, has neither incited, nor encouraged insurrections; but, in recognizing first the independence of South America and in declaring that it would not look with indifference on other nations' acting hostilely in this cause, it has fulfilled a duty that the politics and the moral stance of the United States ordained for it.

A new spirit was introduced, it animated the civilized world; it gave to all men, even the most obscure, the most oppressed, the consciousness of their rights, the will to recover them; each day it made new converts, even in the privileged ranks, and on the very steps to the throne. Will the efforts of some men (who have learned nothing, and forgotten nothing), who dream and who can no longer hope, take that spirit away? Will they be permitted to shut the light in its progress and to make the human spirit go backwards? The planets also seem to the human eye to sometimes have a retrograde movement; but they follow their sure course immutably conforming to the laws of nature from the first impetus given by the Creator: thus, in the moral world, peoples, nobles, statesmen, monarchs, all are presently carried along by the irresistible movement of public opinion and of the ever-growing progress of human knowledge.

Do you want an unanswerable proof of this all-powerful influence? The British Ministry is composed exclusively of men who ten years ago were opposed to all revolutions and quaked at the simple appearance of a slight innovation: it has just, in less than a year, reformed a jurisprudence that was ancient and obscure, and destroyed the monopolistic system in the English Colonies. It recognized the independence of South America; it favors at least, if it does not yet assist, the Greeks; and if we are not misinformed, it is about to emancipate Ireland, that nation friendly to America and oppressed for so long a time.

The flame of freedom has extended from the Peruvian Andes, at the western border of the civilized world, to the other extremity towards the east. Greece, the cradle of European civilization and of ours; Greece, that classical land of liberty, groaned for centuries under the most intolerable yoke; people believed that its sons were entirely degraded by Slavery, degenerate, lost without hope of salvation: their name had become a word of reproach; they themselves an object more of scorn than of pity. Suddenly, they awake from their lethargy, fly to arms, burst their chains; they do not receive any foreign aid. The Christian powers regard them with malevolence; they are surrounded by innumerable dangers and innumerable enemies: one does not ask how many they are but where to join them. Each year, nearly without a navy they destroy formidable ships; each year without trained armies they disperse innumerable enemies; each year they astonish the world, win over its sympathy, in spite of itself, by the worthy acts of triumph of Salamis and Marathon, by exploits that the love of liberty alone can produce, by prodigious acts which would appear incredible to us if they did not happen in our time before our very eyes.

Whence comes this regeneration and its astonishing effects? From the progress of knowledge, from superior intelligence against a brutal force. The Greeks had preserved their immortal language, the memory of their ancestors, their religion, a national character. Fifty years ago some extraordinary patriots had founded schools, established newspapers, employed all means of renewing or extending education. Their stupid oppressors were unable to see, and were not afraid of the progress hardly noticed in Europe. But the seed did not fall on sterile ground, and the scimitar has been less deadly for mankind than the Spanish Inquisition.

The cause is not yet won, a nearly miraculous resistance can still be subjugated by the frightening superiority of numbers; and the civilized world, the Christian world (these two words are synonymous), will it always gaze with an immovable apathy upon the frightening catastrophe that may ensue? A catastrophe that it could, that we ourselves alone could avoid with such great ease, and nearly without danger! But I am swept beyond what I wanted to say. That is due to your presence. Don't I know that everywhere where the man who fights for freedom, or for his life, is in the most danger, that is where your heart is!

I can boldly ask what living man has taken a greater part than Lafayette in the establishment, the propagation and the defense of the principles that have produced so great and glorious results; and among the living and the dead, it has been accorded to him alone to play an equally brilliant role in the two principal theatres of the great struggle, America and France. Can we, after that, be surprised if you are received by a free and enlightened people with an enthusiasm that has not yet been equalled? We share completely the national opinion; we salute in you one of the surviving heroes of the Revolution,

> the energetic defender of the cause of humanity, the rare model of a perfect constancy. Happy to have been on this occasion the spokesman of my fellow-citizens, my private sentiments are easy to declare since the man to whom I address myself is at the same time a personal friend of longstanding, tried and true.

One sees by this speech that Mr. Gallatin is not of the number, unfortunately very large, of those foreigners who, by ignorance or by envy, ceaselessly make no distinction between the legitimate causes and the fortunate results of the French Revolution and the horrible and bloody excesses which some scoundrels afterwards indulged in, scoundrels who were only the instruments of the servile partisans of privileges who, not being able to stop freedom in its noble flight, thought to discredit it by crimes committed in its name. The justice that Mr. Gallatin rendered to the courage and the wisdom of the French patriots of 1789 moved General Lafayette deeply, and he expressed his gratitude in this manner:

> Whatever might have been my constant faith in the power of freedom, and my most cherished hopes as an American patriot, it would have been impossible, at the time when Pennsylvania deigned to give my name to this part of the State, to delude myself that I would live long enough to be the happy witness of the eminent state of prosperity and improvements that I see today with delight. This feeling of delight, my dear Sir, becomes even more intense by virtue of the affectionate reception that I am experiencing in this County, in Uniontown, and by virtue of the particular bliss I enjoy when this welcome is expressed in the name of the people by my old and very intimate friend.
>
> I will dwell on your kind and flattering allusions to the events of both hemispheres insofar as they relate to me only to declare that I feel happy in the highest degree and proud of these marks of approbation given by you, Sir, whose esteem and affection are so precious to me; but in your eloquent discourse, you have acquired rights to my profound gratitude that are even greater and more touching. It is in the name of my companions, my opinions and my conduct through the vicissitudes of the French Revolution that I thank you for the honorable testimonial accorded to us by so enlightened and so respected an observer. We thank you also for the justice that you have rendered to the benefits acquired by the people

of France and to the progress towards the emancipation of Europe which, in spite of subsequent very deplorable circumstances, still remain the result of the first impulsive force and the first years of this great revolution. And is there, Sir, in this multitude of American citizens who surround us, a single one of them whose mind does not feel itself elevated, grateful, and enchanted in listening to your so just and patriotic observations, when you have portrayed the public prosperity and the private happiness without parallel, the honorable, superior degree of political civilization, the national strength gloriously tested, the strong and virtuous opinions, the truly republican spirit upholding institutions founded on the rights of man, all advantages that make of these fortunate States an object of admiration, a noble and indisputable practical model offered to the rest of the world? While you link me with all my heart to your ardent wishes that conform to our principles that the enjoyment of these benefits be extended to the other nations; while you congratulate me for the republican emancipation of the greater part of the American hemisphere, I cannot listen to you speak of classic and heroic Greece without being reminded at what early time, with what interest, with what zeal, we made Greece the subject of our confidential conversations.

But isn't it better that I leave this multitudinous assemblage that listens to us completely won over by the vivid and profound impressions that they received from you? I will only pray then that the people of the County and Town, as well as you, my dear friend, who will be my most capable and agreeable spokesman to them, that you accept the expression of my gratitude and my devotion.

After 24 hours had passed, I will not say in the midst of entertainments, but rather the most tender and fondest displays of affection of the inhabitants of Uniontown, the General acquiesced to the invitation of Mr. Gallatin who urged him to come to take some rest in the bosom of his family; and we left with him for New Geneva, a charming residence situated on the raised and rocky shores of the Monongahela some miles from Uniontown; a detachment of militias from Lafayette County, in the ranks of which appeared a son of Mr. Gallatin, served as our escort; and on the entire route we encountered groups of inhabitants who, in their joyful acclamations, joined to Lafayette's name the name of Gallatin, which was associated with the memory of innumerable benefits lavished on this part of Pennsylvania. We found at New Geneva all that could please us in a stay which, to the advantages of a happily chosen location, joined the charm of pleasant, amiable and enlightened society, such as that of the Gallatin family. But the General was very far from meeting there the solitude that his friend had promised for him. During the 24 hours that we lived in this delightful place, the doors of the dwelling had to stay open constantly to give free access to the good inhabitants of the environs who came in a crowd to greet their well-loved guest.

On May 28, Mr. Gallatin escorted us back to Uniontown to sleep, where we took leave of him in order to proceed to Elizabethtown, a very small burg situated on the banks of the Monongahela. We arrived there towards the middle of the day; there, a boat driven by four oarsmen received us on board, and we descended the river up to the field of the famous Braddock where we only arrived a long time after sunset. Fine weather favored this voyage on which the conversation of our traveling companions, the members of the committee of Uniontown, was very interesting. We traversed shores that formerly reverberated with shouts of victory of the adventurous children of our dear France, and which had also witnessed disasters that the mistakes of a government as arrogant as it was incompetent brought upon them, and the tale of the events of that time captivated our attention up to the moment of our landing. It was nine o'clock in the evening when we landed on Braddock's Field where English troops, under the command of a General of that name, were so totally defeated in July of 1755 by the combined French and Indians. The principal circumstances of this event are too familiar to all those who are interested in American History to retrace them here; I will be content to recall only that it was on this day, so fatal to British arms, that the man who afterwards had the glory of securing the independence of his country gave the initial proofs of his understanding of warfare and his fearless calm in combat. If General Braddock had not disdained the advice of his young aide-de-camp Washington, he would not have engaged his troops so imprudently on a terrain that was to the advantage of his enemies, and he would not have lost his army, his glory and his life there. Although his counsels had been rejected, the young Washington did not fight any less heroically, and it was he who saved the remnants of the vanquished army by his boldness and composure.

On this battlefield where even today the plow cannot trace a furrow without lifting up bones whitened by time and fragments of weapons corroded by rust, stands the vast and elegant residence of Mr. Wallace, into which we were received with the most moving and amiable hospitality, as were our traveling companions. We found already assembled there a large delegation sent by the City of Pittsburgh to meet the General, and on the following morning at daybreak, some voluntary detachments of cavalry arrived to serve as escort to him in his ride towards this City.

Although several miles long, the road that leads from Braddock's Field to Pittsburgh was soon covered by a considerable crowd, in the midst of which the procession advanced slowly towards the City. En route we visited an arsenal of the United States which is found nearly half way. Twenty-four cannon blasts announced the entrance of General Lafayette into the institution in which Major Churchill and the officers under his command offered him breakfast. After having traversed the rooms of arms and the workshops in which a remarkable order and activity reigned, we continued our route to Pittsburgh where the General was welcomed at the entrance of the City by the Magistrates at the head of the people and the militias in battle array.

Until now in the course of the account of this incomparable trip of General Lafayette across the 24 states of the American Union, I have had to describe so many triumphant entrances into great and prosperous cities that I have been obliged, in order not to repeat myself too much, to pass over in silence a large number of these descriptions, or to point out only the principal characteristics of others. This is what I will again be obliged to do here for the arrival of the National Guest in Pittsburgh, although this City did not yield to any other in the United States in the pomp of its fetes, or in the expression of its sentiments of patriotic gratitude. But I have yet before me a long road to traverse and so many things to relate that I see myself forced to imitate Lafayette who, in order not to miss the ceremony of Bunker Hill, was obliged often to abbreviate the delightful times that friendship had prepared everywhere on his passage. I will not quit Pittsburgh, however, without paying my tribute of admiration for the eloquence of Mr. Shaler who addressed the General in the name of his fellow-citizens, and to that of Mr. Gazzam who was charged with presenting the young children of the public schools to him. These two speakers, as remarkable in the loftiness of their thought as in the elegance of their expression, won the approval of their audience and aroused a profound feeling of gratitude in the heart of him to whom they addressed themselves.

Among the people or the public bodies who were officially presented to General Lafayette, one noticed especially a group of old men who, by their enthusiasm in speaking of times passed, one could easily recognize as soldiers of 1776. One of them, addressing his former general, asked him if he still recalled the young soldier who first offered to carry him on a stretcher when he was wounded in the Battle of Brandywine. After having studied him carefully, Lafayette threw himself into his arms, crying out, "No, I have not forgotten Wilson, and it is a great pleasure to be able to embrace him today!..." It was, as a matter of fact, Wilson himself who had just asked the question. This recognition pierced all the spectators with emotion.

General Lafayette also recognized one of his former companions-in-arms of the Revolution in the person of Reverend Joseph Patterson who came to visit him with all the ministers of the different denominations of the City and the neighboring counties. Although a priest, Joseph Patterson had borne arms and had fought for the independence of his country during the two most terrible campaigns of the Revolution, and had been present at the Battle of Germantown.

After having devoted the day of his arrival in Pittsburgh to public ceremonies, the General wanted to use a part of the following day to visit some of the numerous industrial factories that produce glory and prosperity for this manufacturing City which, in the variety and the excellence of its products, deserves to be compared to our St. Étienne or to Manchester, England. He was struck by the excellence and the perfection of the processes employed in the various factories that he visited; but what interested him especially was the production of superb crystal glass. They presented him with some specimens of these that were to be admired in their purity and their transparency even beside the crystals of Baccarat.

Located at the point where the Allegheny and the Monongahela Rivers mingling their flows form a majestic watercourse called the Ohio, Pittsburgh finds in the States of the West, of the South and even on the Atlantic, an easy outlet for the products of its industry, which increases every year, as does its population, with astonishing speed. Today Pittsburgh counts 8,000 inhabitants and a large number of foreign workers who, welcomed by the proprietors of the factories, come each year to communicate to them the secrets of the advancements or improvements due to the knowledge and the activity of European manufacturers.

Chapter XII

Route from Pittsburgh to Erie – Victory of Commodore Perry – Nocturnal Scene at Fredonia – Indian Chief at Buffalo – Niagara Falls – Visit to Fort Niagara – Appearance of Lockport – Trip from Lockport to Rochester – Aquaduct on the Genesee River – Land Route from Rochester to Syracuse – Trip from Syracuse to Schenectady, while Passing by Rome and Utica – Grand Canal.

Upon leaving Pittsburgh, the General was obliged to part company with his old friends from the State of Ohio, represented by Governor Morrow who had accompanied him to that point with his staff. Led by a committee of the City of Pittsburgh and escorted by a detachment of militia, we traveled by Franklin, Meadville, Waterford and Erie in order to proceed to the banks of the great lake that bears this name. This entire western part of Pennsylvania, watered by French Creek, is noteworthy in the beauty and variety of its sites. In each of the towns that we traversed, the General was received for several hours with the honors that had been prepared for him by the citizens and the magistrates. At Waterford, 15 miles from Erie, he met the committee of that Town, with whom he continued his trip. A mile from Erie, a battalion of voluntary militia, the officers of the naval station, the engineers and the civil and military authorities had formed a procession to enter the Town.

The festivities that were provided there were very notable in their good taste, and still more in the sentiments of which they were the manifestation. I will relate only the following circumstance, however: A bridge of more than 160 feet separated State Street from French Street; a tent formed of the sails of the English ships taken by Commodore Perry during the last war covered it completely, and a huge table was set. It was in this chamber of a kind so original and novel, from which the eyes rested agreeably on the vast extent of the lake, that we took our place at the civic banquet at the end of which they made this toast: *"To him who in his youth was a hero, in mature age a sage, in old age an example for the present time and for future generations."* General Lafayette responded to this toast by drinking to the prosperity of the Town of Erie and to the glorious memory of Commodore Perry.

The trophies suspended above our heads, the name of Perry and the sight of Lake Erie necessarily carried the thoughts of the guests back to the events of the last war, and soon the great deeds of the American Navy naturally became the subject of general conversation. As they noticed that General Lafayette took avid pleasure in hearing about the glory of the descendants of his former companions-in-arms, they provided him with all the details of that memorable day in which, after a battle of three hours, an American squadron captured an entire English squadron that was far superior to it in the number of its guns.

> As of the first days of August, 1813, Commodore Perry had arrived to complete the naval war preparations on Lake Erie, and had set sail to search for the enemy squadron after which he sailed in vain for more than one month. He had under his command nine ships, bearing 44 cannons together. Finally, on the morning of September 10, the English squadron, ten ships and 67 guns strong, appeared to be headed towards the American squadron with the wind at its back. The latter, despite the disadvantageous wind, immediately was put under sail and prepared for the fight. Some moments later the wind changed direction, and the Americans could proceed more easily to the encounter with their enemies. At eleven o'clock the two battle lines were formed, and some moments after noon, the ship manned by English Commodore Barclay and another ship of his squadron had engaged in combat against *The Lawrence*, which Commodore Perry was manning. The latter at first received the fire of its adversaries without countering, considering that the cannons with which it was armed did not carry as far as the cannons of the enemy, and the breeze was so weak that the other ships of his squadron could not advance to join it, so that *The Lawrence* had to withstand the efforts of the two strongest enemy ships alone. This unequal combat, in which the Americans displayed the greatest fearlessness, lasted nearly two hours. At the end of this time *The Lawrence*, all of whose cannons were dismounted, all of whose crew with the exception of four or five men were killed or wounded, did not offer any means of defense; in this critical situation the brave Perry made a decision that he executed with rare good fortune and with a presence of mind that earned him the eulogies of the skillful officer against whom he was fighting.
>
> He jumped into a dinghy and proceeded on board *The Niagara* which was commanded by Captain Elliot. At that very moment, the wind having risen, Perry with his new ship rushed on the enemy line, breached it while tacking, and having taken a position within pistol-range of *The Lady Prevost*, he fired on her a volley so fast and so murderous that all the men rushed headlong into the hold. At the same time, all

> the other American ships having approached, the fight commenced on all sides with unequalled relentlessness. Victory did not remain uncertain for a long time; it soon declared itself in favor of Perry. The English, frightened by the loss of nearly all of their officers, made some mistaken maneuvers in which they embarrassed themselves; their vessels collided with each other putting themselves out of condition to respond to the terrible fire of their adversaries; finally, Captain Barclay was obliged to lower the flag, and all the other ships soon followed the example of their commander. This victory, so brilliant and so complete, occasioned yet a new burst of modesty from the intrepid Perry who, in his report to Congress, was content to say: *"We have met the enemy fleet and it is ours."*
>
> The names of Elliot and of Turner deserve to be inscribed beside that of their glorious leader on that glorious day, and the humanity of the conquerors commanded the admiration and gratitude of the vanquished. The English Commodore, Barclay, an officer of great courage, who had already lost an arm in the Battle of Trafalgar and who was again gravely wounded in the Battle of Lake Erie, wrote, in a letter that was made public: *"The generous conduct of the Americans toward their prisoners did them more honor than their victory!"*

In listening to the account of the above facts, Lafayette carried his gaze in turn on the numerous English flags that waved above his head, on the lake, theater of such glorious events, and on the sailors who surrounded him; and his heart was filled with a noble pride in seeing that the Americans of 1813 were shown to be worthy sons of his old companions-in-arms, the immortal Revolutionaries of 1776.

Upon leaving the table the General took leave of the inhabitants of Erie, and departed from his Town at three o'clock in the afternoon with the committee of Chautauqua County, who had come to advise him that a steamship was waiting at Dunkirk to convey him to Buffalo. Before sunset we had already left the territory of Pennsylvania to enter that of New York. As we had 50 miles to travel, and as the General did not want to keep the ship too long, we traveled without stopping until daybreak. In this rapid trip we passed several large villages whose population, pressed together in public places around immense fires, were waiting patiently for the National Guest to pass in order to greet him with patriotic acclamations. These nocturnal scenes have left traces of a profound impression in my mind. I will never forget the magical scene that met my eyes at Fredonia.

Upon leaving Portland, yielding to the fatigue of the preceding days, we were sleeping in our carriage despite the rough jolts caused by the tree trunks that formed the road over which we rolled rapidly; suddenly the loud detonation of an artillery piece awakened us with a start, and our eyes on opening were struck by the brilliance of a thousand sparkling lights suspended from the homes and the trees that surrounded us; they entreated us to step down, and we found ourselves in the middle of a double line formed on one side by old men and young boys, and on the other by young girls and women holding in their arms children of tender years. At the sight of Lafayette the air resounded with shouts of joy, all arms were extended towards him, mothers presented their children to him and requested his blessing for them, and a martial band, blending its tunes with the sound of cannon and bells, played the national song *Yankee Doodle*.

Affected by so moving a reception, the General took some time to be able to master the emotions of his heart; finally, he advanced slowly across the crowd, at each step clasping the hands they held out to him affectionately, and responding fondly to the sweet greeting of the children who shouted *Welcome Lafayette!* on his passage. On a platform built in the middle of an immense public square, which casks of burning resin illuminated, a speaker was waiting to address him in the name of the people of Fredonia who, afterwards, came to file in front of him to greet him once again. However touching this scene was, the General believed, nonetheless, that he had to cut it short so as not to expose to a rather brisk cold for a longer time all the women and young girls who, lightly clad, had passed the entire night waiting for him under the open sky.

It was three o'clock in the morning when, after having taken a light meal, we left Fredonia. The sun was already gilding the top of the trees of the forests that we were passing to our right when we arrived at Dunkirk, a tiny port on Lake Erie where the ship that was to conduct us to Buffalo was waiting for us. A committee from this Town and a large number of ladies had come ahead of the General, and received him on board to the sound of a band whose sweet harmonies were in delightful accord with the beauty of the morning and the romantic look of the bay on which we stood.

At noon we were in sight of the shores of Buffalo; but, our progress having been impeded by a rather violent opposing wind, we could not enter the Port until two o'clock. Although the City of Buffalo had been almost entirely destroyed by the English who burned it during the last war, we were nevertheless struck by its prosperous appearance and by the activity of its Port. We disembarked near one of the ends of that large canal, the other end of which we had visited 500 miles from there near Albany, and which serves as a link between Lake Erie and the great Ocean. After the initial welcoming ceremonies for the National Guest by the citizens and the Magistrates of Buffalo, we went to take some moments of rest at *Eagle Tavern* where they had prepared lodgings for us; there the General received a large number of people who wanted to be presented to him privately; among them we had the pleasure of seeing an old Indian Chief of the Seneca Nation who had acquired a great reputation for courage and eloquence not only among his own people but also among the Whites who knew him under the name of *Red Jacket.*

This extraordinary man, although rather consumed by time and intemperance, preserved still, nonetheless, to a surprising extent the exercise of all his faculties; he recognized General Lafayette immediately, and reminded him that they had been together in 1784 at Fort Schuyler where there was held the great council in which the interests of all the Indian Nations, friends or enemies, who could be found were regulated in relation to the United States. The General answered him that he had not forgotten this great event, and asked him if he knew what had become of that young Indian who had opposed the *burying of the tomahawk*[13] with such great eloquence. "He is standing in front of you," answered the child of the forests with the laconic brevity of his so expressive language. — "Time has changed us much," the General said to him, "for we were young and agile then…." — "Oh!," Red Jacket shouted, "time has not been so hard on you as on me; it has left you a fresh complexion and a full head of hair, while as for me, … look …!" And, untying the kerchief which was covering his head, he showed us with a melancholy air that his head was entirely bald. The onlookers were unable to prevent themselves from smiling at the simplicity of the Indian who seemed not to know of the art of undoing the ravages of time; but they took very good care not to disabuse him of his error; and perhaps they were right, for he might have confused a wig with a scalped head of hair and conceived the idea of restocking his head at the expense of the head of one of his neighbors.

Like all the Indians who have preserved their primitive pride, Red Jacket persists in speaking only his native tongue and puts on a show of great scorn for all the other languages. Though it might be easy to recognize that he understands English perfectly, he refused, nonetheless, to answer General Lafayette's questions before they had been translated into Seneca by

13. To bury the tomahawk is the ceremony by which Indians conclude peace. Red Jacket had spoken for the continuation of war against the Americans with an eloquence which had nearly carried all the Indian Chiefs over to his position.

his interpreter. Having recalled some Indian words that he had learned in his youth, the General spoke them in front of him; Red Jacket appeared to be very sensitive to this courtesy which increased very much the high opinion that he already had of Lafayette in his mind.

The Seneca Tribe is one of the Six Nations formerly known by the name of Iroquois, who live today in the northern part of New York State under the protection of the Government of this State. These six nations are the *Tuscaroras*, the *Onandagas,* the *Oneidas*, the *Cayugas*, the *Mohawks* and the *Senecas*. I would have been very desirous of visiting a large village inhabited by this latter Nation within several gunshots away; but the little time that we spent in Buffalo was so completely and agreeably filled by the fetes that the inhabitants had prepared for their guest that it was impossible to withdraw for a minute.

We spent the night in Buffalo and, on the following day, very early in the morning, we climbed into our carriage and proceeded to Niagara Falls; on the way we had breakfast with the family of General Porter at Black Rock, a pretty little port that rivals Buffalo's port in its activity; and, several hours after, a hollow booming sound that seemed to shake the earth and a thick column of steam which we saw in the distance rising towards the sky announced to us that we were soon going to enjoy the sight of one of the greatest marvels of nature.

At two o'clock we arrived with our traveling companions from Buffalo and Black Rock at Manchester, a little village situated on the right bank of the Niagara near the Falls, where the General was welcomed and addressed by a large delegation from Niagara County. Full of understandable impatience, we abbreviated as much as possible the duration of the public banquet at which it had been necessary to take our places on arriving, and at half-past three we passed on to the large island that separates the Niagara River in two unequal parts at the point where its waters form the falls, hurling themselves into a gulf 150 feet deep. The sight of the bridge that leads to this island, called *Goat Island*, prepares the mind admirably for the contemplation of the imposing scene that one is going to be present at, and provides a great idea of the boldness and the intelligence of the men who constructed it. Built on a bed of rock whose multiple points rise above the surface of the waters, and oppose the current only to increase its force, its wooden pillars are shaken by a continuous tremor that seems to announce that the time is approaching when it is going to collapse and to roll into the abyss. Some moments after having crossed the bridge, we found ourselves in the presence of the great falls.... It is a sublime spectacle; ... but one should not expect to find here the tableau of the sensations that the sight of this gigantic phenomenon made me experience, as they were of a kind unable to be described; besides I abandon this depiction so much more willingly since, in my opinion, the most skilled writers who have attempted it have remained very much beneath their subject. We remained for nearly half an hour on the edge of the gulf, contemplating the rapid fall of the water in silence and as if dumbfounded by the sound of its terrible roar. We would have stayed probably for a longer time still immersed in the waves of our meditations if the voice of one of our companions, no doubt more familiar than we with this frightening wonder of nature, had not pulled us out of there in order to give us some details, very interesting no doubt, but which we would certainly not have had the strength to ask for.

Mr. A. Porter, brother of General Porter, with whom we had stayed at Black Rock, is the owner of Goat Island; he was kind enough to lead the General himself on a tour of all the most picturesque points of this remarkable property, which exists as if suspended above the abyss. From the highest point on the island, we saw a sight less terrifiying than from the lowest point but which was, nonetheless, not without grandeur. Our gazes, being carried into the distance before us, settled agreeably on the beautiful Niagara River which rolls its waters, smooth as a mirror, into a wide bed unencumbered by obstacles, and between low and fertile shores; it is only when approaching the highest point of the island that the speed of the flow is accelerated and prepares for the terrible fall whose noise makes itself heard during the calm of the night, they say, more than 20 miles around.

Woe to the animals or men who would be rash enough to take on this irresistible current; no power could protect them from the insatiable voracity of the gulf! It was only a few years ago that a young Indian furnished a lamentable example of this. He was sleeping stretched out on the bottom of his canoe which he had fastened to the riverbank, a little below the little town of Chippewa; a girl who had responded to his love, but whom he had betrayed for another, came to pass there and noticed him. At this sight the furies of jealousy ignited the desire for vengeance in her heart. She approached, untied the canoe and pushed it gently off the shore; the current took hold of it and carried it along rapidly. Soon the roar of the waves awoke the young Indian who, upon opening his eyes, recognized the imminence of the danger that menaced him; his first action, motivated by self-preservation, was to take the oar to struggle against the current; but he was not long in recognizing the uselessness of his efforts which his pitiless mistress derided from the shore with cries of cruel joy; then, having nothing more to oppose his fate than a courageous resignation, he wrapped himself in his blanket, sat down in the middle of his canoe, fixed his eyes coldly on the gates of eternity that were about to open before him, and moments later disappeared into the deep abyss....

The name Chippewa, mentioned in the tale of the tragedy of the young Indian, stirred up among us the memory of the glorious battles waged by American arms during the last war, on the borders of Canada, from which we were separated at that moment by a branch of the Niagara. And with this memory were naturally intermingled the names of Brown, Van Rensselaer, Ripley, Scott, Porter, Harrison, Pike, Jessup, Miller and very many others who distinguished themselves in these parts by their talents, their courage and their love of country.

After a delightful walk of two hours' duration, we left Goat Island and cast a farewell glance at it over the bridge that joins it to the mainland. From there it appeared to us as an aerial garden, carried on clouds in the middle of which a thunderbolt was rumbling. The General could not tear himself away from this imposing scene, and I believe that, when he learned that Goat Island and its charming buildings were for sale for the sum of $10,000, he regretted greatly that the distance from France did not allow him to acquire it. It would be, as a matter of fact, a delightful habitation; the surface of the ground of about 75 acres is covered with sturdy vegetation whose verdure, constantly maintained by the freshness of the pure and light spray which rises from the Falls, offers an agreeable refuge against the heat of summer. The water currents that surround it offer an incalculable propulsive power that one could easily apply to mills of all kinds. I do not think that Mr. Porter should be a long time in ridding himself of a property that offers the combination of so many advantages.

On leaving Manchester and Niagara Falls, we went to Lewiston, a pretty village situated some miles below the Falls, to sleep, and on the following day, at five o'clock in the morning, we climbed into our carriage to proceed to Fort Niagara where General Lafayette had been invited to breakfast by Major Thompson, commander of the garrison. We found the Major a little way in front of the Fort, as he had come at the head of his officers to welcome the General, who was saluted with 24 cannon blasts at the moment when he entered the surrounding wall of the Fort. Some ladies, wives of the officers of the garrison, helped their husbands do the honors at the banquet and contributed greatly by their amiability to make the time we spent at Niagara appear to us to be very short.

This Fort is built at precisely the point where the river flows into Lake Ontario on which Commodore Chauncey collected laurels similar to those that Perry reaped on Lake Erie. Nearly opposite it on the other bank stands Fort George, occupied by the English. The hostilities between these two points were frequent during the campaigns of 1813 and 1814; but on both sides the fortifications have been rebuilt since, and today it would be difficult to find there any traces of the ravages of the war.

The General greatly abbreviated his visit to Fort Niagara to be able to arrive early at Lockport where we had to embark on the great canal in order to descend to Albany. On a rise in front of Lockport, we encountered a troop of 70 to 80 citizens on horseback; it was with this escort that we entered the village where the General was greeted by artillery of a very extraordinary kind. Hundreds of little pieces of stone, powdered by the workers occupied in cutting the bed for the part of the canal not yet completed out of the rock, exploded at nearly the same time and threw fragments of rock into the air that fell to the sound of the acclamations of the crowd.

The appearance of Lockport struck us with astonishment and admiration. In no other place have I seen the activity and industry of man grappling with nature as in this burgeoning Town. Everywhere one heard the sound of the hatchet and the hammer reverberate. Here, trees fall, are fashioned at the hand of the carpenter and rise in the same place in the form of a house: there, on a public square, which exists still only as a plan, a huge inn already opens its doors to new citizens who have as yet no other shelter. Hardly, in the entire Town, does one find the necessities to satisfy the prime needs of life and, nonetheless, beside a school in which the children come to be taught while their fathers build the dwelling which is to shelter them, stands a printing press which each morning gives birth to a newspaper that teaches the workers, during their rest hours, how the magistrates of the people are responding to the confidence with which they are honored. In streets laid out through the forest and still obstructed by tree trunks and scattered branches, luxury already is shown rolling in the light carriages drawn by superb horses; finally, in the middle of these encroachments of civilization on wild nature, there is nearing completion with a speed that is prodigious, that work of giants, that great canal which, in tightening the bonds of the American Union, is going to spread life and plenty into the wildernesses that it traverses.

Our carriages stopped opposite an arch of greenery, and the General was led onto a platform where he had the sweet satisfaction of being welcomed by one of his former companions-in-arms, the venerable Stephen Van Rensselaer, now president of the board charged with supervising the work on the canal. After having been officially presented to the delegation of Monroe County and to a large number of citizens, we took our places at a public banquet, presided over by Colonel Asher Saxton, at the end of which the General, influenced by the feelings that the sight of such great prodigies had awakened in him, gave the following toast:

> *To Lockport and to Niagara County*: they contain the greatest wonders of Art and Nature, prodigies that can be surpassed only by those of liberty and equality of rights.

The Freemasons of Lockport did not want to allow the General to depart without rendering to him the honors due to his high Masonic rank, and they beseeched him to keep in memory of their lodge the rich ornaments with which they had been clad on his entrance into the temple. They accompanied him afterwards up to the dock where the boat that was going to take us to Rochester was waiting for him. Before we embarked we took pleasure in contemplating the beautiful locks that made the canal rise over the cliff, the canal whose bed was cut into the solid rock, more than 25 feet deep. At the moment when the General set foot on the boat, a multitude of small blasts, buried in the rock, burst above our heads, and their resounding detonation added to the solemnity of the farewells of the citizens of Lockport. Before leaving the dock, we received from Dr. ... a case containing samples of the different kind of rocks through which the canal passes; we accepted this interesting collection with gratitude.

Although navigation by steam may not be applicable to a canal whose sides are not lined with stonework, nonetheless, as the horses and the towing path are excellent, we traveled rapidly, I will even add very comfortably; the boat *The Rochester* that carried us contained all the conveniences of life well beyond what one could have supposed in a small, local boat.

We had left Lockport at seven o'clock in the evening, and during the night we traveled the 65 miles that separated this village from Rochester where we arrived at a rather early hour. We had not yet left our room when suddenly the name of Lafayette, proclaimed in the midst of boisterous acclamations, invited the General to climb onto the deck of the boat; we followed him, and what was our astonishment and wonder at the scene that met our gaze! It was as if we were suspended in the air in the middle of an immense crowd that pressed on the banks of the canal; several falls splashed down while rumbling around us, and the Genesee River rolled below our feet at a depth of 50 feet; we spent some time not understanding our situation, which appeared to us altogether magical; finally, we recognized that the canal on which we found ourselves leapt over the Genesee River on this spot with an incredible boldness, with the aid of an aqueduct more than 400 feet long, supported by arches made of cut stone. Our traveling companions who witnessed our astonishment told us that, in its long course, the canal passes in like manner several times over very wide and deep rivers; that over the Irondequoit, for example, it runs an aerial route more than a quarter of a mile long, at an elevation of 70 feet. This kind of construction appeared to be familiar to the Americans; their bridges have, in general, an elegance and an inconceivable boldness of execution. Not far from Rochester one sees the ruins of a bridge that had been thrown over the Genesee River with a single arch 320 feet wide and 180 feet high above the surface of the water; it collapsed some time ago at the moment when two children were coming to cross it. It was, they say, a masterpiece of the art; but the great fragility of the pieces of wood that supported it prevented it from having a long life.

The General left the canal at Rochester, spent some time with the inhabitants of this City who gave him a reception which, in its affectionate sentiments and elegance, did not yield to any of those which I had attended up to then, and continued his route by land, passing by the villages of Canandaigua, Geneva, Auburn, Skaneateles, Marcellus, etc., in order to rejoin the canal at Syracuse. This route succeeded in convincing us that no part of America, and perhaps the entire world, contains as many wonders of nature as the State of New York. Lakes Canandaigua, Seneca, and Cayuga appeared charming to us in the purity of their waters, the shape of their basins and the fertility of their shores. The sight of all these beautiful things and more still the kindness and the charm of the people whom we met often made General Lafayette regret the necessity of traveling so rapidly. During this journey of more than 130 miles by land, we traveled day and night, stopping only a few moments in each village in order to enjoy the entertainments that the inhabitants had prepared for the reception of their dear guest who, they said, by the simplicity, the pleasantness and the equality of his manners with all classes of citizens, succeeded in charming all the hearts of those whom his devotion to the American cause in particular and to the cause of liberty in general had already won over for him.

From Rochester to Syracuse everywhere we had been struck by the remarkable beauty of the horses that formed our relays; we learned afterwards that they had been furnished free of charge by citizens whose patriotic unselfishness was very much appreciated by the different committees charged with conducting the General; and the committees passed a vote of public thanks to them. Among these generous citizens I heard mentioned particularly Mr. Zeng of Geneva and Mr. Sherwood, owner of public carriages in Auburn.

Upon arriving in Syracuse at six o'clock in the morning, the dying glimmers of the lights and the crowd that filled the streets apprised us that the population of this village had waited for the National Guest the entire night. The splendid supper that had been prepared the night before made us an excellent breakfast, and the General spent three hours in the midst of the affectionate congratulations of the citizens who pressed ardently around him. At nine o'clock he took leave of his friends of Syracuse and embarked on the canal-boat to the sound of artillery and of the good wishes ringing in the air for the successful completion of his trip.

We resumed sailing with so much more pleasure since we had just suffered greatly from the heat and the dust on our last day of traveling by land. Always rushed by the desire to fulfill the promise that he had made to the citizens of Boston, the General resolved to travel day and night as long as he would be on the canal and to stop only in the towns that he would find on his route for the time necessary to display his gratitude to the inhabitants who had made preparations to welcome him. We often had occasion to regret this forced haste especially in seeing the pretty towns of Rome, Utica, Schenectady, etc., and in listening to the patriotic voices of their inhabitants. It was at Rome, which we traversed at night in the brightness of the illuminations, that we met the delegation of Utica, at the head of which the General had the sweet satisfaction of recognizing one of his former companions-in-arms, Colonel Lansing, who fought at his side at Yorktown.

Twenty-four cannon blasts announced his arrival in Utica, and, at this signal, the entire population rushed around him in order to hear the eloquent speech which Judge Williams addressed to him in the name of the people. He was greatly astonished when the speaker told him that this part of the land that he had just traveled through so rapidly and comfortably was the very land that he had traversed with such great difficulty and danger during the Revolutionary War to wrest the garrison of Fort Stanwix from the tomahawk of the Indians allied with the English. He could hardly believe in so great a change and was unable to express all the happiness that he felt about it. We spent only four hours at Utica; but that time would not suffice to recount all the proofs of affection that the General received there. Obliged to divide it between his old companions-in-arms and the school children, between the magistrates and the ladies of the Town, finally, between strangers and Indians who rushed from several miles around to greet him, he found, nonetheless, the means of responding to the enthusiasm of all, and each of them who approached him came away satisfied and persuaded that he had been the object of his particular attention. Three chiefs of the Oneida tribe, Taniatakaya, Sangouxyonta and Doxtator, asked to converse with him in private and reminded him of some circumstances of the campaigns of 1777 and 1778 in which they had rendered services to him. He recognized them, as a matter of fact, but was so much more astonished to meet them again since two of them were already very old at the time of which they spoke and since he did not believe they could still be living; despite their advanced age, their features still retained an expression of great energy; they spoke warmly about the situation of their tribe. "Our hunts are hardly productive any longer," they said to General Lafayette,

> They cannot suffice for our needs, and we are forced to provide for our subsistence by agriculture, a state of affairs that makes us very unhappy; but it is not the fault of our White brothers of the State of New York; they are conducting themselves generously towards us; they allow us to live in peace near the bones of our fathers, which they have not compelled us to carry far away to a strange land, and their Government often comes to our aid when our harvests are bad; also we sincerely love our White brothers, the Americans; we have in former times fought for them with you against the English, and we are prepared to raise the tomahawk again in their favor if the occasion presents itself for it.

The General complimented them on the sentiments that they expressed; he said that he had not forgotten the good services that they had formerly rendered, and he entreated them to regard the Americans as their brothers forever; he made them accept some presents of money, and they withdrew very satisfied.

A delegation of Oneida County came to find the General to seek his attendance at the laying of the cornerstone of a monument that the citizens of the County were proposing to erect over the remains of Baron de Steuben who since 1795 has rested in obscurity at Steubenville. But the time fixed for this ceremony being inconsistent with the public promises the General had made to the citizens of Boston, he found it necessary to refuse this invitation. "If I were able to join you," he answered the delegation,

> To render to the memory of my companion-in-arms and friend, Baron de Steuben, the honors which you are preparing for him and of which no one is more worthy than he, without missing the ceremony at Bunker Hill, it would not be the hardships of a long and speedy trip that would stop me, you should be persuaded; but a single day's delay would make me miss these sacred undertakings, you know; be then kind enough to be the interlocutor of my regrets to the citizens of Steubenville, and be assured that my heart will be with those at this melancholy ceremony that I am compelled to forego in spite of my wishes.

The regrets of General Lafayette were so much more intense and sincere because he had been able, perhaps more than anyone, to appreciate the rare qualities and the noble character of Baron de Steuben who had shared with him the work and the dangers of the Virginia Campaign.

Friedrich Wilhelm Steuben was born in Prussia in 1735. Destined to a military career, his education was entirely military, and he entered the service at an early age. His knowledge, his well-proven courage and his zeal in the accomplishment of his duties did not escape the perception of Frederick the Great who promoted him rapidly and was particularly attached to his person. The young Steuben was not slow in profiting from the lessons of his illustrious master and earned a brilliant reputation among the best generals of the time. But neither the glory that he had acquired nor the favor of the greatest king of the century could counterbalance in his heart the love of freedom. When he learned that the American Colonies, overthrowing the despotism of the Motherland, were making ready to maintain their independence by force of arms, he crossed the Ocean and came to offer his services to them, declaring that he coveted no other honor than that of fighting as a volunteer for a good cause, and that he would accept neither rank nor salary before having proved himself. This noble disinterestedness and the services he rendered to the American Army earned him the friendship of Washington and the confidence of Congress which raised him to the rank of major general. His simplicity and his moderation equaled his skill and his bravery.

After the peace, wanting to enjoy the benefits of that freedom to the conquest of which he had so gloriously contributed, he retired in Oneida County on lands which Congress gave him and, there, cultivating in solitude his mind and his field, he awaited philosophically death which came to strike him down most suddenly in 1795. He was then 60 years old. According to his wishes expressed in his testament, he was wrapped in his cloak, placed in a simple wooden casket and buried without a stone and without an inscription to mark the place of his tomb. He had rested for many years in a thick grove near his home when his ashes were threatened with profanation by the opening of a public road across his property. His old friend Colonel Walker hastened to collect them, and the inhabitants of Steubenville and Oneida County resolved to enclose them within a durable monument, as an expression of the gratitude to and esteem for the German warrior.

The cannon, signal for the departure of the National Guest, had already sounded 24 times; the canal-boat which was to take him to Schenectady was readied, and the people, squeezed together on the piers and the bridges which traversed the canal, waited for his departure in silence. When he had embarked and as our light ship, pulled by superb white horses, had begun to glide over the water, a triple cheer expressed to him the last farewells of the inhabitants of Utica, and children placed on the bridges covered him with a shower of flowers at the moment of his passage. Standing on the bow of the boat, his head uncovered, General Lafayette responded with signs of gratitude for the honorable displays of the esteem of the people. Witnessing this touching scene, his son and I stayed near him, sharing at the same time both the enthusiasm of the people and the happiness of the one who was its object, when suddenly our attention was diverted by the cries of a man who was following the boat while running on the pier, and giving a signal to stop.

His bronze skin, his semi-nude body, his outlandish ornaments made us recognize him as an Indian. Although his intention to board our ship was manifest, our Captain, Major Swartwout, did not consider it appropriate to stop in such a circumstance. Then the Indian, gathering all his strength, accelerated his running with such speed that he had soon passed us by far, and was going to wait for us on the last bridge outside of the town. At the moment when we passed under this bridge, he leaped onto our boat and landed on his feet in our midst with admirable aplomb. "Where is Kayewla? I want to see Kayewla,"[14] he cried excitedly. They pointed out the General to him. His face and his bearing exhibited the most lively satisfaction. "I am son of Wekchekaeta," he shouted, holding out his hand to him, "of him who loved you so much that he followed you to your native land when you returned there after the great war; my father often spoke of you, and I am happy to see you…." The General had already learned that Wekchekaeta had died some time ago, and he was very glad to meet his son, who appeared to be about 24 years old. He had him sit, conversed with him for a few moments and made him very happy by giving him several dollars when he left us. The young Indian was no more troubled in leaving the boat than he had been in entering it. About ten feet separated us from the edge of the canal; he cleared this distance with the nimbleness of a deer and disappeared in an instant. This singular visit greatly excited the curiosity of the numerous witnesses who were aboard with us, and the General hurried to satisfy us in telling the story of Wekchekaeta whom he had taken with him to Europe in 1778 and who, soon disgusted by civilization, returned gladly to his wild forests.

To describe our trip from Utica to Schenectady, a distance of 80 miles, would be to repeat what I have already said about our trip in the upper part of the canal. We arrived in this latter Town on the following day, June 11, at the dinner hour. We stayed there for several hours which the inhabitants made very sweet for the General, and at night we climbed into a carriage to go by land to Albany, which is only a distance of 16 miles away. We lost much, they say, in not continuing our route by the canal which, in all this part, is laid out along the Mohawk River, above which it passes twice in aqueducts 1,800 feet

---

14. Kayewla, in the Indian language, signifies great white warrior. It is in this manner that the tribes who had known Lafayette and who had high esteem for his courage customarily referred to him.

long; but pressed as we were, we had to choose the shortest route: besides, we had traveled nearly 300 miles on the canal since Lockport, and we had been able to judge the beauty and the utility of this great means of communication built in eight years solely by the State of New York without any outside aid. There remains still some small works to finish for the navigation to be open in the entire length of the canal; but they will be completed in several months; then the boats which will go from Lake Erie to Albany will traverse a length of 360 miles while descending a height of 550 feet, with the help of 83 locks built out of cut stone, of which the inside, measuring 30 feet long by 15 feet wide, can contain boats of more than 100 tons. They estimate the total cost for the construction of the canal at a little more than $10,000,000. That sum appears to be enormous at first glance; but it is nonetheless very low if one considers the immense advantages that this construction assures to New York State. The tolls collected for the right of navigation, although they are very low, have nonetheless already produced in 1824 a sum of $350,761; estimates lead one to believe that collections will grow to $500,000 this year, and that in the nine years following they could increase by $75,000 per year: thus, the debts incurred for the completion of this great work will be extinguished at the end of ten years; and, in deducting still $100,000 of annual expenses for the costs of repair, collection and security, the State of New York will have from its canal net revenue of more than $1,000,000, which equals four times the expenses of its Government.

Then the State of New York will present the new spectacle of a community of more than 2,000,000 men not only supporting its Government without taxes but also having money left over originating from the property of the State. The citizens of this State will always have to pay, it is true, the charges that the General Government of the Union will judge appropriate to impose on foreign products that they will have the whim to consume; but the independent farmer who works his property and produces all that is necessary himself can now live without paying any tax, either direct or indirect, either to the State or to the General Government.

I offer this picture of the public prosperity of the State of New York for the consideration of our European politicians and economists.

Chapter XIII

Return to Boston – Lafayette's Reception by the Massachusetts Legislature – Celebration of the Anniversary of Bunker Hill – History of the Revolution Familiar to All Americans – Departure from Boston.

We arrived at Albany before sunrise on the 12th day of June, and several hours later we had already passed the Hudson, and we were advancing rapidly towards Massachusetts whose western border is marked out parallel to the river, only 25 miles from the left bank. We still had 150 miles to go in order to arrive in Boston; but the excellence of the roads that we had to travel on guaranteed us a speedy trip, and General Lafayette was assured of arriving on time to fulfill his commitments from then on. Nevertheless, he decided to stop again only for the time absolutely necessary to take a little rest. Consequently, we entered Boston on the 15th, a little before noon. In publishing this successful arrival, the newspapers spread as much astonishment as joy to the public of all parts of the Union. Very few people had believed in the possibility of General Lafayette's return for the anniversary of Bunker Hill, and each regarded the trip which he had just completed as a tour de force. Indeed, hadn't he traveled a route of more than 5,000 miles in fewer than four months, traversed seas near the equator and lakes near the icy pole, ascended rapid rivers up to the borders of the civilization of the New World, and received the homage of 16 republics! And didn't the astonishment grow greater when they thought that this extraordinary journey was completed by a man 67 years old? The plan of this trip had been, it is true, very wisely and skillfully devised by Mr. McLean, Director General of the Post Office, by General Bernard and by George Lafayette; and this plan had been executed with a precision, a cohesion that could only result from the unanimity of sentiments that animated the people and the magistrates of the States that Lafayette traveled through; but during so long a journey, through so many dangers, how was it possible that an accident did not happen, a single one of which in delaying us only a few days would have upset all our calculations! And yet our good luck was such that we lost not a single one of the days so rigorously computed, and we arrived precisely on the appointed day.

On returning to this City of Boston where so many old and special attachments awaited him, General Lafayette would have felt a most sweet satisfaction if he had not had to lament the loss of two dear friends whom death had cut off during his brief absence; ex-Governor Brooks and Governor Eustis had just departed life, taking with them the esteem and the regrets of those who had known them or who had seen their wise administration. Thus the words of Lafayette's former companions-in-arms began to be realized. All of them had exclaimed on clasping his hand: "We have lived enough, now that we have been given the opportunity to see our old General again!..."

The day after our arrival, on the invitation that had been given to him, the General proceeded to the Capitol where the new Governor, Mr. Lincoln, the Senate, the House of Representatives and the civil authorities of Boston were gathered to welcome him and to congratulate him. After we had taken our places in the midst of the assembly, the Governor rose, and, in the name of the State of Massachusetts, complimented the National Guest on the successful completion of his long trip.

The General responded to the congratulations of the Governor in these words:

> The reception with which I see myself honored by the current representation of the State of Massachusetts in its legislative and executive branches, at the same time as it fills my heart with feelings of the most intense and profound gratitude, recalls to me some old memories, no less cherished and fond; and while, in this magnificent palace of the State your excellency addresses me with a greeting full of kindness, I recall the long-ago time when similar favors were accorded to me in the confines of *Faneuil Hall*, that sacred cradle of American liberty and, I like to hope, of universal liberty.
>
> In the long and happy course of my visits to the different parts of the Union of which you have seen fit to speak, Sir, *Bunker Hill* has always been my North Star; I commend myself now, on this great day of the jubilee anniversary of a half-century, for having arrived in time to join with my companions-in-arms and to appear together as representatives of the early and unwavering dedication of our Revolutionary Army, of the patriotic vows of those of us who are still on this earth, of the final prayers of those of our comrades who have ceased to live. Here, Sir, permit me to grieve over the recent loss of my two friends, your respected predecessors, who were so cordially joined in the last reception that I had the good fortune of experiencing when, after a long absence, I was welcomed by the people of this State and of this well-loved City of Boston, which I have never entered without feeling myself infused with the most intense emotions of affection and gratitude.

> While I have continuously enjoyed with admiration the suddenly appearing marvels of creation and of progress that have been the results of independence, freedom and of those republican institutions to which alone is given the strength to sustain the weight and to spread the powers of a far-reaching empire, I have been particularly delighted to recognize everywhere the sentiments of sympathy and mutual affection that strongly bind the people of each of the parts of the confederation to one union, on which both the security of these States and the hopes of humankind rest.

Hardly had the General finished speaking when the members of the two chambers left their places in a crowd and rushed around him to offer the personal expression of their feelings, and affectionate congratulations were addressed to him tumultuously from the public galleries that were filled by a great number of ladies eager to see him again. Among the visitors of distinction who had been admitted to this session, even onto the well of the hall, we found to our great pleasure Mr. Barbour, having become Minister of War since Mr. Adams had entered into the exercise of his powers as President; Colonel McLane, from the State of Delaware; Dr. Mitchill; Dr. Fisk; General Van Courtlandt and Colonel Stone from the State of New York, all having arrived a few days ago to attend the ceremony of June 17.

On leaving the Capitol, the General was escorted by a large procession of friends to Senator Lloyd's house where we had found our lodgings prepared the night before by the hospitable attentions of his amiable family.

The sun of the 50th anniversary of the Battle of Bunker Hill rose radiant, and thousands of voices joining with the joyous sound of bells and artillery blasts greeted it with patriotic acclamations. At seven in the morning, traversing this crowd excited by the glorious memories of June 17, 1775, General Lafayette proceeded to the Grand Lodge of Massachusetts where delegations from the Grand Lodges of Maine, New Hampshire, Rhode Island, Connecticut, Vermont and New Jersey joined with the officers of the Chapter and the Knights of the Temple to welcome and congratulate him.

At ten o'clock, 2,000 Freemasons, 16 companies of voluntary infantry, a corps of cavalry of the militia and the diverse corporations and civil and military authorities repaired to the Capitol where the procession was formed under the command of General Lyman, while the Grand Masters and deputies of the Masonic Order went to get General Lafayette at Mr. Lloyd's home where he had retired on leaving the Temple.

At ten-thirty, the procession started its march. It was composed of about 7,000 people. Two hundred Revolutionary officers or soldiers marched at its head; 40 veterans, the glorious remnants of the Battle of Bunker Hill, followed them in eight open carriages; they were decorated with a wide ribbon on which was written this inscription: *17 June 1775*. Some had on their shoulders the cartridge pouches that they had emptied on that terrible day, and one of them, who had been a drummer, carried the drum again to the sound of which he had rallied the American battalions, broken by the English columns, several times; behind them marched a long column formed by the numerous subscribers for the construction of the monument in rows of six and by 2,000 Masons clad in handsome ornaments and bearing the instruments and symbols of the order; afterwards came General Lafayette in a superb carriage, pulled by six shining white horses. Then after him, a large number of carriages followed in which were his son, his secretary, the Governor of Massachusetts and his staff and, finally, a large number of distinguished people, national or foreign. This column advanced to the sound of music and bells in the midst of 200,000 citizens gathered from all the States of the Union, while salvoes of artillery and general acclamations saluted it at short intervals. It arrived at Bunker Hill at twelve-thirty, and soon everyone was placed in the correct order on the hill where the monument was to be built, testimony to the national gratitude towards the first heroes of the Revolution.

The modest pyramid formerly raised over the remains of Warren and his companions which we had seen at the time of our first visit to Bunker Hill had disappeared. Out of its principal piece of wood, they had fashioned a cane whose gilded handle bore an inscription which recalled its origin, and stated that it had been presented by the Masons of Charlestown to General Lafayette, who had accepted it as one of the most precious relics of the American Revolution. A large excavation, dug out in the same place, indicated that the new monument was to be raised there.

A few moments after we had taken our places around this excavation, and silence was established in this innumerable crowd that was waiting in religious contemplation for the ceremony to begin, the Grand Master of the Grand Lodge of Massachusetts, accompanied by the principal dignitaries of the Order, by brother Lafayette, Mr. Webster and the principal architect, proceeded to lay the foundation stone of the monument in the manner prescribed by the Masonic Order; they put medals, pieces of money, and a silver plate bearing the program of the dedication of the monument into an iron box; this box was laid under the stone on which the Grand Master scattered corn, wine and oil, while Reverend Mr. Allen, Chaplain of the day, pronounced the benediction. The Masonic order to complete this monument was subsequently given, and a salvo of artillery announced that the first part of the ceremony was concluded.

The procession made its way to a vast amphitheater constructed on the northeast side of the hill; at the center of its base stood a platform from which the speaker of the day was to project his voice to 15,000 listeners located in the amphitheater; all the revolutionary officers and soldiers, some of whom had traveled great distances to attend this solemn ceremony, were seated opposite the platform, the survivors of Bunker Hill forming a small group in front. At the head of this gathering, the only surviving general of the Revolution, General Lafayette, was seated in an armchair; immediately behind them, 2,000 brilliantly dressed ladies seemed to form a guard of honor to these venerable graybeards, and to defend them against the tumultuous waves of the crowd; behind the ladies, more than 10,000 people were seated on the numerous benches which were placed around in a semicircle on the side of the hill, whose summit was crowned by more than 30,000 spectators who, although outside the range of the speaker's voice, stood immobile and in the most profound silence.

After the stirring that inevitably accompanies the movement of so considerable a crowd had been calmed, one heard the sound of the melodious voices of a large number of musicians who, concealed behind the platform, intoned a patriotic and religious song whose sweet and simple harmony exquisitely prepared all minds for the profound impressions of eloquence. This song was followed by a prayer of Dr. Thaxter. When this venerable pastor who had had the honor of fighting at Bunker Hill appeared to the assembly with his white hair falling in long silver curls over his shoulders, when he raised his hands, emaciated by time, towards the sky and when, in a voice still strong, he entreated the benediction of the Eternal Being on the works of the day, the entire audience felt itself infused with an inexpressible emotion. Finally, the speaker of the day, Mr. Webster, presented himself in his turn; … his tall stature, his athletic form, the noble expression of his face, the fire of his gaze put him in perfect harmony with the scene at which he appeared. For a long time already popular by virtue of the spell of his eloquence, Mr. Webster was welcomed by the assembly with great displays of satisfaction; the pleasing murmuring with which he was greeted rose from the bottom of the hill to the summit, and prevented him for some time from beginning his speech. At last, his voice sonorous, though slightly moved, he spoke these words:

> This crowd that surrounds me proves the unanimous feeling which the circumstance that gathers us in this place has excited; these thousands of citizens, glowing with a sympathetic joy, and penetrated by a common feeling of gratitude, raise their eyes towards this immense canopy of a more immense temple still, and proclaim religiously the day, the place, the purpose of this solemn assembly.

Yes, if ever man were to surrender to the influence of places, we can surrender ourselves here to the emotions that stir us. We are in the midst of the sepulchres of our fathers, we tread upon ground consecrated by their valor, their constancy and by the shedding of their blood; it is not then to fix an uncertain date in our annals, or to lend distinction to unknown fields that we join here; for if we had never seen the light of day, if our purpose had never been conceived, the 17th of June, 1775 would nonetheless have shone brilliantly in history, and the place where we stand would have attracted the eyes of all the generations to come. But we are Americans.

The present era will be, so to speak, only the early age of the history of this great continent. We see rolling before us a probable train of great events. The future is full of pleasing promises, and we cannot turn back without interest to the circumstances which, before we were born, were to influence so fortunately our future destiny. It is here, across the passage of time, that our posterity must enjoy and endure; it is fitting to contemplate under what aspect this small portion of eternity presents itself during the time that God allows us to appear on earth.

Can we go back in time to the moment of the discovery of this great continent without feeling an emotion that holds a personal interest? Who could recall with indifference that most touching and pathetic scene that presents to our imagination the great discoverer of America, standing on his shattered bark, in the midst of the shades of night. None around him has found rest. Tossed on the billows of an unknown ocean, agitated by despair and hope that alternate in possession of his troubled, worried mind, pressing his harassed frame on the side of the vessel, and straining his anxious eyes far to the westward he seems to want to approach the horizon, until in a moment of ecstasy, heaven at last grants his audacious genius the vision of the new world.

The settlement of the English Colonies in this country is an event nearer to our times, more closely connected to our present condition, which makes a surer appeal still to our sympathy. We cherish every memorial of our venerable ancestors, we celebrate their patience and their resignation, we admire their daring enterprise, we teach our children to venerate their piety, and we are justly proud of being descended from a race of men who taught the entire world how to succeed in founding civil institutions on the noble principles of human freedom and human knowledge. Will we, their children, be able to stay unresponsive to the story of their labors and sufferings? No, the waters of the Ocean will have ceased to wash the shores of Plymouth before we cast an indifferent look on its banks. The Nation, young and vigorous, the Nation having arrived at a glorious maturity, will not forget the places where, in its infancy, its liberties were defended.

But of all the events, the greatest in the history of the continent is the one that we are met here to commemorate today, that prodigy of modern times, at once a wonder and a blessing, the American Revolution!

Our love of country, the admiration that exalted sights inspire, and sentiments of nearly religious gratitude for distinguished services are the motives uniting us at a time when happiness, prosperity and power all combine to satisfy national pride.

The aim of the Society whose organ I am here was to erect a durable monument to the memory of the early friends of American Independence. No time appeared more propitious to our design than the present prosperous and peaceful period; and this memorable place, and the anniversary of the day when the Battle of Bunker Hill was waged seemed to claim our preference. The work has begun; we have laid the cornerstone of this monument in the midst of this innumerable throng, raising with us thoughts of pious gratitude towards the sky.

We hope that this undertaking will not be abandoned, and that the solid shaft of this massive column, which is to be built into the air with majestic simplicity, will remain as long as heaven permits the works of man to last, as an emblem of the events in honor of which it was raised, and as a reminder of the feelings of gratitude of those who have erected it.

We know that it is only in the universal remembrance of mankind that one must consign the record of illustrious actions. We know that this structure, if it should be raised beyond the azure vault, its broad surface would contain but a small part of knowledge that has been spread over the earth, and which history charges itself with transmitting to posterity.

We know that a pedestal as immense as the earth itself would not carry any farther the renown of the events that we are celebrating, and that no structure, which would not be built to outlive the extinction of knowledge itself, could perpetuate the memorial more surely than history.

Our object, in rendering this homage to the valor of our ancestors, is thus to show that it was justly appreciated. In presenting this work to the eye, we want to keep alive in the generations to come similar sentiments to those which inspire us, and to foster a living and constant regard for the principles of the Revolution.

The human mind is composed of imagination and also sentiment as well as judgment and reason; and it is not useless to give to the one and to the other a noble direction, and to give to the heart a source of generous emotions. Let it not be supposed that our object is to perpetuate a spirit of hostility, or even to nourish military enthusiasm. Our sights are purer, more noble, more elevated; we consecrate this monument to the spirit of national independence, and our sincere wish is that the light of peace brighten it forever! We want to offer also the testimony of our profound conviction that these events, to which we are beholden for the beautiful privileges that we enjoy, have also had happy influences on the general well-being of mankind. We come, as Americans, to make this place conspicuous that will be forever dear to us as well as to our posterity. We wish that the traveler who will trace his steps here may behold here the place where the first battle of the Revolution was fought, and that this trophy may proclaim the magnitude and importance of that event to every class and every age. We wish that childhood may learn the history, the purpose of its erection from maternal lips, and that weary and withered age, in beholding it, be solaced by the honorable recollections it awakens. We wish that the craftsman, the laborer on looking up here may be proud in the midst of their humble toil; and we hope that in those days of disaster that strike all nations and that will doubtless come upon us, desponding patriotism, in turning its eyes to it, may be reassured and be reminded on what solid foundations our national strength reposes. We would wish that this column, rising towards heaven among the steeples of so many temples dedicated to the service of God, may also produce in all minds pious feelings of dependence and gratitude. It will offer itself as the last object to the sight of him who leaves his native land, and, like a beacon of glory and liberty, it will be the first object to gladden his sight on his return. Let it rise until it meets the sun at the beginning of its course; let the earliest light of the morning gild it, and let the lights of the parting day, playing still on its summit, seem to leave it sorrowfully.

What an extraordinary age we live in! Events so various and so important that they might distinguish centuries are compressed within the compass of a single life. When has it happened that history had so much to record in the same term of years as since the 17th of June, 1775? Our Revolution, which might have entailed a war of half a century, has been achieved in a few years; 24 sovereign States have been established, and we are in possession of a government so wise, so free, of such practical beauty that we might wonder that it had been established so rapidly, were it not the far greater wonder that it should have been established at all. Two or three millions of inhabitants have been augmented to 12,000,000 citizens. The great forests of the West are prostrated by the exertions of successful industry, and the dwellers on the banks of the Ohio and the Mississippi have become the fellow-citizens and neighbors of those who cultivate the hills of New England.

There are no seas that our commerce has not explored; our flag is respected everywhere; our revenues are adequate to all the exigencies of government, and we hardly know taxation; and finally, we enjoy peace with all nations, founded on equal rights and mutual respect.

Europe, within the same period, has been agitated by mighty revolutions that not only have been felt in the private affairs of each individual but which, shaking to its core the political fabric, have dashed thrones, unshakable for ages, against one another.

On our continent, our example has been followed and colonies have been transformed into nations. Unaccustomed new sounds of liberty and free government have reached us from regions that the sun hardly visits; and the European dominion is annihilated forever from the place where we stand to the South Pole.

In Europe as in America, the face of the world seems changed; the progress of knowledge has been general; all has been improved; legislation, commerce, the arts and letters proceed under the influence of a need for knowledge that sweeps the century along and which is its distinctive feature.

However great and rapid might be the changes that I have pointed out, the interval that separates us from the Battle of Bunker Hill, during which they have taken place, is only 50 years! And at the very moment when we are gathering the fruits of so prosperous a condition, when we see with satisfaction the brightened prospects that present themselves to the world, we still have among us some of those who took an active part in the scenes of 1775. They are gathered here from all parts of New England to see once more, in a moment so moving for them, this renowned theater of their courage and their patriotism.

Venerable men! You have been bequeathed to us by a former generation; heaven has bounteously lengthened your lives that you might bear witness to this so solemn moment. You are now where you stood 50 years ago, this very hour, with your brothers and your neighbors, pressed shoulder to shoulder for the defense of your country. The same heaven shines above your heads; the same ocean rolls at your feet; but all else, how changed! You hear no more hostile cannons; you see no more smoke and flames rising from the walls of burning Charlestown.

The land strewn with the dead, the impetuous charge, the firm resistance, the loud call to repeated assault, or to a manly and courageous defense; those cohorts who, offering a bosom nearly bared, defied the terrors of death; such was the scene which you witnessed then; now all is peace. From the heights of this metropolis, from its roofs, from its edifices, your mothers, your wives, your compatriots watched for the issue of the combat; today its whole happy population comes out to welcome you here with joyous acclamations. So many ships at anchor at the foot of this mount, which seem to rush to surround it enviously, are not a subject of alarm, but a guarantee of power and independence; all is peace, and God has granted you the sight of your country's happiness, before you slumber in your grave. He has allowed you to receive here the reward of your patriotic toils, and he has allowed us, your children, to thank you in the name of the present generation, in the name of our country, in the name of liberty.

But, alas! You are not all here; time and war have thinned your ranks. Prescott, Putnam, Stark, Brooks, Reed, Pomeroy, Bridge! Our eyes look for you in vain amid this broken band; you have rejoined your fathers, and live only in our remembrance and in the brilliant examples that you have handed down to your sons. But let us not grieve too much; you lived at least long enough to know that your work had been accomplished, and you quit arms and life with joy, for your country was free! To the first rays of liberty, you saw the rays of peace succeed, like a beautiful dawn followed by a brilliant day, and your last gaze rested on a cloudless sky.

But alas! Him, the first great martyr of this great cause! Him, the premature victim of his own devotion! Him, the head of our civil councils, leader of our militias, whom nothing called at that moment but his unquenchable ardor! Him, whom Providence stole from us in the hour of overwhelming doubt, who perished before the star of his country had risen, who poured out his generous blood before he knew whether it would fertilize a land of freedom or of bondage....Warren!... How to control the emotion that I feel in uttering thy name!

The work of this moment may perish, but yours will endure; this monument may tumble down, but your name will soar over the debris.

It is not only on those who hazarded or lost their lives on this consecrated spot that we must fix our thoughts at this time; we are happy to see before us a small number of worthy representatives of the Revolutionary Army.

Veterans, remnant of more than one well-fought field of honor! You who won noble victories at Trenton, Monmouth,

Yorktown, Camden, Bennington and Saratoga! Veterans of the century past, when in your youthful days you put everything at hazard in your country's cause, good as that cause was, shining as were your hopes, they could not promise you an hour like this! Could you foresee that, at a moment of great national prosperity, you would come to receive here with your companions-in-arms, the expression of the intense gratitude of an entire people.

But your agitated countenances, and your heaving breasts inform me that your joy is not unmixed; a tumult of contending feelings trouble your spirits. The images of those who are no more, as well as we, crowd around you; so let us hasten to turn our thoughts from a scene that moves you too profoundly.

May the Father of all mercies smile on your declining years and bless them, and when you shall have rejoined those who, like you, assured the triumph of freedom, then carry your eyes to this lovely land that your young valor so well defended, and contemplate the happiness which it enjoys; cast a look upon all parts of the earth, and see to what station you have placed your country, what value you have given to that word: freedom! And rejoice at the sight of well-being that has become the allotment of so large a part of humanity.

I will not speak in detail of the day of June 17th or of the events that preceded it. These are familiarly known to all. In the controversy that was joined with the British Parliament, Massachusetts and the City of Boston were especially exposed to its displeasure. The Parliament manifested it by shutting up the Port of Boston and altering the form of government of the Province. The impression that these measures produced in America shows how little in England they understood or regarded the spirit of the Colonies, whose conduct brings honor to this early period of our history. It had been anticipated that the other Colonies would be terrified by the severity of the punishment, and that the inhabitants of the seaports, governed by love of gain, would greedily enjoy the advantage that this blow given to the commerce of Boston offered them for enrichment. How they were deceived in their cold calculations! They little knew how deep and intense were the feelings of resistance to illegal acts of power which possessed the whole American People. Everywhere the bait was rejected with scorn; all the Colonies seized this fortunate occasion to show to the whole world that none of them was swayed by selfish or local interest. The people of Salem seemed more than others destined to feel the temptation to profit by the misfortunes of their neighbors, but there, as elsewhere, they spurned the proffer unhesitatingly, in a tone of the most noble self-respect and most indignant patriotism, they said: "We are deeply affected by the public calamities, and the miseries that are rapidly heaping up on the capital of the Province excite our commiseration. By shutting up the Port of Boston, some have thought that we would turn the course of trade to our benefit; but we must be dead to every idea of justice, to all feelings of humanity, could we indulge a thought to raise our fortunes on the ruin of those of our suffering neighbors."

These noble sentiments spread far and wide. In that day of general brotherhood, the blow given to Boston was felt by every patriotic heart from one end of the country to the other. Virginia, the Carolinas, Connecticut and New Hampshire proclaimed the cause to be their own. The Continental Congress, then holding its first session in Philadelphia, expressed its sympathy for the evils that afflicted the inhabitants of Boston and, from all quarters, they received assurance that the cause was a common one, and that they would bring to it common efforts and common sacrifices. The Congress of Massachusetts responded to these assurances, and in an address to the Congress in Philadelphia, bearing the signature of Warren, perhaps among his last, this Colony, notwithstanding the imminent dangers that threatened it, declared that it was ready to hazard all in the cause of America.

But the hour drew nigh that was to put each to the proof, and to reveal those who were willing to seal these professions of devotion with their blood; the cry of war leaving Lexington and Concord instructed that the time was come for action. A heroic spirit pervaded all the ranks, all were inspirited with a fixed, solemn, invincible courage.

Totamque infusa per artus, mens agitat molem, et magno se corpore miscet.

How strange for the peaceful laborers of New England that the roll call of war was transported to the center of their hearths; but their country called them, their consciences were convinced of the necessity for defense, and they did not withhold themselves from this perilous trial. Their daily occupations were abandoned. The plough was forgotten in the unfinished furrow. Mothers gave up their sons, their husbands to all the hazards of a civil war. Death might strike with honor on the field of battle, it might descend from a scaffold; for one or the other, the insurgents were prepared. The sentiment of Quincy was full in their hearts. This distinguished son of genius and of patriotism spoke and our fathers repeated after him: "Blandishments will not dazzle us, nor will threats of death intimidate; for we are determined that in whatever manner, in whatever place, or at whatever time that it pleases God to call us, we will die free men."

The 17th of June saw the four New England Colonies standing here, ready to triumph or fall together; there was then, and would that there be forever among them, only one spirit, one cause, one country.

The Battle of Bunker Hill was attended with the most important effects: the war became open and national. There could no longer be a question of proceeding against individuals as guilty of treason; that distressing crisis had passed. The appeal was to courage, and it was in question whether the energy and the resources of the people would permit the accomplishment of their object. The effect of this military engagement was felt even outside our country. The actions of the Colonies, their appeals, their proclamations, had made their cause known in Europe. We can say that in no age, or country, were the public writings more eloquent, nor did they have more force of argument, or breathe more of that ardent persuasion that exalted feelings and elevated principles can alone bestow. The public papers of that time deserve to be studied, not only for the spirit that inspired them, but for the talent with which they were written.

To these able vindications of their cause, the Colonies had added proof of the devotion and the power that were to defend them; all saw that if America fell, she would not fall without a struggle. They admired with sympathy and surprise this nation still in its infancy, remote, unknown, unaided, struggling against the power of England, and in the first battle that it waged against it, leaving more of its enemies on the contested field, in proportion to the number of combatants, than had been known to fall in the recent wars of Europe.

The tale of these events reached a noble foreigner who hears us today; he has not forgotten that his youthful valor was awakened by the report of the battlefield of Bunker Hill and the name of Warren.

Mr. Lafayette, we have intended on this day to commemorate the establishment of great public principles of liberty and to do honor to their distinguished defenders. We dare not eulogize the living at so solemn an occasion; but your interesting relation to this country and the peculiar circumstances which surround us call on me to express the happiness that we derive from your presence here today.

Fortunate, fortunate man! What measures of devotion do you owe to Providence which has plotted out the circle of your extraordinary life! You belong to both hemispheres, to two generations. Heaven saw fit that the electric spark of liberty should be conducted by you from the New World to the Old; and we, whom duty and patriotism have called here, long ago learned from our fathers to cherish your name and your virtues. You will count, no doubt, in the number of fortunate events of your life, the good luck that enables you to be present at this solemnity. You now behold the field of battle, the report of which reached you in the heart of France and caused a generous ardor in your soul. You see the lines of the redoubt thrown up by Prescott with such incredible diligence and defended by his *lion-hearted* valor. It is within its enclosure that we have placed the cornerstone of our monument; you see where Warren fell, where Parker, Gardner, McClary, Moore, and so many other patriots, fell with him! Those who survived that day, and whose lives have been prolonged to the present hour, are now around you. Some of them you have known in the trials of the war. You see them today wanting to take you in their arms; you hear them raise their voices to invoke God to bless Lafayette and his descendants.

You have helped us in laying the foundation of this structure; you have heard eulogies, very feeble it is true, accompany the names of the noble patriots of 1775. Monuments and eulogies belong to the dead. We give them this day to Warren and to the other citizen-victims of this great victory. On other occasions we have rendered the same honors to your more immediate companions-in-arms, to Washington, to Greene, Gates, Sullivan and Lincoln. We would gladly hold them back for a still longer time from the little remnant of this immortal band. *Serus in coelum redeas*. Let the day be far distant when any inscription shall bear your name, or any tongues pronounce your eulogy.

The principal reflections that present themselves to us on this occasion respect the great changes that have happened since the Battle of Bunker Hill; and, as a result of the character of the age, these thoughts cannot be confined to a single country, so great are the interests of humanity bound together. To the individual progress of a nation is fastened the improvement of all peoples, just as ships of different construction, propelled by a common tide, advance at an unequal rate, but reach the same mark by the same route.

The distinctive character of the age is that community of opinion, of knowledge among men and nations, that was unknown till our time. Acquired knowledge has triumphed and is triumphing over distances, over diversity of languages, customs, prejudices, and religious differences. The civilized and Christian nations know at last that all division of territory does not necessarily entail hostility, and that all contact need not be war. The whole world is becoming an exalted arena where genius and thought come to contend; in whatever language they express themselves they are sure to be heard. A sentiment of sympathetic interest unites the two continents; the winds, the waves cause the intelligence to circulate rapidly from one country to the other; there is a vast commerce of ideas; there exists among all enlightened minds a kind of fraternity from which public opinion emanates. Thought is the great lever by which human ends are reached, and the diffusion of knowledge, adding to the knowledge of each individual, has strengthened the power of the masses.

From these causes important improvements have taken place in the personal condition of individuals. Mankind is not only better fed and better clothed, but they may enjoy more leisure; they join to other kinds of success that of more self-respect. A superior tone of customs, manners and education prevails. This remark, most true in its application to our own country, is not, however, applicable to it alone. Manufacturing and commerce contribute to the comforts of life articles whose consumption has been augmented in a progression much greater than that of the population; and while the incredible improvement of machinery of all kinds would seem to have replaced labor, individual industry still finds its occupation and reward on all sides; so wisely has Providence seemed to combine the capacity and the desires of men.

Volumes would be required to draw a faithful picture of the progress made by us during a last half-century in the Industrial Arts, Commerce, Agriculture, and in Letters and the Sciences. I will not enlarge any longer on this subject, but I will turn for a moment to the contemplation of what has been done on the great questions of Politics and Government, which have intensely occupied men's thoughts for 50 years. They have debated the nature of Government, its ends and its means; old opinions have been attacked and defended, new ideas recommended and resisted. They have deployed in this controversy the greatest power of dialectic of which the human mind is capable. From individual opinion to the public assemblies, the debate has been transferred to the battlefield, and the world has been shaken by wars of unexampled magnitude, and great variety of fortune. A day of peace has at length succeeded; the struggle has ended, the clouds have dissipated, we can recognize what have been the permanent changes affecting the condition of human societies. Without stopping to detail the progress, we may be congratulated that it has been favorable to human liberty and human happiness.

It was in America that the spirit of political revolutions began its course; here its course was prudent, wise, measured. Having arrived at another hemisphere, and carried along by unfortunate but natural causes, it received an irregular and violent impulse; its chariot sprang forward with a dreadful celerity, and, like those that contested for the prize in the races of antiquity, its wheels caught fire from the rapidity of their own motion, spreading everywhere conflagration and terror.

This unfortunate result taught us that much better the value of our fortunate destinies, and we saw how admirably our national character was for setting the example of a popular government. We were not intoxicated by possession of a power by which our self-respect was restored. We had been, as it were, in the habit of governing ourselves. Despite the supremacy of England, a large part of the legislative power has always belonged to our Colonial assemblies. The forms of a representative government were familiar to us. The doctrines inherent in a free government, the balance of power and its division into different branches were known; the character of our countrymen was peaceful, moral, religious, and as there has been nothing destroyed, nothing could shock their feelings, or even their prejudices; we had no thrones to overturn, no privileged orders to cast down; no violent impacts to property to encounter; in the American Revolution they sought only to defend what they possessed, and to assure the right to enjoy it.

Let us not be surprised, however, that under circumstances less auspicious, revolutions begun in the same spirit, have terminated so differently. It is difficult to introduce any principle of liberty whatsoever into governments to which liberty has been long a stranger. The greatest work that the wisdom of peoples could accomplish is to establish a popular government on lasting foundations. Nonetheless it cannot be doubted that Europe has come out of the long contest in which it was engaged, regenerated, and the benefits that it has acquired will be retained, for it consists mainly in a stock of more just and more enlightened ideas: provinces, kingdoms may be wrested from the hands that have conquered them; there exists a perpetual fluctuation in all human affairs; but the glorious prerogative of the empire of knowledge is that what it has once acquired, it never loses; to the contrary, its riches multiply themselves; its ends become means, and its conquests bring new conquests. So abundant a harvest, entrusted like seed to the ground, will provide a new harvesting whose wealth will be incalculable.

Occupied as we are in a time of profound peace in raising a monument to the Fatherland, filled with the sense of our prosperity, will we not turn our thoughts for a moment to that noble land from which the arts have borrowed all their models, and which, in an imposing struggle, fights no longer to protect its masterpieces but to reappear as a nation among nations; let us tell Greece that it is not forgotten, that the universe has its eyes fixed on it, that her efforts are applauded and that our prayers call out for its triumph. We have kept up the consoling hope that no human power can smother a veritable spark of civil and religious liberty. Like the earth's central fire, repressed for a time, its inherent and invincible force heaves at last both the Ocean and the land and, forcing an exit, the volcano lifts it flame towards heaven.

I repeat, let us venture to congratulate ourselves with pride that our example has influenced in so fortunate a manner the liberties and the happiness of the world; let us endeavor to comprehend the grandeur, the importance of the part assigned to us in the great drama of human affairs.

We are placed at the head of the representative system, and we have proved here that such governments are not incompatible with repose, peace, security of personal rights, with good laws, a just administration and great national power.

We are not propagandists for new doctrines, we do not disturb those who, preferring other systems, regard them as better in themselves, or as better suited to existing conditions; we want to prove only that the popular form of government is practicable, that our duty is to preserve so fine an example intact and not to weaken its authority in the eyes of the world. If, in our case, the representative system came to fail, its cause would be lost in the court of reason, for never could a combination of more favorable circumstances be known to facilitate the experiment. The hopes of humanity rest with us, and if our example is a bad argument to offer in favor of popular liberty, it would be universally condemned.

But be it far from my intent to express here any doubt; I want to awaken the emulation of duty: the history of the past time and that of the present time authorizes us to believe that popular governments, however modified in their forms, and not always changing for the better in their details, may yet, in their general character, be as durable, as permanent as other systems.

We know indeed that in our country any other system is inadmissible; the principle of a free government is inherent on American soil; it belongs to it like the mountains.

Let the present generation, then, be infused with the sacred obligations that have been imposed on it; each day sees one of those who established our freedom and our government vanish. It is to us that is now confided this precious trust. Let us ponder the object to which we are to commit ourselves. We do not have to fight for our independence any more; the laurels have already been gathered by hands more worthy than ours. We do not have to place ourselves near Solon, or Alfred, or other founders of states; our fathers have filled these places: it remains to us to share in the defense and preservation of the benefits that we possess. The spirit of the times indicates to us what noble paths we have to pursue; our time is to be one of improvement; in a time of peace, let us dream of advancing the useful arts and the arts of peace; let us develop the resources of our land, and its might; let us maintain its institutions, promote its interests, and let us see if we cannot also merit living in the memory of men: let us cultivate a true spirit of union and harmony, and, in pursuing these great objects which our current condition so clearly points out to us, let us act always with the feeling and the conviction that the 24 States are united as one Nation; let our conceptions be raised to the height of our duties; let us extend our ideas over the vast field of action that is offered to us, and let us have in view only our Country, nothing but our Country! And, with the blessing of God, may that Country offer so beautiful an example of wisdom, peace and liberty that it holds the attention and admiration of the world forever!

During this speech the orator was interrupted at times by bursts of applause from the audience, who could not contain the expression of sympathetic feelings that excited them when Mr. Webster addressed the Revolutionary veterans and General Lafayette; uncovering their venerable heads, they arose to receive the thanks that he gave them in the name of the people. A hymn sung in chorus by the entire assembly followed the speech, and terminated this second part of the ceremony.

At the signal of a cannon blast, the procession formed again, ascended the hill, and they took their places at a banquet that had been prepared on the summit; there, under an immense wooden canopy, 4,000 people took their places without confusion and without the least discomfort; the tables were placed so artfully that the voices of the presiding officer and of all those who made toasts or speeches were easily heard not only by the guests but also by a large number of spectators standing outside; the names of Warren, the orator of the day and of the Nation's Guest were proclaimed in turn during the meal. Before leaving the table, General Lafayette rose to offer his thanks to the members of the Bunker Hill Monument Association, and he spoke in these words:

> I entreat your attention today only to thank you in the name of my Revolutionary companions-in-arms, as well as in my own name, Gentlemen, for the tokens of esteem and affection, I can say filial affection, with which we have been gratified on this great day of anniversary celebration; we offer our most ardent wishes for the maintenance of that republican liberty and equality, of government of the people by the people, of that blessed union among the States of the confederation, objects for which we fought and spilled our blood; it is on these things that the hope of the human race rests today. Permit me to propose to you the following toast:
>
> *Bunker Hill* and the holy resistance to oppression, which has already liberated the American hemisphere. The anniversary toast at the jubilee of the next half-century will be *to liberated Europe.*

This toast was applauded rapturously, and, immediately after, the guests left the table to return to the City.

A delightful evening, pleasantly cooled by a light sea breeze, had succeeded the brilliance and the heat of a fine summer day; in order to enjoy it better, George Lafayette proposed that we return to Boston on foot; I accepted, and we lost ourselves in the crowd that was descending the hill while discussing the day's ceremonies; in these discussions, the name of the National Guest was incessantly mingled, as was the account of the principal actions they have earned him the gratitude of the American people. There, as in nearly all the assemblages in which I had found myself during our trip, I was struck by a very remarkable thing, that is, how completely knowledge of the events of the Revolution is spread in all classes of citizens and even among the children; I often heard little boys of eight to ten years speak to each other about the campaigns of the War of Independence with astonishing accuracy; they recounted to each other what they had read and learned; how, for example, Lafayette had arrived in the United States; how he had been wounded at Brandywine; what he had done at Rhode Island and at Monmouth; how, while he was commander-in-chief in Virginia, he had, after a five-month campaign, entrapped Lord Cornwallis at Yorktown, where the French fleet of Count de Grasse, and Washington, at the head of a corps of Rochambeau's Army and the Lincoln Division, had come to join him and besiege that town where the English and their auxiliaries, the Hanoverians, had capitulated. I am well aware that the receptions given to Lafayette in each town furnished the occasion to recall all these facts, but often I also had proof that the other facts of the Revolution were equally known by all classes of citizens, from the veterans who speak of them incessantly to the schoolchildren who are proud of what their ancestors had done and of the freedom that they have the good fortune to enjoy. Another very remarkable characteristic of the mind of the American public is that, not only are the people free and happy, but they appreciate this freedom and happiness; and what English tourists call vanity is quite simply the inner conviction of the superiority of institutions and civic dignity of which the Americans speak, as a man with a good constitution renders thanks to heaven for his good health; this is so true that American patriotism (one may say the same of French liberalism but not of English patriotism) is completely free of jealousy with regards to other nations whose freedom and prosperity are cordially wished for by the people of the United States.

Yielding to the wishes of the inhabitants of Boston, General Lafayette stayed in their City for several days after the ceremony of Bunker Hill and divided this time between the society of his personal friends and the public, who up to the last moment, gave him evidences of its affection. On the 20th, he accepted a dinner offered to him by the Society of Mechanics, where he met with all the public officials and the most distinguished persons of the State, who had accepted the invitation with equal enthusiasm, so great is the deference that everyone in the United States has for the useful classes of society.

During his stay in Boston, General Lafayette received and, at the same time, accepted the invitations of the States of Maine, New Hampshire and Vermont, where his presence was awaited impatiently by the people; and that of New York City, whose citizens ardently desired that he celebrate July 4th, the anniversary of the Declaration of Independence, with them. To meet all these obligations in so short a time appeared to be a difficult thing; however, the General did not despair of overcoming it, for he knew by experience how, everywhere on his route, the people and the magistrates were in wonderful agreement to make his travels pleasant and speedy.

On the 20th, he went to take leave of his old friend John Adams; he used the entire day of the 21st to make or receive farewell visits in the City, and, on the 22nd, he set out, accompanied by the members of the committee of arrangements, and escorted by a corps of voluntary cavalry.

Chapter XIV

Speedy and Brief Visit to the States of New Hampshire, Maine and Vermont – Return to New York – Celebration of the Anniversary of the Declaration of Independence – The American Longboat – Patriotism and Unselfishness of the Sailors of New York.

In commencing this journal, I had resolved to record in it all the events of this extraordinary trip day-by-day, but their multiplicity, and more still the rapidity of our movements often forced me to renounce the rigorous execution of this initial plan, and it is especially while traversing the States of Maine, New Hampshire and Vermont that I felt even more the impossibility of noting all the interesting facts, all the honorable and moving circumstances that characterized the visit of General Lafayette in this part of the Union. We traveled through these three States with an average speed of 11 miles per hour. Often we passed through so many villages and so many towns on the same day that my memory could not retain all their names faithfully. Therefore, I have not been able to find the time necessary to gather the historical details or statistics that I had amply harvested in most of the other States, and I will be able in this chapter only to recall some of the fetes that the children of the Green Mountains[15] and their neighbors offered to the National Guest of America.

I have said that General Lafayette had left Boston on the 22nd in the early morning. Some hours after his departure, he arrived in Pembroke, on the border of New Hampshire, where he was received by a delegation of this State. At the head of this delegation Mr. Webster, brother of the orator of Bunker Hill, congratulated him in the name of his compatriots. From Pembroke to Concord, capital of the State, his triumphal march was surrounded by a numerous procession formed of citizens who had rushed up in all directions from the furthest points. Upon his arrival in this City, they conducted him to the Capitol, where the House of Representatives and the Senate, presided over by the Governor of the State, were gathered together to welcome him. The speech of congratulations that Governor Morril addressed to him was remarkable for the expression of sentiments of gratitude and attachment of which the people of New Hampshire had just given him so moving evidences. He responded to this speech with the outpouring of a deeply moved heart.

After this first reception, the General was conducted into another room of the Capitol, where General Pierce waited to present to him a large number of his former companions-in-arms who, braving their age and fatigue,

15. Name often used to characterize the inhabitants of Vermont.

had not been afraid to leave their faraway hearths to come to shake his hand in a brotherly manner and to speak with him for a moment about times passed. While they presented them to him individually, as well as the Representatives and Senators who had come to join with them, the people were joyously setting up tables for 600 guests on the public square, and were preparing a civic banquet at which we came to find seats on leaving the Capitol building. The General had the pleasure of being seated in the middle of more than 200 Revolutionary officers or soldiers, who could hardly contain the joy that the presence of their old friend aroused in them. Before leaving the table, many of them expressed in their toasts their feelings of philanthropic liberty. One of them drank *to the holy alliance of Lafayette and liberty!* May it be able to destroy the plots formed against the rights of man! – Another drank to North America, such as it is, and to France, such as it ought to be. – The General responded to these noble wishes by the following toast:

> To the State of New Hampshire, to its representatives, and to this City, home of the organized authorities of the State!
>
> May the citizens of New Hampshire remain eternally possessed of civil and religious freedom; benefits for which the exalted spirit of their ancestors brought them to come to search in a faraway land, and which their fathers have founded on the broad bases of the sovereignty of the people and the rights of man.

A salvo of artillery and unanimous applause of the crowd that gathered around the tables drowned out this toast, and we left the banquet in order to return to the square of the Capitol, where the militias, arranged in battle array, waited until the General had passed them in review in order then to file before him.

Our evening was divided between the musical society, which played an excellent *Oratorio* before the General, and a tea at Governor Morril's house, to which all the ladies pressed in a crowd to take leave of the National Guest who, on the following day, left Concord with a cavalry corps for escort, and took the road to Dover, where he arrived at the end of the day, and where he was received with an enthusiasm that I will not attempt to describe.

A little after having left Dover, we arrived at the borders of Maine where General Lafayette was received by a delegation with whom we made our way to Portland, seat of the Government of this State. On the way we visited Kennebunk, a small town of about 2,500 people, noteworthy in the commercial activity of its Port. The sound of bells and artillery apprised the

General with what pleasure he had been awaited by the inhabitants, with whom he decided to spend several hours. When he entered the Town Hall, where the authorities and the staff of the State Government awaited him, he was welcomed by Dr. Emerson who addressed him in this manner in the name of the citizens.

> You have just traveled the journey of freedom, you have been able to judge its power and its resources, and your heart must have throbbed with joy and happiness at the sight of the result of your efforts. There isn't a single true American who hasn't followed you on your trip in his mind's eye, and who has not experienced an exalted feeling of pride each time that you have expressed your admiration.
>
> This village, as well as thousands of others, has emerged from the forests since that time in which you fought beside Washington; and the children of those brave soldiers, whose bloody feet were supplied with shoes by your generosity when their country had only its courage for everything, pay homage to you today for their well-being, and offer you the testimony of a respect and gratitude that nothing can equal.
>
> General, we learned with profound despair of the persecutions that Germanic despotism practiced against you, and we would have wished to be able to fly to your relief, but the bells that greet your arrival reverberate now in the ears of your persecutors like a horrible alarm bell, a sign of their eternal torment and of the death knell of their tyranny….
>
> Nonetheless, General, your adoptive Fatherland trembles still that it may see you fall back into the power of your enemies. May God inspire you to stay among us until he summons you to enjoy celestial freedom! And may those among us, who will have survived you, have the sad consolation of entrusting you to the same land that covers over the glorious remains of Washington, of Greene, of Lincoln, of Knox, and of all your illustrious companions-in-arms whose glory, joined with yours, can never perish. Such are the wishes of those who welcome you today, and who repeat rapturously *Welcome! Welcome Lafayette!*

These last words of the speaker were repeated with delight by the crowd, and when the first outburst had calmed a little, General Lafayette made the following response:

> I feel a great happiness in seeing myself received with so much affection by the people of Kennebunk and by you, my dear Sir, who has expressed your sentiments in a manner as honorable as it is kind. I thank you, I thank all my friends for wanting to take part in the delightful pleasure that I have had in recognizing, on this long and patriotic journey, the fortunate results of independence, freedom, and of government of the people by the people. While I had the honor of being persecuted by all the Governments of Europe, without a single exception, I gloried also in the thought that I had kept the approbation of, and that I lived in the truly republican hearts of, the American People. Today, Sir, after my happy visit to each of the States of the Union, I will not be restricted to enjoying the spectacle of the salute of this vast empire, to congratulating myself on the already effectuated deliverance of the American hemisphere; I will also bless, by anticipation, the deliverance of the entire human race to whom the United States has given the first example of true and complete national freedom. Accept, my dear Sir, and all of you who press around us with so much enthusiasm and affection, please accept also the expression of my gratitude, my affection and my respect.

Although the General had only a very little time to devote to the citizens of Kennebunk, he nonetheless accepted the public banquet which they had prepared for him, and took his place there on a chair elegantly decorated with flowers by the ladies of the Town; at the end of the meal, each guest expressed the feelings that this patriotic reunion had awakened in him, and Dr. Emerson gave the following toast:

> To our National Guest, *to General Lafayette*; he left Europe to give freedom to America; he returned there to teach his Fatherland the means of achieving happiness; today he comes among us to enjoy the result of his noble efforts.

The General responded to this toast with the following:

> To the village of Kennebunk, on the place where the first tree was felled on the same day that the first shot was fired

> at Lexington, the signal for American and universal freedom! May this glorious date be, for flourishing Kennebunk, a pledge of its republican prosperity, and of its ever-growing happiness.

Upon leaving the table and before departing from the Town, the General proceeded to the house of one of the principal citizens, Mr. Storer, where all the ladies had gathered to be presented to him. He thanked them fondly for the considerate attentions that they had paid to him during his brief stay at Kennebunk, and at four o'clock in the afternoon he set out for Saco, where we slept.

On the 25th, we arrived in Portland, a pretty city located on the sea-coast between the Saco and the Penobscot Rivers. It has been for a long time the seat of the Government of the State of Maine, and its population, nearly entirely mercantile, is about 9,000. The citizens of Portland and their magistrates had acted together to arrange a reception for General Lafayette worthy of their love for him, and one can say that it did not yield in magnificence to any of those that the largest cities of the Union had made for him; the militia corps, having flocked there from all parts of the State, presented an imposing crowd before the City. The schoolchildren filled the streets that the National Guest was to traverse, and they threw flowers on his path. The triumphal arches under which he passed were noteworthy in their good taste and in the delicacy of the inscriptions with which they were decorated. On one of them was a small ship-model under which one read: *I will buy and equip a vessel at my own expense*, words that Lafayette addressed, as one knows, to the American Commissioners in Paris in 1777, when they confessed to him the impossibility of their country providing the means of transporting him to the United States. On others were the names of the battles in which Washington's young companion-in-arms had fought. After having slowly traversed the City in the midst of the acclamations of the crowd, the General arrived at the State House where Governor Parris received and addressed him in the name of the citizens of Maine and in the presence of the representatives and the magistrates of the people. In his speech, the Governor recalled enthusiastically the glorious period that began Lafayette's reputation, and paid a deserved tribute of praise and admiration to the soldiers of the Revolution.

Full of intense emotion, which was shared by all the audience, General Lafayette responded:

> Sir, the honorable resolutions of the two branches of the legislature, your invitations replete with kindness, and I am happy to add, the popular reception that awaited me in each

part of the United States, could only lead me to forecast a pleasant reception in this part of the great federation. But I have been received by the people of Maine, by the citizens of their metropolis, by you, Sir, their First Magistrate, in so affectionate a manner that it arouses in my heart the most intense emotions of pleasure and gratitude. I thank you particularly for the respectful tribute that you have paid to our courageous and virtuous army in which, at the beginning of the Revolution and of my life, I found in *Washington* a father, in *Knox* a brother; you can judge our mutual attachment by the joy that we feel, my old companions and I, when we recognize one another in the midst of the crowd of the new generations. Thus, Sir, in my constant and active dedication to the sovereignty of the people and to the rights of man and their liberties, I am proud to think that my adversaries, as well as my friends, must have acknowledged the pure principles and the republican opinions of a soldier and an American patriot.

From the Senate chamber, the General went to Mr. Daniel Cobb's house, which had been prepared to receive him. There, he was awaited by a large number of delegations that brought him the respects of the surrounding towns and villages. He also found there the high officers of the Masonic Lodge of Portland, and the President of the Academy, who in the presence of the professors and the students, conferred on him the title of Doctor of Law. As soon as he was able to slip away a moment from the common group, he proceeded to Mrs. Thacher, daughter of his illustrious companion-in-arms Henry Knox, with whom he conversed up to the time when they came to advise him that the authorities were waiting for him to take his place at the public banquet prepared by the citizens.

From Portland, the General would have wished to continue his way to the border of the State of Maine, but not having the time, he retraced his steps, and made his way towards Burlington in the State of Vermont, by passing through Concord again, and by traversing Windsor, Woodstock, Montpelier, etc. Although Vermont is covered with high mountains that render the roads most difficult to pass, we traveled nonetheless extremely rapidly. We continued to make nearly always more than nine miles per hour, as relays of horses had been put at our disposal by the inhabitants in order that the General would not experience any delay in his passage to New York.

The day had advanced but little when we arrived on the 28th in Burlington, whose beautiful location on the delightful shores of Lake

Champlain aroused our admiration. While we cast our astonished eyes with pleasure on the beauties of nature that unfolded before us, suddenly we heard loud artillery blasts, and a moment later, we saw advancing toward us a troop of young citizen-soldiers, preceded by the crowd of people who rushed in front of the National Guest. The good order of this militia corps, the proud and assured gait of the men who composed it, corresponded perfectly to the reputation for bravery and patriotism that the inhabitants of Vermont had acquired in the Revolutionary War and during that of 1814. It is known that, in 1777, it was Vermonters who, by their presence, accomplished the embarrassment of the English Army of General Burgoyne who, at the sight of their intrepid troops, had a premonition of his defeat. Several days before surrendering, he wrote the British Ministry: *The inhabitants of the New Hampshire*[16] *grants, a territory uninhabited and nearly unknown in the last war, rush us by the thousands, and bank up on my left like dark clouds*.... His letter had not yet arrived in England when the thunderbolt that these clouds enclosed had struck him. It was also the soldiers of Vermont who, numbering only 800 men led by General Stark, destroyed on the same day two English Army corps, taking from them 700 prisoners, four pieces of artillery and all their camp equipment. Finally, it was again the intrepid children of the Green Mountains who formed the battalions that saved Plattsburg from the pillage of the English on September 11, 1814; and it was their improvised crews, on vessels built in 18 days, who forced an enemy superior in number to lower a flag that pretended to absolute dominion of the seas.

The Governor who had come before the General at Windsor and traveled with him since that Town, presented the General himself to the people and the magistrates of Burlington, who welcomed him with the most fond demonstrations of affection. I will not reproduce here, in spite of their eloquence, the numerous speeches addressed to him by the representatives of the different branches of the administration and the Government, nor his responses in which he congratulated the State of Vermont for its so well-deserved enjoyment of the benefits of the new American social order, so superior to the least vicious institutions of Europe, and for its replacement of *European tolerance* with *religious liberty*; *privilege* with *right*; a shadow of representation and an unequal compromise between the aristocratic families and the people with true representation, the principle of the sovereignty of the nation and self-government. But I cannot dispense with saying some words about the patriotic raptures of those veterans, glorious and living momentos of the Revolutionary War, who presented themselves in a crowd around their chief,

16. The territory of Vermont had first made up a part of the State of New Hampshire from which it had separated in 1764 in order to be annexed to that of New York. It is only in 1791 that Vermont entered the federation as an independent State.

their old comrade in dangers, deprivations and glory, and enthusiastically caused his ears to ring with the names of the battles in which he had aided them in the conquest of the independence of their Fatherland. Formed in a column on the public square, numbering more than a hundred, they listened in silence first to the speech given by Mr. Griswold, President of the Council; then, in their turn, they advanced led by one of their comrades, David Russell, whom they had chosen to be the spokesman of their sentiments, and who acquitted himself in this office with that eloquence of heart that takes its inspiration in love of country and love of freedom. When the General had responded to the professions of attachment of his former companions-in-arms, they came one by one to shake his hand, while reminding him more specifically of the circumstances in which each of them had known him or fought at his side. One, Sergeant Day, showed him a sword while saying to him: "It was nearly half a century ago that I received it from your hands, my General…." And I heard the crowd say that despite his advanced age, Sergeant Day had not found this sword too heavy for his arms in 1814.

After the public dinner, which concluded before nightfall, the General proceeded to the University where he was invited to lay the cornerstone of a new wing intended to enlarge a building that a fire had destroyed a year before, and which the zeal of the inhabitants of Vermont for the propagation of education had completely rebuilt in several months. In the solidity and elegance of this new construction, it was easy to recognize the *hand of the people*. The ceremony of laying the cornerstone took place in the presence of the students of the University, their professors, the magistrates of the City, and a large number of citizens who observed with joy the restoration and enlargement of an establishment designed to assure, more every day, the maintenance of their wise institutions by instructing and enlightening their rising generations. Mr. Willard Preston, President of the University, thanked General Lafayette for the proof of his interest that he had just given, in the education of the youth of Vermont, and we repaired to the house of Governor Van Ness, whose charming home and gardens, arranged with an exquisite taste, were even more delightfully improved by a very numerous gathering of ladies and young people who, during the entire evening party, wrangled over the pleasure of approaching the Nation's Guest in order to express to him their fond sentiments and their gratitude for the services which he had rendered to their country and their ancestors; for in the State of Vermont, as in all the rest of the Union, the women are strangers neither to the principles of government, nor to the obligations of patriotism; their education, more liberal than in any part of Europe, places them in the ranks of thinking beings in a most worthy manner, as it is well known that in all the great events that troubled the United States in different periods, the enthusiasm of the women powerfully supported the energy of the magistrates and the dedication of the warriors. One of the things that has contributed the most to increasing my fondness for the Americans during my stay among them is the profound respect that they have for women of all classes, and the tender solicitiousness with which they surround this sex, which has so great a need to be indemnified for the rigors of nature and the unequal distribution of rights in the social order.

Towards the middle of the night, General Lafayette left the City of Burlington, taking with him the good wishes and the blessings of the inhabitants who accompanied him to the shore where there awaited him two steamships, *The Phoenix* and *The Congress*, both decked with bunting, illuminated and decorated with emblems and transparencies; he boarded *The Phoenix*, which saluted him with 13 cannon blasts on receiving him, and which soon raised anchor to the sound of the farewells of the crowd that lined the shore. *The Congress*, bearing a delegation of Vermont and a large number of citizens, followed *The Phoenix*, and during the entire night, we plowed through the mobile battlefield on which Commodore MacDonough and his intrepid sailors covered themselves with glory on September 11, 1814. We would have been pleased before departing from these places to visit Plattsburg where, on the same day, General Macomb also earned the gratitude of the country by repulsing the veteran British forces with a handful of young volunteers who, at the first report of the invasion of the territory, had come to gather around him; but July 4th was approaching and hastened our pace.

We arrived at Whitehall on the next day, June 30, towards midday and General Lafayette disembarked under a canopy, formed by 200 flags of all the nations, to the sound of artillery, and between two lines of girls who covered him with flowers as he passed before them. Whitehall is a place celebrated in the annals of the Revolutionary War. General Burgoyne had stated openly in Parliament in London that those whom he called the rebels of America were so incapable of resisting that he would undertake, with 5,000 regular troops, to traverse the country from Canada to Boston, where he would take up winter quarters. Indeed, he sailed with his army on Lake Champlain, disembarked at Whitehall, and not far from there, at Saratoga, he was forced to surrender, and it is true, spent the winter in Boston, but as a prisoner of war. At the end of the public dinner that the citizens of Whitehall offered to him, General Lafayette was pleased to recall this remarkable achievement while making the following toast:

> To Whitehall! May this Town enjoy forever the advantages resulting to it from the manner in which the prophecy of the English General was accomplished.

We were able to stay for only a moment with the inhabitants of Whitehall who, having furnished us with good carriages and excellent horses, enabled us to traverse rapidly the 80 miles that separated us from Albany, where we wanted to embark to descend the Hudson up to New York City; after sunset we crossed Fish Creek, and we stopped for a few moments at the home of Mr. Schuyler, built on the very spot where General Burgoyne put his sword into General Gates' hands. At Whitehall they had spoken to us about the English General's boast, and we found ourselves now on the battlefield which saw his pride humiliated; we would have wanted to visit this theater of one of the most glorious events of the Revolutionary War, but the night was too advanced, and we had to give up this pleasure. In order to compensate as much as he could, Mr. Schuyler was kind enough to give us a very detailed outline of the Battle of Saratoga. "The terrain," he told us, "has not undergone any change; the entrenchments, although sunken considerably by time, are nonetheless still easily recognized." Indeed even today, the old patriots of that time can point out to their children the path that the aide-de-camp of General Gates followed in carrying his *ultimatum* to the English General, as well as the road by which the British Army descended in order to lay down their arms in the presence of the *rebels*, who, nearly without arms and without clothing, had just begun so gloriously the conquest of their independence; but these traces will disappear one day. Why not build today a more durable monument, in the midst of these traces, which would recall for future generations the memory of the courage and the patriotism of that glorious generation that time will soon finish reaping?

After some time spent with Mr. Schuyler's family, we left to sleep at a nearby town, and on the following day, we continued our trip by a route that meandered along the Hudson, sometimes to the right, sometimes to the left of the Canal of the North, which runs parallel to the river and at a very short distance from its right bank; upon passing Fish Creek, we re-entered New York State. We crossed the Hudson opposite Waterford; this place is very noteworthy by virtue of the junction of the Canal of the North with the Canal of the West or the Great Canal, which is located right at the confluence of the Mohawk and Hudson Rivers. On July 2, we visited Lansingburg, and we saw Troy for the second time, but without stopping there very long. A steamboat awaited us opposite Albany; it received us at the beginning of night, and at daybreak, it had already transported us to New York City, where we disembarked nearly without being expected.

Nonetheless great excitement reigned in the City, and one noticed a large number of strangers in the streets; at every moment, ships in the Port and carriages on the roads brought still others who appeared to be coming from very far away. Detachments of militia from neighboring towns, inhabitants from the surrounding country, were also increasing the population of New York every minute.

The night did not interrupt this extraordinary traffic, precursor of a great event. Finally, at midnight, a salvo of artillery announced the dawn of a day forever glorious in the annals of the history of the New World, and, some hours after, the sun of July 4th rose radiantly to shine on the 49th anniversary of the Declaration of Independence of a republic whose great lessons will not be lost to the human race.

In the morning, militias stood under arms, the people rushed in a crowd into the streets, on the public squares, and at the doorways of the churches, the air resounded with thanksgiving.... At eight o'clock, the officers and magistrates of New York and Brooklyn presented themselves at the General's lodging place with a large procession of citizens. "We wish," they told him,

> That this day of glorious memory be marked every year by an action that would have as its object the strengthening of the freedom that we owe to the courage of our fathers and to the institutions that we have because of their wisdom; today we are going to lay the foundation of an institution that is to achieve this end, since it will assist in the propagation of enlightenment and education among that class of young citizens who, by the activity of their arms, contribute so strongly to the prosperity of our country; a library for the use of workingmen is going to be built on Brooklyn Heights, the voluntary gifts of our citizens have borne the cost of it; if Lafayette would lay the cornerstone, this institution will be entirely worthy of its intended purpose....

The General yielded readily to the wishes of the magistrates and proceeded at once to Brooklyn where, assisted by the Freemasons of Long Island, he lay the cornerstone of the building, in the presence of a large gathering of citizens, in the first ranks of which the young workers exclaimed their joy and their gratitude; afterwards, he returned to New York, followed by companies of apprentice tailors, shoemakers, bakers, stonecutters, coopers, boatswains, etc., who, preceded by their banners, accompanied him to the church where he attended divine worship. The sermon, which had as its subject the solemnity of the day, was followed by the reading of the *Declaration of Independence*, which the audience listened to with profound contemplation. This declaration, monument of daring and wisdom, whose magical influence saved the Colonies at the moment when, without money, without arsenals, without an army, they were going to undertake a terrible struggle against the colossal forces of Great Britain, affects Americans even today, after half a century, as if they were present on the day when it was proclaimed for the first time.

Not only is it read every year on July 4th in the presence of the people assembled in the churches, but it is also read in a large number of families. It is not rare to find, in entering an American house, the *Declaration of Independence* as well as the immortal names of its signers written carefully and framed luxuriously. Nearly all children know it by heart; it is ordinarily the first subject on which their young minds are exercised; they take pleasure in reproducing it in the different languages that they study; and, when they recite it among a circle of parents or friends, it is easy to recognize that, as their fathers were, they are imbued with the unassailable truth of the principle that "when a long train of abuses and usurpations, pursuing invariably the same object, evinces a design to reduce a people under the yoke of absolute despotism, it is their right, it is their duty to throw off such government and to provide new safeguards for their future security." I have often heard children ten to twelve years old recite this part in English or in French, and it is never without deep emotion that they enumerated the oppressions and the vexations exercised against the American Colonies by the Motherland; it was easy to recognize how patriotism and love of freedom had already thrown down deep roots in their young hearts when they spoke the oath that the last paragraph contains:

> We, therefore, the Representatives of the United States of America, in General Congress, assembled, appealing to the Supreme Judge of the world for the rectitude of our intentions, do, in the name, and by authority of the good People of these Colonies, solemnly publish and declare, that these United Colonies are, and of right ought to be *Free and Independent States*; that they are absolved from all allegiance to the British Crown, and that all political connection between them and the State of Great Britain, is and ought to be totally dissolved; and that as *Free and Independent States* they have full Power to levy War, conclude Peace, contract Alliances, establish Commerce, and to do all other Acts or Things which Independent States may of right do. And for the support of this Declaration, with a firm reliance on the protection of divine Providence, we mutually pledge to each other our Lives, our Fortunes and our sacred Honor.

Upon leaving the church, General Lafayette proceeded to the public square where all the militias and companies of firemen, united together, conducted maneuvers and filed in front of him with great precision. One of the corps that composed this procession marched under a flag remarkable in the brilliance of its colors and by the equestrian portrait of the *National Guest*. After this review, he entered City Hall, where the Governor was waiting to present him to the Senate, which received him with honors that, up to then, had not yet been rendered to anyone. On this entrance, the Senators stood, bared their heads, the President of the Senate advanced towards him and addressed to him, on the occasion of his return, a speech of congratulations in which he expressed the satisfaction of the citizens of New York that he had come to join them in the celebration of the glorious Fourth of July. "It was," he said,

> Your participation in the work of our fathers that earned you the gratitude, the respect and the friendship of this Nation. This friendship has followed you in all the events of your life; it has always found you, in times of trial, faithful to liberty, to order, to a government of laws. The enthusiasm of youth attached you to our cause; the steadfastness of manly age, and the need to resist oppression, sustained you when you suffered in the prisons of Olmutz; but a virtuous love of national freedom could alone make you capable of resisting the seductions of power and the lures of ambition, when a great revolution, placing you at the head of the National Guard of France, invited you to seize power. It was then that you knew how to avoid danger, it was then that the attraction of power was without dominion over the love of principles, and that virtue did not have to fight against ambition. It is in such times, in the presence of the power and the gratitude of the people, who seem to permit everything, that human frailty encounters the most danger. One sees then the Caesars, the Napoleons, the Iturbides fail in their duty; one sees then the Washingtons, the Bolivars, the Lafayettes triumph.

Although his conscience ought to have told him that he was not unworthy of the eulogies he was receiving, the General found himself nonetheless embarrassed for a moment in responding to them; however, after some moments of reflection, he expressed his sentiments in this manner.

> The Fourth of July was the time of a new social order, up to then without example, founded on the sovereignty of the people, on the natural rights of man, and on the total application

> of the principle that a nation has the right to govern itself. Its results have surpassed the most passionate expectations. The problem has been resolved by the achievement and in the most fortunate manner.
>
> You are pleased to congratulate me, Sir, on my visit to the 24 States of the Union. During this happy trip, I was to have admired the wonders of creation and of improvements at each step; but in no part do they excite more than in the State of New York. The Western part of this State, which I had left a wilderness, I found covered with thriving towns, well cultivated fields, factories in full operation, and cut by the wondrous canal that has become the means of an immense commerce, and all of it is only the consequence of the republican spirit and of the establishment of independence and liberty.
>
> The greatest honor that could be bestowed on me was to hear my name associated with those of the two great men whom you have just cited. The first is placed in my filial heart above all other men, and I will always be proud of having been his adoptive son and faithful disciple. As for the second, he has no admirer more ardent than I; and permit me to observe that, what my friends and I only attempted on another hemisphere, has been happily effectuated in South America under the auspices of his talents and his virtues.
>
> But in the displays of benevolence that the citizens of New York and their representatives heap on me, it is very sweet to recognize a kindness which, if it is beyond my deserts, is equaled by the sentiments of eternal devotion, respect and gratitude that I have pledged to them.

From the Senate hall we passed into that of the Governor where the General was awaited by the Society of the Cincinnati, by the European consuls and by a large number of distinguished people whom the municipality had invited to the banquet, whose preparation had been entrusted to a committee which carried out its mission with exquisite taste. All the mementos of glory, patriotism and liberty were found gathered together with an astonishing profusion in the superb chamber of City Hall where the tables had been set up. The busts of Washington and of Lafayette, the portraits of Bolivar and of DeWitt Clinton stood in the midst of trophies above which waved the American and French flags, always joined. The armchair on which

Washington had sat as President was placed in the center and covered with laurel branches and immortelles.... But this chair was vacant now, and it was in vain that the eyes of the veterans of the Revolution looked sadly into the crowd for him who had filled it so worthily.

We sat down to dinner, and we saw exiles from the countries of Europe take their places, which the republican hospitality of the New World had reserved for them, among the happy soldiers of 1776. Among these exiles were members of the Spanish Cortes, driven out of their country by absolutism, German scholars fleeing from punishments as bizarre as atrocious and unjust;[17] French officers[18] reduced to seeking in a foreign land peace of mind, which they had so often sacrificed to their country; and all, in spite of their unhappy past, appeared consoled and reinvigorated by the picture of happiness enjoyed by the free men among which they found themselves.

According to American custom, the meal concluded with a large number of toasts, all of which were stamped with the character of the guests and the solemnity which they were celebrating. After having received the felicitations and good wishes of all those who surrounded him, the General proceeded to the Theater of the Park, where the crowd which awaited him saluted him on his entrance and his departure with three cheers.

After the emotions of such a day, the General had great need of some rest, and the citizens, always attentive to what could be agreeable to him, left him for several days to be delivered up to the attentions, no less sweet but more relaxed, of personal friends. It was with delight that he devoted this time to the friendship of his former companions-in-arms such as Colonel Fish, Colonel Platt, Colonel Willett, Colonel Varick, General Van Courtlandt, and so many others whose names escape my memory, but who would certainly not have escaped his memory if he had written this journal himself, for it never betrayed him in regards to his friends.

He did not then tear himself away from the pleasantries of private life except to go to the New Jersey shore in order to pass some time with his friend Colonel Varick who had invited him to dine with some of the principal citizens

---

17. They have reported that Professor List was sentenced to ten years of *forced literary labors* for having consented to be the spokesman of the citizens to the King of Württemberg.

18. Among these were General Lallemand, whose name is too well known for me to eulogize him, and my two friends, my companions-in-arms, the brothers Peugnet who, pursued for a long time in Europe by persecutions honorable to them, had finally found in New York a safe haven in which American hospitality provided the means of an independent existence. The military academy that they founded on the most extensive and liberal bases already enjoys popular favor.

of New York. The organization of boatmen of the Port claimed the honor of taking him across the Hudson in a longboat whose name, having become popular by a recent occurrence, held the public's attention very much at that time.

An English Captain, Commander of the frigate *The Hussar*, had come to New York in December 1824 bearing on board a longboat remarkable in the lightness of its construction, and with which he had won several prize races in different ports of Europe, notably those of England. Proud of his success and full of confidence in the speed of his boat, he sent a challenge to the sailors of the Port of New York, and proposed to race against them for the sum of $1,000; they accepted the challenge, subscribed together to raise the proposed sum, and chose for the contest a very fine longboat, *The American Star*, having recently left the hands of one of their most skilled shipbuilders. The day, the hour and the place were fixed by agreement between them and the English Captain who, desiring to assure his success by all means which were in his power, chose four of the strongest rowers of his crew to operate his boat, and reserved for himself the important functions of coxswain. The *Whitehallers* (this is how the sailors of the Port of New York call themselves), on their side, entrusted their reputation to four of them, chosen nearly at random, and placed a young boy of 15 at the rudder.

The distance to be traversed, between *Castle Island* and the point of *Long Island*, was about three miles. At the giving of the signal, the two boats shot forward onto the mobile arena. The English sailors, leaning back violently on their benches, and making their oars bend at every stroke of the waves, got off with sudden energy, leaving behind them large eddies of shining foam. The American sailors, seated upright on their benches, with their bodies motionless, and their arms nearly motionless, hardly skimmed the waves with their light oars but, hurrying and multiplying their strokes, leaped forward at the same time as their adversaries, scarcely disturbing the transparent water around them. Several minutes were sufficient to determine the victory, which is sometimes uncertain for so long a time. The two boats, having left from the same point at the same time, were not long in separating. The English, exhausted by the violence of their efforts, could not keep up with the rapid flight of their adversaries, whose prompt arrival at the finish-line was greeted by shouts of joy that emanated from the shore and from all points that were occupied by numerous spectators whom curiosity had brought, not only from all parts of the City but also from all the neighboring towns. Astonished by his defeat, but being unable to hide the fact that it was absolute, the English Captain hastened to acknowledge the superiority of the American boat to his, and displayed a desire to acquire it; he even offered $3,000. But the *Whitehallers* refused to sell it to him. "We want to save it," they said,

> As a monument of the victory that we have had the honor of winning over you; but in order to allay the regrets that our refusal might cause you to have, we propose a new race to you, in which you will board our longboat with your oarsmen; we will board yours, and we will double the prize....

This proposition only left the English Captain astonished, and, fearing a new defeat and the loss of his money, he refused the challenge. On the same evening, the victorious longboat was placed on a triumphal chariot, driven through the entire City and carried to the theater where it was crowned as were its four oarsmen and its young coxswain; and, on the following day, it was placed as a monument on the wharf, with the names of its crew written on its benches and this inscription on its gunnel: *American Star victorious, December 4, 1824.*

It was in this very boat and with the same oarsmen that the *Whitehallers* wanted to conduct General Lafayette to Sandy Hook, on the other side of the North River. In this crossing, we were able to judge its swiftness as well as the skill of those who operated it; the numerous boats that bore the other people invited to the dinner could only follow it from afar. Upon our return, when the General had disembarked, the sailors, joined in a group under the flags of the Association and led by the victors, presented themselves to him to express their gratitude for the services that he had rendered in the past to their country and for the displays of esteem that he had just accorded to them. Then, after having recounted to him a little of the history of the longboat in which he had just crossed the river, they beseeched him to accept it and to have it transported to La Grange so that it would continuously remind him of the memory of his friends of New York, the perfection of the mechanical arts of New York, and the great motto of the American sea service: *Free trade and sailors' rights*.[19]

The nature of the present and the delicacy with which it was offered did not permit the General to turn it down. He accepted it with profound gratitude which he expressed in these words:

> It is with all the pride of a patriotic American that I have already enjoyed the success of your race. It is with all the gratitude of friendship that I accept your generous present. No keepsake could be received by me with more pleasure,

19. The wish of the Whitehallers was fulfilled. *The American Star* is now at La Grange, placed with its oars and its rudder in an elegant structure that the General has had built to provide it with a shelter worthy of the memories that it represents.

> especially when it is offered to me by the five victorious sailors. It will be carefully preserved as a monument dear to my heart.
>
> I pray you, Gentlemen, to accept and to transmit to your companions, the congratulations, the thanks and the good wishes of a veteran entirely dedicated to your great motto: *free trade and sailors' rights*.

Meanwhile, the moment to separate ourselves from the citizens of New York had come, and our hearts were oppressed with sadness. On July 14, we left this City that we were not to see again any more before leaving American soil. The magistrates and the people witnessed the departure of the National Guest. A profound dejection was imprinted on every face, and although the wharfs were covered with a huge crowd, a solemn silence alone reigned during our embarkation, and was only disturbed by our last farewell.

Chapter XV

Mr. Kératry's Letter on the Anniversary of Bunker Hill – Hydraulic Machine of Philadelphia – Germantown – Mr. Watson's Historical Box – Battlefield of Brandywine – The Invocation of Reverend William Latta – Clergy of Lancaster – Return to Baltimore, Lit Up by a Fire.

While the citizens of the United States were exhausting all the means to prove their gratitude to the old friend of their fathers, their Fatherland and their institutions, France was not indifferent to the honors rendered to one of her children in a distant land. By means of her writers, her poets and her orators, she joined her voice to that of republican America to celebrate the principal events of this triumph, equally honorable to the two Nations. It is thus that in a public journal,[20] printed in Paris and sent to the United States, Mr. Kératry, inspired by the ceremony of Bunker Hill, expressed the wishes and the sentiments of every French friend of liberty:

> Nations discharge a sacred debt when they honor the memory of their great citizens; but by that same act they also perform an act of self-preservation, since nothing can arouse a generous devotion to country better than the certainty won by the actor of escaping oblivion.
>
> There is, as a matter of fact, in acclamations of public gratitude something inspiring and almost contagious that removes a man from himself and the interests of daily life. One sacrifices this life in order to ensure himself of another more brilliant and more enduring. If one can tell himself that these approbations would be bestowed on cold ashes, one would feel himself revived to participate in this future glory; and, by a miracle of patriotism, the general security of a country becomes the result of all the individual sacrifices.
>
> Peoples capable of these sacrifices, even when they try to shake off the yoke of oppression, the natural tendency of which is to degrade our species everywhere it submits to it, were never without virtue. We have the deep-seated conviction that, if God waits for men and takes them one by one in order to judge them after their terrestrial life, which is the justice of the after-life, He pronounces such justice on nations in

20. *Courrier Français*.

a body, here below, according to their collective merits, and that is the providential justice of the present economy. According to how he weights them, they prosper or they die out. Thus some peoples have become empires: thus some empires have disappeared.

North Americans, men of a liberated world, here is what has allowed you to constitute the organized body of a nation, here is what has guaranteed a perpetuity of noble existence! Your civic-mindedness is born of your habits of hard work and your domestic virtues. These virtues subsist among you: where the women are chaste, the men are brave: where religion, the free and spontaneous impulse of the creature towards his Creator, has not been transformed into a political lever of worldly interests, salutary beliefs dominate the social order, and fill the soul with strength. You have had a Franklin, a Washington, a Samuel Adams, a Jefferson; in times of need, you will find more of them: the tree is full of sap, why will it not bear new fruits? Your properity does not astonish me any more; it is in the nature of things, divine and human.

Nonetheless, you do well to enhance the renown of the supporters of your liberty, and to provide worthy monuments to those who died for it. The great citizen who in 1765 was one of the founders of that sainted conspiracy of Boston, so influential to your destinies; he whom that City enlisted, on two memorable occasions, to console by his eloquent speeches the shades of your compatriots who were massacred on March 2, 1770; he who in 1775 assisted you in winning the brilliant auguries of the Battle of Lexington, and who succumbed, struck by a deadly shot, at Breed's Hill in the second engagement of your struggle for independence, Doctor Warren, has earned from you and your children a special distinction.

It was perhaps enough for the glory of this citizen-warrior, whose virtue was attested by the regrets of his most ardent enemies, and by the courage to which the entrenched ground that received, with his blood, his last breath, still bears witness: it was perhaps enough, I say, that his gathered remains had found an honorable tomb in the bosom of the City that he wanted to set free. You have resolved more for this hero and his companions-in-arms. Men of North America, I congratulate you that the services of the brave remain full of life in your memory; for it would be foolhardy to be accountable for the future of nations who should forget the past by which they came into being. There are in you some elements of vigor, and you know how to foster them.

You have waited until the hand of one of the first defenders of your freedom should aid you in fulfilling this pious duty: already our thoughts and our eyes had followed this old warrior, celebrated in the annals of two peoples, to Washington's tomb; and I do not believe that the sun has ever illuminated a more noble spectacle on earth. Our eyes shall accompany him again when, on the 17th of next month, he will inaugurate with you the monument that Boston is raising for the brave men of Bunker Hill: well worthy to solemnize with you this great homage, he will be thinking no doubt of his own country while helping you in discharging this obligation of yours: he will offer prayers for us; and, perhaps, without being envious of the prosperous condition that you owe to the civil and military courage of your citizens, he will respectfully ask Providence why it seems to withdraw from the French those beautiful days of which it had allowed them to glimpse the dawn.... No, in his religious grief, he will be silent for fear that the tombstone and the sacred bones that it protects would make a reply to him too severe for us, inhabitants of this old Europe, where they pretend to liberty without sacrifices, to happiness without virtue!

Happy Nation, you count in your annals no other victories than those that have consolidated your independence! You never wish for others; unless a noble sentiment persuades you to interest yourselves in the cause of the oppressed of one of the two hemispheres, because you have been oppressed and been succored.

Do not allow any of your citizens to grow great with a grandeur that would be too personal or that would render small that which would be around him; for a nation must not be a pedestal.

Bestow decorations only on the living who have earned them, and on the dead who possess them without any prejudice to the merit of those ready to rise beside their ashes; for the transmission of glory by way of inheritance is the act of a people of unsound mind who alienate their future to the advantage of strangers.

A simple citizen of another state, I am very brazen to send you these words across the seas which separate us; but my soul has desired to communicate with yours; and I believed that the counsels of a Frenchman who applauds your good fortune will not strike ears too proud or too disdainful, at the same time as a Frenchman is honored with your gratitude. That man, one of those to whom the privilege has been accorded to see himself honored as his like will be honored in the future, is preparing his return to his native land; for you know that his heart does not put itself only in search of the successful men of the age, and that, for him, the just cause will always be the good cause, whether triumphant or not.

May the winds blow propitiously for him! Laden down with your gifts as in the way of ancients, crowned with flowers picked by the hands of your chaste young girls and their virtuous mothers, may he return soon to his hearth! Let him return to us! Ah, be careful not to keep him longer on your shores! You are wealthy enough in citizens. I will only say that they are still included among us, for to speak ill of the Fatherland is never allowed; but when the weak are quaking, the presence of the strong is only that much more necessary.

Swayed by the consciousness of his duties as a citizen, and by his attachments as head of a large family, General Lafayette did not wait for the expression of these vows of friendship to resolve to return very soon to France; but nonetheless it was not without sweet emotions that these words were heard by his heart. They contributed to the mitigation of the sacrifice that he had been obligated to impose on himself in refusing the prayers of the citizens of the United States who, from all regions, had begged him so emotionally and insistently to settle in their midst.

The General's intention was to embark before the return of the inclement season; but before having to leave American soil, he still wanted to fulfill promises that he had made to different towns; to pass some time at the seat of the General Government of the Union, and to pay a last visit to the ex-presidents retired in Virginia. We were already in the middle of July; thus there remained to him barely two months to carry out his plans, and he hastened to return at once to Philadelphia; he traversed New Jersey rapidly in the midst of the customary displays of the veneration of the people. I will speak neither of the fetes that were offered him by the towns that he visited, nor of his second visit to Joseph Bonaparte, while passing through Bordentown, where he had the pleasure of finding Colonel Achille Murat, having returned from a meeting with his brother who was arriving from Spain; but I will tarry yet a moment in Philadelphia to visit the hydraulic works there and to attend a festival that the little republic of Schuylkill wanted also to give to its National Guest.

During our first stay in Philadelphia, we had already visited the fine hydraulic machine built on the Schuylkill to supply water to a population of 120,000 people, and we had been struck by the simplicity of its mechanism, its wonderful power, and the elegance and good taste of the building that enclosed it. But then being a little pressed for time, we had only had a general view, without entering into an examination of the details; and it was to make good this lack of information that we returned a second time with the committee charged with superintendence and the expenses of the institution.

As the tide in the Delaware River is felt well above Philadelphia, it follows that the inhabitants of this City cannot use the water of the river for culinary purposes, and that formerly they had for potable water only what was furnished to them by cisterns that often dried up during the great droughts of summer, or supplied only an unhealthy drink, causing a large number of illnesses. The rapid growth of the population soon rendered obtaining water of better quality and in greater quantity absolutely necessary; a steam-fired pump was built on the banks of the Schuylkill. This pump, having very expensive upkeep and nearly insufficient service, was nonetheless still the sole resource of a population of 80,000 at the end of 1818, the time in which the committee charged with providing water (*watering committee*), composed of citizens distinguished by their knowledge and their love of the public good, was occupied with the means of replacing the old machine by another more powerful and economical. *Fairmont*, on the left bank of the Schuylkill, appeared to be the most favorable spot for the execution of the committee's plans. The Schuylkill Navigation Company, having allowed the damming of the river to obtain a fall of water, on the condition that a canal and locks would be built at the expense of the City on the right bank, so that navigation would not be interrupted, and Messrs. White and Gillingham having consented, for $150,000, to cede their rights in the watercourses, the committee, free of all obstacles, submitted its plans to the City Council, which approved them and immediately voted the sum of $350,000 for the commencement of their execution.

Work had begun on April 19, 1819 under the direction of Captain Ariel Cooley and was concluded in four years. On viewing the canals which it was necessary to open, the embankments that it was necessary to construct, the reservoirs that they were obliged to excavate to a great depth in the solid rock, one can hardly comprehend how so many things were done in so short a time. The money, it is true, was not spared, but money does not always suffice – we know it well among us – to achieve great things; in order to build well and promptly, agents who are honest, skillful, and animated by the love of the public good are required; such a man was Captain Cooley who unfortunately paid with his life for the zeal that he displayed in the accomplishment of his duties. Exposed incessantly either to the heat of the sun or to the cold of the nights, he contracted a mortal illness which did not permit him to enjoy the fruit of his work. Even today the inhabitants of Philadelphia miss in him the good citizen and the artist, as capable as he was disinterested.

Such as we have seen it completed, the hydraulic works at *Fairmont* can supply the needs of the City very abundantly, and offer to the friends of the useful arts a monument worthy of their attention. The building which encloses the machinery is built of hard, brilliantly white stones; it is 230 feet long and 50 feet wide; its architecture is of the Doric order; the lower section is divided into 12 solidly vaulted compartments suitable for the emplacement of eight suction and forcing pumps that are activated by wheels 14 feet in diameter and 14 feet wide; each end of the building is finished with a pavilion of the same architectural order, and one serves for the meetings of the committee, the other for the superintendence of the establishment; of the eight pumps there are only three that operate; they carry by themselves alone nearly 5,000,000 gallons of water per day into the distribution reservoir, which is more than 100 feet above the level of the river; each wheel performs 13 revolutions per minute, their blades are perpendicular to the circumference and turn with an astonishing evenness. Their construction is owed to the talents of Mr. Drury Bromley who, in this circumstance, did not fall short of his reputation as a competent mechanical engineer.

The pumps came out of the workshops of Messrs. Rush and Muhlenberg; they have castings of 16 inches in diameter and have been placed horizontally according to Mr. Graff's plans; their play is so simple and easy that, when they are in motion, one doesn't hear the least sound and one does not notice any friction. In general, all the parts of this admirable monument of American industry are treated with the same care, and it is impossible to visit it without being full of admiration for all those who have contributed to its conception and to its completion. Mr. John Moore, in charge of the masonry, and Mr. Frederick Erdman, in charge of the carpentry, have been the equal of their collaborators, and everyone also pays a tribute of gratitude to the precision of the calculations of Mr. Thomas Oaks in the evaluation and the application of the forces necessary to obtain the most advantageous results with the least possible expense.

The total sum of the expenses for the construction of this establishment stands at $426,330, for which the interest at five percent is $21,316. The annual expense for the salary of the workers, repair of the machines, heating, oil, etc., is only $1,500, which when added to the interest, is only a total sum of $22,816 to distribute to the City of Philadelphia nearly 5,000,000 gallons of water per day. The original steam-fired pump could only supply 1,600,000 gallons of water per day and cost $30,858 per year; in order for it to supply 5,000,000 gallons, it would have been necessary to expend a sum of at least $61,716 each year; thus they have obtained, by the construction of the new machinery, an annual savings of $38,900. To this immense advantage, it is necessary to add, moreover, several others no less precious, such as the health of the City; the increase of resources against fires; the beautification of public places with abundant fountains; the right of each inhabitant to have a water conduit into his house for the reasonable sum of five dollars per year; and finally, the ease of establishing diverse factories or mills driven by water power in the City.

All of these details were heard with a lively interest by General Lafayette, who expressed his satisfaction and admiration by saying that the waterworks of Philadelphia was, according to him, the perfect image of the American Government, in which one finds *simplicity, strength, and economy* at the same time. At the moment when he was going to withdraw, Mr. Lewis, as president and in the name of the committee, offered him a model of the machinery and a vertical section of the building perfectly executed in mahogany wood; the General accepted it with gratitude, and assured Mr. Lewis that he would take true pleasure in showing this proof of the perfection of the mechanical arts in the United States to his friends in Europe.

Although the heat was excessive during our second stay in Philadelphia and the thermometer usually indicated 98 degrees Fahrenheit and rose sometimes to 104 degrees, the General did not go out any less each day, whether to attend gatherings to which he had been invited or to visit the environs of the City, and his health was not affected for an instant.

It was on July 20 that we went to visit the battlefield of Germantown and *Chew's House*, on the walls of which are still found traces of the balls and bullets that prove how important a role it played in the battle that was waged around it. After having breakfasted with Mr. Benjamin Chew, the proprietor of this historic house, the General continued his route up to Chestnut Hill, in sight of Barren Hill, where on May 20, 1778, he effectuated with so much good fortune and success the famous retreat that began his reputation as a tactician; from there, he returned to Germantown to spend some time with the inhabitants who entreated him to visit the university, where the students received him enthusiastically. We found among them the young Fernando Bolivar, adopted son of the Liberator; General Lafayette spoke to him with pleasure of the hopes that the friends of liberty and of humanity were reposing on the character of his uncle, who up to then, had followed with a firm step in the career embarked on by Washington; the young man appeared to be full of gratitude and expressed himself in a manner that led one to hope that it would not be in vain that they should have sent him to study the political institutions of the United States.

At the moment when we were going to leave Germantown, Mr. John Watson offered the General a present made very precious by the nature of the memories that it awakened; it was a box made of several pieces of different woods, the origin and history of which he recounted in this way.

> The body of the box is made of a piece of black walnut, ancient child of the forest that formerly covered the soil of Philadelphia. Contemporary of the trees that lent its shade to William Penn and his companions, it still stood in 1818, its stately branches facing the street where our independence was declared.
>
> The lid is made of an assemblage of four different pieces.
>
> The first was fashioned out of a branch of a forest tree, the last survivor of those that saw the first settlements of Philadelphia excavated. The vigor that still animates its ancient vegetation attests to the rapidity of the growth of the City which it saw the birth of.
>
> The second is made of a piece of oak, remains of the first bridge constructed in 1683 on the little Canard River. This piece was found in 1823, about six feet below the ground.
>
> The third comes from the celebrated elm under which Penn made his first treaty with Shackamaxon. It fell of old age in 1810, but one of its descendants stands today, full of vigor, in

> the garden of the hospital, and our citizens like to discuss its origin under its shade.
>
> The fourth recalls memories even more ancient. It is a fragment of the first house built by European hands on American soil! It is a piece of mahogany from the dwelling constructed and occupied in 1496 by the immortal Columbus! Honor to the Haitian Government that still watches over the conservation of this precious monument with care today.
>
> I offer you these relics with confidence, persuaded as I am that it is with interest that you receive everything connected with the memories of the earliest developments regarding a people which has received so many proofs of your friendship.

General Lafayette was, indeed, very flattered by Mr. Watson's present. He accepted it with gratitude and promised that he would place it among the most precious souvenirs of his trip. To this first present, Mr. Watson added another, no less precious; it was a piece of the frigate *The Alliance*, the American warship on which Lafayette had crossed the ocean twice during the Revolutionary War.

On the 21st, we left Philadelphia to spend the day in the *State of Schuylkill*. But before speaking of the honors that the voyager received there, I must say a word about the history of this *State*.

In 1731 some citizens of Philadelphia joined to form an association the dual object of which was pleasure and beneficence. They purchased an immense terrain near the falls of the Schuylkill; there they constructed a house suitable for their gatherings; elected a governor, a council, a secretary of state, a treasurer and a judge; adopted a particular seal, and constituted themselves *Schuylkill Colony*. More than half a century passed without the existence of the Colony being disturbed by the slightest of mishaps; each day was marked by blessings, and joy and confidence were evident at all the periodic banquets at which the citizens were assembled at the same table. But, subject to the fate common to states all of which have their vicissitudes, Schuylkill Colony was to have its revolution too. In 1783, following a dinner of more than 50 place- settings, the Nation revolted and declared itself independent; it intended to revise its constitution, and Schuylkill Colony became in several hours the *Republican State of Schuylkill*, without the mother country's making the least attempt to oppose it. From that time, the new republic did not stop increasing its strength or its wealth; its pleasures and beneficence have followed the same progression; master today of a more extensive territory that it acquired in a treaty with a farmer, it has transferred the seat of its government, that is to say, its fishing-nets, its kitchen and its cellar, three miles further down the river, under the cool shade trees that the waters of the Schuylkill always irrigate.

It is there that General Lafayette was received by the citizens and the magistrates who, dressed as fishermen, had come to wait for him at the border of the State. In a short but eloquent speech, the Secretary of State recalled the history of the Republic since its founding to the present and ended by notifying him that the title and the rights of citizenship had been bestowed on him by a unanimous vote. As soon as the General had expressed his acceptance and his gratitude, they dressed him in the national costume, and, his head protected with a wide straw hat, he took part in the occupations of the community. Just as George Lafayette and Mr. de Syon, so I too was admitted to share in the work of the day; the people and the magistrates, everyone without distinction, began to work. Having boarded the boats of the republic, we caught an abundance of fish, and at four o'clock, we took our places at a banquet prepared by our own hands. Never was a meal more joyous nor watered by a better wine, and for a long time we will recall the pleasures and the happiness that they enjoy in the State of Schuylkill.

The eight days that we had just passed in Philadelphia, as if in our family, had rested the General completely; and, although the heat continued to be excessive, he set out on the 25th to return to Wilmington where a large number of Pennsylvanians and Virginians were waiting to conduct him onto the Battlefield of Brandywine. This battlefield was not renowned for a victory, as one knows, but its memory is no less dear to Americans who recall with gratitude the blood that their fathers and the young Lafayette spilled on it in the defense of their rights and their independence. Happy is the country in which events are appreciated more for their influence on the destiny of the Fatherland than for the glamour of the moment! The men who prepared the way for the independence of the United States in doing battle at Bunker Hill and on the banks of the Brandywine are no less noble today in the eyes of the Nation than those who consolidated it by the victory of Yorktown.

At the beginning of September of 1777, General Howe, at the head of an 18,000-man English Army, had embarked on the fleet commanded by his brother, and had left New York without knowing precisely the object of his expedition. Several days later, the Americans learned that he had sailed up the Chesapeake and disembarked at Head of Elk in order to proceed to Philadelphia. Immediately Washington traversed this capital of Pennsylvania, where Congress was sitting, and betook himself to meet the enemy, and fought several skirmishes between the point of landing and a little stream called the Brandywine behind which the American Army, very inferior in number and almost entirely composed of militia, came to take its position. It had in front of it the Chadds Ford crossing where they presumed that the battle would be waged; but General Howe, leaving behind a corps in front of this ford to cover his maneuver, marched left to pass by another crossing on the American right. This movement was so much more difficult to recognize since the shores of the river were very wooded and, by a singular unfortunate happenstance, the two parallel roads which led to the two crossings bore the same name, so that the reports reaching Washington from his scouts, although apparently contradictory, were nonetheless equally true. This confusion of names threw the American General into a cruel indecision; he hesitated for too long a time on the course he had to take, and lost time which was invaluable for victory.

Had he been better informed about the movements of the enemy, he would certainly have passed over the ford that lay before him, overwhelmed the English division that had stayed at Chadds Ford under the command of Knyphauzen, and then fallen suddenly on General Howe's corps, who surprised by a flanking attack, would have had very great difficulty in avoiding a complete defeat; but the occasion passed quickly, and soon gunshots fired on his right side apprised Washington of the great danger of his situation. Fortunately, he had positioned three brigades commanded by Sullivan and Stirling behind the second ford; these three brigades withstood the attack vigorously, and stopped the English for a moment with very deadly fire; but their line having been out-flanked on the right and on the left by the superior forces of the English, the wings gave way. The center continued to show a bold front in spite of the hail of grape shot that battered it; but, finally, the center itself tottered, and was going to beat a retreat when the young Lafayette who, in spite of his commission as major general, served only as a simple volunteer with the commander-in-chief, dismounted from his horse, and came to position himself, sword in hand, at the head of a company of grenadiers who held firm for several minutes, revived by this forceful act. Before long, Lafayette received a gunshot below the knee, and was forced to withdraw with his grenadiers; but he had already reaped the advantage of his self-sacrifice; he had given Washington the time to rush up with General Greene's division, and reinstitute combat on a second line. There they fought relentlessly on one side and the other, and one saw the astonishing spectacle of militiamen rallying after an initial defeat and meeting with a firm step an enemy superior to it in number and in discipline. The issue of this second combat was still in doubt when suddenly Washington learned that the Chadds Ford crossing was overrun, and that Knyphauzen was about to attack on his left flank; at that time he hastened to effectuate his retreat to Chester where he arrived in the evening with his entire army.

The battle was lost, but the English had paid dearly for their victory, and the Americans had just augmented their moral force even in their defeat. On this day Lafayette had sealed with his blood his alliance with the principles for which he had crossed the ocean and had just ensured himself forever of the gratitude of a nation among whose people generous sentiments outlive generations.

It was once again to express this gratitude to their old friend that the Revolutionary soldiers of Pennsylvania and Virginia had gathered with their children to conduct Lafayette on the Brandywine Battlefield. On July 26, we left Chester with a new procession at the head of which appeared the two oldest Revolutionary officers of the neighboring counties, Colonel McClellan and Captain Anderson. Numerous militia corps had preceded us and had taken their positions on the former encampment of the American Army where one still finds traces of an old redoubt. It was about noon when we arrived on the shores of the Brandywine which we were to cross at the very point where, they had told us, the army had crossed it; but on approaching the stream, General Lafayette glanced at the surrounding terrain and said: "It cannot be here that we crossed in 1777, it must be a little further upstream." They recognized indeed that the passage had been carried out above the point where we stood. The correctness of his observation and freshness of his memory excited the admiration of the numerous witnesses to the highest degree.

At Chadds Ford, the General learned that one of his companions-in-arms, Gideon Gilpin, at whose house he had passed the night the evening of the battle, was now bedridden by age and infirmities, and despaired not being able to join his homage to those of his fellow citizens; the General hastened to go to the old man, whom he found surrounded by his family. In spite of his extreme weakness, Gideon Gilpin recognized him as soon as he entered and showed him by tears of gratitude and affection how greatly this visit spread charm on his last moments and alleviated them.

Upon arriving on the battlefield, the General recognized in succession and pointed out to us all the principal places on which the two armies had maneuvered and fought on September 11, 1777, and his memories did not lead him astray for an instant. Having arrived at the spot where the initial combat was joined and where he had been wounded, he stopped for a moment; his former companions-in-arms crowded around his carriage, and the militia filed in front of him to shouts of *Long Live Lafayette!* During this entire scene which caused in him a profound emotion and which his modesty sought several times to abbreviate, he spoke to those who surrounded him only of the presence of mind that Washington had shown on that fateful day of September 11 and of the courage with which the soldiers and officers had supported him; but it was in vain that he recounted the names of the more illustrious leaders, and that he attributed to them all the glory of having saved the army; they responded by pointing out to him the soil that he had doused with his blood, and the sight of that indestructible monument exalted to the highest degree the gratitude of the numerous spectators who accompanied him.

In continuing our walk by the route by which the English had conducted their first assault, we arrived at Samuel Jones' house; it had been occupied for some time during the battle by General Howe, and it still bore some traces of the well-directed fire of the American artillery. Following an excellent collation offered by Mr. Jones, they distributed to us several projectiles and debris of weapons that had been collected on the battlefield, and we returned with these precious relics to West Chester, where we concluded the day in the midst of new festivities prepared by the citizens.

In the multiplicitous accounts that I have given of the public fetes that I attended during my stay in the United Sates, one must have been struck by the constant union of religious ideas and patriotic sentiments that characterize the citizens of this republic so strongly; but what is no less worthy of notice is that their religion, stripped of detailed practices, resembles a single *sentiment* as much as their love of liberty resembles a single *faith.* Among the Americans, a political orator never ends a set speech without invoking or thanking the Divine Power, in the same manner as a minister of the gospel, when mounting his pulpit, always begins by reminding his audience of their duties as citizens and of the good fortune that they have to live under wise institutions. Also one can say that this mixture of political morals and theosophy spreads a touch of gravity and deep conviction, of which the charm and power are inexpressible, over all the actions of the Americans. Thus, how can one listen to this invocation, so simple, so touching of Reverend William Latta without being deeply moved and without joining one's pious gratitude to his?... We were about to take our places at the banquet offered to the National Guest by the citizens of West Chester, when the presiding officer of the day remarked that a minister of the Church was present among the guests, and beseeched him to say the *benediction.* Reverend William Latta immediately pronounced the benediction, to which he added the following words:

> All-powerful God, our celestial Father! We give you thanks for the benefits that you have heaped on the American Nation, the memory of which we recall today. We give you thanks for having poured into the bosom of our fathers the pure love of liberty, for having inspired in them, during our infancy, the desire and the strength to conquer it. We give you thanks that

> the very same spirit was carried to a distant land and that you put into the heart of a foreigner, whose presence we celebrate today, the desire to take up our fortunes and our dangers; that in the midst of the trials to which he has been exposed, you have spared his precious life to allow him, after half a century, to revisit our land, to receive in it the tributes of admiration of the people, and to recognize there the fruits of that independence to the establishment of which he contributed so potently.

A committee of the town of Lancaster had come to look for General Lafayette at Chester, which we left on the 27th, after having taken our leave of a large number of soldiers of 1776, who could not receive the last farewell of their former general without shedding tears.

I believe that I have already reported the very remarkable fact that in the South as in the North, in the East as in the West of the United States, we had encountered men of different customs and languages, governed to their common advantage by the same democratic government, and living in good harmony, in the midst of private success and public prosperity under the aegis of the same institutions. From this observation we naturally were led to conclude that neither the grandeur of a state, nor the difference in the customs of the inhabitants of its provinces, present an obstacle to the establishment and the administration of republican government, which is based on an equal appreciation for the interests of all. Perhaps nothing was more suited to confirm General Lafayette in this opinion than the sight of Lancaster and of the county of the same name where one finds a complete union of men from all parts of America and of Europe, nearly all of different religious creeds, but all equally attached to the wise institutions that govern them.

I will not describe the fetes that the citizens of Lancaster offered to their guest and friend, although they were not inferior to those of the most considerable cities of the Union in either splendor or warmth. But I do not want, nonetheless, to pass over in silence facts that by their nature serve to make known the unity of sentiments and principles which characterize all classes of the American people; consequently, I will recount here the actions of the clergy of all the communions of the Town and the neighboring country who, at the news of the General's arrival, joined together spontaneously and came to add their patriotic congratulations to those of the other citizens. Their speech was given by the dean of the religious ministers, in the name of all the communions, without distinction of denomination. If I should report this speech, it would give new weight to that which I have put forward above on the character of the American clergy; but it will be sufficient, I believe, to report only the passage of the General's response in which this opinion is expressed with a force and precision that does not leave any doubt about his conviction. "I accept," he answered, "with profound gratitude, the displays of esteem and kindness that the religious ministers of this Town and the surrounding places have been pleased to bestow on me, and that you have expressed, Sir, in so moving a manner. In my happy journey, I have often had the occasion to observe the veneration that the clergy of all denominations inspire; the members of the Clergy, apostles of the rights of man, are the ever-consistent spokesmen of a religion customarily founded on the principles of liberty and equality, and on the election of ministers of the Gospel by the people."

On leaving Lancaster, we proceeded to Port Deposit on the banks of the Susquehanna, where we found a delegation from Baltimore with whom we embarked to proceed to that latter City. On the way, we visited Havre de Grace, a small town situated on the spot where the Susquehanna flows into Chesapeake Bay. We stopped there for several hours, and we continued our voyage, which the good weather favored and which was shortened by the pleasures that we enjoyed on board. From the ship's deck, we saw spread out before us the beautiful plains and the rich hills of Maryland; our traveling companions, pressed around Lafayette, pointed out to him in the distance the fields on which he once fought for their independence, and at intervals on the shore, groups of citizens attracted by the sound of the national tunes that rang from our deck, displayed the joy that experiencing the presence of the adoptive son of their country occasioned in them by their frequent cheering.

Sunset had long passed when we arrived at the mouth of the Patapsco River, and it was not until midnight that we approached the piers of Baltimore. Despite this advanced hour, a large number of people were waiting for the arrival of the ship, and upon his landing, the General found himself in the middle of a friendly crowd. But at the moment that he set foot on land, a horrible glow suddenly lit up the Port, and to the south of the City we saw flames rising to the sky.... Immediately, the sinister cry – *To the fire! To the fire!* – resounded in all the streets, and the frightened citizens rushed out of their homes. Desirous of being able to offer the first assistance, we left the General in the care of two members of the committee who led him, against his will, to the hotel that had been readied for him, and we ran with all the speed our legs could muster towards the place of the fire; but we found that we had been preceded by four fire trucks that were already in full operation; other fire trucks arrived from all directions driven by young volunteers and took their place beside the first and acted with such promptness that, although the fire had broken out in a warehouse built of wood, the flames were not long in being subdued, and a little later being completely extinguished. Reduced, in spite of ourselves, to the role of useless spectators, we returned to our lodgings at two o'clock in the morning, full of admiration for the zeal and skill of the young volunteer firemen of Baltimore.

ADAMS JEUNE.

Chapter XVI

Return to Washington – Character of the New President – Visit to the Ex-President Now a Farmer and a Justice of the Peace – The Government Offers Lafayette a Warship for His Return to France – Presents Offered to Bolivar through Lafayette – New Homage of the City of New York – Farewell of the President to the Nation's Guest – Departure from Washington City – Boarding the Brandywine – Crossing – Displays of Attachment and Regrets of the Sailors of the Brandywine to Lafayette – Reception at Le Havre – Several Hours at Rouen – Reception of Lafayette at La Grange by the Inhabitants of his Parish.

After having taken two days of rest at Baltimore, we left for Washington City. General Lafayette desired that there be no pomp and circumstance to mark his departure, and the citizens, always eager to satisfy his desires, were content to come in the evening to receive his farewells and to offer him the expression of their regrets. This ceremony lasted several hours and left the imprint of a profound sadness in our hearts. On August 1, we departed with two members of the committee of the City. Several miles from Washington, we encountered an elegant carriage which stopped near ours; a young man climbed out of it and asked for General Lafayette. He was the eldest son of the new President, John Quincy Adams; he had been sent by his father to meet the National Guest, to advise him that he had sought and obtained permission from the citizens of the metropolis to offer him lodging in his house. The General accepted the invitation for himself and his traveling companions, entered the carriage of young Mr. Adams, and we continued on our way. The two members of the committee from Baltimore had not foreseen this circumstance and were thrown into a rather great embarrassment. Zealous partisans of General Jackson, they had declared themselves loudly against Mr. Adams at the time of his election; the latter had not been unaware of it, and today it appeared to be difficult for them to present themselves at his house under the auspices of General Lafayette without exposing themselves to be thought of as men who wanted to make *due apology*. Thus, they decided to separate from us on entering the City and to take lodgings at an inn.

During the electoral contest, I had often heard Mr. Adams' adversaries reproach him for the aristocratic airs that he had contracted, they said, in the foreign Courts where he had spent many years. This accusation appeared to me to be in contrast with what I had seen and what I have reported of his conduct on the steamship which had transported us from Frenchtown to Baltimore; but at last, by dint of hearing it said, I began to fear that with the exercise of power there had come to him what in Europe we call the manners of a prince; so I was very agreeably surprised when, upon arriving in Washington City, I learned that the President had not changed. We found Mr. Adams in Mr. Monroe's place, it is true; but the public man was still the same. The simplicity of the servants, the accessibility of the household did not appear to us to have undergone the least alteration, and in the reception that Mr. Adams gave us, we found all the cordiality of his predecessor.

The President soon learned why our traveling companions had not called on him, and he hastened to send them a dinner invitation which they accepted without hesitation or embarrassment, like men who take account of a courtesy that is extended to them, but who do not believe themselves put under any obligation by accepting it.

The lodgings that the President had prepared for us in his house were simple, but comfortable and in good taste. Eager to have General Lafayette enjoy the rest that Mr. Adams presumed he must have need of after so many and so lengthy travels, after so many diverse and profound emotions, he closeted himself with us in a private mode of living. Aided by Mrs. Adams, his two sons and two of his nieces, he had us enjoy, if I can express it in this manner, the sweetnesses of family life. Rarely during the first days did we see seated with us more than two or three people at a time at the table or at the domestic hearth, and it was ordinarily some of the government officials who, after having worked the entire day with the President, had stayed with him for dinner and for the intimate conversations of the evening. It was during this time, which passed too quickly, that I was able to appraise the character of Mr. Adams, which I knew then only by the eulogies of his friends and the attacks of his adversaries. I found that the former had been justly accurate, and the latter had been led astray by party spirit. It is difficult to have a better cultivated or more righteous mind than that of Mr. Monroe's successor. The beautiful reliefs of the Capitol, in the composition of which he played a role, a treatise of weights and measures written by him, and numerous diplomatic missions that he fulfilled with distinction, evidence his good taste in the Arts, the soundness of his scientific mind, and his political skill. As for the accusation of aristocracy brought against him by some, it is sufficiently rejected by the simplicity of his habits that his elevation to the First Magistracy of the Republic has not changed.

While General Lafayette was preparing his return to Europe each day, but before leaving American soil, he wanted to see again some of his old Virginia friends; he wanted above all to embrace and express his gratitude to the one who, as head of state, had welcomed him at the seat of government and who today, returned to private life, continued to provide to his fellow citizens the example of all the virtues by cultivating his modest patrimony. The General spoke of this to President Adams who offered to accompany him on this visit, while saying, "that he would seize this occasion readily to offer his own tribute of veneration and attachment to his predecessor." On August 6, the day fixed for this trip, we took the route that leads to Oak Hill, Mr. Monroe's retirement home, 37 miles from Washington. Mr. Adams took General Lafayette, George Lafayette and one of his friends in his carriage; I climbed in a tilbury with the President's eldest son, and we left the City in this manner without attendants and without escort. Having arrived at the bridge over the Potomac, we stopped to pay the toll. The collector, after having counted the people and the horses, collected from the President the sum set by the schedule, and we left immediately; but we had hardly gone a short distance when we heard him cry out behind us: "Mr. President! Mr. President! You have given me 11 cents too little!..." Then we saw the collector arrive, all out of breath, holding in his hand the money that he had just collected, and pointing out the error for which he was making a demand. The President listened to him attentively, began to count with him, and agreed that he still owed him 11 cents; at the moment when he put his hand in his pocket to pay them, the collector recognized General Lafayette in the carriage, and wanted to refund the price of his passage, declaring that all the bridges and all the turnpikes were free for the Nation's Guest; but Mr. Adams called to his attention the fact that General Lafayette was not traveling in an official manner, as the National Guest, but simply as a friend of the President, and that, in this capacity, he did not have the right to any favor. This reasoning appeared correct to the collector who withdrew, taking the money with him. Thus, during the entire course of his travels in the United States, the General was subject only one time to the common rule of paying tolls, and it was precisely the day when he was traveling with the head of state, a circumstance that, in every other country, would have probably conferred on him the privilege of not paying.

We arrived at Oak Hill on the day following our departure from Washington. We found the ex-President, having become a farmer, comfortably established with his entire family in a pretty house near his farm, overseeing the agricultural work and engaged in the improvement of his property, abandoned for so long a time for the public interest. Some friends of Mr. Monroe had joined him to assist in welcoming General Lafayette. We spent three days with them; then the inhabitants of Leesburg, a little town in the vicinity, came with the militia of Loudon County to find the National Guest and to invite him to the fetes that they had prepared for him. The President, the ex-President and the

Chief Justice of the United States accompanied him, and received their share of the people's homage; but it was easy to recognize that these respects were accorded to them more on account of the veneration that their virtues inspired than in relation to the titles they possessed.

After the fetes of Leesburg and Loudon County, we returned to Oak Hill, where we took leave of Mr. Monroe to return to Washington. Desiring to make this trip in one day, we left early in the morning, but we soon had reason to rue this plan; toward two o'clock the heat became so oppressive that one of the horses of Mr. Adams' carriage fell in an apoplectic fit. It was in vain that the coachman tried to save his life by abundant bloodlettings; in a few moments, we saw him expire in a ditch into the bottom of which he had rolled upon falling. As soon as the accident had happened, all of us had alighted to help the horse get up, but seeing him dead, we sat down on the grass near his body while a manservant went to look for another horse in the most nearby village. Travelers passed at every moment alongside us and glanced with curiosity at this group in which not a single one suspected the presence of the First Magistrate of the Republic, and of the adopted son of a great nation.... A new horse having been brought to us, we resumed our trip, but the delay that we had experienced because of this accident made us arrive in Washington well after sunset, a fact that prevented us from visiting the Potomac Falls, near which we recrossed the river. They say that these falls are very beautiful to look at, although they are not very high.

A few days later we left the Capital still once again to make a last journey in Virginia. This time we visited Albemarle, Culpepper, Fauquier, Warrenton and Buckland. Although in each of these towns the passage of General Lafayette was marked by popular festivals, he could not avoid a painful feeling in thinking that in a few days he was going to depart, perhaps forever, from this country that contained so many objects of his affection. At Albemarle, we were rejoined by Mr. Monroe who had been invested with a new public office. Faithful to that doctrine that a citizen should always be entirely at the service of his country, he had not believed that his title of former President of the Republic exempted him from still being useful to his fellow-citizens, and he had accepted the office of justice of the peace of his county to which the votes and the confidence of his neighbors had called him. Mr. Madison had also left his retreat at Montpelier and joined us on the way to Monticello, where the General wanted to go to take his leave of his old friend Jefferson, whose frail health now kept in a state of painful inactivity. The reunion at Monticello of three men who, by their successive elevation to the Supreme Magistracy of the State, had given to their Fatherland 24 years of success and glory, and who now offered to it the example of the private virtues, was a rather powerful reason for making us want to stay there for a longer time, but necessary obligations called General Lafayette back to Washington, and he had to take leave of his friends. I will not try to depict the sadness that presided over this cruel separation, which could not be alleviated by the hope that youth ordinarily leaves, for here the men who were bidding each other farewell had all had a long life, and soon the immensity of the ocean was going to increase the difficulties of seeing each other again.

One of the first concerns of Mr. Adams on arriving at the head of the administration had been to persuade the General to accept the service of a ship of state for the return to France. This ship, built in the shipyards of Washington, had been launched towards the end of June and was to be fitted out for the first days of September, the time fixed by the General for his departure. "It is customary in our Navy," the President wrote him,

> To designate our frigates by the names of rivers of the United States; in order to conform to this custom, and to reconcile it with the desire that we have of perpetuating a name that reminds us of that event in our Revolutionary War in which you sealed your devotion to our principles with your blood, we have given the name *Brandywine* to the frigate which has just been completed, and to which we are entrusting the honorable mission of returning you pursuant to the wishes of your country and your family. The command of *The Brandywine* will be given to Captain Charles Morris, one of the most distinguished officers of our Navy, who is under orders to land you, under the protection of our flag, in that port of Europe that you will be pleased to appoint.

This invitation was too honorable and made with too much delicacy for General Lafayette to hesitate a moment in accepting it; so he hastened to return to Washington to express his gratitude to the President, and to consult with Captain Morris on the departure day, which was fixed at September 7. When this decision was known, we saw a large number of citizens who wanted to receive the last farewells of the Nation's Guest rush here from all the surrounding towns, and all the constituted authorities of the Capital decided that they were going to take their leave of him with an official ceremony. From that moment up to the date of our sailing, the General dedicated all his time to the obligations of friendship and to responding to the invitations that had been made to him by very many towns which the time and distance had not allowed him to visit.

The reports of the exploits of Bolivar, fighting for the liberation and independence of the Republics of South America, were reverberating at that time in the United States whose citizens were rapturously applauding his republican patriotism, still free of all suspicion. Mr. Custis,[21] whose ardent soul is ever ready to sympathize with all that is great and generous, conceived a plan to display his admiration for the Liberator by presenting for his acceptance a beautiful portrait of General Washington and a medal of pure gold, which had been awarded to the great citizen by the American Nation at the festival of independence; but he had thought that these gifts, although already precious enough by virtue of their origin, would acquire nonetheless an even greater value in passing through the hands of the veteran of liberty of two worlds, and General Lafayette consented with pleasure to the request that he made of him to be his intermediary to the Liberator. On September 2, Mr. Vallenilla, member of the delegation sent by Colombia to the seat of the Federal Government of the United States, came to receive these presents from the hand of Lafayette, who remitted them to him with the following letter for Bolivar.

> Washington City, September 1, 1825
> Mr. President-Liberator,
>
> My pious and filial devotion to the memory of General Washington could not be better rewarded by his family than by the honorable commission with which I am today charged. In recognizing the exact resemblance of the portrait, I am happy to think that of all men living, and even of all men of history, General Bolivar is the one to whom my paternal friend would have preferred to offer it. What more can I say to the great citizen whom South America has saluted with the name of Liberator, a name confirmed by the two worlds, and who, endowed with power equal to his disinterestedness, bears in his heart the love of liberty without any exception, and the love of the republic without any alloy? Nonetheless, the recent public displays of your benevolence and your esteem justify me in presenting to you the personal congratulations of a veteran of the common cause who, readying to leave for another hemisphere, has followed with all his good wishes the glorious completion of your efforts and that solemn union with Panama,

21. The same one of whom I have already spoken; you will recall that he was raised at Mount Vernon, as an adoptive son of Washington.

> where all the principles and all the interests of independence, liberty and American politics are going to be consolidated and achieved.[22]

On September 6, General Lafayette's birthday, the President gave a grand dinner to which all the government officials and a large number of distinguished persons who were in Washington were invited. The guests were already assembled, and they were about to take their places at the table, when they announced the arrival of a delegation from New York City. It came in the name of the municipal council to present to General Lafayette a book in which were recorded all the acts and all the events of his stay in that great City. This magnificent volume, taken out of its case and displayed to the gathering, excited general admiration. It is, in a word, a masterpiece that can be compared to the most beautiful and richest of the manuscripts that made the glory and the reputation of a library before the discovery of printing. It is composed of 50 pages, each of which is decorated with illustrations drawn and painted with the greatest skill. Some tableaus and portraits complete this work, whose text is by Mr. Bragg and paintings by Messrs. Burton, Inman and

---

22. If we are not deceived by the nature of events which have supervened in Colombia, and if it is unfortunately true that Bolivar should have left the path that he had so gloriously commenced in order to enter that of usurpation and despotism, one must agree that the error of those who put in him their hopes for freedom for the Southerners of the New World was very natural and excusable. Here is how Bolivar responded to the congratulations and encouragements of Lafayette.

> "Lima, March 16, 1826
> General,
>
> I have just had the honor to see for the first time the characters written by your hand, benefactor of the New World. I owe this good fortune to Colonel Mercer who has delivered to me your honorable letter of October 13 of last year.
>
> It is with inexpressible joy that I learn from the public papers that you were kind enough to honor me with a treasure of Mount Vernon. The image of Washington and one of the memorials of his glory are to be offered by you, they say, in the name of the spirit of the great citizen, by the eldest son of freedom of the New World. How can I express how great a value I attach in my heart to such a display of esteem so glorious for me! The family of Mount Vernon honors me beyond my expectations, for Washington given by the hands of Lafayette is the most sublime of the rewards that a man could aspire to. Washington was the courageous protector of social reform, and you, you are the citizen-hero, the champion of liberty, who with one hand served America and with the other served the Old World. What mortal should have dared to believe himself worthy of the honors which you deign to heap upon me! So my confusion equals the immenseness of my gratitude that I offer you with the respect and the veneration that the entire world owes to the Nestor of freedom.
>
> I am, with the greatest esteem,
> Your respected admirer, Bolivar."

Cummings. The view of the Capitol of Washington, of New York City Hall, the portraits of Washington, Lafayette and Hamilton, leave nothing to be desired; and, so that all would be national in this beautiful work, they used only American-made paper, and the binding was entrusted to Mr. Forster of New York, who executed it with an admirable lavishness and elegance.

General Lafayette accepted with gratitude this beautiful present to which the President and his ministers added additional value by placing their signatures on it. Although the dinner joined a large number of guests, and it was intended to celebrate the anniversary of Lafayette's birth, it was nonetheless very serious, I may say almost sad. Each of us was too strongly preoccupied with the day that was going to follow to be able to surrender himself to mirth. We already felt, by anticipation, the regret of separation. Towards the end of the meal, the President, departing from diplomatic customs that prohibited toasts at his table, got up and made the following toast: "To February 22 and to September 6, birthdays of Washington and Lafayette." Profoundly moved to see his name thus associated with that of Washington, the General expressed his gratitude to the President, and gave the following toast: "To July 4, birthday of liberty in the two hemispheres."

Finally, the day that we ardently desired, and the approach of which nonetheless filled us with profound sadness, this day that was to begin to draw us near to our Fatherland, but which was to also take us far away from a nation that now had as much right to our admiration as to our affection, the day of our departure, September 7, dawned radiantly; the workshops were deserted, the stores stayed closed, the people came in a crowd to press around the President's mansion, the militias lined up in battle array on the route that the Nation's Guest was to traverse to go to the riverbank. The magistrates gathered near him to offer him the last respects and regrets of their fellow citizens.

At eleven o'clock, General Lafayette left his rooms, passed slowly through the crowd that silently pressed on his passage and proceeded to the principal vestibule of the mansion, where the President, surrounded by his ministers, various officials of the Government and principal citizens of the City, had waited for him for several moments. He took his place in the middle of a circle which had been formed on his approach; the doors were opened so that the people assembled outside could witness the scene that was about to take place, and upon the soft murmur of regrets that was heard first in the crowd, there followed a solemn and profound silence; then the President, visibly agitated by emotion, addressed these words to him in the name of the American Nation and its Government.

General Lafayette – It has been the good fortune of many of my distinguished fellow-citizens, during the course of the year now elapsed, upon your arrival at their respective places of abode, to greet you with the welcome of the nation. The less pleasing task now devolves upon me, on bidding you, in the name of the nation, adieu.

It were no longer seasonable, and would be superfluous, to recapitulate the remarkable incidents of your early life — incidents which associated your name, fortunes and reputation, in imperishable connection with the independence and history of the North American Union.

The part which you performed at that important juncture was marked with characters so peculiar, that, realizing the fairest fable of antiquity, its parallel could scarcely be found in the *authentic* records of human history.

You deliberately and perseveringly preferred toil, danger, the endurance of every hardship, and the privation of every comfort, in defense of a holy cause, to inglorious ease, and the allurements of rank, affluence, and unrestrained youth, at the most splendid and fascinating court of Europe.

That this choice was not less wise than magnanimous, the sanction of half a century, and the gratulations of unnumbered voices, all unable to express the gratitude of the heart with which your visit to this hemisphere has been welcomed, afford ample demonstration.

When the contest of freedom, to which you had repaired as a voluntary champion, had closed, by the complete triumph of her cause in this country of your adoption, you returned to fulfill the duties of the philanthropist and patriot in the land of your nativity. There, in a consistent and undeviating career of 40 years, you have maintained, through every vicissitude of alternate success and disappointment, the same glorious cause to which the first years of your active life had been devoted, the improvement of the moral and political condition of man.

Throughout that long succession of time, the people of the United States, for whom, and with whom you had fought the battles of liberty, have been living in the full possession of its fruits; one of the happiest among the family of nations. Spreading in population; enlarging in territory; acting and suffering according to the condition of their nature; and laying the foundations of the greatest, and, we humbly hope, the most beneficent power that ever regulated the concerns of man upon earth.

In that lapse of 40 years, the generation of men with whom you cooperated in the conflict of arms, has nearly passed away. Of the general officers of the American army in that war, you alone survive. Of the sages who guided our councils; of the warriors who met the foe in the field or upon the wave, with the exception of a few, to whom unusual length of days has been allotted by heaven, all now sleep with their fathers. A succeeding, and even a third generation, have arisen to take their places; and their children's children, while rising up to call them blessed, have been taught by them, as well as admonished by their own constant enjoyment of freedom, to include in every benison upon their fathers, the name of him who came from afar, with them and in their cause to conquer or to fall.

The universal prevalence of these sentiments was signally manifested by a resolution of congress, representing the whole people, and all the States of this Union, requesting the President of the United States to communicate to you the assurances of grateful and affectionate attachment of this government and people, and desiring that a national ship might be employed, at your convenience, for your passage to the borders of your country.

The invitation was transmitted to you by my venerable predecessor; himself bound to you by the strongest ties of personal friendship, himself one of those whom the highest honours of his country had rewarded for blood early shed in her cause, and for a long life of devotion to her welfare. By him, the services of a national ship were placed at your disposal. Your delicacy preferred a more private conveyance, and a full year has elapsed since you landed upon our shores. It were scarcely an exaggeration to say, that it has been, to the people of the Union, a year of uninterrupted festivity and enjoyment, inspired by your presence. You have traversed the 24 States of this great confederacy: You have been received with rapture by the survivors of your earliest companions-in-arms: You have been hailed as a long absent parent by their children, the men and women of the present age: And a rising generation, the hope of future time, in numbers surpassing the whole population of that day when you fought at the head and by the side of their forefathers, have vied with the scanty remnants of that hour of trial, in acclamations of joy at beholding the face of him whom they feel to be the common benefactor of all. You have heard the mingled voices of the past, the present, and the future age, joining in one universal chorus of delight at your approach; and the shouts of unbidden thousands, which greeted your landing on the soil of freedom, have followed every step of your way, and still resound, like the rushing of many waters, from every corner of our land.

You are now about to return to the country of your birth, of your ancestors, of your posterity. The executive government of the Union, stimulated by the same feeling which had prompted the congress to the designation of a national ship for your accommodation in coming hither, has destined the first service of a frigate, recently launched at this metropolis, to the less welcome, but equally distinguished trust, of conveying you home. The name of the ship has added one more memorial to distant regions and to future ages, of a stream already memorable, at once in the story of your sufferings and of our independence.

The ship is now prepared for your reception, and equipped for sea. From the moment of her departure, the prayers of millions will ascend to heaven that her passage may be prosperous, and your return to the bosom of your family as propitious to your happiness, as your visit to this scene of your youthful glory has been to that of the American people.

Go, then, our beloved friend, return to the land of brilliant genius, of generous sentiment, of heroic valour; to that beautiful France, the nursing mother of the twelfth Louis, and the fourth Henry; to the native soil of Bayard and Colligny, of Turenne and Catinat, of Fenelon and d'Aguesseau. In that illustrious catalogue of names which she claims as of her children, and

> with honest pride holds up to the admiration of other nations, the name of Lafayette has already for centuries been enrolled. And it shall henceforth burnish into brighter fame; for if, in after days, a Frenchman shall be called to indicate the character of his nation by that of one individual, during the age in which we live, the blood of lofty patriotism shall mantle in his cheek, the fire of conscious virtue shall sparkle in his eye and he shall pronounce the name of Lafayette. Yet we, too, and our children, in life and after death, shall claim you for our own. You are ours by that more than patriotic self-devotion with which you flew to the aid of our fathers at the crisis of their fate. Ours by that long series of years in which you have cherished us in your regard. Ours by that unshaken sentiment of gratitude for your services which is a precious portion of our inheritance. Ours by that tie of love, stronger than death, which has linked your name, for the endless ages of time, with the name of Washington.
>
> At the painful moment of parting from you, we take comfort in the thought, that wherever you may be, to the last pulsation of your heart, our country will be ever present to your affections; and a cheering consolation assures us, that we are not called to sorrow most of all, that we shall see your face no more. We shall indulge the pleasing anticipation of beholding our friend again. In the mean time, speaking in the name of the whole people of the United States, and at a loss only for language to give utterance to that feeling of attachment with which the heart of the nation beats, as the heart of one man, I bid you a reluctant and affectionate farewell.

An approving murmur blanketed the last words of Mr. Adams, and proved how greatly the audience sympathized with the noble sentiments that he had just expressed for France and for the one of her children whose entire life and recent triumph ought to increase her glory and her renown. General Lafayette, profoundly moved by what he had just heard, needed to compose himself for a few moments before being able to respond; at last, having exerted himself to steady his voice, which had been impaired by emotion, he expressed himself in this manner:

> Amidst all my obligations to the general government, and particularly to you, Sir, its respected chief magistrate, I have most thankfully to acknowledge the opportunity given me, at this solemn and painful moment, to present the people of

the United States with a parting tribute of profound, inexpressible gratitude.

To have been, in the infant and critical days of these States, adopted by them as a favorite son, to have participated in the toils and perils of our unspotted struggle for independence, freedom and equal rights, and in the foundation of the American era of a new social order, which has already pervaded this, and must, for the dignity and happiness of mankind, successively pervade every part of the other hemisphere, to have received at every stage of the Revolution, and during 40 years after that period, from the people of the United States, and their representatives at home and abroad, continual marks of their confidence and kindness, has been the pride, the encouragement, the support of a long and eventful life.

But how could I find words to acknowledge that series of welcomes, those unbounded and universal displays of public affection, which have marked each step, each hour, of a 12 months' progress through the 24 States, and which, while they overwhelm my heart with grateful delight, have most satisfactorily evinced the concurrence of the people in the kind testimonies, in the immense favors bestowed on me by the several branches of their representatives, in every part and at the central seat of the confederacy?

Yet, gratifications still higher await me; in the wonders of creation and improvement that have met my enchanted eye, in the unparalleled and self-felt happiness of the people, in their rapid prosperity and insured security, public and private, in a practice of good order, the appendage of true freedom, and a national good sense, the final arbiter of all difficulties, I have had proudly to recognize a result of the republican principles for which we have fought, and a glorious demonstration to the most timid and prejudiced minds, of the superiority, over degrading aristocracy or despotism, of popular institutions founded on the plain rights of man, and where the local rights of every section are preserved under a constitutional bond of union. The cherishing of that union between the States, as it has been the farewell entreaty of our great paternal Washington, and will ever have the dying prayer of every American patriot, so it has become the sacred pledge of the emancipation of the world, an object in which I am happy to observe that the American people, while they give the animating example of successful free institutions, in return for an evil entailed upon them by Europe, and of which a liberal and enlightened sense is everywhere more and more generally felt, show themselves every day more anxiously interested.

And now, Sir, how can I do justice to my deep and lively feelings for the assurances, most peculiarly valued, of your esteem and friendship, for your so very kind references to old times, to my beloved associates, to the vicissitudes of my life, for your affecting picture of the blessings poured by the several generations of the American people on the remaining days of a delighted veteran, for your affectionate remarks on this sad hour of separation, on the country of my birth, full, I can say, of American sympathies, on the hope so necessary to me of my seeing again the country that has deigned, near a half century ago, to call me hers? I shall content myself, refraining from superfluous repetitions, at once, before you, Sir, and this respected circle, to proclaim my cordial confirmation of every one of the sentiments which I have had daily opportunities publicly to utter, from the time when your venerable predecessor, my old brother-in-arms and friend, transmitted to me the honorable invitation of congress, to this day, when you, my dear Sir, whose friendly connection with me dates from your earliest youth, are going to consign me to the protection, across the Atlantic, of the heroic national flag, on board the splendid ship, the name of which has been not the least flattering and kind among the numberless favors conferred upon me.

God bless you, Sir, and all who surround us. God bless the American people, each of their States, and the federal government. Accept this patriotic farewell of an overflowing heart; such will be its last throb when it ceases to beat.

Upon uttering these last words, General Lafayette felt his emotion rapidly increasing, and he rushed into the arms of the President, who mingled his tears with his, while repeating sorrowfully these sad words: "Farewell! Farewell!" The spectators, swept along by the same feeling, also let their tears flow, and surrounded their friend to clasp his hand one more time in theirs. In order to curtail this scene that could not be prolonged without exceeding his strength, the General retired for a moment into his rooms where Mrs. Adams, surrounded by her daughters and her nieces, came to express her good wishes and their regrets. Already on the evening before, this lady, whose cultivated mind and charming character had contributed greatly to adorn our stay in the President's house, had offered him a beautiful bust of her husband, and had added to her present a dedication in French verse, whose charm and elegance proved that it was not the first time that she made her muse speak in our language.

Restrained as if by a magic spell, General Lafayette could not decide to separate from his friends; a thousand pretexts served to delay the definitive moment of parting; but finally, the first of 24 cannon blasts that announced his departure having sounded, he threw himself into Mr. Adams' arms again, expressed to him his last good wishes for the American Nation, and climbed into the carriage. From the top of the colonnade, the President repeated to him the sign of farewell, and at this signal the colors of the militia, who were drawn up in battle array in front of the mansion, were bowed to the ground.

Accompanied by the Secretaries of State, Treasury and of the Navy, the General proceeded to the banks of the Potomac where the steamboat *The Mount Vernon* was waiting for him. On a plateau which stands a little above the river, one saw all the militias of Alexandria, Georgetown and Washington City, grouped in long columns, and readying to file in front of the National Guest. Ahead of them were the magistrates of these three towns of the District of Columbia, in front of their fellow citizens, who had just been joined by a large number of foreigners. When the General had arrived to the point from which he could embrace with a single glance this entire scene, General Washington's family came to arrange themselves around him, as well as the principal officers of the Government, and all these diverse groups, who at first were motionless, moved at the sound of the cannon, and came to him, sad and silent, to receive his last farewell. When the last group had departed, the General took leave of his friends who surrounded him, and climbed on board *The Mount Vernon* with the Minister of the Navy and the government officials who were to accompany him to *The Brandywine*. During this time, the innumerable crowd that lined the shore of the Potomac for a great distance, dominated by the painful feeling of regret that this departure inspired, remained in the most profound silence; but, when the steamship gained the open river, carrying the object of their affections, it uttered a cry of grief, repeated from echo to echo, that was mingled with the booming sound of the cannons of Fort Washington. Some moments later we passed in front of Alexandria, and the General received from the people of this Town the same displays of regret. But it was especially while passing in view of the house at Mount Vernon that he felt his heart oppressed, and that he understood still more the greatness of the sacrifice that he was making to his country by leaving American soil, that hospitable soil on which he could not take a step without encountering memories that were dear to him.

In a few hours, we reached *The Brandywine*, which was anchored at the mouth of the Potomac, where it awaited only our arrival to set sail. The General was welcomed on board with the greatest honors; the crew lined up on the yards, the gunners at their cannon, and the marines in battle array on deck. Of all the people who had come from Washington with us, it was only Mr. Southard, the Secretary of the Navy, who went on board *The Brandywine* with the General in order to introduce him and commend him to Commodore Morris in the name of the American Nation and its Government. During our stay in Washington, Mr. Southard had given us so many marks of kindness that it was not without true sorrow that we took leave of him. Hardly had he received our final embraces than he reboarded *The Mount Vernon*, and our Commodore gave the orders to get underway; but, at that moment, we saw arriving near us another steamboat that appeared to have communications for us; we soon recognized it as *The Constitution*, which was arriving from Baltimore, carrying a large number of citizens of that City, who had wanted to see General Lafayette one more time before his departure, and to express to him their best wishes as well as those of their fellow citizens. We felt very great pleasure in recognizing among them most of the people with whom we had had the most intimate relations during our different stays in Baltimore. Their presence at this time, by returning our thoughts to the happy time when we were with them, made us forget for a moment that we had already left American soil, perhaps forever, and our illusion was prolonged up to the moment when the evening gun signaled the breaking of all communication between their boat and ours.

The night was then too far advanced to be able to get underway, and Commodore Morris waited for the next day to lift anchor. It was September 8. We entered Chesapeake Bay under full sail, sailing at the center of a brilliant rainbow, one of whose feet pressed against the Maryland shore, and the other against that of Virginia. Thus, the same sign which had appeared in the skies the day when Lafayette landed on American soil appeared again at the moment when he was leaving it, as if nature had reserved to itself the task of constructing the first and the last of the numerous triumphal arches which had been dedicated to him during his wonderful journey.[23]

23. The day of our arrival in Staten Island, while the General received the congratulations of the people on the balcony of the Vice President's house, a rainbow, one of whose feet enveloped and speckled *Fort Lafayette* with a thousand colors, appeared in view of the multitude who, struck by the beauty of this scene and its timeliness, cried out that "the sky was in agreement with Americans in celebrating the happy arrival of the friend of their country."

The wind blowing strongly and in a favorable direction, we had soon passed the capes of Virginia, and in a little while we gained the high seas. It was only then that our Captain, extricated from the concerns that an always difficult navigation near the coasts required, made us more fully acquainted with his officers and our new home. In the character of the former, and in the comfortable arrangement of the latter, it was easy to recognize that the American Government had neglected nothing which could contribute to the safety and the pleasure of Lafayette's return to his native land. The Captain announced to the General that the last instructions that he had received from the President were to put himself entirely at his disposal, to conduct him to that port in Europe that it would suit him to designate, and to land him there under the protection of the American flag; that he should, from the present time, regard himself as absolute master on board, and should be assured that his orders would be carried out with the greatest dispatch. The General was moved, but not surprised, by this fresh evidence of the interest of the American Government, and declared to the Captain that he would exercise such honorable rights only to ask to be conducted to Le Havre. Two reasons, he added, led him to desire to return to France by this City; his family was to come to greet him there, and his heart felt the need to see first those who had received his farewells with such kindness at the moment when, the previous year, he had left his Fatherland.

Meanwhile, the wind blew violently and, in the barely 48 hours that had passed since our leaving Chesapeake Bay, we were already in the current of the Gulf of Mexico, whose waves, opposed by the wind, made us experience all the agony of *rolling* and *pitching,* horribly combined. Soon to the seasickness that had overtaken nearly all of us was added a rather strong concern. The frigate was taking on water without anyone being able to recognize where the leak was; the pumps were insufficient to drain it in spite of their use, and already some people seemed to regret that we should have been so far from the coast; but our Captain and his officers were not the type of people to allow themselves to be intimidated by so little a matter; after a close examination of our situation, Mr. Morris opined that his vessel, being too deep in the water to begin with, needed to be lightened, and he had the crew throw 32,000 weights of iron that were part of its ballast into the sea. This single operation, carried out in several hours, remedied all our troubles. The frigate, now lighter, was in better trim, and in being elevated several inches more above the water, it permitted the discovery of the source of the leak, which was only a little below its initial water-mark; from that moment, the danger, which had never been very serious, disappeared entirely, and our voyage was accomplished without the slightest anxiety.

Just as the President had told the General while offering him the service of *The Brandywine* for his return to France, we had as Captain one of the most distinguished men of the American Navy. As early as his youth, Captain Morris had called attention to himself in several battles before Algiers under the command of Commodore Rodgers. Later, in the last war against England, he had added more to his reputation by the skill of several of his maneuvers before an enemy who nearly always had the advantage of numbers; and his comrades generally agreed to attribute to him a large part of the victory of the American frigate, *The Constitution,* over the English frigate, *The Guerrière*; the latter, proud of her formidable artillery and of the experience of her numerous crew, had challenged all those American ships who should have the courage to confront her, and seemed to wait impatiently for one of them to answer her call, when *The Constitution* appeared and made her regret her presumption.[24]

The officers who served under the command of Captain Morris on board *The Brandywine* had all also fought with distinction in the last war, and each of them could justifiably boast of having added to the glory of the annals of the American Navy by his actions. I regret being unable to name all of them here and relate some of the deeds by which they earned the gratitude of their country and the esteem of their fellow citizens, but these details would carry me beyond the bounds that I have prescribed for myself, and I hope that one would see in my silence only the sense of my incapacity as a historian, not that of my indifference towards men whose company had so much pleasure for us during a voyage that no doubt would have appeared very short to us, if it had not been bringing us back to our country.

The Government of the United States does not have a theoretical school for its young naval officers, but each warship, on entering the service, receives on board a certain number of candidates (*midshipmen*) and in this manner forms a practical school, not very expensive for the treasury and fruitful in its successful results. When the rumor spread that *The Brandywine* had been assigned to conduct Lafayette to France, all the parents who intended their children for the Navy coveted a place as *midshipmen* aboard this frigate for them, and the President found himself overwhelmed with requests sent from all parts of the Union. Not being able to satisfy all, but nonetheless wanting to reconcile as much as possible private interests with the good of the public service, he decided that each State would be represented in Lafayette's service by one candidate, so that *The Brandywine* received on board 24 students, instead of the eight or ten that ships of its class ordinarily receive. It was very sweet

24. The frigate *The Constitution* was then commanded by Captain Hull, a man of great courage, celebrated for his actions in the last war. One knows that this battle, which lasted less than an hour, ended with the capture of the English frigate.

satisfaction for the General to see himself thus surrounded by young representatives of the republics that he had just traveled through with so much pleasure; not only did their presence remind him of the places that he loved, but some of them, sons of former Revolutionary soldiers, furnished him with still another occasion to speak of his former companions-in-arms; and the young people, on their side, proud of the mission with which they were associated, sought to render themselves worthy of it by devoting themselves passionately to study and to the accomplishment of their duties. The entirely paternal friendship that the General displayed towards them during the crossing earned their affection towards him to such a degree that they were not able to separate from him without shedding tears. They beseeched him to permit them to get up a subscription amongst themselves to offer him a lasting token of their filial attachment that would remind him, at the same time, of the days spent with them aboard *The Brandywine*.[25]

The winds did not stop blowing strongly during the entire crossing, but often fluctuated, and this made our voyage rather arduous. Nonetheless, in spite of their changeableness, Captain Morris found the secret of making us proceed rapidly, and, on October 3, we arrived in sight of the shores of Le Havre, that is to say 24 days after leaving the waters of Chesapeake Bay. This crossing can be regarded as very short, especially if one considers that the ship that we boarded was making its first voyage, and consequently required to be studied with greater care by those who navigated her.

I will not speak of the feelings that agitated us at the sight of our Fatherland. There is, perhaps, not a man who has not experienced them on seeing his native land again, even after a short separation, and for the one who has never known the torments of absence and the sweet emotions of return, I should fear that my words would appear only exaggerated or ridiculous.

As the sea was swelling and the wind variable, the Captain did not want to jeopardize the frigate by approaching too close to land at the beginning of the night; consequently, he sent one of his officers to Le Havre to procure a pilot, and tacked back and forth while awaiting his return. At midnight, a fishing vessel approached us, and delivered letters by which we learned that

---

25. This present, which General Lafayette received some time after his return to Paris, is a silver urn of antique form and very skillfully embossed. It rests on a base of the same metal, whose three faces are decorated with exquisite pictures, representing the Capitol of Washington, the visit of Lafayette to Washington's tomb, and the arrival of *The Brandywine* at Le Havre. On the fourth face is inscribed in relief the offering of the young *midshipmen* to their paternal friend. This magnificent work was executed at Paris under the direction of the consul of the United States, Mr. Barnett, who answered the confidence of the young sailors with that zeal which he brings to everything which relates to the glory of his country or the interests of his fellow-citizens.

a large part of General Lafayette's family and very many of his friends, among whom was my father, had been waiting for several days at Le Havre and would join us in a few hours.

As one can well imagine, such news kept us awake all night, waiting impatiently for the return of the day that was to bring us to our friends, our families and our country. At six o'clock in the morning, the pilot was at our side, directing the frigate cautiously towards the Port of Le Havre which we saw slowly becoming larger on the horizon. In three hours, we stopped, restrained by the impossibility of approaching the coast any more with a ship of our size.[26] Captain Morris then fired a salutation of 24 cannon shots, to which the fort that protected the Port responded some moments later. At eleven o'clock, a steamship had come alongside us, and we enjoyed the happiness of being among our family and friends....

We also received on board some citizens of Le Havre, among whom was Mr. de Laroche, who came to entreat the General to accept lodgings in his house for the entire time that it would please him to stay in the City. Mr. Beasley, the American Consul at Le Havre, was also among the visitors. Our Captain and his officers received them with honor and had them visit every part of the frigate whose beautiful proportions and wonderful appearance excited their admiration.

However, the time passed rapidly, and the moment to separate ourselves from our companions of the voyage had arrived. It would be difficult to depict the expression of grief and regret that reigned on the faces of all the crew at the moment when they came to clasp, for the last time, the hand of the man whom they had conducted with such pride across the ocean. The officers milled around him for a long time while pressing him in their arms, not being able to find it in their heart to allow him to depart; their first lieutenant, Mr. Gregory, who had been charged by them to express their sentiments, felt such great emotion that his voice faltered from the first words that he uttered; but then, impelled as if by a sudden inspiration, he rushed towards the national flag that waved behind the vessel, detached it precipitously and presented it to the General while exclaiming:

> We cannot entrust it to more glorious hands. Take it, dear General; may it remind you forever of your alliance with the American Nation; may it remind you sometimes also of

26. *The Brandywine* carried sixty 32-pounder cannons, ready to fire, and a crew of 450. If one adds to this number the officers, the garrison of infantry and the passengers, we had more than 500 on board.

> those who will never forget the pleasure that they had to spend 24 days with you aboard *The Brandywine*; waving two times each year above the towers of your hospitable home, may it remind your neighbors of the anniversary of two great dates whose influence on the entire world is incalculable, the birth of Washington and the Declaration of Independence of our country!

"I accept it with gratitude," responded the General,

> And I intend that, displayed on the most visible place of my home at La Grange, it witness each day, to all those who shall see it, the kindness of the American Nation to its adopted and devoted son. And I hope that, when you and your compatriots shall come to visit me, it will remind you that at La Grange you are not on foreign soil....

At this moment, the sound of cannon and the *huzzahs* of the crew lined up on the yards drowned out the final farewells, and we passed on board the steamship, from which we saw *The Brandywine* spread its sails and move off with the majesty of a floating fortress.

Captain Morris, who was to accompany the General to Paris; Captain Reed, a distinguished officer of the American Navy, charged by his Government with a scientific mission in Europe; and Mr. Somerville, envoy of the United States to the Court of Sweden, left *The Brandywine* at the same time as we, and the vessel, now under the command of Lieutenant Gregory, was to go to reinforce the Mediterranean squadron.

At the moment of his landing, General Lafayette must have noticed that the sentiments that the citizens of Le Havre had displayed to him at the time of his departure had not changed, and his heart was wonderfully moved. As for the authorities, they were what they should have been the preceding year, that is to say, they allowed free range to the expression of public opinion, and on his route from the Port to Mr. de Laroche's house, the General did not have the pain of seeing his friends threatened by the sword of the gendarmes, or humiliated by the presence of foreign soldiers.

General Lafayette impatiently desired to see again those of his children who had not been able to come to meet him and who were waiting for him at La Grange; consequently, he decided to leave Le Havre the day after his arrival. His son embarked on the Seine with his family and his friends in order to go to wait for him at Rouen; while, accompanied by Captain Morris and the author of this journal, Lafayette took the land route. On his leaving the outlying part of the City, his carriage was surrounded by a large procession of young citizens who asked his permission to accompany him for a distance. After an hour's march, the General stopped to thank his escort, who did not separate themselves from him until after having expressed to him the most honorable sentiments through the voice of their young leader, Mr. Etesse, to whom his fellow citizens had also given proof of their esteem and friendship on that day by placing themselves under his command.

Upon arriving at Rouen, we alighted at the house of Mr. Cabanon, an honorable merchant whom the people have always entrusted with the representation of the interests of his department in the Chamber of Deputies, so far as his fellow citizens have been free in their choices. An old colleague and friend of General Lafayette, he had claimed the right of receiving the Guest of America at his table and had prepared for him the pleasure of being seated in the midst of his family and a large number of the most distinguished citizens of the ancient capital of Normandy. Towards the end of the dinner, someone came to advise the General that a large crowd, joined together in the street and accompanied by a band of musicians, wanted to salute him; he repaired hurriedly onto the balcony to respond to this mark of esteem of the people of Rouen; but hardly were the first acclamations heard when we saw arrive from the two ends of Crosne Street, where Mr. Cabanon's house was situated, detachments of the Royal Guard and the gendarmes who, without prior notice, prepared to disperse the crowd. The moderation with which the Royal Guard executed the orders, which it had received from an impudent and blind authority, proved how repugnant this expedition was to it; but the gendarmes, eager no doubt to show themselves the worthy instrument of the power that employed them, *bravely* charged the unarmed citizenry, and were not stopped by the cries of women and children overrun by the hooves of their horses…. A manufacturer of Bolbec, an old man of Rouen and several other people were gravely wounded…. Many others were illegally and brutally arrested…. After these glorious exploits, the gendarmes, masters of the terrain, waited for the General to depart, and swords in hand, insults in their mouths, they accompanied the carriage to the hotel where we were to spend the night…. But there, their success ended; some young people, standing at the door, blocked the entrance of this sanctuary where many of those who had been obliged to flee Crosne Street had come to take refuge. Thus, General Lafayette was able to receive in peace the honorable congratulations of these peaceable citizens who had just committed, in the eyes of the authorities, the wrong of displaying the satisfaction that the return of a man made them enjoy, a man who, by virtue of the triumph that a free nation had just bestowed on him, had added so much to the brilliance of the French name, made them enjoy.

This shameful conduct of the authorities and their servile instruments affected us so much more deeply since, a few days earlier, we had still had before our eyes the tableau of the free expression of opinions and of the enthusiasm of the American people, and since, in spite of ourselves, we surrendered ourselves to a comparison that was far from being favorable to our country. The presence of Captain Morris, and some of his compatriots who were accompanying us up to Paris, added more to our embarrassment and our sorrow. We seemed to read on their severe countenances the expression of feelings that the sight of a people once so energetic in their love of liberty, today so timidly submissive to the despotism of the bayonette, inspired in them. As soon as I found the occasion to converse with them for a moment, I hastened to tell them that they must really guard against confounding prudence and moderation with weakness which, here, was only apparent. That, in this circumstance, the citizens could not have imagined that the local authorities would be senseless enough to oppose the expression of sentiments so inoffensive to them, and so natural, and that, consequently, no one should have thought to prepare a resistance whose necessity could not be foreseen. Some young people who were around us, hearing this conversation, added heatedly:

> We hope that our moderation will not be misinterpreted by those who know us, and that they will understand that we resigned ourselves to retreat before the gendarmes in this manner only because we wanted to spare our friend General Lafayette the pain of being the occasion of a great disturbance....

The American officials applauded the courage and the delicacy of this sentiment, and understood that, in every other circumstance, the triumph of the police and the gendarmes over the citizens of Rouen would not be so easy.

On the following morning, October 8, the courtyard of the hotel was filled by young people on horseback, intending to form an escort to the General up to the first postal station. Their bearing, and some words that I overheard, proved to me that they still had on their mind the scene of the night before and that they were very resolved not to allow it to recur with impunity. The infantry posts and those of the gendarmes had been doubled during the night, as if the day was to bring great happenings, but the authorities confined themselves to these ridiculous demonstrations, and General Lafayette left the City peacefully while receiving on his passage numerous displays of the goodwill of the citizens. At the outskirts of Rouen, the escort was augmented by some other young horsemen who accompanied him up to the first postal station, where they took their leave of him, after having presented him with a crown of immortelles that was placed in his carriage on the sword that the militias of New York had given to him.

This same evening we slept at Saint Germain-en-Laye, and the next day, October 9, we arrived at La Grange where for three days the inhabitants of the neighboring townships had been busy with preparations for a fete for the reception of him whom they had been waiting for impatiently for so long a time.

At a certain distance from his house, the carriage stopped, the General descended and suddenly found himself in the middle of a crowd whose raptures and enthusiasm would have deceived the eye of a stranger, making him believe that all of them were his children. Until the evening, the house was filled by the crowd, which had difficulty separating from the General. The citizens only withdrew after having led him, by the brightness of the illuminations and to the sound of music, under a triumphal arch bearing an inscription in which they had bestowed on him the title *Friend of the People*. There he received anew the expressions of joy and happiness that his return gave rise to in his good neighbors.

On the following day, the General was occupied all day long in receiving the young girls who brought him flowers and sang couplets to him, the company of the National Guard of Court Palais, as well as a delegation of the Town of Rozay. The inhabitants of this Town, in offering a box of flowers to their friend, spoke to him through Mr. Fricotelle, the leader of the delegation, as follows:

> When we learned that in defiance of a long voyage, you were going to brave, under a sky that was unknown to you, a climate that they told us was dangerous, our hearts were seized with fright, and we shed tears on the departure of a father. Soon we received the news of the glorious reception that the good American people gave you, so worthy of the freedom that you helped them to win, and, in our joy, our prayers were raised to the sky for them and for you; but when we learned that, in the midst of the triumph of those displays of affection, and urgent solicitations of the Americans to stay with them, your thoughts turned to us, to our country, then our admiration for your virtues increased even more; today our gratitude is boundless.

After his speech, they all rushed into the arms of the General; they left him only to hurl themselves into the arms of his son, George Lafayette.

The following Sunday, the inhabitants of Rozay and the environs presented the General with a brilliant festival, for which a subscription, to which everyone contributed, defrayed the expenses. The preparations, which had required several days of labor, were the work of a part of the citizenry which had not wanted to be helped by any paid hands. At five o'clock in the evening, more than 4,000 people, very many of whom having come from some miles away, filled the rooms and the courts of the castle of La Grange in order to salute the man whom all were calling the *Friend of the People.* At seven o'clock, a troop of young girls, marching at the head of the people of Rozay, came to present to the General a basket of flowers, while chanting in chorus some simple and moving couplets. Mr. Vigné, in the name of the district, gave a speech full of generous sentiments. "We see you again at last," he said to the General,

> Rejuvenated by the air of freedom that you have just breathed, and by the sight of the happiness of a strong and grateful people whom you have just beheld. Like the Americans, how can we describe to you our love, our admiration, and the pleasure that we take in seeing you again! But, General, this love, this pleasure and this admiration, while stirring our hearts, forces us into silence.

The General answered him:

> The touching reception that awaited me here at the moment of my arrival, the fresh displays of friendship that you have heaped on me today, complete the satisfaction that I feel in finding myself in the midst of my family, and in your midst, my dear neighbors and friends. While I was traversing the free and flourishing regions of the United States, it was sweet for me to think that the voices of that admirable and excellent people were echoing up to you, and that you were taking pleasure in these voices on my behalf.
>
> The enemies of the popular cause reproached me in that, in the meetings with the Americans, while expressing to them my feelings, I was thinking also of you. They have had reason to believe that, indeed, in sight of the miracles of public prosperity and private happiness that have been the result of liberty, equality and of legal and national order in that vast land, it was difficult for me to forget the prayers of my whole life that my French compatriots should exercise the same rights and gain the same happiness.

> Here I am now returned to this retreat of La Grange, which is as dear to me as honorific titles, and to those agricultural occupations to which you know that I am so attached, and that, for many years, I have shared with you, my dear neighbors, and with most of the friends who surround me. Your affection, well-reciprocated on my part, makes them all the more dear to me. Receive, I beg you, my thanks for the beautiful and moving fete that you have prepared for me, which fills my heart with joy, love and gratitude.

After this response, which was received rapturously, the General was led in triumph on the meadow where an elegant tent had been set up for him and his family. Illuminations artfully laid out, fireworks prepared by Ruggieri, animated dances, a large number of booths of all kinds and a population of more than 6,000 people, all, in a word, contributed to recall to Lafayette some of the beautiful scenes of his American triumph – with so much more verity since he found a great similarity in their sentiments and in their expression.

The dances lasted the entire night, the shouts of *Long live the Friend of the People!* reverberated until daylight, and, on the following day, Lafayette, returned to the bosom of his family, enjoyed the happiness and peace that only the memory of a life well-spent produces.

END OF SECOND AND LAST VOLUME

Presented by the
MIDSHIPMEN of the U.S. FRIGATE
BRANDYWINE
as a Testimonial of individual esteem
and collective admiration a Tribute to
the private Worth and public Excellence of
GENERAL LAFAYETTE.

ACKNOWLEDGMENTS

I am very grateful to Diane Windham Shaw, Special Collections Librarian and College Archivist at the David Bishop Skillman Library of Lafayette College, for sharing her knowledge and insights about General Lafayette, introducing me to the college's fine collection of "Fayettabilia," providing encouragement to me during the entire time I worked on this book, consenting to read the manuscript, and favoring me with her jacket comments. Diane also graciously allowed me to reproduce the image of the wonderful "Welcome Lafayette" scarf that adorns this publication.

I am indebted to Michiko Okaya, Director of the Williams Gallery at Lafayette College, for letting me use the image of the fine Thomas Sully painting of Lafayette during his Farewell Tour that graces the book jacket.

I was privileged to have Professor Edmund S. Morgan, Sterling Professor of History, Emeritus, Yale University, whose instruction instilled in me a love of American history, review the manuscript and write a comment for the jacket.

Betsy Bailey of BaileyDonovan of Manchester, New Hampshire, designed the book jacket and other features of the publication; she was a pleasure to work with and her work is a pleasure to look at.

Jay and Edmond Girard of Lafayette Press were at all times congenial, flexible and easy to work with. I hope they are as proud of the end product of our collective work as I am.

I want to acknowledge the important role that Mary Tetreau, my astute copyeditor, played in preparing the manuscript for publication. Her dedication to this project was indispensable to its success.

I am also indebted to Jill MacDonald, Ruth Welch, Robin Reale and Mary Zoza, who collaborated to word-process a barely legible handwritten draft translation into usable, readable text.

I am grateful to a number of publishing and museum professionals whose advice helped me bring this project to fruition. Among them are: Ellen Wicklum, Editor at the University Press of New England in Lebanon,

New Hampshire; Tordis Ilg Isselhardt, Principal of Images from the Past in Bennington, Vermont; and my cousin, Noah Amstadter of Sports Publishing in Champaign, Illinois. Special thanks are also due to Stacey Pomeroy Draper, Curator of the Rensselaer County Historical Society in Troy, New York, and Rosalind Magnuson, Archivist of the Brick Store Museum in Kennebunk, Maine, for their help in identifying the full names of various people whom Levasseur only identified by surname.

I want to thank my nephew, David Myers, who took the photograph of me that appears on the jacket and whose work belies the expression: "I'm only a photographer, not a plastic surgeon." I am indebted to his parents, Anne Hoffman and Phil Myers, who provided moral, technical, and proofreading support to this project.

Finally, I am deeply appreciative of my wife Marilyn's important role in this work. Marilyn encouraged me and served as my "in-house" consultant throughout the process of creating this book. Her fluency in the French language and her experience with publishing art catalogues, as a former museum curator and director, were invaluable. She also became a sounding board for my reading long passages of the translation aloud, and, by osmosis or otherwise, became nearly as "Fayettophile" as her husband.

Alan R. Hoffman
Londonderry, New Hampshire
August 2006

INDEX

C

D

K

L

M

O

P

Q

R

Y

Z